ILLUSTRATED TREES
OF BRITAIN & EUROPE

ILLUSTRATED
TREES
OF BRITAIN & EUROPE

Second Edition

DAVID MORE JOHN WHITE

BLOOMSBURY
LONDON · NEW DELHI · NEW YORK · SYDNEY

First edition published by Cassell in 2003

Second edition published in 2013 by
Bloomsbury Publishing
50 Bedford Square
London WC1B 3DP

www.bloomsbury.com

ISBN 978-14081-2366-9

A CIP catalogue record for this book is available
from the British Library

© in the paintings, David More and Domino Books Ltd., 2013
© in the text, John White and Domino Books Ltd., 2013

A **Domino** book. All rights reserved. No part of this publication
may be reproduced or transmitted in any form or by any means,
electronic or otherwise, without prior written permission from Domino Books Ltd.

Frontispiece: In Memoriam, the English Elm

Printed and bound in China by Toppan Leefung

This book is produced using paper that is made from wood grown in managed sustainable forests.
It is natural, renewable and recyclable. The logging and manufacturing processes conform to the
environmental regulation of the country of origin.

10 9 8 7 6 5 4 3 2 1

CONTENTS

FOREWORD 7

INTRODUCTION 9

Ginkgo Family · Ginkgoaceae
   MAIDENHAIR TREE 21

Yew Family · Taxaceae
   YEWS 23
   NUTMEGS 31

Plum Yew Family · Cephalotaxaceae
   PLUM YEWS 33

Huon Pine Family · Podocarpaceae
   PODOCARPS, TOTARAS 35

Monkey Puzzle Family · Araucariaceae
   MONKEY PUZZLE 37
   NORFOLK ISLAND PINE 37

Cypress Family · Cupressaceae
   INCENSE CEDARS 39
   LAWSON CYPRESSES 41
   FALSE CYPRESSES 53
   LEYLAND CYPRESSES 59
   CYPRESSES 61
   JUNIPERS 71
   RED CEDARS, THUJAS 83

Swamp Cypress Family · Taxodiaceae
   REDWOODS 91
   JAPANESE CEDARS 95
   DAWN REDWOOD 101
   SWAMP CYPRESSES 101
   TASMANIAN CEDARS 105
   CHINESE FIR, UMBRELLA PINE 107

Pine Family · Pinaceae
   SILVER FIRS 109
   CEDARS 147
   LARCHES 155
   SPRUCES 167
   HEMLOCKS 195
   DOUGLAS FIRS 201
   PINES 205

Willow Family · Salicaceae
   POPLARS 263
   WILLOWS 285

Walnut Family · Juglandaceae
   WING NUTS 293
   WALNUTS 295
   HICKORIES 299

Birch Family · Betulaceae
   BIRCHES 303
   ALDERS 317
   HORNBEAMS 325

Hazel Family · Corylaceae
   HAZELS 333

Beech Family · Fagaceae
   BEECHES 335
   SWEET CHESTNUT 349
   OAKS 351

Elm Family · Ulmaceae
   ELMS 395
   ZELKOVAS 415
   NETTLE TREES 417

Mulberry Family · Moraceae
   MULBERRIES 421

Magnolia Family · Magnoliaceae
   MAGNOLIAS 427
   TULIP TREES 437

Laurel Family · Lauraceae
   GUTTA-PERCHA, BAY 439
   SASSAFRAS 443
   CALIFORNIAN LAUREL 443

Cercidiphyllaceae, Moraceae
   KATSURA TREE, FIG 441

Witch-Hazel Family · Hamamelidaceae
   SWEET GUMS 445
   PARROTIA 447

CONTENTS

Plane Family · Platanaceae
   PLANES   449

Rose Family · Rosaceae
   MEDLAR, QUINCE   455
   THORNS   457
   ROWANS   465
   WHITEBEAMS   483
   APPLES   491
   PEARS   513
   CHERRIES   523

Pea Family · Fabaceae
   JUDAS TREE, YELLOW-WOODS   569
   REDBUDS, SILK TREE   571
   WATTLES   573
   LOCUST TREES   575
   HONEY LOCUSTS   583
   LABURNUMS   587
   KENTUCKY COFFEE TREE   589

Orange Family · Rutaceae
   EUODIA, CORK TREES   591

Tree of Heaven Family · Simaroubaceae
   TREES OF HEAVEN   593

Smoke Bush Family · Anacardiaceae
   VARNISH TREE, SUMACH   595

Box Family · Buxaceae
   BOX   597

Holly Family · Aquifoliaceae
   HOLLIES   599

Maple Family · Aceraceae
   MAPLES   609

Horse Chestnut Family · Hippocastanaceae
   HORSE CHESTNUTS   663

Mallow Family · Malvaceae
   LIMES   677

Tamarisk Family · Tamaricaceae
   TAMARISKS   703

Eucryphia Family · Eucryphiaceae
   EUCRYPHIAS   705

Tea Family · Theaceae
   STEWARTIAS   707

Araliaceae, Meliaceae, Flacourtiaceae
   KALOPANAX, TOONA, IDESIA   709

Soapberry Family · Sapindaceae
   GOLDEN RAIN TREE   711

Olive Family · Oleaceae
   ASHES   713
   OLIVE, LIGUSTRUM   761
   FRINGE TREES   763

Pittosporum Family · Pittosporaceae
   PITTOSPORUM   733

Tupelo Family · Nyssaceae
   TUPELOS   735

Myrtle Family · Myrtaceae
   GUMS   737

Davidia Family · Davidiaceae
   HANDKERCHIEF TREE   745

Dogwood Family · Cornaceae
   DOGWOODS   747

Heather Family · Ericaceae
   STRAWBERRY TREES   753
   OXYDENDRUM   757
   RHODODENDRON   757

Storax Family · Styracaceae
   HALESIA, STYRAX   759

Ebony Family · Ebenaceae
   PERSIMMONS   765

Bignonia Family · Bignoniaceae
   CATALPAS   767

Foxglove Family · Scrophulariaceae
   PAULOWNIAS   773

Palm Family · Palmae
   PALMS   775

Some Southern Trees   778-803

GLOSSARY   804

SHOOTS, BUDS AND LEAVES   806

INDEX OF SCIENTIFIC NAMES   816

INDEX OF ENGLISH NAMES   825

FOREWORD

This book began and for many years quietly proceeded as DM's personal project to record in detail as many tree species, varieties and cultivars as he could find in the British Isles and Ireland. It was not a formal undertaking with the benefits (and sometimes limitations) of a whole background of foresters, gardeners, dendrological and taxonomic advisers, publishers, contracts, budgets, deadlines, of sizes decreed and designs imported. It was the private work of an artist obsessed by trees.

The trees constantly being added were thus those to be found in temperate north-western Europe, including those that could not survive the rigours of a continental winter but not those restricted to Mediterranean, let alone subtropical zones. In effect it represented something approaching an illustrated analogue of Krüssmann's great work of reference, whose English translation (now alas out of print in both German and English) was one of DM's principal guides.

Eventually, Philippa Mitchell, widow of the late, great dendrologist Alan Mitchell, mentioned the project to one of Alan's past editors, to whom DM showed a considerable mountain of paintings, already thigh-high on the floor of his Camberwell flat. With a publishing contract arranged, but still a hazy finishing date, the work pursued its placid course while widening its girth to the present 800 pages. Soon after, JW joined the team, to contribute the brief texts for which DM had left an upper right-hand corner of each painting and particularly to resolve some problems of naming. These last, which lie like serpents in the way of all tree students, derive partly from the constant revision of scientific names that afflicts all branches of natural history, but also and particularly from mis-labelling. Of the millions of mature trees to be seen in British and Irish tree collections, both public and private, a considerable number were planted and subsequently labelled in the 19th or even earlier centuries. Time moves on, taxonomists are untiring, the rest of us are prone to human error, old labels get forgotten: it is all too easy to find two patently different trees carrying the same name, and others with names invalid or forgotten, but still fixed to the tree's trunk since the days when transport involved a horse.

A further problem for DM lay in frequently finding a further and striking form of a tree already painted several plates ago. Where possible, he accommodated these by repainting earlier pages: where not, he would sometimes find a home for the latecomer in pages covering related species. In such cases, the texts carry cross-references directing the reader to and from these isolated out-stations, and both occurrences are referred to in the indexes of English and Latin names.

The sequence of trees described is broadly that of their conventional scientific order, but this is primarily a book for pleasure – far from a botanical text-book.

Similarly, JW's texts aim simply at indicating a tree's distinctive characteristics of form, growth, history or points of general interest. A minimum of technical terms is used, and these are explained in the glossary on pages 804-6. Concise additional notes as to heights attained, hardiness and values are at the end of each tree's description, as explained on pages 18-19.

Of course, no work of illustration such as the following, whatever its faults, can be made without years of help from many arboreta, botanic gardens and other institutions, from their directors and staff, from gardeners and other friends – far more than the artist can individually thank here. And no descriptive text, however cursory, can be written without extensive reference to the whole body of dendrological literature, and again a lifetime of help and instruction from other tree enthusiast friends, professional and amateur.

In particular, though, we jointly want to acknowledge special kindnesses and generous help over the years from the following friends and institutions: David Alderman, Tree Register of the British Isles; Alice Holt Lodge, Farnham; Hugh Angus; Bedgebury National Pinetum; Mrs Arabella Binney-Killander, Pampisford Hall, Cambs.; Cambridge University Botanic Garden; Cardiff City Parks Department; Sidney J. Clarke; Allen Coombes; Edinburgh Botanic Garden; Endsleigh Gardens; David Elgy; Charles Erskine; Mark Flannigan; The Forestry Commission and its Research Agency; Forest Enterprise; David Gardener; National Botanic Garden, Glasnevin, Dublin; Duncan Goodwin; the Harold Hillier Gardens, Arboretum and Library; Tom Hudson; Anne Hyde; Royal Botanic Gardens Kew, and its library; Alan Jackson; Andy Jackson; Kilmun Forest Garden; Mr Maclachlan, Batsford Park, Gloucs.; the late Alan Mitchell; Philippa Mitchell; Colin Morgan; Grace Pasley; David Paterson; Jim Paterson; Keith Rushforth; Harry Smith Horticultural Collection; Richard Stone; Adonal Synott; Tradespark, Nairn; Tregrehan Gardens, Cornwall; Norman Villis; Wakehurst Place, Sussex; Westonbirt Arboretum; John Wilkinson; Richard Wooster.

The book's producers and publishers in both Britain and America have also been endlessly patient (at least, we fear that it must have seemed endless to them, with both of us incessantly altering and adding material – a process that still looks unlikely ever to stop). And at a more personal level, DM will be ever grateful to Neal Jackson for his kindness, encouragement and support, and JW to his wife Jill for both tolerating his frequent fits of dendro-abstraction and for typing and retyping his outpourings.

But most books can be improved, and we will both be very grateful for any criticisms or suggestions. Please email them to us at: mswalter32@aol.com.

INTRODUCTION

Paradoxically, although more tree species can be found growing today in Britain and Ireland – and usually growing better – than in any comparable area of the temperate world, the *native* tree flora of our area is notably small. Natural woodlands across North America and other continents regularly exhibit a rich array of different tree species all growing together. But European woods tend to be dominated by a few or sometimes monotonously only a single species.

The reason for this difference lies in the last Ice Ages and in the conformation of our European mountains and valleys. In other regions of the northern hemisphere where the principal mountain ranges run north-south, as the ice descended from the north, plants were able to retreat before its advance, and then repopulate their old territories once the ice retreated. In Europe, however, the major physical barriers lie east-west: the Alps, Pyrenees, most other ranges and the northern shore of the Mediterranean all barred the way to plants' retreat before the ice, condemning the majority of warmth-needing species to extinction. When the ice retreated, far fewer plants had survived to advance northwards again. Of those that did, the trees most adaptable to different soils and conditions were able to form dominant colonies with less competition. For the time being, the post-Ice Age botanical landscapes were established – great variety in North American and other northern hemisphere woods and forests, not in the European. And away from parks and gardens, this is still the situation today.

But in compensation, the Europeans have been active for centuries in collecting trees from other parts of the world and bringing home the seeds of unfamiliar species – to Germany, France, Holland and particularly to the British Isles. From the late seventeenth century onwards a passion for new trees provided commercial impetus for collecting expeditions launched by individuals, botanic gardens or the tree nurseries themselves. And warmed by the Gulf Stream and favoured by a moist maritime climate without extremes of heat or cold, Britain and Ireland offered perfect growing conditions for most of these exotic arrivals. The great majority of trees growing in the great European gardens and arboreta, both public and private, are therefore exotic, and far outnumber European natives.

This book offers a record of some 2,000 trees, both native and exotic, to be found in north-western Europe, with an added survey on pages 776-803 of some conspicuous species too tender for Europe north of the Alps but to be seen in the Mediterranean zone.

Note that throughout this book, we exclude of course the tropics, where over three-quarters of the world's flowering plants are to be found – but see page 15.

TREES

Flowering plants (Angiospermae) began to appear about 120 million years ago. They completely dominated the earth's vegetation in the following 30 million years. There are reckoned to be now over 250,000 species, three quarters of which are tropical. All trees are classified as flowering plants. Even conifers have primitive structures that resemble flowers and serve the same reproductive purpose.

Many garden trees are '**cultivars**'. This means in broad terms that they have been first produced by human selection from chance seedlings and have ever after been propagated vegetatively so that their individual characteristics are perpetuated rather than lost again in a genetic 'soup'. They may be grafted, layered, grown from cuttings or replicated from their tissues in a laboratory. It is as if a red-headed Scotsman could be selected and conveniently reproduced, a process now less distant if not yet imminent. A new vegetatively produced plant will furthermore begin flowering at an early age, unlike many seedlings which go through a lengthy juvenile stage. A twig on a flowering tree behaves in exactly the same way whether it remains on its parent or finds itself grafted on to an entirely new set of roots. It cannot know that its circumstances have changed. However, the lifespan of a vegetatively produced plant is likely to be shorter than that of a seedling.

Breeding new flowering trees has been practised for hundreds of years. There is always the prospect that two good trees crossed with each other under controlled conditions may produce an even better plant. It might have superior flowers, more (or less) vigorous growth, sweeter scent or greater resistance to disease. However, the production of spectacular new progeny without careful prior selection of the parents is an unusual occurrence. It does not often result from unmethodical or arbitrary seed collecting.

Within naturally occurring variations, rather than the human-induced, botanists recognise certain subdivisions of the actual **species**: notably **subspecies**, **varieties** and **forms**. These, representing successively less significant changes from the species' normal characteristics, are normally signalled in a scientific name by the abbreviations (not in italic type) subsp., var. and f. A **hybrid** between two different species (or less often genera) is indicated by the multiplication sign ×. Cultivars are accorded names with initial capitals, printed within single inverted commas, not in italic type.

Thus nurserymen's selections of the hybrid Black Italian Poplar have names such as *Populus* × *canadensis* 'Serotina'; and the shrubby northern populations of the European Bird Cherry are *Prunus padus* subsp. *borealis*. It is useful to remember that italic type is reserved for names of naturally occurring plants themselves rather than names of 'man-made' cultivars or of categories used by botanists to indicate relationships. Plant names are far from stable, and the complexities of scientific nomenclature mercifully beyond the scope of this brief introduction.

GARDENING WITH TREES

Trees in a garden give it permanence, depth and vertical interest. Unlike ground-hugging flower beds, which left alone will repeat themselves with only minor changes each year, trees develop character as they grow. Week by week and year by year, trees constantly change – in colour, form, light and shade, in trunk, branches, bark, shoots, foliage and flowers.

Of course, they also provide shelter from extremes of heat, cold and wind. They purify the air, protect and mulch the ground around them, extract soil moisture but reduce waterlogging, conserve warmth, harbour wild life and generally benefit everything living in their immediate vicinity: not just ourselves.

A long time is required for a tree to reach maturity, but not to grow. Trees in fact grow at the same rate as herbaceous garden plants, anything from 10cm to one metre each year according to the species and its age. A tree may stand in one place for 100 years and each year it will stack upon itself the equivalent of a whole new flower bed.

Planting such a phenomenal vegetable deserves more thought and planning than it is usually given. The first decision is the choice of species. With so many to choose from, start by eliminating those groups which you do not want, for instance very large, very small, non-flowering evergreens, conifers or poisonous trees. Those that are tender in the neighbourhood are seldom worth bothering with: sooner or later a cold winter will probably kill them. Conversely some alpine species cannot take too much heat. If your site is acid or alkaline, of course discount trees that like the opposite conditions. Check on the health of other people's trees nearby. See what grows well, then also call to mind all the other species in the same genus. Be positive about what you want from your tree; is it shade, colour, foliage texture, flowers, bark, fruit (decorative or edible), scent, shelter, conservation value (e.g. good for bees) or at what time of the year is it to be at its best?

Finally, having found a tree you like, try to be sure that you will still like it in the future when its size and shape is dramatically changed. Visualize it in 10 years time, or 20 or 50 years if you can. The kind of tree a garden can accommodate obviously depends on the space available, and walls, buildings, paths, roads, neighbours, light and windows must all be considered. Services under and above ground too: some species are adept at seeking out your leaky drains and poor foundations, will bring down your power cables or wreck your television reception. Areas close to doors and windows may not be the place for scented trees that attract biting or stinging insects, or become tenanted by unwanted roosting birds.

Some trees create unpleasant smells, cast too-dense shade, produce irritating seed fluff, drop copious squashy fruit or slippery dead leaves on your paths or sticky honey-dew on your car. Then they may be blown down or struck by lightning. As a rule it is not wise to plant a tree closer to a dwelling than 80% of its own ultimate height. On shrinkable clays the distance should be greater and species that sucker or

INTRODUCTION

have spreading roots should be avoided altogether. But the commonest error is simply planting too close to a house for comfort. Drive out of any town to see houses in the process of disappearing in their little thickset, self-made forests: in 100 years they will be invisible, perhaps unreachable.

Changing the view. If the above has not put you off altogether, remember that any large established tree will mightily obstruct a view. If the view is to be retained, then either the tree should not be planted there, or as it grows its lower branches should be progressively cut off to reveal the view again. (This can actually be attractive: enhancing a view by framing it. Blue sky always appears more intense when seen next to green foliage.) True, sometimes the object of planting a tree is positively to obstruct an unpleasant view. The view then becomes the tree itself.

Now consider the lighting. For example, brown autumn leaves look muddy and dull lit from the front, but can be transformed to gold when back-lit. White blossom all but disappears when back-lit but shines out when lit from the front. Trees with large or two-coloured leaves show off their foliage well with side light. The best way to determine a tree's 'best side' is to walk right round an existing specimen on a sunny day and see the different effects for yourself.

Shade is another obvious factor. Observe the path of the sun round your garden and calculate how far and in which direction at different times of day a new tree would cast its shade. Garden flowers below a tree will usually be concentrated on its sunny side, with the tree planted on the shady side of a border.

PLANTING A TREE

The hole. Digging the hole to plant a tree is your only opportunity to cultivate and improve a piece of ground that will not be touched again for a very long time. It is well worth taking extra trouble to do it properly. Your tree will grow much better from the start and for a long time after. Don't attempt the job until the weather and the season are right. Choose an overcast day in the dormant season with no wind and no risk of frost. If something unexpected appears in the hole, such as water, stop. Look again at your design and try somewhere else nearby.

The most important factor is certainly not fertilising (see below) but the size of the hole. The more broken-up congenial soil around the roots, the less resistance to their rapid growth and the more oxygen available to them. This is true however large or small your tree may be. The hole must be substantially larger than the root-ball of your plant. None of the ordinary roots should need bending to fit them in – though excessively long side roots can be cut back to a sensible length. The tree should also be planted on the same day that the hole is dug. Leaving a hole open in sun, rain or frost changes the soil structure and kills organisms in the immediate vicinity, many of which might have been beneficial to the tree. On heavy soils, surface drainage away from the pit may be needed to save the refilled hole from filling with rain-water. Double digging outwards from below the site is often enough to avoid this.

Staking. If a wooden tree stake is to be used, drive it in to the bottom of the empty hole on the windward side in exposed situations. But in a sheltered garden the stake can be placed behind the tree if it will be mainly viewed from one direction. If many trees are planted together it does look better if all the stakes are on the same side. Stakes that have not been pressure-treated with preservative may not last for long and they can carry diseases such as honey fungus. Do not cut the stake to its final length until the tree is planted.

Planting. The tree, which should have remained in its packing, or its pot, in the shade, can now be inspected. Trim off any damaged shoots with sharp secateurs and inspect for signs of disease. Unpack the root ball, even from a so-called biodegradable container, and cut any damaged roots off cleanly. Pull out any roots that are coiled around the rest. Either make them point outwards or cut them off. Replace some of the excavated soil to form a mound in the bottom of the pit. Build this up until the tree, when placed on the top of it, will have its root collar level with the natural surface of the ground. As quickly as possible begin to fill the hole. Shake the tree occasionally and press the soil *gently* round the roots to expel air. Do not skin the roots or compress the soil by treading or pressing too hard.

Good natural topsoil should go into the hole, *without adding peat or any other organic material*. This is almost as important, and as disregarded, as digging a big enough hole. The point is that the decomposition of organic material changes the nature of the soil near the roots. It can cause anaerobic conditions by holding excess moisture and restricting soil air movement. It can reduce the supply of oxygen to the roots through its own oxidation as it decomposes; and of nitrogen as the population of micro-organisms (which absorb nitrogen) is increased to break down the organic material. Farmyard manure can also encourage diseases and weed seeds. Generally speaking, fertilizers can encourage strong competitive weed growth and promote top growth of the plant. This leads to root/shoot imbalance and then shoot tip death as the tree struggles to redress the equilibrium which is essential for its sustained growth.

So leave the tree well alone without dosing its immediate soil with anything. Only on notably infertile sites may a little slow-acting manure such as bonemeal be acceptable. Otherwise give any feeding as a mulch in a few years time when the tree has established a new root-system. But mulching with some inert substance, such as bark chips so long as they have been well composted, or indeed black plastic, can help greatly from the start, both in retaining moisture and suppressing weeds.

Lastly, do not tie too rigidly to the stake. It is good for stem diameter growth if the plant can flex in the wind. If the plant is small enough to have a flexible stem no stake should be needed and the tree will be better for that. Rigidly tied plants do less well.

PLANT COLLECTORS

Even in prehistoric times, men took useful plants with them when moving around the world. We know, for example, that the English Elm was brought to England from eastern Europe by neolithic farmers. The Romans introduced many trees, such as wild cherries from Asia, first to Rome and then to outlying regions of their empire, and extended the range of many European species, especially those with edible fruits such as Sweet Chestnut and the Stone Pine – which until recently was wrongly thought not to have reached Britain until the sixteenth century.

Before the mid eighteenth century and the foundation of all modern naming by the great Swedish naturalist Carl von Linné, the naming of trees was often confused. Furthermore, little attention was paid to their provenance, so that the first seed to be sent back to Europe was thought to be typical of the species. Even today new kinds of some trees are still being discovered which contradict accepted ideas of their form.

The eighteenth century, however, saw the rise of serious botanical collecting in remote countries, often by doctors, missionaries or soldiers. At first the chances of bringing even dry seeds back safely were slim. Journeys took months, storms soaked packets in salt water, ships were sunk, inhabitants were wary or hostile. One of the first successful European collectors had been Englebert Kaempfer (1651-1715) a German doctor who visited Japan around 1689 with the Dutch East India Company. Although not allowed to collect plants by the Imperial Japanese Court he occasionally managed to hide seeds in his handkerchief. Two of these were Ginkgo and the Japanese Larch which bears his name – *Larix kaempferi*, and he also brought back the first Japanese Flowering Cherries. It was 85 years before anyone else went plant-hunting in Japan.

By 1700 other expeditions had been bringing back trees from Asia, Turkey and the Middle East, such as Cedar of Lebanon, Manna Ash, Cork Oak, Syrian Juniper. John Tradescant the elder, gardener to Charles I, brought back European Larch from Russia – although it had always been a native tree in most of mainland Europe. In 1698 James Cunningham, a Scottish botanist and surgeon, had travelled to China, collected Japanese Cedar and Chinese Fir, surviving revolutions, massacres and thefts, but died on his way home in 1709.

Meanwhile Tradescant's son (another John) began to collect and introduce trees from America, including Black Locust, Tulip Tree and Swamp Cypress. Henry Compton (1632-1713), Bishop of London, began his own arboretum at Fulham Palace, sending missionaries out to America to convert the native Indians and at the same time to look out for exotic trees and collect seeds wherever they could. Peter Collinson, a London linen merchant in collaboration with an American botanist, John Bartram (1699-1777), discovered and introduced most of the remaining tree flora from the Great Lakes to Georgia. In return, he introduced Cedar of Lebanon and Horse Chestnut to America.

Throughout the eighteenth century the flood of new plants increased. The French were very successful in China, trading skills such as glass-blowing, engineering and clock-making for permission to explore and collect. Father Pierre d'Incarville, working for the Jardin des Plantes in Paris, remained in China for 15 years.

The Dutch were successful in Japan, mostly trading through the Dutch East India Company. Captain Cook sailed from Britain to Australia and Francis Mason began collecting in South Africa. William Roxburgh travelled in India and French botanists began to explore Peru. European gardeners had developed a passion for exotic plants and the commercial boom stimulated research much as it does today.

The momentum increased in the nineteenth century. Nurserymen began to fund special expeditions. John Gould Veitch (1839-1870) went to Japan in 1860 for the Veitch Nurseries in England, organizing teams of native collectors, but died aged only 31 on his way back from Australia and Pacific Islands. The next Veitch Nurseries collector in the Far East was the famous Ernest Wilson, the greatest collector of them all. He was funded by the Arnold Arboretum in America but his plants were distributed to botanic gardens world-wide. In 1902 he returned home with 305 new Chinese plants including Paper-bark Maple and the Dove (or Handkerchief) Tree.

In America the search was now on for commercial forest trees. The leader in this field was David Douglas (1799-1834) a truly intrepid Scottish explorer. His epic trip in 1824 was to the Pacific coast and Rocky Mountains, where he collected around 500 specimens, though harassed by hostile Indians and enduring injuries and great hardship. After discovering huge trees such as Sugar Pine, in 1827 he travelled on into Canada. By the time he returned to England via Hudson Bay he had collected 210 more plants, including Douglas Fir and Sitka Spruce. On his next trip to Western America in 1830 he sent home another 670 new plants, including Monterey Pine from California and Mexico, and by 1833 he was in Hawaii. But here he came to a sad end. After several expeditions to the island's volcanic mountains he fell into a bull pit and was gored to death by a wild bull already caught in it.

The twentieth century saw continual work by breeders in hybridising and in selecting cultivars from seedlings of those trees which tend towards variation in these ways. This is found very much more in some trees than in others. For example, there are now over 500 named varieties of Lawson Cypress on the market, and an endless profusion of new types of cherries and of other trees of the rose family. The Black Mulberry, on the other hand, appears to have resisted change altogether. Over many centuries, it has shown no appreciable variation at all. The Tree of Heaven is another single type. But breeders naturally concentrate on trees important in forestry, horticulture, or for their valuable fruits or timber.

Perhaps surprisingly, a great many new trees able to survive our temperate-zone winters still await discovery, the more so with global warming. Collecting in Mexico and down the length of South America has a long way to go. In the southern hemisphere and throughout the tropics wherever altitude produces temperate conditions, there are riches to be found.

TREES FOR PROBLEM SITES OR SPECIAL NEEDS

CLAY SOILS
Aesculus indica Indian Horse Chestnut
Alnus incana Grey Alder
Carpinus betulus Hornbeam
Crataegus laevigata 'Paul's Scarlet' Hawthorn
Eucalyptus gunnii Cider Gum
Fraxinus excelsior Ash
Populus nigra Black Poplar
Salix alba White Willow
Catalpa bignonioides Indian Bean Tree
Platanus orientalis Oriental Plane

VERY WET GROUND
Quercus palustris Pin Oak
Salix alba White Willow
Alnus species Alders
Populus tremula Aspen
Populus × canadensis Hybrid Black Poplar
Betula nigra River Birch
Pterocarya fraxinifolia Caucasian Wingnut
Fraxinus pennsylvanica Green Ash
Nyssa aquatica Water Tupelo
Eucalyptus glaucescens Tingiringi Gum

SEASIDE CONDITIONS
Acer pseudoplatanus Sycamore
Eucalyptus gunnii Cider Gum
Eucalyptus pauciflora subsp. *niphophila* Snow Gum
Prunus spinosa Blackthorn
Laurus nobilis Sweet Bay
Phillyrea latifolia Phillyrea
Populus alba White Poplar
Tamarix (all kinds)
Quercus ilex Holm Oak
Hippophae rhamnoides Sea Buckthorn

ACID SOILS
Arbutus menziesii Madrona
Oxydendrum arboreum Sorrel Tree
Halesia carolina Snowdrop Tree
Quercus petraea Sessile Oak
Magnolia denudata Lily Tree
Eucryphia × nymansensis
Abies concolor Colorado White Fir
Abies pinsapo Spanish Fir
Castanea sativa Sweet Chestnut
Fitzroya cupressoides Patagonian Cypress

DRY SOILS
Ailanthus altissima Tree of Heaven
Betula pendula Silver Birch
Castanea sativa Sweet Chestnut
Cercis siliquastrum Judas Tree
Gleditsia triacanthos Honey Locust
Robinia pseudoacacia Black Locust
Tamarix (all)
Cupressus glabra Smooth Arizona Cypress
Pinus nigra Black Pine
Fraxinus texensis Texas Ash

POOR SOILS, LANDFILL etc.
Populus × canescens Grey Poplar
Quercus cerris Turkey Oak
Alnus incana Grey Alder
Sambucus nigra Elder
Robinia pseudoacacia Black Locust
Populus tremula Aspen
Betula pubescens White Birch
Prunus avium Wild Cherry
Ailanthus altissima Tree of Heaven
Alnus cordata Italian Alder

LIME RICH SOILS
Acer campestre Field Maple
Buxus sempervirens Box
Sorbus aria Whitebeam
Cornus mas Cornelian Cherry
Taxus baccata Yew
Morus nigra Black Mulberry
Fraxinus ornus Manna Ash
Fagus sylvatica Beech
Juniperus communis Juniper
Carpinus betulus Hornbeam

COLD EXPOSED PLACES
Acer pseudoplatanus Sycamore
Betula pubescens White Birch
Hippophae rhamnoides Sea Buckthorn
Salix daphnoides Violet Willow
Larix kaempferi Japanese Larch
Picea abies Norway Spruce
Pinus sylvestris Scots Pine
Sorbus intermedia Swedish Whitebeam
Abies lasiocarpa Alpine Fir
Populus tremula Aspen

WEEPING FOLIAGE
Alnus incana 'Pendula'
Salix × pendulina Weeping Willow
Betula pendula 'Youngii' Young's Weeping Birch
Fagus sylvatica 'Aurea Pendula' Golden Weeping Beech
Fagus sylvatica 'Pendula' Weeping Beech
Fagus sylvatica 'Purpurea Pendula' Weeping Copper Beech
Pyrus salicifolia 'Pendula' Weeping Willow-leaved Pear
Prunus subhirtella 'Pendula'
Fraxinus excelsior 'Pendula' Weeping Ash
Ilex aquifolium 'Pendula' Weeping Holly

UPRIGHT TREES
Ginkgo biloba 'Sentry'
Carpinus betulus 'Fastigiata'
Fagus sylvatica 'Dawyck' Dawyck Beech
Populus nigra subsp. *afghanica*
Juniperus communis 'Hibernica' Irish Juniper

INTRODUCTION

UPRIGHT TREES (contd.)

Cupressus sempervirens 'Green Pencil'
Tilia cordata 'Greenspire'
Pyrus calleryana 'Chanticleer'
Chamaecyparis lawsoniana 'Stricta'
Betula pendula 'Obelisk'

FOR INTERESTING BARK

Zelkova serrata Keaki
Quercus suber Cork Oak
Acer griseum Paper Bark Maple
Arbutus andrachne Greek Strawberry Tree
Betula utilis var. *jacquemontii*
Betula albo-sinensis var. *septentrionalis*
Eucalyptus pauciflora subsp. *niphophila* Snow Gum
Platanus orientalis Oriental Plane
Prunus serrula Tibetan Cherry
Pinus bungeana Lace-bark Pine

FOR ATTRACTIVE SHOOTS

Salix × 'Basfordiana'
Salix daphnoides Violet Willow
Salix alba 'Vitellina' Golden Willow
Acer pennsylvanicum 'Erythrocladum' Red Moosewood
Tilia platyphyllos 'Rubra' Red-twigged Lime
Fraxinus excelsior 'Jaspidea'
Corylus avellana 'Contorta' Corkscrew Hazel
Salix babylonica 'Matsudana Tortuosa' Corkscrew Willow
Acer palmatum 'Sangokaku' (Senkaki) Coral-barked Maple
Acer 'Silver Vein' Snake-bark Maple

FOR GOOD AUTUMN COLOUR

Taxodium distichum Swamp Cypress
Betula neoalaskana Yukon White Birch
Quercus coccinea 'Splendens' Scarlet Oak cv.
Liriodendron tulipifera Tulip Tree
Cercidiphyllum japonicum Katsura Tree
Liquidambar styraciflua Sweet Gum
Parrotia persica Persian Ironwood
Sorbus commixta 'Jermyns' Japanese Rowan cv.
Pyrus calleryana 'Bradford'
Acer japonicum 'Vitifolium' Vine-leaved Japanese Maple
Acer palmatum 'Osakazuki'

FOR GOOD FLOWERS

Salix daphnoides 'Aglaia'
Magnolia × *soulangiana* cvs.
Magnolia wilsonii Wilson's Magnolia
Liriodendron tulipifera Tulip Tree
Sorbus sargentiana Sargent's Rowan
Malus 'Magdeburgensis'
Prunus padus 'Colorata'
Prunus sargentii Sargent's Cherry
Prunus lannesiana 'Sarasa'
Prunus 'Tai-haku' Great White Cherry of Japan

FOR ORNAMENTAL FRUIT

Malus hupehensis
Abies koreana Korean Fir
Corylus maxima 'Purpurea' Purple Filbert
Maclura pomifera Osage Orange
Broussonetia papyrifera Paper Mulberry
Ficus carica Fig
Mespilus germanica Medlar
Cydonia oblonga Quince
Crataegus crus-galli Cockspur Thorn
Sorbus cashmiriana Kashmir Rowan

ORNAMENTAL CONIFERS

Ginkgo biloba Maidenhair Tree
Cupressus glabra Smooth Arizona Cypress
Juniperus drupacea Syrian Juniper
Metasequoia glyptostroboides Dawn Redwood
Athrotaxis selaginoides King William Pine
Abies veitchii Veitch's Silver Fir
Abies concolor 'Candicans' Colorado White Fir cv.
Pseudolarix amabilis Golden Larch
Picea pungens 'Koster' Koster's Blue Spruce
Pinus sylvestris subsp. *scotica* Scots Pine

UNUSUAL GARDEN TREES

Aesculus pavia Red Buckeye
Tilia kiusiana
Acer griseum Paper Bark Maple
Koelreuteria paniculata Golden Rain Tree
Betula grossa Japanese Cherry Birch
Nothofagus antarctica Antarctic Southern Beech
Fagus sylvatica 'Aurea Pendula' Golden Weeping Beech
Magnolia liliiflora
Eucommia ulmoides Gutta-percha Tree
Crataegus laciniata Oriental Thorn

CHOICE EVERGREENS

Araucaria araucana Monkey Puzzle
Nothofagus betuloides Oval-leaved Southern Beech
Quercus myrsinifolia Bamboo-leaved Oak
Quercus ilex Holm Oak
Quercus canariensis Mirbeck Oak
Magnolia grandiflora 'Exmouth'
Laurus nobilis Sweet Bay
Umbellularia californica Californian Laurel
Prunus lusitanica Portugal Laurel
Buxus balearica Balearic Islands Box

TOWN STREETS

Catalpa ovata Yellow Catalpa
Acer platanoides 'Crimson Sentry'
Acer platanoides 'Elsrijk'
Ligustrum lucidum Chinese Privet
Betula lenta Cherry Birch
Corylus colurna Turkish Hazel
Quercus × *turneri* Turner's Oak
Sorbus × *thuringiaca* 'Fastigiata'
Robinia pseudoacacia 'Bessoniana'
Gleditsia triacanthos 'Sunburst' Golden Honey Locust

TEXT NOTES

Throughout the book, notes are included at the end of each description. They apply to the principal species or form described, rather than to any cultivars or other subsidiary forms – such selections being usually made for their *un*typical characteristics.

Height generally attained is indicated by 3 figures: the heights (in metres) that the tree may be expected to reach in 10 years, in 20 years, and eventually. They assume a healthy isolated specimen, growing in its appropriate conditions and climatic range. They are *not* necessarily the heights reached by a tree in its natural habitat: some alpine species, for example, will be stunted and smaller where found in the wild, while some forest trees will be drawn up to great heights – much taller than cultivated plants would achieve. The initial 10 year measurement also assumes a good planting or re-planting, with minimal check on growing: subsequent growth may also be influenced by untoward stress or change of environment, for example by the sudden removal of adjacent shelter.

Hardiness. Cold tolerance is suggested by a percentage, from zero tolerance of frost (0%) at freezing point to effectively total resistance (100%) at -40°C or -40°F. We chose 40° because this is the one point at which the Celsius and Fahrenheit scales obligingly 'cross', and a degree of cold which no garden tree is ever likely to suffer.

For the mathematical, $(-40 - 32) \times 5/9 = -40$. And $(-40 \times 9/5) + 32 = -40$.

For the gardener, if a tree will take -40° below freezing, it will take anything (certainly more than he or she can). These figures are only indications: the approximate minimum temperatures (including wind chill) that a cultivated tree will tolerate without sustaining lasting damage. But the provenance of seed can have a considerable effect on the ability to withstand cold, as also may unseasonal weather conditions: in cultivation even the hardiest alpine or Arctic species may be seriously damaged by a late spring frost.

Degrees C	Hardiness	Degrees F
-40	100%	-40
-36	90%	-33
-32	80%	-26
-28	70%	-18
-24	60%	-11
-20	50%	-4
-16	40%	+3
-12	30%	+10
-8	20%	+18
-4	10%	+25
0	0%	+32

Choice. A tree's garden value is indicated by figures referring to four categories of usefulness below, from the most desirable to the least. But these are only personal assessments, and tastes differ. Some people find the foliage of copper beeches or cherries detestable, gloomy drainers of light. Others like them for their warmth or contrast. Moreover, in choosing a tree for any site or purpose, we should never forget its suitability for the soil and situation, its eventual height, root-spread, shade thrown and effect on the view.

1. Excellent. Among the finest trees for ornament – with perhaps also some special practical value.
2. Good. Trees which are less decorative, but still have some particular use, such as for shade from sun, shelter from wind, urban screening from noise, dust or ugly sights, or for planting on derelict and re-formed sites.
3. Of lesser garden merit. But these may be good trees for offering food and shelter for wild life. Others may be interesting for their rarity or age, or for providing non-wood benefits such as bark products (cork), oils, nuts, food, tannins, cosmetics, forage (for domestic livestock, silkworms etc.) or medicines.
4. Not recommended for gardens, for reasons such as:
    * Susceptibility to disease.
    * Invasive tendencies, suckering habits or very extensive roots.
    * Unpleasant characteristics (smell, irritant, poisonous foliage or fruit, the fallen leaves, fruits or aphids' honeydew a nuisance).
    * Potentially dangerous, as for instance from dropping branches.
    * Not sufficiently well tried or unpredictable in cultivation.
    * – or even extreme dullness.

    Though here again a tree in this category may have some redeeming feature, such as bearing edible seeds.

Wood. Five categories are suggested, again from 1 as the best:

1. High quality wood for cabinet making, veneers and decorative work.
2. Good structural timber, for domestic or industrial use, including sea defences, construction, piling, boat-building.
3. Less valuable timber, but good for fencing, gates, garden and other non-structural use, pallets and packaging.
4. Wood used in making fibre-board, particle board, hardboard or paper pulp.
5. Inferior wood but used for fuel.

When no mention is made of the wood, this may be because its particular merits have been described in the text, or because the wood has no particular use to cite, not even as fuel; or because the tree remains too small in size for its wood to be of any consequence.

GINKGO FAMILY · Ginkgoaceae

Maidenhair Tree *Ginkgo biloba*

This is the only surviving species of the plant order Ginkgoales, which dominated the tree flora of the world 150-200 million years ago. When first brought to the west from a cultivated source in China in 1689 it was thought to be extinct as a wild plant. Subsequently limited numbers have been found growing naturally in Zhejian and Guizhou provinces in eastern China. Wild examples of Ginkgo are believed to have occurred in Europe before the current ice ages.

This is a rather gaunt spiky tree capable of growing to 40m in height but generally achieving much less. It is deciduous with 7cm leaves shaped like duck's feet: ya-chou-tze (duck's foot) is a Chinese name for it. The bark is corky, ridged and light earthy grey-brown. Male and female flowers occur on separate trees, the males consisting of 2-3cm solitary drooping yellowish-green catkins which grow in the leaf axils. Females also occur in the leaf axils but each one has a long, 4-5cm, thickened stalk. These primitive solitary flowers, which in the strict botanical sense are not true flowers at all, are pollinated by a self-propelling (motile) sperm. This is thought to have disadvantaged the family in the evolutionary competition with conifers and almost brought Ginkgoaceae to extinction. The fruits are plum-like and edible, but with an unpleasant smell. Seeds germinate well and transplant easily.

Ginkgo is highly valued as a town tree: in America it is grown as a pollution resistant city shade tree from Montreal to New Orleans, a huge geographic and climatic range. The brilliant golden autumn foliage colour is greatly appreciated, and the curious leaves. In recent years there has been a revival of interest in the medicinal uses for Ginkgo, known to the Chinese for centuries.

The upright form sometimes known in the trade as '**Sentry**' can actually be one of several named or unnamed clones. Once established upright specimens tend to develop occasional long horizontal or sharply angled branches which may spoil the effect.

The pretty French clone '**Variegata**' originated in 1854. Unfortunately it is female and likely to produce obnoxious smelling fruit. Odd leaves with some yellow stripe variegation frequently occur on individual branches, particularly during a hot dry summer. There is also an insignificant weeping form, 'Pendula', first cultivated in 1855. It is seldom over 3m tall and requires constant pruning and training to keep it in shape.

Growth: 2-5-25. Hardiness: 60-70%. Choice: 2, 4.

'**Variegata**'   autumn leaves   fruit

YEW FAMILY • Taxaceae

Common Yew *Taxus baccata*

Although called 'Common' this tree only occurs naturally in parts of Europe and Asia Minor, and it is only locally common in the wild. In America and south-east Asia it is replaced by other species. It tolerates a wide range of soils and climatic conditions, including chalk and limestone in very dry areas. This is a long-lived tree, especially where vigour is limited by inhospitable conditions: specimens are sometimes measured in thousands of years. On religious sites ancient trees usually pre-date the current theological use and are often older than the existing buildings. A dense, compact evergreen, it will tolerate shade and grows perfectly well under the canopy of large deciduous forest trees. Although generally small and spreading, trees sometimes exceed 20m in height. Yew foliage and bark are poisonous to most domestic livestock and to people, dried needles are very toxic. Trees are normally dioecious with separate male and female trees, however occasionally a single branch of the opposite sex to the rest of the tree may be randomly produced.

There are many cultivated forms, some of which are difficult to distinguish. '**Lutea**' (see also p. 27) is obvious when in fruit, it has yellow berries and is probably the same thing as 'Xanthocarpa' which was produced some time later (1864) in Germany. '**Aurea**' the Golden Yew, is a yellow-needled form first cultivated in 1866 but many selections have been made since then so this name now refers to several similar-looking clones.

The Irish Yew '**Fastigiata**', found in County Fermanagh in 1780, is a familiar sombre green, upright tree favoured in cemeteries. The original was a female tree but since 1927 males have appeared in cultivation. Seed can not be relied upon to come true to type. Irish Yews seldom exceed 7m in height and gradually thicken to around 5m wide. At which point, or before, snow often breaks off occasional boughs. The golden form '**Fastigiata Aurea**' (also illustrated on p. 24) occurred at least twice, firstly in 1868 in France and then in 1875 in Britain. A very much brighter yellow form, '**Fastigiata Aureomarginata**', produced in Sheffield in 1881, is now preferred in the nursery trade. All of the fastigiate yews have probably arisen from the original Irish Yew of 1780.

Growth: 2-4-20. Hardiness: 60-70%. Choice: 2, 3, 4. Wood: 1, 3.

'Aurea'   'Fastigiata Aurea'   'Fastigiata'

Taxus baccata cultivars

There are over 200 forms of *Taxus baccata* listed in the World Conifer Data Pool (1993), though many have now invalid names or are no longer in cultivation. This bewildering diversity comes from yews being dioecious – either male or female – and therefore necessarily crossing with another plant to set seed.

The Westfelton Yew, *Taxus baccata* '**Dovastoniana**' discovered in Shropshire in 1777 by John Dovaston, is a distinctive small tree. Although it has a straight vertical stem its wide spreading branches often make it broader than it is high. The branchlets are pendulous but rather sparse.

The golden form '**Dovastonii Aurea**' was raised in France and named in 1868. It is similar to the Westfelton tree but produces orange-yellow growth in the spring. This recedes to the margins of the needles and fades to dull yellow in the summer.

The unmistakable short-needled form of yew '**Adpressa**' is a dense female tree up to 10m tall. The foliage resembles that of Tsuga (p. 195) and consists of blunt ended deep green needles between 5 and 10mm long. They usually form two ranks along the shoot facing upwards towards the light. 'Brevifolia', as it was called, was first cultivated in 1828 at Chester. It was eventually renamed 'Adpressa' in 1850 so avoiding confusion with the American species *Taxus brevifolia*. Inevitably there is a yellow-leaved form 'Adpressa Aurea' raised in 1885 and a variegated form '**Adpressa Variegata**' described in 1866.

A female seedling of Golden Yew was raised by William Barron in Derby, and called '**Barronii**' in 1868. It is a particularly striking golden bushy plant. The foliage colour has a bronze tint when it is young. Branches and twigs are short and dense and tend to grow sideways rather more than upwards.
Growth: 2-4-12. Hardiness: 60%. Choice: 1, 4.

Taxus × *hunnewelliana*

This hybrid between Canadian Yew (p. 28) and Japanese Yew (p. 28) has been repeated many times to produce new hardy ornamental plants. The cold resistance and compact form of Canadian Yew results in improved progeny from the Japanese plant and its numerous cultivars. The original cross is believed to have been made at the Hunnewell Pinetum in Massachusetts. It was described in 1925 by Alfred Rehder.
Growth: 2-5-24. Hardiness: 60%. Choice: 1, 4.

'Barronii'   'Barronii'

Taxus baccata cultivars

'**Aureovariegata**'
Each year's growth starts green but then develops yellow-edged needles. Britain, 1865.

'**Semperaurea**'
(see below)

The Fulham yew '**Erecta**'
A female seedling from 'Fastigiata', the Irish Yew (p. 23), in 1838.

'**Summergold**'
Just as bright as 'Semperaurea' but more of a low spreading bush. Holland, 1968.

'**Semperaurea**' has golden-yellow foliage from the beginning of the season but shaded needles turn green. Male. Britain, before 1908.

'**Standishii**'
Slow-growing and less brightly-coloured but with very dense foliage. Female. Britain, 1908.

YEWS

A distinctive large form '**Glauca**' with slightly bloomed blue-green foliage at first. Britain, 1855.

'**Aldenhamensis**' a rare cultivar producing clear yellow young growths. One of many similar golden cultivars. Many of these burn when planted in full sun. Britain, 1926.

'**Rushmore**' Needles stunted and short and the whole plant is never more than a low spreading bush. Britain, 1978.

'**Lutea**' see p. 23

'**Neidpathensis**' An attractive male form. It has graceful shoots and relatively long needles. Male. The original plant was found in the grounds of Neidpath Castle in Scotland in the 1850s.

'**Paulina**', or 'Cheshuntensis' Twisted shoots and curved needles. A good hedging plant. Britain, 1923.

Japanese Yew *Taxus cuspidata*. A very hardy species introduced to the west by Robert Fortune in 1855. It now has 90 named forms, and over 130 hybrids with Common Yew. *Growth: 1-2-8. Hardiness: 70%. Choice: 2, 4.*

Taxus × media '**Hatfieldii**' commemorates T. D. Hatfield who first made the cross in Massachusetts. This 1923 cultivar is a compact upright male plant with green needles.

Chinese Yew *Taxus chinensis*. This species is taxonomically uncertain. Some authorities called it *Taxus celebica* but others include up to six obscure species in the Chinese Yew group. Occasionally planted as a curiosity but not notably ornamental.
Growth: 1-2-8. Hardiness: 60%. Choice: 2, 4.

Canadian Yew *Taxus canadensis*. This extremely hardy bush is monoecious, which is unusual in yews. Seldom over 1.8m and hardly more than prostrate in its natural habitat. The French cultivar '**Variegata**' has white needles at first, becoming yellow and finally green by the end of the summer.
Growth: 1-1-2. Hardiness: 80%. Choice: 3, 4.

YEWS

The rare cultivar *Taxus × media* '**Skalborg**' is of Swedish origin but was raised in Denmark and named in 1956.

Himalayan Yew *Taxus wallichiana*. Closely related to Common Yew, this small tree occurs in the Himalayas from Afghanistan to Sikkim. Except for its strongly pointed needles it is very difficult to distinguish from Common Yew.
Growth: 2-4-16. Hardiness: 60%. Choice: 4.

Taxus × media '**Hicksii**'. A female American shrubby tree raised in 1923. It has dark glossy green needles on sinuous shoots making it an ideal evergreen hedging plant.
Growth: 1-2-4. Hardiness: 60%. Choice: 2, 4.

'Sargentii'

fruit

Taxus × media '**Sargentii**' is another erect tree, female, selected at the Arnold Arboretum.

The Kelsey Yew, *Taxus × media* '**Kelseyi**', or 'Kelsey's Upright', is a bushy female plant from America which fruits abundantly, its popular name is Kelsey Berrybush.

Hybrid Yew *Taxus × media*. The cross between Japanese and Common Yew first took place at the Hunnewell Pinetum in Massachusetts around 1900. Many of the resulting cultivars are so close that identification is only possible when detailed historical notes are available.
Growth: variable. Hardiness: 60%. Choice: 1, 2, 4.

NUTMEGS

Californian Nutmeg *Torreya californica*

There is no connection between this tree and the spice nutmeg (*Myristica fragrans*). *Torreya* is a member of the yew family. The fruits, however, usually produced on separate female trees, do bear some resemblance to the culinary nutmeg. After two years they are 3-4cm long with a green fleshy outer husk and a hard ridged yellowish-brown core. They smell rather unpleasant. This is a fairly large tree usually with a straightish single stem and a conical outline. The branches of older trees spread widely like a Yew (*Taxus*). American Indians used the flexible strong wood to make bows. Rigid evergreen needles up to 7cm long with sharp points occur mostly in two ranks facing up to the light. The foliage is reminiscent of some long-needled Silver Fir species (*Abies*). Mountain and coastal valleys in central and northern California are the natural range of this species. On the western side of the Sierra Nevada it extends to over 1800m mostly in mixed coniferous forest. William Lobb brought the species to Europe in 1851 and it was described in 1854. It is a fine specimen tree in cultivation and it tolerates chalky soils very well.
Growth: 2-5-20. Hardiness: 60%. Choice: 1, 4.
Wood: 1, 3.

Japanese Nutmeg *Torreya nucifera*

From Japan this 6-14m tree (in cultivation) differs only slightly from Californian Nutmeg. It is smaller in virtually all its parts. The needles are only 3cm long and the fruits are a little over 2cm long. Crushed foliage and fruits have the same rather unpleasant resinous smell as the Californian Nutmeg. Cultivated plants often flatten out and spread in preference to growing upwards. Native trees in Japan are more shapely (as illustrated) and can attain 25m in height. The physician and plant hunter Englebert Kaempfer discovered this plant in 1712. It was introduced to Europe in 1764 but not finally named until 1846.
Growth: 1-3-14. Hardiness: 50-60%. Choice: 3, 4.
Wood: 1, 3.

Torreya grandis

Similar in most respects to Japanese Nutmeg this 25m tree from eastern China was introduced to Europe by Robert Fortune in 1855 and described and named by him two years later. It is rare and often stunted in cultivation, with yellowish-green needles. The disagreeable smell of Japanese and Californian Nutmeg trees is absent.
Growth: 1-2-8 (25 in native region). Hardiness: 30-40%. Choice: 4.

Torreya grandis   **Japanese Nutmeg**   underside

PLUM YEW FAMILY · Cephalotaxaceae

Plum Yew *Cephalotaxus harringtonia*

The Plum Yews have opposite shoots and dense spirally arranged spined needles which form two ranks on side shoots facing upwards. There are two glaucous-grey bands of stomata on the underside and a keeled midrib on the upper side of each needle. Male and female flowers usually occur on separate trees. The brown fruits are around 2.5cm long and shaped like a nutmeg. They take two years to reach maturity. The origin of this plant is unknown. Most authorities suggest it came from China but it has been in cultivation in Japan for centuries. It was originally named *Cephalotaxus pedunculata* and introduced to the west in 1829. The present name was published in 1873.

The variety *Cephalotaxus harringtonia* var. *drupacea* "Cow's Tail Pine" is an interesting plant from Japan and central China. It is a compact shrub in cultivation with dense foliage. Originally it was considered to be a species, and *harringtonia*, then called *pedunculata*, was a variety of it. The Chinese form was also given separate variety status. So too was *nana*, now *harringtonia* **var. nana**, a suckering bush cultivated in Japan and introduced to Europe in 1830, a year after **var. *drupacea***.

The upright form '**Fastigiata**' has strongly ascending branches and spirally arranged upward facing needles. It has long been cultivated as an ornament in Japan and was introduced to Europe in 1830 as a variety of *Cephalotaxus drupacea*. Only in 1913 was its present cultivar designation allocated to it.
Growth: 1-2-9. Hardiness: 50%. Choice: 1, 2.

Chinese Plum Yew *Cephalotaxus fortunei*

Robert Fortune introduced this large open shrub from China in 1849 and it is named in his honour. However, the plant's status and name are still being challenged by some taxonomists. In the wild it may reach 10m in height, but it is seldom restricted to a single stem. The long 6-8cm pointed needles are spread horizontally in two ranks. Ovoid 2.5cm fruits ripen to bloomed purplish-brown after two years. This is a very hardy plant though with little decorative appeal. In European gardens it thrives best under partial shade of deciduous trees. The evergreen foliage appears to be more healthy out of strong sunlight. It is tolerant of dry soils but resents vigorous competition from other ground cover species.
Growth: 1-2-9. Hardiness: 50%. Choice: 4.

Chinese Plum Yew

HUON PINE FAMILY • Podocarpaceae

Plum-fruited Yew *Podocarpus andinus*

In 1978 the name of this plant was changed to *Prumnopitys andina* but there seems to be little support in the horticultural trade for this change. It is a small untidy tree similar to Common Yew (p. 23) except for the fruits. These are ovoid, 2cm long and yellowish-brown. It was introduced from Chile in 1860.
Growth: 2-5-15. Hardiness: 30-40%. Choice: 4. Wood: 5.

Willow-leaf Podocarp *Podocarpus salignus*

Wild plants in Chile are up to 20m tall, but in cultivation this size is hardly ever achieved. The glossy grey-green needles are 5-15cm long, slender and slightly twisted. They are held on drooping shoots. The ovoid fruits are around 8mm long. This tender plant was introduced in 1853.
Growth: 2-5-20. Hardiness: 20-30%. Choice: 4.

Acute-leaved Totara *Podocarpus acutifolius*

Also known as Needle-leaved Totara, this small New Zealand tree was described and named in 1873. In cultivation it is usually only a dense evergreen shrub with sharply pointed needles. A curiosity but certainly not a choice garden subject.
Growth: 1-2-4. Hardiness: 10%. Choice: 4.

Totara *Podocarpus totara*

In New Zealand this is a 30m tall tree but in Europe it is hardly ever as tall, requiring warmth and shelter. Totara is the local Maori name.
Growth: 2-5-15. Hardiness: 10%. Choice: 4. Wood: 2, 3, 4, 5.

Podocarpus hallii

A rare and tender plant from New Zealand, capable of growing to 20m in height; however, most cultivated specimens are shrubby bushes. The evergreen 3-5cm needles and the peeling bark are attractive.
Growth: 2-4-10. Hardiness: 10%. Choice: 4.

Large-leaved Podocarp *Podocarpus macrophyllus*

Grown on a moist acid site this is one of the most rewarding podocarps. It is from south-east Asia and fairly hardy. The distinctive bark, on stems up to 20m tall, is fissured and shreds vertically. The linear-lanceolate 8-12cm needles spiral round vigorous shoots. They are dark glossy-green above and dull pale yellowish-green on the underside. The fruits, 1cm long, are green, sometimes with a purplish cast on a fleshy purple receptacle reminiscent of a small acorn cup. The upright shrubby variety **maki** is popular in Japanese gardens.
Growth: 1-5-20. Hardiness: 60-80%. Choice: 1. Wood: 5.

Chilean Podocarp *Podocarpus nubigenus*

A slow-growing shrubby plant from Chile southwards to Patagonia, is moderately hardy in cultivation. The sharp-pointed densely-packed needles are 3-5cm long spirally arranged on strong shoots. The fruits are nut-like seeds held on a fleshy receptacle. The genus name is a reference to this, meaning literally (from the Greek) foot-fruit.
Growth: 1-2-4. Hardiness: 40%. Choice: 2.

Large-leaved Podocarp — underside

Chilean Podocarp

Totara old tree

Monkey Puzzle Tree

♀ flowers

♂ flowers

fruit

leaf detail

seed

Bunya-Bunya

old bark

Monkey Puzzle Tree

MONKEY PUZZLE FAMILY • Araucariaceae

Monkey Puzzle Tree *Araucaria araucana*

This species occupies a large natural range in Chile and Argentina. It grows in hill country, including volcanic slopes up to 1500m above sea level. On Llaima volcano natural regeneration of the burnt-out forest gets under way almost before the ground has cooled. Monkey Puzzle is now cultivated throughout the temperate world; it is a familiar sight in parks and gardens everywhere. Such trees seldom exceed 25m in height but native forest trees in the better parts of their natural range can reach 50m. The original introduction to Europe occurred soon after 1795. In that year Archibald Menzies raised a few plants on board ship from seed given to the Vancouver expedition as food by South American Indians. The most obvious feature of this tree is its outline. It always produces a single straight stem. The horizontal branches are sinuous and in distinct whorls, producing a dense evergreen dome of foliage. Often this is confined to the top of the tree as lower branches are shaded out and shed. The overlapping evergreen leaf scales are rigid and viciously spined, completely obscuring the shoot. The cones are the size of a coconut, male and female on separate trees. In three years they disintegrate on the tree and shed the heavy edible seeds.

Growth: 2-6-25. Hardiness: 60-70%. Choice: 1, 3. Wood: 1, 2, 3.

Norfolk Island Pine *Araucaria heterophylla*

This tender symmetrical tree, usually in cultivation as a pot plant with only juvenile foliage, can grow to over 40m in its native Norfolk Island in the Pacific. It has tiered branches on a persistently straight stem.

Growth: 2-4-8. Hardiness: 10%. Choice: 1.

Bunya-Bunya *Araucaria bidwillii*

This Australian tree is native near the coast of Queensland. It is similar to the Monkey Puzzle Tree except the 5-10cm leaf scales are set wider apart. The horizontal branches occur in distinct whorls up a stem that may reach 50m in height. The huge 30cm cones contain edible seeds much prized for centuries by the Aborigines.

Growth: -50 in native region. Hardiness: 0%. Choice: 1. Wood: 2.

Norfolk Island Pine old tree

fruit

juvenile foliage

Bunya-Bunya old tree

♀ flower   ♂ flowers

Incense Cedar

leaf detail

'Aureovariegata'

closed cone

open cone

Chilean Cedar
leaves enlarged

seed   seedling

Incense Cedars   young tree   **Chilean Cedar**   closed cone

CYPRESS FAMILY · Cupressaceae

Incense Cedar *Calocedrus decurrens*

From western Oregon south to Baja California this big, 46m tall, tree usually grows on cool mountain sides, often in a mixed coniferous forest habitat. In the south of its range it extends to over 2000m. Traditionally its aromatic wood was used to manufacture pencils. It is soft, straight and does not splinter. The foliage, which resembles Thuja (p. 83), is dense, resinous and deep glossy green. In cultivation, particularly when it is grown on dry sites, the outline of the tree remains very narrow. At Blenheim Palace near Oxford, for example, open grown trees have reached almost 30m in height with a crown width of little more than 4m. Incense cedar stems have red-brown bark reminiscent of Wellingtonia (p. 93) but unlike the redwoods it is not spongy.

A smaller variegated form, '**Aureovariegata**', was cultivated in 1894. It has occasional splashes of golden foliage but this variegation is not spectacular. Better gold forms have since been developed from it.
Growth: 3-6-30. Hardiness: 50-60%. Choice: 1.
Wood: 1, 2, 3.

Chilean Cedar *Austrocedrus chilensis*

This small evergreen tree, 10-15m in height, comes from cool moist forests in central Chile and western Argentina. It is closely related to Incense Cedar and has much in common with that species. The branches are ascending and dense, supporting flat sprays of tiny, hard scale-like, pale green leaves in opposite pairs. It was introduced to Europe in 1847 but is usually very slow-growing and requires shelter.
Growth: 1-3-15. Hardiness: 20-30%. Choice: 4.
Wood: 3, 4, 5.

Prince Albert's Yew *Saxegothaea conspicua*

From southern Chile, an evergreen conifer intermediate between Podocarpus (p. 35) and Araucaria (p. 37). It either grows to 15-20m tall with a conical top or remains low and bushy depending upon the immediate environment. Plants with a properly formed stem have bark that is smooth at first becoming scaly. It is reddish-purple, turning to brown as it matures and then bleaching grey-brown in old age. The foliage is superficially like yew but the undersides of the needles have two silvery bands of stomata. The 1.5cm cones consist of overlapping pointed green scales. This tree, introduced by William Lobb in 1847, was named in honour of Prince Albert, Queen Victoria's consort. The Genus name commemorates his original home Saxe-Coburg-Gotha in northern Germany.
Growth: 1-3-15. Hardiness: 20%. Choice: 4.
Wood: 3, 4, 5.

Lawson Cypress

old cones

leaf detail

young cone, enlarged

cone, enlarged

seed

♂ flower detail

♀ flower detail

seedling

'Lombartsii'   'Glauca Lombartsii'   Lawson Cypress

Lawson Cypress *Chamaecyparis lawsoniana*

The limited range of this North American forest tree includes south-west Oregon and north-west California from sea level on the coast to over 900m inland. Specimens with straight stems may reach 50m in height. Trees of this species were introduced to Europe by the Scottish botanist Andrew Murray in 1854 from the upper Sacramento Valley in California. Seed was sent to the Lawson Nursery in Edinburgh. Lawson soon distributed the plant widely as an evergreen ornamental rather than as a forest tree. He, and subsequent growers, found huge variations in foliage colour and vigour which did not occur in the native American forests. Its low nutrient requirements and shade tolerance made this an indispensable urban decorative tree, wind-break and hedging plant. Seeds germinate in about three weeks and young saplings transplant easily. Clipping is tolerated from an early age if required. When grown as a forest tree this species produces timber which is soft but durable. It is pale orange-brown with attractive darker brown streaks and knots. See p. 261 for cone.

Growth: 2-8-40 (50 in native region). Hardiness: 80%. Choice: 2, 3. Wood: 2, 3.

Chamaecyparis lawsoniana cultivars

Of the many cultivars '**Lombartsii**', raised in Holland in 1904, is particularly large. It has a straight stem and conical top. The foliage is yellowish-green but with the typical Lawson Cypress bluish bloom on it. Strongly bloomed plants within this cultivar are called '**Glauca Lombartsii**', first described in 1925. From 1887 *glauca* was recognized as a distinct form but it is only used now in a collective sense. Named glaucous trees were often prefixed 'Glauca', as in 'Glauca Lombartsii', but this is no longer permitted in the rules of cultivated plant taxonomy.

'**Grayswood Pillar**' and '**Hillieri**' (also illustrated on p. 45) are two of the finest Lawson Cypress selections to come from the Hillier Nurseries. 'Grayswood Pillar', described in 1971, is a narrow columnar tree with grey-blue foliage. It arose as a sport on 'Blue Jacket' (p. 46) originally produced at Young's Nursery in Surrey. 'Hillieri', which was produced in 1910 and named in 1928, has feathery sprays of foliage which are bright yellow at the extremities. This is also a columnar tree and one of the most reliable golden Lawson Cypresses, provided it is planted in full light.

Growth: variable. Hardiness: 50-70%. Choice: 1.

'Lombartsii'

'Hillieri'

'Grayswood Pillar'

forma *glauca*

'Stricta'
(Waterer's tree)

'Westermannii'

'Columnaris'

'Erecta Viridis'

'Pottenii'

'Alumii'

← **'Pottenii'** →

'Alumii'
old tree

'Erecta Viridis'
old tree

LAWSON CYPRESSES

Chamaecyparis lawsoniana cultivars (continued)

The cultivar '**Pottenii**' is a columnar tree first described in 1923. It has slender upright branches which are often damaged by snow and even nesting birds, such as jackdaws. On old specimens the neat vertical outline is often broken and unsightly brown patches of inner crown are exposed to view. The original plant was produced at the Potten Nursery in Kent.

Two cultivars which started out as columnar specimens but have proved with time to be rather spreading in maturity are '**Alumii**' and '**Erecta Viridis**'. 'Alumii' was described in 1891 but its actual origin is obscure. Possibly it arose as a sport on the lost 1872 clone 'Erecta Glauca', either at Worcester or somewhere in Germany. The foliage is dull grey-green as 'Erecta Glauca' must have been.

'**Erecta Viridis**', named in 1867, is a product of the famous Anthony Waterer Nursery in Surrey. This is one of the brightest green upright forms of Lawson Cypress, even in mid-winter. Originally, in 1850, it was called 'Erecta' but this (now invalid) name was also applied to several other cultivars, including various yellow sports loosely referred to as 'Erecta Aurea' (see p. 46). These are all potentially very large trees and in old age branches do tend to 'fall apart'.

Semi-juvenile foliage is a permanent feature of '**Ellwoodii**', a pre 1929 seedling raised at Swanmore Park in Hampshire. It was named in honour of the head gardener there. Originally promoted as a dwarf rockery plant 'Ellwoodii' has proved itself to be quite unsuitable in this role. Trees over 10m tall are known in England. The dark grey-green foliage is tightly packed on ascending branches producing an impenetrable column. Eventually several main stems develop producing multiple pointed tops.

Narrow cultivars of Lawson Cypress are very common. '**Stricta**' is another Waterer Nursery tree named in 1888. Unfortunately the name 'Stricta' had already been assigned to a completely different tree elsewhere in England. '**Stricta Glauca**' is a 1937 Belgian plant. It is a narrow 10m tree with blue-green foliage. A more feathery blue-green clone is '**Columnaris**' a Dutch selection made around 1940. It was formerly called 'Columnaris Glauca'. Another Dutch cultivar is '**Westermannii**' named in 1890. It has pale yellow tipped sprays of foliage on a broadly conical medium-sized tree.

Growth: 2-6-15 variable. Hardiness: 50-70%. Choice: 1.

'Ellwoodii'   'Stricta Glauca'   'Stricta'   'Columnaris'

'Wisselii'

'Youngii'

'Fletcheri'

leaf detail

'Wisselii'
old tree

'Wisselii'
flowering profusely

'Triompf van Boskoop'

Chamaecyparis lawsoniana cultivars (continued)

The curious cultivar '**Wisselii**' is a distinctive Dutch clone of Lawson Cypress named in 1893. It was produced by and named after F. van der Wissel. It has stout ascending branches and shoots densely clothed in short compact but irregular foliage which appears to be somewhat spirally arranged. The minute scale leaves are blue green. Some individuals produce copious amounts of red male strobili (flowers) in spring. This is a fast-growing columnar tree easily able to exceed 15m in height.

'**Triompf van Boskoop**' was produced by F. J. Grootendorst at Boskoop in Holland around 1890. In shape and almost in size it resembles the true Lawson Cypress but it has glaucous blue-green foliage. It is a very fertile clone which produces a range of brightly-coloured seedlings, some of which are glaucous like the parent.

The golden Lawson Cypress '**Hillieri**' is described on p. 41.

The drooping green cultivar '**Youngii**' is a vigorous tree produced in England by L. M. Young, at the Milford Nursery in Surrey. It was named in 1900 as 'Youngs variety'. Many specimens develop distinctly pendulous shoots on a rather open conical branch arrangement, others resemble the species (illustrated).

'**Fletcheri**' is an interesting cultivar found originally as a sport on a normal tree growing in Surrey in 1911. It has permanently semi-juvenile foliage which was 'tested' for reversion in the nursery for 12 years before a name was assigned to it in 1923. Nevertheless cuttings taken from low down on 'Fletcheri' trees behave quite differently to cuttings taken from leading shoots. Typical plants have ascending branches densely arranged on a columnar multi-stemmed tree 10-15m tall. The foliage is light grey-green. The many informal golden varieties of 'Fletcheri' including seedlings, are now being replaced in cultivation by the yellowish-grey cultivar '**Somerset**' described in 1967 and produced by Scott's Nursery in Somerset.

Growth: 2-6-20. Hardiness: 50-70%. Choice: 1.

'Hillieri'   'Youngii'   'Somerset'   'Fletcheri'

LAWSON CYPRESS CULTIVARS

'Lycopodioides' A curious 5m shrub with densely deformed irregular blue-green foliage. Holland, 1890.

'Erecta Aurea' see p. 43

'Blue Jacket' Fine glaucous adult foliage. Milford Nursery, Surrey.

'Moerheimii' A conical 10m tree with pale-yellow-tipped green foliage. Holland, before 1934

'Kilmacurragh' Narrowly fastigiate, short-branched, found originally growing in Ireland, 1951.

'Albo-spica' A narrow tree with pale yellowish-white tipped foliage. Now considered to be identical to 'Argenteovariegata' (see p. 51). England, 1975.

'Henry Dinger' More yellow than 'Albo-spica'. Holland, 1968.

'Golden King' A vigorous lax 10-15m tree with bright yellow shoot tips. Holland, 1931.

Growth: 1-5-12 variable.
Hardiness: 50-70%.
Choice: 1.

'Green Hedger'
Densely conical, discovered in a nursery in Surrey in 1939. Formerly called 'Westermannii'.

'Silver Tip' has distinctly variegated foliage. Selected in Holland before 1968.

'Elegantissima'
A conical tree with more than one cultivated origin. It is greenish in summer and golden-yellow in winter. (Illustrated is a twig from the William Barron tree, UK).

'Winston Churchill' keeps its distinctive conical shape for at least 20 years. England, 1965.

'Aurea'
Slow-growing and compact. Britain, 1862.

'Slocock'
A conical tree. England, 1989.

'Tamariscifolia'

'Chilworth Silver'
A slow-growing blue green form of 'Ellwoodii'. England, 1971.

'Ellwood's Gold'
A distinctive but dull yellow slow-growing compact upright tree. It is a mutation from 'Ellwoodii' (p. 43) and only has semi-juvenile foliage. Britain, 1968.

'Tamariscifolia'
A domed 4-5m spreading bush with a dense canopy supported by bare multiple stems. England, 1923.

'Erecta
Filiformis'

'Filiformis'

'Intertexta'

'Kestonensis'

'Green Pillar'

'Stewartii'

'Filiformis'

'Intertexta'

'Stewartii'

LAWSON CYPRESSES

Chamaecyparis lawsoniana cultivars (continued)

'**Filiformis**' is a curious tree from Belgium, described in 1877, although several earlier introductions were made. It is an open spreading tree over 10m in height. The shoots hang down in long deep green tresses. In 1896 an upright stiff-twigged form of the same thing was produced in Germany and named '**Erecta Filiformis**'.

Another 'drooping' cultivar is '**Intertexta**' but it does not have filamentous foliage. Although young trees are usually conical and symmetrical, they may eventually develop rogue branches which stick out sideways for no apparent reason. All the foliage turns downwards at the extremities. This cultivar was produced in Worcester from 1872 but probably originated at the Lawson Nursery in Edinburgh in 1869.

Similar in many respects is '**Pendula**' which has softer foliage and a more regular shape. Only the shoot tips are strongly pendulous. It was first cultivated in 1870 and named in 1891.

Three golden forms are illustrated here, '**Lutea**' is the standard bright yellow type from which most of the others have probably come. '**Stewartii**' is a subtle yellow form changing to greenish-yellow in winter. The fronds of foliage are held more or less horizontally. It was cultivated by Stewarts Nursery, Bournemouth around 1900. '**Green Spire**' is a fairly upright tree with yellowish-green young shoots. Its origins are curious. In the world conifer data pool its name is described as synonymous with 'Green Pillar'. This probably accounts for some of the variation often found in that cultivar today (p. 51).

'**Kestonensis**' is a plant surrounded by taxonomic intrigue. It originated around 1920 but the name was applied to different cultivars by several authors. The original plant was said to be a compact rounded bush and it was described and named in 1935. Subsequently it was lost from cultivation and a new plant appeared which was described, quite differently, as a compact form of 'Ellwoodii'. The Reuthe Nursery at Keston in Kent later claimed this was not correct and the original plant was a dwarf form of 'Fletcheri' (p. 45). Some authorities dismiss the whole saga and suggest the name should not be used at all.

Growth: 2-6-20. Hardiness: 50-70%. Choice: 1.

'Lutea'   'Green Spire'   'Pendula'   'Kestonensis'

'Pembury Blue'

'Pembury Blue' leaves enlarged cone

'Naberi'

'Fraseri'

'Stardust'

'Argenteovariegata'

'Lutea Smithii'

'Merrist Wood'

'Pembury Blue'   'Argenteovariegata'   'Lutea Smithii'   'Merrist Wood'

Chamaecyparis lawsoniana cultivars (continued)

Of the glaucous cultivars '**Pembury Blue**', named in 1968, has become a popular garden tree in a relatively short time. It was developed by the Jackman Nursery in Surrey in 1965. The foliage is silvery-blue in the first year darkening to grey-blue after the second year. The outline of the tree remains neat and conical for the first 20-30 years. A much older blue-grey form is '**Fraseri**' which was cultivated by Lombarts Nursery in Holland before 1887. The foliage, unlike 'Pembury Blue' stands vertically on the branches showing off flat sprays of light and darker grey. This is a big tree and old specimens are often seen in landscaped parks and arboreta.

'**Naberi**' is a 1929 Dutch selection, finally named in 1949. It is a variegated form which is not easy to separate on the ground from many other similar-looking variegated plants. The foliage is dull green with yellow shoot tips which become pale creamy-grey in winter. The tree is usually conical but it does not grow vigorously and is slow to recover if inadvertently damaged.

The Dutch cultivar '**Stardust**' varies from season to season. It produces yellow spring growth, on a deep green background, which becomes bronze later in the year. The much older clone '**Argenteo-variegata**' is a strong-growing cultivar with creamy-white variegation on grey-green foliage. It arose in the Lawson Nurseries in Edinburgh, Scotland, in 1875.

'**Green Pillar**', originally produced by Hoggers Nursery in England and named 'Hogger', is a conical tree with vertical foliage which is yellowish in spring and green later on. It was cultivated around 1960 but renamed in 1965 as 'Green Pillar'. Another cultivar dating back to 1940 was already called 'Green Pillar', probably named 'Green Spire' (p. 49) originally, so individuals in cultivation today appear to vary depending on their origins.

'**Merrist Wood**' is a green foliage tree similar to the species but selected for its resistance to the root-rotting disease *Phytophthera*, which can be a serious killer of Lawson Cypress. Merrist Wood is an agricultural college in southern England.

'**Lutea Smithii**' was produced in Derbyshire around 1898. In full sun it is perhaps a little brighter than most other 'golden' forms of Lawson Cypress. Probably this is because the foliage tends to be more tightly packed than it is on 'Lutea' and 'Aurea'. Some authorities still list this clone as 'Smithii' but this is a confusing mistake because two trees were listed as 'Smithii' for a time, the other being 'Darleyensis'. Both of these cultivars were created by Smith's Nursery at Darley Dale.

Growth: 2-6-20 variable. Hardiness: 50-70%. Choice: 1.

'Green Pillar'   'Fraseri'   'Stardust'   'Naberi'

Sawara Cypress

'Squarrosa Aurea'

'Filifera Aurea'

'Gold Spangle'

underside   closed cone

'Squarrosa'

'Strathmore'

'Plumosa'

'Plumosa' leaf detail

'Squarrosa'

'Plumosa'

FALSE CYPRESSES

Sawara Cypress *Chamaecyparis pisifera*

Ultimately this is a large tree; specimens 50m tall have been recorded in its native Japan. In cultivation, where it is seldom seen as the true species, most specimens do not achieve half this height. It was introduced to England in 1861 by Robert Fortune, the former gardener at the Chelsea Physic Garden in London. From seed young Sawara Cypress plants pass through three stages of juvenility. Each of these is marked by a different kind of foliage, from an initial squarrose (feathery) form, to a plumose, compact, soft, acutely spiky form to the final adult scaly leaves. Even these are not always of one single type. Some individuals remain fixed in either of the first stages of development, giving rise to numerous cultivars.

'**Squarrosa**' is a common tree up to 25m tall from Japan. It was described in 1844 and introduced, to Belgium, in 1861. The soft spiny juvenile foliage is bunched on long spreading branches. Although the red-brown stem is usually straight, the conical outline becomes open and untidy with age. Patches of brown dead foliage frequently appear. There are numerous named 'Squarrosa' cultivars of every size, shape and colour from silvery-green to yellow ('**Squarrosa Aurea**').

'**Filifera**' is a small conical tree with spreading branches and a pendulous elongated form of adult foliage. It was introduced to England from Japan in 1861. A golden type '**Filifera Aurea**' was cultivated in England in 1889. It is very slow-growing and needs good light to produce its characteristic golden threads of foliage. '**Gold Spangle**' is a sport of 'Filifera Aurea' produced in Holland around 1900. The foliage is partly adult and partly plumose, a good example of the unstable nature of this species and showing how it is also able to regress to a semi-juvenile state. A more recent golden form is '**Strathmore**' described in 1975. This may actually be identical to the lost cultivar 'Aurea Nana' (1891), which is supposed not to be in cultivation. It is a bushy plant with green and yellow adult foliage.

'**Plumosa**', described in 1867, is a Japanese tree with all-juvenile foliage. It was introduced to Britain from Japan by John Gould Veitch. The very soft foliage becomes dense and eventually thick 'mats' of live and dead material build up among the branches making them prone to snow damage. There are many named 'Plumosa' clones of every shape and size. Several cultivars so-called by plant breeders have progressed, years later, to adult foliage, making their names invalid.

Growth: 3-8-30. Hardiness: 80-90%. Choice: 2 (cvs). Wood: 1, 2 (species)

open cone

'Filifera' leaf detail

Sawara Cypress

'Filifera Aurea'

White Cypress

Nootka Cypress

'Glauca'

Chamaecyparis thyoides 'Variegata'

'Variegata'

cones

Taiwan Cypress

Chamaecyparis nootkatensis 'Variegata'

White Cypress
old tree

White Cypress
bark

FALSE CYPRESSES

Nootka Cypress *Chamaecyparis nootkatensis*

Also known as *Xanthocyparis nootkatensis* and *Cupressus nootkatensis*, this incredibly hardy tree extends northwards from Oregon into Alaska to 61°N. In the south of the range it grows up to an altitude of 1800m. It occurs either as pure dense forests or mixed with other forest conifers such as Sitka Spruce (p. 191) and Mountain Hemlock (p. 197). It is a big 30m straight tree with a symmetrical conical outline and a deeply fluted stem. Nutrient requirements are low but a good supply of moisture is essential. This species was discovered by Archibald Menzies between 1791 and 1793. It was sent to Hamburg and Leningrad around 1850 and arrived in Britain from Germany in 1853. The medium-sized cultivar of it '**Variegata**' has cream-coloured shoots scattered throughout the foliage. It was produced around 1873 in Germany but the original clone is probably no longer in cultivation. '**Pendula**' is as large as the species but less symmetrical with lax pendulous branch tips. There are several different clones in cultivation and new pendulous seedlings continue to appear.
Growth: 2-5-30. Hardiness: 80%. Choice: 2. Wood: 2, 3.

White Cypress *Chamaecyparis thyoides*

Also known as White Cedar and in America Swamp-cedar, this 15-27m tree has a straight stem, slender crown and short horizontal branches. It grows on wet peaty acid soils usually in swampy conditions close to the North American coast from central Maine south to northern Florida and Mississippi. In cultivation its branches spread more widely than in the wild. It was introduced by Peter Collinson in 1736. The cultivar '**Glauca**' was first described in 1847 but new blue-green seedlings continue to occur. Finally '**Variegata**' is an 1831 Irish cultivar described in 1855. It has occasional small bright yellow patches among the foliage.
Growth: 1-3-25. Hardiness: 90%. Choice: 2. Wood: 2, 3.

Taiwan Cypress *Chamaecyparis formosensis*

In Taiwan this is a huge forest tree up to 65m tall. It grows in mountainous areas at 1000-2900m in central and northern parts of the island. Ancient specimens exist which are said to be over 1000 years old. In cultivation it is generally a small to medium-sized tree with open spreading branches and a broad conical outline. The scratchy green foliage darkens and becomes bronzed in the winter.
Growth: 2-6-15. Hardiness: 60%. Choice: 3. Wood: 2, 3.

White Cypress
young tree

'**Pendula**'

Taiwan Cypress
bark

Hinoki Cypress

cones

'Aurea'

leaf detail

underside

'Crippsii'

'Aurea'   Hinoki Cypress   'Crippsii'

FALSE CYPRESSES

Hinoki Cypress *Chamaecyparis obtusa*

In its native Japan this is one of the most highly respected forest trees. Its wood is usually reserved for fine furniture and lacquer work. It is also used for top quality house interiors and for Shinto temples. It grows in mixtures, with spruces and *Zelkova serrata* (p. 415), or sometimes in pure stands which occur from sea level to 1500m in altitude. It is hardy to -40°C and resistant to snow damage. The outline is broadly conical when grown in the open. Eventually it becomes ragged when trees become ancient. Most of the flexible horizontal branches are relatively thin so the wood contains very few large knots. Since its introduction to horticulture in 1861 a vast number of cultivated forms have been developed from it. These now far outnumber the true species except in Japan. Many are slow-growing dwarf forms which resemble bonsai plants.

Golden Hinoki Cypress '**Aurea**' was sent to England from Japan by Robert Fortune in 1860. Originally it was called 'Argentea' but the name was changed to 'Aurea' in 1862. It is a conical tree with rather open flat sprays of yellow foliage. A much brighter yellow tree, '**Crippsii**', has dense foliage but is slow-growing. This cultivar was raised in England before 1899 and named in 1901.

'**Lycopodioides**' is a peculiar bush or small rather gaunt tree with widely spaced out branches and truncated tufts of distorted green foliage. It was introduced to the west by Philipp von Siebold in 1861. Several surviving early plants appear to have been grafted on to Lawson or Hinoki Cypress rootstocks which vastly outgrow the 'Lycopodioides' scion.

'**Tetragona Aurea**' is another plant with truncated mossy foliage. It was introduced around 1870 and is thought to be a golden-leaved sport from the 'Fernspray Cypress', 'Filicoides'. The cultivar '**Filicoides**' itself is usually only a bushy plant with an irregular outline. The short green foliage resembles some species of club-moss. It too was introduced to Germany from Japan by Philipp von Siebold around 1860.

Growth: 3-6-20 (40 in native region). Hardiness: 90%. Choice: 2 (cvs), 3 (species). Wood: 1, 2, 3 (species).

'Tetragona Aurea'

leaf detail

'Lycopodioides'   'Lycopodioides'   'Filicoides'

leaf detail

'Haggerston Grey'

cone

seeds

'Castlewellan'

'Naylor's Blue'

leaf detail

leaf detail

'Leighton Green'

'Haggerston Grey'

'Naylor's Blue'

'Robinson's Gold'

58

Leyland Cypress × *Cupressocyparis leylandii*

The parents of this intergeneric hybrid, *Chamaecyparis nootkatensis* (p. 55) and *Cupressus macrocarpa* (p. 67), are American species but the cross does not appear to have occurred in America. The natural ranges of the species do not overlap. Leyland Cypress originated, quite by accident, in central Wales on two occasions, in 1888 and in 1911. It is a fast-growing plant which resembles the *Cupressus macrocarpa* parent but is more hardy. Genetic instability within the plant has resulted in numerous variations. A lucrative bonus for keen eyed nurserymen. The green forms are particularly large trees, over 36m tall, which produce very durable timber. However, clonal forests of dense *leylandii* are probably unacceptable in the natural environment, being hostile to wildlife and ground vegetation.

'**Haggerston Grey**' was one of the first clones to be developed in 1888 although it was not named until 1964. The open, rather lax, foliage is green with a greyish cast. '**Leighton Green**' a 1911 Welsh plant (also known as clone 11) has more compact glossy green foliage. It is widely used for evergreen hedging.

The golden *leylandii* '**Castlewellan**' (often wrongly called 'Castlewellan Gold') was produced in Northern Ireland in 1962. Its parentage is slightly different from other green clones, in so far as golden cultivars of both parents were used to produce it. Although young plants may be stunted and 'bronzed' by cold weather this is a strong-growing tree which is likely to reach formidable heights.

'**Naylor's Blue**' is another original 1911 plant. It is a compact tree with a dark slightly blue-grey appearance.

Probably the best variegated form of *leylandii* is '**Silver Dust**', raised in America in 1976 as a sport of 'Leighton Green'. The foliage is evenly marked with creamy white. '**Golconda**', which is a bright yellow form of 'Haggerston Grey', was raised in England in 1977. So far it seems to keep its colour well and is moderately hardy. In the same year a new Irish golden form, '**Robinson's Gold**', was developed. It is a neat conical tree but does not have such bright yellow foliage as 'Golconda' or 'Castlewellan'.

Growth: 5-20-40. Hardiness: 50-60%. Choice: 2, 3. Wood: 2, 3.

'Silver Dust'

'Castlewellan'

'Golconda'

cone

leaf detail

West Himalayan Cypress

Gowen Cypress

leaf detail

cone

leaf detail

Kashmir Cypress

West Himalayan Cypress

Gowen Cypress

Kashmir Cypress
young tree

West Himalayan Cypress *Cupressus torulosa*

Although its natural range in Nepal, Tibet and north-west India extends to 3300m, this species is not particularly hardy in cultivation. In northern regions it often looks sick, with brown and yellowish fronds among its naturally drooping foliage. The best specimens are around 20m tall with a columnar outline and conical top. On old trees the dull brown bark peels off in vertical strips. Clusters of bluish-green 1.5m cones ripen in the autumn to bloomed chestnut brown. The species was introduced to the west in 1824 but has never become popular in cultivation.
Growth: 2-5-20. Hardiness: 30%. Choice: 4. Wood: 2, 3.

Gowen Cypress *Cupressus goveniana*

This rather sombre narrow dark green tree grows up to 20m in height. It has grey brown rough flaky bark which is mostly hidden by the dense strongly scented foliage. The globose glossy brown cones are 1.5cm across. This species was named in 1849 in honour of James Gowen, a notable British rhododendron grower. Its natural range extends along the coastal mountain ranges of central and northern California. The variety *pygmaea*, Mendocino Cypress (see p. 65) is smaller, but by no means a dwarf as the name suggests. Its natural range is limited to Mendocino County on the Pacific coast of North America.
Growth: 2-5-20. Hardiness: 20%. Choice: 1. Wood: 2, 3.

Kashmir Cypress *Cupressus cashmeriana*

Closely related to the West Himalayan Cypress and presumed to have come from Kashmir, this popular conservatory plant has no known wild origin. Its strongly pendulous sea-green foliage is very distinctive, particularly when growing under glass and free of any environmental stress. Unfortunately it is capable of rapidly reaching 20m in height and will outgrow all but the grandest greenhouses. First cultivated in 1862, it was described in 1867.
Growth: 4-9-20. Hardiness: 0%. Choice: 1. Wood: 2, 3.

Chinese Weeping Cypress *Cupressus funebris*

There is still taxonomic controversy about this Chinese tree. Some authorities place it in the genus *Chamaecyparis* because of its flat scaled foliage and small number of seeds in each 2cm cone. Unlike *Chamaecyparis* though the seeds take two years to ripen. Growth is erect but the fronds of foliage hang down, a feature which is accentuated with age. Young plants have juvenile foliage in short spiky glaucous-grey tufts, quite unlike the adult form. This tree, also known as "Mourning Cypress" was introduced to the west in 1894. Although it has a long history of cultivation in Chinese religious sites it remains rare in cultivation and will only grow in mild areas.
Growth: 2-6-15. Hardiness: 20%. Choice: 1.

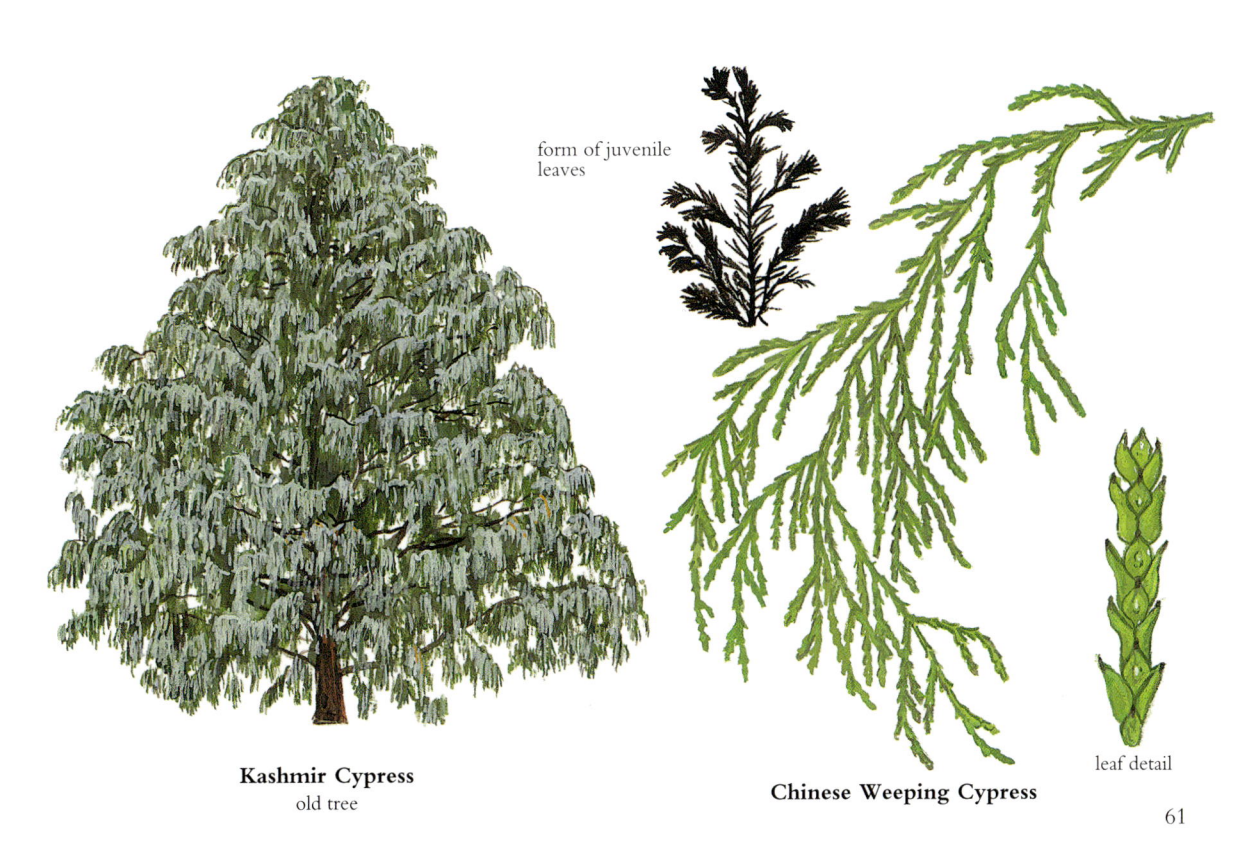

form of juvenile leaves

Kashmir Cypress
old tree

Chinese Weeping Cypress

leaf detail

Mexican Cypress

cone

leaf detail

♂ flowers

'Glauca'

Mexican Cypress

Bentham Cypress

leaf detail

'Glauca Pendula'

Mexican Cypress *Cupressus lusitanica*

Also known as "Cedar of Goa" this large tree, often over 20m tall, occurs in central Mexico, Guatemala and Honduras. Its complicated history is reflected in its unexpected mixture of names. It was thought by some to have originated in Portugal, hence the name Lusitanica and the reference to Goa, a former Portuguese colony in western India. The introduction dates are also complex, the first recorded date, around 1640, was probably only to Portugal. General cultivation elsewhere appears to have been from 1682. The species was eventually described in 1768.

The cultivar '**Glauca**' has bluish-green foliage. The original clone, introduced in 1910, was said to have originated either in Portugal or in Montserrat in the West Indies. New glaucous seedlings from different origins frequently occur. There is a beautiful weeping blue form, '**Glauca Pendula**', first cultivated by the Hillier Nurseries in 1925.

The variety *benthamii*, "**Bentham Cypress**" is a regional variation from north-east Mexico. It was named and described in 1867 but has been in cultivation since 1838. The outline is narrow and conical with foliage in flattened lacy fronds.

Growth: 3-6-20. Hardiness: 30%. Choice: 3. Wood: 1, 2, 3.

Piute Cypress *Cupressus nevadensis*

Named as a species in 1919 this desert plant from the Piute Mountains in the Sierra Nevada is now considered to be a variety of *Cupressus arizonica*. The foliage is silver-grey with tiny clear or reddish secretions of resin all over it. Now rare in cultivation, it is fairly tender and difficult to grow.

Growth: 2-5-15. Hardiness: 0%. Choice: 1. Wood: 3, 4, 5.

Sargent Cypress *Cupressus sargentii*

This medium-sized tree comes from the coastal mountain ranges of Mendocino, Colusa and Santa Barbara Counties in California. It is closely related to *Cupressus goveniana* (p. 61) and intergrades with *Cupressus macnabiana*. The species name, published in 1909, commemorates the American dendrologist Charles Sprague Sargent. Narrow-crowned or wide-spreading trees occur, but the foliage is always glaucous-green and resinous. The bark is thick and fibrous with vertical fissures.

Growth: 3-6-20. Hardiness: 20%. Choice: 1, 3. Wood: 3, 4, 5.

Piute Cypress

Sargent Cypress

narrow form

seeds

closed cones

young cone

'Swane's Golden'

Italian Cypress

Santa Cruz Cypress

Guadalupe Cypress

Italian Cypress
old tree

'Green Pencil'

'Swane's Golden'

Guadalupe Cypress

64

CYPRESSES

Italian Cypress *Cupressus sempervirens*

The natural range of Italian Cypress extends from the north-east coast of the Mediterranean to Iran in the east and as far as Tunisia in the south. It has been cultivated for its fragrant and moth repellent timber and as an ornamental tree in horticulture all round the warm temperate world, especially in its narrow form (*Cupressus sempervirens* var. *stricta*). In ideal conditions huge trees 45m tall have been recorded. In Cyprus and Crete specimens of the variety *horizontalis* grow to over 30m. Introductions were made all over Europe before 1500 and trees now grow in sheltered localities as far north as Edinburgh. Plants have often been collected in Israel and planted in the grounds of religious establishments world-wide.

The cultivar '**Swane's Golden**' is a beautiful clear yellow-coloured tree with good vertical form. It was developed in Sydney, Australia around 1944 and described in 1959. '**Green Pencil**' which was originally called 'Greenspire' is one of the best selections of the upright variety *stricta*. It was raised by the Hillier Nurseries.

Growth: 3-6-45. Hardiness: 20%. Choice: 1. Wood: 1, 2, 3.

Guadalupe Cypress *Cupressus guadalupensis*

From Mexico, this tender 20m tree was first described in 1879. In Mexico it is called Tecate Cypress but confusingly so is the closely related *Cupressus forbesii*. The outline is more or less oval with strongly upswept branches and a rounded top. The aromatic foliage is grey-green or blue-green on some individuals and held in thin slender bunches. Cones, around 3cm across, are distinctly spiny and often stay on the tree in clusters for several years.

Growth: 2-5-20. Hardiness: 10%. Choice: 3. Wood: 1, 2, 3.

Santa Cruz Cypress *Cupressus abramsiana*

Morphologically very little separates trees from California and from Mexico. This is a 20m tree with strong green foliage. It only grows in the Santa Cruz Mountains and was named originally in 1948 but its status was re-examined in 1970 when it was re-classified as a variety of *Cupressus goveniana*.

Growth: 2-5-20. Hardiness: 20%. Choice: 3. Wood: 1, 2, 3.

Tecate Cypress *Cupressus forbesii*

In 1922 this rare tree from the mountains of south-west California was named and described. Since, it has been re-classified as a variety of *Cupressus guadalupensis* (1970).

Growth: 2-5-20. Hardiness: 10%. Choice: 3. Wood: 1, 2, 3.

Cuyamaca Cypress

Cupressus arizonica var. *stephensonii*

Named in honour of J. Bert Stephenson from the US Department of Agriculture, Forest Service, this rare tree comes from the mountainous areas of southern California. Originally thought of as a true species in 1948 it was reduced to variety status in 1966.

Growth: 2-5-20. Hardiness: 20%. Choice: 1, 3. Wood: 2, 3.

Mendocino Cypress (see p. 61)   **Santa Cruz Cypress**   **Tecate Cypress**   **Cuyamaca Cypress**

Monterey Cypress

open cone

cones

seeds

old bark

'Horizontalis Aurea'

'Goldcrest'

seedling

'Lutea'

young tree

Monterey Cypress
native spreading form

66

Monterey Cypress *Cupressus macrocarpa*

The limited natural distribution of this species is of special interest. It occurs only around Monterey on the Pacific coast of California and on Guadalupe Island. Following the retreating ice after the last glaciation it failed to migrate any further northwards because of the geography of these areas. Consequently it is now in a region which is very hot and dry, so growth is stunted and slow. When seed is taken from these unfortunate bushy plants (illustrated) and grown in cool moist areas of the world large, straight, luxuriant trees over 25m tall are often produced.

The first introductions were in 1838. Seed was sent to Europe from Russia, then direct imports from California were made by Karl Hartweg the head gardener at Schwetzingen in Germany, who collected plants for the Royal Horticultural Society in London. In Britain many huge trees were killed by freak cold weather in the 1970s. Only specimens growing close to the coast survived. It is potentially a productive timber tree although the heavy branches do produce large defects and spoil the form of some stems. As a living tree it withstands salt spray and some salinity in the soil, so it is valuable as a wind break close to the sea. Its main claim to fame, however, is that it is one parent of the ubiquitous Leyland Cypress (p. 59).

Golden Monterey Cypress '**Lutea**' is a large tree with yellow tipped fronds of foliage. Individuals over 25m in height are known with massive rough pale grey stems over 70cm thick. It was produced by Dicksons Nursery at Chester in 1893 and named in 1896.

Growth: 3-7-25. Hardiness: 40%. Choice: 2, 3. Wood: 2, 3.

There are also two stunted golden forms both called '**Horizontalis Aurea**' which originated in Australia around 1873 and were named in 1898. The 'second form' (illustrated) can eventually grow quite tall if not pruned back. In Ireland '**Donard Gold**' was produced before 1940. It is a beautiful greenish-gold plant with upswept fronds of vigorous foliage. The brightest of all golden foliage, however, occurs on the English cultivar '**Goldcrest**' described in 1948 and produced by Treseder Nurseries of Truro in Cornwall.

Growth: variable. Hardiness: 30-40%. Choice: 1.

'Horizontalis Aurea' 'Goldcrest' 'Donard Gold'

Smooth-barked
Arizona Cypress

Rough-barked
Cypress

'Conica'

open cone

'Pyramidalis'   'Conica'   Rough-barked Cypress

68

CYPRESSES

Smooth-barked Arizona Cypress
Cupressus glabra

From central Arizona in the USA this tough, 18m tall tree prefers dry conditions. Its waxy blue-green foliage is designed to keep transpiration to an absolute minimum. Although it is able to grow in hot semi-desert conditions it is also able to withstand severe cold. In Europe it will grow as far north as lowland Scotland. The exact date of introduction and precise identity are uncertain. In America, since 1966, it has only been given variety status and regarded as part of the *Cupressus arizonica* alliance. The original species designation was given to it in 1910 by George Sudworth of the US Forest Service. Seeds arriving in Britain from the Arnold Arboretum in the USA as early as 1882 were probably of this species.

A superior dense foliage type called '**Pyramidalis**' was selected by the Hillier Nurseries in 1928. There is also a fine ornamental form '**Conica**' which has a narrow outline and thin lacy grey foliage. Growers recently have been clipping glaucous forms of Arizona Cypress into topiarian pot plants. In this unfortunate state they produce abundant sulphur-yellow male flowers in late winter.

Growth: 2-6-18. Hardiness: 40%. Choice: 1, 3.
Wood: 1, 2, 3.

Rough-barked Cypress *Cupressus arizonica*

Although closely related to Cupressus glabra this rare species in cultivation has a wide natural distribution from Texas to New Mexico and Arizona. It is a mountain side tree with greener foliage, a straight 20m stem and a neat conical outline. In tree collections it is often confused with *Cupressus glabra* and intermediate forms almost certainly exist.

Growth: 2-6-20. Hardiness: 40%. Choice: 1, 3.
Wood: 1, 2, 3.

Patagonian Cypress *Fitzroya cupressoides*

This South American tree was discovered by Europeans during Charles Darwin's epic 1834 voyage in the Beagle. The genus name commemorates Captain FitzRoy of the British Navy. In its natural habitat huge trees were found with stems up to 290cm in diameter and heights up to 48m. Some individuals are thought to be 3000 years old. The first live material to reach Europe was collected by William Lobb in 1849. It is still rare in cultivation and grows slowly except in high rainfall areas. Snow bends down the flexible stems and branches of young trees and many become permanently deformed. This is a very ornamental plant and it may have some potential in commercial forestry perhaps as a good, long-lived hardy alternative to Lawson Cypress (p. 41).

Growth: 2-8-25. Hardiness: 40%. Choice: 1, 3.
Wood: 1, 2, 3.

Patagonian Cypress

♂ flowers ♀ flowers

Common Juniper

fruit

seedling

seed

underside

'Pyramidalis'

'Seil Island'

'Graciosa'

Swedish Juniper

'Hibernica'

Common Juniper　　Scottish form

Common Juniper *Juniperus communis*

This species has transglobal distribution in the north temperate and sub-Arctic zones. It is extremely variable, due mostly to the particular environment in which it originated. Wild specimens are often prostrate but when taken into cultivation they resume normal upward growth. Only the subspecies *alpina* and *depressa* have compact dense foliage which does remain constant when plants are moved to another environment. The foliage of Common Juniper is entirely juvenile. It consists of silver-backed 1cm sharp spiny leaves set in whorls of three along the shoot. The berries are 5-6mm across ripening to bloomed purplish-black in two or three years. Ancient specimens several hundred years old are known. Trees will grow on the most hostile acid ground that it is possible to find but they will also thrive equally well on dry chalky soils.

Growth: 2-5-10. Hardiness: 100%. Choice: 2, 3.

Juniperus communis forms and cultivars

The world conifer database lists around 170 named types of Common Juniper. Many of these are poor horticultural specimens which are replicated within the natural wild population. Many bear the names of nurserymen or locations where they were collected. '**Seil Island**' for example is good west Scottish stock but it is not officially registered as a cultivar and has no reason to be. '**Graciosa**' is a Dutch selection made before 1968. It is a shrubby bush with pale green foliage.

The **Swedish Juniper** (*Juniperus communis* f. *suecica*) is native in Scandinavia. It is an upright 10m tall tree with dense foliage usually obscuring the whole stem. The shoot tips extend unevenly or may droop slightly. This form, often listed as a cultivar, was first introduced to horticulture in 1768. The Irish Juniper '**Hibernica**' is a cultivar or more precisely a single clone. It has Irish origins but was actually raised by Loddiges Nursery in 1858. Its growth is strictly upright, resulting in a tight narrow column of compact blue-green foliage over 5m tall. Unfortunately old specimens tend to fork and produce several leading shoots. Eventually snow or wind pulls these apart to reveal unsightly dead foliage inside the plant. '**Pyramidalis**' is similar to 'Hibernica' raised by Hermann Hesse in Germany in 1908 and listed by him as a variety. The antithesis of Irish Juniper is the cultivar '**Oblonga Pendula**', an unpredictable semi-pendulous tree reminiscent of *Juniperus rigida* (p. 75). It appeared in cultivation in Britain in 1838 but is seldom seen now.

Growth: 2-4-8 variable. Hardiness: 90-100%. Choice: 1, 3.

'Oblonga Pendula'

Swedish Juniper   'Hibernica'

adult leaves

Chinese Juniper

'Iowa'

juvenile leaves

fruit

'Variegata'

'Aurea'

detail of juvenile leaves

'Jacobiana'

'Kaizuka'

'Leeana'

Chinese Juniper

'Keteleeri'

'Leeana'
bushy specimen

72

Chinese Juniper *Juniperus chinensis*

Across its extensive range in China, Mongolia and Japan this species occurs in many forms and sizes, from narrowly conic to flattened and shrubby. The juvenile and adult leaves usually occur together but on separate male and female plants. In some individuals only juvenile or only adult foliage can be found. This plant was first cultivated in the west before 1767 but it has been re-introduced many times since then from different locations.

Growth: 2-6-18. Hardiness: 70%. Choice: 1.
Wood: 1, 2, 3.

Juniperus chinensis cultivars

Such a diverse geographic range produces a wide variety of forms which nurseries have been quick to exploit. Furthermore because this species is dioecious every new seedling has to be the product of two different trees. Once selected, new plants are easy to raise from cuttings.

'**Iowa**' named in 1948 is a female tree grown from seed at Iowa State College around 1937. '**Jacobiana**' was in cultivation before 1887 but it has now become confused with more modern selections and the name is often misapplied to almost any narrow, dense-leaved blue-green Chinese Juniper. The name '**Variegata**' now covers a whole range of old named forms such as 'Argentea' and 'Albovariegata'. Unfortunately many of the old names referred to plants of quite different kinds and their original identity has been lost. Some had upright ascending shoots, others were slow-growing and bushy. Only cuttings with some yellow leaves on them will perpetuate variegation. '**Aurea**' is an old cultivar raised in England in 1855 and named in 1865. It has golden tipped shoots in full light, but may suffer from sun scorch. '**Kaizuka**' is a female Japanese plant first sent to America around 1920 and called the Hollywood Juniper. In addition to its distinctive spiky foliage it produces violet-blue berries. There is also a variegated form of it in cultivation. '**Keteleeri**' is another female selection which produces a shapely narrow conical tree. It was raised in Belgium around 1910. '**Leeana**' is a male form but it is no longer in cultivation. Finally '**Obelisk**', which is one of the best upright Chinese Junipers, has ascending blue-green shoots but seldom exceeds 4m in height. An ideal tree for a garden or where space is restricted. The original plant was raised in Holland from seed collected in Japan around 1930. It was named and introduced to the horticultural trade in 1946.

Growth: variable. Hardiness: 60-80%. Choice: 1.

'Obelisk'   'Kaizuka'
             variegated form

'Aurea'   'Jacobiana'   'Iowa'

Syrian Juniper

Temple Juniper

♂ flowers

fruit

adult leaves

Mexican Juniper

fruit

juvenile leaves

Grecian Juniper

Syrian Junipers
various forms

JUNIPERS

Syrian Juniper *Juniperus drupacea*

The awl-shaped 2cm juvenile needles on this tree have viciously sharp points which will draw blood if touched. A good defence against browsing goats in its native south-west Asia and south-east Europe. The species was described and named in 1791 and brought into cultivation in 1854. It is hardy as far north as the British Isles. Although wild trees are often ragged and even stunted, cultivated specimens are mostly columnar with a single persistent but hidden stem.

Growth: 2-6-18. Hardiness: 40%. Choice: 1.
Wood: 1, 2, 3.

Temple Juniper *Juniperus rigida*

In Japan this is a sacred tree planted close to religious temples. Its natural range also includes Korea and northern China. Although perfectly hardy, the foliage tends to brown off in winter. Temple Juniper was introduced to the west through the Veitch Nursery in 1861.

Growth: 2-8-16. Hardiness: 60%. Choice: 1, 3. Wood: 1.

Mexican Juniper *Juniperus flaccida*

Also known as the Mexican Weeping Juniper this species has pendulous foliage often in long sprays of adult scale leaves. It is fairly tender in cultivation, including plants that originated towards the northern limit of the range in Texas. Trees 12m tall are known but they are generally much less. The bark has attractive long narrow scales. Branches spread horizontally producing an uneven outline. This species has male and female flowers on the same tree but on separate branches.

Growth: 2-5-10. Hardiness: 20%. Choice: 1.

Grecian Juniper *Juniperus excelsa*

This is a small shapely tree or large shrub. Ancient specimens in Greece several hundred years old have become very picturesque. The aromatic foliage consists of thin thread-like adult scale leaves. On female trees the fruits, which take two years to ripen, are 9-12mm round berries that are deep purplish-brown with white bloom. The brown bark strips off in long vertical ribbons. The species occurs in mountainous areas in south-west Europe, Asia Minor and the Caucasus, occasionally as pure forest. It is perfectly hardy and was introduced into cultivation in 1806, after being described and named in 1800. An upright form 'Stricta' has only juvenile foliage. In cultivation it is often confused with *Juniperus chinensis* 'Pyramidalis'.

Growth: 2-6-15. Hardiness: 30%. Choice: 1, 3.
Wood: 1, 2, 3.

Temple Juniper
showing winter bronzing

Grecian Juniper
old Mediterranean tree

Drooping Juniper

♂ flowers

inner surface

Drooping Juniper var. *coxii*

juvenile leaves

fruit

adult leaf detail

'Castlewellan'

fruit

Wallich Juniper

Drooping Juniper var. *coxii*

Wallich Juniper

juvenile leaves

JUNIPERS

Drooping Juniper *Juniperus recurva*

Also known as Himalayan Juniper, this variable 10m monoecious tree has a broad natural range extending eastwards to the Pacific coast and including Japan. It was introduced to the west through the Veitch Nursery in 1861 although it had been described in 1825. It intergrades with Flaky Juniper (*Juniperus squamata*) where their natural distribution overlaps. Several cultivars of *recurva* have been re-classified as *squamata* and some confusingly appear to be hybrids between the two.

The variety ***coxii*** is probably more familiar in cultivation than the species. It has a narrow conical outline, with a persistent straight stem, curved branches and open very lax shoots. The vertically peeling bark is greyish-orange. It occurs naturally in Burma and south-west China.

An Irish cultivar '**Castlewellan**' is a taller tree with filiform pendulous foliage described as 'whip-like' or 'thread-like'. It was described and named in 1965.

Growth: 2-5-10. Hardiness: 50%. Choice: 1.

Wallich Juniper *Juniperus wallichiana*

This species is still occasionally called Black Juniper which is the common name for *Juniperus indica*, a shrubby Himalayan bush. Wallich Juniper is a small tree often with a regular conical outline and ascending branches. The foliage is a mixture of juvenile and adult leaves. Male and female flowers occur on the same tree. It was introduced in 1849 by Sir Joseph Hooker, director of Kew Gardens in London. The natural range extends into the Himalayan mountains but nevertheless it is a tender plant in cultivation.

Growth: 2-8-15. Hardiness: 20-30%. Choice: 1. Wood: 5.

Prickly Juniper *Juniperus oxycedrus*

'Oil of Cade', used to treat certain skin diseases, is produced from the wood of this species. Large bushy examples of Prickly Juniper up to 14m tall, occur from the north Mediterranean coast to western Asia. The foliage resembles Common Juniper but is more drooping. Male and female flowers occur on the same tree. The red-brown berries are 10-12mm long and take two years to ripen. It has been cultivated at least since 1739 and was described by Linnaeus in 1753.

Growth: 2-7-14. Hardiness: 20-30%. Choice: 1, 3.

Prickly Juniper

Drooping Juniper

Alligator Juniper

Western Juniper

fruit

juvenile leaves

'Meyeri'

var. *fargesii*

adult leaves

One-seed Juniper

fruit

fruit

'Meyeri'

Alligator Juniper
old tree

Alligator Juniper *Juniperus deppeana*

The reddish-brown bark of this tree is divided into regular 'chequer-board' squares which resemble the pattern of alligator skin. It is also the brightest glaucous-green of any juniper, particularly when the foliage is young. The conical outline gives way to a flat or rounded stout specimen 20m tall at maturity. It grows in the south-west USA and Mexico on dry limestone hillsides with Ponderosa Pine (p. 241). The first cultivated plants appeared in Europe in 1904 although the species had been described 64 years earlier. In 1946 a segregate variety (*pachyphlaea*) was suggested as the true Alligator Juniper but this variety name is now considered to be invalid.

Growth: 3-10-20. Hardiness: 40-50%. Choice: 1. Wood: 1, 2, 3.

Flaky Juniper *Juniperus squamata*

As a species this Asiatic plant is not well known in cultivation but several of its cultivars are very popular garden plants. '**Meyeri**' is an old 1914 favourite from a Chinese garden named in 1922 in honour of Frank Meyer from the US Department of Agriculture. It is a vigorous ascending but dense shrub with deep glaucous green foliage. By contrast the variety *fargesii* is a slow-growing plant with drooping shoots covered in dense apple green awl-shaped leaves. It was first cultivated outside China in 1908.

Growth: 1-3-8. Hardiness: 70%. Choice: 1.

One-seed Juniper *Juniperus monosperma*

Also known as Cherrystone Juniper, this plant from south-east USA and Mexico is tender in cultivation. It is a dense shrub or small tree with grey-green adult foliage.

Growth: 1-4-8. Hardiness: 30-40%. Choice: 1.

Juniperus scopulorum '**Skyrocket**'

This fast-growing narrow evergreen cultivar of the Rocky Mountain Juniper was popular with gardeners and landscape planners almost from the day it was introduced in 1949. Of Dutch origin, it is a hardy substitute for Italian Cypress (p. 65) in cold countries and has grey-green foliage.

Growth: 5-15-ultimate size not yet achieved. Hardiness: 50%. Choice: 1.

Juniperus × media

This hybrid between Chinese Juniper (p. 73) and *Juniperus sabina* (Savin) a variable dwarf species, has resulted in around 85 named cultivars and forms. '**Blue and Gold**' is a Dutch selection made in 1972 and named in 1984. It has pretty blue-grey foliage splashed with cream shoot tips. Several former *Juniperus × media* cultivars are now classified as Chinese Junipers. '**Blaauw**' is one, a vigorous shrubby rather untidy spreading bush with feathery grey-blue adult foliage.

Growth: 1-2-3. Hardiness: 60%. Choice: 1.

Western or Sierra Juniper *Juniperus occidentalis*

Identified in 1839, this rare tree in Europe is from the mountains of western North America, particularly California. It withstands severe dry conditions.

Pencil Cedar adult leaves

juvenile leaves

adult leaves
juvenile leaves

'Canaertii'

unripe fruit

'Glauca'

'Globosa'

'Pseudocupressus'

Pencil Cedar old tree

'Cupressifolia'

'Burkii'

JUNIPERS

Pencil Cedar *Juniperus virginiana*

Although somewhat variable this tree is usually straight-stemmed and neatly conical when young. In old age the horizontal branches may extend outwards in a haphazard way. The bark is very colourful and shreds into long vertical strips. The deep green foliage is mostly the adult scaly type, but strangely very old trees tend to produce a preponderance of 10mm prickly juvenile leaves. Male and female flowers appear on the same tree and the fruit, dark blue glossy 6mm oval berries, ripen in one year. This species, as the name suggests, comes from eastern and central North America, from Canada to Florida and westward to the foothills of the Rocky Mountains. It was introduced into cultivation before 1664 and named by Linnaeus in 1753.

There are a large number of cultivated forms of Pencil Cedar many of which are blue-grey upright trees. '**Pseudocupressus**' named in 1932, is one of the best of these. It was raised in France and has all juvenile foliage. '**Canaertii**' is a Belgian clone raised in 1868. It is a compact bright green tree bearing a profusion of blue berries. '**Glauca**' is a French cultivar, a columnar form with silvery-green, mostly adult, foliage. It was first cultivated and described in 1855. '**Globosa**' is an 1891 German clone, a dwarf rounded compact plant consisting almost entirely of adult leaves. '**Burkii**' is a very good ornamental form with a straight stem and ascending branches. The foliage is silvery blue-green in summer and purplish-brown in winter. It was produced in the USA around 1932 and originally called 'Burk Red Cedar'.

Two Pencil Cedars have been named '**Cupressifolia**' one in 1932 and another in 1946 (illustrated). It has compact 'whip-cord' foliage and a dense conical outline. Finally '**Pendula**' which is now a group name for several similar clones. These have arisen as seedlings and sports since 1852. The name covers several elegant small and medium-sized trees with pendulous branch tips although the main limbs are upright or arched.

Growth: 3-7-25. Hardiness (species): 80-90%. Choice: 1 (cvs), 2 (species). Wood: 1, 2, 3 (species).

'Burkii' 'Canaertii' 'Pendula'

♂ flower ♀ flower

Western Red Cedar

cones

seed

cone

underside

'Zebrina Extra Gold'

seedling

'Fastigiata'

Western Red Cedar

RED CEDARS

Western Red Cedar *Thuja plicata*

Cedarwood garden sheds, greenhouses and other outbuildings all come from the wood of this rot resistant tree. In America even roof tiles (shingles) are traditionally made from it. It is a very large straight-stemmed forest tree up to 60m tall in its native western North America. It has a split distribution on either side of the Rocky Mountains from south-east Alaska to north-west California and from south-east British Columbia to Montana. American Indians made totem poles and 'dug-out' war canoes from Western Red Cedar. The inner bark is fibrous, like lime bark, and was used for blankets, clothing, rope and even thatching. See p. 261 for cone.

Growth: 7-15-40. Hardiness: 50%. Choice: 2, 3. Wood: 1, 2, 3.

Thuja plicata cultivars

The species was introduced into cultivation in 1853 by William Lobb, having been discovered in the 1790s and described in 1824. An early cultivar with a columnar outline like an evergreen Lombardy Poplar is '**Fastigiata**', also grown as '**Stricta**'. In time the upright branches droop under the weight of dense foliage and those which meet the ground often take root. Eventually a ring of layered trees can be produced round the original plant. All Western Red Cedars are capable of doing this. Rings of trees often remain after the original has gone.

There are several golden foliage forms although in Thuja this is never a radiant colour. The most popular is '**Zebrina**' selected in Britain in 1923. It has pretty zebra stripes of green and pale yellow across the fronds of scale leaves. Eventually it makes a big tree over 20m tall and thrives in a whole range of soil and site types. '**Zebrina Extra Gold**' is an improved form of it developed in 1987 in Ireland. It is sometimes found in collections still labelled with the invalid name 'Irish Gold'. Probably the strongest golden foliage colour Thuja can produce is on the vigorous cultivar '**Aurea**' produced in France in 1868. This too is ultimately a fairly large tree which is seldom seen in cultivation now. The dwarf form 'Stoneham Gold' is much more popular.

Growth: 4-8-15. Hardiness: 50%. Choice: 1.

'Zebrina'

3 year seedling

'Aurea'

'Zebrina'

White Cedar — open cone — underside — stem

Chinese Thuja — underside

'Douglasii Pyramidalis'

'Waxen'

'Holmstrup Yellow'

'Lutea'

'Spiralis'

White Cedar

White Cedar *Thuja occidentalis* (see also p. 89)

Also known as the American Arbor-vitae this hardy species has a natural range extending from eastern Canada to New York State. It is a good species on poor swampy ground, which in cultivation makes it ideal for damp lowland sites. The shape of the tree is usually slender with a straight buttressed stem. It only grows to 15m, half the height of its western counterpart in America. See p. 261 for cone.

Growth: 3-7-15. Hardiness: 80-90%. Choice: 2. Wood: 2, 3.

Thuja occidentalis cultivars (see also p. 89)

There are approximately 300 named forms of White Cedar dating back to its early introduction to Europe in 1536 and Britain around 1596. In 1891 '**Douglasii Pyramidalis**' was obtained by the Späth Nursery in Germany from the Arnold Arboretum. In outline it is very like the species but has slightly shorter twigs and less vigour.

'**Waxen**' also from the Arnold Arboretum in the same year has greenish-yellow foliage in summer and drooping foliage. Before 1873 an early golden form '**Lutea**' was produced at Maxwell's Nursery in New York. It is another slender 10m tree with yellow foliage in full light, which fades to green in shade. A smaller golden plant is '**Holmstrup Yellow**' which is unlikely to exceed 4m in height. This garden cultivar originated in Denmark. It was discovered by Asger Jensen and described in 1965.

The much larger cultivar '**Spiralis**' is an interesting slender conical tree up to 15m tall. It has short twigs and compact foliage, producing a spiral effect. The exact origin of it is uncertain but it is believed to have come from the Atkins Nursery in New Jersey in 1920. It was described in 1923.

The cultivar '**Fastigiata**' was originally produced in Germany in 1865. However, it is unlikely that the original plant is still in cultivation. In the nineteenth century there was considerable debate about what to call it. At one time the same plant had three or four different names depending upon which authority was consulted. Furthermore the fastigiate form comes true from seed so it is impossible to identify present day specimens with any certainty.

Growth: variable. Hardiness: 60-80%. Choice: 1.

Chinese Thuja *Thuja orientalis* see p. 89

'**Bonita**' is a slow-growing cultivar with yellow foliage in spring, gradually fading to pale green.

Growth: 3-10-15. Hardiness: 40-60%. Choice: 2.

'Spiralis'   'Fastigiata'   'Lutea'   'Bonita'

♂ flower   ♀ flower

Japanese Arbor-vitae

cones

under-side

cone

'Hiba'

underside

open cone

Japanese Arbor-vitae   **'Aurea'**

Japanese Arbor-vitae *Thuja standishii*

This 20-30m tall tree has a straight stem and wide spreading branches which ascend towards the extremities. The foliage is lax and open always letting some light shine through. In northern areas the young scale leaves are occasionally scorched by frost. The name Arbor-vitae, means 'Tree of Life' and is also applied to many other Thujas. This species, from central Japan, was introduced to the UK Standish Nurseries in 1860.

Growth: 5-12-25. Hardiness: 50%. Choice: 2. Wood: 2, 3.

Hiba *Thujopsis dolabrata*

This close relative of Korean Thuja is the only species in a monotypic genus. It is often called False Arbor-vitae. The scale leaves are dark glossy green with bright white markings on the underside. In its native Japan it is a forest tree up to 30m tall. In cultivation it is generally grown in isolation as a specimen so its height is usually somewhat less. In an open situation it makes a broad pyramid of dense foliage reaching to the ground. Large bottom branches appear to layer and then set off upwards again, as happens with Western Red Cedar.

There are several cultivars of Hiba, although the species is such a good tree that horticultural improvement hardly seems justified. 'Variegata' is the most common, but the amount of variegation is often limited and has to be searched for. '**Aurea**' is a yellowish-green form developed in Britain in 1866. The back of the foliage has a lovely silver and gold effect to rival the finest and most intricate jewellery.

Growth: 3-12-25. Hardiness: 40-50%. Choice: 1. Wood: 2, 3.

Korean Thuja *Thuja koraiensis*

Korean Arbor-vitae is a small tree, often only an untidy shrub in cultivation. At a glance the foliage looks very ordinary, like other Thujas but shorter than most and somewhat thicker. However, when it is lifted up to reveal the underside it is far from ordinary. Each scale is bright silver outlined delicately in pale green. Its native range is north and central Korea where it was described in 1834. It appears to have not reached western nurseries until 1917.

Growth: 3-6-12. Hardiness: 50%. Choice: 1. Wood: 5.

Chinese Thuja

open cone

closed cone

seed

Chinese Thuja

'Flagelliformis'

'Filiformis'

'Wareana Lutescens'

'Elegantissima'

RED CEDARS

Chinese Thuja *Thuja orientalis*

This is usually a small tree not exceeding 15m in height, often with multiple but fairly straight vertical stems. The main ascending branches also subdivide frequently to form a dense cylindrical evergreen crown. Reddish-brown bark eventually exfoliates in fibrous scales but it is usually hidden from view by low branches. The dark green scaly leaves are difficult to distinguish from other Thujas but when crushed they do have a pungent scent, reminiscent of pine resin and disinfectant. The small 1.5cm cones have about six scales with a peculiar extension on the end of each one shaped like a rhinoceros horn. The species is native to China, Japan, Manchuria and Korea. It was brought into cultivation in 1752 and named, by Linnaeus in 1753.

There are a large number of cultivars of Chinese Thuja some of which are tender. '**Flagelliformis**' has thread-like foliage and was first described in 1837. The original plant was often grown close to temples in Japan but it is probably no longer in cultivation. Its integrity has been eroded by other similar-looking filamentous forms including new spontaneous seedlings which appear from time to time. '**Elegantissima**' is a small columnar tree with golden-yellow foliage. This turns greenish-yellow in summer and brownish or bronze in the winter. It was produced by Rollinson's Nursery in London around 1862.
Growth: 3-10-15. Hardiness: 40-60%. Choice: 2. Wood: 3.

Thuja occidentalis cultivars (see also p. 85)

In 1536 this tough subalpine 12-20m forest tree from Eastern Canada and the adjacent states of the USA was introduced to Paris, the first Thuja to reach Europe. Cedar oil is distilled from the twigs and vitamin C-rich tea was once brewed from the foliage. Although perfectly adapted to its hostile upland or swampy habitat in America, it has not been successful in European plantations, but it is represented in horticulture by many diverse cultivars.

'**Filiformis**' is a small bushy tree with filamentous foliage which may be erect or bend outwards. It is easily confused with other plants with similar foliage including the Chinese Thuja cultivars. This clone was produced in Germany and described in 1901. Another German cultivar is '**Wareana Lutescens**' the golden version of 'Wareana' a small dense 7m tree named after G. Weare from Coventry. The golden plant is compact with pale yellowish-green foliage first produced at the Hesse Nursery in 1884. These cultivars produce fertile seed so some deviation from the original has been inevitable.
Growth: variable. Hardiness: 40-60%. Choice: 1.

'Elegantissima'   **'Wareana Lutescens'**   **'Filiformis'**

♀ flowers

♂ flowers

underside

underside

fruit

old bark

Coast Redwood

sprouting burr

SWAMP CYPRESS FAMILY · Taxodiaceae

Coast Redwood *Sequoia sempervirens*

The world's tallest tree is a Coast Redwood, 112m measured in 1988. It is thought to be 400-500 years old. The largest number of rings counted on a cut stump is 2200. This species is able to re-grow from basal shoots when an original tree is broken or harvested, so root systems may be much older than the visible part of the tree. The native range is mostly on coastal alluvial soils from the extreme south-west corner of Oregon to central California, from sea level up to 900m. In this region it is possible for the forest trees to supplement their supplies of water by intercepting Pacific sea fog. Once extensive forests in that region are now much reduced by timber cutting. The warm pinkish-brown wood is of high quality. The reddish-brown bark is fibrous and spongy, divided up into soft vertical ridges and furrows. It is thick and heat resistant. Although not entirely fireproof it does resist forest ground fires sufficiently to enable many trees to survive. This is a fire climax species which requires the heat of fire to initiate cone opening and seed dispersal. It could be argued that the US Forest Service, by their efficient fire prevention procedures, are not actually helping conservation of this particular species.

The foliage is of two sorts – scale leaves on the leading shoots and flat 1-2cm pointed needles in two ranks elsewhere. They are dark green above and greenish-white on the undersides. Burrs form in the bark of some individuals. These readily sprout when removed from the tree and planted. See p. 261 for cone.

There are over 25 named varieties of Coast Redwood. One of the best known is '**Adpressa**' a French plant described in 1867 but now thought to be a variant of 'Albospica' which only dates back to 1903 and was raised in Italy. It produces numerous young creamy-white leafy shoot tips in spring. Although sometimes described as a 'dwarf' it would certainly out-grow a small garden.

Another good ornamental form is '**Cantab**', a modern sport which occurred in the Cambridge University Botanic Gardens in 1977. It has compact foliage, and at first appeared to be diminutive, but most specimens have actually grown quite tall. A specimen in Kent for example has exceeded 14m (1997).

Growth: 4-18-40. Hardiness: 30-40%. Choice: 1 (requires space). Wood: 2, 3.

'Adpressa'

underside

'Cantab'

old cone

seeds

♂ flowers

♀ flowers

young cones

seedling

Wellingtonia

92

Wellingtonia or Sierra Redwood
Sequoiadendron giganteum

This is one of the world's largest, oldest (over 3200 years) and most impressive trees. It is well known for its soft reddish-brown bark, huge stem thickness and great height (up to 76m). Old parkland stems develop great curving buttresses. If not grazed off, massive lower branches sweep down to the ground, layer, and then curve upwards again. Sometimes forming a complete ring of new trees. In natural conditions along the western slopes of the Sierra Nevada, this does not occur. Passing forest fires and suppression have removed all traces of low branches leaving bare cathedral-like columns supporting minimal tops. The dense evergreen foliage consists of overlapping pointed scales which completely obscure the shoots. The oval 5-7cm cones have flat ended scales. They accumulate in bunches for several years on the tree waiting for hot enough conditions to crack them open. In nature forest fires, usually caused by lightning strikes, to which redwoods are particularly prone, produce this heat. Burning also ensures that the competition is eliminated, the ground cleared, cleansed of disease or predators and furnished with a nutritious layer of wood ash.

Growth: 4-20-50. Hardiness: 40-50%. Choice: 1 (requires space). Wood: 3.

Sequoiadendron giganteum cultivars

Out of many named varieties two are of special note. **'Pendulum'** an 1871 French clone is a very curious form that is both fastigiate and pendulous at the same time. When growing upwards it is ridiculously narrow. So much so that it can not always support itself and leans or falls, or has to be supported artificially. It then seems content to produce curtains of very pendulous side shoots. An arched specimen at the Hillier Arboretum in Hampshire is nicknamed 'the carwash'. Following this unpredictable life-style it can suddenly set off in another direction, sideways or straight up.

A more conventional Redwood is **'Aureovariegatum'** raised in Ireland in 1856. It is a smaller conical version of the species with golden-yellow shoots. At its best as a young tree it tends to develop a diseased or nutrient-deficient look once the symmetrical shape is lost.

Wellingtonia
young tree

'Pendulum'

'Aureovariegatum'
young tree

'Elegans'

'Cristata'

'Aurescens'

'Elegans'

'Pyramidata'

autumn

'Elegans'
bush form

Japanese Cedar

Japanese Cedar *Cryptomeria japonica*
(see also p. 99)

This big 30-40m valuable forest tree has for many years been a fruitful source of ornamental cultivated forms and varieties. In Japan 337 races were listed at one stage. The species belongs to a monotypic genus occurring only in Japan and southern China. The evergreen foliage is reduced to thin woody, awl-shaped, pointed scales up to 1.2cm long, completely obscuring the shoot. The bark is coppery-red exfoliating in fibrous vertical strips. See p. 261 for cone.
Growth: 3-8-30. Hardiness: 50-60%. Choice: 1 (cvs). Wood: 1, 2, 3.

Cryptomeria japonica cultivars

'**Elegans**' is an untidy bush or small tree up to 10m tall. It has glaucous juvenile foliage which turns purple-brown in winter. In harsh winters quite alarmingly because it looks half dead. The leaf scales are extended to over 2cm long. They are pointed but soft. This cultivar was imported to England from Japan in 1854 by Thomas Lobb for the Veitch Nursery. There are now several different clones under this name in the nursery trade.

'**Cristata**' is a peculiar form with fasciated foliage among otherwise normal shoots, giving it a deformed and quite unhealthy look. It may achieve 8m in height but is very slow-growing. It was imported from Japan to Germany as 'Sekka-sugi' in 1900 and re-named 'Cristata' in 1901.

'**Aurescens**' may be as close as this species comes to a golden form. It makes a small compact tree which is greenish-yellow darkening in the winter to lime green. It is of Dutch origin, developed by the Blijdenstein Pinetum in 1937 and named in 1949.

'**Yoshino**' is an upright form with pale green foliage which tends to 'bronze' in cold winters. The outline is columnar with a conical top and relatively short even branches. It is of Japanese origin raised in the Yokohama Nursery around 1928.

'**Pyramidata**' is a short rather ragged pyramidal tree which is usually very narrow. The foliage is similar to the species, glaucous to deep green, but densely packed round the shoot. It was selected in France at the Paillet Nursery near Paris in 1891.
Growth: variable. Hardiness: 30-50%. Choice: 1.

'Aurescens'   'Yoshino'   'Pyramidata'

'Viminalis'

'Viminalis'

'Compacta'
old tree

96

JAPANESE CEDARS

Cryptomeria japonica 'Viminalis'
('Lycopodioides')

The European form of this cultivar (illustrated) is still called 'Lycopodioides' but it should more properly be called **'Viminalis'** which means 'with long slender shoots'. It has extended young growth, like lengths of cord 30cm or more long, but the plant is generally bushy and slow-growing. The leaf scales are short and tightly packed round the shoots. The cultivar 'Selaginoides' raised at the Rovelli Nursery in Italy in 1923, but no longer distinguishable, is the same.

The Japanese plant called 'Lycopodioides' is quite different. It has tufted compact shoots and short branches. The leaf scales are densely arranged and dark green. In Japan this plant is called 'Ikari-sugi' or 'Kusari-sugi' it was imported to the Mazel Nursery in France and named in 1875. Due to the confusing situation with names in Europe the true Japanese 'Lycopodioides' (meaning 'like a wolf's foot') is seldom available in the nursery trade.

'**Compacta**', in spite of its name, is a tree up to 15m tall with a cylindrical but open outline and conical top until old age causes it to spread out. The foliage is in dense clusters consisting of short, hard leaf scales that are blue-green. In old age the foliage thins out and is suppressed around the base, exposing multiple stems and untidy branches (illustrated). It is a French selection raised near Paris in 1877 and named by Elie Abel Carrière, head gardener at the nursery of the Natural History Museum in Paris in 1878. Confusingly this name was used again in Britain in 1972 to describe a completely different yellow-green bushy form growing at Wakehurst in Sussex.

The cultivar '**Sekkan**' – the Japanese name means 'snowcrowned' which describes the creamy-white tipped foliage – is of Japanese origin, but was raised in America in 1970. As is so often the case with Cryptomeria cultivars this form has been confused in horticulture with 'Sekka-sugi' which is actually a synonym for 'Cristata', quite a different plant with no variegation.
Growth: 1-2-4 variable. Hardiness: 40-60%. Choice: 1.

'**Compacta**'

'**Sekkan**'

'**Compacta**'
bark

Cryptomeria fortunei
underside
closed cone
young cone
♀ flower
♂ flowers

'Lobbii'

seedling
seed

Japanese Cedar 'Lobbii'
parkland specimen

Cryptomeria fortunei
old tree

Japanese Cedar *Cryptomeria japonica*
(see also p. 95)

This species is split between Japanese and Chinese varieties. The Chinese form, which should be called **Cryptomeria fortunei**, is found across central and southern China. It is a neat conical plant in its youth gradually opening out with age. Trees over 30m tall with straight stems are known. In many respects, red-brown vertically stripping bark for example, it is very similar to the Japanese species. It was introduced in 1842 by Sir Edward Hume and named (as a variety *sinensis*) in 1844. See p. 261 for cone.

'**Lobbii**' is a full-sized tree up to 30m tall, similar to the species except for having 'bunched' foliage especially at the branch ends. It is as common and as magnificent in ornamental collections as the true species. The first plants were sent from Java to England by Thomas Lobb in 1853.

'**Ashio-sugi**' is another full-sized forest tree. It is actually a clone of the variety *radicans* which was identified in 1941 as a superior type and widely planted in Japanese forests. The stems are slender and particularly straight. It is only propagated by cuttings so although the genetic base is narrow, all originating from a single plant, the pedigree is very pure. *Cryptomeria japonica* var. *radicans* deserves more attention from the forest industry in the western world. The potential for producing high quality straight softwood timber is good.

'**Dacrydioides**' has foliage that is not bunched at the branch tips. The shoots are somewhat sinuous and spreading, but often forming a tangle of foliage. It is a bushy plant usually green to the ground because of the pendulous branches. In winter the dark green foliage turns brown. This species originated in Japan and was named by Elie Abel Carrière in Paris in 1867.

'**Pungens**' was sent to England in 1861 by Robert Fortune, who worked in Japan from 1860 with John Gould Veitch and Philipp von Siebold. It is a curious dwarf form with compact, hard short-leaved foliage. The outline is usually conical unless damaged. The deep green foliage does not go brown in winter.

Growth: variable (Lobbii: 3-8-30). Hardiness: 40-60%. Choice: 1.

'Ashio-sugi'

Japanese Cedar

cones

open cone

'Pungens'

'Dacrydioides'

new leaves

♂ flower

♀ flower

autumn

closed cone

seed

seedling

autumn

Dawn Redwood

100

Dawn Redwood *Metasequoia glyptostroboides*

There is one species remaining in this genus which, until 1941, was thought to be extinct. Palaeontologists were able to distinguish fossils of *Metasequoia* from those of true Redwoods (*Sequoia*), by their opposite and decussate shoots. In 1941 live specimens were discovered in south-west China. Dawn Redwood is a large, 40m tall, deciduous conifer with a narrow conical outline and light ascending branches. The original introduction to the west in 1948 was of clonal material raised vegetatively from cuttings. As timber trees these were flawed because the stems and lower branch intersections became deeply fluted. In the 1980s new seed imports from Chinese trees without this defect were made. The potential for Dawn Redwood as a plantation species appears to be good although it has not been tested on a large scale. It also makes an attractive tree, with its light green feathery foliage in summer and rusty brown autumn colour. A handful of ornamental clones with compact or lighter-coloured foliage have been selected in Canada and Holland.

Growth: 3-10-25 (40). Hardiness: 50%. Choice: 1 (requires space), 3. Wood: 2, 3.

Chinese Swamp Cypress
Glyptostrobus pensilis

The exact distribution of this monotypic genus in south-east China has been obscured by years of extensive planting. The one remaining species thrives with its roots close to, or in, water. It is an ideal tree for stabilising river banks and providing shelter in wetlands where little else will grow. Outside China it is seldom seen in cultivation, its place usually being taken by Swamp Cypress (p. 103), which is larger, faster-growing and less tender. The two are not closely related, Chinese Swamp Cypress, although deciduous, is allied to Cryptomeria (p. 95).

Growth: 2-4-15. Hardiness: 20%. Choice: 1.

Taiwania cryptomerioides

Potentially this is a huge tree, up to 60m tall in the wild, which grows on the island of Taiwan. Enormous stems like those of Wellingtonia (p. 93), 10m in diameter, have been recorded. The juvenile foliage is very similar to *Cryptomeria japonica* (p. 95) to which it is related. Adult foliage is scale-like and completely obscures the shoot.

Growth: 2-5-16 (60). Hardiness: 20-30%. Choice: 1. Wood: 1, 2, 3.

cones

Chinese Swamp Cypress

Taiwania cryptomerioides

young tree

Swamp Cypress

flower
♂ flowers
shoot
'Nutans'
autumn
seedling
winter
'knees'
cone
summer

Swamp Cypress

SWAMP CYPRESSES

Swamp Cypress *Taxodium distichum*

The natural range of this distinctive wetland tree extends from Texas and New Jersey northwards along the main river basins to Tennessee and southern Delaware. It is potentially a 30m tall deciduous conifer with soft pale green needles arranged alternately along the shoot. In the autumn these turn through brick red to golden-brown before falling late in the season. The surface roots produce vertical extensions (knees) above the ground in permanently wet conditions, and help the oxygen supply when the ground water is stagnant.

The species was introduced to Europe around 1640 but it has never had more than a limited role. Although it thrives in very wet conditions it will grow perfectly well on drier sites. It is completely hardy except that terminal buds are never formed and this can make young trees vulnerable to frost damage. As a timber producer the fluted stems are a disadvantage. However, the soft, light, non-resinous wood is easy to work and durable. In the past it was used in America for house building and furniture. Felled trees coppice easily, so once they are established a sustainable source of timber is assured.

Growth: 3-8-30. Hardiness: 60-70%. Choice: 1, 3. Wood: 2, 3.

Pond Cypress *Taxodium ascendens*

This 20m tree occurs along the American coastal plain from Louisiana to Virginia and Florida. It is a close relative of Swamp Cypress but occurs on higher ground in parts of its range. In some places they grow together in or out of standing water. Pond Cypress is capable of producing 'knees' but it rarely does so. It is a deciduous erect narrow-crowned conifer producing golden brown autumn foliage colour. The common form in cultivation is '**Nutans**' (illustrated) meaning nodding: a reference to the drooping shoot tips. In America this tree is called *Taxodium distichum* var. *nutans*. It is not common in cultivation and is frequently mistaken for Swamp Cypress: there are no reliable ways to distinguish the two. The species and the cultivar appear to have been introduced to Europe in 1789. At that time they were probably regarded as the same thing.

Growth: 3-7-20. Hardiness: 50-60%. Choice: 3. Wood: 2, 3.

'Nutans'
winter

Swamp Cypress
autumn

♂ flower ♀ flower **Summit Cedar** **King William Pine**

young cones

♂ flowers

♀ flower

young cone

old cone

old cone

new cone

young tree **Summit Cedar** **King William Pine**
old tree, artificially pruned

TASMANIAN CEDARS

Summit Cedar *Athrotaxis laxifolia*

Also known as 'Tasmanian Cedar' this moderately hardy 15m tree grows in the mountains of western Tasmania. It occurs in open wooded country with other mixed species. In cultivation on a good site it may grow taller with a rounded-conic top and straight stem. The bark becomes vertically shredded in old age. Awl-shaped, thick, evergreen, incurved scale leaves cover the shoots. They are spirally arranged and 4-6mm long with free tips. The cones are 2cm across with pointed scales. Tiny seeds similar to those of Wellingtonia (p. 93), each with a pair of rudimentary wings, are freely produced, but are seldom fertile in cold areas.

Growth: 2-7-12. Hardiness: 20-30%. Choice: 1. Wood: 5.

King William Pine *Athrotaxis selaginoides*

This is a temperate rain forest species from western Tasmania. It occurs with Cider Gum (p. 741) and other Eucalyptus species at around 1000m elevation in mountainous country. Trees vary in height from 15-35m. In cultivation it is moderately tender but will grow in moist areas such as western Ireland. It was described by David Don, professor of botany in London in 1839 and introduced to Europe in about 1857. The bark is fibrous, peeling and reddish-brown similar to the Redwoods (p. 91). The thick awl-shaped evergreen leaves are about 1cm long and held out from the shoot. They are spirally arranged and have bright white stomatal bands on the inner surfaces. The cones are 2.5cm across with many pointed scales. The foliage is reminiscent of Japanese Cedar (p. 95).

Growth: 3-8-15. Hardiness: 10%. Choice: 1.

Smooth Tasmanian Cedar

Athrotaxis cupressoides

A tender 12m tall tree from western Tasmania which is rare in cultivation. It has peculiar foliage which consists of deep green adpressed 3mm scales tightly packed round cord-like shoots. These densely clothe the short branches, which form a ragged conical outline. The cones are globular, 1cm across, woody with a short spike on the end of each scale. Although described in 1839 and introduced into cultivation in 1848, this tree has never become universally popular.

Growth: 2-6-10. Hardiness: 10%. Choice: 1.

Smooth Tasmanian Cedar

Chinese Fir

'Glauca'

young cone

closed mature cone

flower

flowers

underside

Chinese Fir

Japanese Umbrella Pine

Chinese Fir *Cunninghamia lanceolata*

This forest tree, with potential for much wider commercial use in western plantations, occurs right across China. It was first discovered by a European in 1701, but not introduced to Europe until 1804 when William Kerr brought material from Canton. In China, and in cultivation, it makes a medium-sized (10-20m) tree on a fat, more or less straight stem. The outline is columnar but bulging out of shape with great age. The suppressed bare lower branches are retained for many years. Any dead foliage on them turns conspicuously orange-brown. The bark is reminiscent of Redwood (p. 91) but harder. The evergreen leaves are lanceolate, 7cm long and 0.5cm across the base. Although flexible they have a very sharply spined tip. Most occur in two ranks but tend to curve upwards over the shoot on strong well lit branches. The colour is brilliant green, one of the brightest greens of any conifer, enhanced by a glossy upper surface and two broad white bands below. The female cones are 3-4cm long, ovoid with pointed scale tips, green at first maturing to pale brown. Male cones in terminal short-lived clusters occur on separate trees.

The cultivar '**Glauca**' described in 1931, produces silvery-green current shoots which droop to give a pleasing weeping effect when the plant is young.
Growth: 3-7-20 (species). Hardiness: 30-40%.
Choice: 1 (requires space), 3. Wood: 2, 3.

Japanese Umbrella Pine
Sciadopitys verticillata

This is the one surviving plant in a genus which is otherwise extinct. It has a primeval appearance befitting its precarious status. Fossil evidence suggests a widespread distribution. It occurs in coal measures in Europe. Now living trees are confined to southern Japan where they remained undiscovered by outsiders until 1776. One plant was brought to Britain in 1853 by Thomas Lobb. Others followed in the 1860s. It is a rare slow-growing conical specimen with unique foliage. The 10cm stiff evergreen needles appear to be in pairs that are fused together, although botanically this is not strictly true: they are arranged in regularly spaced whorls like the spokes of an umbrella. The 7cm cones are oval or nearly round like those of Wellingtonia (p. 93).
Growth: 2-6-14. Hardiness: 50-60%. Choice: 1. Wood: 3, 5.

Japanese Umbrella Pine

King Boris Fir

underside

cone of King Boris Fir

Cilician Fir

underside

Cilician Fir

cone of Cilician Fir

King Boris Fir

PINE FAMILY • Pinaceae

King Boris Fir *Abies × borisii-regis*

Some authorities consider this tree to be a natural hybrid between *Abies alba* (p. 137) and *Abies cephalonica* (p. 131), which is the designation accepted here. Others consider it to be a legitimate species in its own right. It occurs in its own distribution area in the central part of the Balkan peninsula. Within this natural range it comes true from seed. Superficially it resembles *Abies alba* with deep green glossy 3cm needles and 15cm upright cones. These are cylindrical with rounded ends and exserted bracts between the scales. Trees over 25m tall are known. This taxon was first cultivated in 1883 and named in honour of the King of Bulgaria.

Growth: 4-18-30. Hardiness: 50-60%. Choice: 3. Wood: 2, 4.

Cilician Fir *Abies cilicica*

This large 30m tree is rare in its native range and in cultivation. It comes from southern Turkey, parts of Syria and the Lebanon – a southern extension of the range of the closely related Caucasian Fir. The large upright cones, sometimes over 20cm long, are deciduous but leave conspicuous woody spines fixed to the tree when they break up.

Growth: 3-15-30. Hardiness: 40-50%. Choice: 3. Wood: 2, 4.

Tienshan Fir *Abies sibirica* var. *semenovii*

Siberian Fir (*A. sibirica*) is a native tree over a huge diverse part of central and eastern Asia. This hardy variety of it is confined to the Tienshan area. It differs only in minute details of foliage. In cultivation it is rare and its status is uncertain. This is partly because the same plant is listed under different names, such as *Abies semenovii*.

Growth: 1-2-10. Hardiness: 90-100%. Choice: 1.

Sakhalin Fir *Abies sachalinensis*

Also closely related to Siberian Fir, this species is limited to northern Japan, Sakhalin and the Kurile Islands. Presumably it is a segregate population isolated during the Tertiary Period. It makes a neat tree around 15m tall with pale grey scaly bark. The rich green needles are soft and rather haphazard in direction and length. They have two greenish white stomatal bands on the underside. The cones, which may be up to 8cm long, occasionally have exserted bracts. There are two naturally occurring varieties. *Mayriana* has thinner bark and exserted cone bracts, and **nemorensis** has smaller cones and short needles.

Growth: 2-7-15. Hardiness: 90%. Choice: 3. Wood: 3.

Tienshan Fir

var. **nemorensis** underside

underside

Sakhalin Fir

new growth

Shensi Fir

underside

♀ flower

Veitch's Silver Fir

♂ flowers

Veitch's Silver Fir

Veitch's Silver Fir *Abies veitchii*

This extremely hardy fir is from the mountains of central Japan, where it grows in sub-alpine (-40°C) conditions up to 2400m. It is beautifully symmetrical and conical when grown in the open and retains a conical top even in plantations. Only the great productivity of the main American species has prevented this species from having a much wider role in modern European forestry. It was discovered by the English nurseryman, John Gould Veitch, on Mount Fujiyama in 1860-61 but appears to have been sent to America before Europe in 1876. In 1879 Charles Maries, who worked for the Veitch Nursery, sent seed to England. One of the resulting trees was planted in 1881 in Kent, and it survived until 1951.

The 2cm flexible needles are dark glossy green with two broad brilliant white bands on the underside. This dramatic white foliage is usually hidden from view until the branch tip is lifted up. The bluish-purple upright cones are 7cm long with exerted bracts. Situated on the topmost branches, they mature in one season, turn pale brown and disintegrate, showering down a rain of winged seeds and cone scale debris. The central spine of the cone remains on the tree for several years. The bark is olive-brown at first, very smooth with sporadic resin blisters. It becomes pale-coloured and then fissured with age. Although best in a moist climate with relatively acid soil, this species will tolerate a wide range of conditions including urban situations.

Growth: 4-9-25. Hardiness: 80-90%.
Choice: 1 (requires space), 2, 3. Wood: 2, 4.

Shensi Fir *Abies chensiensis*

The species *chensiensis* from northern China is extremely rare in cultivation and its status in the wild is uncertain. Most plants encountered now are subspecies *salouenensis*, the **Salween Fir**. Originally from the mountains of northern Yunnan to Burma and the eastern border of India, it is an evergreen tree, seldom exceeding 18m in height. The distinctive needles spread out each side of the shoot. They are up to 7.5cm long, longer on the subspecies than the type. Cones up to 10cm long turn from blue-purple or blue-green to light brown on ripening. Although quite hardy these trees will only thrive in moist sheltered areas.

Growth: 3-8-18. Hardiness: 60%. Choice: 4. Wood: 2, 4.

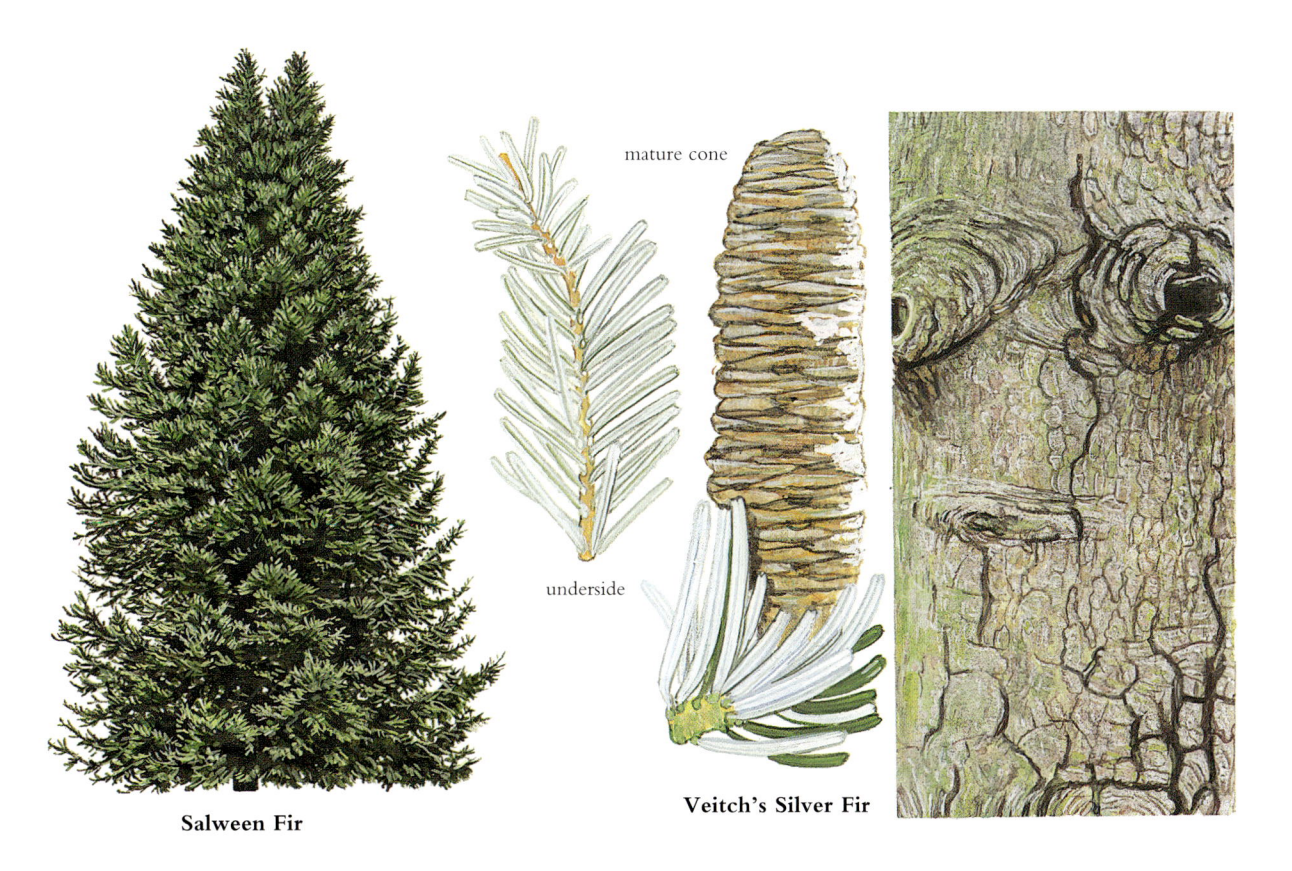

Salween Fir

mature cone
underside

Veitch's Silver Fir

Min Fir

leaves pointing back

leaves pointing forward

underside

Min Fir

Min Fir cone

Abies fargesii var. *sutchuenensis*

112

Min Fir *Abies recurvata*

This large 40m tree is from western China in the mountainous Min valley. In cultivation it seldom achieves half this height. It becomes a spreading rather untidy tree after early upright growth. The dense foliage is glossy green and retained on the shoots and branches for several years. The needles are acutely pointed, 1.5-3.5cm long and recurved or bent backwards (hence the species name) along the upper side of the shoot. Deciduous cones ripen and disintegrate in one season. They are violet to dark brown, about 7cm long, ovoid oblong with a short pointed tip. The tips of pointed bracts sometimes project beyond the scales towards the base of the cone. The species was named by Maxwell Masters an English botanist in 1906 and was introduced to Britain in 1910. It is not popular in collections although extremely hardy.

Growth: 3-7-20 (40). Hardiness: 50-60%. Choice: 3. Wood: 2, 4.

Abies fargesii var. *sutchuenensis*

Although this variety still occurs in named collections, as *Abies sutchuenensis*, it is no longer considered to be botanically distinct. Even in 1911 when introduced it was thought to be 'close' to *Abies fargesii* (p. 119). It occurs slightly to the west of the species in central China. Adrien Franchet from the Natural History Museum in Paris named it as a variety. He was then overruled for a time in favour of a species designation by Ernest Wilson, who was probably familiar with the plant in China, and Alfred Rehder the dendrologist at the Arnold Arboretum in the USA. Now it is simply considered to be a segregate of the *Abies fargesii* population.

Growth: 4-7-18. Hardiness: 60%. Choice: 2, 3. Wood: 2, 4.

Maries' Fir *Abies mariesii*

Charles Maries, an English plant collector for the Veitch Nursery, introduced this sub-alpine Japanese tree to Europe in 1879. It was named in his honour by Maxwell Masters in 1897. It grows in close association with Veitch's Silver Fir in the northern and central regions of Honshu, Japan, to around 20-25m in height with a straight stem and neat conical outline. The 1-2cm needles are crowded above the shoot and parted below it. The upper surfaces are glossy-green and there are conspicuous white bands beneath. Young cones are violet-purple in summer turning blackish-brown at maturity and then disintegrating. (See also following page.)

Growth: 4-8-22. Hardiness: 60%. Choice: 2, 3. Wood: 2, 4.

underside

Abies fargesii var. **sutchuenensis**

Maries' Fir

underside

Maries' Fir

underside

♂ flowers

♂ flowers

underside

expanding buds

Sacred Fir

Sacred Fir

114

Maries' Fir (continued from previous page)

This species is the Japanese counterpart of *Abies amabilis* (p. 125) across the Pacific ocean in America. They both have rusty brown velvety hairs on the shoots.

Sacred Fir *Abies religiosa*

This tender species comes from central and southern Mexico and northern Guatemala. It was originally named in 1830 and brought into cultivation in 1838. In Europe it almost died out before a new consignment of seed was brought to Britain in 1962. In Mexico it is a 30m tree with a short branched conical top. The bark is greyish-brown and smooth for many years before cracking in old age. Needles are parted above the shoot but bend forwards and outwards. Below the shoot they turn downwards. The length may be variable, 2-3.5cm, the stomatal bands can be pale grey or white. Tips are yellowish running to a fine point. In most respects they are superficially like Douglas Fir (p. 201). The cones are barrel-shaped narrowing towards the tip, around 10cm long and blue-black becoming brown at maturity. The long exserted bracts with reflexed tips are distinctive. Sacred Fir was formerly used in Mexican religious festivals, hence the name.

Growth: 3-8-15. Hardiness: 40%. Choice: 3. Wood: 2, 4.

Vejar Fir *Abies vejari*

Closely related to Sacred Fir, this tree comes from north-east Mexico where it grows in mixed forests with *Pinus hartwegii* and *Pinus rudis* (p. 257). It is a mountain species but tends to always shelter below the pine canopy and never extends to the edge of the tree line. There are variations in the foliage colour and cone size. Northern plants have blue-green needles and larger cones. Some authorities suggest variety *macrocarpa* for this form. The plant illustrated is the more typical type. It was named in 1942 by Martinez and introduced into cultivation (in Britain) in 1962. The pointed 2cm needles are evenly packed round the shoot except for a parting on the underside of weak side shoots. The 6-15cm barrel-shaped cones are purplish-black, with spots of white encrusted resin.

Growth: 3-8-20. Hardiness: 30-40%. Choice: 3. Wood: 2, 4.

young tree

Vejar Fir

underside

underside

Abies forrestii var. *smithii*

Forrest's Silver Fir

♀ flower

underside

leaf section underside

undersi

♂ flower

Faber Fir

Abies forrestii var. *smithii*

Abies fabri subsp. *minensis*

under

116

Delavay Fir *Abies delavayi* (complex)

This plant named in 1899 and introduced to the west from its native China, west Yunnan, north Burma and northern India in 1918, has been subjected to rigorous taxonomic scrutiny. In the early 1900s it was considered appropriate to regard several closely related species as varieties of Delavay Fir. Subsequently these varieties reverted to species status again, or became varieties of other species. It could be argued now that the name *Abies delavayi* is no longer valid. However, trees bearing this name are still to be found. They are variable but medium-sized, with deep green glossy needles with rolled down edges round a white underside. The 10cm barrel-shaped cones are violet-blue ripening to dark brown.

Growth: 4-9-25. Hardiness: 40-50%. Choice: 1 (requires space), 3. Wood: 2, 4.

Abies forrestii var. *smithii*

Formerly *Abies delavayi* var. *georgei* this 25m straight tree is distinguished by its reddish hairy twigs. The deep green glossy needles are up to 2cm long and white on the underside. The 9cm cones have exerted bracts.

Growth: 3-7-25. Hardiness: 50%. Choice: 1 (requires space), 3.

Forrest's Silver Fir *Abies forrestii*

Originally another variety of Delavay fir this species comes from north-west Yunnan, western China and south-east Tibet. It is a small straight tree seldom reaching 20m in height. The variable 2-4cm needles are pectinate, dark glossy green above and silvery white on the underside. The violet-black 12cm cones have short exserted bracts. George Forrest is credited with its introduction to Britain in 1910.

Growth: 4-9-20. Hardiness: 50%. Choice: 1 (requires space), 3. Wood: 2, 4.

Faber Fir *Abies fabri*

This large 40m tree is from western China. It was introduced to Europe in 1901 but remains rare in cultivation. It too has been classified in the past as a variety of Delavay Fir. The bark is distinctly scaly and dark-coloured. The irregular needles are 2-3cm long and more or less pectinate, deep glossy-green above and brilliant white beneath. The 6-8cm cones are blue-black with exserted and reflexed bracts.

This species is closely related to Forrest's Silver Fir and difficult to distinguish with certainty. **Abies fabri subsp. *minensis*** is almost the same. The shoots are slightly more pubescent. The needles, in two ranks are 1.5cm above the shoot and 2.5cm to the side. This subspecies has been classified as *Abies faxoniana*, *Abies fargesii* (p. 119) and *Abies delavayi* var. *faxoniana*. In cultivation trees labelled with all these names can still be found.

Growth: 4-15-40. Hardiness: 40-50%. Choice: 3. Wood: 2, 3, 4.

Abies forrestii var. *smithii*

Forrest's Silver Fir

Abies fabri subsp. *minensis*

Gamble Fir

underside

new growth

underside

underside

Korean Fir

Gamble Fir

Taiwan Fir

Korean Fir

Gamble Fir *Abies gamblei*

One of a series of closely related Himalayan silver firs, this species was originally considered to be a variety of *Abies pindrow* (p. 129). The original plant came into cultivation, in 1860, from northern India but it is now thought to be extinct in the wild. It was named in 1929 but its true taxonomic identity still seems to be in doubt. The foliage is rich glossy green and the 8-12cm cones are violet-blue in the summer.
Growth: 4-9-25. Hardiness: 50%. Choice: 4. Wood: 3.

Korean Fir *Abies koreana*

This small 10m tree has a straight stem and strikingly dark-coloured bark. The needles are short, seldom over 1.5cm, with very blunt notched ends giving a 'clipped' look, deep glossy green above with two brilliant silver bands of stomata on the underside. Seen from below the foliage has a silvery-green appearance. The cones are bloomed purple, maturing to dull brown in the autumn. They are around 6cm long, cylindrical, but with rounded ends. They appear on plants as young as five years which gives the tree considerable garden appeal. However, heavy coning does result in the proliferation of bare leafless branches, which spoils the plant's appearance in subsequent years. Originally from Korea and its neighbouring islands, this species was discovered and introduced around 1905 and finally named in 1920.
Growth: 2-4-10. Hardiness: 50-60%. Choice: 1.

Taiwan Fir *Abies kawakamii*

Another relative of Korean Fir, this species is from high ground in Taiwan. It is a small but generally straight tree, up to 15m tall, with interesting pale corky bark. The purple cones are 8cm long and cylindrical with rounded ends. The species was named in 1909 and introduced to Europe before 1930.
Growth: 2-5-12. Hardiness: 30-40%. Choice: 1. Wood: 3.

Farges's Fir *Abies fargesii*

The silver firs of northern China are a difficult group to identify and classify. Even within this single species there is variation. It has been named and re-named as a species and also as a variety of *Abies delavayi* (p. 117). It is a strong-growing tree, but only likely to reach 15m in height. The parted and notched evergreen needles are dark glossy green with twin white bands on the underside. The purple cones which are around 7cm long turn brown and disintegrate on ripening, a characteristic of all *Abies* species. It was discovered by and named after Père Farges in 1899 and introduced to the west by Ernest Wilson in 1901. See also p. 113, *Abies fargesii* var. *sutchuenensis*.
Growth: 3-7-15. Hardiness: 50%. Choice: 4. Wood: 3.

Momi Fir

♂ flowers

♀ flower

underside

Momi Fir   **Cheng Fir**

Momi Fir *Abies firma*

This large 30m tree occurs in Japan from Honshu southwards to Kyushu and Shikoku. It is closely related to Nikko Fir (p. 123) from part of the same location. The crown is conical but the whorled branches continue to extend each year until the whole tree becomes very broad. The bark is pale pinkish-grey, especially on young branches. It develops an uneven surface as resin blisters form and then becomes corky and lightly fissured in old age. The 1.5-2.5cm leathery evergreen needles are pectinate but turn upwards to more or less cover the top of the shoot. They are yellowish green and lustrous on the upper side and grey-green, in two distinct stomatal bands, below. The needle tips are rounded or strongly notched. On young vigorous shoots this notch is in the form of two individual points, and an old name for the species, *Abies bifida*, reflects this characteristic. The 12cm cones have bracts only slightly exposed towards the base. They ripen to yellowish-brown and disintegrate in the autumn.

This species has been in general cultivation since 1861 when it was introduced to England by John Gould Veitch. A short-needled form was discovered in Sussex and called 'Tardina', but this name is invalid. It is possible that variants of Momi Fir exist, but it is equally likely that hybrids have occurred, especially between it and the Asiatic group of Silver Firs.

Growth: 4-18-30. Hardiness: 40-60%. Choice: 2, 3. Wood: 2, 3, 4.

Cheng Fir *Abies chengii*

There is some doubt about the authenticity of this medium-sized (15-20m) straight tree. It is closely related to several other Asiatic firs and may be a hybrid between *Abies forrestii* and *Abies chensiensis* subspecies *salouensis*. It was named and described in 1987 by Keith Rushforth. The type specimen was a tree at Westonbirt, collected by George Forrest around 1931 and planted as *Abies forrestii*. Although perfectly healthy in 1987, it died soon after. This tree had a dense dark evergreen crown of branches on a persistent single stem. The shoots were mahogany red, becoming paler in subsequent years. The needles parted below the shoot and formed a V above it. They ranged from 2.5 to 4cm long, with a distinct notch in the tip. The violet-brown cones ripened in one season and disintegrated. This species, presumed to have come from Yunnan in China, is rare in cultivation and still likely to be confused with other similar Silver Firs.

Growth: 3-8-15. Hardiness: 50%. Choice: 4. Wood: 3.

Cheng Fir

Momi Fir
cone

Nikko Fir

ripe cone

Nikko Fir bark

young cones

underside

'Tomomi'

underside

Nikko Fir

Manchurian Fir

122

Nikko Fir *Abies homolepis*

This species belongs to a closely related group of Silver Firs from low altitude locations in south-east Asia. Nikko Fir is from southern Japan including Shikoku and Honshu. It was named in 1842 and brought into cultivation, in the west, in 1861. The stem is straight and up to 30m tall supporting mainly horizontal branches in regular whorls. A conical outline gradually develops with maturity into an irregular, somewhat open columnar shape. The 2-3cm deep green needles are pectinate below the pale-coloured shoot but crowd upwards and forwards above it. Each one has two bright white bands on the underside. The beautiful violet cones occur all over the tree. They are around 10cm long and stand upright, often in clusters or rows along the branch. This is an outstanding ornamental specimen tree, not only for its general appearance but also because it withstands some lime in the soil and is tolerant of urban air pollution.

The cultivar '**Tomomi**' was a peculiar form with short needles and spreading branches. It was produced in the USA in 1909 but the original clone is no longer in cultivation.

Growth: 4-20-30. Hardiness: 70%. Choice: 2, 3. Wood: 2, 3, 4.

Manchurian Fir *Abies holophylla*

Closely related to Nikko Fir, but much smaller, this species has a maximum height of only 15-20m. The outline is columnar, retaining a conical top for many years. Needles are carried all round the shoot but tend to turn upwards and forwards on side branches. They are 2-4cm long, with two pale bands on the underside. Cones, up to 14cm long, are bluish-green with a faint grey bloom in the summer, turning brown before disintegrating at the end of the season.

The species is native to Korea, northern China and Manchuria. Some strains are extremely hardy. It was named in 1866 and introduced to the west in 1908. Specimens can occasionally be found in arboreta and gardens in Europe, but it is uncommon.

Growth: 3-7-20. Hardiness: 50-60%. Choice: 2, 3. Wood: 2, 3, 4.

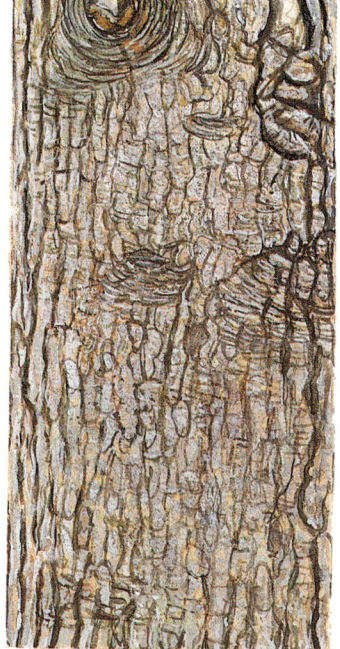

Manchurian Fir

underside

Red Fir

Californian Red Fir

♀ flower

♂ flowers

Red Fir | underside | **Californian Red Fir** | underside | **Californian Red Fir** bark

old American trees

124

Red Fir *Abies amabilis*

Also called the Pacific Silver Fir in its native northwest America, this tree is very large but remarkably slender. It grows to a spire-like point with short branches which develop a downward tendency. David Douglas, the Scottish plant hunter discovered it and named it *amabilis*, meaning 'lovely', in 1839. The dark green glossy evergreen needles are 2-4cm long with two bright white bands of stomata on the underside. The big upright cones are up to 15cm long and always found at the very top of the tree.
Growth: 5-20-40. Hardiness: 50-60%. Choice: 2, 3. Wood: 2, 4.

Californian Red Fir *Abies magnifica*

Perhaps Albert Murray, the American botanist who named this tree in 1863, regretted that the name 'Amabilis' had already been used by Douglas for another Silver Fir. However, he settled for 'Magnifica' for what is a truly magnificent tree. The common name is a reference to the colour of the bark. The curved needles are pectinate but bend upwards over the shoot. They are 2-3.5cm long and 4-sided with pale lines of stomata. The upright cones, on the top of the tree, are up to 20cm long. This American species grows at high elevation (1800-2700m) in the Cascade Mountains and through the Sierra Nevada to central California. It withstands dry summers and bitterly cold winters.

The only other Silver Fir with distinctly curved needles is Noble Fir (p. 145). There is a hybrid between Noble Fir and this species called Shasta Fir, *Abies × shastensis*. Some authorities consider it to be a variety of *Abies magnifica*. It occurs in nature between Lassen Peak, California, and Crater Lake, Oregon.
Growth: 5-20-40. Hardiness: 50%. Choice: 2, 3. Wood: 2, 4.

Fraser's Fir *Abies fraseri*

Although common in the Great Smoky Mountains, this tree has a fairly limited range in the USA. It extends only to south-west Virginia, western North Carolina and eastern Tennessee. Discovered by John Fraser from Scotland in 1811 and named in 1817, it is extremely hardy and grows to above 2000m in the mountains. The needles are very pectinate, spreading out in two distinct ranks. The undersides are silvery-white. The upright cones are 4-6cm long, dark purple in summer with yellowish bracts showing between each scale. This species is used locally as a Christmas tree.
Growth: 3-7-20. Hardiness: 60-70%. Choice: 2, 3. Wood: 2, 4.

Fraser's Fir

underside

Californian Red Fir cone

epicormic shoot

Himalayan Fir

underside

Himalayan Fir

var. *brevifolia*

Himalayan Fir *Abies spectabilis*

Sometimes known as East Himalayan Fir this evergreen species is from Afghanistan eastwards across the Himalayas to Bhutan. Usually it occurs in forests with *Abies pindrow* (p. 129) extending 1000m higher up the mountain sides. It was introduced into cultivation in 1822 and named at first *Abies webbiana* and then in 1824, *Abies spectabilis*, which means beautiful.

This is a spreading 20m tree with massive side branches which frequently die or break off only to be replaced by strong epicormic growth from the main stem. Quite a useful diagnostic feature in mixed collections of Silver Firs. The deeply notched needles are long (6cm) and held flat in two ranks. Outer ones tend to curve downwards under the shoot. The 7-15cm cones are grey-blue, becoming darker at the end of the season but remaining on the tree until the following spring. A purple dye was once made from the cones. In cultivation this tree often suffers damage from late frosts and cold drying winds.

The variety **brevifolia** is of uncertain taxonomic status, but it is quite unlike the species. It is a neat, short-branched conical tree with a straight 20-30m stem. The needles are short, as the variety name suggests, and deeply notched at the tip, 2-4cm long, strongly parted below the shoot but with only a narrow groove along the top side. They are grey-green with twin lines of paler stomata on the underside. This variety extends higher up into the mountains than the species. Variety status was suggested, for what in the strict botanical sense is a segregate of the species, by Alfred Rehder in 1919. It remains rare in cultivation in spite of being completely hardy.

Growth: 4-14-20. Hardiness: 40-60%. Choice: 2, 3. Wood: 2, 3, 4.

underside

Himalayan Fir

var. *brevifolia*

Pindrow Fir

var. *intermedia*

Pindrow Fir

underside

cone of Pindrow Fir

Flaky Fir

Pindrow Fir *Abies pindrow*

Also known as the West Himalayan fir this species grows in mixed forests with *Abies spectabilis* high up in the Himalayas from Afghanistan to western Nepal. Generally it occurs at lower elevation than *spectabilis* and there is a hybrid population (*Abies pindrow* var. **intermedia**) where the two overlap. Pindrow Fir can grow to 40m in height in ideal cool moist conditions. It has a columnar outline, usually with a conical top. Branches tend to be short and fairly light. The evergreen needles are long, up to 6cm, and widely parted in two layered ranks. They have a distinctly notched tip and two greenish-white bands of stomata on the underside. Cones are violet-blue without any extending bracts. The largest may just exceed 14cm long.

In addition to the variety **intermedia**, which inherits characteristics of both parents, there is another variety *Abies pindrow* var. *brevifolia*. It appears that all of the 'long-needled' silver firs also have a short-needled form. Confusingly these are usually called *brevifolia*. This one occurs in north-west India and is considered by some authorities to be a legitimate species, *Abies gamblei* (p. 119).

Growth: 4-20-30. Hardiness: 40-50% (species). Choice: 2, 3. Wood: 2, 3, 4.

Flaky Fir *Abies squamata*

A unique feature of this high elevation Chinese Fir is its red-brown bark which exfoliates in thin scales from stems and branches over five years old. On a good healthy tree this may hang thickly from large branches like peeling birch bark. Old stems become less flaky and fade to grey-brown. The stiff needles are parted below the shoot but spread and point upwards and sideways above it. The uppermost needles and those towards the shoot tip are only 1cm long. To the sides they may be up to 2.5cm long. The cones are purple in summer becoming brown at maturity. This very hardy species withstands dry conditions in cultivation. However, it grows very slowly in isolation and has only limited ornamental value.

Growth: 2-6-12. Hardiness: 50-60%. Choice: 2, 3. Wood: 3.

Flaky Fir

seed scale

seed

leaf detail

♂ flowers

♀ flower

Algerian Fir

Algerian Fir **Greek Fir**

Algerian Fir *Abies numidica*

This important North African counterpart of Spanish Fir (p. 133) occurs in north-east Algeria on lime-rich mountain sides. It is a large 25m tree with a straight persistent stem and conical top until old age or a harsh environment flattens it out. The evergreen needles are parted beneath the shoot but crowded sideways and upwards above it. They vary between 1 and 2cm long, the shortest point directly upwards. The 16cm cones (see p. 260) are slender, pale green flushed with a hint of purple, becoming light brown at maturity and then disintegrating. Algerian fir was brought into cultivation in France in 1861 and named by Elie Abel Carrière, head gardener at the Natural History Museum in Paris. The one advantage this tree has over most other silver firs in cultivation is its tolerance of lime in the soil.

Growth: 4-14-25. Hardiness: 50-70%. Choice: 2, 3. Wood: 2, 3, 4.

Greek Fir *Abies cephalonica*

The natural range of this huge bulky tree is the island of Cephalonica to northern Greece. It prefers well-drained rocky limestone slopes and extends high up into mountainous country. Although perfectly hardy it tends to come into leaf early in the spring and may be damaged by frost. Perhaps for this reason it becomes an untidy tree with several leading shoots and spreading forked branches. The evergreen needles have pointed translucent tips. They are dark glossy green with pairs of grey stomatal bands on the undersides. The cones are 10-16cm long.

This species is one of several segregates of European Silver Fir (p. 137). The variety *graeca*, **Apollo Fir**, is almost identical to it. Some authorities however, retain an alternative name *apollinis*. It grows in the region of Mount Parnassus in southern Greece, and has blunt shorter dense needles. The Trojan Fir (see p. 135) is also considered to be this variety although it grows some way off in north-west Turkey. Clearly all of the south-east European Silver Firs are closely related. Their precise classification is made more difficult by the inherent variability within each group, which has led to plenty of confusion over names.

Growth: 5-20-32. Hardiness: 50%. Choice: 1 (requires space). Wood: 2, 3, 4.

♂ flowers

underside

stem detail

new leaves

Spanish Fir

underside
stem

Sicilian Fir

Spanish Fir bark

Spanish Fir

'Glauca'

132

SILVER FIRS

Spanish Fir *Abies pinsapo*

The foliage of this 20m tree is unique among Silver Firs and instantly recognizable. The blunt stiff 1.5cm needles stick out all round the shoot like the spines on a hedgehog. They are deep grey-green giving the whole tree a rather sombre appearance. The native range is now confined to just three sites in southern Spain, but cultivated specimens have been planted all over Europe. It is hardy as far north as southern Sweden. The ornamental cultivar '**Glauca**' raised in France in 1867 has paler grey-green foliage. It was originally a selection from the naturally variable native population.
Growth: 4-9-20. Hardiness: 40-50%. Choice: 1 (requires space). Wood: 2, 3, 4.

Vilmorin's Fir *Abies × vilmorinii*

This hybrid between *Abies pinsapo* and *Abies cephalonica* (p. 131) was first cultivated in France in 1867 and eventually named in 1901. The cross occurs spontaneously, either way round, wherever the parent species are planted in close proximity to each other. It develops into a magnificent shapely tree with glossy deep green foliage, exhibiting the best ornamental qualities of the parents.
Growth: 3-6-20. Hardiness: 50%. Choice: 1. Wood: 3.

East Siberian Fir *Abies nephrolepis*

Also known as Khinghan Fir, this 15m tree is outstandingly hardy. It comes from a harsh environment in Manchuria and northern China. Separate populations can also be found in Korea and close to the east coast of Russia. Across the Pacific Ocean in North America this tree's close relatives Balsam and Alpine Firs (p. 141 and p. 139) are found, suggesting a single primeval population that was in existence before the sea intervened. Distinguishing features are small (7cm) cones and the very narrow needles.
Growth: 3-8-15. Hardiness: 90%. Choice: 2.

Sicilian Fir *Abies nebrodensis*

This close relative of European Silver Fir (p. 137) has almost been exploited to extinction in its native northern Sicily. It is a relatively small tree, seldom reaching over 14m in height. The finely shredding bark is orange-brown. The short, 1.5-2cm, needles are densely packed more or less in two horizontal ranks along the shoot. They are dark green above and have two light grey stomatal bands on the underside. The erect deciduous cones in the very tops of trees are cylindrical and about 10cm long. Most trees are now in ex-situ collections where they have been in cultivation since 1908.
Growth: 5-10-15. Hardiness: 40-50%. Choice: 1 (requires space). Wood: 3.

underside

Vilmorin's Fir

underside

East Siberian Fir

stem detail

♂ flowers

Caucasian Fir

♀ flower

underside

Caucasian Fir

closed cone

SILVER FIRS

Caucasian Fir *Abies nordmanniana*

This hardy verdant form of European Silver Fir, also known as Crimean Fir, comes from the Caucasus Mountains and north-east Turkey. It has a huge straight persistent stem, up to 60m tall, and a columnar outline. The dark glossy green foliage is retained for longer than any other fir. Up to 14 years is commonplace, and sometimes trees will hold green needles for 20. This creates a dense effect that immediately identifies Caucasian Fir from some way off. The individual evergreen needles are about 3cm long and crowded round the shoot, almost covering the upper side. The greenish-brown 20cm cones, always at the top of the tree, have exerted reflexed bracts between the scales. The tree has a long history of forest use in Eastern Europe, but was not introduced to the west until 1848. In Britain, where large imports of seed arrived in 1854, this species has largely been ignored as a forest tree because more productive American conifers became available at the same time. As an ornamental specimen it found favour from the start and it is now in almost every arboretum, park and stately garden. Lime-rich soils do not preclude it, although better growth may be expected on moist, slightly acid ground. In recent years it has been increasingly used as a Christmas tree, its ability to 'hold' its needles for a long period in warm dry conditions being an advantage.

There are several cultivated forms of Caucasian Fir although none are superior to the true species. 'Aurea' has yellowish foliage of little merit. It was raised in Germany in 1891. The variety *equi-trojani*, the Trojan Fir, which dates back to 1883 is still named in collections. It should actually be called *Abies cephalonica* var. *graeca*, the **Apollo Fir**, which is a regional type of Greek Fir (see p. 131).

Growth: 5-20-40. Hardiness: 60-70%. Choice: 1 (requires space). Wood: 2, 3, 4.

Bornmueller Fir *Abies × bornmuelleriana*

This cross, possibly between Caucasian Fir (p. 135) and Greek Fir (p. 131), produces a big tree superficially not unlike the parents. It appears to grow naturally in Turkey but was not recognized as a hybrid until 1925. There is still some doubt about the true identity and taxonomy. It has 2-3cm needles densely packed above the shoots. The cones, with reflexed bracts, are up to 15cm long.

Growth: 4-20-30. Hardiness: 50%. Choice: 2, 3. Wood: 2, 3, 4.

Apollo Fir

Bornmueller Fir

European Silver Fir

shoot detail

cone scale

♀ flower

♂ flowers

mature cone

seed

seedling

European Silver Fir

rachis of cone

European Silver Fir *Abies alba*

The natural range of this species has been obscured by centuries of cultivation for timber. The mountains of central and southern Europe are native strongholds, especially the Vosges, Jura and the Black Forest. In the south-east it tends to intergrade with Greek Fir (p. 131) and in the east with Caucasian Fir (p. 135). It is not a native tree in the British Isles but it was the first silver fir to be introduced there, around 1603. It continued to be favoured in Britain until the mid-nineteenth century, then became subordinate to highly productive American imports. Increasingly it became preyed on by the aphid *Adelges nordmannianae*. Heavy infestations are eventually fatal. These occur in close-planted forest conditions rather more than where individual specimen trees are planted in isolation or mixed with completely different species. Despite the insect problem this remains a popular ornamental plant and specimens up to 50m tall are known with stems almost 2m in diameter. In its native range and in other parts of Europe where the climate suits it, disease and predation are not limiting. Huge pure and mixed forests still exist.

It is a straight tree with a persistent stem and light branches. These are brittle and soon break off to give a clean stem resulting in high quality softwood timber. The bark is smooth becoming silvery-grey and only lightly fissured in old age. The evergreen needles, up to 3cm long, are spreading and forward pointing. They are soft, blunt tipped and deep glossy green, but vary from tree to tree in size and density. Cones (see p. 260), which often occur in upright pairs or clusters, are deciduous, cylindrical and up to 15cm long.

A large number of ornamental forms of European Silver Fir have been produced. None of them are particularly striking. '**Pyramidalis**' is a British cultivar raised in 1851. It has distinctive fastigiate branches when young but tends to mimic the ordinary species later on. Its French rival '**Columnaris**', discovered on Mount Pila in 1859, appears to develop a more spreading top. It is no longer in cultivation. Trees listed as 'Columnaris' now are probably different selections made more recently.

Growth: 5-20-40. Hardiness: 60-70%. Choice: 2, 3, 4. Wood: 1, 2, 3, 4.

'Pyramidalis'
leaf variation

'Pyramidalis'

'Columnaris'

♀ flower

Santa Lucia Fir

Corkbark Fir

underside

♂ flowers

Santa Lucia Fir

cone

'Compacta'

Alpine Fir

SILVER FIRS

Santa Lucia Fir *Abies bracteata*

In its native range, the Pacific edge of the Santa Lucia Mountains in southern California, this tall, 20-30m, tree is also known as Bristlecone Fir. It is rare in the wild and in cultivation. The original introduction to Europe was by William Lobb in 1852, although at that time the species name appears to have been *Abies venusta*. This is a long-branched cylindrical tree with a conical top and a persistent single stem. The evergreen pectinate foliage consists of flat 4-6cm long needles, which are dark glossy green above and twin striped brilliant white below. Deciduous cones up to 10cm long occur on the top branches like erect candles. Each scale has a bract ending in a long bristle. Unfortunately they are hardly ever seen because they disintegrate on ripening and flutter down in pieces.

Growth: 4-20-30. Hardiness: 30-40%. Choice: 2, 3. Wood: 2, 3, 4.

Alpine Fir *Abies lasiocarpa*

In North America this species is also known as the Subalpine, or Rocky Mountain Fir. It occurs in two forms, sometimes designated as varieties, representing the north and the south of the huge range. This extends from south-east Alaska to New Mexico. Trees in cultivation exhibit extreme provenance differences. Some specimens are tall and slender while others are quite stunted and short. In the wild Rocky Mountain landscape this is the alpine tree that so often enhances the view, its narrow deep green spires contrasting with brilliant white snow, blue sky and grey rock. The upright cones are hairy, which explains the species name *lasio*, meaning woolly, and *carpa*, fruit.

Growth: 3-7-20. Hardiness: 60-80%. Choice: 2, 3. Wood: 3, 4.

Corkbark Fir *Abies lasiocarpa* var. *arizonica*

This segment of the Alpine Fir population comes from Arizona and Colorado. In order to survive the heat there, it grows as high in the mountains as it can. The bark, as suggested by the name, is corky and buff-coloured to pale brown. The foliage, which is particularly striking in cultivation, is silvery bluegreen. The variety was named in 1898 and introduced as a garden tree in 1903. A more compact form '**Compacta**' was developed in Holland in 1979. It is now a favourite ornamental plant where ground and climatic conditions suit it.

Growth: 3-7-18. Hardiness: 60%. Choice: 1. Wood: 4.

Alpine Fir

Alpine Fir

Santa Lucia Fir

♂ flowers

♀ flower

Grand Fir

underside

cone scale

seedling

mature cone

seed

cone rachis

Grand Fir

Grand Fir *Abies grandis*

In America and Europe this is one of the tallest (90m) and most productive Silver Firs. It comes from southern British Columbia and along the Pacific seaboard to California. A separate inland population occurs in the Rocky Mountains, centred on Idaho, and there are others in eastern Oregon. It prefers cool mountain and hill slopes where humidity is high and the soil is moist. In cultivation, usually as an initially shade tolerant timber tree, it also thrives best in these wet conditions. Huge 60m straight stems support a narrow crown of whorled branches. The bark is olive-brown and thin at first with prominent resin blisters. Eventually towards the base of large stems it becomes fissured but remains fairly smooth and fades to pale grey. The 3-5cm evergreen needles are parted horizontally to present a flat deep glossy green surface towards the sky and a grey-green side to the ground. The deciduous cylindrical cones (see p. 260) in the tree tops are pale green turning to light brown as the season advances. They are 5-10cm long with a fairly smooth outline. David Douglas discovered Grand Fir on the Columbia River in 1825. He introduced it to Britain in 1830. By 1883 it was considered to be one of the best trees to grow in Scotland and it remains the most productive conifer there.

Growth: 8-22-55. Hardiness: 50%. Choice: 3. Wood: 2, 3, 4.

Balsam Fir *Abies balsamea*

Balsam is a reference to the liquid resin which occurs profusely in 'blisters' under the young bark of this tree. 'Canada balsam' is obtained from it. This is used for mounting microscopic specimens and optical work. Its aromatic properties are valued by aroma therapists. The range of this species covers much of eastern and central Canada. It also extends into the USA to Pennsylvania, Minnesota and parts of Iowa. Local pockets of it, at high elevation (1200m), can be found in Virginia and West Virginia. In North America it is a major producer of low grade timber and paper pulp. The evergreen needles are around 2cm long and more or less parted on the shoot. Upward pointing cones, up to 8cm long, are produced on the top branches. They are deep purplish-grey, but never fall to the ground in one piece so are seldom seen.

Growth: 2-5-12. Hardiness: 80%. Choice: 3. Wood: 4.

Balsam Fir

Low's Fir

♂ flowers

♀ flower

Colorado White Fir

Colorado White Fir bark

'Wattezii'

Low's Fir bark

Low's Fir northern form

cone

'Violacea'

Low's Fir

Colorado White Fir *Abies concolor*

This sub-alpine species is from southern California, Utah, Colorado and north-west Mexico. In the south it grows up to 3300m in order to escape the intense heat and dryness. As it is the foliage is sage grey and specially adapted to minimise transpiration. The bark is light grey, becoming furrowed and corky towards the base. Cylindrical 8-12cm cones occur at the top of the tree. They are pale green with a bloomed purple tint just before they disintegrate in the autumn. The needles are strongly pectinate and longer than most other silver firs, up to 5cm. William Lobb introduced the species to Europe in 1851 but in most forest situations it has been outclassed by the variety *lowiana*. However, the strikingly grey needles assure its place in ornamental horticulture.

The cultivar '**Candicans**', which is a selection of the form *argentea*, has brilliantly silver-grey foliage. It was produced in 1929 at the Arboretum les Barres in France. The name '**Violacea**' was attributed to it in 1875, but similar-coloured seedlings have frequently occurred since then. The cultivar '**Wattezii**' is a 1900 Dutch selection with pale cream new growth in the spring.

Growth: 3-8-22. Hardiness: 60-70%. Choice: 1 (requires space). Wood: 2, 3, 4.

Low's Fir *Abies concolor* var. *lowiana*

In Britain this variety (although not recognized as such at the time) was probably introduced in 1851. At first it was confused with Colorado White Fir. Variety status was confirmed in 1862 and trees were distributed by Messrs. Low, the English nurserymen. Potentially it is an important forest tree, having a straight stem up to 50m tall (in Scotland). It is less prone to drought and frost crack than Grand and Noble Firs (p. 141 and p. 145). However, care is still needed to choose provenances wisely. In Britain, northern forms with dark relatively smooth bark are clearly the most productive. Trees from Oregon and the Sierra Nevada compare well with Grand Fir. They are hardy and also planted commercially in the USA as far north as Boston.

Growth: 7-18-50. Hardiness: 70%. Choice: 2, 3. Wood: 2, 3, 4.

'Candicans'

f. glauca

underside

Noble Fir underside

♂ flowers

♀ flower

cone scale

seedling

Noble Fir

seeds

f. glauca

Noble Fir *Abies procera*

Noble Fir has become an important forest species far beyond its natural range, which is restricted to the Cascade Mountains in Oregon and Washington State in the USA. It grows there on mountain sides between 600 and 1500m. A huge tree 84m tall has been recorded. In Scotland, where the species was only introduced in quantity in the 1850s, trees already exceed 50m in height.

The stem is straight and stout, 1.8m diameter is commonplace, with smooth silver-grey bark which only fissures lightly in old age. The foliage is deep grey-green, or blue-green in the glaucous form. The flexible needles are variously curved to give a flat coverage above the shoot and a parting beneath. To achieve this some rows of individuals are twisted into the shape of a letter S, a feature shared only with Californian Red Fir (p. 125). The undersides have two pale green lines of stomata. The female flowers on this species are quite spectacular but out of sight in the tree tops. They are bright pink miniature upright cones, often several in a row along the branch. They develop into fat heavy 25cm cones (see p. 260) which change through straw-yellow to brown. The down-turned tips of papery bracts project from between each scale forming an intricate pattern of diagonal crossed lines over the whole surface of the cone. The beauty of this is totally lost in the autumn when the whole lot disintegrates to shed the seed. Often the sheer weight of massed cones can break the brittle branches, giving the tree a gaunt-looking top.

David Douglas discovered Noble Fir in 1825 on the south side of the Columbia River. He sent seed back to his native Scotland soon after. Large consignments were later exported through the Oregon Association in the 1850s but many of these had been predated by a species of seed wasp. William Lobb sent more seed independently to the Veitch Nursery in London. In Britain this species became a significant forest tree after 1919. From the start Noble Fir also became a popular ornamental park and estate tree where conditions were right. It requires prodigious amounts of rain and poor, moist acid soil. The species is totally hardy and always grows straight, even in severely exposed places.

Timber is usually produced in vast quantities, but it is soft and weak. There is a tendency for it to crack spirally up the stem, a problem usually attributed to drought or frost. Whatever the reason, spiral cracking renders it useless when it is milled. Sawn boards simply fall to bits behind the saw blade. Forms with particularly glaucous foliage, f. **glauca**, have been selected and perpetuated by horticulturists for many years.

Growth: 7-18-50. Hardiness: 80%. Choice: 2, 3. Wood: 3, 4.

Noble Fir

Cedar of Lebanon

♀ flower

♂ flower

old cone

Cedar of Lebanon

Cedars

The genus Cedrus, the true cedars, contains only four species, some authorities suggest fewer, spread across North Africa and into Asia. Each species consists of a geographic segregate occupying a particular sector of the range. Some interaction between these can make precise identification extremely difficult.

Cedar of Lebanon *Cedrus libani*

The natural range of this species extends along the eastern coast of the Mediterranean and into Asia Minor. Its strongholds were always Lebanon and Syria. Originally a mountain species growing between 1400 and 2000m above sea level, it is now grown in numerous different habitats and responds favourably to lush lowland conditions. It usually makes a spreading tree, often with huge low branches, themselves as large as tree trunks, growing outwards almost horizontally. In cultivation it seldom confines itself to a single stem but prefers several. They reach upwards like organ pipes to a potential height of 40m. Among the few remaining native trees stems over 4.5m in diameter are on record. Such specimens are estimated to be 2500 years old. It was introduced in Britain, one of the first countries to grow Cedar of Lebanon as an ornament, in 1683. The largest recorded stem diameter, which was measured when the tree was only 230 years old was 2.86m.

The layered branches are characteristically level almost to the tip. Soft evergreen needles 2-3cm in length occur singly on current shoots and in whorls on short spur shoots. Like most cedars they vary slightly in length and colour according to the provenance of the tree. Some are dark green while others are much lighter and easily confused with the closely related Atlas Cedar. The conspicuous upright male catkins are yellow and appear in the autumn. Females are almost hidden at the tips of spurs. The 10cm cones (see p. 261) are barrel-shaped but widest below the half way mark. They are bloomed green at first, becoming purplish-grey the second year. After three years they start to break up. The first indication of this is when the scales start to bulge and the sleek symmetrical outline is lost.

Most of the nineteenth-century cultivars of Cedar of Lebanon were produced in France. Probably the best is '**Glauca**' which dates back to 1855. It is a compact replica of the species with silvery green foliage. There is also a similar yellow type 'Aurea' (1868) but it is often more green than yellow and rather disappointing.

Growth: 2-8-35. Hardiness: 40%. Choice: 1 (requires space). Wood: 1, 2, 3.

'Glauca'

Atlas Cedar

Blue Atlas Cedar

'Aurea'

Atlas Cedar bark

Atlas Cedar

'Aurea'

'Glauca Fastigiata'
old tree

Atlas Cedar *Cedrus atlantica*

Snow lies for three months of the year where this hardy tree grows in North Africa. Its natural range is the Atlas Mountains, at 1200-2100m, in Morocco and Algeria. This is in part dry limestone; consequently the species is tolerant of chalky soils in cultivation. The best specimens produce a vertical stem, or series of stems, reaching to around 40m in height. The branches set off at 45° but become horizontal as they extend. The evergreen foliage is thick and persistent. It occurs in a range of colours from green to grey-green. Needles around 2cm long are produced singly on current shoots and subsequently in whorls of 30-45 on spur shoots. Conspicuous erect 5cm male flowers appear in early autumn while 1cm female flowers, which are difficult to find, hide away among the needles on spur shoots. Cones are freely produced, often in rows along the shoots. They are 8cm high by 4cm wide, smooth and barrel-shaped. After three years they disintegrate on the tree to shed the winged seeds. This species was discovered in 1827 and described by the eminent Italian gardener Guiseppe Manetti in 1844.

Growth: 2-10-35. Hardiness: 40%. Choice: 1 (requires space). Wood: 1, 2, 3.

Blue Atlas Cedar *Cedrus atlantica* f. *glauca*

This spontaneous powdery blue form of Atlas Cedar occurs within the wild population. It is more commonly planted as an ornament than the species. The original clone was distributed in 1867 from France, and since then many similar individuals have been cultivated. Most of them are morphologically like the species but slightly smaller.

Growth: 2-10-30. Hardiness: 40%. Choice: 1 (requires space). Wood: 1, 2, 3.

Cedrus atlantica cultivars

Over 40 named selections of this species are available. Many of them are derived from the blue form. They make excellent hardy evergreen park and garden trees because of their tolerance of poor soils. '**Aurea**' is a 1900 Dutch selection – a medium-sized tree with shorter yellowish needles. '**Glauca Fastigiata**' is an invalid name given to a narrow-crowned American plant in 1972. There are several similar forms of blue Atlas Cedar. '**Glauca Pendula**' is a good blue weeping form grown at Chatenay, France in 1900.

Growth: variable. Hardiness: 30-40%. Choice: 1.

Blue Atlas Cedar

♂ flower

spur leaves

'**Glauca Fastigiata**'
young tree

'**Glauca Pendula**'
old tree

Deodar Cedar   **'Argentea'**

♀ flower

Deodar Cedar   seedling   **'Verticillata'**

twig detail

CEDARS

Deodar Cedar *Cedrus deodara*

This Himalayan species marks the eastern limit of cedar distribution world-wide. It occurs from western Nepal to east Afghanistan between 1200 and 3000m above sea level. Such a wide range of habitats and elevation results in a quite variable species. Strains from some regions are hardy, others less so. Most tolerate poor dryish limestone or moderately acid soils. In the best conditions a substantial timber tree 35m tall is produced. The outline is smooth because of the soft dense foliage. Trees are conical at first then become gracefully rounded with age. Major side branches level out to roughly horizontal with nodding tips. The flexible needles are blue-green at first, darkening when the tree reaches about 25 years of age. They are around 4-5cm long, the longest of all cedars, occurring singly on current shoots then in whorls on older spurs. Each needle ends in a translucent point. This long, soft foliage is a good identification feature in the field. The vertical male catkins are 8cm tall when they ripen in late autumn. Tiny female flowers only occur on a limited number of trees. The upright stout barrel-shaped cones are around 9cm tall and 5-6cm wide. Traditionally Deodar timber was used in India for ship building. A nineteenth-century plan to grow it for this purpose in Britain failed because the timber grown so far north lacked durability in sea water.

Growth: 3-10-30. Hardiness: 30%. Choice: 2, 3.
Wood: Europe 5, Himalaya 1, 2, 3.

Cedrus deodara cultivars

'**Argentea**' is a silvery-green-needled form which keeps its colour fairly well. It was raised in France and described in 1866. It is an interesting curiosity but is no match for the Blue Atlas Cedar in garden and landscape design. '**Verticillata**' was produced in France in 1887. As a young plant it has a neat formal appearance with a single stem and evenly spaced whorls of horizontal branches. Each branch has a slightly upswept tip and short curtains of pendulous side shoots. Unfortunately, as the illustration shows, it does not age well. The Golden Deodar '**Aurea**' flushes golden-yellow then turns green in the summer. The original cultivar raised in Britain in 1866 is now often confused with newer selections which closely resemble it.

Growth: variable. Hardiness: 30-40%. Choice: 1. Wood: 3.

'Aurea'
young tree

'Verticillata'

Cyprian Cedar

♀ flower

'Gold Mound'

underside

Cyprian Cedar

Deodar Cedar

'Robusta'

'Pendula'
young tree

Cedrus deodara cultivars (continued)

This species is described on p. 151. It varies considerably in the wild and has given rise to a large number of cultivated selections. They have the characteristically long 5cm needles of Deodar in a range of muted colours from cream to blue-green. '**Robusta**' described in 1852 is a British clone similar in size and appearance to the species but having bright blue-green foliage. '**Gold Mound**' is a relatively new cultivar produced in Canada in 1986. It is a spreading plant usually growing to a broad point with clear yellow foliage. '**Albospica**' is an old Northern Irish selection made in 1899. It is a medium-sized conical tree with pale cream young needles which turn yellow and then green before the end of the growing season. '**Pendula**' is a well known little weeping tree in collections. It originated in Germany before 1900. Unless trained up a stake in its youth it will simply creep along the ground.

Although magnificent at maturity, this tree is often a great disappointment in the garden for perhaps 20 to 30 years. Most specimens are ungainly and shapeless at first.

Growth: variable. Hardiness: 30-40%.
Choice: 1 (except 'Pendula').

Cyprian Cedar *Cedrus brevifolia*

A tough tree or large shrub, this species is found wild in only two places on the island of Cyprus itself. It grows in mainland Greece on the upper slopes of Mount Paphos. The illustration shows the tree at its best. It is more often seen as a stunted and sparse individual with an open crown of horizontal branches. These may be short or disproportionally long. Cedars produce two kinds of evergreen needles, they appear singly in the first year on long shoots and subsequently as tufts on short spur shoots. This particular species has thick, stiff slightly curving needles up to 2.5cm on the long shoots and 1-2cm on the spur shoots. These are in whorls of up to 20. On old trees or specimens standing in severely exposed conditions the needles are shorter. The shortest of any cedar. The cones are similar to Cedar of Lebanon (p. 147) but smaller, often with an irregular point. This species was considered to be a variety of Lebanon Cedar until it was described separately in 1908 by Joseph Hooker, the retired director of the Royal Botanic Gardens at Kew.

Some Lebanon Cedars in cultivation do produce very short needles and generally these are more commonly found than true Cyprian Cedar.

Growth: 2-4-15. Hardiness: 40%. Choice: 1 (requires space).
Wood: 1, 2, 3, 5.

Deodar Cedar

'Albospica'

♀ flowers

European Larch

♂ flowers

♀ flower

old cone
(from above)

European Larch
parkland tree

Carpathian Larch

154

Larch *Larix*

There are about ten species of larch distributed throughout the cold temperate regions of the northern hemisphere. They are deciduous conifers with soft flexible single needles which, after the first year, are produced in rosettes on short spur shoots. Extensive natural and artificially planted forests of larch provide supplies of durable, heavy, softwood timber. This serves a whole range of purposes, particularly in wet conditions.

European Larch *Larix decidua*

The native range of this species extends across much of Europe, especially the European Alps and Carpathian Mountains. It is a more or less straight tree, up to 45m tall (but generally much less), with a conical top and light horizontal or down-turned branches. The twigs are pendulous, especially low down on old trees. Like all larches this is a light-demanding tree so the lower branches are soon suppressed and die. They become brittle and break off easily. This produces a clean looking stem but results in the dead knots in the timber falling out when it is dried. In European forestry four distinct types are recognized, Alpine, Sudeten, Polish (subsp. ***polonica***) and selections from the Carpathian and Tatra Mountains. Alpine trees should usually be avoided, as they are variable and prone to disease. Polish seed has in the past come from lowland areas, so failure occurs when it is planted on severe upland sites. Sudeten Larch and **Carpathian Larch** have consistently proved to be the best types for British conditions. Nevertheless, disease resistant origins are the only safe ones to plant.

European Larch is not native to the British Isles. It appears to have been introduced sometime before 1620. A tree 'of goodly stature' was observed growing in south-east England in 1664. Specimens were cautiously tried in Scotland from 1725. By 1788 it had become fashionable and extensive forests were established from then on.

This species, which is the only deciduous conifer native in Europe, has soft, thin, grass-green needles. They appear very early in the spring, almost before the end of winter in mild districts. Also at this time the flowers begin to show. Males are tufts, 1cm across, of cream-coloured stamens, often occurring in huge numbers and sending out clouds of pollen when conditions are right. The females, all over the same tree, are upright miniature cones, with brilliant pink scales. They develop into cones (see p. 261) in the course of one season which are ovate, straw-coloured, about 3cm long and open to shed the winged seeds in the autumn. Several years' empty cones stay behind on the tree, often until the whole branch dies and falls off. Unlike Japanese Larch, the cone scales are rounded and not reflexed. However, this is not a good aid to identification. The presence of straw-coloured or buff first year shoots is much safer.

Growth: 5-12-30. Hardiness: 80-90%. Choice: 2, 3. Wood: 1, 2, 3.

Carpathian Larch

subsp. ***polonica***

European Larch

autumn

winter

♂ flowers ♀ flowers

Hybrid Larch

spring growth

♀ flowers ♂ flowers

Japanese Larch

seed

2yr old seedling

'Pendula'

156

Hybrid Larch *Larix × marschlinsii (eurolepis)*

The name *'eurolepis'* is retained here because it is so familiar to foresters, plant breeders and nurseries though the botanically correct name for this hybrid between European and Japanese Larch is now *Larix × marschlinsii*. The first recorded tree originated at Dunkeld in Scotland, where the parent species were planted side by side. An avenue of Japanese Larch planted in 1887 produced the first F^1 seed from around 1904. The hybrid was described in 1919. There have been numerous other crosses since then, using either parent as the mother tree. Back-crosses have also occurred, resulting in a mixed selection of inferior progeny. An authentic hybrid larch is an ideal forest tree. It carries the attributes of fast growth from Japanese Larch and strong durable timber from European Larch. In 60 years the best specimens on record have exceeded 40m in height, with stems more than 120cm in diameter.

Growth: 8-20-35. Hardiness: 70%. Choice: 2, 3. Wood: 2, 3.

Japanese Larch *Larix kaempferi*

Although Japanese Larch only occurs in a small region of central Japan, Honshu Island, it has been planted as a forest tree all over the cool temperate world. Even though the native range is limited, the elevation within it, 1200 to 2800m, gives rise to considerable provenance variation. By good fortune the original introductions to Europe in 1861 by the Veitch Nursery happened to be good. Even so, the species was shunned for over 30 years in favour of European Larch. Not an unjustified reaction, because young trees tend to produce wood that is inferior. Only when a high proportion of heartwood is present in the timber does the quality begin to compare favourably with European Larch. It is a potentially large tree, 30m in height, and has a fairly straight stem. The branches are strong and spreading towards the base of the tree. The top is conical at first, becoming ragged or flattened with age. The foliage is sea-green, with orange-red shoots which show up in the winter when the needles are off. The autumn colour is gold and the subsequent carpet of needles on the ground is a valuable source of nutrition for other species planted or growing near the larch. The 2-3cm cones (see p. 261), which develop in one season from carmine-pink flowers, are pale brown with reflexed scales. The cultivar '**Pendula**' is one of many ornamental forms. It first appeared in Germany in 1896, but several weeping selections have been made since then.

Growth: 7-18-30. Hardiness: 50-70%. Choice: 2, 3. Wood: 2, 3.

Japanese Larch
in winter

parkland specimens

Hybrid Larch
in spring

Subalpine Larch

open cone

♀ flower

♂ flower

Tamarack Larch

autumn

Subalpine Larch   **Tamarack Larch**

158

LARCHES

Tamarack Larch *Larix laricina*

This 'eastern larch' of North America, like the Western Larch, is also called 'Hackmatack'. It is an extremely hardy, straight, 20-24m tree, which grows close to the limit of trees in the sub Arctic, from Alaska to Labrador. Further south it extends to New Jersey and Maryland, growing on a range of soils and site types from sea level to 1200m up mountain sides. It is a short-lived but slow-growing pioneer species. Nevertheless, the timber is strong and durable. American Indians once used its thin roots to sew strips of birch bark on to canoes. The stem is usually straight but increasingly truncated towards the north of the range. The open branches are light, horizontal or pendulous. In severe exposure they may be very short. Soft blue-green needles appear early in the year on trees in cultivation. They are about 3cm long and 3-sided. Male flowers droop beneath the shoot and rose pink females stand in erect clusters above it. Consequently the cones often occur in small bunches. They are around 1.5cm long with very few scales.

Growth: 2-8-20. Hardiness: 80-100%. Choice: 2, 3. Wood: 3.

Subalpine Larch *Larix lyallii*

This is a tree of high mountainsides from British Columbia to Alberta and south to Washington. It occurs as a pioneer timberline species, demarcating bare rock and scree slopes from shrubby vegetation and alpine fir forest. For much of the year in this situation it remains leafless and in a semi-moribund state. When brought into cultivation – it was discovered by David Lyall, a Scottish surgeon, in 1858 – it makes a good conical tree 15m or more tall. The foliage appears at the proper time of year in the spring. The needles are 3cm long, 4-angled, stiff, pointed and bright pale green. On second and subsequent years' spur shoots they are numerous and crowded together. The whole tree in summer has a tufted look about it which can be recognized from some way off. The yellow autumn colour is attractive especially when viewed against blue sky. Elliptical cones are produced singly or in small clusters. Narrow twisted trident bracts extend from between each scale, giving the cone a ragged outline.

Growth: 2-4-15. Hardiness: 80-90%. Choice: 4. Wood: 3.

Tamarack Larch

Western Larch

Weeping Larch

young cone

♀ flo

♂ flower

leaf section

summer   seed   winter

Weeping Larch   **Western Larch**

LARCHES

Weeping Larch *Larix × pendula*

The exact parentage of this hybrid is uncertain. It is presumed by most authorities to be *Larix decidua × Larix laricina* – a cross between a European and an American species. It is a broad-headed wide-spreading tree with level or down-turned branches and pendulous shoots. In other respects it is like European Larch (p. 155). Its origin appears to have been in London, in the garden of Peter Collinson at Peckham, where the parents must have been growing close to each other, around 1839. The first seedling appeared in his other garden at Mill Hill in north-west London soon after.

It was a common nineteenth century practice to train it over an iron framework with cross members set just above head height. This produced a mysterious grotto effect and could eventually cover an area some 20m across. Many larches in cultivation with pendulous shoots are wrongly ascribed to this hybrid.
Growth: 2-2-3. Hardiness: 90%. Choice: 1.

Western Larch *Larix occidentalis*

This big tree, up to 60m tall, occurs in western North America between the Cascade and Rocky Mountains in British Columbia, Oregon and Idaho. Known locally (like the Tamarack Larch) as 'Hackmatack', it is often in dense forests in the company of Lodgepole Pine (p. 255). Where fires or natural disasters occur this is one of the first pioneer species to cover the resulting bare ground with a carpet of new seedlings. The first European to discover Western Larch was David Douglas in 1826 on the Columbia River. It was brought into cultivation in 1880 and taken to Kew in London in 1881 by Charles Sprague Sargent from the Arnold Arboretum in the USA. The needles are grey-green, 2.5-4cm long, produced singly on new shoots and subsequently in clusters on spur shoots. They are triangular in cross section and keeled on the lower side. Although pointed they are not viciously sharp. The ovoid cones are 2.5-3.5cm long, they are held in an upright position on the branch and ripen in one season. They have distinctive protruding pointed bracts between the scales. The bark is reddish brown and scaly: with age it becomes increasingly grey and roughly furrowed. The timber is of excellent quality, close grained, heavy and durable. It is streaked with warm brown and speckled with small dark brown knots.
Growth: 6-12-24 (in cultivation). Hardiness: 70%. Choice: 2, 3. Wood: 2, 3.

Western Larch

Himalayan Larch

Himalayan Larch

Japanese Larch 'Dervaes'

var. *principis-rupprechtii*

♀ flower

leaf section

Dahurian Larch

var. *japonica*

Dahurian Larch

♀ flower

♂ flowers

Dahurian Larch *Larix gmelinii*

The range of this hardy species is eastern Siberia and northern China, a climactically testing area where it may only develop into a cowering bush. In better conditions it may grow 20m tall. The stem is then straight and the top conical. Branches spread widely on cultivated specimens. The needles are bright green, blunt, 2-3cm long and appear early in the year, so frost damage is a serious problem in Europe. The cones are small, up to 3cm long, with few scales. The variety ***japonica*** (Kurile Larch) from Sakhalin Island has dense foliage and very small cones, 1-2cm long. The needles are also particularly short and prone to spring frost damage. The variety ***principis-rupprechtii*** (now regarded as a legitimate species by some authorities) comes from west of Beijing. It has bloomed shoots and longer needles (up to 3.5cm, occasionally longer in cultivation). The cones are 2-3.5cm with notched scales.

Growth: 2-4-15. Hardiness: 100%. Choice: 4. Wood: 3.

Himalayan Larch *Larix griffithiana*

Sir Joseph Hooker, director of the Royal Botanic Gardens, Kew, introduced this elegant 20m tree from west Nepal in 1848. Its natural range extends from Nepal, Sikkim, Bhutan to south-east Tibet. William Griffith discovered it 10 years earlier and it was eventually named in his honour in 1854, as *Larix griffithii*. The cone distinguishes this from other larches. It is cylindrical, 5-11cm long, and pointed at both ends, with long bracts extending from between each scale.

Growth: 2-5-20. Hardiness: 20-40%. Choice: 4. Wood: 3.

Larix kaempferi 'Dervaes' Japanese Larch cv

This Belgian clone of Japanese Larch (p. 157) was recognized in 1949. It is a pendulous form, usually grafted on to a standard stock. The scion material is identical to 'Pendula' a German cultivar produced in 1896 (p. 157).

Growth: 2-2-3. Hardiness: 60%. Choice: 1.

Chinese Larch *Larix potaninii*

In south-west China this is a huge, 50m tall tree growing at very high elevations of between 2500 and 3000m. It is native in Sichuan and Gansu provinces and in adjoining parts of Tibet. Père David, the French missionary and plant collector, discovered it in 1884. It was named in 1893 and introduced into cultivation, in Germany, in 1899. Another five years passed before it reached America. It remains a rare tree and in cultivation somewhat variable. It is possible that the original introduction might have actually been the variety ***macrocarpa***. Some individuals have dense foliage, others do not. The 2-3cm keeled needles are bright green, highlighted by silvery stomatal bands on the underside. The distinctive oval cones are 3-5cm long with exserted bracts between each scale. The cone changes from red-brown to violet and finally grey-brown when ripe.

Growth: 2-4-15. Hardiness: 80%. Choice: 4. Wood: 3.

Himalayan Larch

var. ***macrocarpa*** cone

Chinese Larch

♀ flowers

underside

♂ flowers

Golden Larch

side shoot leaves

cone

Golden Larch
winter

'dragon's eye'

autumn

164

LARCHES

Golden Larch *Pseudolarix amabilis*

This deciduous conifer is a close relative of the true larches. It has the same needle arrangement, spiral on first year shoots and in rosettes subsequently. In its native southern China trees 30-40m tall occur, but in cultivation it is more likely to be small, sometimes little more than a large bush – a definite advantage when the tree is intended to be seen at close quarters, as this species must if it is to be fully appreciated. The main feature, the autumn colour, produces what is known as the 'dragon's eye' effect. During the summer the soft needles are light green with blue-green backs. In the autumn they turn yellow and golden-brown progressively from the needle tip to its base. This occurs simultaneously over the whole plant. The rosettes of needles on spur shoots are very regular and fairly flat when viewed from above. The following year's bud is already formed in the centre. The 'dragon's eye' is a rosette of 15-30 needles with the pale bud in the centre, light-green around it, yellow beyond that and a fringe of golden-brown round the whole lot. This intriguing effect is repeated all over the tree. The flowers are produced in spring. Males are small yellow clusters of catkins made up of stamens; they form on a leafless spur shoot. The females are pale yellowish-green with white bloom on them, developing into unique artichoke-shaped cones with tough projecting fleshy triangular scales. They ripen to golden-brown and disintegrate in the autumn to release the seeds.

This species was introduced into cultivation by Robert Fortune in 1852 after one of his trips to China looking for tea plants. It is difficult to establish and the first consignments of Chinese seed may have failed to grow. However, by 1860 there were live plants at Kew and in America. Acid soil is essential for this slow-growing but reasonably hardy tree.

Growth: 1-3-15. Hardiness: 50%. Choice: 1.

Siberian Larch *Larix russica*

This 30m tall tree is from a vast area in north-east Russia and western Siberia, it is extremely tough and hardy. In outline it varies with its situation. Most specimens start conical with upswept branches; towards the Arctic they stay slender but further south they spread out and the lower branches become horizontal or even slightly pendulous. The soft, 2.5 to 4cm needles, dark-green above and grey-green on the underside, appear early in the spring, but drop early in the autumn. The cones are smooth, around 4cm long and leathery.

Growth: 3-15-30. Hardiness: 100%. Choice: 2. Wood: 3.

Golden Larch
summer

cone

cone scale

Siberian Larch

Morinda Spruce

♂ flower

♀ flower

Morinda Spruce

closed cone

new leaves

Morinda Spruce

Schrenk Spruce

Spruces *Picea*

Mostly straight single-stemmed trees, often growing to considerable heights in dense forests. The shoots are characteristically rough, covered in sharp woody pegs, retained for many years after the stout, pointed evergreen needles have been shed.

Morinda Spruce *Picea smithiana*

This Himalayan spruce, like Brewer Spruce in America, is a snow-shedding adaptation with pendulous foliage. Unlike Brewer Spruce it has long (4cm) needles which are pale green. Occurring from Kashmir to Nepal and west to Afghanistan, mostly between 2100 and 3600mn, it was introduced into cultivation in 1818 at Hopetoun house in Scotland. After some debate and name changes it was finally described in 1884, over 60 years later.

In cultivation it suffers from spring frost damage. Although perfectly hardy, it begins to grow early in the year when planted on a lowland site, and is then hit by inevitable late frosts. Young trees are very decorative with their long branch tresses and conical shape, but they do not age well: crowns spread, stems bend and foliage thins out. In Britain many specimens die after 60 years or so. The best trees achieve 40m.

Needles are produced all round the flexible shoots. The leathery cones are 10-20cm long, cylindrical and glossy. Plants collected in west Nepal have hairy shoots and are given separate variety status, var. *nepalensis*.

Growth: 5-18-30. Hardiness: 30%. Choice: 1 (requires space). Wood: 3.

Schrenk Spruce *Picea schrenkiana*

A rare Chinese tree closely related to Morinda Spruce, this species comes from the border between Russia and China, a harsh cold region. The resinous foliage is less pendulous than Morinda Spruce and the needles are shorter (2-3.5cm). The cones are about 9cm long, dark purplish-brown and often encrusted with resin. Stems are usually straight and up to 30m tall. Occasional trees are on record that have reached 40m. It occurs in pure dense forests exclusively of this species. Some authorities consider it to be related to the Siberian Spruce (p. 171) and consequently Norway Spruce (p. 175).

In cultivation it is not an easy species to identify. It often develops poor form due to its susceptibility to late spring frost damage. It was described by Friedrich von Fischer and Carl von Meyer of St Petersburg Botanic Garden in 1842. Although introduced to European horticulture in 1877 it has never become popular.

Growth: 3-10-25. Hardiness: 50%. Choice: 4. Wood: 3.

♂ flowers

Schrenk Spruce

underside

Sikkim Spruce

♂ flowers

Sikkim Spruce

♀ flower

Mexican Spruce

Sikkim Spruce

168   **Japanese Bush Spruce**   var. *senanensis*

SPRUCES

Sikkim Spruce *Picea spinulosa*

This rare and graceful tree comes from Sikkim and Bhutan. It is a Himalayan species with a fragmented distribution. Inherent variability means that specimens are not all identical. One form is probably related to an obscure type of Likiang Spruce. In cultivation it makes a 20-25m tree with a conical outline until it becomes rounded in old age. Some individuals have lax foliage reminiscent of Morinda Spruce (p. 167) and rather heavy pendulous 7-8cm cones.

Growth: 4-15-22. Hardiness: 30%. Choice: 1. Wood: 3.

Japanese Bush Spruce *Picea maximowiczii*

Also called Maximowicz Spruce after Carl Johann Ivanovitch Maximowicz, curator of St Petersburg Botanic Garden, this tree can easily be mistaken for Norway Spruce (p. 175). The foliage in particular is very similar. In cultivation it tends to cone heavily and the cones are small, 3-5cm long. It is native around Mount Fujiyama in Honshu and was described in 1880 but remains rare.

The variety **senanensis** has longer needles, up to 1.5cm long, and larger cones. It comes from the same region of Honshu but from different mountains, and was described and separated from the species in 1969.

Growth: 4-15-20. Hardiness: 40%. Choice: 2, 3. Wood: 3, 4.

Mexican Spruce *Picea engelmannii* var. *mexicana*

There is confusion about the taxonomy of this hardy variety. Some authorities regard it as a subspecies and others as a true species, *Picea mexicana*. It is from a limited area in north-east Mexico, where it was discovered in 1962. It is a rare tree with glaucous-green, sharply pointed 3cm needles. The soft pendulous cones are around 6cm long. Usually it has a conical outline on a single stem 20m tall, or up to 30m in the wild, (see *Picea engelmannii* p. 189).

Growth: 3-10-20. Hardiness: 10-30%. Choice: 1. Wood: 3.

Wilson Spruce *Picea wilsonii*

Many of the specimens grown from Wilson's original seed collected in the Hubei province of China and introduced into cultivation in 1901, are still alive (1999). This is a tough, hardy, fairly slow-growing tree with dense spreading branches and a straight 10-15m stem. The needles resemble those of Norway Spruce (p. 175), but the shoots are distinctly white on the underside. The 7cm pendulous cones are leathery and cylindrical, but rounded at each end.

Growth: 3-7-15. Hardiness: 50%. Choice: 3. Wood: 3.

Wilson Spruce

♀ flower

twig detail

♂ flower

Tigertail Spruce

Siberian Spruce

♀ flower

♂ flower

Tigertail Spruce

Siberian Spruce

SPRUCES

Siberian Spruce *Picea obovata*

This sub-Arctic tree was described by Carl von Ledebur in 1833 and brought into cultivation in 1852. It occurs from north-west Europe across northern Asia to the northern extremities of China – an eastern extension of the range of Norway Spruce (p. 175), to which it is closely related. Some authorities regard it as a subspecies of Norway Spruce, *Picea abies* subsp. *obovata*. It can grow to 35m tall with a straight stem, flaky grey-brown bark and slightly pendulous branches. The needles are mostly in two ranks, dull green and pointed. Most are less than 2cm long. Leathery, pendulous, 6-10cm cones are purple at first. This species freely crosses with Norway Spruce to produce Finnish Spruce (*Picea* × *fennica*) in Scandinavia and Finland. Like many Arctic species, Siberian Spruce often suffers from spring frost damage when moved to a mild district. It is quick to begin growth in response to increasing day length and starts to grow before the risk of cold weather is over.

Growth: 5-18-30. Hardiness: 90%. Choice: 4. Wood: 2.

Tigertail Spruce *Picea polita*

This conical tree from central and southern Japan inhabits volcanic sites. It was described in 1855 and introduced by J. G. Veitch in 1861. At its best it is 25m tall with a straight stem and exfoliating bark. The branch tips are pendulous like tiger tails. The rigid, vertically flattened, glossy-green needles have the sharpest spine tips of any spruce: they will draw blood at the slightest touch. The 7-12cm cones are leathery, pendulous and sessile.

Growth: 6-12-20. Hardiness: 50%. Choice: 1.

Hybrid American Spruce *Picea* × *lutzii*

First noticed in Alaska in 1950, this hybrid is a natural cross between White Spruce (p. 185) and Sitka Spruce (p. 191). It has potential as a forest tree, so additional artificial hybridization has also been tried. Botanically it has intermediate characteristics between the parents. The hybrid produces fertile F^2 seed. Since 1962 this has been imported to various countries from Iceland. However, vegetative propagation of original trees seems likely to be more reliable. The advantage of the cross appears to be an injection of White Spruce hardiness into Sitka Spruce, a proven timber producer.

Growth: 5-12-30. Hardiness: 60%. Choice: 4 (experimental forest tree). Wood: 2, 3, 4.

Candelabra Spruce *Picea montigena*

Although recognized as a species in 1906, this is more likely to be a variety of Likiang Spruce (p. 193). It is a spreading, 30m, conical tree from western Sichuan. The 1-1.5cm needles are 4-sided with blunt tips. The pendulous cones are 7-10cm long, glossy and leathery.

Growth: 4-12-30. Hardiness: 70%. Choice: 4. Wood: 2, 3.

Hybrid American Spruce

Candelabra Spruce

Dragon Spruce

♀ flower

♂ flower

♀ flower

♂ flower

closed cone

Northern Sargent Spruce

underside

leaf section

open cone

underside

leaf section

Dragon Spruce

Northern Sargent Spruce

172

SPRUCES

Dragon Spruce *Picea asperata*

In the wild state, and to some extent in cultivation, this is a variable species. Its natural range extends through north-west China. This is the Chinese equivalent to Norway Spruce (p. 175), which it superficially resembles. A conic outline eventually develops into a spreading open-branched, more or less straight-stemmed tree around 20m tall. The bark is purplish-brown and scaly; it retains curled flakes for a long time before shedding them. In the open the bark is bleached grey in the sun. The branches are approximately horizontal with upturned ends. The rough (*asperata* means rough) shoots are lax and droop from the lower limbs. The needles are grey-green, around 2cm long, and sharply pointed on some individuals. Other forms are much less pointed and the amount of grey varies from silvery to almost nothing. Like Norway Spruce the needles are 4-sided. The female flowers are bright red and in one summer develop into leathery pale brown pendulous 12cm cones.

Several named varieties were introduced with this species at the beginning of the twentieth century. Their validity is questionable as the whole lot will inter-breed in cultivation, and also cross within the Norway Spruce group. Dragon Spruce was discovered in China in 1903. It was named by Maxwell Masters in 1906, and brought into cultivation by Ernest Wilson in 1910.

Growth: 4-10-18. Hardiness: 50-60%. Choice: 2, 3. Wood: 2, 3, 4.

Northern Sargent Spruce *Picea brachytyla*

Once, vast 40m tall forests of this species extended from central and western China to eastern India. It is a hardy species inhabiting high mountainous sites between 2000 and 4000m. A spreading open conical tree with a straight stem, in cultivation it will only reach half the height of the original forest trees from which it came. The bark is smooth but finely scaly, resinous and pale pinkish-grey at first, becoming darker and roughly cracked in old age. The distinctive shoot is pure white on the underside in the first year, with silver-backed 1.5cm flat needles. The species was introduced in 1901 but remains rare in cultivation.

The southern form var. **complanata** from western China also appears in several different forms in cultivation. It is similar to Northern Sargent Spruce except that the cones are larger, to 16cm long, and the needles are an even brighter silvery-grey on the underside. The pendulous shoots, fairly slow rate of growth and neat conical shape make this a good, but rare, ornamental tree.

Growth: 4-15-22. Hardiness: 40-50%. Choice: 3. Wood: 2, 3, 4.

var. *complanata*

var. *complanata* leaves

type leaves

Northern Sargent Spruce bark

Norway Spruce

♀ flower

♂ flower

closed cone

stem detail

Norway Spruce
parkland specimen

North Swedish type

forest form

open cone

174

SPRUCES

Norway Spruce *Picea abies*

Most of Europe, but not the British Isles, is home to this common species. It occurs from the Pyrenees to the Balkans, across Scandinavia, the Baltic and western Russia. Further east it intergrades with Siberian Spruce (p. 171). It was introduced to Britain around 1500. It is one of the most widely used softwood timber and pulpwood trees in Europe, marketed under such names as Baltic Whitewood and White Deal. It grows best in cool moist regions where late spring frost is unlikely. With such a broad natural distribution this tree can be any shape from tall and slender to broad and spreading. Sub-arctic trees are small but further south specimens 50m tall are known. In forest conditions it is shade tolerant and stands for years in close proximity. Tops become relatively small and lower branches are shaded out. See p. 261 for cone.

There are many named forms (over 350 listed in the World Conifer Data Pool 1993) – some are illustrated here and on the next page. The cultivar name '**Pyramidata**' was listed in 1836 but later expanded to take in all similar upright forms. '**Pendula**' was introduced even earlier, in 1836, and it too now consists of several different clones. The original is considered by some authorities to be the same as '**Inversa**' an 1855 Belgian selection. '**Cupressina**' is a medium-sized tree with up-swept branches. A German clone was described in 1908 but there are now others.

Illustrated on the next page: '**Viminalis**' is a 1741 Swedish selection found growing wild near Stockholm. It is a tall open branched individual with pendulous side shoots. '**Pendula Major**' is one of the few completely weeping cultivars to remain distinct ever since it was described in 1868. '**Tuberculata**' is a curious Dutch cultivar with swellings at the base of old branches. '**Argentea**', was originally a German 1891 clone but is now confused with numerous similar sports. A tree rather like it, '**Finedonensis**', is still identifiable. It has creamy-yellow young shoots but by mid-summer they revert to green. '**Laxa**' is a short needled clone selected at the Royal Botanic Gardens Kew in 1972. '**Cincinnata**' is a strange German weeping tree with particularly long curving needles it was described in 1897. '**Cranstonii**' is a peculiar, often quite vigorous, shrubby tree, first cultivated in 1855. It is reluctant to produce side shoots so the branches produce a snake-like effect. '**Will's Zwerg**' is a 1956 German selection. A small conical dense-needled slow-growing form, seldom exceeding 2m in height.

Growth: 2-18-40. Hardiness: 70%. Choice: 1 (cvs), 3. Wood: 1, 2, 3, 4 (species).

cone scale

seeds

seedling

'Pyramidata'

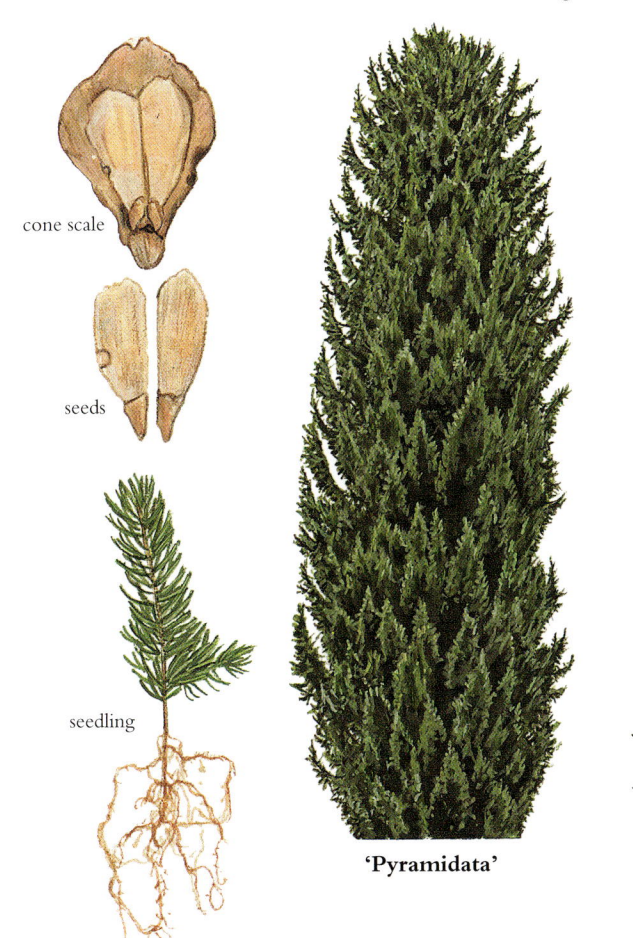

'Pendula'

'Cupressina'

'Viminalis'

'Pendula Major'

'Tuberculata' bark

'Tuberculata'

'Argentea'

'Argentea'

NORWAY SPRUCE FORMS

'Finedonensis'

'Inversa'

'Cincinnata'

'Laxa'

'Cranstonii'

'Will's Zwerg'

♀ flowers

♂ flowers

Oriental Spruce

'Aurea'

'Gracilis'

Oriental Spruce

'Gracilis'

Serbian Spruce

178

SPRUCES

Oriental Spruce *Picea orientalis*

North-east Asia Minor, Anatolia and the Caucasus Mountains are home to this 40m straight-stemmed forest tree. It can easily be identified among other spruces by its very short 8mm deep glossy green needles. Black Spruce (p. 187) also has short needles, but they are grey-green. In addition to its obvious potential as a forest timber producer, this species is tolerant of some lime in the soil and dryness beyond the limits of most other spruces. Its outline is columnar with a conical or rounded top. The dense foliage has a neat appearance and branches seldom break off except in very old age. The slender pendulous violet-brown cones are 9cm long and remain on the tree for longer than many spruces. The species was introduced to Europe around 1837 and described in 1847. In cultivation it appears unable to reach anything like the age of wild trees, some of which are reputed to be over 390 years. Nevertheless it is extensively planted in parks and gardens as an ornamental specimen. It withstands air pollution in urban situations.

There are over 50 named varieties in cultivation (1993). '**Aurea**' is an 1873 German selection with bright yellow foliage which lasts all year. A very dense foliage type, '**Gracilis**', was selected in Belgium in 1903. It grows more slowly and is more compact than the species.

Growth: 2-10-40. Hardiness: 70%. Choice: 2, 3. Wood: 2, 3, 4.

Serbian Spruce *Picea omorika*

This endangered species is confined to a small area in the Drina River valley in the Balkans. It is a last remnant of flat needled spruce which was common in Europe in pre-glacial times. In the harsh icy environment of its last refuge it has developed a natural snow shedding outline. The short downward-pointing branches and very narrow shape ensures that the tree is seldom damaged even in the most severe weather. Also this is perhaps the most lime tolerant of all the spruces. For this reason, and its extreme hardiness, it has frequently been used on a limited scale as a plantation tree. It is good in this role, but is less rewarding financially than hardwood species, such as beech, which can grow on similar ground. As an ornamental it succeeds because it is totally hardy and tolerant of industrial pollution. It will grow on almost any site, wet or dry. As well as cold in winter, summer temperatures over 30°C are endured without damage. Trees 30-40m tall are known with a maximum branch spread of only 5m. It is also sold as an alternative Christmas tree.

Growth: 3-12-30. Hardiness: 70%. Choice: 1, 3. Wood: 2, 3, 4.

underside

seed

Serbian Spruce

♀ flowers

♂ flowers

Hondo Spruce

underside

Koyama Spruce

♀ flowers

Hondo Spruce

♂ flowers

SPRUCES

Hondo Spruce *Picea jezoensis* var. *hondoensis*

The Jezo Spruce (*Picea jezoensis*) from Japan and the Pacific coast of Asia is a close relative of Sitka Spruce (p. 191). It is a fine straight 25–30m forest tree. The population from Honshu (once called Hondo) is regarded as a separate variety, var. *hondoensis*. It is a larger tree, up to 45m tall. The outline is slightly ragged but the stem is generally straight. The shoots are reddish, unlike the species, which has pale brown shoots. Flat 1.2cm needles, with grey stomatal bands on the underside, point forward all round young shoots and occur in two ranks on weak side shoots. The cones are 5–7cm long, leathery and pendulous. The first true Hondo Spruce seed was introduced to Britain in 1871. It was found to be less frost tender than earlier introductions of Jezo Spruce from Manchuria and Siberia. At Vivod arboretum in Wales an outstanding timber tree has resulted from an artificial cross between this variety and Sitka Spruce (p. 191).

Growth: 3-12-30. Hardiness: 70%. Choice: 3. Wood: 2, 4.

Koyama Spruce *Picea koyamai*

This tree has a limited range around Mount Yatsuga in central Japan, where it is now an endangered species. In cultivation it makes a 10–20m conical tree with dark green foliage. The upper stem and branches have reddish-brown bark like Norway Spruce (p. 175). The 1.2cm needles are also like Norway Spruce with which it will hybridize. It was discovered and named after Mitsua Koyama in 1911 and introduced to Europe by Ernest Wilson in 1914. He also found the same species cultivated in a garden in Korea. Interestingly this species is often confused with Korean Spruce (*Picea koraiensis*, p. 239).

Growth: 2-8-18. Hardiness: 50-60%. Choice: 3. Wood: 2, 3.

Taiwan Spruce *Picea morrisonicola*

This spruce occurs in the mountainous parts of Taiwan. It is moderately tender in temperate collections away from there. Superficially there is some resemblance to Wilson Spruce (p. 169) in so far as the shoots are pale-coloured. They are, however, far less stout. The slender pointed needles are between 0.8 and 1.4cm long. They point forward and cover the top of the shoot but are parted below except on the most vigorous extremities. The pendulous leathery cones are around 6–8cm long.

Growth: 2-8-20. Hardiness: 30-40%. Choice: 3. Wood: 2, 3.

Koyama Spruce

new leaves

Taiwan Spruce

underside

cross-section

Alcock's Spruce

open cone

underside

Alcock's Spruce
(with ivy)

Picea shirasawae

182

Alcock's Spruce *Picea bicolor*

This tree from central Japan (Honshu) was discovered and collected by John Gould Veitch in 1861. He named it in honour of his travelling companion Rutherford Alcock, the British Consul at the time. Together they explored the sacred mountain Fujiyama where they also discovered Veitch's Silver Fir (p. 111). They appear to have been the first Europeans to obtain permission to visit the area. Plants were grown at the Veitch family nurseries (as *Picea alcoquiana*) and quickly distributed to collections round the world. Nevertheless Alcock's Spruce is still not common in cultivation. It is perfectly hardy and tolerates a range of soil types but it has little to offer as an ornamental specimen. A well grown tree generally has a straight vertical stem up to 25m tall and spreading branches. The outline is conical for some years and then the symmetry is lost as some limbs grow to excess and others break off. The shoots are pale cream or buff on the shaded side and orange-brown on top. Bi-coloured needles give the tree its species name. They are 1-2cm long, 4-sided, and mostly forward pointing. The upper faces are deep glossy green and the lower ones are blue-green. On old or shaded branches they become parted below the shoot, otherwise they are packed tightly along its length. The foliage resembles Hondo Spruce (p. 181) except in needle cross section. Unlike Hondo Spruce, Alcock's has needles which can be 'rolled' between the finger and thumb. The virtually stalkless cones are about 10cm long, purple at first becoming pinkish-brown. They are pendulous and after opening to shed the winged seed, clearly show reflexed scale tips.

Growth: 2-8-25. Hardiness: 50-60%. Choice: 2, 3. Wood: 2, 3, 4.

Picea shirasawae

Formerly considered to be a variety of Alcock's Spruce (var. *acicularis*) this rare tree comes from central Japan. Its natural range is confined to Mount Yatsuga in Honshu where it grows in company with Koyama's Spruce. Some authorities actually consider this species to have originated as a hybrid between Koyama's and Alcock's. It has dense thick glaucous-green needles which curve over the shoot. The stem is straight but height seldom exceeds 14m. The upper bark is flaky like Dragon Spruce (p. 173) but it thickens up and becomes rugged with age. The cone scales are rounded and smooth and not reflexed at the tip.

Growth: 3-10-14. Hardiness: 50-60%. Choice: 2, 3. Wood: 2, 3, 4.

Picea shirasawae

Alberta White Spruce

species leaves

♂ flowers

var. *albertiana* leaves

♀ flowers

leaf section

underside

open cone

Alberta White Spruce   **Red Spruce**

184

White Spruce *Picea glauca*

This is found across the whole of North America, mostly in Canada. It is extremely hardy and extends northwards to the Arctic tree line. Growth is generally slow and cultivated specimens in warmer climates suffer from spring frost damage. (See p. 261 for cone).

The variety illustrated is the **Alberta White Spruce**, *Picea glauca* var. *albertiana*, found in Alberta and Montana, mostly in the Rocky Mountains. It is an upright tree with a straight stem and glaucous-green needles. The branches spread more widely than in the species and the 2cm needles are longer. It was introduced by Henry Elwes in 1906 and described in 1919, but remains rare in collections. The clone of this variety, named 'Conica', is extensively planted in gardens. It is a neat, slow-growing pyramid of short tightly packed shoots.

Growth: 2-8-20. Hardiness: 90%. Choice: 1. Wood: 2, 3, 4.

Red Spruce *Picea rubens*

This widespread tree in eastern North America grows on wet acid soils in mountainous areas. Its natural range extends southwards from Ontario and Nova Scotia along the Appalachian Mountains and then to Tennessee and Georgia. Stands of it are preserved in the Great Smoky Mountains National Park. It is a shade-tolerant species that thrives in dense forest conditions. In the south it grows between 1300 and 1900m where the air is cool and moisture is abundant. In America and in the timber industry generally it is called Eastern Spruce or Yellow Spruce. The name 'red' is said to refer to the cones but this description does leave a lot to the imagination. They are 3-4cm long, cylindrical, and have rather stiff papery brown scales. After shedding the seed they quickly fall off the tree. The glossy evergreen 1.2-1.5cm needles are slender and twisted round until they cover the upper side of the shoot. They are 4-angled with white stomatal bands on the inner surfaces. When they fall, after 3-5 years, they leave a sharp wooden peg on the twig. The small (1cm) flowers are crimson at first.

Where this species overlaps the range of Black Spruce (p. 187) intermediate forms occur and seed from these has produced rogue plants with shorter grey needles, suggesting some connection with Black Spruce. Clearly, hybrids and back crosses occur naturally. Good Red Spruce has a variable outline depending upon where it grows, but the stem is usually straight. The best trees reach 25m in height. Although introduced to Europe before 1755 it is still uncommon: not particularly ornamental and although completely hardy, it can not compare commercially with existing forest species such as Sitka Spruce (p. 191).

Growth: 2-15-25. Hardiness: 90%. Choice: 3. Wood: 2, 3, 4.

Red Spruce

Brewer Spruce

leaf section

closed cone

cone scale

♀ flowers ♂ flowers

Hybrid Spruce

Brewer Spruce

Hybrid Spruce

Brewer Spruce *Picea breweriana*

Designed by natural selection to minimise snow damage, the branches of this hardy species are flexible, with long pendulous shoot tips. The outline is conical and on old trees the stem becomes buttressed and strengthened towards the base. In cultivation specimens seldom exceed 20m in height but in the wild 40m has been recorded. The natural range is limited to high ground (1000-2200m) on mountainsides in mixed coniferous woodland in south-west Oregon and north-west California. The soft needles are evergreen and spread all round the shoot. They are up to 2.5cm long, flat and pointed. The overall effect is of sombre dark green layered curtains. After 3-5 years the needles fall leaving their sharp basal 'pegs' on the slender branches. The pendulous cones are 6-10cm long but quite narrow until they open up to shed the winged seed. This tree was discovered in the Siskiyou Mountains by William Henry Brewer, professor of agriculture at Yale University. It was subsequently described in 1855.

Growth: 2-8-18. Hardiness: 60%. Choice: 1. Wood: 2, 3.

Hybrid Spruce *Picea × hurstii*

This hybrid between Englemann Spruce (p. 189) and Colorado Spruce (p. 189) is of unknown origin. It is intermediate between the parents but has the potential to grow to 45m in height. Fertile seed is produced but the resulting F^2 plants are variable. The needles on the original hybrid are soft and flexible, up to 2.5cm long, curving upwards over the shoot. Although cultivated since 1938 this plant remains rare. Its potential as an alternative forest tree has not yet been fully tested.

Growth: 3-15-30 (45). Hardiness: 70%. Choice: 4 (experimental forest tree). Wood: 2, 3, 4.

Black Spruce *Picea mariana*

This Arctic/alpine tree is best known for its short branches and very short, tightly packed needles which are only 6-12mm long. It may achieve 18m in height on a prime site but is a prostrate shrub at high elevation and in the sub Arctic. It is at home in cold acid peat bogs, wet clay or gravelly soils. The natural range covers much of Canada and part of the USA around the Great Lakes. It extends almost to the Arctic Circle, as far as the northerly limit for trees of any sort. This neat little tree was described in 1888 but brought into cultivation at a much earlier date, in 1700. The fine blue-grey needles and numerous small (3-4cm) pendulous cones are extremely decorative features. However, like many Arctic species it does not always thrive in mild conditions and is prone to aphid attack.

Growth: 2-4-15. Hardiness: 80%. Choice: 1, 2. Wood: 2, 3.

♀ flowers ♂ flowers

Black Spruce

Blue Engelmann Spruce

cone scale

♀ flowers

type   underside

Colorado Spruce

♀ flow[ers]

type

open cone

'Moerheim'   'Endtz'

'Koster'   **Colorado Spruce 'Glauca'**

188

Blue Engelmann Spruce
Picea engelmannii 'Glauca'

The blue form of this species is common in cultivation but the ordinary green-needled species is hardly ever seen. In its wild state this species produces straight-stemmed narrow conical trees 24-30m tall. It is native in a long north-south region from British Columbia south-east to New Mexico, mainly confined to cool moist high ground in the Rocky Mountains. The evergreen needles, up to 2.5cm long, are spread all round the shoot. Each one is 4-sided, flexible and sharp pointed. They tend to be grey-green but in the cultivar 'Glauca' they are particularly glaucous, with white stomatal bands on the inside faces. The pendulous papery cones are 4-6cm long and often produced in large numbers at the top of the tree. The species name commemorates George Engelmann, a German doctor and botanist from St Louis.

Growth: 3-12-30. Hardiness: 70%. Choice: 1. Wood: 2, 3.

Colorado Spruce *Picea pungens*

Also known in its native America as Blue Spruce, because of its glaucous tendencies, this species has produced some vivid blue-needled ornamental forms in cultivation. The true species has a fairly scattered natural range from southern Wyoming and eastern Idaho southwards to parts of Arizona and New Mexico. Although it is confined to the southern United States it grows at high elevation (1800-3300m) and is extremely hardy. It makes a large straight tree, normally up to 30m tall but exceptional specimens 45m have been known.

The cultivar '**Koster**' produced in Holland and named in 1901 is perhaps the best known garden form. Sold under several names including 'Pungens Koster' and Koster's Blue Spruce, it is a medium-sized conical tree with silvery-blue needles. Young trees are best because the lower branches on old specimens eventually loose their vigour and rapidly become defoliated if shaded. The form **glauca** is a natural variant of Colorado Spruce. Some specimens of it are intensely glaucous but most are just grey-green. Cultivation of large numbers recently for the Christmas tree market has high-lighted the huge amount of variation within the form. The cultivar '**Endtz**' is another Dutch clone described in 1933. It is very similar to an average grey-blue f. *glauca*. A rival to 'Koster' for dramatic colour since 1912 is '**Moerheim**', cultivated and named in Holland. It is more compact than 'Koster' and still one of the best blue-needled conifers for ornamental use.

Growth: 3-15-30. Hardiness: 80-90%. Choice: 1 (cvs decorative). Wood: 2, 3 (species).

Colorado Spruce 'Glauca'   **'Koster'**   **Blue Engelmann Spruce**

Sitka Spruce

leaf details

opening cone

closed cone

young cone

cone scale

♀ flower

♂ flower

Sitka Spruce

Sitka Spruce *Picea sitchensis*

This remarkable forest tree has probably been the most successful and productive woody plant cultivated in the twentieth century. Upland forestry, particularly in the British Isles, has been transformed by it. Originally it came from a long north-south range running down the Pacific coast of North America, from Kodiak Island in Alaska to California. Within this natural range it grows from sea level to 900m. Huge trees, up to 60m tall, the world's largest spruce, occur in pure stands or mixed forest with Western Hemlock (p. 195). In the hot dry south it hugs the coast and relies on Pacific sea fog to provide enough moisture to survive. It was discovered by Archibald Menzies in Washington State in 1792 and introduced to Europe in 1831 by David Douglas. Plants from the Queen Charlotte Islands, British Columbia, where the largest and best trees grow, are ideal for British forestry. In cool moist regions on poor mineral or peaty soils it makes a fast-growing straight tree. In dense plantations the lower branches become suppressed and soon defoliate. However, they are reluctant to fall off and develop into an impenetrable wall of tough, sharply abrasive brown twigs. The bark is thin and flaky, variable in colour between purplish-grey brown and silvery-brown. In old age it becomes rough and fissured, often swelling the base of the tree until it is reminiscent of a huge bottle. The 1.5-2.5cm needles are flat, glaucous-green when healthy, and have a vicious point. When shaded or in poor health they are dull green or yellowish, shorter and less sharply pointed. Cones (see p. 261) are pendulous and usually confined to the tree tops. They start bright pink and change to pale green, straw yellow and finally pale brown as they mature. The crinkled scales are thin like parchment. Sitka spruce is hardy to below -20°C, withstands salt spray and some salinity in the soil, but does not like atmospheric pollution or low phosphate levels. Spring frosts can cause shoot death, especially on young northern trees planted out of context. Unhealthy plants are susceptible to predation by aphids and beetles. The long fibre length timber is ideal for paper making. Straight-grained clean lengths are strong and lightweight. Formerly used for aircraft frames.

Growth: 7-20-60. Hardiness: 50%. Choice: 3.
Wood: 1, 2, 3, 4.

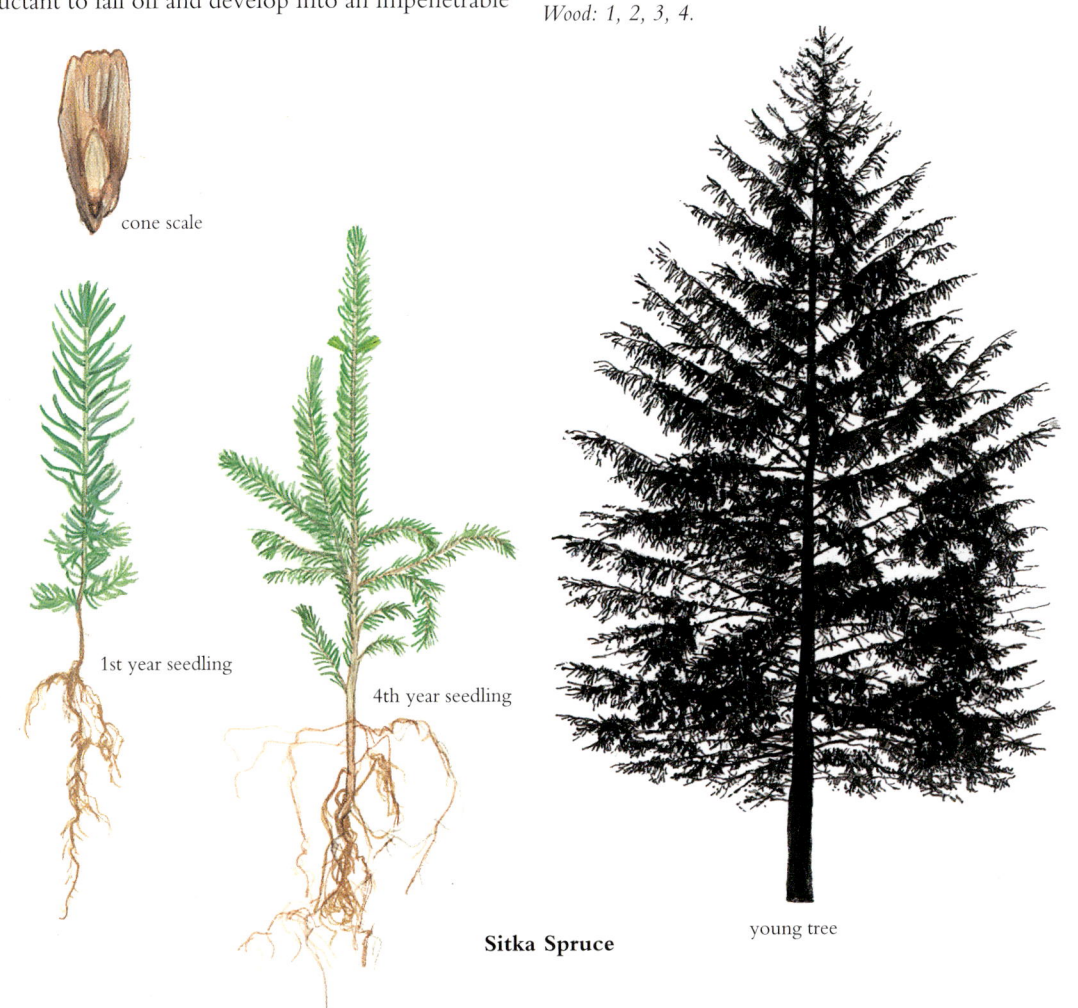

cone scale

1st year seedling

4th year seedling

young tree

Sitka Spruce

♀ flower

Likiang Spruce

new leaves

♂ flowers

actual size

Purple-cone Spruce

leaf section

underside

underside

Likiang Spruce

actual size

Likiang Spruce

Likiang Spruce *Picea likiangensis*

This obscure group of Chinese spruces has been subject to taxonomic debate ever since they were collected by Ernest Wilson and Harry Smith in the early 1900s. First given species names, later the whole group became varieties of Likiang Spruce. Now – with the exception of Candelabra Spruce (p. 171) – they are species again. Strangely the most distinct tree of all, '**Yunnan Form**', has no official name allocated to it at all since var. *yunnanensis* has been dropped.

Picea likiangensis is a variable tree up to 30m tall from north-west Yunnan, Sichuan and south-east Tibet. It has been extensively cultivated as an ornamental in Europe and America since 1900. Most of the trees in European collections are the '**Yunnan Form**' which has wide spreading branches and a moderately straight vertical stem. The main attraction is the brilliantly-coloured spring flowers (although they are not strictly flowers in the botanical sense). Male and female are bright crimson. The females then develop into 13cm cones, turning through shades of bloomed purple-red as they do. They bend from the vertical to become pendulous when fully expanded. Fortunately they occur all over the tree and can easily be seen from the ground. The pointed 1.5cm needles have blue-grey lines of stomata on the underside.

Growth: 3-10-20 (30). Hardiness: 60%. Choice: 1 (requires space). Wood: 2, 3.

Purple-cone Spruce *Picea purpurea*

This hardy 30m tree is quite different in general appearance to Likiang Spruce. It has a dense crown of deep green foliage reminiscent of Norway Spruce. Shoots sweep upwards towards the conical top. The 1.2cm needles are sharply pointed or rounded. As a species it was first described in 1906. The 1923 variety designation *likiangensis* var. *purpurea* has now been discredited.

Growth: 3-15-30. Hardiness: 60-70%. Choice: 2, 3. Wood: 2, 3, 4.

Balfour Spruce *Picea balfouriana*

This species resembles Purple-cone Spruce. The needles are slightly longer (1.5cm) and greyish-green in colour. Branches are rather more spreading but this is influenced to a large extent by the immediate environment. The native range is a very diverse region between south-west Sichuan and eastern Tibet. Seed was first collected by Ernest Wilson and the tree was described by him and Alfred Rehder in 1914.

Growth: 3-10-20. Hardiness: 40-50%. Choice: 3. Wood: 2, 3.

Balfour Spruce

'Yunnan Form'

Western Hemlock

closed cone

♂ flowers

seed

open cone

♀ flower

underside

1 year old seedling

seedling

Western Hemlock

Carolina Hemlock

194

HEMLOCKS

Western Hemlock *Tsuga heterophylla*

This tree has a huge native range extending from Alaska along the Pacific coast and the slopes of the Rocky Mountains to north California. It is a high quality timber producer, particularly in Oregon and Washington. Straight stems 70m tall can still be found there today. Plantation grown trees tend to have fluted stems and exaggerated buttresses which reduce productivity. When grown for pulp it yields cellulose material of high quality, suitable for the manufacture of rayon and cellophane. This is an exceptionally shade-tolerant species, so individuals thrive in close proximity. Branches in this situation are small and soon suppressed so the resulting timber is not spoiled by having large knots in it.

Western Hemlock was discovered by David Douglas in 1828. It was described by Lewis and Clark in 1832, but not brought to Europe until 1852. At one point the species name was changed to *albertiana* at the request of Queen Victoria because she had such a high regard for it. It is a relative of the spruces, having single flat evergreen needles, each one borne on a small wooden peg. The foliage is soft and there are no sharp points; even the shoots are fine and flexible. Young nursery plants of this species must be raised away from intense light. In Britain a common practice was to grow them only in the damp misty west of the country. See p. 261 for cone.

Western Hemlock has not produced many cultivated forms. The peculiar selection '**Laursen's Column**' was discovered at the Hillier Nursery by Mr Asger Laursen in 1968.

Growth: 5-15-45. Hardiness: 50%. Choice: 3. Wood: 2, 4.

Carolina Hemlock *Tsuga caroliniana*

This rare tree in cultivation is from a limited area in the eastern United States, south-west Virginia, north-east Tennessee and just into the Carolinas. It is slow-growing, to around 18m, with a conical outline. The needles are 1-2cm long and point in all directions on the shoot, unlike Western Hemlock which has needles more or less in two ranks. As the natural range of Carolina Hemlock joins that of Eastern Hemlock (p. 197) there is some confusion about its identity. It was not discovered as a distinct species until 1850, and was finally described and named by Georg Englemann from St. Louis in 1881.

Growth: 2-6-18. Hardiness: 70%. Choice: 4. Wood: 2, 4.

Carolina Hemlock

'Laursen's Column'

Eastern Hemlock

flower
♂ flowers
cone scale
closed cone
underside

'Aurea'

'Fremdii'

'Macrophylla'

'Taxifolia' 'Microphylla'

Eastern Hemlock 'Sargentii'

HEMLOCKS

Eastern Hemlock *Tsuga canadensis*

Although in the wild state this is a straight tree, in cultivation it often produces multiple crooked stems. It has particularly drooping shoot tips and lax foliage. The flat soft evergreen needles are round-tipped and 1-1.5cm long. Most of them occur in two ranks, presenting their deep glossy green side to the sky and their glaucous underside downwards. Trees have chestnut-brown bark which develops close vertical fissures with age. This hardy species occurs in North America from Nova Scotia to southern Ontario and southwards to northern Alabama and Minnesota. In the south it grows on high ground up to 1500m.

This species has provided a large number of horticultural forms since its introduction by Peter Collinson in 1736. Many are pendulous in the extreme. 'Pendula' was first raised in Germany in 1891 but the actual plant is now unknown. Specimens in cultivation now tend to be called '**Sargentii**', or as previously 'Sargentii Pendula'. There are clearly many slightly different pendulous types, some making trees around 6m tall and others barely leaving the ground. An early compact rounded form that still survives in cultivation is '**Fremdii**' found in Holland, but raised in the USA in 1932. Cultivars with variable needle lengths are called '**Macrophylla**' (1930), the clones with long needles, and '**Microphylla**', first isolated in 1864, with short needles. Several different types now share this name. Another needle variant is the American cultivar '**Taxifolia**' which resembles yew (p. 23). The Golden Eastern Hemlock, originally called '**Aurea**' now comes in many different forms.

Growth: 3-15-25. Hardiness: 80%. Choice: 1 (cvs). Wood: 2, 3, 4 (America)

Mountain Hemlock *Tsuga mertensiana*

This lovely tree comes in various shapes and sizes almost all of them picturesque. The range is from a lean slender alpine tree with short down-swept branches, to a conical or rounded dense bushy plant. A common factor is the grey-green rosemary-like foliage. Short crowded evergreen needles of variable lengths (0.5-2cm) occur together on the same shoot. The trees natural range is southern Alaska along the Pacific coast then southwards and high up (over 3000m) in the Rocky Mountains to California.

Growth: 3-8-25. Hardiness: 70%. Choice: 1 (requires space, variable). Wood: 2.

Hybrid American Hemlock *Tsuga × jeffreyi*

This tree was first raised artificially in Britain in 1919 but was subsequently discovered growing wild in America where the range of the parents Western Hemlock and Mountain Hemlock meet. It is a yellowish to grey-green needled plant resembling Mountain Hemlock, but less attractive in cultivation.

Growth: 3-7-18. Hardiness: 60%. Choice: 4. Wood: 2.

♀ flower   ♂ flowers

Hybrid American Hemlock   **Mountain Hemlock**   young tree

underside underside
Himalayan Hemlock

Eastern Himalayan Hemlock

underside

♀ flower ♂ flowers

Northern Japanese Hemlock

Northern Japanese Hemlock

under

seed

cone scale

Northern Japanese Hemlock

Himalayan Hemlock *Tsuga dumosa*

This is a huge tree up to 50m tall in its native range between north-west India and China. It occurs up to 3300m in Bhutan. In cultivation it is generally disappointing, small and untidy. This is probably due to the provenance of the original plant, which may have been forgotten. Since its introduction in 1838 trees have been confused with Chinese Hemlock. The needles are pointed and up to 3cm long with silvery grey undersides.

Growth: 3-15-25 (50). Hardiness: 40%. Choice: 3. Wood: 2, 4.

Eastern Himalayan Hemlock
Tsuga yunnanensis

Although this plant occurs in collections and minor distinctions may be found, it is now considered to be part of *Tsuga chinensis*. Some specimens may have a lot in common with cultivated *Tsuga dumosa*.

Growth: 3-10-20. Hardiness: 50%. Choice: 3. Wood: 2, 4.

Northern Japanese Hemlock
Tsuga diversifolia

If it were not evergreen and coniferous this tree could easily be mistaken by its outline for a small broadleaved species. Its top is bushy and domed on a short stem. The height seldom reaches 15m. The short blunt needles are mostly in two ranks except for the occasional stray that points forward above the rest. In general the whole tree resembles a small version of a cultivated Eastern Hemlock (p. 197). It comes from northern Japan, from Honshu to Hokkaido, and is extremely hardy. Although introduced as early as 1861 it remains rare in cultivation.

Growth: 2-7-15. Hardiness: 50%. Choice: 4. Wood: 2, 4.

Southern Japanese Hemlock *Tsuga sieboldii*

This rare plant, introduced from the southern islands of Japan in 1861, may reach 20m in height. However, it seldom confines itself to a single stem in cultivation and may become twisted and very untidy. The outline is broadly conic becoming quite open and irregular. The drooping shoots have a double rank of 1.5-2cm flat notched needles. They are deep glossy green above and grey below but less bright than *Tsuga diversifolia*.

Growth: 2-8-20. Hardiness: 50%. Choice: 4. Wood: 2, 4.

Chinese Hemlock *Tsuga chinensis*

Although still uncommon as a cultivated tree this species is less rare now that *Tsuga yunnanensis* is included within the same name. Its native range includes the mountains along the course of the Yangtse River in China. The outline is more or less conical on one or several vertical stems up to 15m long. The needles are parted below the shoot and tend to flatten out above it. They are blunt ended and sometimes notched, with pale, though not very distinct, grey-green bands on the underside. The margins may be minutely toothed. For a *Tsuga* the whole tree has a rather pale appearance.

Growth: 2-8-15. Hardiness: 50%. Choice: 4. Wood: 2, 4.

underside
bud
underside

seedling seed parkland tree **Douglas Fir** forest tree

♂ flowers

♀ flowers

♂ flower

cone scale cone bract

Douglas Fir *Pseudotsuga menziesii*

Also known in the timber trade world-wide as Oregon Pine, this great forest tree has a huge north-south range in Western North America. The species is split into two varieties. This, var. *menziesii*, is the green or coastal Douglas fir which occurs from central British Columbia down the Pacific side of the Rocky Mountains to California. Blue Douglas Fir var. *glauca* is described on p. 203. Douglas Fir grows on freely draining rocky or sandy non-calcareous ground to an altitude of 1800m in the south. In high rainfall areas the best trees exceed 50m with straight stems. The tops are conical until excessive height exposes them to the wind which breaks them up. The evergreen needles are soft and flexible, up to 3cm long, flattened and mostly spreading all round the shoot. The leathery 5-9cm cones (see p. 261) hang downwards as they expand. Between each rounded scale there is a prominent exserted trident bract. The cones ripen, shed seed and fall to the ground in a single season of about six months. This species was discovered by Archidald Menzies at Nootka Sound in British Columbia in 1792 and introduced to Europe by David Douglas 35 years later. It has a different chromosome number to most other conifers including the other species in the *Pseudotsuga* genus.

The cultivar '**Stairii**' was first described in 1871. It is a smaller tree with cream-coloured needles in the spring changing to pale green in summer. The name commemorates the Earl of Stair on whose estate, Castle Kennedy in Scotland, this spontaneous sport was first noticed.

Growth: 7-20-55 (species). Hardiness: 40-60%. Choice: 3. Wood: 1, 2, 3.

Japanese Douglas Fir *Pseudotsuga japonica*

This very hardy but rare tree in cultivation is from two small regions of south-east Japan, the islands of Honshu and Shikoku. It is smaller than the American tree with shorter distinctly white banded needles but generally less luxuriant foliage. Genetically it is closely related to Bigcone Douglas Fir (p. 203). Douglas Firs probably all originated in the same area of the World but during its evolution this species became separated from the rest. It drifted away on the western tectonic plate when the Pacific Ocean split Asia and America apart. The tree illustrated is growing on an unsuitable site, lacking moisture and acid soil.

Growth: 2-5-10. Hardiness: 50%. Choice: 4.

'Stairii' underside

Japanese Douglas Fir underside

Bigcone Douglas Fir

Bigcone Douglas Fir

Blue Douglas Fir

♂ flow

202

Bigcone Douglas Fir *Pseudotsuga macrocarpa*

This species grows outside the range of ordinary Douglas Fir in the mountains of southern California. It occurs in mixed woodlands and pure forests on dry rocky slopes up to 2400m above sea level. The branches are wide-spreading, but height varies between 12m and 24m depending upon the local environment. The thick corky bark is moderately fire resistant, and a surprising number of trees survive forest fires. Bigcone Douglas Fir differs from the more familiar species by having much larger cones (9-15cm long). These are similar to the common species except the trident bract only just shows beyond the rounded scales. The needles are longer, 3-5cm, exceptionally up to 8cm, with a sharpish point. Most of them are set in two ranks and not all round the shoot, they are blue or grey-green.

Growth: 3-15-24. Hardiness: 30-40%. Choice: 3. Wood: 2, 3.

Blue Douglas Fir

Pseudotsuga menziesii var. *glauca*

Away from the Pacific coast from Montana to New Mexico Douglas Fir is represented by a regional variant with conspicuously glaucous foliage. Also known as Rocky Mountain Douglas Fir it tends to be narrow, conical and up to 25m tall. The cones are slightly smaller than green Douglas fir with extended or reflexed bracts. In cultivation, for forestry or ornament, this variety is more lime tolerant but also more prone to leaf-cast, a serious and widespread fungal disease.

Growth: 6-15-25. Hardiness: 80%. Choice: 3. Wood: 2, 3.

Fraser River Douglas Fir

Pseudotsuga menziesii f. *caesia*

The northern extension of the variety *glauca* into British Columbia was redefined in 1950 by Joao Franco, a Portuguese taxonomist, as f. *caesia*. It has blue-green foliage, slightly longer flattened needles and erect cone scales.

Growth: 5-12-25. Hardiness: 60-80%. Choice: 3.

Pseudotsuga menziesii cultivars

By 1993 over 120 cultivated forms of Douglas Fir had been recognized. Many of these have arisen from 'witches brooms' and have stunted growth. Some of the blue needled varieties are very attractive. All Douglas Firs are evergreen. '**Brevifolia**' is a British 1930s selection with truncated foliage and bright red-brown buds during the winter. '**Fretsii**' is a 1905 Dutch plant raised at Boskoop. It has thick tangled creeping shoots with short grey-green needles.

Growth: 1-2-4 (variable). Hardiness: 60%. Choice: 1.

Blue Douglas Fir 'Brevifolia' 'Fretsii' Fraser River Douglas Fir (underside)

Stone Pine

♂ flowers

♀ flower

conelet

seeds

♂ flowers

Heldreich Pine

cone scale   cone bract

Stone Pine

bud

204

Stone Pine *Pinus pinea*

The familiar sight of these domed evergreen trees along the north coast of the Mediterranean has given them their alternative name of Umbrella Pine. For centuries Stone Pines have been planted for their edible seeds (Stone is a reference to the seed). Roman invaders brought stone pine cones to Britain almost 2000 years ago. Artificial planting has been so extensive that the exact natural distribution is now uncertain. The stout cones 8-15cm long take three years to ripen. Needles, in pairs, are around 12cm long, slightly twisted and armed with a sharp tip. The short (3-4cm) juvenile leaves, which occur singly like Douglas Fir (p. 201), occur on young plants for five or six years. These are sold as Christmas ornaments.

Growth: 3-10-20. Hardiness: 50%. Choice: 1 (requires space). Wood: 3.

Arolla Pine *Pinus cembra*

Also called Swiss Stone Pine, this species occurs in the central European Alps, north-east Russia and northern Asia. It is a slow-growing pyramidal tree up to 25m tall. In old age the top spreads unevenly. The bark is smooth dark grey at first becoming deeply fissured between flat red-brown plates. The needles, in fives, are 7-9cm long. The cones (see p. 261) are quite unlike those of most other conifers. They do not open on the tree to shed the wingless seeds. After 2-3 years the whole cone, a truncated 7cm cylinder, falls to the ground and is eventually broken up, usually by animals. Many cultivated forms of *Pinus cembra* have been developed, 'Aureovariegata' (1868) has patchy golden yellow foliage on a narrow upright tree. The variety *chlorocarpa* (1899) is a yellow coned variant. This name was also used in 1964 for another form now called *Pinus pumila* 'Compacta'.

Growth: 5-12-25. Hardiness: 70%. Choice: 3. Wood: 2, 3.

Heldreich Pine *Pinus heldreichii*

Described in 1863 and in cultivation since 1891 this species is native in the Balkans, northern Italy and Greece. Trees there are believed to be 1000 years old. The stem is straight, the top conical, up to 20cm tall and the bark is pale grey at first then flaky and developing yellowish-grey patches reminiscent of a plane tree. The stiff needles are 6-9cm long with blunt ends. Ovoid cones around 8cm long are bluish-purple for almost two years, ripening to rusty-brown.

Growth: 5-12-25. Hardiness: 50%. Choice: 3. Wood: 2, 3.

bud

Foxtail Pine

Bristlecone Pine

bud

resin dots

Limber Pine

♂ flowers

♀ flowers

open cone

closed cone

Foxtail Pine

Foxtail Pine *Pinus balfouriana*

This small tree, 5-15m tall, inhabits a limited area in northern California. Dry rocky hillsides up to 3500m in the Klamath Mountains. It shares this inhospitable place with Whitebark Pine, *Pinus albicaulis* (p. 223). Foxtail Pine has very short needles, less than 3cm, mostly arranged in fives, which crowd the shoot and often curve inwards like the hair on a foxes tail. The cylindrical cones have spine tipped scales, they are 9-13cm long. The seeds, which are distinctly mottled have a persistent wing. The bark is light grey and smooth at first becoming deeply furrowed and reddish-brown.

Growth: 3-10-15. Hardiness: 50%. Choice: 1. Wood: 2, 3.

Bristlecone Pine *Pinus aristata*

World famous for its great age, over 4600 annual rings have been counted, this hardy tree occurs in eastern California, Colorado and New Mexico. It is unable to achieve great height in the severe conditions where it grows naturally. Specimens range from only 3-12m. In cultivation it will exceed this in a relatively short time. This is another Foxtail Pine with short, 3cm, blunt-ended needles in fives, curving in towards the shoot. They produce numerous tiny white resin flecks from ruptured resin canals situated just below the surface. The ovoid 6-10cm cone has a distinctive bristle-like spine on the end of each scale, hence the name. The seeds are mottled fawn and brown with a detachable wing. Two varieties have been identified, the Colorado Bristlecone Pine and the Intermountain Bristlecone Pine, **var *longaeva*,** which is found from Utah, Nevada and eastern California. Remnants of the native populations of this variety are conserved in various Forest Parks. Some authorities consider this to be a species in its own right.

Growth: 1-4-12. Hardiness: 50%. Choice: 1, 3.

Limber Pine *Pinus flexilis*

Although superficially similar to a Foxtail Pine this is a relative of the white pines. It has a long north south range from south-east British Columbia and Alberta to New Mexico in the foothills of the Rocky Mountains where it grows to elevations of 3600m. It hybridizes freely with the Southern Limber Pine, *Pinus reflexa* and South-western White Pine, *Pinus strobiformis* (p. 237). Specimens in cultivation may show characteristics of these species. It is a small tree 5-15m tall, up to 25m in cultivation, with short tough branches. The twigs are so flexible that they can be tied into a knot. This is reflected in the species name. The needles, in fives, are crowded along the shoots. They are often short, 3-4cm, but may make 9cm on some trees. The cones, which are 15cm long, sometimes more, contain almost wingless edible seeds. The bark is light grey becoming dark brown and roughly divided into deep furrows and squarish plates.

Growth: 3-1-20. Hardiness: 40-70%. Choice: 4. Wood: 2, 3.

Bristlecone Pine
American form

var. ***longaeva***

Chinese White Pine

♀ flower

♂ flowers

open cone

crinkle base

Chinese White Pine closed cone

Chinese White Pine

Chinese Red Pine

208

Chinese White Pine *Pinus armandii*

In cultivation this is a neat upright tree while it is young with a fairly straight stem and whorled horizontal branches. After maturity it becomes unevenly extended and more open. Trees usually do not exceed 20m in height, but specimens up to 40m have been recorded. This is a variable species from a huge natural range which includes Burma, south-east Tibet and western China. Further east a variety (var. *mastersiana*) occurs in Taiwan. At the eastern end of the range there is a clear affinity with Korean Pine (p. 239) and Arolla Pine (p. 205). The lax needles, in fives, are 10-15cm long. They point forward in the first year then droop below the shoot. Some bundles bend sharply or become kinked towards the base which accentuates this floppy posture. The cones, on a stout 3cm stalk, are around 14cm long with thick incurved scales except at the base. They usually occur in clusters of two or three and develop obliquely to fit in with each other. The seeds have virtually no wing, they fall out of the cone before it fully opens, and take their slim chance of survival directly under the parent tree. They are over 1cm long and edible. This species was discovered by the French missionary the Abbé Armand David in 1873 and named in his honour by Adrien Franchet. It was introduced into cultivation by another French missionary Père Farges in 1895.

Growth: 3-10-20. Hardiness: 50%. Choice: 1 (requires space). Wood: 2.

Chinese Red Pine *Pinus tabuliformis*

This is a rare tree in cultivation, it is a native species in northern China. Although not usually large, specimens 30m tall are known. It becomes wide spreading and, as illustrated, often leans or falls over but continues to grow in a bushy form. The needles, in pairs or sometimes threes, are 10-15cm long crowding all round the shoot. More or less oval woody cones up to 9cm long, but frequently much less, have spikes on the tip of each scale. Most provenances of this tree are very hardy. It was first described in 1867 but has been the subject of taxonomic revision and argument since then. Several former varieties have now been designated as species in their own right. *Pinus yunnanensis*, the Yunnan Pine, for example, which grows to 30m in height but is more tender. The needles are in threes, and the 8cm ovoid-conic cones do not have spines.

Growth: 2-6-12 (30). Hardiness: 50%. Choice: 4. Wood: 2.

Gaoshan Pine *Pinus densata*

Formerly classified as a variety of Chinese Red Pine this species occurs in central China and is rare in cultivation. Confusingly it has needles in twos and in threes, often on the same shoot. The oblique ovoid cone has a down curved spike on the tip of each scale. This group of Chinese Pines are extremely difficult to tell apart out of context, particularly as they come from such a wide range of different environments.

Growth: 2-6-12. Hardiness: 50%. Choice: 4.

Sugar Pine

Western White Pine
bark

Sugar Pine

Sugar Pine

open cone

210

Sugar Pine *Pinus lambertiana*

Regarded as the 'King of the pines' by American lumbermen, this tree is truly magnificent. One specimen called the Champion in 1997 was 73m tall and 3m across the stem. It occurs in cool moist places, usually in mixed woodlands, from west Oregon to Baja California. The stem is usually straight and often branch free for a good height. Young bark is thin, smooth and grey but it becomes rough and fissured in old age. The evergreen needles point forward for the first year, spread out in the second and fall after 3. They are 5-10cm long, in bundles of 5, rigid, but slender and sharply pointed. The cones are spectacular, 30-50cm long, hanging down from the branch ends. The seeds with their long aerodynamic wings were once eaten by American Indians. They also relished the edible sweet resinous sap which exudes from cut or partly burned heartwood. Hence the name Sugar Pine.

The species was discovered by David Douglas in 1826 and named in honour of A.B. Lambert, secretary of the Royal Horticultural Society in London. Like all white pines, Sugar Pine is susceptible to white pine blister rust (*Cronartium ribicola*) a fungus that spends part of its life cycle on currant bushes.

Growth: 4-18-40. Hardiness: 40%. Choice: 3. Wood: 1, 2, 3.

Western White Pine *Pinus monticola*

Closely related to Sugar Pine but less spectacular, this important timber tree extends from British Columbia to California. It grows on both sides of the Rocky Mountains up to 2900m in the south. It is a narrow, rather open conical tree with horizontal branches and upward curving shoots. Stems are generally straight at first with smooth bark as illustrated, but in old age this becomes deeply fissured between angular plates. The evergreen needles are 7-10cm long in bunches of five, remaining on the tree for about four years. Cones up to 25cm long, with thin un-spined scales, hang down on long stalks.

This is an important timber tree in America. In addition to structural softwood its straight even grain makes it ideal for matches. White pine blister rust, a fatal disease spread round the world from Asia, is a serious problem in America and also where this tree is used in forestry plantations and ornamental collections in other countries.

Growth: 4-18-40. Hardiness: 50%. Choice: 3, 4. Wood: 2, 3.

Western White Pine

old cone

young cone

♀ flowers

Western White Pine

Japanese White Pine

'Glauca'

young cone

♀ flowers

♂ flowers

'Tempelhof'

Japanese White Pine

'Saphir'

Lacebark Pine
bark

Japanese White Pine *Pinus parviflora*

This is a complex Japanese species which causes considerable argument among botanists. Its classification and nomenclature are by no means straightforward. Furthermore a huge number of 'Bonsai' trees have been created from it and given new invalid cultivar names. The species, in the broad sense, was first described in 1844. It is a hardy straight-stemmed tree up to 20m tall, with tiered spreading foliage. The curved glaucous-green needles emerge in spring from bright pale orange buds. They are in fives and up to 6cm long. The cones are small, only 6cm long, with very few scales. Originally from Honshu, Kyushu and Shikoku, it has been cultivated for so long that its wild distribution is now confused. Most arboretum trees world-wide are probably of garden origin.

The cultivars of Japanese White Pine are often muddled by the use of a host of different graft understocks. These can cause a variety of apparently different results from a single scion. '**Glauca**', described in 1909, is a low silver-needled tree of great beauty. '**Saphir**' is a slow-growing Dutch selection made in 1982 with short bluish foliage, and '**Tempelhof**' is similar but stronger-growing. It was originally from a specimen tree found in the Dutch Gimborn Arboretum in 1969. It has become very popular with gardeners recently.

Growth: 3-10-20 (species). Hardiness: 50%.
Choice: 1 (requires space). Wood: 2, 3 (species).

Lacebark Pine *Pinus bungeana*

Originally from northern China this tree has unique bark among pines, reminiscent of a plane tree or Eucalyptus, having patches of bloomed grey, brown and olive-green when large enough to exfoliate. The species has been a temple garden favourite in China and Korea for centuries. Specimens may grow to 20m, but are generally much lower and inclined to be bushy. The needles, in threes, are 6-8cm long. The oval cones, around 5cm long, are viciously spiny. Although very hardy, it is quite difficult to establish and the 'lace bark' pattern takes many years to develop.

Growth: 2-8-12. Hardiness: 60%. Choice: 1 (bark feature).

Maritime Pine

bud

♂ flowers

♀ flowers

Maritime Pine
(storm damaged tree)

Macedonian Pine

214

Maritime Pine *Pinus pinaster*

This species is native in southern Europe and North Africa. Close to the sea it is often a wild, twisting, even prostrate tree but still capable of growing to an impressive size. In sheltered locations and where it has been cultivated for forestry, particularly in France and Portugal, straight stems and heights to 35m have been achieved. The Portuguese subspecies *atlantica* is a particularly good fairly hardy timber producer that deserves wider use in forestry. Even in Britain stems over 120cm in diameter are known.

The bark can sometimes be more brightly-coloured than the example illustrated, with pink and light reddish-brown and purple-brown in squarish smooth plates between deep fissures. The needles, in pairs, are stiff, straight or gently curved, and up to 25cm long. The hard woody cones, often in clusters, are oblique-conic, up to 18cm long, and often retained on the branches for several years. Cones on trees planted among dunes may become highly polished by the blowing sand. Seeds germinate readily but young seedlings quickly develop a long tap root, making them difficult to transplant. This species has been cultivated in western Europe at least since the sixteenth century. It was described by the English botanist William Aiton in 1789. As well as providing shelter and timber, it has always been an important source of resin in western France.

Growth: 6-15-30. Hardiness: 30%. Choice: 2, 3. Wood: 1, 2, 3.

Macedonian Pine *Pinus peuce*

This is a tough columnar tree which is native to the Balkans, Bulgaria and northern Greece. It generally produces a good straight stem and specimens approaching 30m in height are common. Rarely for a pine it will grow well in the cold wet acid peaty conditions usually reserved for spruce in the forestry industry. The foliage is distinctly dense, deep green and retained well down the tree in semi-shade, even in plantations. The thin needles, in fives, are around 8cm long and are retained on the branches for at least four years. The drooping cones are leathery, cylindrical and 10-15cm long. Young stems are smooth, resinous and grey-green reminiscent of silver fir. Unlike most pines in the 'white pine' group they are not brittle and do not break easily. They are also resistant to the disease white pine blister rust. When it was discovered in 1839 by August Heinrich Grisebach, professor of botany at Göttingen, he spelt the name 'peuke', which is an indication of how it should be pronounced. He described the species in 1844, and it was brought into cultivation in 1863 by the Greek botanist Theodoros Orphanides.

Growth: 5-15-25. Hardiness: 70%. Choice: 3. Wood: 2, 3.

Macedonian Pine

♂ flowers

♀ flowers

needle detail

♂ flowers

♀ flowers

Mexican White Pine

Mexican White Pine
young tree

Pinus ayacahuite
var. *veitchii*

Mexican White Pine *Pinus ayacahuite*

The true species *ayacahuite* is native to southern Mexico and Guatemala and is doubtfully hardy outside this climatic band. Within its native range trees can occasionally reach 45m in height. Specimens that are seen in cooler temperate areas have usually come from upland sites or the most northerly sector of the population. The lax 14-20cm needles, in bunches of five, point forwards along the shoot and droop below it in a characteristic way. The flexible pendulous cones are cylindrical, up to 40cm long and 12cm wide. They are relatively soft and leathery, quite unlike woody pine cones. The seed is 9mm long with an efficient 3cm wing that allows it to travel some distance in a favourable wind. This tree has been in cultivation since 1838. It was named and described by Christian Ehrenberg, professor of botany in Berlin, and by Diederich von Schlechtendal from Halle-Saale.

An artificial hybrid between this species and the closely related but geographically remote Macedonian Pine (*Pinus peuce*) also exists. This is a rare tree not in general cultivation. It has intermediate morphological characteristics and is probably considerably more hardy than *Pinus ayacahuite*.

Growth: 3-10-20. Hardiness: 50%. Choice: 1 (requires space), 4. Wood: 2, 3.

Pinus ayacahuite var. *veitchii*

This variety of Mexican White Pine from central Mexico is the tree most often seen in temperate collections and plantations. Many planted specimens credited with the species name *ayacahuite* should probably be listed as this variety. It is one of the parents of Holford's Pine (p. 247). Benedikt Roezl, an Austrian botanist working in Central America, originally classified it as a species, *Pinus veitchii*. Herbert Airy Shaw working at Kew Gardens much later confirmed its variety status in 1909. The cones are large and contain seeds over 12mm long but with shorter wings. The needles may extend to around 20cm long with the same lax tendency as the species. The shape of the tree, a heavy, more or less straight stem and spreading top, is similar, but ultimate size is generally less. Keith Rushforth in 1987 suggested that this taxon might be better treated as a subspecies of *Pinus strobiformis* (p. 237), but even *strobiformis* has in the past been considered to be a variety of *ayacahuite*. A confused situation prevails still within this closely related group.

Growth: 3-10-20. Hardiness: 50%. Choice: 1 (requires space), 4. Wood: 2, 3.

young cones

type cone

Pinus ayacahuite* var. *veitchii

Weymouth Pine

♂ flowers

♀ flower

young cones

old bark

opening leaf sheath

'Radiata'

Pinus × *schwerinii* cone

Pinus × *schwerinii*

Weymouth Pine

Eastern White Pine or Weymouth Pine
Pinus strobus

In its native eastern North America this is a large and important timber tree. The wood formally had numerous uses including ship masts. Straight stems 30m long are known. The original Eastern White Pine forests contained trees 75m tall. In Britain it is called Weymouth Pine. There are conflicting arguments about why this should be. Lord Weymouth at Longleat was an advocate of the species in the early 1700s, but in 1605 it had been brought to Britain from Maine by Captain George Weymouth RN. At first conical, then round-topped, it grows very well in the close company of other trees. The 6-13cm needles are in bunches of 5. The narrow, leathery, pendant cones (see p. 261) are 10-20cm long, often spotted with white resin. Unfortunately the enthusiastic use of this valuable forest tree in Europe in the nineteenth century encouraged the spread of white pine blister rust, a fatal disease from Asia. This has destroyed any plantation potential the tree might have once had. The disease spreads by way of an alternative host, *Ribes* species (currants). Nowhere that provides suitable growing conditions for the pine is far enough away from a currant bush to be safe.

Numerous ornamental forms of Weymouth Pine have been cultivated, some of which appear to be resistant to blister rust. '**Contorta**' developed in 1932 at Rochester NY, is a curious plant with twisted branches and needles. An older cultivar '**Fastigiata**' is a German plant created in 1884. It is an erect columnar clone said to be particularly resistant to rust. '**Radiata**' is one of many semi-dwarf forms. It originated in England in 1923 and usually grows wider than it is tall.

Growth: 6-15-30 (species). Hardiness: 80%. Choice: 4. Wood: 2, 3.

Pinus × schwerinii

This artificial *Pinus strobus* × *Pinus wallichiana* hybrid exhibits a range of intermediate characteristics between the parents. The foliage illustrated is close to *Pinus strobus*. The first plant was raised by Count von Schwerin in Berlin in 1931. It was described and named in his honour by Jost Fitschen, a schoolmaster from Hamburg, in 1931. The hybrid is likely to occur whenever the parent species is planted within wind-blown pollen range of each other. A point to bear in mind if collecting any seed in an arboretum and expecting authentic progeny.

Growth: 2-8-15. Hardiness: 40%. Choice: 4.

'Contorta'

'Fastigiata'

♂ flowers   ♀ flower

Blue Pine

bud

Blue Pine
closed cone

Blue Pine bark

Blue Pine

220

Blue Pine *Pinus wallichiana*
(formerly Bhutan Pine)

The Blue, or western Himalayan Pine, once known as *Pinus excelsa* and for a time as *Pinus griffithii*, occurs in Asia from Afghanistan to Nepal. The old name Bhutan Pine now describes *Pinus bhutanica*, a recently described close relative. It seems possible that trees in ornamental collections may have actually originated from either species. In the most favourable conditions, dryish sheltered valleys, Blue Pine may reach around 40m in height on a straight slender stem. Elsewhere, particularly in the high (4000m) Himalayan foothills it is more diminutive. The soft wood and foliage breaks easily causing serious deformities. However, when young this is an elegant conical plant with long (12-18cm), lax glaucous-green needles in fives, which droop from the upwardly curving branches. Even in cultivation it tends to become ragged and untidy in old age, especially when planted in a cold or exposed place. The pendulous cylindrical cones are leathery and spotted with dry resin. The largest may reach 30cm long.

Artificial hybrids involving Blue Pine have been developed to test potential growth, timber production and disease resistance. Some of these are occasionally found in collections. See also *Pinus × schwerinii* and *Pinus × holfordiana* (p. 247) for example.
Growth: 4-12-40. Hardiness: 40%. Choice: 3. Wood: 2, 3.

Siberian Stone Pine *Pinus sibirica*

This very tough resilient relative of the Arolla Pine (p. 205) occurs in moist areas from the Ural Mountains eastwards across Siberia and into northern China. It is a shrub in the most severe conditions but may develop into a large tree where the climate and soils are more favourable. It has been in cultivation since 1803 but remains rare. The branches are generally short with tightly packed tufts of needles. These are in fives, with grey inner surfaces which only show up when the needles twist. They are between 6 and 10cm long depending on climatic conditions. The disproportionately large oval cones, up to 12cm long, contain edible seeds.
Growth: 2-8-20. Hardiness: 90%. Choice: 3. Wood: 3.

Pinus hwangshanensis

A recently introduced tender pine from China. Possibly a segregate population of Taiwan Black Pine, *Pinus taiwanensis* (p. 225).
Growth: 1-5-? Hardiness: 30%. Choice: 4.

Blue Pine cone

♂ flowers

Siberian Stone Pine

Pinus hwangshanensis

bud

♂ flowers

closed cone

Whitebark Pine

young cones

Whitebark Pine

♂ flowers

Mexican Pinyon Pine

conelet

open cone

Mexican Pinyon Pine

Whitebark Pine *Pinus albicaulis*

This extremely hardy North American shrub or small tree grows along the line of the Rocky Mountains from central British Columbia and Alberta through Wyoming to California. It climbs to over 1000m in the north and 3600m in the south. In dry rocky inhospitable places it only grows to around 6m in height, but may reach 15m. The twisted stem and branches support a spreading dome of foliage. The bark is grey-white, thin and smooth at first, becoming darker and rough in old age. The flexible strong twigs and short, 4-7cm, needles in fives, can withstand the ravages of the wind. The cones are non-opening, 4-8cm long and stalkless. Clark's Nutcracker, a crow-like American native bird, expertly picks the wingless seed from the rotting fallen cones, no doubt distributing a few to grow on in the process.

Growth: 2-6-15. Hardiness: 80%. Choice: 2. Wood: 3.

Mexican Pinyon Pine *Pinus cembroides*

Another shrubby tree of hot dry rocky places, this species occurs in limited areas of Texas, Arizona and southwards into Mexico. The bark, on twisting stems and branches, is light grey at first becoming grey-brown and rough with age. Needles in threes, 2-6cm long, are tightly packed along the shoots. The resinous 2-5cm roundish cones open on the tree to release the wingless seeds which are relished by rodents and birds. People too enjoy the seeds called 'pinyon nuts' which are sold commercially in Mexico and exported round the world.

Growth: 2-4-7. Hardiness: 20-30%. Choice: 3.

Single-leaf Pinyon Pine *Pinus monophylla*

Formerly classified as a variety of *Pinus cembroides*, this is another shrubby stunted plant with edible wingless seeds. It is tender but survives on dry mountainsides in the 'Great Basin region', Idaho, Utah, southern California and northern Mexico. It has almost unique needles, for a pine, occurring singly. Occasionally pairs can be found. They are stout and more or less straight. The 5-7cm ovate stalkless cones shed edible seeds that are sold locally. They have a dry mealy taste.

Growth: 2-7-14. Hardiness: 20-30%. Choice: 3.

Colorado Pinyon Pine *Pinus edulis*

Another former variety of *Pinus cembroides*, this compact 4-10m tree or sprawling shrub occupies local pockets of dry hillside in Utah, Arizona, Wyoming and northern Mexico. The contorted branches have smooth grey-brown bark which becomes rough and deeply furrowed. The short needles, in twos, are only around 3cm long. The ovate resinous 4-5cm cones shed their wingless seeds. These are oily, nutritious and good to eat.

Growth: 2-5-10. Hardiness: 30%. Choice: 3.

young cones

Single-leaf Pinyon Pine

open cone

Colorado Pinyon Pine

Japanese Red Pine

'Aurea'

young cone

'Oculus-draconis'

type needles

Japanese Red Pine

224

Japanese Red Pine *Pinus densiflora*

Throughout Japan, Korea, northern China and along the Pacific coast of Russia this hardy species is the equivalent of Scots Pine (p. 227). It is narrow and conic when young, spreading out in old age to a flat or domed top. In ideal conditions it may reach 30m, but it is generally much less, even becoming stunted and bushy in climatically extreme conditions. The needles, in twos, are 8-12cm long, slender and slightly curved or twisted. The small, woody, short-stalked cones are about 4cm long, ovoid and slightly oblique especially when they occur in clusters. Japanese Red Pine has been in cultivation since 1842 but because it has little merit as a decorative tree, it remains rare in collections. However, a large number of ornamental varieties have been produced from it, particularly in Japan. Akamatzu, which is the Japanese name for the species, appears in the names of many selections but horticulturally it is invalid. Three cultivars, all described in 1890 by the professor of botany in Munich Heinrich Mayr, are important. '**Aurea**' has rather acid yellow needles. The colour is strongest in a harsh winter. '**Oculus-draconis**' (Dragon's-eye Pine) is an interesting plant. The green needles are curiously marked with yellow, giving – when viewed from above – a banded effect which explains the name. This effect can also be seen in the autumn colour of the Golden Larch (p. 165). There is a pendulous form of Dragon's-eye Pine in which the 'eyes' are easier to see. Finally '**Umbraculifera**' which is a small slow-growing tree shaped somewhat like an umbrella. Its ultimate height is only about 4m and its width is a little more. The needles are short, and the cones are tiny versions of the parent species.

Growth: 3-12-20. Hardiness: 40-60%. Choice: 1 (cvs), 3. Wood: 2, 3.

Taiwan Black Pine *Pinus taiwanensis*

This tender species can only be grown in the most sheltered and mild places in the temperate zone. It is therefore seldom seen in cultivation. In the subtropical valleys of Taiwan it may grow up to 35m tall, with a conical outline and tiered horizontal branches. The stiff but twisted needles, in pairs, are 8-10cm long. The 6cm cones are ovoid. Bunzo Hayata, the Japanese botanist who wrote the flora of Formosa (Taiwan) described this species in 1911.

Growth: 2-10-15. Hardiness: 10%. Choice: 1. Wood: 2, 3.

'Umbraculifera'

Taiwan Black Pine

Scots Pine

base of leaves

open cone seeds

Scots Pine var. *lapponica* seedling young tree

226

Scots Pine *Pinus sylvestris*

This is a totally hardy native tree in much of Europe and northern Asia, extending north almost to the Arctic circle and south to Spain and Turkey. Regional variations occur within this huge and widespread population. However, other than dwarf ornamental forms, trees are constant in a persistent single stem, up to 36m tall, and conical tops until old age causes them to cease upward growth and flatten out. The slightly peeling bark is distinctly orange-brown when young, becoming rugged, grey and fissured with age. The evergreen slightly twisted needles are dark grey-green, occurring in pairs, and around 9cm long, more on young plants, less on old trees. The woody, slightly oblique cones (see p. 260) are produced in abundance. They are about 5cm long and fall in the summer after shedding the winged seed. The range of this species was even greater in the pre-boreal period, 9500 years ago. Subsequently it migrated northwards into harsher conditions but was replaced in the south by broad-leaved forest. It will thrive on dry sandy sites, fertile agricultural land and will even tolerate wet acid conditions.

A tall narrow-crowned form occurs in Sweden, and indeed most other sub Arctic regions. This is an environmental adaptation designed to cope with snowfall and wind resistance. The short branches hold little snow and soon shed it. Resistance to wind is minimal. Many such trees have grown slowly and stand, or have stood, in close company with others for a very long time. The variety (technically a sub-species) **lapponica** is such a tree. It was described by the Swedish botanist Robert Fries in 1888. Another slender form from the Baltic Coast is var. *rigensis*, described by John Loudon the Scottish dendrologist in 1838.

Growth: 3-12-36. Hardiness: 90%. Choice: 3.
Wood: 1, 2, 3, 5.

Pinus sylvestris var. *engadinensis*

This is a very local type of Scots Pine found in the Engadine Alps in Switzerland and the Tyrol. It is a tough tree, often with a curved stem and very short needles. It was first described in 1862, but its variety status is questionable. Trees of this sort can be found wherever the range of the species is climatically severe.

Growth: 2-8-15. Hardiness: 70%. Choice: 4. Wood: 3.

Pinus sylvestris* var. *engadinensis

Scots Pine

Pinus sylvestris subsp. *scotica*

bud

Mongolian Scots Pine

summer

Pinus sylvestris '**Aurea**'
autumn/winter

Pinus sylvestris subsp. *scotica*

Scots Pine *Pinus sylvestris* subsp. *scotica*

The subspecies from which Scots Pine takes its name is indigenous in Scotland. Since 1978 considerable efforts have been made by the British Forestry Commission to ensure that trees for new planting are from authentic local sources. About 12,000 hectares of the once extensive 'Forest of Caledonia', a name used by the Roman historian Tacitus, remain intact. The best of the extant trees may be 400 years old. The genetic integrity and diversity of Scots Pine seed gathered from the original Caledonian forest is good. There has never been a need, or will, to import alien seed from outside the region. Young trees of the subspecies are straight and conical for many years with clearly defined annual whorls of branches. Ancient specimens develop a full rounded head of branches as the illustration shows. Often, though, ground fires and 'shading out' will have led to the removal of most lower branches, resulting in clean exposed stems. The needles are generally shorter than the species, although they do vary in this respect. Most are distinctly glaucous, stiff and slightly twisted. The cones too are smaller than the species, often less than 5cm long. They may be slightly oblique or uniformly ovate.

Growth: 3-12-30. Hardiness: 90%. Choice: 3. Wood: 1, 2, 3, 5.

Mongolian Scots Pine

Pinus sylvestris var. *mongolica*

This variety is from the eastern limit of the species range. Its status is questionable. There is some doubt whether it is a Scots Pine or whether it is a Mongolian form of Chinese Pine, *Pinus tabulaeformis*. It was first described by the Russian botanist Dimitri Litvinov in 1905. It is a medium-sized tree with stout twisted needles in pairs around 10cm long. The conelets may persist for several years before developing into seed-bearing ovoid symmetrical or slightly oblique 8cm cones.

Growth: 2-7-15. Hardiness: 60%. Choice: 4. Wood: 3.

Pinus sylvestris cultivars

Ornamental Scots Pine '**Fastigiata**' is a slender columnar form. It was described by the French gardener Elie Carrière in 1856, but originated in Britain. F. ***aurea*** is a yellow-needled tree at its best in winter. It was first described in 1876 but several different clones exist. There are also examples of variegated trees, but they are not spectacular. 'Variegata' is an 1855 French selection, 'Argentea' (1990) is from Trompenburg Arboretum but it appears to be exactly the same as 'Inverleith' an earlier Scottish selection made in 1979.

Growth: variable. Hardiness: -%. Choice: 1.

Pinus sylvestris '**Aurea**'
spring

Pinus sylvestris
'**Fastigiata**'

Pinus sylvestris subsp. *scotica*
old bark variation

Aleppo Pine bark

Calabrian Pine

cone formation

Aleppo Pine

♀ flowers

cone formation

bud detail

Aleppo Pine

Calabrian Pine

230

Aleppo Pine *Pinus halepensis*

This is a tree which may grow to 20m tall, but is usually much less as it adapts to wind and heat in southern Europe. It thrives on dry sites and will root deeply into sand dunes. Planting has obscured its original natural distribution. Old trees become characteristically rugged and gnarled. The needles, in pairs, rarely threes, are slender and around 11cm long. They may be gently curved or markedly twisted. The woody cones are 10cm long. The species was first described by Philip Miller, Director of what was to become the Chelsea Physic Garden in 1768.

Growth: 2-6-12. Hardiness: 10-30%. Choice: 2, 3. Wood: 3, 5.

Calabrian Pine *Pinus brutia*

Once treated as a variety of *Pinus halepensis*, which it closely resembles, this tree is now considered to be a species in its own right. It replaces *halepensis* around the eastern Mediterranean. The foliage is sparse on young specimens but thickens up on maturity. Needles, in pairs, are 10-16cm long. The 10cm cones are stalkless and not reflexed.

Growth: 3-10-18. Hardiness: 10-20%. Choice: 4. Wood: 3, 5.

Mountain Pine *Pinus uncinata*

This native of the European Alps and Spanish mountains has been widely planted for shelter elsewhere. It is hardy as far north as the sub-Arctic. It is variable in form but can develop into a straight-stemmed specimen 20m tall where conditions are favourable. The bark is dark grey-brown (black when wet), ultimately cracking into small squarish plates. The paired needles are hard and short, 6cm long, and they cling to the shoot in exposed conditions. Cones (see p. 260) are woody, one-sided, 6cm long, and occur in clusters or complete whorls. Each cone scale bears a sharp pointed hook at the tip. *Pinus uncinata* var. *rotundata* is a natural shrubby form often confused with *Pinus mugo*.

Growth: 3-10-20. Hardiness: 50-60%. Choice: 2. Wood: 3.

Dwarf Mountain Pine *Pinus mugo*

Barely making a tree at all – 3m is exceptional – this species is common throughout alpine central Europe and, through commercial shelter planting, much further north. It was once widely used by the British Forestry Commission to shelter upland plantations. Its role now is largely in horticulture, where numerous ornamental selections have been made. The tough, dense 4-7cm needles in pairs, hug vertical shoots which dissipate the strength of the wind with their flexibility. The sharply-spined cones are symmetrical, around 5cm long, and occur in clusters.

Growth: 2-3-4. Hardiness: 100%. Choice: 2.

Mountain Pine

cone scale

Dwarf Mountain Pine   **Mountain Pine**

Crimean Pine

bud detail

leaf section

immature cone

♀ flower

♂ flower

seedling

Crimean Pine   **Corsican Pine**

Crimean Pine *Pinus nigra* subsp. *pallasiana*

As the name suggests this black pine is found in the Crimea. It also occurs naturally in Turkey, the Balkans and the Carpathian Mountains. It is a geographical race of black pine which extends right across southern and central Europe. This subspecies was widely known in the past as var. *caramanica*. The top of the tree is typically spreading and rounded usually supported by a series of huge vertical stems. Specimens 40m tall are frequent. The needles, in pairs, are around 16cm long, forward pointing, stiff and sharply pointed. This is a rough individual best planted as a forestry tree, and its excessive size and alarmingly rapid growth limit its uses.

Growth: 3-20-40. Hardiness: 70%. Choice: 3. Wood: 2, 3.

Corsican Pine *Pinus nigra* subsp. *laricio*

In forestry circles this subspecies is still generally known as var. *maritima*. The two epithets, *laricio* and *maritima*, seem to have alternated several times since the tree was introduced by Philip Miller in 1759. The botanical and morphological minutiae of black pines across their range do not vary much, but this subspecies has a reliable tendency to produce a single straight stem. This may be 50m tall and supporting a narrow conic head of branches. An ideal forest tree, and a producer of very high quality timber in a remarkably short time. In dense forest the deeply ridged bark remains dark, almost black when wet. In the open scaly plates of light grey, pink and orange develop. The needles, in pairs and slightly twisted, are usually around 12cm long. The woody 8cm oblique cones are copiously produced and carpet the ground when they fall in late summer.

This small segment of the black pine population occurs on the island of Corsica and also in southern Italy from Calabria to Sicily. It is an alpine species growing mostly between 1100 and 1600m. In forestry plantations it likes sandy sites and withstands marine exposure very well. The deep root system draws in moisture from a wide area so periods of drought are tolerated. In cold northern districts the fungal disease *Gremmeniella* (*Brunchorstia*) can cause stunted growth and death. The foliage is full of volatile oils, so the danger of forest fires in hot dry conditions is also serious.

Growth: 3-18-45. Hardiness: 50-60%. Choice: 3. Wood: 2, 3.

young tree

Corsican Pine

Austrian Pine

basal sheaths detail

♂ flowers

♀ flowers (emerging needles removed)

closed cone

tall form

Austrian Pine

234

Austrian Pine *Pinus nigra* subsp. *nigra*

Austrian Pine is geographically in the centre of the black pine range which extends across central and southern Europe from the Atlantic to western Asia. None of the subspecies within this huge population stand out as botanically different. They have, however, adapted to the environmental conditions which prevail in each region. Austrian Pine grows in lower Austria and western Hungary, through the Balkans, Greece and parts of Italy. It merges with other black pine subspecies and introgression occurs, resulting in intermediate hybrids and back-crosses. The tall form illustrated suggests an affinity with Corsican Pine in Italy.

The foliage within Austrian Pine varies from tree to tree even where hybridization is not suspected. Provenances from the highest elevations (1600m) tend to produce shorter stiff needles and flexible branches better able to withstand severe exposure. The typical form, on a good site, may grow to 40m with a wide spreading top. The leaves are almost straight, about 12cm long, stiff and sharply pointed. The 5-8cm woody slightly oblique cones (see p. 260) have ridged scale tips.

Introduction dates, to America in 1759 and Britain in 1835, are uncertain because so many early introductions have turned out to be Corsican Pine. Austrian Pine is represented in many nineteenth and early twentieth century arboreta by a branchy, even multi-stemmed type with huge ascending limbs, reminiscent of great organ pipes.

Growth: 3-16-30. Hardiness: 60%. Choice: 3. Wood: 2, 3.

Pyrenean Pine *Pinus nigra* subsp. *salzmannii*

The most western of black pines, Pyrenean Pine, grows in southern France through the Pyrenees and into central and eastern Spain. It may also be identical to the subspecies growing in Algeria and Morocco. It is a smaller tree generally, seldom over 20m tall. The stem starts off straight but usually becomes forked and deformed in response to environmental pressures. Branches spread outwards in old age and foliage tends to droop at the lower extremities. The blunt tipped grey-green pairs of needles are longer, up to 15cm, and more flexible than other black pine subspecies. Several ornamental cultivars have been developed from this form, notably the dwarf plant 'Nana'.

Growth: 3-12-20. Hardiness: 30-40%. Choice: 3. Wood: 2, 3.

closed cone

Pyrenean Pine

Big-cone Pine

♀ flowers

♂ flowers

cones relative to leaves

Big-cone Pine
tall form

236

Big-cone Pine *Pinus coulteri*

This is one of the American trees which provides the ubiquitous building trade product 'pitch pine'. Flat sawn boards are used for every conceivable purpose in the construction industry. The stem is straight, the branches sparse and stout, and the foliage tends to bunch towards the extremities. In its native south-west North America, usually at elevations between 300 and 2000m on dry rocky slopes, height growth is restricted to less than 20m. In ornamental collections greater heights (30m) have been recorded. The stiff, sharply pointed evergreen needles, in threes, are usually over 20cm long. They crowd together on thick terminal shoots. The huge ovoid woody cones, which may be up to 30cm long and weigh over 2kg, point downwards in heavy clusters or singly. They usually remain on the tree for some years after the reflexed scales have opened. The seeds are edible, they once provided a valuable supplement to the native American Indian's diet. The Irish botanist Thomas Coulter discovered big-cone pine in 1831. It was described and brought into cultivation in 1836.
Growth: 4-18-25. Hardiness: 30%. Choice: 1 (requires space), 3. Wood: 2, 3.

Gregg Pine *Pinus gregii*

This is a rare tree restricted in its native range to cold upland areas in northern Mexico. It is closely related to *P. patula* but lacks the pendulous foliage. Trees up to 30m tall are known but that is more than would normally be expected. The needles, in bunches of three, are around 10cm long. The glossy light-brown 12cm cones remain on the tree in clusters for several years.
Growth: 2-7-12. Hardiness: 20%. Choice: 4.

South-western White Pine *Pinus strobiformis*

A rare medium-sized straight tree with a conical head of level branches. The slender evergreen needles, around 7cm long, are in bunches of 5. The bark is smooth pale grey at first becoming dark grey-brown with rough vertical ridges and furrows. Cylindrical curved cones are produced on short stalks. This is an upland species occurring naturally in parts of Texas, Arizona and northern Mexico.
Growth: 3-10-20. Hardiness: 20%. Choice: 3. Wood: 2, 3.

Nelson Pinyon Pine *Pinus nelsonii*

This somewhat shrubby species, often with multiple straight stems, occurs locally in north-east Mexico. The 8cm needles are particularly interesting. They are in bunches of three but held tightly together by a persistent basal sheath. The 12cm cones tend to stick out horizontally from the branch and then curve downwards. Fertile seeds develop a bright red end. Although in cultivation since 1904 specimen trees are rare and seldom thrive.
Growth: 2-5-8. Hardiness: 20%. Choice: 4.

Japanese Black Pine

♂ flowers

♀ flowers

ripening cones

Japanese Black Pine

Chilgoza Pine

238

Japanese Black Pine *Pinus thunbergii*

This untidy 'branchy' tree is a coastal species in Japan and South Korea where it is native. When it does produce a single straight stem it invariably leans, sometimes quite alarmingly. It grows to 25m tall and in exceptional circumstances may top 40m. Very often, though this state of affairs, is reversed since Japanese Black Pine is a favourite subject for Bonsai. Numerous variants of the species have been selected for this trade. Unfortunately, since 1890, some of them have been given invalid names. These include 'Kuromatsu' or just 'Matsu', which is the Japanese name for the species.

The needles, in pairs 8-15cm long, are bunched together but shoots often have short sections that are bare and exposed. These are where past clusters of male flowers have been. The cones are ovoid, up to 7cm long, with a small spine on each prominent scale tip. Occasionally an individual tree will be found that produces cones profusely. Single tight clusters of over 50 cones may occur, sometimes pulling down branches with their weight.

Growth: 3-14-25. Hardiness: 50-70%. Choice: 1 (bonsai), 3. Wood: 2, 3.

Korean Pine *Pinus koraiensis*

Another relative of the Arolla Pine (p. 205), this alpine species has edible seeds around 1.5cm long. It is a tough hardy tree native to north-east Asia and Japan. Its size and shape varies according to the environment where it is growing, although often quite small, exceptional specimens 50m tall have been reported. Such trees provide fine quality timber and edible nuts. The foliage is like Arolla Pine, the needles, in fives are blunt-ended and up to 12cm long. The large more or less oval and pointed woody cones are 9-16cm long. Of the many cultivated types 'Variegata', described in 1890, is interesting. It has wholly pale yellow, patchy yellow and green or yellow fringed needles. It was produced in Japan in 1887.

Growth: 2-10-18. Hardiness: 10-20%. Choice: 3.

Chilgoza Pine *Pinus gerardiana*

Dry valleys and mountain sides in the Himalayas are home to this small round-headed tree. It will occasionally grow to around 15-20m. The bark exfoliates in patches in the way Lace-bark Pine (p. 213) does, but it is less spectacular. The foliage is dense: needles 6-10cm long in bunches of three crowd together along shoots. The large woody oval cones may be up to 20cm long and 11cm wide. This species is very rare in ornamental collections even though it has been known in horticulture since 1832.

Growth: 2-10-15. Hardiness: 20%. Choice: 1. Wood: 2, 3.

Korean Pine

Korean Pine

Ponderosa Pine

♀ flowers

♂ flowers

young cone

seed

open cone

Ponderosa Pines
forest trees

Ponderosa Pine
parkland tree

240

Ponderosa Pine *Pinus ponderosa*

Also known as the Western Yellow or Blackjack Pine this lofty tree (up to 40m tall) is probably the most widely distributed pine in its native central and western North America. Its range extends from British Columbia and North Dakota to Texas and Mexico. Forests occur from sea level up to 2500m. Typically the stiff evergreen needles, in bunches of three, are 10-20cm long. The hard woody cones may be 10cm or more long and virtually stalkless. The seeds, which are edible, are relished by squirrels and chipmunks, and their unfound winter hoards aid the tree's natural dispersal. The species was discovered (by non-native Americans) in 1804 by Lewis and Clark, and described by David Douglas in 1826. He sent seed to Britain where the first plants appeared in 1827. In America this is an important timber tree. The name recalls the ponderous (heavy) wood. In Europe it has not been able to compete commercially with European black pine for a significant place in forestry. Such a widely distributed species has many regional and environmental forms, some of which are cultivated as ornamentals. Some have been re-classified as relatives of *P. engelmannii*.

In the south of its range the species is replaced by the variety *arizonica*, described in 1909 by Herbert Airy Shaw at Kew Gardens. This tree is now considered to be a species in its own right (*Pinus arizonica*). It is distinct because its needles are in bunches of 5, not 3. The natural range is southern Arizona, mostly in hot dry conditions.

Growth: 4-20-35. Hardiness: 60%. Choice: 3. Wood: 1, 2, 3.

Apache Pine *Pinus engelmannii*

This medium-sized, generally straight-stemmed tree seldom exceeds 20m. It has wide spreading branches. The magnificent evergreen needles, which usually occur in bunches of three, but occasionally four or five, are 20-30cm long. Their exceptional length causes them to droop on side shoots. Rocky mountain sides in Apache country, southern Arizona, New Mexico State and northern Mexico, is where this tree grows naturally. It is seldom seen in cultivation elsewhere, for ornament or commercial forestry.

Growth: 3-15-20. Hardiness: 30%. Choice: 3. Wood: 2, 3.

Apache Pine

♂ flowers

♀ flowers

Jeffrey Pine

open cone

Jeffrey Pine

Mexican Weeping Pine

Jeffrey Pine *Pinus jeffreyi*

Also known in America as Western Yellow Pine, this long-lived tree has an extensive range from south-west Oregon to California. It prefers high cool mountain sides and dry rocky valleys. The best trees are found, often in pure stands, between 1500 and 1900m. It was named after the Scottish botanist John Jeffrey, who discovered it and sent seed back to Britain in 1852. At the time it was considered to be a variety of Ponderosa Pine (p. 241) which, confusingly, is also called Western Yellow Pine. Strangely, in Britain authentic Jeffery Pine does not grow well. So it is possible that any thriving specimens in ornamental collections might be wrongly identified forms of *Pinus ponderosa*.

The bark and twigs are aromatic. The stem is straight and flawless making it a perfect timber producer (in America). The grey-green needles, in threes 13-25cm long, are stiff, slightly twisted and relatively short lived. Big woody cones 15-30cm long with a reflexed prickle on each scale contain numerous seeds. It is quick to establish itself on devastated ground and fire sites. In parts of its natural range ancient trees 600 years old have been reported.

Growth: 2-15-25. Hardiness: 50-60%. Choice: 3. Wood: 3.

Mexican Weeping Pine *Pinus patula*

This is a tender tree only able to thrive in warm temperate or sub-tropical conditions. Within the most favourable parts of its Mexican range it becomes a productive timber producer 30-50m tall. Elsewhere it is short and stunted in comparison. The stem is often twisted and multiple stems, usually caused by past frost damage, are common. Vertically rolled up flakes of orange-brown peeling bark persist on branches and young stems. The long level branches with drooping tips give the tree a billowing rounded appearance. The long slender needles (15-30cm) droop from the extremities. Although normally in threes, sometimes bundles of four or even five occur. The cones are oblique and stalkless, 6-10cm long, with a fine prickle on each scale tip. The species was described in 1831 but has never become common on account of its poor survival rate.

Growth: 3-10-15. Hardiness: 20%. Choice: 4.

Mexican Weeping Pine

Shortleaf Pine

closed cone

Shortleaf Pine

Shortleaf Pine

Pinus echinata × *rigida*

Shortleaf Pine *Pinus echinata*

This American tree is the most widely distributed of the southern yellow pines, covering an area from New York to Florida and west to Texas. It is a native species in 21 American states. In favourable conditions it reaches 30m with a conical then rounded top. The slender shoots bear flexible 10cm needles in pairs (sometimes threes). Internodal whiskery shoots often occur even on the stem down to ground level, a helpful initial aid to identification in mixed pine collections. The 3-8cm cones are short-stalked with a spine on the tip of each scale: the name *echinata* meaning 'hedgehog-like'. The seeds are often released by the heat of forest fires. They rapidly germinate and cover the ground.

Shortleaf pine will cross naturally with Pitch Pine (*Pinus rigida*, p. 251) where their natural ranges overlap in Kentucky, Tennessee and North Carolina. This meeting of two of the most important timber producers in the world is potentially valuable. Pitch Pine has high quality, and Shortleaf Pine has greater size. Typically the hybrid (**Pinus echinata** × **rigida**) is vigorous with thick foliage. It is well adapted to poor gravelly sites and even swampy ground.

Growth: 3-15-20. Hardiness: 20-40%. Choice: 3. Wood: 3.

Washoe Pine *Pinus washoensis*

Named as recently as 1945 after the Washoe Indians, who shared its native habitat, this slow-growing 18m tree is tough and hardy. It occurs in west Nevada and north-east California, but at immensely high elevations (2000-2500m). Although Indians once hunted in extensive forests of this species it is now rare and local. It was only discovered and described in 1938. The needles, in bunches of three, are 10-15cm long. Stalkless woody cones around 8cm long have a sharp hooked prickle on the tip of each scale. They are reluctant to fall from the tree after shedding seed, but eventually break away, often leaving a ring of basal scales behind.

Growth: 2-10-18. Hardiness: 50-70%. Choice: 4. Wood: 3.

Pinus echinata × *rigida*

Washoe Pine

♂ flowers →

Bosnian Pine

♀ flowers

bud detail

maturing cone

Bosnian Pine

Holford's Pine

246

Bosnian Pine *Pinus heldreichii* var. *leucodermis*

This species takes its name from its country of origin. It also occurs naturally in the rest of the Balkans and on lime-rich soils in Italy, Bulgaria and Greece. It is closely related to Heldreich Pine (p. 205) and indeed the black pines (pp. 233-235). In cultivation they are easily confused. Bosnian Pine is a very symmetrical tree in its youth, but it develops a more uneven outline with age. Although the shoots are pale grey, even bloomed for a time, the foliage generally has a dark appearance. In plantations trees grow straight with a single stem up to 30m tall. The 8cm needles, in twos, are stiff, sharply pointed and packed densely round the shoot. Sometimes gaps occur in the foliage along young shoots where clusters of male flowers have been. The cones (see p. 261) are blue for one year, as they mature the following season they turn purplish-brown and light brown. They are ovoid-conic, 5-8cm long with hooked spines. This tree was described in 1868 by Franz Antoine, director of the Imperial Gardens in Vienna.

Growth: 3-15-25. Hardiness: 50-60%. Choice: 3. Wood: 2, 3.

Holford's Pine *Pinus* × *holfordiana*

This hybrid between a Mexican White Pine (var. *veitchii*, p. 217) and Blue Pine (p. 221) arose artificially, but quite unintentionally, at Westonbirt Arboretum in about 1904. The parent trees were planted in a small grove of conifers some 15m apart in 1852. Robert Holford, after whom the tree is named, collected seed from the Mexican tree around 1904. The resulting progeny were clearly unlike either parent. These were planted out in groups in the collection and distributed to other establishments. The hybrid was officially recognized in 1933 and described by Albert Bruce Jackson the English conifer authority. The original plants have grown rapidly up to about 20m tall, but the stems and branches are rather coarse. The foliage is variable but more like Mexican White Pine than Blue Pine. The 14-18cm needles, in fives, are slender, curved and lax. The pale brown resin-spotted cones are variable but always leathery and pendulous. Some may exceed 25cm long with a 4cm stalk. Fertile seed is produced but second generation seedlings are extremely variable.

Growth: 3-16-20. Hardiness: 50%. Choice: 4. Wood: 3.

old cones

young cone

♂ flowers   ♀ flower

Holford's Pine

♂ flowers

Jack Pine

open cone

♀ flowers

young cone

Scrub Pine

young cone

closed cone

♂ flowers

Jack Pine

Scrub Pine

248

Jack Pine *Pinus banksiana*

This is a functional rather than ornamental tree. It occurs in several forms, including the narrow sub-Arctic forest type illustrated and down to scrubby bushes cut back by the wind. The broad natural range extends from Nova Scotia to the Yukon and south to New Hampshire. It grows further north than any other conifer in Arctic Canada. This is a pioneer species quickly seeding into dry sandy soils devastated by climatic disasters. It is also a 'fire Climax' species keeping its cones closed on the tree until scorched by a forest fire. The resinous foliage adds ferocity to fires; the buds in particular are rich in volatile resins. The stout evergreen needles are in twos, flattened, twisted and spread out. They are seldom over 4cm long. The oblique woody cones (see p. 260) are around 5cm long. Unusually for pine they point forwards along the shoot.

Growth: 3-12-15. Hardiness: 90%. Choice: 4.

Scrub Pine *Pinus virginiana*

Almost as hardy as the closely related Jack Pine this species occupies the same pioneer niche but on lower ground and much further south. It occurs naturally in the south-eastern United States from New York to Alabama and the Mississippi Basin. The form is variable but never impressive. The bark becomes roughly ridged and eventually shaggy. Needles, 4-7cm long in twos, are flattened and twisted. The cones are symmetrical, narrow-ovate, and spined; they point straight out from the shoot or may be inclined slightly backwards.

Growth: 2-6-12. Hardiness: 50%. Choice: 4.

Durango Pine *Pinus durangensis*

This rare tree has only been in cultivation since 1962. It was described in 1942. The natural range is within limited areas of Mexico. It is related to the more widespread but still rare Arizona Pine (*Pinus arizonica* p. 241). The possibility of hybrids in cultivation can not be ruled out. Plants tested near Plymouth in 1962 could not be separated from Arizona Pine with certainty. These particular trees were unable to survive in southern England. In Mexico this is a tree 20-40m tall with needles, in fives, between 10 and 20cm long. They are slender and flexible terminating in a point. The cones are ovoid-conic, 8-10cm long, and spiny.

Growth: 3-12-20. Hardiness: 20-30%. Choice: 4. Wood: 3.

Durango Pine

Scrub Pine

'green' form

'blue' form

♂ flowers

♀ flowers

Bishop Pine

old cones

Bishop Pine

Pitch Pine bark

Bishop Pine *Pinus muricata*

This vigorous, but often coarse-branched tree, occurs in a small number of locations along the Pacific coast of California; also on Santa Cruz and Santa Rosa Islands, although the status of the latter is in question. Forms of *muricata* also occur in Baja California and Cedros Island in Mexico. In the wild it is a tree usually under 16m tall, but in cultivation it will grow very much larger. It is a pioneer species, quick to colonize disturbed or burnt ground. The needles occur in pairs with a persistent basal sheath. They are around 14cm long and often twisted. The oblique, woody and viciously spined cones are 9cm long. They remain unopened on the tree until heated by fire or extremely hot weather. The foliage is of two colour types: southern forms have bright green needles, and northern trees have foliage that is visually glaucous green. This 'blue' form is considerably more hardy than the 'green' form. It can be grown in lowland conditions in Europe as far north as Scotland, whereas the green form barely survives north of the southern coast of Ireland and south-west England. This is an ideal species for coastal planting, it withstands salt spray and roots deeply into sandy soils and dunes. Bishop Pine timber is rough and knotty, but other more valuable timber producing species can benefit tremendously from the shelter Bishop Pine provides when planted on the windward side of plantations.

Growth: 6-15-20. Hardiness: 30%. Choice: 2. Wood: 3.

Pitch Pine *Pinus rigida*

This hardy American pine tree ranges from southern Maine to New York State, then south to Georgia. Fringes of the population occur over the US border in southern Canada. It is tolerant of a wide range of site types from the coastal plains to 1300m mountain sides. Consequently the form of the tree is extremely variable. Now used for wood production, Pitch Pine was formerly an important source of resin from which turpentine and pitch were made. Even on good ground trees seldom exceed 18m in height. The stout evergreen needles are around 10cm long in bunches of three, they are usually twisted. The ovate woody, and sharply pointed cones are 4-6cm long.

Growth: 3-10-15. Hardiness: 80%. Choice: 3. Wood: 2, 3.

Monterey Pine

open cone

♂ flowers

♀ flowers

Red Pine bark

Monterey Pine   young **Monterey Pine**

Monterey Pine *Pinus radiata*

The natural post-glacial movement of this species to cooler northern latitudes was curtailed by its geographical position. It became confined to isolated localities along the Californian coast and Guadalupe Island. Further northerly movement especially from Monterey is obstructed by the Pacific Ocean on one side and mountainous desert on the other. Wild specimens are stunted and baked by excessively hot dry conditions. When moved artificially to a more temperate climate the species thrives. Growth over 1m per year may be expected for 30 years and trees 40m tall are frequent. In old age the top billows out in a huge cloud of bright green. The needles, in threes, are up to 12cm long. The big woody 14cm cones are almost as wide as they are long. An immediate feature of this tree is the way it holds heavy clusters of cones strung out along its branches for many years. Eventually whole branches may break under the immense weight. Monterey Pine was discovered by David Douglas in 1831. Seed was taken to Chiswick, London the following year. Consignments continued to arrive in England until 1851. In recent years this species has become very important as a timber producer, especially in Australia, New Zealand, South Africa and parts of South America. In Europe it is planted in the south and mild central areas and it is able to withstand the maritime climate very well.

Growth: 7-22-35. Hardiness: 30%. Choice: 2, 3. Wood: 1, 2, 3.

Red Pine *Pinus resinosa*

Red Pine is closely related to Scots Pine in Europe. It is a common North American species native between south-east Manitoba and Nova Scotia and southwards to West Virginia. Like Scots Pine the young bark is reddish-brown becoming rough and fissured with maturity. The foliage, which resembles Corsican Pine, is sparse. Needles, in twos, are brittle and easily broken by the wind. Liquid, resinous sap exudes from these breakages, sometimes covering the whole tree, making it sticky and strongly aromatic. They are up to 15cm long, slender, and more or less straight. The ovate cones are 4-6cm long, spineless and glossy when first ripe.

Growth: 3-12-20. Hardiness: 90%. Choice: 3. Wood: 2, 3.

Red Pine

Shore Pine

♀ flowers

bud

Shore Pine

♂ flowers

♂ flowers

var. *latifolia*

snow-damaged lower branches removed

young cone

young cones

Shore Pine

var. *latifolia*

var. *bolanderi*

Shore Pine *Pinus contorta*

This species occurs in western North America as three distinct geographic races. The differences are in tree form rather than botanical detail. Shore Pine, more correctly *Pinus contorta* var. *contorta*, is from the Pacific coast of Alaska, western Canada and the United States south to northern California, never extending naturally to more than 160km from the sea. It thrives on dunes and marine edge environments. It is a pioneer species coning at around five years of age and quickly re-seeding devastated and burned areas. Growth is rapid but the tree's energy is directed towards heavy branchwood or multiple curving stems, not a massive single trunk. Height growth seldom exceeds 10m. The specimen illustrated is an exceptionally large tree at Westonbirt.

The needles, in pairs, are bright green and usually 7cm or more long. They twist slightly and have hard pointed tips. The small woody cones are 4-5cm long, oblique-ovate, stalkless and sharply spined on the scale tips. Individuals and small clusters point backwards along the branches.

In forestry Shore Pine has been used to shelter plantations of timber trees on very poor acid peaty sites. It requires minimal nutrition and is hardy, particularly trees from the northern end of the range. A variety ***bolanderi***, the Mendicino Shore Pine, is a local shrubby form from Baja California.

Growth: 5-15-16 (species). Hardiness: 50%. Choice: 2.

Lodgepole Pine *Pinus contorta* var. *latifolia*

So called because its stems were used by American Indians to support their lodges, this variety covers a wide range of variable mountainous terrain. Some forms formerly growing at high elevations have washed down rivers (presumably as seed) to new lowland estuarine habitats. Some authorities define two varieties. The Rocky Mountain form, **var. *latifolia***, extends from south-east Alaska along the Rocky mountains to Baja California. The Sierra Lodgepole Pine, (var. ***murrayana***) occupies a parallel range to the east of the Rockies, along the Cascade Mountains and the Sierra Nevada to central California up to 3500m in the south. The foliage is similar to Shore Pine, but the needles are generally shorter, considerably shorter on high altitude trees, and more of a dull green, or in some instances yellowish-green. See p. 261 for cone. Slender trees grow up to 25m tall. This is a good timber tree but it is less productive than several other coniferous species in the same area, e. g. Ponderosa Pine (p. 241) and Sitka Spruce (p. 191).

Growth: 3-12-20. Hardiness: 60%. Choice: 2, 3. Wood: 3.

old tree

Lodgepole Pine

young cone

var. *murrayana*

Montezuma Pine

Montezuma Pine

Hartweg Pine

Montezuma Pine *Pinus montezumae*

From central Mexico southwards to Guatemala this beautiful rounded 20m tree is named in honour of Montezuma the last ruler of the Aztec empire until 1520. Since its introduction to Europe in 1839 it has been planted widely as a curiosity, but harsh weather conditions usually kill it off at an early age. The bark is reddish-brown on young stems, gradually cracking into scaly plates and weathering to dark grey. The 15-25cm needles, mostly in bundles of 5, point forwards along the shoot but their length and weight cause them to flop downwards and fan out gracefully. Cones, which take two years to mature, are 12-15cm long by 3-4cm wide with glossy brown woody scales. The species is rare because it is tender and also because many specimens in cultivation are actually *Pinus rudis* or *Pinus hartwegii* which were often mistaken for Montezuma Pine. For a long time they were wrongly thought to be varieties of it. Both come from high elevations in Mexico and seem to survive quite well in cultivation.

Growth: 5-15-20. Hardiness: 20%. Choice: 1 (requires space). Wood: 3.

Hartweg Pine *Pinus hartwegii*

Closely related to Montezuma Pine, this species grows in pine forests on high volcanic slopes in Mexico, Guatemala and north-west El Salvador. It was collected and sent to London in 1836 by Theodor Hartweg. Most specimens in cultivation are stiff and shapeless with 10-15cm needles in bundles of 3-5, pointing forwards along the shoot. The dark brown woody cones are 7-17cm long. Often when they fall a few basal scales are left behind on the tree.

Growth: 3-14-20. Hardiness: 20%. Choice: 4. Wood: 3.

Endlicher Pine *Pinus rudis*

Many of the early so called Montezuma Pines in cultivation are this species. It is a less decorative tree often with a bare lower stem and irregular outline. The 15-25cm needles, in fives, are not so lax and darker green. It is more hardy because it comes from high cool mountainous sites in central and northern Mexico. Few specimens exceed 15m in height, although growth is usually quite fast. The earliest trees appeared in Europe in 1855. The last original specimen known in England, at the Westonbirt Arboretum, died in 1963. New material has been imported to Europe since then.

Growth: 3-10-15. Hardiness: 30%. Choice: 4. Wood: 3.

stem detail

Hartweg Pine

Endlicher Pine

Digger Pine

♂ flowers

new growth

♀ flowers

Digger Pine   **Knobcone Pine**

Digger Pine *Pinus sabiniana*

Often this 12-20m tall tree is an ugly specimen in cultivation with twisted branches and a forked stem. It is a native species in California, along the coast and through the centre of the state. In the Sierra Nevada it thrives on dry rocky ridges and hill sides to above 1000m. The name is a reference to the Digger Indians, a collective term for all Californian Indians, who used to dig up the fibrous roots of this pine and also eat the seeds. The slender 20-30cm evergreen needles are in bundles of three which form pendulous clusters all over the tree. Ovate cones, 15-26cm long and slightly one sided, have curved or straight spines on the scales. They point downwards and remain on the tree after shedding their seed, which is thick-skinned and large with a deciduous wing. David Douglas the Scottish plant collector introduced Digger pine to Europe in 1832.

Growth: 4-10-20. Hardiness: 20-30%. Choice: 3. Wood: 3.

Knobcone Pine *Pinus attenuata*

Limited to a few areas in Oregon, California and parts of Mexico, this is one of the 'closed cone pines'. It requires great heat to liberate any seed, and usually it must be the intensity of a forest fire. The woody 8-15cm reflexed ovate cones are clustered in rings along the branches. Seeds inside them may remain viable for 30 years. Some cones remain on the tree for such a long time that the developing stem or branch wood thickens and gradually overwhelms them. Knobcone pine reaches 24m in the most favourable conditions, but on poor dry sites 9m is more likely. Plants survive at over 1200m in the south of the range. The grey-green needles in bundles of three are between 10 and 15cm long. Young trees have up-swept branches but they spread out and arch downwards with ascending tips in old age. The first trees in cultivation in Europe arrived from America around 1847.

Growth: 2-14-24. Hardiness: 50%. Choice: 3. Wood: 3.

Cooper Pine *Pinus cooperi*

Found in low rainfall areas of north-west Mexico, this fairly hardy pine was introduced to Europe as recently as 1960. In its natural environment it is a round-headed tree, often with a clear stem and drooping branch tips. The needles are packed in tight bundles of 5, occasionally 4, or sometimes 3, on the same tree at the same time. Cones are 5-9cm long, ovoid and slightly one sided, with a sharp reflexed prickle at the end of each seed-bearing scale.

Growth: 3-12-15. Hardiness: 40%. Choice: 4.

Knobcone Pine

bud

Cooper Pine

CONIFER CONES

scale — outer
bract — inner (seeds)
scale — side

Noble Fir
p. 145

Algerian Fir
p. 131

Silver Fir
p. 137

Jack Pine
p. 249

Austrian Pine
p. 235

Scots Pine
p. 227

Mountain Pine
p. 231

Grand Fir
p. 141

CONIFER CONES

White Spruce
p. 185

Sitka Spruce
p. 191

Douglas Fir
p. 201

Western Hemlock
p. 195

European Larch
p. 155

Japanese Larch
p. 157

Western Red Cedar
p. 83

White Cedar
p. 85

Lawson Cypress
p. 41

Norway Spruce
p. 175

Japanese Cedar
p. 95

Coast Redwood
p. 91

Cedar of Lebanon
p. 147

Lodgepole Pine
p. 255

Bosnian Pine
p. 247

Arolla Pine
p. 205

Weymouth Pine
p. 219

Grey Poplar

leaf from sucker

White Poplar

underside

leaf from young tree

Grey Poplar

White Poplar

262

WILLOW FAMILY · Salicaceae

Grey Poplar *Populus × canescens*

This hybrid between White Poplar and Aspen (p. 265) is widely distributed throughout Europe and western Asia, including the south of Russia. It is a variable tree intermediate between the parents, but as it is fertile it also occurs as F^2 back crosses. The best specimens may reach 35m in height and these can be reproduced clonally, although propagation can only be successful using semi-ripe cuttings under glass. The most striking feature of this hybrid is the foliage. The leaves are deep grey-green on the upper side and felted greenish-white beneath. Shoots and leaf stalks are also covered with grey woolly tomentum at first. Individuals that are closer to Aspen are less grey. The leaves are extremely variable in shape. Not only do they change from the juvenile 'maple' outline to a more rounded less lobed adult form, they are also influenced to some degree by parental dominance. Stems are creamy-grey with rough dark brown patches developing as the tree matures. They sucker freely so thickets are common and many of these lean 'collectively' away from the prevailing wind. This hybrid is often unstable because it has a very heavy top in summer and minimal roots. Just a single lateral root for a time if it is in a line of suckers. In late winter male trees produce a good display of 10cm pendulous crimson catkins.

The rare cultivar '**Macrophylla**' (p. 283), Picart's Poplar, is a large-leaved (15cm on long shoots) form, which grows rapidly with a persistent usually straight stem to around 25m in height.

Growth: 5-18-25. Hardiness: 80%. Choice: 2. Wood: 3, 4 (species).

White Poplar *Populus alba*

Native to central and southern Europe then extending to western Siberia and round the Mediterranean, this tree is both ornamental and commercially important. The foliage differs from Grey Poplar in that it is much whiter and more woolly. The leaves are mostly five-lobed, markedly so on young growth. It is a good tree for coastal areas but often leans or falls away from the direction of prevailing gales. It suckers freely which provides additional ground cover when used as a shelter-belt. In the autumn the leaves turn bright yellow for a brief time, giving a unique yellow-and-white effect.

The cultivar '**Pyramidalis**' or Bolle's Poplar is an interesting tree. It is an upright form which originated in Uzbekskaya in southern Russia in the 1870s, it has the potential to out-grow the species but it is not entirely disease resistant. '**Richardii**' is a 1918 Dutch selection with superb white-backed golden leaves in summer.

Growth: 4-15-20. Hardiness: 80%. Choice: 2, 4 (invasive suckers). Wood: 3, 4 (species).

'**Macrophylla**' bark

'**Pyramidalis**'
winter

'**Richardii**'

♂ flowers

Aspen

underside

♀ flowers

fruiting catkin

top of sucker

Aspen

Weeping Aspen

young bark

POPLARS

Aspen *Populus tremula*

The range of this species extends from the British Isles to North Africa, eastwards to Central Asia and Siberia. In order not to confuse it with **American Aspen** (*Populus tremuloides*) it is sometimes called European Aspen. It is a suckering tree 15-25m in height, usually with numerous stems of various sizes. A tree near Chepstow, in Wales, has over 1000 stems and covers an area of around 1 hectare. The rootstock age of such a plant must be hundreds, if not thousands, of years. The deciduous foliage is of two kinds. On new seedlings and fresh sucker growth juvenile leaves are ovate with a curved pointed tip. Adult leaves, up to 7cm across, are round with a wavy edge. The stalks, also some 7cm long, are compressed laterally so the leaf becomes unstable in the slightest wind and flutters in a characteristic way, hence the traditional name 'Quaking Aspen'. Trees are either male or female, which also applies to whole woodland populations if they have originated from sucker growth over a long period. Flowers appear in late winter, male and female catkins are about 4cm long. Pollination, by wind, is a hurried process and the male catkins are quickly shed. Females produce minute seeds in a mass of seed fluff as soon as the spring weather warms up. The fluff transports the seed away on the wind and then heavy rain is urgently required to push it into contact with damp ground. Germination begins within hours if conditions are right. Closely related species occur in the Himalayas, China and also in North America from Canada to northern Mexico.

American Aspen is famous for its golden quivering autumn foliage colour and silvery-white birch-like stems. It is the most abundant broadleaved tree in North America. Beavers like to use it for their dams.
Growth: 4-15-25. Hardiness: 90%. Choice: 3. Wood: 3, 4.

Weeping Aspen *Populus tremula* 'Pendula'

This strange little tree enjoys sporadic periods of popularity as an urban landscape plant. It is quite unlike normal Aspen mainly because the foliage is all juvenile and it does not flutter in the breeze. It is a male clone so it does produce purplish-grey catkins in late winter before the leaves appear.
Growth: 4-8-10. Hardiness: 70%. Choice: 1.

American Aspen

Fruiting ♀ flowers

autumn

underside

fruit

**Japanese
Balsam Poplar**

underside

Populus 'Oxford'

fruit

underside

Populus purdomii

Japanese Balsam Poplar

underside

Chinese Aspen

POPLARS

Japanese Balsam Poplar
Populus maximowiczii

One of the largest trees in south-east Asia this 30m, straight, very productive plant provides most of the raw material for the match industry. It is also very decorative. The leathery 6-14cm leaves are deep green above and pale on the underside. Unlike most poplars they give a good but brief display of golden-yellow autumn foliage colour. Female trees bear interesting 20-25cm long strings of seed capsules in the summer which do not shed seed until the autumn. This species was introduced to western Europe, from Russia, in 1913. It is frost tender and most provenances appear to be susceptible to bacterial canker. Programmes of hybridization with other species have produced vigorous progeny since the 1920s. One in particular, 'Androscoggin' growing in Somerset, reached 30m in only 12 years.

Growth: 5-20-30. Hardiness: 50%. Choice: 2, 4. Wood: 3, 4.

Populus 'Oxford'

Originally grown for the Oxford Paper Company of Maine, USA, in the 1920s, this is a hybrid between *Populus* × *candicans* (p. 271) and *Populus* × *berolinensis* (p. 277). This complex cross brought together four individual taxa, two species, a variety of another species and Lombardy Poplar. The resulting trees introduced to Britain in 1937 produced veneer quality logs in just 11 years. Since 1966 this clone has been used in Holland where it is particularly resistant to leaf cast.

Growth: 6-25-30. Hardiness: 50%. Choice: 3. Wood: 4.

Populus purdomii

Originally from north-west China this rare tree is related to *Populus cathayana* (p. 269). The ovate pointed leaves are 10-13cm long with long stalks. They are rounded or sub-cordate at the base and have prominent veins giving the leathery appearance. The species was introduced to America in 1914.

Growth: 6-25-30. Hardiness: 50-60%. Choice: 4. Wood: 2, 3, 4.

Chinese Aspen *Populus adenopoda*

From central and western China this species grows to 25m in height. It is rare in cultivation although it was introduced (to America) in 1907. The foliage is variable, particularly between long and short shoots. On vigorous growth the leaves may be up to 15cm long.

Growth: 4-15-25. Hardiness: 50%. Choice: 2, 3, 4 (invasive suckers). Wood: 2, 3, 4.

Populus yunnanensis

This Balsam Poplar from southern China has deep green 15cm leaves with bright red veins and petioles. In Europe it tends to be short lived and prone to frost damage. It was introduced before 1905.

Growth: 6-20-25. Hardiness: 50%. Choice: 4. Wood: 2, 3, 4.

Populus yunnanensis

Chinese Aspen

Populus szechuanica var. *tibetica*

Populus wilsonii

Populus cathayana

underside

Populus simonii

Populus szechuanica var. *tibetica*

Populus szechuanica var. tibetica

This species is capable of growing to a large size, 40m tall, but in cultivation it is slightly tender and often stunted by frost. The species came from west China and was introduced by Ernest Wilson in 1908. About four years earlier the variety *tibetica* was introduced from the same area. It is more vigorous with large red veined silvery-backed leaves which are similar to *Populus yunnanensis* (p. 267). Young branches are purplish brown at first so the whole ornamental effect of young trees or cut back coppice in cultivation is magnificent.

Growth: 6-20-30. Hardiness: 50-60%. Choice: 4. Wood: 3, 4.

Populus wilsonii

Ernest Wilson's own poplar was introduced from China by him in 1907 and named in his honour by Camillo Karl Schneider the prominent German dendrologist and garden designer. It is a 25m tree which keeps a symmetrical shape until maturity. The sticky buds give way to large leaves up to 18cm long and 15cm broad. Fruits on female trees are in pendulous strings up to 15cm long. In this and many other respects *Populus wilsonii* is similar to *Populus lasiocarpa* (p. 271).

Growth: 6-20-25. Hardiness: 50%. Choice: 4. Wood: 3, 4.

Populus simonii

This south-east Asian tree seldom exceeds 12m in height in cultivation but may reach 30m in the wild. It is early into leaf and therefore subject to frost damage when planted away from its natural habitat. *Populus simonii* is light branched, wind-firm and hardy, although it only produces a slender crown it is used extensively in China as a shelter-belt species. After being introduced to France in 1862, it was often planted in upland regions. The species itself is susceptible to bacterial canker but its more frequently planted ornamental cultivars '**Fastigiata**' and '**Pendula**' (illustrated) are usually disease free.

Growth: 4-8-10. Hardiness: 90%. Choice: 4. Wood: 3, 4 (species).

Populus cathayana

In its native north-west China, Manchuria and Korea, this is a large, vigorous 30m tree with strongly ascending upper branches. Leaves at the top of the tree may be over 20cm long, those on lower short shoots are only 6-10cm. They are narrow-ovate, with a rounded or subcordate base, bright green on the upper side and distinctly pale-coloured below, with 5-7 curved parallel veins. Glutinous winter buds smell of balsam. In Europe it is subject to bacterial canker. The species was described by Alfred Rehder and introduced around 1908 by Ernest Wilson.

Growth: 3-8-25. Hardiness: 50%. Choice: 4. Wood: 3, 4.

Populus simonii 'Pendula'   **Populus wilsonii**   **Populus cathayana**

underside

Western Balsam Poplar

Balsam Poplar

underside

Western Balsam Poplar

Balm of Gilead

'Aurora'

270

POPLARS

Western Balsam Poplar *Populus trichocarpa*

Also known as 'Cottonwood' in its west North American range, this tree is a vital component of the world's forest industry, both in its own right and as a component of many highly productive hybrids. Specimens 35m tall with stems up to 1m in diameter occur frequently and in a relatively short time. In the open the outline may be ragged but in plantations the tops are narrow and the stems perfectly straight. The foliage has a lovely balsam smell especially after rain. Provenances of this species particularly from the Mount St Helen's area are free of disease. Named clones such as 'Fritzi Pauley' (p. 282) and 'Scott Pauley' have been developed in America and Europe for their resistance to bacterial canker and leaf cast.
Growth: 8-25-30. Hardiness: 60%. Choice: 3, 4 (invasive). Wood: 1, 3, 4.

Balsam Poplar *Populus balsamifera*

Only in recent years has the colourful American Indian name for this species 'Tacamahacca' been replaced by *balsamifera*. It is a large 30m erect tree with upright branches. The big sticky balsamic buds give off a delicious clean scent just before the leaves appear in spring. It suckers strongly from surface roots especially if damaged or cut down. A hybrid clone between this and the previous species, named 'Balsam Spire' (see p. 282), has been extensively used as a forest tree in Britain and Europe.
Growth: 6-18-30. Hardiness: 60%. Choice: 4 (invasive). Wood: 3, 4.

Balm of Gilead *Populus × candicans*

This 15–20m tree has a narrow top and straight stem. Its origins are obscure, it may be a form of Balsam Poplar or more likely a hybrid between it and *Populus deltoides* var. *missouriensis*. Unfortunately it is decimated in cultivation by bacterial canker. The well known variegated cultivar '**Aurora**' (p. 283) is a striking ornamental plant developing white, yellow, pink and green foliage in summer. It too suffers from bacterial canker which soon renders whole limbs dysfunctional.
Growth: 7-20-25. Hardiness: 60%. Choice: 4.

Chinese Necklace Poplar *Populus lasiocarpa*

This curious tree grows rapidly to 15 or 20m in height. It produces huge 35 x 25cm heart shaped slightly leathery leaves. Male catkins are yellow and 20-25cm long often extending from a female section, which is a rare occurrence in poplars. The fruit consists of strings of green capsules 'beads' until they burst in mid-summer to release copious amounts of white fluff and tiny seeds.
Growth: 8-16-18. Hardiness: 50%. Choice: 1. Wood: 3, 4.

Balsam Poplar

Chinese Necklace Poplar

Populus × *generosa*

underside

Lance-leaf Cottonwood

Populus × *canadensis* 'Lloydii'

underside

Populus × *generosa* 'Beaupre'

POPLARS

Populus × *generosa*

This entirely artificial cross was first made at Kew Gardens in London in 1912. The Dutch name, which is still used in the commercial poplar growing industry, is 'Interamericana'. This describes the origin of the hybrid which is *Populus deltoides* × *Populus trichocarpa* from eastern and western North America respectively. A cross between completely different species, a balsam and a black poplar. One of the resulting extremely vigorous clones 'Rap', produced annual shoots up to 4m long and had the potential to produce veneer logs in 11 years. Unfortunately it became susceptible to bacterial canker and was withdrawn from cultivation. New clones have since been developed in Belgium, with names such as '**Beaupré**' and 'Boelare', which are almost as productive and appear to be canker resistant. They are already transforming the appearance and productivity of poplar plantations everywhere.

Growth: 10-25-30. Hardiness: 50-60%. Choice: 3. Wood: 3, 4.

Lance-leaf Cottonwood *Populus acuminata*

This small Balsam Poplar comes from the eastern side of the Rocky Mountains from Alberta, through the USA to New Mexico where *Populus angustifolia*, the Narrowleaf Cottonwood, and *Populus deltoides* var. *occidentalis*, the Plains Cottonwood, overlap. It tolerates dry stony ground but is seldom productive. It was introduced to Britain in 1916 but has never been popular either as an ornamental specimen or for commercial timber. Some authorities list it as a hybrid between *Populus angustifolia* and *Populus sargentii* var. *texana*, but this seems unlikely in a tree with such an extensive range.

Growth: 6-10-12. Hardiness: 90%. Choice: 4.

Populus × *canadensis* 'Lloydii'

This hybrid between *Populus deltoides* and *Populus nigra* subsp. *betulifolia* (p. 275), is a female clone which is easily confused with the Black Poplar parent. It is no longer grown as a commercial timber tree and its present status is uncertain.

Growth: 6-20-30. Hardiness: 50%. Choice: 2, 3. Wood: 3, 4.

Populus × *generosa*
young tree

Lance-leaf Cottonwood

***Populus* × *canadensis* 'Lloydii'**

Black Poplar

subsp. *betulifolia*

'Variegata'

fruiting ♀ flowers

ivy on stem

fruiting ♀ flowers

Black Poplar

Populus nigra 'Vereecken'

Black Poplar *Populus nigra* subsp. *betulifolia*

The 'Atlantic' form of European Black Poplar is native in western France, the Low Countries and the British Isles. In most areas it is a rare endangered tree. Its traditional uses, heavy timbers for barns and fire resistant floor boards, have become obsolete. Its form is less straight and true than modern hybrids and it is less productive. More insidiously it has been adulterated by genetic pollution. No seed of this subspecies can now be relied upon to be true to type. Hybridization with compatible commercial hybrids is almost inevitable. Pollen has been judged to be capable of travelling up to 15 kilometres and very few native Black Poplars are beyond the range of a compatible hybrid.

In Britain at least 90% of the mature population are male trees because females have traditionally been discouraged due to the seed fluff nuisance they cause. Many specimens in Britain thought to be female are actually hybrids between this subspecies and other cultivated poplars, for example *Populus × canadensis* 'Lloydii' (p. 273). Several fastigiate Black Poplars are genetically close to *betulifolia* and have similar foliage characteristics.

In eastern and central Europe the subsp. *nigra* replaces *betulifolia*. It is a similar-looking tree but is distinct in some important botanical details, for example it has completely glabrous shoots.

There are several ornamental forms of Black Poplar (see also p. 277), the little known '**Variegata**' has mottled and blotched leaves. It is not a particularly robust clone. The variety *thevestina* is a fastigiate type now regarded as part of another species *Populus afghanica*.

Growth: 6-20-25. Hardiness: 50%. Choice: 3.
Wood: 1 (burrs), 2, 3.

Populus nigra 'Vereecken'

This male clone of Black Poplar was cultivated in Holland before 1959 but probably arose in Belgium. In the 1960s and 1970s it was the fastest-growing Black Poplar available to the timber industry. Final crop size (60cm diameter stems) was routinely achieved in 32 years on lowland alluvial sites. Modern hybrids have now exceeded this remarkable productivity. See also p. 282.

Growth: 8-20-25. Hardiness: 50%. Choice: 3. Wood: 2, 3.

Black Poplar subsp. ***betulifolia***
♂ flowering

Black Poplar

Lombardy Poplar

♂ flowers

aphid gall →

Populus nigra 'Plantierensis'   'Italica'   'Italica Foemina'   'Elegans'

Lombardy Poplar *Populus nigra* 'Italica'

This familiar fastigiate tree is believed to have originated as a variety of Black Poplar (p. 275) in northern Italy at the end of the seventeenth century. It was first cultivated in Britain in 1758, where it is regarded as a cultivar, because almost the entire population is clonal and male. Other variants have also been given individual cultivar names. Trees over 40m in height are known, although crown diameter seldom exceeds 5m.

'**Italica Foemina**' is a female form of Lombardy Poplar. It is instantly recognizable, especially in winter, by its more open shape and often broad top. Also, in winter its orange-ochre glossy twigs show up very well in some lights. Some authorities regard this clone as a hybrid but there is no definite proof of this. '**Elegans**' is another very slender clone of Lombardy Poplar but the name is probably invalid. '**Lombardy Gold**' is a yellow-leaved form which is often difficult to establish but is a good plant when it gets going.
Growth: 6-20-30. Hardiness: 60%. Choice: 2.

Populus nigra 'Plantierensis'

This fastigiate male tree arose at Metz in north-east France at the end of the nineteenth century. It is thought to be a hybrid between Lombardy Poplar and *Populus nigra* subsp. *betulifolia* (p. 275). It has the typical hairy young growth of *betulifolia*. The foliage is usually more dense than Lombardy Poplar. Similar to this is *Populus nigra* subsp. *afghanica* (not illustrated) which is found all over eastern Europe and Asia Minor: it is distinctive in its narrow shape and silver-grey stem. The ubiquitous presence of this subspecies in south-east Europe casts some doubt on the origins of many fastigiate poplars in cultivation.
Growth: 6-20-30. Hardiness: 60%. Choice: 2.

Berlin Poplar *Populus* × *berolinensis*

In 1865 Lombardy Poplar crossed with *Populus laurifolia*, the central Asian Balsam Poplar to produce this productive but slender female hybrid. The same cross occurred later on, in 1750, in France, which resulted in a male clone that was extensively used in Europe and North America for windbreaks. It withstands hot dry conditions in summer and also severe winter cold. Unfortunately in recent years it has become susceptible to leaf cast and has now become rare.
Growth: 8-22-30. Hardiness: 50%. Choice: 2, 3. Wood: 1, 4.

'Lombardy Gold'

Berlin Poplar

Black Italian Poplar

♂ flower

bud detail

'Serotina Aurea'

'Serotina Aurea' *bark*

bract ♂ flower

Black Italian Poplar

***Populus* × *canadensis*
'Serotina Aurea'**

POPLARS

Black Italian Poplar
Populus × canadensis 'Serotina'

This was the earliest commercial poplar resulting from a cross between the European and American Black Poplars. It occurred, probably spontaneously, in France in the early part of the eighteenth century. At first it was wrongly called Swiss Poplar and then Canadian Poplar. Even Black Italian Poplar is a misleading name because it has no connection whatever with Italy. Although it has now been superseded by more productive clones, it became an important timber and pulp producing tree. Stems 30m tall and up to 1.8m in diameter were regularly produced. The best way to identify this otherwise typical black poplar is to note its colour and 'flushing' date in the spring. The leaves, which are the last to appear on poplars (*serotina* means late), are deep bronze when they emerge (flush).

Numerous named clones of 'Serotina' have been bred in Belgium, Italy and France to meet various commercial requirements. Some were given lyrical names like 'Serotina de Champagne' and the upright form 'Serotina de Selys' (p. 283), recalling their origins.
Growth: 8-22-35. Hardiness: 50%. Choice: 2. Wood: 2, 3.

Populus × canadensis 'Serotina Aurea'

In ornamental situations this great golden 'cloud' of a tree dominates the summer landscape wherever it occurs. It has the kind of impact Copper Beech has in another part of the arborial spectrum. The original plant arose at Kalmthout in northern Belgium in 1871. It is frequently planted in urban situations but the spreading and thirsty roots can be a problem. The foliage is clear yellow for most of the summer. Heights around 30m are known and the crown spread can exceed 20m.
Growth: 6-15-25. Hardiness: 50%. Choice: 1 (requires space), 2.

Populus × canadensis 'Regenerata'

Female poplars, like this one, are not usually very popular because of the nuisance caused to people and some soft fruit crops by the seed fluff, which can travel many kilometres in early summer. However, this productive tree did find favour for a time in the shelter-belt and timber industry. A cross between 'Serotina' and the American female Black Poplar 'Marilandica', it arose in Arcueil near Paris in 1814. See also p. 282.
Growth: 8-22-35. Hardiness: 50%. Choice: 2, 3. Wood: 1, 3, 4.

summer

spring

'Regenerata'

Populus × canadensis 'Regenerata'

fruiting ♀ flowers

Prince Eugene's Poplar

'Marilandica'

Prince Eugene's Poplar bark

'Marilandica' bark

Prince Eugene's Poplar

Populus × *canadensis* 'Marilandica'

spring leaf

Prince Eugene's Poplar
Populus × canadensis 'Eugenei'

This clone arose spontaneously in Plantières-les-Metz, north-east France, in 1832. It was imported into Britain in 1888 where it became an important forest tree. Its parentage involves Lombardy Poplar, and probably *Populus × canadensis* 'Marilandica' as the mother tree. The straight stem and narrow crown of fairly light branches make this an ideal wind-firm timber producer. It also tolerates drier sites than most other poplars. Trees up to 40m in height are known. Although resistant to bacterial canker, this hybrid may be prematurely defoliated by a fungus in some areas.

Growth: 8-20-30. Hardiness: 50%. Choice: 2, 3. Wood: 1, 2, 3.

Populus × canadensis 'Marilandica'

A female clone which has been extensively used in tree breeding, this poplar is tolerant of fairly dry alkaline soils. Its origin is uncertain but 'Serotina' appears to be the pollen parent, back-crossed with a Black Poplar. The cultivar name suggests an American connection but this is disputed. It is slightly susceptible to bacterial canker and although frequently planted in Holland and England in the past, it is hardly used at all now. In its day it reached 37m in height with a stem 173cm in diameter but it is now heading for extinction.

Growth: 8-20-30. Hardiness: 50%. Choice: 3, 4. Wood: 1, 2, 3.

Populus × canadensis 'Robusta'

Although generally regarded as a cultivar, there are several different clones of 'Robusta'. The original was another product of Plantières-les-Metz in France appearing in cultivation around 1890. It has been grown all over Europe and at one time accounted for half of all the commercial poplars planted: the first plantations in Britain were at Ryston Hall in Norfolk in 1928. The unfolding bronze foliage is the first of any hybrid poplar to emerge. By early summer it turns deep green, and becomes characteristically dense.

Growth: 7-20-30. Hardiness: 50%. Choice: 2, 3. Wood: 1, 2, 3.

Eastern Cottonwood *Populus deltoides*

Also known as American Black Poplar, this is one of the original parents of the ubiquitous hybrid *Populus × canadensis*. It is 30m tall in its native eastern and central North America, from Quebec to Texas. It was brought into cultivation before 1750. Although its hybrid progeny are known world-wide, the species itself is rare in cultivation. Some named clones are grown in Italy, Germany and France.

Growth: 6-18-25. Hardiness: 60-70%. Choice: 2, 4. Wood: 1, 2, 3.

young tree in spring

***Populus × canadensis* 'Robusta'**

Eastern Cottonwood

POPLAR CULTIVARS

'Vereecken'
old tree

(see p. 275)

'Balsam Spire'
(see p. 271)

'Fritzi Pauley'
(see p. 271)

'Regenerata'
(see p. 279)

'Balsam Spire'
young tree

POPLAR CULTIVARS

Grey Poplar 'Macrophylla'
(see p. 263)

Populus × canadensis **'Florence Biondi'**
A 1925 American hybrid

Populus × candicans **'Aurora'**
(see p. 271)

'Serotina de Selys'
(see p. 279)

♀ flower
♂ flower
Bay Willow
fruit (enlarged)

underside
Grey Sallow
underside
Violet Willow
Bay Willow
underside
Almond-leaved Willow

♀ flower
underside
♂ flower
Goat Willow

284

Bay Willow *Salix pentandra*

Although widely distributed throughout Europe this species prefers cool northern latitudes. It is absent, as a native species, from the Mediterranean region and even southern Britain and Ireland. Trees up to 12m tall occur but this species tends to be rather bushy. The foliage is deep glossy green on 'varnished' shoots. Leaves have glandular teeth which exude yellow slightly aromatic gum. The name, given to it by John Ray in 1690, reflects the similarity of the leaves to the Bay tree (*Laurus nobilis*).

Growth: 4-12-18. Hardiness: 80%. Choice: 3.

Almond-leaved Willow *Salix triandra*

A 12m, spreading, bright green deciduous tree, native in Europe and eastern Asia. It has a long history of cultivation for 'heavy grade' basket manufacture. In a single year rods 3m long and 2cm thick at the base can be grown from selected clones. As a tree this willow has unusual exfoliating bark.

Growth: 6-12-20. Hardiness: 80%. Choice: 3. Wood: 3, 5.

Grey Sallow *Salix cinerea*

This European pioneer wetland species comes in two forms. The mainland eastern subspecies *cinerea* and the Atlantic subspecies *oleifolia*. The latter tends to have smaller leaves with rust-coloured hairs on the back. As male and female trees are distinct, the seedlings are always variable. Where the ranges of the subspecies overlap, intermediate types occur.

Growth: 4-5-7. Hardiness: 90%. Choice: 3.

Violet Willow *Salix daphnoides*

Although grown as a cultivated garden plant over a wide area, this is in the wild an upland species, thriving particularly in peaty ground and on mountain slopes and valleys. The plum-coloured young shoots are covered at first with white dusty bloom which rubs off as the twigs and leaves blow about in the wind. It is a native species in parts of central Europe from the Baltic to the Balkans.

Growth: 6-15-20. Hardiness: 80%. Choice: 1.

Goat Willow *Salix caprea*

This rounded tree up to 10m tall grows in woodland and on dryish ground often well away from open water. It is a broad-leaved tree unlike most of the narrow-leaved wetland willows. Unable to propagate itself naturally from cuttings, it relies on its outstanding ability to produce copious quantities of minute seeds. These travel on the wind among 'seed fluff' for huge distances and colonize any available freshly disturbed ground. Ideal climate conditions for seeding goat willow consist of a gale to distribute the fluff and a rain storm to press the seeds on to the surface of the ground. Germination begins virtually at once.

Most Goat Willows encountered today are hybrids between this species and other sallows. The peculiar garden plant '**Kilmarnock**' is a weeping form usually grafted on to a standard stock. It is a male clone giving a fine display of silky upright catkins in early spring.

Growth: 3-4-4 (cv), 6-10-10 (species). Hardiness: 80%. Choice: 1 (cv).

Goat Willow

'Kilmarnock'
(enlarged)

flowers

detail

♂ flowers

Golden Weeping Willow

summer

Crack Willow

autumn

underside

♀ flower

fruiting catkin

Golden Weeping Willow
spring

Crack Willow
pollarded

286

Golden Weeping Willow

Salix × sepulcralis 'Chrysocoma'

A fast-growing pendulous tree which has bright yellow twigs and young leaves, which subsequently turn green. A hybrid between White Willow (p. 291) and the fairly tender Chinese species *Salix babylonica* (see also p. 289) produced this well-known weeping form in 1888. It rapidly replaced a similar clone, 'Salamonii', produced from the same cross in 1864. In recent years in Europe it has suffered severe attacks of leaf-cast and canker. Disease has become so prevalent in some urban areas that the tree is no longer worth planting. There is no other willow with golden twigs, but there are several other disease-resistant weeping willows, notably the *Salix × pendulina* (*babylonica × fragilis*) cultivars 'Blanda' and the much larger 'Elegantissima', both with glossy brown stems. These are both often wrongly called *Salix babylonica* in the nursery trade.

The advantage of planting 'Elegantissima' is its disease resistance; the disadvantages are its potentially large size (20m, with a 1m diameter stem) and its wide-spreading, moisture-seeking roots. The twig fragility of Crack Willow does not seem to occur in this cultivar. The leaves are exactly like those of Crack Willow.

Growth: 6-18-20. Hardiness: 60-70%. Choice: 1, 4.

Crack Willow *Salix fragilis*

In Europe and northern Asia this species is one of the largest willow trees, often rapidly growing to 20-25m in height and producing a stem over 1.5m in diameter. There are several different forms of crack willow depending on the region in which they are growing. Huge identical populations develop along river valleys. This species has perfected the technique of vegetative propagation. The brittle shoots 'crack' off at a joint when they are disturbed, especially by winter gales. Pieces of debris which fall into water or on to wet mud instantly root when the temperature is right. These rapidly grow into new trees, compensating to some extent for the lack of longevity inherent in the species. Clonal reproduction is perfected to such an extent that whole single sex populations never resort to seed production. Some authorities regard some segregates of Crack Willow as hybrids with White Willow (p. 291) and also Almond-leaved Willow (p. 285). In its natural habitats it frequently crosses with White Willow to form the hybrid *Salix × rubens*, which has itself become stable and produced extensive populations of large trees. The clone 'Basfordiana' is a popular red winter twig form from Belgium.

Growth: 6-20-25. Hardiness: 80%. Choice: 4. Wood: 3.

rooting twig

Crack Willow

'Crispa'

'Tortuosa' branch system

♀ flowers

'Tortuosa'

Common Osier

'Tortuosa'

Common Osier

♀ flower detail

♂ flower detail

WILLOWS

Salix babylonica cultivars

The Chinese species *babylonica* is only hardy in mild districts. However, many of its hybrids and cultivars will tolerate much colder conditions. The Ringleaf Willow '**Crispa**' is a strange, rather sickly plant that produces straight slender shoots and normal-sized *babylonica* leaves, but these immediately spiral as if rolled round a finger and remain in that position.

The Corkscrew Willow, '**Tortuosa**', formerly known as *matsudana* 'Tortuosa', has contorted branches, twigs and leaves. It grows vigorously to form a tangled tree up to 10m in height and almost as wide.

There is an increasingly popular red-twigged form *Salix* × *sepulcralis* 'Erythroflexuosa', a cross between 'Tortuosa' and a red-twigged White Willow. It originated mysteriously in Argentina.

Growth: 4-10-15. Hardiness: 30%. Choice: 1 (cvs).

Common Osier *Salix viminalis*

This shrubby bush or small tree produces long current seasons shoots but only remains vigorous if it is repeatedly cut back. For centuries it has been cultivated for medium to heavy basket rods. Growth in a single season is generally around 1.5m. Throughout its natural range, Europe, north-east Asia and the Himalayas, it has been moved around and planted wherever agriculture required strong baskets. There are over 100 named clones and probably many more favoured types without names in the basket-making industry.

Growth: 5-6-7. Hardiness: 80%. Choice: 3. Wood: 5.

Hoary Willow *Salix elaeagnos*

This close relative of the Common Osier comes from southern Europe and western Asia. It was cultivated in 1820 as a light basket willow and as an ornamental garden plant. The foliage is very fine like rosemary. A former species name for it was *rosmarinifolia*.

Growth: 3-4-5. Hardiness: 70%. Choice: 1. Wood: 5.

Caspian Willow *Salix acutifolia*

First cultivated in 1798 this small Russian tree, originally called *violacea*, is closely related to the Violet Willow. It has purplish-red spreading first year shoots covered in white bloom. These are slender and in spring support silvery 3cm upright catkins. On male trees they become golden-yellow with pollen. The 15m long, slender, lanceolate leaves droop from mature branches in a distinctive way. The equivalent in America is *Salix irrorata*, introduced to Europe in 1898.

Growth: 7-8-10. Hardiness: 70%. Choice: 1 (as coppice).

Hoary Willow

Caspian Willow
♂ flowers

White Willow

autumn

Cricket Bat Willow

Silver Willow

♂ flowers

♀ flowers

White Willow

White Willow winter

Coral-bark Willow pollarded

White Willow bark

290

White Willow *Salix alba*

There are many races of White Willow distributed throughout Europe and western Asia. Most of them are moderate to large trees with distinctive silvery-green foliage. They require moist ground if they are to thrive. The short-lived minute wind-blown seeds must fall on to wet mud or gravel to germinate, so natural populations are confined to freshwater habitats, river sides or lake margins. The young lanceolate leaves are silky-hairy on both surfaces. Later in the year fine hairs are retained on the underside only. The flexible twigs often droop when trees reach maturity. The species was introduced to America in the eighteenth century and has become naturalized in some areas there.

Growth: 6-20-25. Hardiness: 80%. Choice: 2, 3. Wood: 3.

Cricket Bat Willow *Salix alba* var. *caerulea*

Sometime around the year 1700 a single tree was selected in Norfolk which was considered to be the ultimate plant for the production of cricket bats. This specialized process still begins with a rapidly grown stem thick enough to be cleft into 8 bat blades. The face of each blade has to be along the radius of the log. Usually three or four blade lengths can be cut from a single tree. Cricket Bat Willows are always grown vegetatively so the original plant lives on to this day. There are a small number of different clones also in cultivation which may be appropriate in different locations.

Growth: 8-15-20. Hardiness: 80%. Choice: 3. Wood: 1.

Silver Willow *Salix alba* var. *sericea*

Bright silver foliage forms of White Willow have been selected for ornamental use for many years. Several differently named clones, such as forma *argentea*, have been developed, but the tendency now is to lump them all together under the variety name *sericea*. There is no finer tree in early summer when the wind exposes the silver-backed leaves.

Growth: 6-14-18. Hardiness: 80%. Choice: 1 (requires space).

Coral-bark Willow *Salix alba* 'Britzensis'

The young shoots of White Willow vary naturally from clone to clone. Usually they are glossy olive-brown but occasionally yellow, orange and even shades of waxy red can be found. Several red clones have been brought into cultivation and named. 'Britzensis' is an upright tree which is usually coppiced every 2nd or 3rd year. It produces a haze of striking red winter shoots. It was of German origin, raised from seed at Britz.

Growth: 4-12-15. Hardiness: 80%. Choice: 1 (as coppice).

Cricket Bat Willow

Silver Willow

Coral-bark Willow

Caucasian Wing Nut

fruit detail

naked bud

winged rachis detail

Hybrid Wing Nut

Hybrid Wing Nut

Caucasian Wing Nut

Chinese Wing Nut bark

WALNUT FAMILY • Juglandaceae

Caucasian Wing Nut *Pterocarya fraxinifolia*

This member of the walnut family is a fast-growing 30m tree from the east Caucasus and northern Iran. It was introduced into cultivation in France in 1782 by the French botanist André Michaux. With the turbulent Anglo-French relationships of the time it did not reach Britain until 1810, and even that date shows considerable botanical indifference to politics and war. In its natural range it is a tree of damp woodlands. In cultivation it is best known for its habit of producing numerous sucker shoots which, given some freedom, soon develop into a thicket of new trees. The pinnate leaves are up to 60cm long with around 19-21 oblong pointed leaflets. The largest of these may be 15cm long. Pairs of semi-orbicular wings on the nuts are a distinctive feature of this tree in summer hanging among the foliage in 50cm strings. In winter *Pterocarya* can be identified by its naked buds often flanked by small pale brown scaly leaves.

Growth: 6-25-30. Hardiness: 50%. Choice: 4. Wood: 2, 5.

Hybrid Wing Nut *Pterocarya × rehderiana*

Produced in the Arnold Arboretum, Boston, USA, in 1879, this suckering fast-growing 25m tree is more or less intermediate between its parents (Caucasian and Chinese Wing Nuts). The pinnate leaves have a slightly winged rachis and 11-21 dark green leaflets.

Growth: 8-20-25. Hardiness: 50%. Choice: 4. Wood: 2, 5.

Chinese Wing Nut *Pterocarya stenoptera*

Native to wet woodlands in China, this species was first introduced to the west in 1860. It is a large vigorous tree with deeply fissured grey-brown bark. The pinnate leaves often have serrate wings on each side of the rachis, and the terminal leaflet is often missing. The remaining 7-21 un-toothed leaflets vary considerably in size. The fruits, in clusters, are on 30cm pendulous strings. The wings on the nuts are narrow and usually held erect.

Growth: 6-25-30. Hardiness: 70%. Choice: 4. Wood: 2, 5.

Japanese Wing Nut *Pterocarya rhoifolia*

In its native Japan this is a tree of wet ground, usually on mountain-sides. The first cultivated plants were produced in the west in 1888. The finely toothed elliptic leaflets, 11-21 on each 30cm pinnate leaf, colour well to shades of bright yellow in the autumn. The flowers, males on second year wood and females on current shoots, are 6-8cm long. Females develop into 20-30cm strings of winged nuts. The name *Pterocarya* is from the Greek 'Pteron' meaning wing and 'Karya' meaning nut.

Growth: 6-20-25. Hardiness: 50-60%. Choice: 4. Wood: 2, 5.

mature fruit (enlarged)

Chinese Wing Nut

Japanese Wing Nut

Common Walnut

'Laciniata'

'Monophylla'

underside

Black Walnut

Black Walnut

294

Common Walnut *Juglans regia*

Walnuts all have a distinguishing feature that separates them from other pinnate-leaved trees: if the shoot is cut in half along its length, the pith can be seen to be divided into compartments which resemble the rungs of a ladder.

The natural distribution of Common Walnut has been confused by centuries of cultivation, firstly for nuts and then for the decorative wood. Its western limit is reckoned to be Greece. From there it extended eastwards within the warm temperate zone as far as China and Japan. The Romans also imported trees from Greece to much of their Empire over 2000 years ago. The original stocks have been improved, for example in Britain by the great monastic houses, and good fruiting cultivars still prevail near some of them. The familiar nut is contained in a 5cm globular green husk which is both aromatic and staining while still green. This is a tree for warm dryish soils, it hates cold wet clays. Frost and cold weather are also damaging. Good trees can exceed 30m in height. When grown for timber they are best started off in a group so they are almost branch free and drawn up straight towards the light. However, there has always been a market for crooked material with decorative wavy grain. Even the roots produce good material for ornamental work and veneers. Once properly seasoned, which may take six years, walnut wood will not warp or swell.

The cultivar '**Laciniata**', Cut-leaved Walnut, has deeply toothed and indented leaflets and pendulous branch ends. Originally it was described and named as a separate species. The One-leaved Walnut '**Monophylla**' is a peculiar form with simple or only tri-foliate leaves.

Growth: 3-10-30. Hardiness: 50%. Choice: 3. Wood: 1.

Black Walnut *Juglans nigra*

From eastern and central North America this 30-40m forest tree produces deep chocolate-brown wood of very high quality. The best trees were originally from North Carolina and Tennessee. The long, evenly spaced-out pinnate leaves tend to be inclined downwards. In the autumn they turn to golden yellow for 2-3 weeks before falling. The strongly aromatic fruits are encased in a 3cm green husk. Forests of this tree once covered tracts of fertile land in America. It was introduced to Britain by John Tradescant before 1656.

Growth: 3-12-30. Hardiness: 50-60%. Choice: 1 (rquires space). Wood: 1.

Common Walnut

Butternut

Arizona Walnut

Japanese Walnut

var. *cordiformis*

Manchurian Walnut

WALNUTS

Butternut *Juglans cinerea*

The species name *cinerea* is a reference to the grey fissured bark, when compared to Black Walnut which shares this tree's natural range in east and central North America. The best specimens are around 30m tall but they are never as good as Black Walnut. The pinnate leaves consist of 11-19 oblong-lanceolate 6-12cm leaflets. Thick shelled nuts each with four prominent ridges are encased in an oblong pointed viscid-pubescent green husk around 6cm long.
Growth: 3-10-30. Hardiness: 70-80%. Choice: 3. Wood: 1.

Arizona Walnut *Juglans elaeopyron*

Since 1894 this ornamental walnut has been widely cultivated, especially for its golden-yellow autumn foliage colour. Its origin is complex because the species is probably a small segregate of a much wider population. In its native south-western deserts of North America it is still listed as *Juglans major*, which is considered to be a variety of *Juglans microcarpa* by some authorities. It is a small to medium-sized tree with a rounded outline and delicate pinnate leaves. The leaflets are narrow and distinctly toothed.
Growth: 2-7-15. Hardiness: 30%. Choice: 1. Wood: 1.

Japanese Walnut *Juglans ailanthifolia*

The sticky 5cm seed husk of this Japanese tree is poisonous. In former times it was used in Japan to catch fish. The pinnate leaves have larger (15cm) and wider leaflets than most other walnuts giving the tree a more 'solid' appearance from some distance away. It thrives best in sheltered wet areas preferably close to water. The variety **cordiformis** differs only slightly from the species. The leaflets and the seeds are narrower.
Growth: 3-8-18. Hardiness: 40-50%. Choice: 4. Wood: 1.

Manchurian Walnut *Juglans mandshurica*

The broad range of this species, from north-east Russia through northern China to Korea, makes it a variable but rugged hardy tree. The largest specimens may be 20m tall with a broad head of spreading branches. The leaves on some provenances are large, up to 60cm long, with 9-17 leaflets from 7-18cm long. The fruits are encased in an ovoid pointed husk around 5cm long. The 4cm nut is reinforced with 8 sharp edged woody ridges. Although it was introduced to the west in 1859 this remains a rare tree in cultivation. It is sometimes confused with Chinese Walnut (*Juglans cathayensis*) which is much larger in all its parts.
Growth: 3-8-20. Hardiness: 70-80%. Choice: 3. Wood: 1.

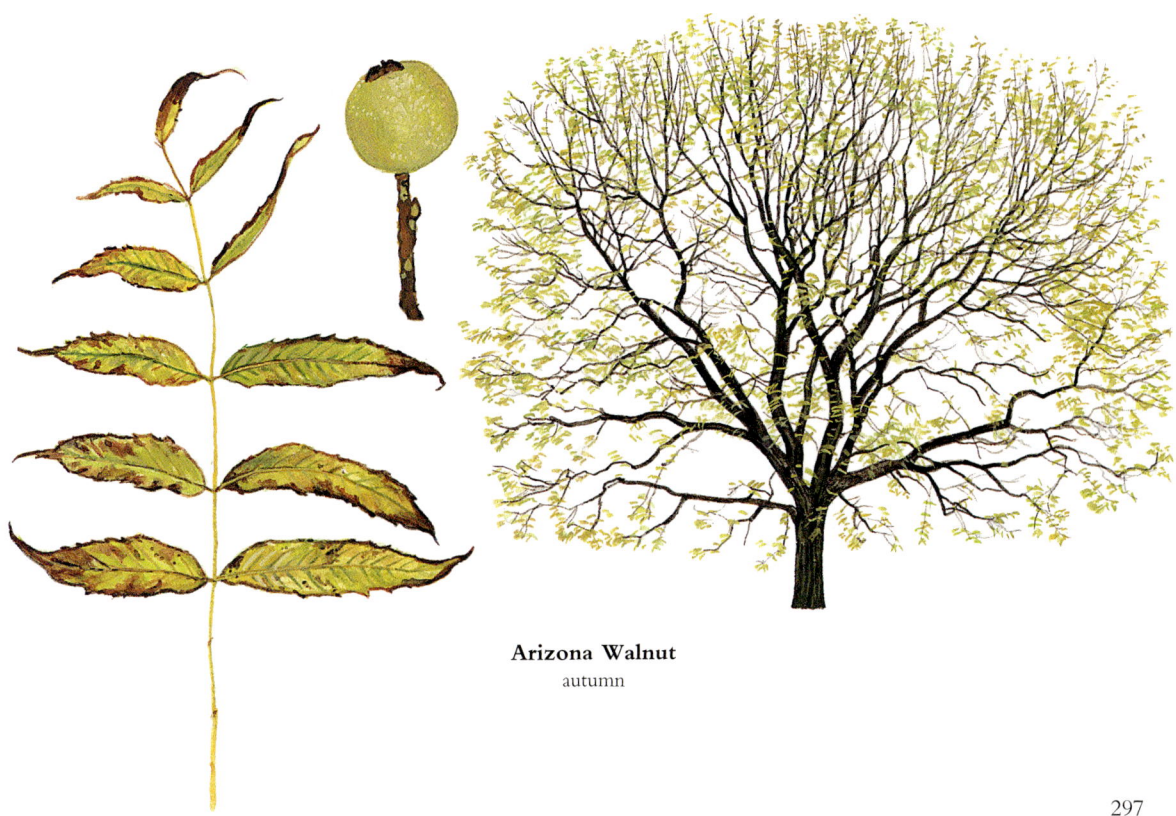

Arizona Walnut
autumn

nut

bud

leaflet variation

Shellbark Hickory

old bark

Shellbark Hickory

bud

nut

Pignut

underside

fruit

leaflet variation

underside

nut

Pecan

nut

Mockernut

298

HICKORIES

Shellbark Hickory *Carya laciniosa*

The name 'hickory' comes from 'pawcohiccora' the American Indian word for the oil produced from crushed nut kernels. The natural range of this species is wet land in the Mississippi Basin to Oklahoma and northwards as far as Ontario. It is also be found along the Alabama River and into Louisiana. Nowhere is it abundant and 40m straight-stemmed trees are now rare. The distinctive bark is shaggy with hard curling vertical flakes up to 1m long which are retained for years. Laciniosa means 'with flaps' which describes it exactly. This tree has the largest leaves of any *Carya*, over 60cm long, and the largest nuts, 5-6cm long. The valuable timber is heavy, very hard and flexible. Dark brown heartwood contrasts with cream-coloured sapwood, making it both decorative and functional. The autumn foliage colour is golden-yellow.

*Growth: 6-18-30. Hardiness: 50-60%. Choice: 1.
Wood: 1, 2, 3.*

Mockernut *Carya tomentosa*

Of all the hickories the timber of this one is most highly prized. It once provided functional handles for every kind of tool and agricultural implement, giving reliable strength and elasticity. Today it also has a place in furniture manufacturing and sports equipment. Waste makes excellent 'aromatic' firewood or wood chips for smoking hams or finishing barbecued food. Its broad natural range is eastern North America. The silvery-grey bark is smooth and then slightly fissured at maturity.

*Growth: 6-20-30. Hardiness: 60-70%. Choice: 1.
Wood: 1, 2, 3, 5.*

Pecan *Carya illinoinensis*

This is the source of the pecan nut. Good fruiting trees have been selected since around 1760 and grown in orchards. It is naturally a riverside tree thriving in moist fertile soils throughout the southern and central United States, especially along the Mississippi, Missouri and Arkansas Rivers. The heavy wood is brittle and less valuable than most hickories but it still makes acceptable flooring, veneers and good firewood. Trees 30m are known, with more or less straight stems and spreading branches. The foliage in the autumn is bright yellow.

Growth: 6-18-30. Hardiness: 50-60%. Choice: 3. Wood: 3.

Pignut *Carya glabra*

In the nineteenth century this tree was put to the most humble uses by North American settlers. Its nuts were fed to pigs and the wood was finely split to manufacture traditional broom heads. This species has a broad range in the eastern United States. It extends into drier country than many other hickories. The tough heavy wood is flexible enough for tool handles, wagons and agricultural equipment. The bark is smooth until shallow interlocking vertical fissures develop in old age.

*Growth: 6-20-30. Hardiness: 60-70%. Choice: 4.
Wood: 1, 2, 3.*

Shellbark Hickory
old tree

Mockernut
young tree

Pignut
young tree

♂ flowers

bud

underside

bud

Shagbark Hickory

new leaves

Bitternut old bark

Bitternut   split husk   ♂ flowers

300

Shagbark Hickory *Carya ovata*

Perhaps the best known of the rough-barked hickories, this species has been grown in temperate tree collections world-wide. The distinctive bark has very hard fixed curling flakes which through time project a long way out from the tree but never seem to fall off. Originally from Quebec to Maine and southwards to Georgia, south-east Texas and north-east Mexico, Shagbark Hickory was brought into cultivation in 1629. It is one of the best nut-producing trees in the United States. The nuts are 4-6cm long with a sweet kernel. The pinnate leaves, with 5 or occasionally 7 leaflets, are yellowish-green in summer. They are often over 30cm long depending on the shelter round the tree and the moisture in the soil under it. In autumn the foliage turns to bright cadmium yellow for two or three weeks. The flowers, which in all hickories begin to develop before the leaves fully open, are green and small. Males are drooping 12cm catkins while the females, in clusters of 2-5, are almost hidden at the shoot tips. In cooler countries the flowers suffer damage from spring frost and nuts are seldom produced. In cultivation trees over 21m are known. In 1906 a tree in the original American hickory forest measured 23.7m to the first branch and its total height was estimated to have been 70m.

Growth: 3-14-25. Hardiness: 60-70%. Choice: 1.
Wood: 1, 2, 3.

Bitternut *Carya cordiformis*

As the name suggests the seeds of this tree are very bitter and compressed. The alternative name 'pignut' describes about all they are fit for. The husks round the nuts, which are 3-5cm long, have four equally spaced stiff wings extending from the apex to around the middle. The tree grows on dry or swampy ground in eastern North America from Florida to the Canadian border and southern Quebec to eastern Texas. The 15-25cm leaves are pinnate with 5-9 sharply toothed leaflets. They colour well to golden-yellow in the autumn. Stems, up to 28m tall, have thick vertically ridged grey-brown bark. The species was introduced to horticulture in 1766 but it has little value as an ornamental tree and is seldom planted. In America it is a common timber tree. Much of it has grown as coppice from cut-over forest. The timber is strong and flexible. It is used where strength and elasticity is essential, notably for tool handles. Wood grown as coppice appears to be even stronger than original trees. Early settlers finding the nuts inedible, crushed them to produce lamp oil. This oil was also thought to give relief from rheumatic pain.

Growth: 4-15-28. Hardiness: 60-70%. Choice: 3.
Wood: 1, 2, 3.

Bitternut

Shagbark Hickory

Erman's Birch

catkin scale

winged seed

Betula albo-sinensis var. *septentrionalis*

winged seed

catkin scale

type

'Grayswood Hill'

seed

scale

Blue Birch

'Grayswood Hill'
young tree

type

type

Monarch Birch

BIRCH FAMILY · Betulaceae

Erman's Birch *Betula ermanii*

The range of this hardy tree extends from Japan to Siberia from sea level to the tree-line. In some situations it is an opportunist pioneer and in others it is a long-lived forest tree. In cultivation its diverse natural range has resulted in considerable variation, particularly in tree size and bark colour. Furthermore several different species hybridize with it to create numerous beautiful but unidentifiable specimens. There are also distinct varieties such as *japonica*, and a superb white-barked cultivar called '**Grayswood Hill**' which is often listed (wrongly) in collections as *Betula costata*.
Growth: 4-12-18. Hardiness: 50-60%. Choice: 1. Wood: 1, 4.

Betula albo-sinensis var. *septentrionalis*

The best examples of this variety of Chinese Red Birch have smooth orange-grey bark, which is bloomed with a thin layer of white wax. It is shed in large sheets to reveal a burnished coppery layer underneath. Botanically it would appear to be intermediate between the species and Erman's Birch. They are closely allied. Chinese Red Birch and the variety *septentrionalis* were both introduced to the west by Ernest Wilson in 1901 and 1908.
Growth: 4-15-25. Hardiness: 50%. Choice: 1.

Monarch Birch *Betula maximowicziana*

The Pacific coast of Japan, from the Kurile Islands to Honshu and Hokkaido, is home to this big magnificent tree. It occurs in mixed forests and is frequently planted as an ornamental specimen. In any collection of birches, provided the site is fertile and moist, Monarch Birch always stands out from the rest. It rapidly grows to 20-25m in height with a smooth fat stem up to 1m thick. The bark is not spectacular but it is unmistakably birch with horizontal bands of grey and dull white. The foliage is bold with leaves 10-15cm long which colour to bright yellow in the autumn.
Growth: 5-18-25. Hardiness: 40%. Choice: 1 (requires space). Wood: 1, 4.

Blue Birch *Betula* × *caerulea*

This hybrid between Grey Birch (p. 309) and Mountain Paper Birch (*Betula papyrifera* var. *cordifolia*) was formerly called *Betula caerulea-grandis* by William Blanchard, an American botanist. It is still occasionally found under this name. In America where the ranges of the parents overlap it occurs naturally. Cultivated specimens are prized for their blue-green foliage and papery white and pale orange bark. The first introduction to Europe was in 1905.
Growth: 3-8-10. Hardiness: 80%. Choice: 1. Wood: 1, 4.

Monarch Birch

Betula albo-sinensis* var. *septentrionalis

'Jermyns'

'Grayswood Ghost'

Himalayan Birch

'Silver Shadow'

Japanese Cherry Birch

Japanese Birch

Asian Black Birch

'Doorenbos'

underside

Himalayan Birch *Betula utilis*

This deciduous 15-20m tree has a broad range across the Himalayas, often reaching high into the foothills close to the tree line. Consequently it is extremely variable when brought into cultivation. The horizontally peeling papery bark is usually brown but occasional specimens are pink, copper-coloured and even white. The variety ***jacquemontii*** (illustrated on p. 306) is a white barked form, but it is often produced from seed and then the colour is not constant. It grows in northern India and parts of Nepal. Plants of this variety first arrived in the west in 1880, some 30 years after the species.

Grafted white bark forms of *Betula utilis* have been pioneered by the Hillier Nursery. Grafted plants of variety *jacquemontii* were distributed by them under the name '**Silver Shadow**'. Perhaps the best known Hillier plant though is '**Jermyns**' which was selected from a batch of *jacquemontii* seedling received from Belgium. It retains its smooth creamy white bark on large stems up to 50cm in diameter. Another fine white form is '**Grayswood Ghost**', like 'Silver Shadow' it seems to glow in the half light of early morning and late evening. There has been a plethora of new named selections of white-stemmed birches in recent years each claiming to be the best. They include 'Moonbeam', 'Inverleith', 'Silver Queen' and '**Doorenbos**'.

Growth: 5-12-20. Hardiness: 50-60%. Choice: 1.
Wood: 1, 4. (species)

Japanese Cherry Birch *Betula grossa*

The stem of this tree is reminiscent of wild cherry, with horizontal stripes of grey-brown bark exfoliating in thin papery curls. It grows naturally in mixed woodland on hill and mountain sides in Honshu, Shikoku and Kyushu. There is some affinity between it and the American species *Betula lenta*, including the aromatic foliage. Although rare in cultivation it has been available in the west since 1896.

Growth: 5-10-20. Hardiness: 60-70%. Choice: 1.
Wood: 1, 4.

Japanese Birch *Betula platyphylla* var. *japonica*

The variety *japonica* and not the species is the tree in general cultivation. They are very similar but come from different areas. The species, from mainland Asia, intergrades with Silver Birch (p. 311). Japanese Birch, from Japan, is a 15-20m tree with white and brown peeling bark also like Silver Birch. The 4-7cm leaves are less deeply toothed and glaucous-green on the underside.

Growth: 5-10-20. Hardiness: 60-70%. Choice: 1.
Wood: 1, 4.

Asian Black Birch *Betula davurica*

This tree from northern China, Manchuria and Korea, was introduced in 1882, and has distinct rough silvery-grey bark. It is very hardy, withstanding cold but intolerant of exceptionally warm conditions. In favourable parts of its range trees up to 30m tall have been recorded, but half this is more likely in most other places.

Growth: 5-10-20. Hardiness: 50-70%. Choice: 1.
Wood: 1, 4.

'Jermyns'

Japanese Birch

Betula utilis var. *prattii*

10-14 veins

7-9 veins

'Fetisowii'

♂ flowers

Transcaucasian Birch

Dwarf Birch

underside

'Fetisowii'

autumn

7-9 veins

Betula utilis var. *jacquemontii*

Betula utilis var. *jacquemontii*

Transcaucasian Birch

autumn

306

BIRCHES

Betula utilis var. *prattii*

Of the many forms of Himalayan Birch (p. 305) this is one of the most striking. It was brought into cultivation from west China in 1908. The bark is bright orange on the best specimens but may vary between pale grey to orange-brown. The deep green lustrous leaves have silky hairs on the midrib and veins on the underside.

Growth: 5-12-20. Hardiness: 50-60%. Choice: 1.

Dwarf Birch *Betula nana*

This very tough sub-Alpine shrub has dense twiggy branches and small (5-15mm) round leaves, each with a short petiole. It occurs world-wide through northern Asia, Europe, Greenland and west to Alaska. In cultivation since 1789, it grows slightly larger but will not tolerate hot sun.

Growth: 1-1-2. Hardiness: 100%. Choice: 4.

Betula utilis var. *jacquemontii*

This variety is described on p. 305. Closely related to var. *jacquemontii* is '**Fetisowii**' from Central Asia. Plants in cultivation all appear to be seedlings of wild, mostly Chinese, origin but they are remarkably similar in appearance. A slender, flexible, thin-branched tree, with peeling white bark usually developing on quite young specimens. Some authorities suggest hybrid origin but uncertain parentage. The name is sometimes spelt 'Fetishowii'.

Growth: 5-10-unknown. Hardiness: 50-60%. Choice: 1.

Transcaucasian Birch *Betula medwediewii*

Grown chiefly for its glorious yellow autumn colour and big, 8-12cm leaves, this small tree was introduced in 1897. It has distinct more or less upright stout twigs and branches, and big sticky buds. As with many other trees from the Caucasus region, everything about this plant is big and vigorous.

Growth: 4-10-14. Hardiness: 70-80%. Choice: 1. Wood: 1, 4.

Manchurian Birch *Betula platyphylla*

Less well known in cultivation than the variety *japonica* (p. 305) this species is a substantial tree in its native Manchuria and Korea. Heights over 20m are known. The bark is greyish-white and the shoots are glandular and sticky. The leaves are deltoid-ovate and 4-6cm long. These too are covered in raised glandular dots. This species was thought at first to be a subspecies of Silver Birch (p. 311). Then it was named as a species *Betula mandshurica* for a time and some authorities argue quite convincingly that it should have remained so. Its actual date of introduction to horticulture is unknown.

'**Whitespire**' is a cultivar of *Betula platyphylla* var. *japonica* (p. 305), the Japanese White Birch. It is a strikingly narrow tree when young but the branches spread outwards as it matures. The stem and foliage resemble the species.

Growth: 5-12-20. Hardiness: 60-70%. Choice: 1. Wood: 4 (species).

'Whitespire'

Manchurian Birch

River Birch

fruit & scale

Grey Birch

fruit

scale

Yellow Birch

fruit

scale

var. *fallax*

Cherry Birch

young bark

old bark

scale

fruit

Yellow Birch
autumn

Cherry Birch

River Birch *Betula nigra*

In its native eastern North America this tree extends further south than any other birch. It inhabits low-lying swampy ground and river banks and has been extensively used for erosion control. The natural range extends from New Hampshire to northern Florida and west to east Texas and Iowa. In America it makes a tree 15-24m tall with pinkish-brown bark exfoliating in a mass of curled papery scales then becoming thick, dark brown and fissured. As ornamental specimens, trees are often cut back to ground level from time to time to encourage multiple stems which show off the distinctive young peeling bark to good effect. It was originally sent to Europe by Peter Collinson in 1736.

Growth: 4-12-24. Hardiness: 60-70%. Choice: 1. Wood: 3, 4.

Grey Birch *Betula populifolia*

The species name refers to the similarity of the foliage to a poplar leaf. In America this is a native species from Cape Breton Island to southern Ontario and southwards to eastern Virginia. In the wild state it is usually a small bushy tree not more than 9m tall. It rapidly reinstates derelict ground and fire sites to woodland by prolific seeding but is short-lived and gives way to other species which easily establish themselves under its light shade. In cultivation it is an elegant but tough little tree with fluttering foliage and good yellow autumn colour. It was introduced to Europe in 1750.

Growth: 4-8-10. Hardiness: 60-70%. Choice: 1.

Yellow Birch *Betula alleghaniensis*

Although named *Betula lutea* in 1812 and changed to *alleghaniensis* as long ago as 1904 the old invalid name *lutea* still persists on labels in some collections. In its native North America this is one of the most valuable hardwood lumber trees. It grows to 30m in height with stems up to 80cm in diameter. The bark is horizontally marked silvery-grey to pale yellowish-brown, an interesting feature in cultivation. The twigs are aromatic especially when gently crushed. The long yellow male catkins in spring are another desirable feature. In the autumn the foliage turns golden-brown. The variety **fallax** was first described in 1966 but it is obscure and virtually unknown in cultivation.

Growth: 5-18-30. Hardiness: 80%. Choice: 2. Wood: 1, 3, 4.

Cherry Birch *Betula lenta*

Arguably this is one of the finest birches for ornamental and forest use. It has light aromatic foliage which smells of wintergreen if crushed. It grows to a good size, 15-24m tall, on a slender stem and has superb golden autumn colour. The dark brown bark on mature trees resembles American Black Cherry. It is a native species from southern Quebec and southeast Ontario to northern Alabama. In former times oil of wintergreen was distilled from the wood.

Growth: 4-15-24. Hardiness: 80%. Choice: 2. Wood: 1, 3, 4.

Yellow Birch
forest tree

River Birch

Grey Birch

Silver Birch

♀ flower

♂ flowers

♂ flowers

'Purpurea'

'Dalecarlica'

'Youngii'

Silver Birch
old tree

'Dalecarlica'

'Youngii'

310

Silver Birch *Betula pendula*

Silver Birch (see also p. 313) is common throughout the whole of Europe, Asia Minor and Russia. It is widely planted in North America giving it transglobal distribution throughout the northern temperate and sub-arctic world. There is considerable variation within the species, which has been eagerly utilized by the nursery trade ever since the eighteenth century.

This graceful tree is familiar to almost everyone, with its light airy foliage and distinctive white and pink peeling bark. The young branches are glossy mahogany brown and the slender shoots are rough and warty. The golden-yellow autumn foliage colour is brilliant on a sunny day against a blue sky.

There are numerous traditional and present day uses for birch. The creamy-brown wood is of high quality for internal joinery, although it is not durable out of doors. The sap can be used to make a fine potent wine and also birch beer. In the environment Silver Birch is food and shelter to numerous invertebrates and as a pioneer species it extends woodland into otherwise barren or treeless areas. It thrives best on sandy soils where the seedlings can germinate easily, but it will tolerate a wide range of sites and it is completely hardy. Light is essential for healthy growth, shaded trees soon dying out.

Growth: 5-18-25. Hardiness: 90-100%. Choice: 2. Wood: 1, 3, 4.

Betula pendula cultivars

'**Purpurea**' is a good ornamental tree with purplish-brown leaves that are subtle in colour rather than garish. It tends to grow slowly, because the leaves are not green and photosynthesis is restricted, but in other respects it is like the species. The first plants appeared in cultivation in 1872.

'**Dalecarlica**', the Swedish Birch, is a narrow tall tree with pendulous shoots and deeply cut leaves. It is often confused with 'Laciniata' which is more pendulous but has less deeply cut leaves. Swedish Birch was originally found in Sweden in 1767. Similar cut-leaved individuals still turn up in the wild and in cultivation from time to time.

The ultimate weeping birch is '**Youngii**', Young's Weeping Birch, which takes the pendulous characteristic to almost grotesque limits. Top grafted trees look ridiculous when the stem is straight and all the branches grow directly downwards from the top of it. Properly trained trees can produce a dome, or series of domes, of foliage on crooked stems with hanging curtains of twigs which are quite pleasing in the landscape. Specimens over 60 years of age look best. This cultivar was introduced in the late 1860s.

Growth: variable. Hardiness: 80-100%. Choice: 1.

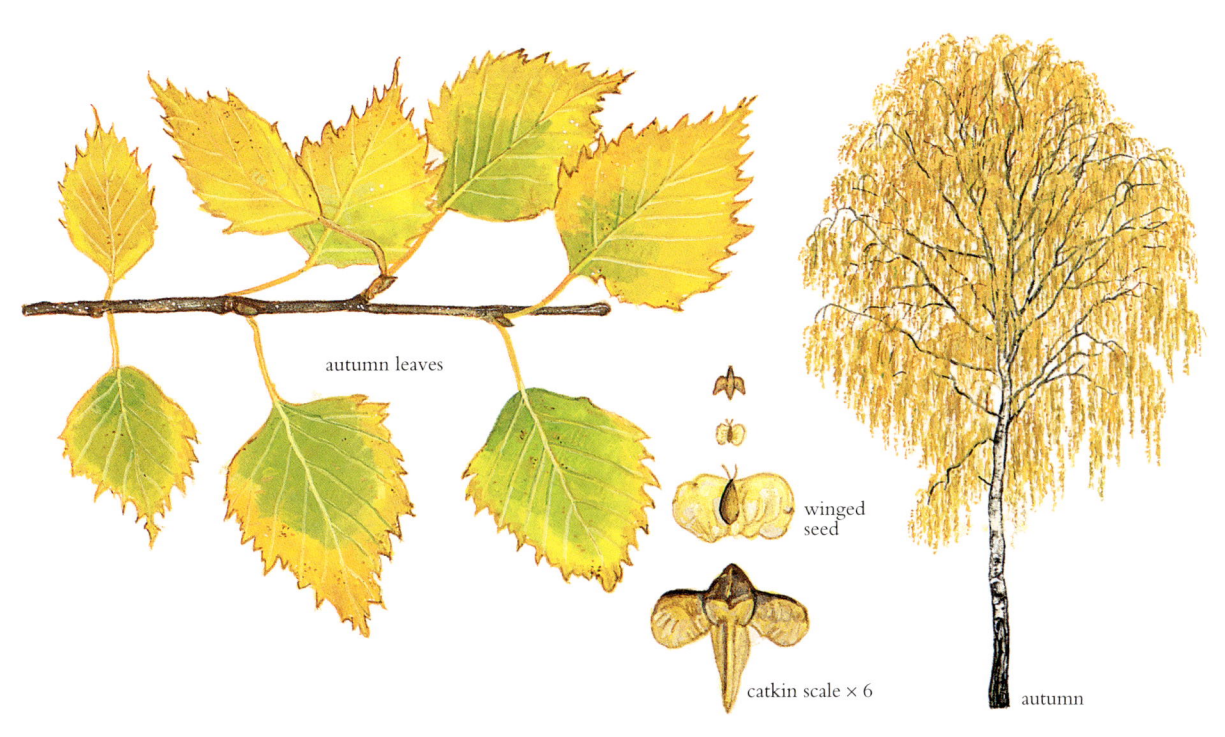

Silver Birch

'Birkalensis'

'Gracilis'

'Tristis'

'Viscosa'

'Birkalensis'

'Obelisk'

'Fastigiata'

young tree

312

Betula pendula cultivars (continued)

'**Birkalensis**' is an elegant tree found originally in Finland and brought into cultivation in 1877. Its form is narrow and semi-pendulous with a white and dark grey peeling stem and deeply double toothed leaves. It is seldom seen now because similar-looking seedlings have obscured the identity of the original cultivar to such an extent that it is probably no longer in cultivation.

'**Gracilis**' is one of several 'cut-leaved birches' in cultivation. It is a small tree seldom over 10m tall, with pendulous branches, clustered twigs and deeply cut leaves. Often it is difficult to distinguish from 'Laciniata' which in turn is frequently mistaken for 'Dalecarlica'. Although the taxonomy of cut-leaved birches has become confused the trees are very distinct and highly ornamental.

'**Tristis**', Weeping Silver Birch, is a tall tree with thin spreading branches and arching pendulous shoots. The leaves are exactly like the species and they colour well, to golden yellow, in the autumn. There appears to be conflicting evidence about the origin of this cultivar, including two widely different dates of introduction, 1867 and 1904. Possibly more than one clone is in cultivation and pendulous-twigged trees are common in the wild. It was common practice to call any tree with pendulous twigs, forma *tristis*. These generally come true from seed but the effect may not be obvious in young plants.

'**Obelisk**' is an upright form of Silver Birch with a very narrow outline and good scattering of 'silver' bark on the stem. '**Fastigiata**' is more or less the same but generally becomes slightly wider in the crown. It was first cultivated in 1870. As a proportion of seedlings from it also show upward tendencies, the exact identity of the original cultivar is often questionable. It seems a contradiction to call this cultivar *Betula pendula* 'Fastigiata'. Although the crown is relatively narrow and the main branches are upswept, the extremities eventually become pendulous.

'**Viscosa**' is a small bushy tree with very sticky young foliage and twigs. The leaves are small, 2-3.5cm long, and crowded together. It was first cultivated in 1912 and is also distributed under the name 'Dentata Viscosa' a reference to the deeply toothed leaves.

Growth: variable. Hardiness: 80-100%. Choice: 1.

'Tristis'

'Gracilis'

Betula szechuanica bark

var. *commutata*

underside

White Birch

seed ×7

bract

Paper Birch

White Birch

Paper Birch

autumn

White Birch *Betula pubescens*

Most wet moorlands and sub-arctic wastelands throughout Europe, Scandinavia and Russia are inhabited by this ubiquitous species. Its form varies from a stunted shrub in the north to a tree over 20m tall in more favoured areas. In outline it is similar to Silver Birch (p. 311) but the twigs are silky hairy and not rough to the touch. The bark on young trees is often dull brown and grey but the branches are copper-coloured and quite glossy. Male catkins are pendulous and up to 6cm long while females are erect on short spur shoots. When ripe these disintegrate showering tiny winged seeds and scale debris over a wide area. Often shedding is delayed and seeds can frequently be found on the surface of winter snow. White Birch hardly ever hybridizes with Common Birch, being genetically distinct, but it will cross with several Asiatic birches. This often causes serious taxonomic and identification headaches for botanists and arboretum curators.

Growth: 5-15-20. Hardiness: 90%. Choice: 2. Wood: 3, 4.

Betula szechuanica

Originally thought to be a variety of *Betula platyphylla* (p. 307), this very ornamental tree is now considered to be a species in its own right. It came from western China and south-east Tibet in 1908. Another of Ernest Wilson's collections. The bark is white and chalky and the foliage is glossy blue-green. In the autumn this turns golden yellow.

Growth: 4-10-15. Hardiness: 40-50%. Choice: 1.

Paper Birch *Betula papyrifera*

Also known in North America as Canoe Birch, because Indian canoes were made from it, this tree is a native species from the Pacific coast to the Atlantic coast in Canada and the northern United States. Modern, less noble, uses for the wood now include broom handles, toothpicks and lollipop sticks. It is also a major source of pulpwood. The species was introduced to Europe in 1750 and since then ornamental forms have often been cultivated. Best known is the variety **commutata** which has broad heart-shaped leaves and white bark. The variety *humilis*, now properly called **Betula neoalaskana**, The Yukon White Birch, has attractive red-brown peeling bark. In much of its native Alaska it is hardly more than a bush. In cultivation, where it appeared in 1904, it becomes a sturdy cold tolerant small tree with glorious golden-brown autumn foliage.

Growth: 5-15-25. Hardiness: 90%. Choice: 1. Wood: 3, 4.

Betula neoalaskana
autumn

var. *commutata*
winter

♀ flowers
♂ flowers
developing flowers
♂
♀
old cones
seeds

Common Alder

underside

'Quercifolia'

Common Alder
old tree in winter, formerly coppiced

'Imperialis'

Common Alder *Alnus glutinosa*

The natural range of this wetland species includes the whole of Europe, Russia including Siberia, western Asia and North Africa. It has traditional uses which go back to the dawn of history. This is a tree of watery places and the wood was used for every conceivable purpose to do with water management. Pumps, troughs and even small boats were made from it. In heavy waterside engineering it provided baulks of timber for piles and sluices. Alder faggots were even buried in lines end-to-end to provide land drainage. In contrast to all this, dry alder wood makes superb charcoal which in its day was favoured for the manufacture of gunpowder. Perhaps the most widespread use for the wood though was for clog making. Alder clogs mainly for industrial workers were water- and grease-resistant, they absorbed impact very well and lasted a long time. Furthermore they were light and comfortable to wear. In Britain "cloggers", who cut the blanks by hand out in the wood, moved from coppice to coppice on a 10-12 year cycle. A good example of a totally sustainable supply of raw material for an important industrial process.

As a living plant this alder is beneficial to all of the other species which grow nearby. It can root into and break up wet compacted soil where free oxygen is limited and by a symbiotic relationship with a bacteria-like organism on the roots it can convert atmospheric nitrogen into a usable form. This is a pioneer species: its role in life is to colonize derelict land by seeding to establish shrub and tree cover, and then be shaded out by more enduring species. Its life is naturally short and it can only thrive in full light. However, some make large trees 25m tall, with stems 1m thick. Coppice, which is constantly being rejuvenated by cutting, can exist for hundreds of years if it is not neglected.

Growth: 5-18-25. Hardiness: 70%. Choice: 4.
Wood: 1, 2, 3, 4, 5.

Alnus glutinosa cultivars

There are several ornamental cultivars of Common Alder. They are valuable in horticulture because of their ability to thrive in wet conditions. The leaves show various amounts of deep toothing. '**Quercifolia**' has indented rounded teeth reminiscent of an oak leaf. '**Laciniata**' has more deeply cut leaves with pointed lobes. It was produced originally in France in 1819. The ultimate "cut-leaf" effect occurs on the leaves of the 1859 cultivar '**Imperialis**', lobes extend almost to the midrib and the points are long and narrow. The lacy effect is pretty when the trees are planted by a river or lake.

Three more cultivars are shown overleaf.

'Imperialis'

'Laciniata'

Common Alder
young tree

'Pyramidalis'

'Aurea'

'Incisa'

'Pyramidalis'

Alnus japonica

Alnus hirsuta

Alnus glutinosa cultivars (continued)

Common Alder has thrown up a myriad of tree shapes and foliage types from time to time. Several of these have been selected for ornamental use. The upright tree '**Pyramidalis**', formerly called 'Fastigiata' is frequently used in parks and large gardens in damp places. There are several clones of it and the original selection is probably no longer identifiable. The golden form '**Aurea**' is very distinct. It was raised in 1860 and has soft yellow foliage which fades to light green by the end of summer. Another variant is '**Incisa**' which has cut leaves but the lobes are rounded. There are several clones of 'Incisa' in the nursery trade and the cultivar is usually reduced to "group" status.

Growth: variable. Hardiness: 70%. Choice: 1.

Alnus japonica

From north-east Asia and Japan this 25m tree has unusual narrow-elliptic leaves around 12cm long. It was introduced to the west before 1880 but remains rare in tree collections. Closely related to it is ***formosana*** which is very rare and no longer in cultivation.

Growth: 4-15-25. Hardiness: 50%. Choice: 4. Wood: 5.

Alnus hirsuta

This species is similar to Grey Alder, a pioneer wetland species which extends the range of Grey Alder eastwards into north-east Asia and Japan. It was introduced to the west in 1879 by Charles Maries, plant collector for the Veitch Nursery.

Growth: 4-14-20. Hardiness: 60-70%. Choice: 3. Wood: 5.

Sitka Alder *Alnus sinuata*

The huge range of this tundra and subalpine shrubby tree is from the Arctic Ocean through Alaska and down the west side of North America to California. In the south it is restricted to high mountain sites. It was introduced to Europe by Charles Sprague Sargent, director of the Arnold Arboretum in 1903. In cultivation it suffers badly from excessive heat and drought. As an upland 'nurse' species for plantations of forest trees it is ideal, soon forming thickets of vegetation which provide shelter above ground and fix atmospheric nitrogen in the soil. Research is also under way to explore the possibility of producing new cold-resistant hybrid alders using Sitka Alder as one parent. Like the other pioneer alders this species grows easily and quickly from seed, which incidentally floats on water, and it is responsive to regular coppicing. The counterpart of it in Europe is *Alnus viridis*.

Growth: 4-10-12. Hardiness: 100%. Choice: 1. Wood: 4, 5.

Alnus formosana

Sitka Alder

underside

new cone

developing ♀ flowers

old bark

Italian Alder

old cone

seeds

young bark

Caucasian Alder

Italian Alder

Caucasian Alder

Italian Alder *Alnus cordata*

Of the 35 species of alder world-wide Italian Alder is the least dependent upon permanent standing water in close proximity to its roots. It is native to Corsica, southern Italy and parts of Albania where it grows in dry woodlands up to 900m. It also occurs in lowland areas if conditions are right. Trees over 30m tall are known with stems around 1m thick. Although the timber is not of high quality it is good for low grade joinery, charcoal and pulp. Early growth may be fast, over 1m each year. The deciduous glossy green foliage, like a vigorous pear tree, makes this a particularly handsome tree. The species was introduced to horticulture outside its local range in 1820.

Growth: 8-20-30. Hardiness: 50%. Choice: 2. Wood: 2, 3, 4.

Caucasian Alder *Alnus subcordata*

From along the Caspian Sea coast, the Caucasus and Iran, this species grows in mixed damp woodland or as a pioneer species on bare devastated ground following floods or land-slips. It is closely related to Italian Alder, but generally makes a smaller tree. The leaves may be up to 16cm long but they are dull green. Caucasian Alder was introduced to Britain around 1838 and France in 1861 but very few specimens were ever planted. There is renewed interest in selected vigorous provenances of it for wood production. In its native region there is some introgression with Common Alder (p. 317).

Growth: 8-14-20. Hardiness: 40%. Choice: 2. Wood: 2, 3, 4.

Green Alder *Alnus viridis*

This is a variable mostly shrubby species from alpine locations in south-east and central Europe. It was introduced to Britain in 1820 but was seldom planted. Recently it has been tried as a soil improver and shelter species on harsh upland forestry sites. The Ascomycete fungus *Frankia* produces nodules on alder roots which are able to fix atmospheric nitrogen in the soil. This nourishes the host plant and eventually other species growing nearby.

Growth: 2-4-6. Hardiness: 70-80%. Choice: 2.

Alnus × spaethii

This is an artificial hybrid made between Japanese and Caucasian Alders in 1908 purely for ornamental purposes. It has the rapid growth of the Caucasian parent combined with hybrid vigour and the narrowish leaves of Japanese Alder, which emerge coppery-purple. The late winter male catkins are highly decorative.

Growth: 8-18-20. Hardiness: 40%. Choice: 1.

Alnus maximowiczii

From Japan and the adjacent mainland of south-east Asia this alder is small in size but it has thick shoots, large leaves and stout yellow catkins. It is closely related to *Alnus sinuata* (p. 319) from across the Pacific Ocean in Alaska. Plants were introduced to the west in 1914.

Growth: 2-8-10. Hardiness: 50-60%. Choice: 1.

cone

bud

Green Alder   *Alnus maximowiczii*   *Alnus × spaethii*

young cones

Grey Alder

old cones

'Aurea'

'Laciniata'

'Ramulis Coccineis' twig

♀ young flowers ♂

'Angustissima'

Grey Alder
underside

Grey Alder

'Pendula'

'Aurea'

Grey Alder *Alnus incana*

The grey pubescent shoots and leaf undersides give this aggressive hardy pioneer species its name. It is native to mainland Europe, Russia and the Caucasus. It grows closer to the Arctic tundra in the north of its range than Common alder. Its counterpart in North America is *Alnus incana* subsp. *rugosa*. Trees almost 30m tall are known but growth is usually restricted to low thickets. In cultivation it has been known to grow incredibly fast, for example 9m in nine years after planting. Suckers are common and cut or naturally broken stems recover by coppicing freely. It is an ideal pioneer species to plant on reformed derelict land or capped rubbish tips.

There are several interesting cultivars of Grey Alder including '**Laciniata**' which has deeply dissected leaves. '**Angustissima**' has leaves reduced to just a strip of green along the midrib and the main veins. The cultivar '**Aurea**' has good yellow foliage especially in the spring. Its catkins are deep pink for about three weeks before the leaves emerge. '**Ramulis Coccineis**' is a selection of the same thing. The Dutch clone '**Pendula**' is a superb strongly weeping tree which at present is under used in landscaping. It is a picturesque water-side feature plant.
Growth: 5-18-22. Hardiness: 90%. Choice: 2. Wood: 5.

Red Alder *Alnus rubra*

The whole length of the North American west coast is home to this hardy pioneer species. Gravel workings, road lines, land slip sites and devastated areas, especially after flooding, are all colonized immediately by this tree if there is a seed source nearby. Provenances from the Cascade Mountains in particular have been imported to Europe. They have potential as forest trees and as site-improvers for other timber producing species. Complete tree cover to 'thicket' stage can be achieved in plantations only five years old.
Growth: 8-18-20. Hardiness: 50-70%. Choice: 2.
Wood: 1, 2, 3, 4, 5.

Alnus nepalensis

From the eastern Himalayas and western China, this 18m tree has elliptic-lanceolate leaves up to 18cm long. It was described by David Don in the nineteenth century but is extremely rare in cultivation.
Growth: 5-9-18. Hardiness: 40-50%. Choice: 4.

Alnus cremastogyne

Potentially huge, 40m in height, this tree is from western China. It was introduced to the west in 1908 but is very rare in cultivation. The elliptic finely toothed leaves are 6-14cm long. The solitary strobiles are on 6cm slender stalks.
Growth: 4-8-20. Hardiness: 40-50%. Choice: 4.
Wood: 1, 2, 3, 4, 5.

Red Alder

cone scale

seed ×3

Alnus nepalensis

Alnus cremastogyne

♂ flowers

♀ flowers

fruit

autumn

ripe fruit

seedling

Common Hornbeam

324

HORNBEAM FAMILY • Betulaceae (syn. Carpinaceae)

Common Hornbeam *Carpinus betulus*

There are over 30 species of hornbeam recognized world-wide, distributed throughout all of the north temperate regions. There is little variation between species and many are difficult to distinguish when grown in cultivation. The Common Hornbeam is a typical type, slightly larger than most at around 20-25m in height and width. The deciduous leaves are up to 12cm long with 10-14 straight parallel veins and unevenly fine toothed margins. This tree can be instantly distinguished from broadly similar-looking beech by the presence of teeth on the leaves. In the autumn the foliage, including numerous clusters of seed wings, turns to golden yellow with a grand finale of brilliant orange. Male and female flowers are separate but on the same tree. Females develop into small nuts, in drooping clusters, each with a trident wing, the central lobe being longer than the other two. Individual trees may live for several hundred years, particularly if they are pollarded. Stems can exceed 1m in diameter and frequently develop a slightly oval cross section. The bark is smooth, thin and silvery-grey throughout the life of the plant. Old trees often become heavily fluted like Zelkova (p. 415).

The natural range of Common Hornbeam extends right across central Europe including south-east England and southern Sweden to Asia Minor. It has become naturalized over a wide area following cultivation for its hard heavy wood in former times. It was traditionally used for ox yokes and heavy beams. The wood is so hard that it was unpopular among woodmen using sharp edged hand tools. As firewood it has a calorific value almost equal to coal. In order to keep on harvesting poles of manageable size trees were often pollarded. Branches 10-15cm in diameter were relatively easy to cut with a heavy axe, and they re-grew in about 20 years. This already sustainable management system was improved further by keeping stems at wide spacing and grazing domestic animals on the pasture below. Hornbeam is resistant to bark damage when it is chewed by animals, including rabbits and squirrels, even when the outer surface is completely removed, exposed cambium often heals over completely.

Regeneration of hornbeam is a slow process. Most seed is taken by animals and birds. Mice and voles find it an acceptable size to take away or eat on the spot. Seeds that do reach the soil may take one to three years to germinate, thus providing further opportunities for predation. Once germinated early growth of young seedlings is slow and suppression by weeds is often fatal in the first year. This is an excellent hedging plant. Like beech, clipped hedges will retain dead pale brown leaves for much of the winter.

Growth: 4-10-20. Hardiness: 50%. Choice: 2, 3. Wood: 1, 2, 5.

underside

Common Hornbeam
autumn

Weeping Hornbeam

fruit

'Quercifolia'

'Quercifolia'

Carpinus betulus 'Incisa'

Weeping Hornbeam

Carpinus betulus 'Fastigiata'

Weeping Hornbeam
Carpinus betulus 'Pendula'

This cultivar is an ideal weeping tree for garden landscaping where water may not be present. It does not rely on a pond or lake-side situation to thrive. Although nursery catalogues often list it as a slow growing or dwarf tree, it can easily reach 10m in height and much the same in width. Young trees on a good site will exceed 4m in 10-15 years but, unlike weeping willows, strongly weeping shoots do not develop at an early age. The summer shade cast by a weeping hornbeam can not be surpassed. Furthermore the foliage is seldom infested by insects which habitually rain down debris and honeydew. In the autumn the leaves turn to orange-brown before falling.

Growth: 5-10-12. Hardiness: 50%. Choice: 1.

Carpinus betulus 'Fastigiata'

The upright form of hornbeam is a valuable town park and street tree. For 20-30 years it remains narrow with upright branches and a persistent stem. Later in life it slowly broadens, eventually resembling the species but with uniformly dense foliage. This cultivar was introduced in 1883, probably as 'Pyramidalis'. A form selected in Holland, 'Frans Fontaine', appears to remain narrow for much longer. It is widely distributed as an urban street tree. Although the narrow potentially weak branch forks are a possible disadvantage in town planting, the twigs are thin and light and the wood is strong, so branches seldom fall. There is also a slower growing fastigiate form of hornbeam called '**Columnaris**', first cultivated in 1891.

Growth: 5-12-20. Hardiness: 50%. Choice: 1, 2.

Carpinus betulus 'Incisa'

Various clones with deeply toothed leaves have often occurred in cultivation since the first recorded plant in 1789. They are not strictly 'cut-leaved' as beech and alder might be, but they have leaves which are twisted and finely serrated around a series of exaggerated teeth. These are sometimes drawn to a fine point and sometimes rounded. '**Quercifolia**', the Oak-leaved Hornbeam, is no longer recognized as a separate cultivar but is included in the 'Incisa group'. These make full-sized trees around 15m tall, usually with a broad head of branches. Most specimens insist on reverting to normal foliage which is difficult to control when the trees are large.

Growth: 5-14-22. Hardiness: 50%. Choice: 1.

'Columnaris'

Carpinus betulus '**Fastigiata**'
old tree

Carpinus × *schuschuensis*

Carpinus henryana

Carpinus tschonoskii

fruit

fruit

Carpinus × *schuschuensis*
young tree

Carpinus tschonoskii

Carpinus polyneura

Carpinus × schuschuensis

The natural range of this Caucasian hybrid also includes northern Iran. It is a cross between Common Hornbeam (p. 325) and Oriental Hornbeam (p. 331). The leaves are usually smaller than Common Hornbeam but otherwise it is difficult to distinguish from either parent. It has arisen from natural introgression between the species.
Growth: 4-10-20. Hardiness: 50%. Choice: 2. Wood: 1, 2, 3, 5.

Carpinus henryana

In its native China this is a 15m tall tree, but in cultivation it is usually much less. The 5-6cm leaves are smaller than Common Hornbeam and more lanceolate, with 12-16 pairs of parallel veins. Ernest Wilson introduced it to the west in 1907.
Growth: 4-12-15. Hardiness: 50%. Choice: 1. Wood: 5.

Carpinus tschonoskii

From Japan, north-east China and Korea, this tree also closely resembles Common Hornbeam. It is probably only a regional variant which occurs under various names across the world. It was introduced to the west in 1901 but remains obscure or unidentified.
Growth: 3-9-12. Hardiness: 50%. Choice: 2. Wood: 1, 2, 3, 5.

Carpinus polyneura

This name was allocated to two fairly indistinct trees by different authorities in the late nineteenth century. The leaf illustrated is from the plant at present in the nursery trade in Britain, which is probably an earlier Chinese introduction of *Carpinus turczaninowii* (p. 331). It is a graceful shrub or small rounded tree.
Growth: 3-8-10. Hardiness: 50%. Choice: 4.

American Hornbeam *Carpinus caroliniana*

Known in America as Blue Beech or Water Beech, where the wood of this tree is used for tool handles and other small items for which a strong hard material is needed. The name beech, wrongly applied to this member of the birch family, was given to American Hornbeam because of its similar-looking smooth, thin grey bark. In its native eastern North America this is usually a small rounded tree, often with several stems. Heights over 8m are seldom seen but trees this wide are frequent. The leaves are 8-10cm long with double-toothed margins and 8-12 straight parallel veins. This is a tree of moist woodlands, especially stream and lake sides. Within its huge north-south distribution, from Ontario to Florida, it encounters a wide range of different environmental conditions which influence its size and shape. It was introduced to Europe in 1812 by Frederick Pursh, a German botanist who lived in America.
Growth: 4-12-14. Hardiness: 40-70%. Choice: 2, 3. Wood: 1, 5.

underside   fruit

American Hornbeam

European Hop Hornbeam

Oriental Hornbeam

Carpinus turczaninowii

fruit

fruit

fruit

European Hop Hornbeam

Carpinus fangiana

fruit

Carpinus fargesiana

330

European Hop Hornbeam *Ostrya carpinifolia*

Closely related to the hornbeams and still part of the Birch family, this deciduous 20m tree comes from southern Europe and Asia Minor. It was first cultivated as an ornamental specimen tree in 1724. The 5-10cm leaves are doubly toothed, ovate to oblong with an acuminate tip. Each one has 12-15 pairs of parallel veins. The distinctive fruits are in tight 3-5cm drooping clusters with overlapping papery scales reminiscent of a hop (*Humulus*). Young trees are broadly conical, then many of them spread out in middle age until they are wider than they are high.
Growth: 5-16-20. Hardiness: 50%. Choice: 1, 2. Wood: 1, 5.

Oriental Hornbeam *Carpinus orientalis*

A tree or large shrub, up to 16m tall, with dense foliage and branches. The leaves are 2-6cm long with distinct irregular teeth. The fruits are held in broad bracts which tend to overlap in a similar way to the Hop Hornbeam. The species was introduced in 1735 but has remained rare in cultivation.
Growth: 5-12-16. Hardiness: 50%. Choice: 2. Wood: 5.

Carpinus turczaninowii

From Korea, northern China and Japan this rare tree, seldom more than 10m tall is broadly similar to Oriental Hornbeam. It has 5cm serrate leaves and tight clusters of seeds. The variety *ovalifolia* has slightly larger and distinctly toothed leaves. These are bright red when they first appear.
Growth: 3-8-10. Hardiness: 50%. Choice: 2.

Carpinus fangiana

This remarkable Chinese hornbeam has relatively large leaves up to 30cm long with 24-34 pairs of parallel veins. The female catkins may be in 50cm strings followed by equally long clusters of winged fruits. The bracts, or wings, bend round to protect the seeds. Trees 18m are known but there are very few of them in cultivation.
Growth: 3-10-15. Hardiness: 50%. Choice: 1. Wood: 1, 5.

Carpinus fargesiana

This 6m shrubby tree has ovate-lanceolate leaves up to 7cm long. It originated in western China but is very rare in cultivation. It should not be confused with the Japanese tree originally named *Carpinus fargesii* which is now *Carpinus laxiflora* var. *macrostachya*.
Growth: 2-4-6. Hardiness: 50%. Choice: 4.

Carpinus cordata

This small south-east Asian tree has scaly fissured bark and large leaves up to 12cm long with 15-20 pairs of veins. The leaf base is strongly cordate (heart-shaped). It was introduced to the west in 1879.
Growth: 3-10-15. Hardiness: 50%. Choice: 1.

Japanese Hornbeam *Carpinus japonica*

The narrow elliptic leaves of this 15m tall Japanese tree are quite distinctive. They are 5-10cm long with 20-24 pairs of veins. The seed bracts overlap one another, like the Hop Hornbeam, in drooping 6cm clusters. It was first introduced to the west in 1879.
Growth: 4-12-15. Hardiness: 50-60%. Choice: 2. Wood: 1, 5.

Carpinus cordata

Japanese Hornbeam

♀ flower

♂ flowers

wild fruit

cultivated fruit (Filbert)

Common Hazel

'Purpurea'

'Aurea'

'Heterophylla'

fruit

Turkish Hazel young tree

underside

Turkish Hazel

332

HAZEL FAMILY · Corylaceae

Hazel *Corylus avellana*

Usually this is a multi-stemmed shrubby plant, seldom over 7m tall, but 15m trees are known. It is native in much of Europe, western Asia and parts of North Africa. As a component of ancient forest it prefers moist lowland soils and is often found growing in the shade of deciduous trees, especially oak. The bark is smooth, glossy-brown and peeling slightly. On old stems, which seldom exceed 18cm in thickness, it is rough, grey and scaly. The rough-textured 10cm leaves are more or less round with double teeth, sometimes with a suggestion of shallow pointed lobes. Male flowers are showy late winter catkins, but females, on the same plant, are minute jewel-like pink extensions to ordinary looking buds. The fruits, familiar hazel nuts, are ovoid and half enclosed in a ragged-edged calyx. The name *Corylus* from the Greek 'horys' meaning helmet, refers to this.

The cultivar '**Aurea**' has yellowish-green foliage and cultivated as an ornamental garden plant since 1864. '**Contorta**' (Corkscrew Hazel), discovered in England in 1863, has grotesquely twisted twigs and deformed leaves. '**Heterophylla**', which still appears under several alternative descriptive names, has well developed teeth and lobes on otherwise normal hazel leaves. '**Pendula**' is an old 1867 plant with weeping shoots.

Growth: 7-12-15. Hardiness: 60-70%. Choice: 3.
Wood: 3 (species).

Filbert *Corylus maxima*

Hazel bushes cultivated especially for fruit belong to this genus. There are many named fruiting varieties. In addition there is an ornamental cultivar called '**Purpurea**' which is quite outstanding (if you like purple foliage). It rivals any other species of tree in this colour range and even produces purple-tinted nuts.

Growth: 5-8-10. Hardiness: 50%. Choice: 3.

Turkish Hazel *Corylus colurna*

This large conical tree, up to 25m tall, is both ornamental and productive. Its pinkish-brown hardwood timber is of fine quality and good for cabinet making. Even the decorative root can be used for inlay work and veneers. The original range is south-east Europe and Asia Minor, but it has been cultivated over a much wider area since before 1580. As an ornamental specimen it is a tidy tree, usually with a straight stem. The late winter male catkins are decorative and the summer foliage is a strong green. The nuts occur in clusters, each one around 1cm across.

Growth: 5-18-25. Hardiness: 50%. Choice: 1, 2, 3.
Wood: 1, 5.

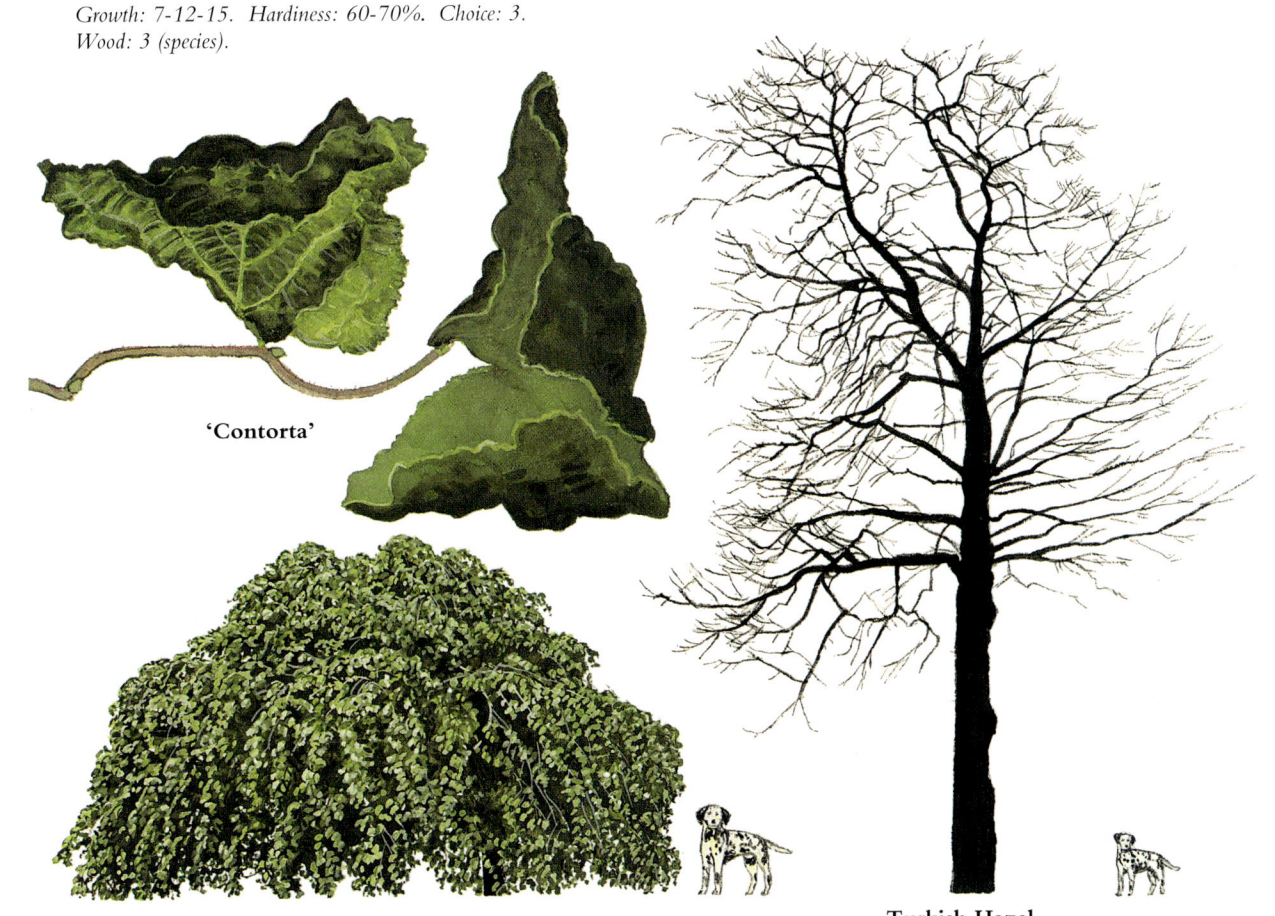

'Contorta'

'Pendula'

Turkish Hazel

fruit

seeds

Rauli

Roble Beech
bark

underside

spring leaf

undersid[e]

autumn

Rauli

Roble Beech

BEECH FAMILY • Fagaceae

Rauli *Nothofagus nervosa*

Formerly known as *Nothofagus procera*, this is a forest tree from central Chile and western Argentina. It was introduced to Britain in 1913 and has gradually become accepted as a valuable timber producer, provided frost-hardy strains are chosen. Rapid growth in plantations to around 20-25m in height may be expected on moist, slightly acid rocky hillsides.

The smooth bark is like beech. After several years long shallow vertical fissures develop. Ascending twigs have alternate zig-zag buds like beech. Each of these is about 1cm long, sharply pointed and red-brown in colour. The 8-10cm deciduous leaves resemble hornbeam. They have 14-18 pairs of straight impressed veins. The male flowers are small and produced singly. Females, on the same tree, are in threes in tiny glandular tufts in the leaf axils. Through the summer these become spiky green fruits consisting of three nuts in a husk. Two triangular ones either side of a flattened one forming a diamond shape in cross section. The tree produces very good autumn foliage colour.

Growth: 8-18-25. Hardiness: 30-40%. Choice: 2, 3. Wood: 1, 2, 3, 5.

Roble Beech *Nothofagus obliqua*

Roble in Spanish means oak and this tree has much in common with several deciduous oaks. The timber is hard and durable, the stem is rugged and the twisted branches reach up to about 30m. The scalloped oval 4-7cm leaves have 8-11 straight veins.

Roble Beech is native in Chile and Argentina including cold southern districts. In cultivation it is more hardy than Rauli but less elegant. It was introduced, possibly by William Lobb, in 1849 and again by Henry Elwes in 1902.

Growth: 6-16-28. Hardiness: 40%. Choice: 2, 3. Wood: 2, 3, 5.

Oval-leaved Southern Beech
Nothofagus betuloides

This hardy evergreen forest species grows in southern South America down to Tierra del Fuego. It was introduced into cultivation in 1830. The dense 2-3cm dark shining green leaves make this a very ornamental small tree. Multiple twisted stems are often produced. The shoots are resinous and sticky. In spring the tiny male flowers have bright red anthers and just before the exhausted evergreen leaves fall they turn bright yellow.

This species is often confused in cultivation with the closely related *Nothofagus dombeyi*, introduced in 1916. *Dombeyi* is ultimately a larger shapely tree with slightly larger leaves. It is also more likely to have a single main stem.

Growth: 4-10-18. Hardiness: 30-40%. Choice: 2, 3. Wood: 3, 5.

fruit

Roble Beech

Oval-leaved Southern Beech

Common Beech

underside

♀ flower detail

♂ flower detail

autumn

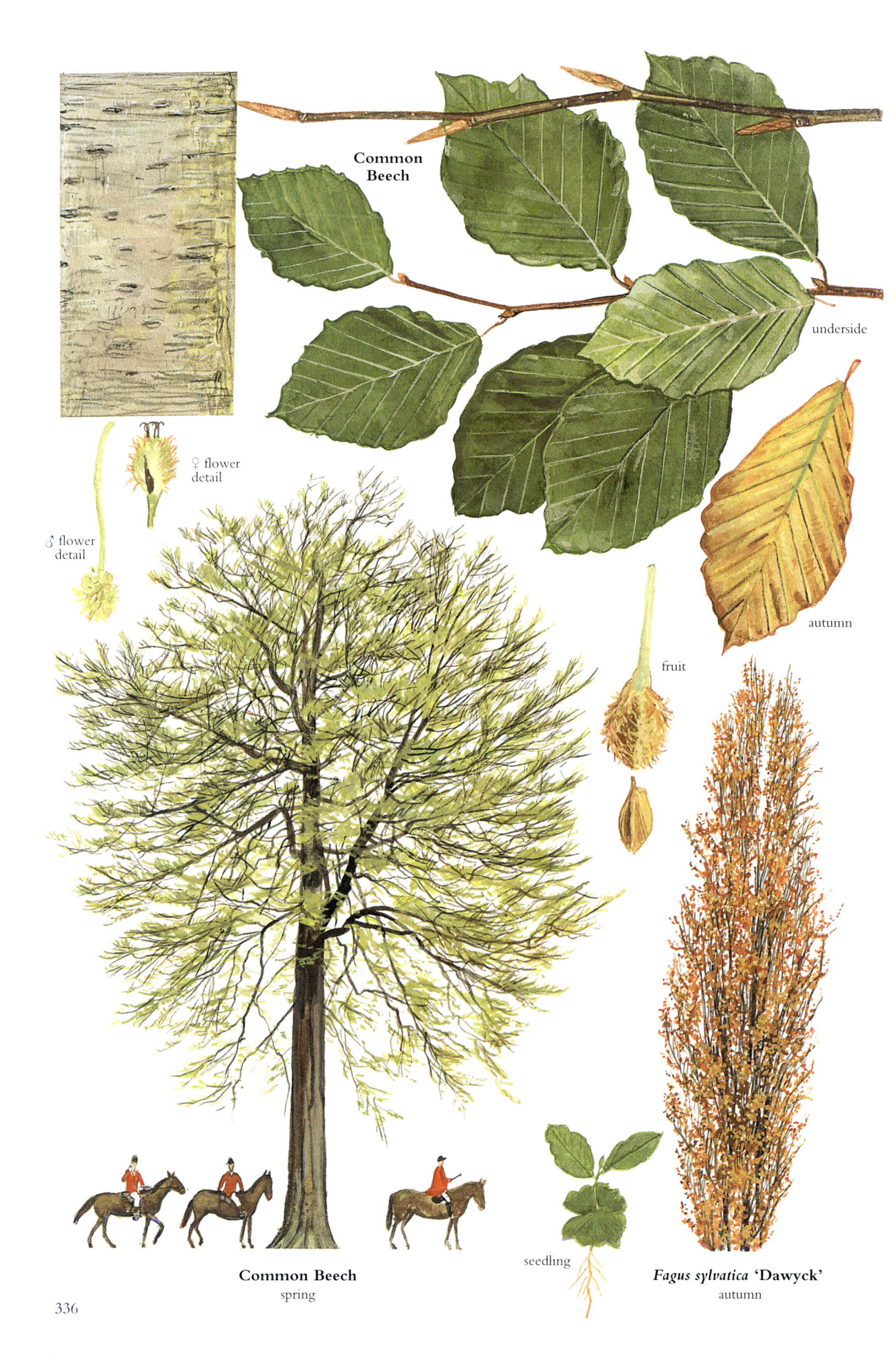

fruit

seedling

Common Beech
spring

Fagus sylvatica **'Dawyck'**
autumn

Common Beech *Fagus sylvatica*

The natural range of Common or European Beech includes most of Europe northwards to southern England, Denmark and just into Russia. In the south it extends from the Pyrenees to Turkey. It has been planted extensively far beyond this region. It is a shade-tolerant deciduous forest tree which will grow at close spacing and casts dense shade in summer. Few plants, except fungi, will survive under it. Perhaps the most distinctive feature of beech is the smooth thin silvery-grey bark typically on a straight stem supporting a broad head of branches. Trees up to 35m tall are frequent and a specimen 46m high, and another with a 231cm diameter stem have been recorded. Although non-durable, the wood of beech has many domestic uses, notably for furniture. Alien animals in Europe, including rabbits and grey squirrels, cause severe damage to young and middle aged trees by chewing the bark.

In former times pigs and deer were allowed to feed on fallen beech nuts (mast). In France nuts were also used to fatten poultry, especially turkeys, giving the meat a particular flavour. They are bad for horses in large amounts. Oil from pressed ripe nuts was used for cooking and for oil lamps.

A large number of forms and cultivars have been propagated: some of the more widespread are covered here and on the following pages.

Growth: 4-10-35. Hardiness: 50%. Choice: 2, 3.
Wood: 1, 4.

Fagus sylvatica 'Dawyck'

Sometime before 1850 this upright tree appeared on the Dawyck Estate in southern Scotland. It is a tall, 25m narrow tree reminiscent of Lombardy Poplar (p. 277). The foliage is bright green and held in dense upward pointing sprays. In winter the red-brown buds and young shoots give the tree a distinctive warm purplish-brown colour, which distinguishes it from Lombardy Poplar.

Growth: 5-15-25. Hardiness: 50%. Choice: 1.

Fagus sylvatica 'Pendula'

Although strongly pendulous, with all the shoots apparently pointing straight downwards, this tree manages to grow to huge dimensions. Specimens 20m tall are not unusual, some have a single stem and others develop a cluster of low branches or secondary stems. Given space and time some individuals will layer their branch tips and develop a ring of mature stems round the original tree. First cultivated in 1836, it makes a highly ornamental specimen for gardeners with enough space to grow it.

Growth: 4-10-20. Hardiness: 50%. Choice: 1 (requires space).

Fagus sylvatica 'Zlatia' is described on p. 345.

Fagus sylvatica 'Pendula'

Fagus **sylvatica 'Zlatia'**
spring

'Rohan Pyramid'

'Rohan Gold'

'Cochleata'

'Rohan Pyramid'

'Tortuosa'

Fagus sylvatica Rohan cultivars

The original purple form of Fern-leaved Beech 'Rohanii' (p. 343) was produced around 1894. It produces fertile nuts so seedlings are often produced from it. By using controlled pollination entirely new plants can be raised. '**Rohan Pyramid**' is just such a plant. It has cut leaves, although the degree to which they are incised is variable, and a columnar outline. The parentage probably involved a tree from the 'Dawyck' group (p. 337). '**Rohan Gold**' was raised in Holland in 1970 using a similar technique. 'Rohanii' was crossed with the Golden Beech (p. 345) to give a fern-leaved golden beech. It does not keep its golden colour all summer, but is a delight in the spring.
Growth: variable. Hardiness: 50%. Choice: 1.

Weeping Purple Beech
Fagus sylvatica 'Purpurea Pendula'

This small domed pendulous tree was created in 1865 by grafting a prostrate purple scion on to a stock at least 2m high. Except for occasional reverting twigs, which should be quickly cut off, it grows outwards and downwards until it reaches the ground. The original selection was of a very dark-leaved form so the tree is quite unmistakable and makes a strong landscape statement.
Growth: 3-4-5. Hardiness: 50%. Choice: 1.

Fagus sylvatica aberrant cultivars

'**Tortuosa**' is a tangled spreading tree which is reluctant to grow upwards but cannot be accurately described as pendulous either. It was cultivated in 1861 by grafting some deformed growth from a sport or 'Witch's broom', on to a standard stock. Unlike the shoots the green deciduous foliage is not usually contorted. '**Cristata**', the Cockscomb Beech, is a slow-growing tree raised in 1811, probably in the same way as 'Tortuosa'. Its leaves are distorted (see p. 344), usually pale green and packed tightly together on short shoots. '**Cochleata**' is another bushy slow-growing plant raised in 1842. It has quite deeply toothed leaves.
Growth: variable. Hardiness: 50%. Choice: 1.

Weeping Purple Beech

'Cristata'

Cut-leaved Beech

'Purpurea Tricolor'

Fagus sylvatica 'Remillyensis'

Fagus sylvatica 'Remillyensis'

'Albovariegata'

Cut-leaved Beech *Fagus sylvatica* 'Heterophylla group'

With the exception of 'Aspleniifolia', which is always grafted, cut-leaved green beeches should now all be placed in this group. It includes the old cultivars 'Incisa' and 'Laciniata' and the numerous cut-leaved seedlings they produce. It is impossible to separate them morphologically. The advantage of growing a 'Heterophylla group' tree is its inability to revert. This is because it is on its own roots. The main disadvantage is that most specimens have leaves which are less deeply cut than 'Aspleniifolia', (p. 343).

Growth: 4-15-30. Hardiness: 50%. Choice: 1 (requires space).

Fagus sylvatica 'Remillyensis'

This pendulous tree with twisted branches is usually grafted at or above head height, is a good smaller alternative to 'Pendula', the Weeping Beech. 'Pendula' (p. 337) itself has the potential to grow to a very large size and quickly runs out of space in a restricted garden situation. 'Remillyensis' has reached 15m in height but seems unlikely to grow much larger. It has a dense green billowing top with tresses of lax branch tips.

Growth: 3-10-15. Hardiness: 50%. Choice: 1.

Fagus sylvatica variable foliage cultivars

The cultivar 'Tricolor' has leaves that are splashed with white on a green background with a pink margin. **'Purpurea Tricolor'** is the purple form of the same thing, formerly called 'Roseomarginata' and produced in 1888. **'Albovariegata'** is an old 1770 selection with green leaves streaked with white and yellow. Shaded leaves tend to revert to green. It was formerly called 'Argenteovariegata', a reference to the silvery-white variegation. **'Luteovariegata'** is very similar except the colour is deeper yellow and it is sharply defined around the margins of the leaves. Grafted trees often revert to ordinary green foliage and this quickly outgrows the variegation. Huge old beech trees, originally of this cultivar, are sometimes seen with just one or two variegated branches remaining. Further investigation will generally reveal a faint graft line near the base of the stem. The interesting and rare cultivar **'Quercifolia'** is a small shade-tolerant tree with green leaves which are deeply indented. These resemble an ornamental oak's and at a glance the tree can easily be confused with some species of oak. This is not a spectacular plant and must be regarded as a curiosity rather than an ornamental tree.

Growth: variable. Hardiness: 50%. Choice: 1.

'Quercifolia'

'Luteovariegata'

'Spaethiana'

'Rohanii'

'Ansorgei'

Fern-leaved Beech

Fern-leaved Beech

'Rohanii'

342

Purple Beech *Fagus sylvatica*

Purpurea group

Purple, or Copper, Beeches raised from seed fall into this group. Ordinary seeding beech trees may produce 1 in 1000 plants with coppery leaves. Most are pale and suffused with green, others turn out muddy brown. Occasionally a deep rich purple-leaved plant is produced. Existing Copper Beech trees seed freely and produce a far greater proportion of copper-coloured seedlings but these can seldom be relied upon to retain good colour, especially if planted in shady situations.

Growth: 4-15-30. Hardiness: 50%. Choice: 1 (requires space).

Fagus sylvatica purple-leaved cultivars

Almost black leaves are produced on the grafted cultivar '**Spaethiana**' but it does not seem to be fashionable at present and has become rare in cultivation. The best and most readily available Copper Beech now is '**Riversii**' produced in 1880. In addition to having rich dark colouring the leaves are larger than common beech. Even in partial shade they keep their colour. Young shoots bear wine-red foliage which can be perpetuated by summer pruning or encouraged on a hedge by trimming. '**Dawyck Purple**' has similar foliage but on a narrow columnar tree.

The cultivar '**Rohanii**' is a cut-leaved form of Copper Beech. It is slow growing but produces a good looking straight tree. There are several named selections. The cut-leaved feature is taken to its limits in '**Ansorgei**' which has purple foliage reduced almost to the midrib with just a fringe of leaf on either side. It originated in 1891 but is not popular as a decorative specimen. Young grafted trees often produce one or two long untidy gangling shoots with dark skeletal leaves which look as if they have been eaten by caterpillars.

Growth: variable. Hardiness: 50%. Choice: 1.

Fern-leaved Beech
Fagus sylvatica 'Aspleniifolia'

Since it was first cultivated in 1804 this has remained the best cut-leaved beech. The leaves (as illustrated) vary between deeply cut and almost reduced to nothing. The effect is of misty green foliage spread over a billowing round-topped tree often up to 20m tall. This cultivar is always grafted close to ground level and its identity can often be confirmed by finding the graft union. A disadvantage is that occasional branches, on old established trees in particular, revert to plain leaves originating from the rootstock. It is often impossible to remove these because the extremities of the crown can not be reached and more drastic tree surgery would spoil the shape of the tree.

Growth: 4-10-20. Hardiness: 50%. Choice: 1 (requires space).

'Dawyck Purple'

young tree

'Riversii'

Fagus sylvatica
'Prince George of Crete'

'Miltonensis'

'Cristata'

'Grandidentata'

'Rotundifolia'

'Zlatia'

Fagus sylvatica 'Prince George of Crete'

The largest beech leaves of all, up to 17cm long, occur on the 1898 selection of Common Beech named in honour of Prince George of Crete. It actually appears to be a cultivar of *Fagus sylvatica* forma *latifolia*, recognized as a distinct east European type some 34 years earlier. It is possible that in the eastern part of the range of Common Beech there is introgression with Oriental Beech (p. 347), which usually has larger leaves than the European tree.

Growth: 4-10-20. Hardiness: 50%. Choice: 2.

Fagus sylvatica green cultivars

'**Miltonensis**' is one of the many intermediates between 'Tortuosa' (p. 339) and 'Pendula' (p. 337). It was formerly regarded as a variety (*miltonensis*). The leaves resemble Common Beech but the branches tend to twist and droop. Another similar cultivar, probably with the same antecedents, is '**Grandidentata**' but it has distinctive indented leaves like those of 'Cochleata' (p. 339).

Growth: variable. Hardiness: 50%. Choice: 1.

Fagus sylvatica golden cultivars

There are yellow-leaved beech trees in cultivation of every shape and size, most are potentially large. '**Zlatia**', the Golden Beech, is a big 20m tree which produces golden foliage in the spring (illustrated on p. 337), but fades to pale green through the summer. It is said to have appeared in Serbia (zlatia meaning gold), and was brought into cultivation in 1890. Some authorities place it in *Fagus moesiaca*, an intermediate species between Common and Oriental Beech. '**Dawyck Gold**' is an upright yellow-leaved cultivar produced in Holland in 1969 by crossing 'Zlatia' with 'Dawyck'. It becomes very tall and the slender fastigiate branches eventually tend to lean or break out of the column when it is old. In complete contrast, '**Aurea Pendula**', is a slender tree with thin, down-turned branches supporting curtains of golden-yellow foliage. Although in full light this cultivar produces some of the best yellow leaf colour, it suffers from sun scorch in hot summers and turns green in the shade.

Growth: variable. Hardiness: 40-50%. Choice: 1.

Fagus sylvatica small-leaved cultivars

'**Rotundifolia**' is a semi-fastigiate tree with small, 3cm, almost round leaves. It was first cultivated in 1872 and remains fairly popular, although the superb selection made from it at the Hillier Nursery in 1960 called '**Cockleshell**' is more widely planted. It is an upright plant with bright green, even smaller, round leaves.

The cultivar '**Cristata**' is described on p. 339.

Growth: variable. Hardiness: 50%. Choice: 1.

'Dawyck Gold' young tree

'Aurea Pendula'

'Cockleshell'

Oriental Beech

fruit

bud

autumn

Engler Beech

Fagus taurica

Oriental Beech

Engler Beech

Oriental Beech *Fagus orientalis*

This species extends the natural range of beech eastwards from Europe into the Caucasus, where it grows up to 1800m, and Asia Minor, Bulgaria and Persia. It is said to have more leaf veins, 7-10, but this feature is not constant or reliable for identification. On a good site this tree is larger in every respect than European Beech. It was introduced to horticulture before 1880 but at that time its precise identification appears to have been unclear. **Fagus taurica** is an intermediate between this and European Beech; its status is uncertain and some authorities regard it as a hybrid.

Growth: 4-16-30. Hardiness: 50%. Choice: 2, 3. Wood: 1, 5.

Engler Beech *Fagus engleriana*

Also known as Chinese Beech this species has sea-green foliage and a small, 10-15m, rounded outline. It occurs in mixed woodlands in central China and was introduced to the west in 1907 by Ernest Wilson.

Growth: 4-12-15. Hardiness: 50%. Choice: 1.

American Beech *Fagus grandifolia*

American Beech covers a huge range from Nova-Scotia to Florida and Texas. There are considerable provenance differences resulting from this wide distribution. Unlike many beeches it can easily spread through root suckers, so it regenerates itself freely if cut down or severely damaged. It was introduced to Europe in 1766 initially from southern locations but these introductions did not become popular and were probably tender. Later introductions of more hardy strains fared better.

Growth: 4-15-30. Hardiness: 70-80%. Choice: 2. Wood: 1, 5.

Siebold's Beech *Fagus crenata*

In its native Japan this beech grows from sea level to 1200m. On good ground it grows to 30m high, usually in mixed broadleaved and conifer woodland. Even in Japan it is not highly regarded as a timber tree. It was introduced to Europe in 1892 but is seldom planted.

Growth: 4-15-30. Hardiness: 40-60%. Choice: 2. Wood: 1, 5.

Japanese Beech *Fagus japonica*

Although able to grow to 25m, this hardy species is usually seen in cultivation as a large shrub. It has a tendency to produce multiple stems which lean outwards from the base. Japanese Beech, which is also an alternative name for *Fagus crenata*, was introduced to America and Europe in 1905 but it remains rare and confined to specialist collections.

Growth: 3-12-25. Hardiness: 50%. Choice: 2.

Fagus lucida

From western China this small 10m tree was introduced to the west in 1905. As the species name suggests it has bright glossy green 5-8cm leaves. Although completely hardy, it remains rare.

Growth: 2-5-10. Hardiness: 50%. Choice: 1.

Sweet Chestnut

twig detail

♂ flowers

♀ flower

fruit

Sweet Chestnut

summer

winter

Sweet Chestnut *Castanea sativa*

This south European tree is grown for its fruit and timber over a huge area, after being carried around the Roman Empire 2000 years ago. Originally it came from the Mediterranean coastal regions and eastwards to Asia Minor and the Caucasus, and closely allied south-east Asian species extended this natural range to China and Japan. Sweet Chestnut is a big, heavily-branched tree with vertically-ridged rough grey bark. The ridges may spiral round the tree trunk in either direction or simply point straight upwards. Trees dating back to the twelfth century are known, some with stems over 4m in diameter. The deciduous 20cm elliptic leaves have about 20 pairs of straight parallel veins each terminating in a 'saw' tooth. The flowers are bisexual catkins, female at the base and male towards the tip. The prominent male section, around 15-20cm long, matures in mid-summer. It is dull creamy-white with a strong, slightly unpleasant smell. After shedding pollen it falls away leaving small clusters of developing females which produce full-sized chestnuts in less than four months. Some trees are wholly male or female.

Chestnut timber has always been used as a cheap substitute for oak. It is, however, more durable than oak when used out of doors in contact with the soil. Large timbers have a tendency to 'shake' (crack) when they are sawn. Research indicates that on most sites trees over 50cm in diameter are most liable to shake. If poles, including coppice material, are harvested before that critical size is reached they are usually sound.

Growth: 5-20-30. Hardiness: 50%. Choice: 2, 3.
Wood: 1, 2, 3.

There are two notable ornamental forms of Sweet Chestnut. The cultivar '**Albomarginata**' has leaves similar to the species but with a creamy white edge which to a greater or lesser extent extends into the leaf between the veins, but old specimens tend to revert and then strong green growth soon obliterates any variegated foliage. The Cut-leaved Sweet Chestnut is listed under various names, '**Heterophylla**' is probably correct, although 'Laciniata' and 'Asplenifolia' are still used. The foliage varies considerably even between branches on the same tree. Some leaves are deeply incised while others only have exaggerated teeth. Cut leaves are not a persistent feature and trees tend to revert back to normal Sweet Chestnut.

'Heterophylla'

'Albomarginata'

Sweet Chestnut bark

Willow Oak

Ludwig's Oak

new leaves

Quercus × *schochiana*

2nd year   1st year
fruit

Willow Oak

summer   winter

Willow Oak *Quercus phellos*

The ovate-lanceolate 10cm × 2cm deciduous unlobed leaves are quite unlike ordinary Common Oak. They resemble a long-leaved willow except for the entire wavy margins. Each leaf is pale green with fine greyish pubescence on the underside. This is a swamp margin species in eastern North America although it does also tolerate dry sandy soils. Its love of moisture makes it a good street tree. The roots thrive in the damp conditions under paving and tarmac. It is widely used as an urban tree in America but tends to out-grow available space and often becomes a nuisance. European landscapers seldom use it, although it has been available in Europe since 1723. The little acorns are almost round and held in shallow flat cups. They mature in two years and are eagerly consumed by squirrels.

Growth: 3-8-20. Hardiness: 50%. Choice: 2, 3.
Wood: 1, 2, 3, 5.

Quercus × *schochiana*

This rare cross between Willow Oak and Pin Oak (p. 361) results in a rounded medium-sized tree. The leaves have the glossy finish of Pin Oak but more or less retain the Willow Oak shape except that some have occasional haphazardly arranged lobes. In the autumn they may colour bright yellow or in a mild year stay green and hang on well into the winter. This hybrid occurs in the wild in America and has been in cultivation since around 1894.

Growth: 3-8-20. Hardiness: 50%. Choice: 2, 3.
Wood: 1, 2, 3, 5.

Ludwig's Oak *Quercus* × *ludoviciana*

A tiny segment of American Red Oak which grows in small areas of Louisiana, south-east Virginia and north-west Florida, has crossed with Willow Oak to produce this pretty hybrid. The Red Oak parent is now called *Quercus falcata* var. *pagodifolia*. Ludwig's Oak is another wetland tree in the wild and a good city tree in cultivation. It was introduced to Europe in 1880 but has never become popular. The leaves vaguely resemble Red Oak with a lustrous green upper surface and sharply pointed lobes. In the autumn they turn to bright golden-brown and scarlet. This hybrid, Willow Oak and all its other hybrid forms, thrive best on moist acid soils.

Growth: 3-8-20. Hardiness: 40-50%. Choice: 2, 3.
Wood: 3, 5.

new leaves

Ludwig's Oak

var. *grosseserrata*

Quercus aliena

Quercus aliena
var. *acuteserrata*

Mongolian Oak
(not to scale)

Daimio Oak

Chinese Cork Oak

Sawtooth Oak underside

OAKS

Mongolian Oak *Quercus mongolica*

This small to medium-sized deciduous tree from south-east Asia has thick vigorous shoots and large 25cm leaves. Rare in cultivation, it is usually represented by the variety **grosseserrata** from Japan, which has more irregular leaves with forward-pointing tapered teeth. Introduced to the west by Charles Sprague Sargent in 1893.

Growth: 4-10-25. Hardiness: 60-70%. Choice: 2, 3. Wood: 1, 2, 3, 5.

Quercus aliena

Closely related to the American Chestnut Oak (p. 393), this species grows to around 20m with rich lustrous green foliage. The 20cm leaves have parallel veins and distinct pointed teeth. The undersides are closely felted and pale-coloured. Native to Japan, Korea and China and introduced to the west in 1908. The variety **acute-serrata**, which is the type usually represented in collections, has more pointed bristle-tipped teeth.

Growth: 3-8-20. Hardiness: 50%. Choice: 1, 3. Wood: 2, 3, 5.

Daimio Oak *Quercus dentata*

Of all the 'Chestnut Oaks' this 20m spreading branchy species has leaves least like Chestnut. However, they are very large, 25-30cm long, and held on strong stout shoots. Still rare in cultivation, it was introduced from south-east Asia in 1830.

Growth: 4-10-20. Hardiness: 50%. Choice: 1, 3. Wood: 2, 3.

Chinese Cork Oak *Quercus variabilis*

Although the leaves of this species are very like Sweet Chestnut this is not a 'Chestnut Oak', it is closely related to Sessile Oak (p. 381). A large tree with thick pale-coloured corky bark. The deciduous foliage often stays on until late in the year. The acorns are almost obscured by the cup, which has free reflexed scale tips. Robert Fortune first brought this species from China in 1861, but there have been several subsequent introductions.

Growth: 3-8-18. Hardiness: 50%. Choice: 1. Wood: 1, 2, 3, 5.

Sawtooth Oak *Quercus acutissima*

A relative of Turkey Oak (p. 369), this tree from south-east Asia was introduced in 1862. It has Chestnut-like leaves with bristle-tipped teeth.

Growth: 3-8-20. Hardiness: 50%. Choice: 2, 3. Wood: 2, 3.

Bamboo-leaved Oak *Quercus myrsinifolia*

This lovely little evergreen oak is a good alternative to Bamboo where space is limited. It is picturesque in a neat oriental way. The original cultivated plant was introduced to the west by Robert Fortune in 1854.

Growth: 2-8-18. Hardiness: 30-40%. Choice: 1.

Quercus lanuginosa

The status of this oak is uncertain. It is extremely rare and is no longer in cultivation. It was described by Jean de Lamarck (1744-1829) but the same species name was also given to a form of Sessile Oak.

Quercus ithaburensis

A small obscure tree from south-west Asia, probably an eastern extension of the 'Valonia Oak' (*Quercus macrolepis*) from further west in Asia. The angular, lobed, bristle-tipped deciduous leaves are often narrow-waisted.

Growth: 2-8-15. Hardiness: 20-40%. Choice: 1.

underside

Quercus lanuginosa

new leaf

Bamboo-leaved Oak

underside

Quercus ithaburensis

Chinkapin Oak

Quercus × *heterophylla*

Overcup Oak

Post Oak

new leaves

Spanish Oak
(see p. 357)

354

Chinkapin Oak *Quercus muehlenbergii*

Gotthilf Muhlenberg (1753-1815) a minister and botanist living in Pennsylvania first described this species, although 'Chinquapin' is the much older American Indian name for it, and also for Chestnut (*Castanea*). It makes a substantial tree up to 24m tall, usually growing on rocky limestone ground. Its natural range includes a large area of the United States south of the Great Lakes almost to the Gulf of Mexico. It was introduced to Europe in 1822.

Growth: 3-10-24. Hardiness: 50%. Choice: 3. Wood: 1, 2, 3, 5.

Quercus × *heterophylla*

This cross between Red Oak (p. 363) and Willow Oak (p. 351), occurs naturally with the parents in America. It was described from a specimen growing on John Bartram's property on the Schuylkill River near Philadelphia in 1812 by Francois Michaux. Jean de Lamarck also described a species *Quercus heterophylla* which he called Bartram's Oak. These two obscure plants are either the same thing or usually regarded as such in cultivation.

Growth: 3-8-20. Hardiness: 50%. Choice: 2, 3. Wood: 1, 2, 3, 5.

Overcup Oak *Quercus lyrata*

The species name refers to the lyre-shaped leaf, and the common name to the acorns being almost enclosed by a large round cup. It is a wetland tree from the southeast United States. Introduced in 1786.

Growth: 3-8-20. Hardiness: 40-50%. Choice: 1, 3. Wood: 1, 2, 3, 5.

Post Oak *Quercus stellata*

Posts and railway sleepers were made from the strong durable wood of this tree by settlers in America. It is native in the United States from the Atlantic coast, south of Massachusetts, west to Texas and Iowa. The species is divided into regional varieties on the southern edges of its range. The 2.5cm acorns are half enclosed in a deep cup and the rough leaves are covered with stiff stellate hairs. Post Oak was introduced to Europe in 1800 but is rare in cultivation.

Growth: 3-8-20. Hardiness: 50%. Choice: 2, 3. Wood: 1, 2, 3, 5.

Quercus × *falcata* var. *triloba*

This trident-leaved form of Spanish Oak (p. 357) is of uncertain botanical status. Three-lobed leaves are common within normal populations of *Quercus falcata* and there seems little justification for the variety designation.

Growth: 3-8-20. Hardiness: 40-50%. Choice: 4. Wood: 1, 2, 3, 5.

Quercus × *bushii*

This uncommon hybrid between *Quercus marilandica* and *Quercus velutina* occurs in a limited range around Oklahoma, Mississippi and the Alabama River.

Growth: 2-7-15. Hardiness: 50%. Choice: 4. Wood: 3, 5.

Water Oak *Quercus nigra*

From the southern United States of America this wetland tree can reach 30m in height with stems almost 1m thick. Apart from being wedge-shaped towards the base the 5-12cm leaves are totally unpredictable, some ovate and entire, others with occasional lobes. The almost round acorns are 1.5cm long and wide in a flat saucer-shaped cup. Water Oak, or 'Possum Oak' was introduced to Europe in 1723.

Growth: 4-10-30. Hardiness: 40-50%. Choice: 2, 3. Wood: 1, 2, 3, 5.

Quercus × *falcata* var. *triloba*

autumn

Quercus × *bushii*

Water Oak

Shumard Oak

Northern Pin Oak

autumn

Blackjack Oak

var. *pagodifolia*

1st year
2nd year

Shumard Oak

California Black Oak

Shumard Oak *Quercus shumardii*

Benjamin Franklin Shumard, the State geologist of Texas, was commemorated in the name of this south-west North American tree in 1860. It comes in two forms, one of which, variety *texana* the 'Texas Oak', is restricted to an area in and around the State of Texas. In cultivation Shumard Oak is generally a small to medium-sized tree with typical Red Oak leaves subdivided into pointed lobes. Autumn foliage turns a superb shade of glowing deep red.
Growth: 4-10-25. Hardiness: 50%. Choice: 2. Wood: 3, 5.

Northern Pin Oak *Quercus ellipsoidalis*

The species name *ellipsoidalis* is a reference to the shape of the mature acorns which are elliptical or almost round and held in a deep cup. The range of this oak in North America is concentrated around the Great Lakes from Ontario to Ohio and northern Missouri. It is a northern segregate of Pin Oak (p. 361) but seldom exceeds 20m in height. Trees first appeared in Europe after 1902.
Growth: 4-10-25. Hardiness: 60%. Choice: 2, 3. Wood: 3, 5.

Spanish Oak *Quercus falcata*

Also more descriptively called 'Cherrybark Oak' or 'Bottomland Red Oak', this species is a southern form of American Red Oak (p. 363). The variety **pagodifolia** has the most decorative foliage with leaves shaped like a pagoda. It was given variety status in 1824 but this has been challenged by botanists several times since. See also p. 363.
Growth: 5-10-25. Hardiness: 30-40%. Choice: 2, 3. Wood: 3, 5.

Blackjack Oak *Quercus marilandica*

This south-east North American species has very distinctive leaves which are roughly triangular and up to 16cm long and 10cm wide at the top. It is a dry upland and prairie edge species which was described in 1704 and introduced to cultivation in Europe in 1739.
Growth: 3-8-18. Hardiness: 50%. Choice: 2. Wood: 3, 5.

California Black Oak *Quercus kelloggii*

The physician and botanical artist Albert Kellogg is commemorated in the name of this west North American tree. It grows to 24m in height with a stem almost 1m thick. This is never a dominant tree in America but rather a component of deciduous or mixed conifer forest, particularly with Ponderosa Pine (p. 241). It was introduced to Europe in 1873 and is a brilliant golden-brown autumn colour feature.
Growth: 4-10-24. Hardiness: 40-50%. Choice: 2, 3. Wood: 3, 5.

Laurel Oak *Quercus laurifolia*

Semi-evergreen leaves like Laurel (*Laurus nobilis* p. 439) distinguish this 18-24m tree from other oaks in its native south-eastern United States of America. It prefers moist but well drained bottomlands and river banks. Cultivated plants arrived in Europe in 1786.
Growth: 3-8-20. Hardiness: 30-40%. Choice: 1.

Spanish Oak

Laurel Oak

'Magnifica'

'Nobilis'

Shingle Oak

new leaves

fruit variations

Black Oak

bud detail

Shingle Oak

Black Oak winter

Black Oak bark

Black Oak *Quercus velutina*

Two features mark this tree out in a mixed collection of oaks. It has the most shiny upper surfaces to the deciduous leaves of any oak. Even when lying on the ground in late winter the dead leaves remain brilliantly glossy and dark brown. The other, less obvious, feature is bright yellowish-orange inner bark. This was formerly used as a yellow dye. In America it is sometimes called Yellow Oak or Quercitron Oak. This is typically a tree of upland rocky sites in mixed or pure woodlands. Its natural distribution extends from southern Ontario and south-west Maine to Florida and Texas.

It is a medium-sized to large tree up to 24m tall with 10-20cm leaves. These have variable numbers of very angular lobes each terminating with a fine bristle. The acorns are up to 2cm long, half enclosed in a deep cup. Black Oak was introduced to Europe in 1800 but remains rare in cultivation. There are various cultivars with leaves of many shapes and sizes, including '**Nobilis**' and '**Magnifica**'.

Growth: 4-10-30. Hardiness: 60%. Choice: 2, 3.
Wood: 3, 5.

Shingle Oak *Quercus imbricaria*

Roof tiles (shingles) are made from cleft sections of this wood in central North America. It is a native species from Pennsylvania to North Carolina and west to Iowa and south Michigan. It grows in company with Black Oak and Post Oak (p. 355). The 8-15cm leaves are entire with wavy edges. Nearly round 1.5cm acorns are held in flat cups. They take two years to ripen. Shingle Oak was introduced to Europe by John Fraser in 1786.

Growth: 4-8-25. Hardiness: 50%. Choice: 2, 3.
Wood: 2, 3, 5.

Lea's Hybrid Oak *Quercus × leana*

The hybrid between Black Oak and Shingle Oak is a big vigorous tree which occurs with the parents in the wild. It has good features from both of them, including high quality hard timber and decorative qualities. The leaves are almost as glossy as Black Oak, and they too stay shiny after they have been on the ground for most of the winter. They are 10-15cm long, sometimes with angular bristle-tipped lobes but sometimes short toothed or more or less entire. The dark-coloured bark is smooth for many years, eventually becoming vertically cracked and rough.

The hybrid population consists of many different forms, some of which are probably back crosses with either Black or Shingle Oaks. It appears to have been first cultivated in Europe in 1850.

Growth: 4-8-25. Hardiness: 50%. Choice: 2, 3.
Wood: 2, 3, 5.

Lea's Hybrid Oak fruit

leaf variations

Shingle Oak

Lea's Hybrid Oak

new leaves

Pin Oak

1st year fruit

2nd year

autumn

Scarlet Oak

Pin Oak

Scarlet Oak

Pin Oak *Quercus palustris*

Few oaks can withstand flooding and wet ground as well as this species. It inhabits poorly drained and flat land throughout the eastern-central United States of America. Long-stemmed trees over 30m tall are common and nineteenth-century records show even larger specimens, 63m tall and 146cm in diameter, from the lower Ohio River region. The 'pins' in the name are short sharp spur shoots, especially on young trees, which show up very well in winter when the deciduous leaves are off. The bark is smooth and dark grey becoming pale like Red Oak (p. 363) for many years. It eventually becomes lightly fissured. The smooth leaves are deeply cut, with between 3-4 pairs of angular lobes each of which has several bristle-tipped points. They are glossy green in summer then turn rich brown or fiery-red in the autumn. The acorns are 1.2cm long and almost round, held in thin flat cups.

Pin Oak is a shallow rooting species because in its natural habitat it has adapted to adequate soil oxygen being limited to near the surface. This tree is easy to transplant even when quite large. It is ideal for city landscaping where space permits, because conditions under tarmac and paving closely resemble oxygen-starved marshy ground. The species was described in 1770 and sent to Europe soon after. It did not arrive in Britain until 1800.

Growth: 4-10-30. Hardiness: 60-70%. Choice: 1 (requires space), 2, 3. Wood: 2, 3, 5.

Scarlet Oak *Quercus coccinea*

This well known American Red Oak is a superb tree for autumn colour, especially the cultivar '**Splendens**'. As the name suggests, the leaves turn scarlet before they fall in the autumn. It makes a big billowing tree up to 25m tall with long bare main branches and an open top. The smooth dark grey bark eventually roughens and becomes fissured on the stems of old trees. The inner bark is bright orange-red. Like Red Oak (p. 363) the leaves are divided into angular lobes, each with several sharp bristle-tipped points. Some leaves are deeply cut almost to the midrib, resembling Pin Oak. The upper surface is glossy, more so than Red Oak, which is a useful identification feature. The 2-3cm acorns are half enclosed in a deep cup and take two years to mature.

This tree grows on a whole range of poor soils. It prefers sandy ridges and hillsides and is often found in mixed forests. The natural range extends from Maine to Georgia and west to north-east Mississippi and Indiana. It was sent to Europe in 1691 but – due to widespread confusion in the botanical world concerning American Red Oaks – not described and named until 1770.

Growth: 5-10-25. Hardiness: 60-70%. Choice: 1 (requires space), 2, 3. Wood: 2, 3, 5.

'Splendens'

1st year

2nd year

autumn

young tree in autumn

Scarlet Oak

old bark

bud detail

new leaves

♂ flowers

Red Oak

2nd year

1st year

autumn

young bark

Red Oak

'Aurea' spring

362

OAKS

Red Oak *Quercus rubra*

From Nova Scotia to Georgia this fast-growing hardy tree is both a timber producer and an ornamental specimen. In North America vast natural Red Oak forests containing 45m tall trees have been cut over by European settlers, had sufficient time to regenerate, and been cut over again. It is an upright tree usually with a single straight stem and a huge billowing top. The bark is silver-grey and smooth like Beech. The leaves are large, up to 22cm long, with 3-6 pairs of pointed angular sub-divided lobes on each side, each point terminating with a fine bristle tip. Upper surfaces are slightly lustrous but not as shiny as the similar-looking Scarlet Oak (p. 361). The solitary or paired ripening acorns, after two years, are egg-shaped and up to 2.5cm long, held in broad flat cups. Taxonomists have been rather unhelpful with this species which was given its present scientific name in 1753, then re-named *rubra maxima* in 1785 and *borealis* in 1817. In 1904 *Quercus rubra* var. *borealis* was put forward but this only remained until 1916. Botanists have also split the southern forms away from the rest in 1824 as *Quercus falcata* var *pagodifolia*, the 'Bottomland Red Oak' or 'Spanish Oak' (p. 357).

Red Oak is often planted in America as a park or shade tree. It is rather large for most street planting. In Europe, where it arrived in 1724, it thrives very well usually as a parkland specimen depending to some extent on the provenance. There are also limited plantations for timber. Growth and productivity are very rapid in favourable conditions but the untreated heavy wood is not particularly durable out of doors. It is pinkish-brown with some silvery figure on the radius. The sapwood is creamy-brown and relatively soft.

The cultivar '**Aurea**' is usually a smaller tree with butter-yellow foliage in the spring. As the summer progresses it gradually turns green and by early autumn is indistinguishable from the species. Strong sunlight can spoil the early foliage and frost may also be damaging. First cultivated in Holland in 1878, there appears to be more than one clone distributed under this cultivar name.

Growth: 5-10-25. Hardiness: 60-70%. Choice: 2, 3.
Wood: 1, 2, 3, 5.

'Aurea'
late spring

Red Oak
autumn

Chestnut-leaved Oak

autumn

underside

Cambridge Oak

Chestnut-leaved Oak

Quercus castaneifolia × *macranthera*

Chestnut-leaved Oak *Quercus castaneifolia*

Although closely related to Turkey Oak (p. 369), this tree actually resembles the Chestnut Oaks of America and indeed Chestnut (*Castanea*) itself. It comes from the Caucasus Region and Iran where good specimens reach 25m in height with a rounded outline. It was introduced into cultivation in 1846 but remains uncommon. Main stems often have a tendency to fork low down and to keep on forking as they extend. The bark is smooth for around 30-40 years then it fissures into small rough plates. Leaves up to 15cm long are oblong with 6-12 pairs of parallel veins and coarse forward-pointing teeth. The acorns are 2-3cm long and half enclosed in a cup which has recurved scales. The range of this species extends into North Africa as subspecies *incana* which is similar but has broader leaves.

Growth: 3-8-25. Hardiness: 40-50%. Choice: 2, 3. Wood: 3, 5.

Cambridge Oak *Quercus warburgii*

The first tree named Cambridge Oak arose in the University Botanic Garden in Cambridge before 1869. It is a fine semi-evergreen tree up to 20m tall but its origin is uncertain. The early specimens at Kew and Cambridge were then grafted on to Common Oak, but the tree at Bath in western England which is about the same age appears to be on its own roots. Its foliage is grey-green and persists on the tree through all but the most severe winters. Leaves around 13cm long have shallow irregular lobes with occasional mucronate teeth. The acorns are stalked like those of Common Oak. This tree is probably an artificial or accidental hybrid, which may have occurred first in the Genoa Botanic Garden in Italy.

Growth: 3-7-20. Hardiness: 50%. Choice: 1.

Quercus castaneifolia × *macranthera*

This is thought to be a hybrid between trees in two different and usually incompatible sections within the genus *Quercus*, although their geographic distribution does overlap where it was found. However, this is a vigorous plant with downy shoots and obovate leaves up to 20cm long with 8-12 pairs of parallel veins and rounded forward pointing shallow teeth. Acorns were collected for the Hillier Nurseries by Roy Lancaster in Iran around 1980 from *Quercus castaneifolia*.

Growth: 4-8-. Hardiness: 50%. Choice: 4.

Cambridge Oak

Quercus × *hispanica* **'Ambrozyana'**

Cork Oak

underside

Macedonian Oak

Cork Oak

Fulham Oak
French type

Lebanon Oak

var. *pinnata*

stripped bark

Cork Oak

Quercus × *hispanica* 'Ambrozyana'

This hybrid between Turkey Oak (p. 369) and Cork Oak arose in the arboretum of Count Ambrozy at Mlynany in the former Czechoslovakia before 1909. Although similar to Turkey Oak in most other respects it has semi-evergreen leaves. They are dark lustrous green above and pale grey on the underside. Once established the tree is tolerant of exposure and is quite hardy in northern Europe.

Growth: 3-7-18. Hardiness: 50%. Choice: 1 (requires space).

Fulham Oak   *Quercus* × *hispanica* 'Fulhamensis'

This cultivar is described on p. 371. These leaves (illustrated) are of the French, Trianon Garden, Paris, type described in 1783.

Cork Oak   *Quercus suber*

From southern Europe and North Africa Cork Oak has been extensively cultivated for centuries. Cork is harvested by removing a layer of thick soft bark from the stem from time to time. This can be done carefully without killing the tree. In many southern wine-growing regions of Europe, especially Spain and Portugal, Cork Oaks and vines were often grown side by side to meet the requirements of the wines and spirits industry. Sadly, synthetic "cork" may make the traditional use of real cork a thing of the past. The Atlantic race of Cork Oak, var. *occidentalis*, is more hardy and less persistently evergreen than the species. Strangely it also tends to flower all summer. Most ornamental trees cultivated in colder northern regions belong to this variety.

Growth: 3-8-22. Hardiness: 40%. Choice: 1, 2, 3. Wood: 4 (cork).

Lebanon Oak   *Quercus libani*

This close relative of Turkey Oak grows in Syria and adjacent areas of Asia Minor. The lanceolate leaves have distinct bristle-tipped teeth. It is a small tree in cultivation, where it was introduced before 1855. The variety **pinnata** has ragged, deeply indented leaves.

Growth: 3-7-18. Hardiness: 50%. Choice: 2. Wood: 5.

Macedonian Oak   *Quercus trojana*

Young trees have a narrow pyramidal outline: with age they spread out stiffly but never become very large. The semi-evergreen foliage is dull grey-green. Each leaf is ovate-oblong with 9-12 pairs of parallel veins, terminating in a short triangular tooth. They are 3-7cm long with a short stalk. The acorns are 2-3cm long in deep cups with free-tipped scales. This species is closely related to Lebanon Oak but the leaves are smaller and more grey. Its natural range, the Balkans and south-east Italy, is a north westerly extension of the distribution of Lebanon Oak. It was first cultivated in England in 1890, where it appears to be quite hardy.

Growth: 3-5-10. Hardiness: 40-50%. Choice: 4.

underside

Macedonian Oak

Turkey Oak

new leaves

♂ flowers

leaf from young tree

Turkey Oak

368

Turkey Oak *Quercus cerris*

Vigorous straight stems and great size give the impression that Turkey Oak is a good timber tree. On many sites, however, it is not. The wood is often shaken and cracked by the time it reaches the sawmill. Trees over 40m tall are known with stems over 2m thick. The silvery-grey bark is roughly cracked and broken into small hard squarish plates. Deciduous leaves are variably shaped with deep or shallow lobes. The upper surface is lustrous dark green, which on some individuals looks as if the foliage could be evergreen. The 3-4cm long acorns, which take two years to mature, are held in cups that are thickly covered with long whiskery and twisted scales.

The natural range of Turkey Oak is not well defined because it has been planted for centuries over a wide area. It is also very hardy and easily becomes naturalized in new locations. Native trees and woods occur across central southern Europe from south-east France to the Czech Republic, Rumania and Turkey. It is on record as 'in cultivation' by 1735 but clearly it was moved around and planted locally long before that. Fortunately it does not seem to hybridize with Common and Sessile Oak otherwise the whole European high quality oak timber stock would have been adulterated long ago.

As an ornamental tree this species is fast-growing and attractive on a grand scale. For avenues it rapidly makes a bold statement and produces a line of substantial trees in one human generation. Environmentally it is probably less valuable than Common Oak and it is host to an early stage of *Andricus quercuscalicis*, a damaging seed wasp which subsequently moves on to Common Oak, causing deformation of the acorn cup and subsequent abortion of the acorn.

There are several subspecies and cultivars of Turkey Oak. Across south-west Europe the variety *austriaca* is prevalent. It has distinctly grey-backed leaves. Forma *laciniata* has deeply indented leaves and a subspecies *tournefortii* occurs in the extreme east. The cultivar '**Variegata**' has some deep green leaves bordered with pale yellow, others with yellow tips and some only lightly flecked with colour.

Growth: 4-16-40. Hardiness: 60%. Choice: 2, 3. Wood: 3, 5.

'Variegata'

Turkey Oak

Lucombe Oak

new leaves

winter leaves

♂ flowers

underside

Lucombe Oak winter

Fulham Oak bark

370

Lucombe Oak

Quercus × hispanica 'Lucombeana'

There is a complex group of hybrids between Turkey Oak (p. 369) and Cork Oak (p. 367). Most of them have artificial, or accidental, origins and spontaneous crosses also occur. Lucombe Oak in its original eighteenth-century form was a straight forward hybrid found growing close to a Cork Oak at Exeter in 1765. It is a big semi-evergreen tree, like Turkey Oak but with somewhat softer bark. It was grown by the Lucombe Nursery in Exeter by grafting on to Turkey Oak root stock. Several thousand of these clonal plants were distributed and some of them still survive. In 1792 three distinct forms were available and two others arose in 1830. This tree can produce fertile seed so numerous seedlings have arisen subsequently. They represent a whole range of types with characteristics ranged between the parents, from completely evergreen to completely deciduous. Notable among the recognized named forms is 'Crispa', one of the original 1792 seedlings with a short stem, spreading branches and distinctive crisp leaves often much reduced towards the centre. It is said that Mr. Lucombe in Exeter had his first tree cut into planks for his own coffin. The timber is hard and heavy and shows a beautiful figure on the radius.

Growth: 4-16-30. Hardiness: 50%. Choice: 1 (requires space), 2, 3. Wood: 1, 2, 3, 5.

Fulham Oak

Quercus × hispanica 'Fulhamensis'

Quite distinct from all the Exeter trees is 'Fulhamensis', the Fulham Oak, produced from the same parents but at Osborne's Nursery in London around 1760. It is completely evergreen and only sheds its leaves in late spring. The stem, which has thick ridged soft corky bark, is usually short, supporting massive spreading branches and a deep green, almost black, head of foliage. Today original Lucombe and Fulham Oaks are becoming increasingly rare because so many F^2 seedlings are available on their own roots. These produce an unpredictable range of tree sizes and foliage types. It is often impossible to know what a new tree will ultimately be like when a sapling is planted. Unfortunately few nurseries grow plants vegetatively now, and in time the originals may become extinct. See also p. 367.

Growth: 5-10-25. Hardiness: 50%. Choice: 1 (requires space). Wood: 1, 2, 3, 5.

Fulham Oak

Holm Oak

underside

subsp. *rotundifolia*

'Fordii'

subsp. *rotundifolia*
leaf variations

Turner's Oak

Coast Live Oak

Holm Oak

Holm Oak bark

Holm Oak *Quercus ilex*

Often forked and with multiple heavy branches, this medium-sized rounded evergreen tree has a natural range from Spain along the Mediterranean fringe and eastwards to West Pakistan. Specimens 27m tall are on record but most individuals are a lot less. Trees especially from Corsica and Italy have been grown elsewhere in mild districts in northern Europe since the late 1500s. They thrive and regenerate along many coasts as far north as England. Holm Oak tolerates alkaline soils, strong winds and low rainfall. The waxy foliage has a low transpiration rate and it also resists salt burn. In many areas trees grow perfectly well immediately behind the high tide mark and among sand dunes. They also thrive in city conditions where they are particularly useful for winter screening. A proportion of the leaves normally drop in spring as a new generation begins to emerge. Sometimes in very cold conditions trees completely defoliate in late winter and do not produce new leaves for at least six months.

The fastigiate form of Holm Oak '**Fordii**' has smaller leaves and a slender outline. It was raised at Exeter around 1843.

The round-leaved form, subspecies ***rotundifolia***, occurs naturally within the wild population especially towards the western end of the range. Conversely, trees which naturally produce narrow leaves are called subspecies *angustifolia*.

Growth: 2-8-20. Hardiness: 40-50%. Choice: 2, 3. Wood: 3, 5.

Turner's Oak *Quercus × turneri*

Produced artificially by crossing Holm Oak with Common Oak in the 1780s at Turner's Nursery in Essex, this much neglected tree has huge potential in urban situations. It looks like everyone's idea of an oak tree, if rather small, but when winter comes the leaves do not fall off. This provides a perpetual eye-level screen and a good degree of shelter.

Growth: 3-9-25. Hardiness: 50%. Choice: 2. Wood: 3, 5.

Coast Live Oak *Quercus agrifolia*

From California, Mendocino County to northern Baja, this is the most characteristic oak tree of the Pacific seaboard. It is evergreen and bushy with a domed top and crooked branches. Some gnarled specimens are thought to exceed 250 years of age. Like Holm Oak this species will grow directly above the high tide line. It was introduced to Europe in 1849 but remains rare in cultivation.

Growth: 2-8-18. Hardiness: 30-40%. Choice: 3. Wood: 3, 5.

Turner's Oak   **Coast Live Oak**

Mirbeck Oak

buds

Downy Oak
leaf variations

Mirbeck Oak

subsp. *palensis*

Mirbeck Oak *Quercus canariensis*

Also known as Algerian Oak, this superb tree comes from North Africa, southern Portugal and parts of Spain. Although its origins are in southerly latitudes, it survives very well in northern Europe, where it was first introduced in 1845. In the landscape this is a majestic oak tree with fresh green 10-15cm leaves, each with around 10 pairs of evenly spaced rounded lobes. The leaves do not fall in the autumn, but mostly stay on the tree, keeping their bright green colour until the following spring. Few broadleaved trees give such a good display of summer foliage in mid-winter. The rough bark is dark grey-brown with deep vertical furrows and horizontally broken ridges. As it is in almost perpetual shade it is seldom heavily colonized and obscured by epiphytes, especially lichens. The flowers and new season's leaves emerge pinkish-green in the spring. Acorns ripen in one year. They are around 2.5cm long, held in deep cups which are downy on the outside. In cultivation most seed is adulterated by closely related Common Oak pollen, giving an interesting but usually less decorative array of semi-evergreen progeny. In future it may be difficult to say whether Common Oak trees retaining their foliage for longer than usual is a consequence of climate change or a past brush with Mirbeck Oak genes.

Growth: 4-8-28. Hardiness: 50%. Choice: 1 (requires space), 2, 3. Wood: 3, 5.

Downy Oak *Quercus pubescens*

Downy Oak, which is closely related to Sessile Oak (p. 381), is a difficult species to define. It is tempting, but botanically irresponsible, to lump all the hairy-leaved trees that are vaguely like Sessile Oak into this species. However, confusing hybrids between the two occur within the natural range, from northern Spain to the Caucasus, and positive identification of the resulting intermediate forms is virtually impossible. Generally the tree is only medium-sized, around 15m tall at best, with a ragged open outline. The leaves are infinitely variable in shape but always densely hairy, especially on the underside. The acorns, produced in one season, are stalkless. The subspecies **palensis** comes from the Pyrenees; its leaves are smaller, under 7cm long and some of the scales around the acorn cup have distinctive free tips. Trees from Greece and Turkey are now described as a separate species called *Quercus brachyphylla*; and some trees in Italy producing edible acorns are now described as *Quercus virgiliana*.

Growth: 2-6-15. Hardiness: 40-50%. Choice: 2, 3. Wood: 1, 2, 3, 5.

leaf variations

underside

Downy Oak

Hungarian Oak

Hungarian Oak
'Hungarian Crown'

Pyrenean Oak

Hungarian Oak *Quercus frainetto*

The deciduous leaves of Hungarian Oak are unique among oaks. Each one has an intricate pattern of lobes and deeply rounded teeth; they are broadest above the centre and can be as much as 20cm long and 12cm wide. The dark green upper surface is lustrous with minute stellate hairs, making it rough to touch. The underside is grey-green and downy, remaining distinctly pale-coloured even when the leaves have died and fallen to the ground. Tall trees without low branches can be identified by the persistent dead leaves around the base of the stem. This is a big tree, up to 35m tall, with a mature stem over 1m thick on a good site. However, grown outside the natural range, the timber is often shaken and cracked when it reaches the sawmill.

Hungarian Oak is native to much of south-east Europe. It was brought into cultivation in 1838. In many respects the tree resembles Sessile Oak, to which it is closely related, but the foliage is more ornate. A common form in cultivation in Britain and Western Europe is '**Hungarian Crown**' originally produced by the Hillier Nurseries.

Growth: 4-10-30. Hardiness: 50%. Choice: 1 (requires space), 3. Wood: 3, 5.

Pyrenean Oak *Quercus pyrenaica*

With a native range from France, Spain and Portugal to Morocco this woodland tree extends the distribution of closely related species such as Hungarian and Caucasian Oak (p. 379) westward to the Atlantic. It can grow to 20-25m in height with a domed but open outline and drooping lower branches. The variable leaves are around 15cm long with wedge shaped rounded lobes. The undersides are densely hairy and pale grey-green. The male catkins are attractive in early summer. This species, or to be more exact the pendulous form of it, was introduced into cultivation in 1822. The cultivar '**Pendula**' has strongly weeping shoots and narrower leaves which are often arched, slightly obscuring the downy underside. In the past plants were often top-grafted on to long 3-4m Common Oak stocks. Many of these specimens are now spoiled by Common Oak regrowth, particularly at the top of the stem. Once established, 'Pendula' often produces a normal upright head of top branches and only droops at the bottom. The usual plant in cultivation resembles *Quercus pubescens* (p. 375) and Sessile Oak (p. 381) so its taxonomic status could be open to question.

Growth: 3-8-22. Hardiness: 40-50%. Choice: 2, 3. Wood: 3, 5.

Pyrenean Oak 'Pendula'

Hungarian Oak winter

Caucasian Oak

Caucasian Oak

underside

Caucasian Oak

Golden Oak of Cyprus

Caucasian Oak *Quercus macranthera*

Of all the deciduous Old World oaks this is perhaps one of the finest. It grows up to 30m tall in ideal conditions, moist broadleaved forest, and has a rounded outline and up-swept branches. The lush foliage, resembling that of *Quercus canariensis* (p. 375), consists of big dark green leaves as much as 14cm long and 9cm wide. They are broadest towards the top end with 6-10 pairs of forward-pointing rounded lobes. Smaller, more irregular leaves can also be found on some specimens. This is sometimes due to introgression with other species, notably Sessile Oak, to which the species is related. The young shoots are stout and thickly pubescent, and the chestnut brown terminal winter buds are unusually large, up to 1.5cm long. The stalkless acorns are around 2.5cm long and held in deep cups. Acorns on a leaf-stalk, as illustrated, are an unusual occurrence but many strong-growing plants occasionally produce such abnormalities. Some cherries, for example, have leafy bracts among the flower petals. This oak is from the Caucasus and around the Caspian Sea coast. It was introduced into cultivation in 1873 but has never become common.

Growth: 3-9-30. Hardiness: 50%. Choice: 2, 3. Wood: 1, 2, 3, 5.

Golden Oak of Cyprus *Quercus alnifolia*

A small, unremarkable evergreen oak around 7m tall at maturity, which on closer inspection reveals bright golden felted backs to the leaves. The rarely seen acorns are tapered towards the base. Introduced from Cyprus in 1815.

Growth: 2-5-7. Hardiness: 40%. Choice: 4.

Quercus 'Macon'

A modern vigorous Dutch hybrid between Caucasian Oak and Hungarian Oak. It is like a very good specimen of Caucasian Oak except for the more ornate sub-divided lobes on the leaves.

Growth: 4-10-30. Hardiness: 50%. Choice: 1 (requires space).

Armenian Oak *Quercus pontica*

Cultivated specimens of this very rare tree resemble small 8-10m tall broad-leaved chestnuts (*Castanea*). They have stout shoots and large deep green parallel veined leaves, as much as 25cm long and 5-15cm wide on vigorous specimens. The stalkless 3-4cm acorns, which are rarely seen in cultivation, are in clusters of two or three maturing in one season. It is native to northern Turkey, Armenia and adjacent areas of Russia. Its status in the wild is largely unknown but it is almost certainly vulnerable. Specimens in cultivation seldom set seed at all and when they do it is often hybridized with Common Oak. Plants have been available since 1885.

Growth: 2-5-10. Hardiness: 50%. Choice: 4.

Quercus 'Pondaim'

This artificial hybrid between Armenian Oak and *Quercus dentata* from south-east Asia was created in Holland around 1960. In general appearance it is like Armenian Oak with sharply pointed teeth on the leaves.

Growth: 2-6-. Hardiness: 40-50%. Choice: 1.

Quercus 'Macon'

Armenian Oak

Quercus 'Pondaim'

Sessile Oak

Sessile Oak

Sessile Oak
underside

'Mespilifolia'

'Insecata'
leaf variations

Sessile Oak

380

Sessile Oak *Quercus petraea*

Sessile Oak is a valuable native timber tree across Europe from the British Isles to Asia Minor, inhabiting upland, rocky, cool moist areas in preference to lush fertile lowland sites. It is closely related to Common Oak and frequently grows alongside it. Quite often it is difficult to distinguish them from each other, particularly as intermediate forms are common. True hybrids are seldom found. The best identification feature of Sessile Oak is its stalkless acorns. Also, the leaves usually have longer stalks, 1-3cm long, but this is not always so. Wedge-shaped (cuneate) leaf bases and upswept branches are less reliable identification features. Stems are often straight and fairly persistent: they reach maturity from about 80cm in diameter but may go on to exceed 3m. By the time trees reach that size they could be 800 or more years old. Heights over 40m are known but in stormy exposed upland situations 10-15m may be the upward limit. Sessile Oak timber is strong and durable. The heartwood resists penetration by liquids. This, and straight close grain, makes it ideal for barrel and cask making. When used in this way the wood imparts a particular flavour to wines and spirits. It is also used for construction work, ship building and fine furniture.

Growth: 4-15-30. Hardiness: 60-70%. Choice: 2, 3. Wood: 1, 2, 3, 5.

Quercus petraea cultivars

The cultivar '**Mespilifolia**' is also a big tree, but it has forsaken lobes for crinkled, more or less entire leaves up to 20cm long. They are gently tapered at both ends and mostly stalked. Much thinner 15cm leaves occur on '**Insecata**', formerly known as 'Laciniata', which may have individual leaves reduced to just a thread around a midrib vein. The foliage of this cultivar does vary and occasionally normal Sessile Oak leaves appear on it. This is an unhealthy slow-growing curiosity which gives every appearance of having been severely attacked by caterpillars. '**Columna**' is a fastigiate tree, especially when young, which has narrow leaves like 'Mespilifolia'. It may be worth growing as a curiosity but as a landscape feature there are many superior alternatives.

'Columna'

'Mespilifolia'

♀ flower detail

♂ flower detail

auricles

underside

autumn

seedling

Common Oak

OAKS

Common Oak *Quercus robur*

This great familiar tree has a broad natural range extending across Europe and Asia Minor from Scandinavia and Ireland to the Caucasus. It comes in many forms but is mostly a rugged branchy 20-30m tree with hard grey fissured bark. The deciduous short-stalked leaves are variably lobed with entire margins and a pair of emarginate auricles at the base. Acorns, which ripen in one season, are held singly, or up to 3, in cups on a slender stalk. Vigorous buds are five sided in cross-section.

Common Oak is usually a lowland species growing on a range of soils from clay to gravel, but not peat. Damp slightly acid sites suit it best but good drainage is essential. The timber quality varies according to the ground on which the trees grow, but ideal conditions appear to be so complex as to defy exact description. Longevity also appears to be site-dependent. The most ancient trees, up to 1000 years old, are found on acid sands and gravels but curiously these sites are renowned for causing longitudinal cracks and 'star' shakes (radial cracks) in the timber as it matures. Perhaps some mature trees have become 'ancient' because they were simply not worth felling for their wood.

Traditionally in Britain oak provided people with four essential products: bark for tanning leather, acorns for fattening pigs, small wood for fuel or charcoal and massive timbers for constructional work and, especially, ship building. Sadly none of these seem essential to us any more, but as tropical hardwood resources become depleted oak may once again regain its place as a timber producer. In nature this species supports, feeds and shelters a vast range of organisms. It is also a good wind-break, particularly by the sea where it tolerates some salinity in the soil.
Growth: 3-15-25. Hardiness: 60-70%. Choice: 3. Wood: 1, 2, 3, 5.

Quercus robur cultivars

There are several upright cultivars of Common Oak. Forma **fastigiata**, the Cypress Oak, has fastigiate branches, short side shoots and dense vigorous foliage. After about 50 years and 15m of height growth most specimens sustain some sort of damage from wind or snow and loose their symmetrical shape, but they continue to grow steadfastly upwards. Several named slender cultivars are listed. '**Hungaria**' is possibly the narrowest of them all, reminiscent of a small Lombardy poplar. Wider, but still with fastigiate branches is '**Raba**'. There is also a more open slow-growing form, '**Tortuosa**', which has twisted shoot tips.

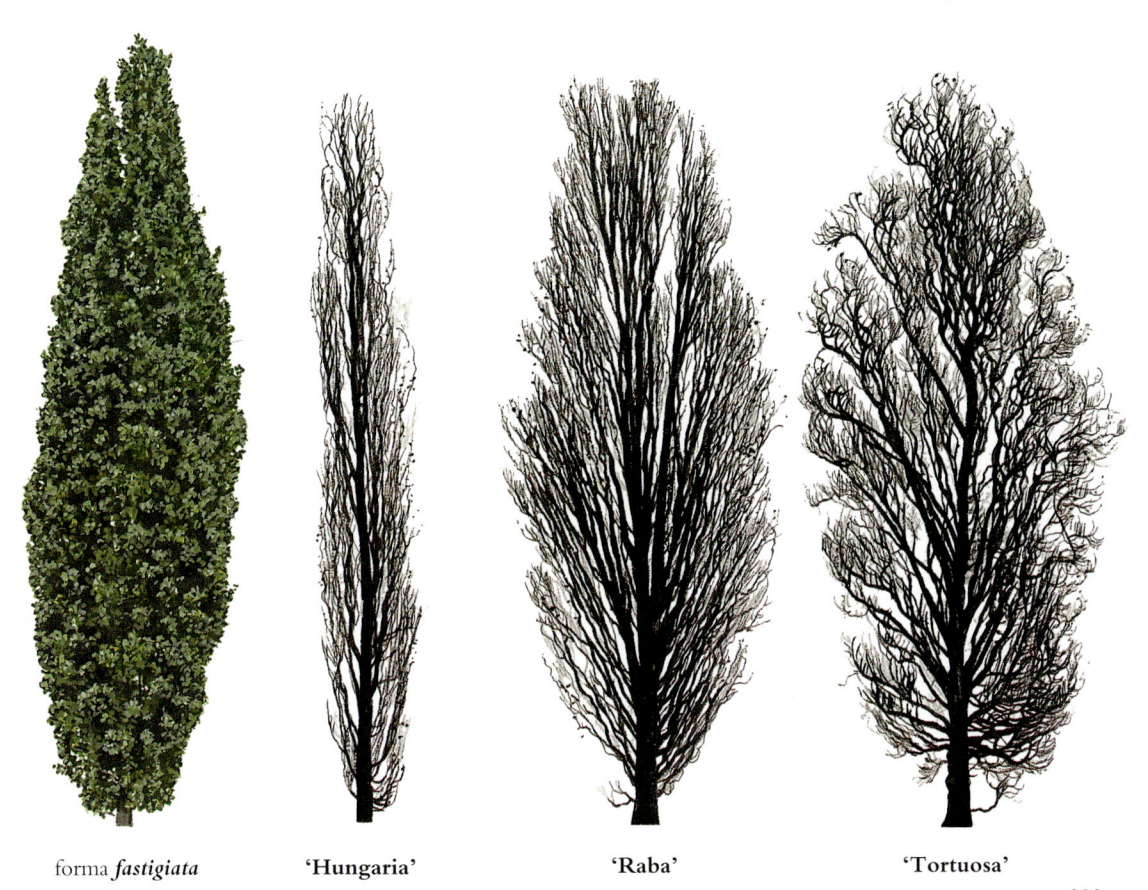

forma *fastigiata*   'Hungaria'   'Raba'   'Tortuosa'

Quercus × *rosacea*

'Argenteovariegata'
leaf variations

'Atropurpurea'

'Filicifolia'

'Atropurpurea'

'Filicifolia'

Quercus × *rosacea*

There is often fierce debate, particularly among foresters, about the status of this hybrid between Common and Sessile Oak. Some say that most oaks resembling these species are hybrids, but genetic experiments suggest that a true hybrid is quite a rare occurrence. The problem lies in the fact that both Common Oak and Sessile Oak produce a whole range of variants. Profound morphological differences occur, especially in leaf shape, sometimes on the same tree. There is also regional variation within populations. Studies of Common Oak trees over 500 years of age in England show that several distinct regional leaf types exist depending upon which ancient forest the trees were part of. Any specimens labelled *Quercus* × *rosacea* in collections should be regarded with some caution unless their genetic make-up has been investigated.

Growth: 3-15-25. Hardiness: 60%. Choice: 3.

Quercus robur cultivars (continued)

The variegated cultivar '**Argenteovariegata**' has fairly standard Common Oak leaves mottled and splashed with silver. The dark red shoots are also marked with white. It is becoming very uncommon in cultivation. '**Atropurpurea**' is quite different, the leaves and shoots are wine-red at first maturing to purplish-green later in the year. Not a spectacular tree, although it may reach 18m in height. Fertile acorns are produced but most, if not all, seedlings have predominantly green foliage.

At the other end of the spectrum '**Concordia**', the Golden Oak, has yellow leaves all through the growing season. Raised in Belgium in 1843 it is popular in cultivation but tends to be a sickly plant. Specimens grafted on to Common Oak rootstocks may suffer badly from basal growth which soon overwhelms them.

Cut-leaved Common Oaks come in several shapes and sizes. The 1854 German cultivar '**Filicifolia**', which may really be a hybrid with Sessile Oak, has lobes deeply divided almost to the midrib. Specimens are not large and they grow very slowly.

'**Strypemonde**' is a curious plant. The leaves are all to some extent reduced, many extremely so, but they can not be strictly described as 'cut-leaved'. The whole plant usually looks as if it has been devastated by locusts. When growing in full light the leaves are mottled yellow which adds to the tree's already unhealthy appearance.

Growth: variable. Hardiness: -%. Choice: 1 (some cvs).

'**Strypemonde**'
leaf variations

'**Concordia**'

'Cristata'

'Pendula'

Quercus pedunculiflora

'Fastigiata Grangei'
winter

'Granbyana'

Quercus robur cultivars (continued)

Common Oak cultivars fall into two broad categories: foliage aberrations often associated with variegation, and variants in tree shape. Colours such as purple or gold in foliage are generally weak features. Very upright forms (p. 383) are often spoiled by ravages of the climate and end up with a series of untidy vertical spikes. Pendulous plants that have to be grafted on to a long rootstock tend to become incongruous as the stem expands and the top fails to keep up.

'**Cristata**' is a very peculiar tree with dense bunches of tightly packed, deformed leaves. These appear to be stalkless upper halves of normal flat leaves rather than strictly contorted foliage. It arose as a sport on a tree in the ancient forest of Savernake before 1917 but has never been common in cultivation. Diminutive acorns are produced and when they ripen properly they are said to come true to type.

'**Pendula**' the 'Weeping Oak' is a small tree entirely dependent upon the size of stock on which it is grafted. Without a tall rootstock it would only creep around close to the ground. The foliage is like Common Oak, but probably less vigorous. It has been in cultivation since 1733 and there are many different clones.

'**Fastigiata Grangei**' is a variant of forma *fastigiata* (p. 383) that is difficult to distinguish in its early years, after which it more or less reverts to a Common Oak shape at maturity. '**Granbyana**' is a very rare plant which tends to be pyramidal rather than fastigiate. More popular in cultivation is the similar-looking form 'Koster'.

The Dutch cultivar '**Holophylla**', formerly called 'Salicifolia', is quite unlike Common Oak. The leaves are ovate-oblong or lanceolate and more or less unlobed. They tend to be bunched together at the shoot tips.

Growth: variable. Hardiness: -%. Choice: 1.

Quercus pedunculiflora

This rare tree is from south-eastern Europe and Asia Minor. It has leaves broadly similar to Common Oak but pubescent on the underside and more glaucous above. It was named *Quercus haas* by the Austrian botanist Karl Kotschy and first cultivated in 1870. Another oak was also called 'Haas' by a German botanist Theodor Wenzig, but they have so much in common, they are probably the same thing.

Growth: 4-8-20. Hardiness: 40-50%. Choice: 4. Wood: 1, 2, 3, 5.

'Holophylla'

'Pendula'

♂ flowers

new leaves

White Oak

autumn

underside

Burr Oak
winter

Burr Oak

White Oak *Quercus alba*

In its native North America this is one of the most important commercial timber trees. In America it is also called 'Stave Oak' because the close grained impervious wood is good for making watertight barrel staves. Ships were also made from it by the early European settlers. The natural distribution extends from Ontario to south-west Maine and then a huge range south to Texas and the Gulf States but excluding most of Florida. In this varied territory their preferred habitat is moist but well drained lowland soils and hillsides up to 1600m in the south. White Oak leaves can be extremely variable even on the same tree. It will hybridize with several compatible species so variants are common and identification out of context is difficult. If there is a 'standard' leaf it is 15cm long and 8cm wide with 4-9 lobes. Upper surfaces are glabrous and bright green when fully extended. Undersides are greyish and also become more or less hairless at maturity. The bright red and brown autumn colour is dark or light depending on which way up the leaves fall. Ovate acorns, 1-3cm long, are held in shallow almost stalkless cups. White Oak, probably the variety *latifolia*, the common northern form, was introduced to Europe in 1724. This is why most old trees in Europe do not have the deeply divided leaves so often seen on trees of other forms in the United States.

Growth: 4-10-25. Hardiness: 60%. Choice: 3.
Wood: 1, 2, 3, 5.

Burr Oak *Quercus macrocarpa*

The outstanding feature of this tree is its huge acorns. They are up to 5cm long and wide, broadly elliptical, and held in a big deep cup which may easily obscure half the nut. An alternative American name 'Mossycup Oak' is a reference to the acorn cup scales, which are hairy and form a grey fringe around the rim. The leaves too can be very large on a favourable site, up to 25cm long and 13cm wide. Each one has 5-7 lobes on the lower part and deep teeth towards the rounded tip.

This North American species has a broad range through southern Canada then southwards through the United States in an inverted triangle terminating in central Texas. Towards the south and west it is a shrubby prairie edge pioneer species. In better cool moist conditions it can grow to 20m in height usually with crooked branches and an open rounded top. The wood is heavy and durable sometimes with dark brown heartwood. In Europe, where it was introduced in 1811, it tends to be a smallish tree, sometimes with even larger leaves but very few acorns.

Growth: 3-8-20. Hardiness: 50%. Choice: 3.
Wood: 2, 3, 5.

autumn **White Oak**

Valley Oak

Swamp White Oak

Swamp White Oak

Valley Oak

Swamp White Oak

390

Valley Oak *Quercus lobata*

This Californian species of White Oak has exaggerated lobes on the leaves, hence the Latin name, and grows in moist valleys and foothills throughout California. Shasta Lake and southern San Joaquin are important regions for it, but the most impressive trees are in the Coast Ranges, for example in Mendocino County. Specimens up to 600 years old are on record. Such ancient trees are able to resist wind, drought and even fire because of the thick rugged heat resistant bark. This is the largest of the Californian Oaks, easily reaching 30m in height with stems 1.2m in diameter. The deciduous leaves, up to 10cm long, are deep green with paler felted undersides. The acorns, which are up to 6cm long, are slender and pointed. They are edible and said to be sweet. Local wildlife and domestic animals certainly relish them. Californian Indians also ground a kind of flour from them. In 1796 George Vancouver compared Valley Oaks in California to Common Oaks in an English stately park. In 1874 the species was introduced to Europe where it tends to grow slowly. Most of the best trees in California have now been lost to agricultural clearance and urban expansion. Those which are left may be at risk from damage by water abstraction and air pollution.

Growth: 3-15-30. Hardiness: 30-40%. Choice: 3. Wood: 1, 2, 3, 5.

Swamp White Oak *Quercus bicolor*

From eastern North America this relative of the Chestnut-leaved Oak grows in mixed woodlands that are often subject to flooding. Its natural range runs from Quebec and Maine to Virginia in the south and west to Missouri following river valleys and stretching across wetlands. It is a fairly narrow but rounded tree with drooping lower branches. Most mature specimens are between 16-20m tall. Stems struggle to reach 80cm in diameter. The 10cm leaves are obovate, broadest towards the tip, with 5-8 pairs of shallow rounded lobes. They are deep lustrous green above and softly downy grey-green on the underside. Before falling in the autumn they turn red and chestnut brown above and pink below. The acorns are up to 3cm long in deep scaly cups. The species name, given to the tree in 1801 by Karl Willdenow, is a reference to the two-coloured leaves.

Growth: 3-10-20. Hardiness: 80%. Choice: 3. Wood: 3, 5.

underside

Swamp White Oak
spring

Chestnut Oak

autumn

Swamp Chestnut Oak

Chestnut Oak

Swamp Chestnut Oak
winter

Chestnut Oak *Quercus prinus*

In its native North America the bark of this species was once used for tanning leather. It is the best of all American oaks for the purpose. The timber, called 'White oak' in the trade, is also highly valued. The actual range of Chestnut Oak extends from southern Ontario to Maine and south-westward across the United States to Michigan and Mississippi. It is an upland tree most at home on dry acid rocky soils up to 1500m. It has been in cultivation since 1688 but remains rare in Europe. Trees up to 24m tall with spreading branches have big 15-20cm deciduous leaves, very like those of Chestnut (*Castanea* p. 349). The 2-3cm acorns which ripen in one year are held in deep cups.

Growth: 3-12-24. Hardiness: 50-60%. Choice: 3.
Wood: 1, 2, 3, 4, 5.

Swamp Chestnut Oak *Quercus michauxii*

This wetland counterpart of Chestnut Oak is a native tree from the valleys and flood plains of eastern North America, from New Jersey to Florida and westwards to Illinois and eastern Texas. It was introduced to Europe in 1737, where it prefers moist acid soils. An alternative American name is Basket Oak, because baskets for carrying cotton were made from finely split wood. It is also called Cow Oak because the sweet edible acorns were fed to cattle. The deciduous leaves are up to 23cm long with 10-14 rounded teeth. The acorns, up to 3cm long, are held in rather stout cups which give the impression of being a size too large for the seed.

Growth: 3-15-30. Hardiness: 50%. Choice: 3.
Wood: 1, 2, 3, 4, 5.

Oregon White Oak *Quercus garryana*

In western North America this is the most important commercial producer of oak timber. It resembles the eastern White Oak, hence the name. The close-grained wood is ideal for structural work, shipbuilding and furniture. The sweet acorns are fed to domestic livestock. They are up to 3cm long and each one is held in a small thin short-stalked cup. The deciduous leaves are deep green and glossy on the upper side. In a good autumn they turn red. This is a tree of mountain slopes and rocky valleys, usually in deciduous forest. Its long north-south range, from British Columbia to central California, means that a variety of tree types and sizes occur. Provenances from Washington and Oregon produce the best specimen trees, up to 30m tall.

Growth: 3-15-30. Hardiness: 60-70%. Choice: 3.
Wood: 1, 2, 3, 5.

Oregon White Oak

European White Elm

fruit

fruit

English Elm

English Elm

young tree infected with Dutch Elm Disease

394

ELM FAMILY · Ulmaceae

English Elm *Ulmus minor* var. *vulgaris*

The origin of this variety, formerly *Ulmus procera*, is not entirely certain, but it is not English. Populations in northern Spain do appear to be native, though, and possibly the 'English Elm' in England came from there. People have carried useful plants with them on their migrations since before Neolithic times. In this way English Elm which provided cattle fodder, shelter and heavy timber reached England and other locations beyond its natural distribution. Archaeological evidence suggests that elm wood was even carried to many improbable places where the tree certainly would not grow, for example to ancient Egypt.

In Britain English Elm is one of the oldest living links with the past. It was used by Bronze age farmers and, because it seldom produces viable seed, propagation since then has been vegetative, mostly through naturally spreading root suckers. Root systems under hedges around settlements may still consist of clonal material that was planted over 3000 years ago. By repeatedly harvesting the timber and cutting hedges, farmers inadvertently rejuvenated the elm so that it never reached biological old age and died out.

In the second half of the twentieth century English Elm has been affected by 'Dutch Elm Disease' a microscopic fungus (*Ophiostoma novo-ulmi*) which blocks vessels in the metabolic system of the tree. It is transmitted from tree to tree by two species of flying Scolytus bark beetles, and then directly through adjoining communal root systems. Commercial transportation of logs has now spread the disease throughout the world. However, past epidemics of similar pathogens in elms failed to eliminate the genus completely.

There are several ornamental cultivars of English Elm. '**Viminalis**' is a slow-growing picturesque tree with semi-pendulous branches and small leaves. The golden form of it '**Viminalis Aurea**' has yellow leaves in spring which turn green by late summer. '**Silvery Gem**' has yellow-margined leaves which remain coloured all through the season. Persistent yellow leaves also occur on the Dutch cultivar '**Louis van Houtte**'.

Growth: 4-16-30. Hardiness: 50%. Choice: 4.
Wood: 1, 2 (species).

European White Elm *Ulmus laevis*

Through central Europe to western Asia this is a common elm species. It is a large tree up to 35m tall with stems 1.5m across. The outline and foliage are reminiscent of Wych Elm (p. 399). The flowers and fruits are distinct because they are long-stalked and flutter in the slightest breeze, giving rise to the alternative name 'Fluttering Elm'. It has been in cultivation for a very long time but is difficult to identify except when flowers and fruit are present.

Growth: 4-18-35. Hardiness: 60-70%. Choice: 4.
Wood: 1, 2.

'Viminalis'

'Viminalis Aurea'

'Silvery Gem'

'Louis van Houtte'

American Elm

fruit

underside

Slippery Elm

new leaves

corky twig

Rock Elm

fruit

Rock Elm

396

American Elm *Ulmus americana*

Also known as White Elm or Soft Elm, the American commercial names for its wood in America, this widespread tree occurs from Saskatchewan to Cape Breton Island, south to Florida and then west to central Texas. Before 1930 it was abundant everywhere in the countryside and also in urban planting schemes.

Then Dutch Elm Disease appeared on the east coast and the American Elm was decimated. Trees 30m tall with stems 1.2m thick were once commonplace. Reproduction is by seed, which has a characteristic 1.2cm oval wing with a deep notch in the end and in-curved points. Introduced to Europe in 1752, it was never widely planted and very few specimens have survived Dutch Elm Disease.

Growth: 3-15-30. Hardiness: 90%. Choice: 4.
Wood: 1, 2, 3, 5.

Slippery Elm *Ulmus rubra*

The slippery part of this tree is the inner bark which has medicinal properties and has been used effectively as a poultice. It is fragrant and sticky and claimed to be edible. The natural range of this species is slightly less extensive than American Elm.

It makes an open-branched 20m tree with deciduous elliptical long-pointed neatly toothed leaves. They are unequal at the base and held on a very short stalk. The bark is dark brown and eventually ridged. The almost round flat fruits consist of a membranous wing with a single seed held in the centre. At first, in 1753, it was named as part of *Ulmus americana*, then in 1793, it was properly identified as a species and introduced to Europe in 1830.

Growth: 3-10-20. Hardiness: 80%. Choice: 3.
Wood: 2, 3, 4.

Rock Elm *Ulmus thomasii*

Named after David Thomas, a civil engineer and horticulturalist in the United States in 1902, this tree is famous for its tough wood. Huge amounts of timber were exported to England in the nineteenth century for shipbuilding and agricultural implements. The natural range of the species forms a wide crescent round the southern side of the Great Lakes.

An impressive tree, it usually has a straight stem up to 1m thick and 15-30m tall. The branches tend to be short and droop at the extremities. The leaves, 5-9cm long, are ovate with distinct teeth, a short point and an oblique base. They are leathery and shiny on the upper surface but downy and pale green on the underside. The twigs have corky wings like young Field Maple (p. 625). Seeds, up to 2cm long, are enclosed within a flat drooping lemon-shaped wing. Plants were introduced, as *Ulmus racemosa*, to Europe in 1875.

Growth: 3-12-25. Hardiness: 90%. Choice: 4.
Wood: 1, 2, 3.

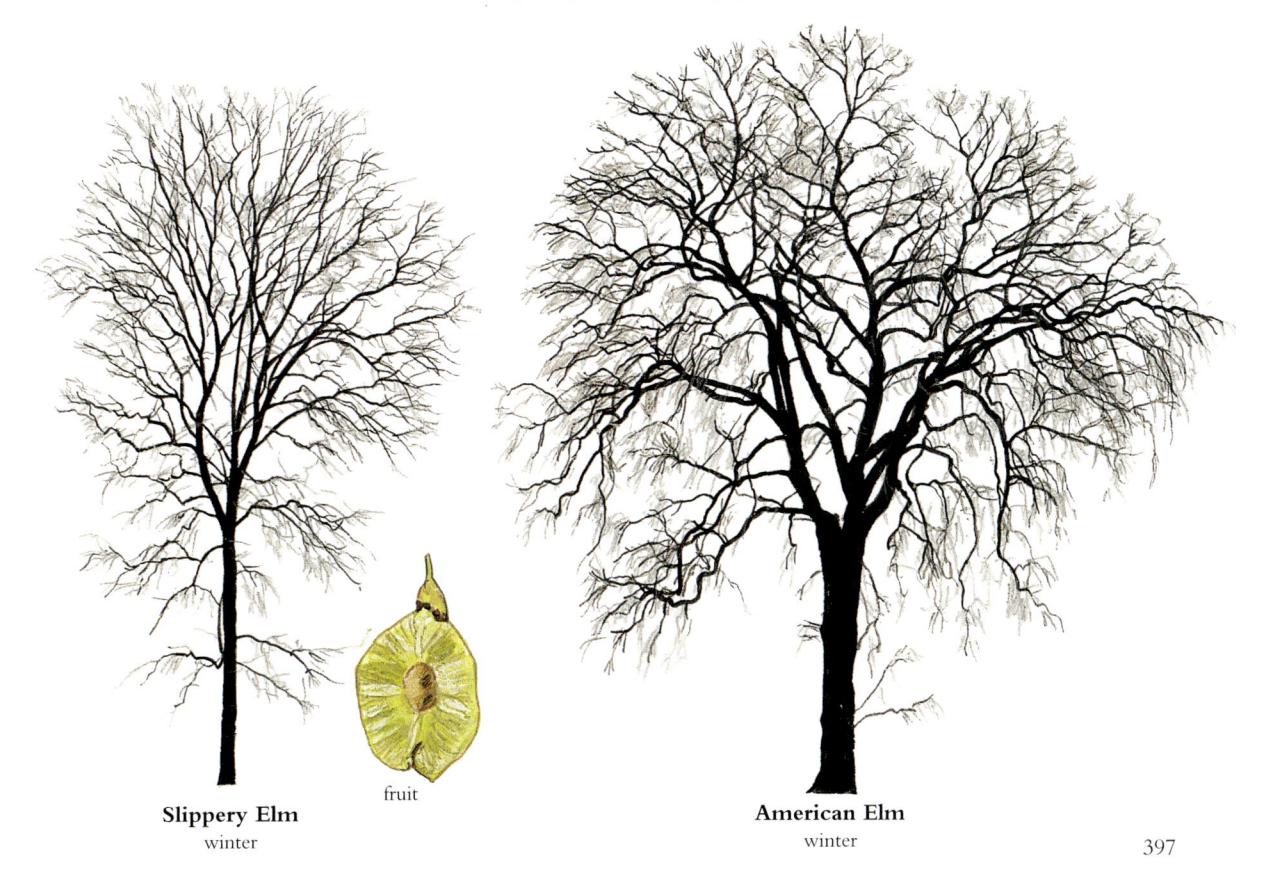

Slippery Elm
winter

fruit

American Elm
winter

Weeping Wych Elm

fruit

flower detail

Wych Elm

398

Wych Elm *Ulmus glabra*

Over much of its natural European range this is a tree of mountain sides, hence a former name *Ulmus montana*. It is a native species in Europe as far north as Scotland, southern Scandinavia including Finland, and into Russia. To the south it is found in Switzerland and the Carpathian Mountains. In Scotland it is called 'Scotch Elm' but the Gaelic name for it is 'Leam'. 'Leamanonius Lacus' meaning 'the lake of the elms' is Loch Lomond, out of which flows the River Leven. The town of Leven in Fife also owes its name to the Wych Elm. In Ireland the vernacular name for it is 'Leamhan Sleibhe'.

This is potentially a huge sinuous tree, often with a short stem and wide-spreading, rather gaunt branches. Heights up to 40m are known but on exposed rocky crags and high up stony valleys it may struggle to rise above any surrounding shelter. Flowers appear on short spur shoots in late winter before the leaves. They may be bisexual or single sex but all together on the same tree. The 5-6 maroon anthers on male flowers give the tree an early flush of colour when they are plentiful. Big, 10-16cm, long rough leaves taper towards the unequal base and come to an abrupt point, sometimes with subsidiary points flanking it on one or both sides. The margins are prominently toothed with double or even triple points on each tooth. Clusters of 2mm fruits consist of a seed in the centre of a round, flat, membranous wing with a notch in the top. Wych Elm bark is grey and smooth for many years eventually becoming fissured and scaly.

The wood had numerous traditional uses based upon its great strength, tight twisted grain, durability and ability to withstand many years under water. It was prized for boat building and wheel stocks. Even water pipes were made from hollowed out poles, a painstaking process carried out with rather primitive hand tools. Strips of the inner bark made strong cordage and woven chair seats. Like English Elm the foliage was used for feeding and bedding domestic animals. Although this species can be grown from cuttings it is usually propagated from seed. This has to be carefully timed because the seed ripens in mid-summer and goes into dormancy within a matter of days.

Growth: 4-16-30. Hardiness: 60%. Choice: 4. Wood: 1, 2, 3.

Weeping Wych Elm
Ulmus glabra 'Horizontalis'

Also known as *pendula*, but not 'Camperdownii' (p. 401), this cultivar originated around 1816. It is a flat spreading plant which only makes a standard tree when it is grafted on to a tall rootstock. It was discovered in a batch of seedlings at a nursery in Perth, Scotland.

Growth: 3-4-4. Hardiness: 60%. Choice: 1, 4.

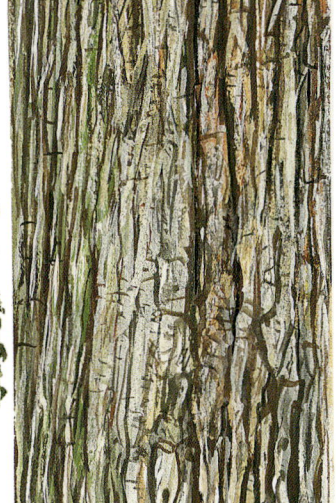

Weeping Wych Elm

'Nana'

'Camperdownii'

'Exoniensis'

underside

'Lutescens'

'Exoniensis'

'Lutescens'

Ulmus glabra cultivars

Wych Elm has produced some interesting ornamental types in 150 years of cultivation. Most of the variants are to do with tree shape. One 'Crispa' has deformed leaves and another '**Lutescens**' has yellow foliage.

The dwarf Wych Elm '**Nana**' is a neat compact bush seldom as much as 5m tall but often wider. Its precise origin is uncertain and few nurseries still grow it. The tree at Kew Gardens (illustrated) has grown little since it was described in 1884 as having probably originated from a 'witch's broom' (a deformed dwarf shoot), and in 1906 by Elwes and Henry, as "a slow-growing hemispherical bush, which has not increased appreciably in size for many years."

The Camperdown Elm, '**Camperdownii**', is a famous tree with well documented origins. Camperdown House near Dundee, in Scotland is where the original tree appeared in 1850. Like 'Horizontalis' (p. 399), which appeared in cultivation before it in 1816, it needs to be grafted on to a standard stock, usually about 1.5m tall. Wych Elm and English Elm are suitable stocks, although the latter tends to sucker after a while. It has large leaves and most specimens produce a neat rounded outline with arched branches and weeping shoots down to the ground. Even where Dutch Elm Disease is rife this cultivar often escapes unscathed.

The Exeter Elm, '**Exoniensis**', was discovered near Exeter in 1826 and immediately cultivated vegetatively at the nursery of W. Ford in that city. This is an upright variety, although it can not be described as strictly fastigiate. The leaves are peculiarly twisted but not deformed or excessively contorted. Upper surfaces are deep green and rough to the touch with 'feathered' teeth and an abrupt point. Leaf fall is often late because of the large number of leaves that have folded themselves round the shoot for support and resist the autumn winds. It is ultimately a big tree up to 17m tall which appears, in England, to be resistant to Dutch Elm Disease. An 1875 tree at Westonbirt Arboretum in Gloucestershire survived for many years after all the other elms around it had been killed. Unfortunately it subsequently died from Honey Fungus.

The Golden Wych Elm '**Lutescens**' is seldom seen in cultivation now, perhaps because its pale yellowish-green colour is surpassed by alternative deeper yellow foliage plants. It has much larger leaves than the Golden English Elm 'Louis van Houtte' (p. 395). Growth is rapid and trees often exceed 20m in height. Named in 1903 as a variety, the original tree was know as the Gallows Elm, because it was located close to the gallows in York. This is probably the same tree as the Golden-leaved Elm raised by Calmpthout Nursery in Belgium, named by them *Ulmus americana aurea*.

Growth: variable. Hardiness: 60%. Choice: 1, 4.

'Nana'

'Camperdownii'

Huntingdon Elm

fruit

Huntingdon Elm
winter

fruit

Dutch Elm

402

Huntingdon Elm *Ulmus × hollandica* 'Vegeta'

In 1750 seed from elm trees growing at Hinchingbrook Park, Huntingdon, produced what has become one of the most successful urban trees of all. That is until Dutch Elm Disease put a stop to elm planting. Huntingdon Elm proved to be more resistant to the disease than English Elm but not entirely immune to it. Wild elms in the region around Huntingdon are similar to this cultivar, probably hybrids involving Wych Elm (p. 399) and Smooth-leaved Elm (p. 407). The outline of this tree is narrow for many years eventually spreading out with numerous, often nodding, fine shoots. Leaves, usually offset at the base are similar in shape and size to Wych Elm.
Growth: 4-15-30. Hardiness: 50%. Choice: 2, 4. Wood: 1, 2.

Dutch Elm *Ulmus × hollandica* 'Major'

Natural hybrid elms involving Wych Elm are frequent in Western Europe and the British Isles. Their parentage is complex and still not entirely understood. The segment of this population which occurs in the Low Countries has been subjected to considerable research and horticultural selection. Although all *Ulmus × hollandica* hybrids are called 'Dutch Elm' by some authorities, the cultivar 'Major' is a convenient reference to the particular type that was usually planted in England. This provides a horticultural distinction between Dutch Elm and Huntingdon Elm, or indeed the Belgian Elm 'Belgica'. 'Dutch Elm' is a large tree prone to epicormic shoot growth on the stem and sucker growth from its surface roots. In outline it is reminiscent of Cornish Elm (p. 407) and the leaves are intermediate between Wych and English Elms. Fertile seed is produced but the progeny are unpredictable.
Growth: 4-15-30. Hardiness: 50%. Choice: 2, 4. Wood: 1, 2.

Ulmus × hollandica 'Dampieri'

Selected for urban use, especially around 1864, this tree has upright branches and a narrow outline. In summer the foliage is dense and luxuriant. The tough 6-8cm ovate leaves are double toothed and crowded on the glabrous shoots. This cultivar is thought to be of Continental European origin. Resulting from it is a tree with bright yellow foliage, **'Dampieri Aurea'** which is of similar size and shape. It was popular in late nineteenth-century parks and gardens.
Growth: 4-15-25. Hardiness: 50-60%. Choice: 2, 4. Wood: 1, 2.

Dutch Elm   *Ulmus × hollandica* **'Dampieri'**   **'Dampieri Aurea'**

Ulmus parvifolia 'Plantjin'

Ulmus 'Dodoens'

fruit

Ulmus minor var. *diversifolia*

Ulmus × *hollandica* 'Groenveldt'

404

Ulmus parvifolia 'Plantjin'

This cultivar of Chinese Elm is of unknown hybrid origin. The Royal Horticultural Society in London regard it simply as *Ulmus* 'Plantjin'. It was bred in Europe for its resistance to Dutch Elm Disease. Several Asiatic elms have been used in this role with promising results. It has a narrow flexible outline but does not look much like a European elm in the countryside.

Growth: 3-10-20. Hardiness: 50%. Choice: 2, 4.

Ulmus 'Dodoens'

Released in Holland in the 1960s this clone was artificially bred for its resistance to Dutch Elm Disease. It grows quickly and is resistant to wind damage but is only moderately resistant to the aggressive strain of the disease.

Growth: 4-15-. Hardiness: 50%. Choice: 4.

Ulmus × hollandica 'Groenveldt'

Attributable to 'Dutch Elm', this vigorous 1960s hybrid has lush healthy foliage and fast up-swept growth at first. Trials suggest that it slows down as it matures. It too is only moderately resistant to Dutch Elm Disease and planting is no longer recommended in Britain.

Growth: 4-15-. Hardiness: 50%. Choice: 4.

Ulmus minor var. *diversifolia*

Dr. R Melville named this plant *Ulmus diversifolia*, and a tree labelled *diversifolia* by him has been grown at Kew in London. However, its validity is now questioned and its origin seems uncertain. The Royal Horticultural Society suggest it is synonymous with *Ulmus carpinifolia* (see also p. 407), the 'Smooth-leaved Elm', but unhelpfully in this case, *carpinifolia* has now been swallowed up in the *Ulmus minor* complex. The foliage certainly resembles Cornish Elm and Guernsey Elm, which are forms of the old *Ulmus carpinifolia* group. This plant is no longer in cultivation and would seem to be a prime candidate for extinction. It is not distinct enough to be instantly recognizable in the field and its present legitimate name places it in a large group of difficult taxa.

Growth: 4-16-30. Hardiness: 70%. Choice: 4.

Ulmus × hollandica 'Groenveldt'

Ulmus 'Dodoens'
young trees

Ulmus parvifolia 'Plantjin'

fruit

Smooth-leaved Elm

Cornish Elm

Guernsey Elm

Smooth-leaved Elm

Cornish Elm

Guernsey Elm

406

Smooth-leaved Elm *Ulmus minor* subsp. *minor*

Also called the Field Elm, and until recently *Ulmus carpinifolia* (see also p. 405), this big, 30m tall, graceful tree was once common across Europe to North Africa and western Asia. Like English Elm (p. 395) it was transported around by Bronze Age and Iron Age farmers. Young trees have a conical outline but this broadens with age and lower branches often become pendulous. The bark is silvery-grey and smooth for many years. Oval leaves, 5-10cm long, are oblique at the base and distinctly double toothed. The upper surface is smooth and shiny with 10-13 pairs of parallel veins. Flowers with purple anthers appear in early spring followed by seeds held in the centre of a flat papery oval wing. This species was extensively used in the past for cattle food. Most valuable in late summer when the leaves stay green during periods of drought. Variable native hybrids with Wych Elm are common, notably in eastern England. These are mostly resistant to Dutch Elm Disease.

Growth: 3-16-30. Hardiness: 50%. Choice: 3, 4. Wood: 2, 3.

Cornish Elm *Ulmus minor* var. *cornubiensis*

Confined to south-west England and adjacent regions of France, this isolated population of Smooth-leaved Elm once contributed much to the rural landscape. Now it has been reduced by Dutch Elm Disease to remnants of shrubby suckering re-growth. Young plants are conical with steeply ascending branches, flattening out as they age, usually cut back by the salt-laden sea winds in their native regions. The leaves are like Smooth-leaved Elm but generally a little smaller. It is possible that Cornish Elm survived the last glaciation in the British Isles on ice-free land to the immediate south now covered by the sea.

Growth: 4-16-25. Hardiness: 50%. Choice: 3, 4. Wood: 2, 3.

Guernsey Elm *Ulmus minor* 'Sarniensis'

Although treated now as a cultivar, this tree, also known as Wheatley Elm, probably arose as another isolated population of Smooth-leaved Elm. The Guernsey population has been wrecked by Dutch Elm Disease. Urban Wheatley Elm trees, mostly a clone from Northern France, have survived rather better. A golden form, **'Dicksonii'**, is a slow-growing narrow upright tree with bright yellow leaves. It was raised in Chester by Dickson's Nursery in 1900 and called 'Golden Cornish Elm'.

Growth: 4-16-25. Hardiness: 50%. Choice: 3, 4. Wood: 2, 3.

Lock's Elm *Ulmus minor* var. *lockii*

Also known as Plot's Elm, this stiff upright tree has short side branches and an open appearance. Some specimens resemble Cornish Elm. Before Dutch Elm Disease it was common in central and northern England where it is considered to be a native species. The hybrid between this variety and Wych Elm (*Ulmus × elegantissima*) is an important British native tree.

Growth: 4-16-25. Hardiness: 50-60%. Choice: 3, 4. Wood: 2, 3.

Lock's Elm

'Dicksonii'

Ulmus villosa

Ulmus 'Karagatch'

bud detail

leaf detail

Ulmus villosa

Ulmus 'Karagatch'

Ulmus villosa

Rare in cultivation, this tree is from the western side of the Himalayas, where it can grow to 30m. The leaves, which are reminiscent of Zelkova, are pale green and softly pubescent. It appears to be a western counterpart of *Ulmus parvifolia*, the Chinese Elm (p. 411).
Growth: 3-15-30. Hardiness: 40-50%. Choice: 1, 4. Wood: 2, 3.

Ulmus 'Karagatch'

Originally from Turkestan this intriguing and beautiful tree is intermediate between *Ulmus pumila* (p. 411) and *Ulmus androssowi*, which is really a larger spreading variety of *Ulmus pumila*. The cultivar is of uncertain origin but it was probably a selection of *androssowi* made before 1915, although the variety was not introduced until 1934. It makes a shapely tree with the dense foliage which is typical of the Asiatic elms.
Growth: 2-9-18. Hardiness: 80%. Choice: 1, 4. Wood: 2, 3.

Ulmus 'Lobel'

An artificial Dutch cultivar of uncertain botanical origin, selected for its resistance to Dutch Elm disease. After a promising performance in the nursery and test beds, it has only grown slowly in field trials and seems likely to remain fairly small. Furthermore it appears to be only moderately resistant to the aggressive strain of the disease. Further planting is not recommended in Britain.
Growth: 4-12-18. Hardiness: 60%. Choice: 4.

Ulmus 'Pinnato-ramosa'

Although now considered to be a cultivar in British horticulture, this pyramidal open branched tree may be better known as the variety of Siberian Elm, *Ulmus pumila* var. *arborea*. An earlier invalid species designation *pinnato-ramosa* dates back to 1895. The German gardener Georg Dieck is credited with its introduction from western Siberia in 1894. It is very similar to Siberian Elm except for its larger ultimate size. The selected cultivar, generally grown from cuttings, is quite vigorous and capable of rapidly making a moderate to large tree. The 4-7cm leaves are ovate-lanceolate, double toothed and finely pointed.
Growth: 2-10-20. Hardiness: 80%. Choice: 2.

Ulmus 'Lobel'

Ulmus 'Pinnato-ramosa'
spring

Japanese Elm bark

Siberian Elm

Japanese Elm

Ulmus 'Sapporo Autumn Gold'

fruit

fruit

'Jacon'

Siberian Elm

Japanese Elm

410

Siberian Elm *Ulmus pumila*

Often this is a shrubby bush but strains from different regions vary so much that occasional shapely trees do occur in cultivation (var. *arborea*). The natural range, across a huge part of northern Asia, includes many diverse sites and different environments. The leaves are elliptic, usually equal at the base and only 2-6cm long. They are smooth on the upper side and leathery when mature. The fruits, in a flat membranous wing, are 1-1.5cm long with a closed notch at the tip. Introduced in 1860 in America and 1870 in Europe, this plant was recommended for planting in cold dry areas where few other trees would grow well.

Growth: 2-7-15. Hardiness: 90%. Choice: 2, 4. Wood: 5.

Japanese Elm *Ulmus japonica*

Closely related to *Ulmus davidiana*, of which it was originally thought to be a variety, this big 30m tree comes from north-east Asia including Japan. The young branches are densely pubescent and sometimes with corky wings. The leaves are obovate, 8-12cm long with double toothed margins.

Japanese Elm was first cultivated in the west in 1895. Plant collectors such as Professor Miyabe, who sent material to the Arnold Arboretum concentrated on the area around Sapporo in Japan. The cultivar 'Jacon' has been selected for its suitability for urban planting and resistance to Dutch Elm Disease.

Growth: 3-10-25. Hardiness: 50%. Choice: 2, 4. Wood: 2, 3, 5.

Ulmus 'Sapporo Autumn Gold'

Selected at the University of Wisconsin for its resistance to Dutch Elm Disease, this is a hybrid between Siberian and Japanese Elms. It arose as a Siberian Elm seedling pollinated by the Japanese species in Japan. Although disease resistant, it does not look like any of the European Elms. The golden autumn foliage is attractive.

Growth: 3-8-15. Hardiness: 70%. Choice: 1.

Chinese Elm *Ulmus parvifolia*

Usually a small tree less than 15m tall, but larger specimens do occur. The pubescent shoots bear small elliptic 2-6cm leaves, at first accompanied by stipules, which remain on the tree until early winter. Flowers appear in late summer in axillary clusters. From northern and central China, Taiwan, Korea and Japan, this tree was introduced to Europe first by French plant collector, the Abbé Gallois, who thought it was a tea plant. James Main, an English botanist, brought verified material into cultivation in 1794.

Growth: 3-8-15. Hardiness: 50%. Choice: 1, 4. Wood: 2, 3, 5.

Ulmus 'Sapporo Autumn Gold'

Chinese Elm

underside

fruit

Chestnut-leaved Elm

Ulmus laciniata

fruit

Ulmus bergmanniana

Ulmus bergmanniana

fruit

Chestnut-leaved Elm *Ulmus castaneifolia*

Although still occasionally found in some collections, this small, shrubby, long-leaved tree is no longer available in cultivation. Its origins are obscure, probably Asiatic, and its taxonomy appears to be dubious.

Growth: 2-5-10. Hardiness: 50%. Choice: 4.

Ulmus laciniata

A close relative of Wych Elm, formerly regarded as a geographical variety of it, this usually makes a small tree with very vigorous foliage. The 14-18cm leaves are deep green, like the Exeter Elm (p. 401), and rough to touch. The margins are excessively toothed and end in three or more distinct serrated points. Seeds are held in an oval wing 2cm long.

It is a common tree in its native eastern Asia, but has never been widely grown in the West since its introduction in 1905. Exceptional trees in Japan have reached 30m in height. The inner bark can be made into coarse rope and rough cloth after treatment in water and chair seats and baskets can be woven from long, thinly cut strips.

Growth: 2-6-15. Hardiness: 50%. Choice: 3, 4.

Ulmus bergmanniana

Coming from Central China, this small spreading tree has very short stalked 7-12cm leaves similar to Wych Elm. It was introduced to cultivation in the west in 1900 but remains rare.

Growth: 2-6-15. Hardiness: 40-50%. Choice: 4.

Large-fruited Elm *Ulmus macrocarpa*

The obovate fruits on this small tree are up to 3cm long and covered in bristles like the leaves. Pubescent young branches have corky wings on them like Field Maple (p. 625). Native to northern China, this species was introduced to the west in 1908. It is restricted to just a few specialist collections.

Growth: 2-5-10. Hardiness: 50%. Choice: 4.

Ulmus davidiana

Introduced from northern China in 1895, this small-leaved tree is very similar to the Large-fruited Elm. It is also a close relative of the Japanese Elm (p. 411). Young branches have broad corky wings, usually in pairs. A feature shared with *Ulmus alata* in the southeast United States.

Growth: 2-6-12. Hardiness: 50%. Choice: 4.

fruit

corky twig

underside

Large-fruited Elm

Ulmus davidiana

Caucasian Elm

Caucasian Elm

underside

Caucasian Elm

Cretan Zelkova

fruit

Chinese Zelkova

Cut-leaved Zelkova

fruit

Keaki

subsp. *stipulacea*

Caucasian Elm

414

Caucasian Elm *Zelkova carpinifolia*

This large forest tree, 25-35m tall, is from the Caucasus and northern Iran. In most respects it resembles Hornbeam (p. 325), but it has smooth pale greyish-buff bark on a fluted and buttressed stem. In Britain where it was introduced in 1760, most of the older trees in cultivation have a short thick bole and a massive multi-stemmed top, very like a pollarded tree that has been neglected. The deciduous leaves are oblong-elliptic with distinct rounded teeth and parallel veins. Usually there are only 7-10 teeth on each side of the leaf which also has a pointed tip. The insignificant flowers appear in the vein axils of new growth.

Growth: 4-17-30. Hardiness: 50%. Choice: 1 (requires space). Wood: 3, 5.

Cut-leaved Zelkova *Zelkova × verschaffeltii*

The origin of this tree, and to some extent its horticultural status, is uncertain. It is believed to be a hybrid between Caucasian Elm and Keaki first cultivated in 1886. Some authorities still regard it simply as a cultivar of Caucasian Elm. It never makes a large tree and it has narrow leaves with 5-8 pairs of pronounced triangular teeth.

Growth: 3-8-15. Hardiness: 50%. Choice: 1.

Chinese Zelkova *Zelkova sinica*

Introduced by Ernest Wilson from China in 1908, this species is still rare in cultivation, although it has found a modern use in bonsai. It has the potential to grow into a medium-sized tree, with grey bark which gradually roughens with age and then sheds occasional small roundish flakes. The colour revealed under each of these is light orange at first. The delicate, 3-6cm, coarsely-toothed and pointed leaves are light pink when they first appear in spring.

Growth: 3-10-20. Hardiness: 50%. Choice: 1. Wood: 2, 3, 5.

Keaki *Zelkova serrata*

From Taiwan and China this medium to large-sized tree has a rounded outline and tends to spread outwards. The bark is grey-brown and flakes off to reveal orange-brown beneath. The deciduous 6-12cm leaves are ovate with an acute point. The subspecies ***stipulacea*** is similar except for the leaves, which are ovate-lanceolate with an extended tip. The species was sent from China to the Veitch Nursery in 1862. It has proved to be a good pollution-resistant town tree but is not suitable for street planting.

Growth: 3-12-30. Hardiness: 50%. Choice: 1, 2. Wood: 3, 5.

Cretan Zelkova *Zelkova abelicea*

This rounded 15m tree comes from the islands of Crete and Cyprus. It is closely allied to Caucasian Elm and is probably an isolated segregate of that species. The leaves are smaller with fewer teeth. When young the shoots are covered in white downy hairs. It was introduced around 1924 and was thought at first to be an oak.

Growth: 2-8-15. Hardiness: 20%. Choice: 1. Wood: 3, 5.

autumn

Keaki

Hackberry

Nettle Tree

fruit

underside

Mississippi Hackberry

var. *smallii*

Hackberry

416

NETTLE TREES

Hackberry *Celtis occidentalis*

From a large part of America, Ontario to New England and North Dakota to Georgia, this 15-25m tall tree is a close relative of the elms. In addition to being a useful timber producer it is environmentally valuable, providing numerous sweet red and then purple berries for birds, and supporting a wide range of galls and mites on the foliage. The deciduous leaves are pointed and toothed, around 10cm long with three main veins emanating from an unequal base. Hackberry was first grown as decorative trees in 1656, but it is not spectacular and has never been in great demand. The variety **cordata**, formerly called *crassifolia*, is a more vigorous and luxuriant plant.

Growth: 3-10-25. Hardiness: 90%. Choice: 3.
Wood: 1, 3, 5.

Nettle Tree *Celtis australis*

In its native range, southern Europe and Asia Minor, this deciduous tree may reach 25m in height. When cultivated in cooler northern regions, 10m is more likely. It has thin zig-zag shoots and toothed narrow leaves which come to a slender point. The 1cm sweet-flavoured berries are green turning through orange and red to black. The bark is pale grey and smooth, rather elephantine. Nettle trees were first cultivated in England in the sixteenth century but they remain uncommon.

Growth: 2-6-15. Hardiness: 60%. Choice: 3. Wood: 3, 5.

Mississippi Hackberry *Celtis laevigata*

Most specimens have a broad rounded top and drooping branch ends. The greenish early spring flowers in the leaf axils are under 3mm wide and fairly insignificant producing one-seeded, orange-red to black 6mm fruits by the end of summer. This species extends the range of common Hackberry in North America southwards to Florida and Texas. Plants appeared in cultivation some time after 1811. The variety **smallii** has sharply serrate leaves, 7cm long on pubescent shoots. It occurs on the southern fringe of the species range.

Growth: 3-12-30. Hardiness: 40%. Choice: 3.
Wood: 1, 2, 3, 5.

Celtis tournefortii

Often only a large shrub, this plant has reddish-brown twigs with white downy hairs. The 5-7cm long alternate leaves are oval with a more or less rounded base, a short point and blunt teeth. The fleshy fruits are ovoid, around 1cm long and ripen brownish-red. The single stone has four distinct ridges running from the base to the apex. From the Balkans, Sicily and the Crimea this species was first cultivated in 1738.

Growth: 1-3-6. Hardiness: 50%. Choice: 1, 3.

var. *cordata*   *Celtis tournefortii*    **Nettle Tree** bark

Caucasian Nettle Tree

old bark

Caucasian Nettle Tree underside

Japanese Hackberry

Celtis bungeana

Caucasian Nettle Tree

NETTLE TREES

Caucasian Nettle Tree *Celtis caucasica*

This vigorous tree has downy young twigs and coarsely toothed 5-9cm obovate to ovate-lanceolate leaves. The fruits are yellow turning to orange-brown. Each consists of a thick-shelled nutlet encased in a thin layer of fleshy pulp, held in place by a tough outer skin. This species is usually dioecious. Its natural range extends across Asia Minor but it is rare in cultivation. It was introduced to the west around 1885, having been considered to be a form of the closely related *Celtis australis* (p. 417) before that date. The variable nature of the foliage makes these trees extremely difficult to identify.

Growth: 4-12-20. Hardiness: 40-50%. Choice: 3. Wood: 1, 3, 5.

Japanese Hackberry *Celtis sinensis*

From eastern China, Korea and Japan this medium-sized, 15m tall, tree has a rounded open outline. The serrated leaves are around 8cm long and fairly broad with a short point. Fruits are dark orange and fleshy. A fairly tender plant, it was introduced to the west in 1910, about 15 years after the closely related and very similar *Celtis biondii* from the same area in China.

Growth: 3-6-15. Hardiness: 40-50%. Choice: 3. Wood: 1, 3, 5.

Celtis koraiensis

A rare bushy tree, seldom reaching 12m in height has dark grey bark and glabrous shoots. The 5-15cm oval leaves have teeth which are exaggerated towards the end. Most are offset at the base with some pubescence along the veins on the underside. The globose 1cm fruits are orange-brown when ripe, held on a 2cm pedicel – some of the largest fruits in the genus. From Manchuria, Korea and northern China, it is very hardy but seldom seen in cultivation even though it was introduced to western horticulture in 1923.

Growth: 2-5-12. Hardiness: 50%. Choice: 3.

Celtis bungeana

The smooth bark on this 15m tree is pale grey and the tree's outline is rounded. The 5-8cm deciduous leaves are dark glossy green on the upper side, petioles are less than 1cm long. Insignificant greenish flowers in spring are followed by purplish-black 1cm fruits. Originally it came from central and northern Asia, and is quite hardy. Although in general cultivation since 1868, this species has never become popular. It is closely related to the slower-growing *Celtis tournefortii* (p. 417) and *Celtis glabrata* which was introduced from western Asia at about the same time.

Growth: 2-5-15. Hardiness: 50%. Choice: 3.

Celtis koraiensis

Caucasian Nettle Tree fruiting twig

♂ flowers

White Mulberry

♀ flowers

'Venosa'

'Pyramidalis'

unlobed leaf

White Mulberry

fruit

underside

White Mulberry
lobed leaf

Morus mongolica

420

MULBERRY FAMILY · Moraceae

White Mulberry *Morus alba*

This Chinese species, long cultivated for its leaves to feed silkworms, has spread round the temperate world. It is a small tree, seldom reaching 15m in height with spreading branches and a rounded top. Traditionally trees were planted like Cricket-bat Willows (p. 291). Branches of about ankle thickness and cut to around 1.5m long were hammered into moist ground, where they proceeded to grow into instant trees. White Mulberry leaves are variable in shape and size. They may be anything between 6 and 16cm long and heart-shaped or variously-lobed. The upper surface is quite smooth and bright green. Margins are toothed with soft, coarse, rounded and rather blunt teeth. The leaf stalk, or petiole, is only 1-2.5cm long. The fruit which resembles an elongated blackberry can be white, pink or purplish-red. It is edible but not particularly pleasant and not recommended in any quantity.

There are several cultivated forms, all of which make good garden plants. '**Pendula**' which dates back to 1897 is a superb weeping tree. It tends to be rather more hardy than the species. The leaves are 4-8cm long and frequently lobed in a haphazard kind of way. This clone produces inferior fruit which may be white, pink or dark red. Another interesting cultivar is '**Venosa**', which is exactly like the species except the leaf veins are white. '**Pyramidalis**' is the antithesis of 'Pendula': it resembles a small Lombardy Poplar with up-swept branches and bright green foliage.

Growth: 3-6-15 (species). Hardiness: 40-50%. Choice: 1, 3.

Morus mongolica

Introduced in 1907 this very rare tree or large shrub up to 8m tall is closely related to *Morus australis*. They both come from China and Korea and may have frequently been confused in cultivation. The 8-16cm leaves are oblong-ovate with a pointed tip and sometimes a cordate base. They have coarse cuspidate teeth and a short, 2-4cm petiole. Lobes, as illustrated for white mulberry, do occur but they are not usually common. The fruit is red, ripening to dark red or black. It is edible but not as good as Black Mulberry (p. 423). An obscure variety *Morus mongolica* var. *diabolica* has rough leaves that are wildly-lobed and sculptured into irrational shapes.

Growth: 2-4-8. Hardiness: 50%. Choice: 3.

'Pendula'

White Mulberry

underside

Black Mulberry

Black Mulberry **Chinese Mulberry**

fruit

Black Mulberry *Morus nigra*

Few trees can claim to be as rewarding in cultivation as this one. It lives for a long time and soon develops an aged appearance. The deciduous foliage is vivid green, dense and largely free of insect predators. The pleasant picturesque rounded shape is of manageable garden size, 10m is quite exceptional. As a shade tree it is ideal – cool and thick with no obnoxious smells, honeydew or falling limbs. When ripe, the dark red 2.5cm fruits are deliciously sweet. The only complaint most owners voice is about the mess fallen berries make when it becomes impossible to eat them rapidly enough.

Originally from western Asia this species has been spread across the whole of temperate Europe reaching Britain in the early sixteenth century and finally America by 1548. Black Mulberry tends to be deceptive in terms of age. Gnarled, leaning and even fallen specimens generally appear to be much older than they actually are. Most trees that fall right over usually make a full recovery, especially when they are cut back. In this situation they tend to fruit in abundance; furthermore, in a reclining position the berries are easier to pick. Like White Mulberry new trees can be produced by simply hammering trimmed-out, 10cm thick, branches into the ground in winter. Branches forced into the ground when a tree falls over also take root.

Black Mulberry leaves are broadly ovate, 6-12cm long, exceptionally 20cm, with a pointed tip, cordate base and 1.5-2.5cm petiole. They are rough on the upper side and pubescent below. The margins are coarsely serrate with occasional lobes on some individuals.

Growth: 3-8-10. Hardiness: 60%. Choice: 3. Wood: 1.

Chinese Mulberry *Morus cathayana*

This rare, 8m, spreading rounded tree is from an extensive area in central and eastern China. Environmental variants may grow to 15m in height while others remain short and bushy. The leaves are ovate, pointed and coarsely toothed. Leaf bases may be truncate or cordate, and petioles do not exceed 3cm. The upper surface is rough like a stinging nettle. Occasionally lobed leaves are produced but they are infrequent. The fruit is narrow, about 3cm long and only up to 0.7cm across. Colour varies between white, red and black but at any stage they are not particularly good to eat.

The species was brought out of China in 1907 by Ernest Wilson, the same year as two other Chinese mulberries. There seems to be confusion in some collections about exactly which species they actually have.

Growth: 2-7-8. Hardiness: 50%. Choice: 4.

Chinese Mulberry

Black Mulberry

old bark

♀ flowers

fruits

Paper Mulberry

♂ flowers

leaf variation

underside

Paper Mulberry

autumn

MULBERRIES

Paper Mulberry *Broussonetia papyrifera*

Paper was once made from the inner bark of this tree in Japan and female plants bear fruits which are orange-red and vaguely resemble mulberries. Male trees have catkin-like flowers. This is a close relative of the true mulberries and like them it has rough bristly leaves of various shapes.

Originally from eastern Asia, since the eighteenth century this good urban species has become naturalized in parts of the United States. It tolerates poor soil and polluted air and is quite hardy. It spreads like *Robinia* (p. 575) by root suckers and may become a persistent nuisance once it is established.
Growth: 3-12-16. Hardiness: 40-60%. Choice: 1, 3, 4.

Osage Orange *Maclura pomifera*

Another member of the Mulberry family, this monotypic species grows to around 14m in height with a rounded head of branches. The stem and main limbs are often contorted. The thick brown shoots contain milky sap. Occasionally a sharp spine is produced at the base of a leaf. The 5-8cm leaves are ovate and pointed at both ends. They are deep glossy-green above and paler beneath. Male and female flowers in clusters occur in early summer on separate trees. Female trees produce spectacular fruits like oranges up to 13cm across. They are green, ripening to yellow and actually consist of many individual fruits fused together. Each of these contain a pale brown nutlet, enclosed in a thin layer of succulent flesh, rich in milky juice. Isolated female trees also produce full-sized fruits, but no seeds.

This was probably originally a wetland species. It prefers moist riverside situations. The native range is no longer clearly defined but it would have included parts of Texas, Oklahoma and Arkansas.

Local American Indians once used the springy wood for bows and clubs. A local American name for the tree is Bow Wood. Early settlers used the brightly-coloured roots to dye fabrics yellow. They also fed the fruits to livestock. A common use for this species in America was for hedging where it made a sustainable alternative to barbed wire. In parts of the United States it is still known as Hedge-apple. The wood is strong, hard and heavy and its durability made it ideal for fence posts and other uses in wet conditions.
Growth: 3-9-14. Hardiness: 50%. Choice: 1, 2. Wood: 1, 3.

fruit

spine

Osage Orange

'Exmouth'

'Goliath'

underside of type leaf

Bull Bay Magnolia

Bull Bay Magnolia

Veitch's Hybrid Magnolia

Cucumber Tree

Magnolia officinalis var. *biloba*

underside

Cucumber Tree

Large-leaved Cucumber Tree

MAGNOLIA FAMILY · Magnoliaceae

Bull Bay Magnolia *Magnolia grandiflora*

Bull Bay was probably the first magnolia to be illustrated in Britain when it was drawn by Georg D. Ehret in 1737. In the American hurricane belt this wind-firm tree was often planted in gardens. Branches were pegged down to take root and increase their resistance to the wind. The late summer flowers appear 20 years after planting, The cultivar '**Exmouth**', raised in the English town of that name, is one of the oldest cultivated evergreen magnolias. The big deep green leaves are pale brown and felted underneath at first. The 25cm flowers are light yellow. '**Goliath**' is a white-flowered form with smaller (20cm) evergreen non-felted leaves. It was raised in Guernsey in 1910.

Growth: 3-12-25. Hardiness: 30-40%. Choice: 1, 3.

Veitch's Hybrid Magnolia *Magnolia × veitchii*

This cross between *Magnolia denudata* and *Magnolia campbellii* was first made at the Veitch Nursery in Exeter in 1907. Only two seedlings were retained, 'Isca' and Peter Veitch', which is illustrated on p. 429.

Growth: -. Hardiness: 50%. Choice: 1.

Large-leaved Cucumber Tree

Magnolia macrophylla

From the mountains of the south-east United States, this bushy tree can produce leaves 90cm long. They are deciduous, papery and white on the underside. The infrequent flowers are up to 30cm across. It was discovered and named by the French explorer André Michaux.

Growth: 3-9-18. Hardiness: 40-50%. Choice: 1.

Cucumber Tree *Magnolia acuminata*

A substantial deciduous tree that is at first not obviously a Magnolia. It develops a broad head of branches up to 12m tall. Flowers, mostly hidden among the foliage, are metallic blue and dull yellow, followed by green cucumber-like seed pods.

Growth: 3-5-12. Hardiness: 60%. Choice: 1.

Magnolia officinalis var. *biloba*

This rare Chinese species is probably only known in cultivation. The variety *biloba* is most often seen. It was introduced to Britain by Sir Harold Hillier and planted in his Hampshire garden in 1936. It grows rapidly and has deciduous leaves with distinctive notched tips. It requires moist fertile soil and a sunny position.

Growth: 4-12-15. Hardiness: 50%. Choice: 1.

Chinese Evergreen Magnolia *Magnolia delavayi*

A tender Chinese Himalayan evergreen with large 36cm long, dark, matt green leaves with sea-green backs. It was discovered by, and named after, the French plant collector Père Jean Delavay in 1886. The disappointing ephemeral flowers only come out at night.

Growth: 4-7-12. Hardiness: 40%. Choice: 1.

Japanese Big-leaf Magnolia *Magnolia hypoleuca*

This Japanese and Russian Pacific coast species is usually only a small upright specimen in cultivation, but a large forest tree in the wild. The 20cm deciduous leaves are silver-backed when young. The scented pinkish-cream flowers occur in early summer.

Growth: 3-5-10 (in cultivation). Hardiness: 50%. Choice: 1.

Magnolia
'Wada's Memory'

'Heaven Scent'

'Picture'

Magnolia
'Wada's Memory'

'Brozzonii'

Magnolia 'Wada's Memory'

This outstanding plant was selected at Seattle in 1940 and named in honour of Mr. Koichiro Wada of Yokohama, Japan. Probably it is a form of *salicifolia* or a hybrid between it and *Magnolia kobus*. The pure white flowers are fragrant.

Growth: 3-6-10. Hardiness: 50%. Choice: 1.

Magnolia 'Heaven Scent'

A Gresham hybrid (created by D.Todd Gresham of Santa Cruz in 1955) using *Magnolia × veitchii* and *Magnolia liliiflora* 'Nigra'. A small tree, producing an abundance of strongly scented flowers.

Growth: 3-6-8. Hardiness: 50%. Choice: 1.

Magnolia × soulangiana cultivars

'**Picture**' is a strong-growing Japanese clone bred by Koichiro Wada in 1930. It is purple outside and white inside its erect flowers.

'**Rustica Rubra**' is another vigorous plant this time closely related to 'Lennei'. It is one of the most tolerant of all magnolias for garden use.

'**Brozzonii**' is about the best selection ever made from a *Magnolia denudata × Magnolia lilliflora* cross. It has big white flowers, shaded purple towards the base, which appear over an extended period through spring and summer.

'**Sayonara**' is perhaps the ultimate small garden Magnolia. It is actually a 'Gresham' hybrid produced in Santa Cruz, California in 1955, with stunning flowers which are creamy-pink gradually darkening in colour to pinkish-gold in the centre. This plant started life as a seedling from *Magnolia × soulangiana* 'Lennei Alba' crossed with *Magnolia × veitchii* 'Rubra'.

Growth: variable. Hardiness: 50%. Choice: 1.

Magnolia × veitchii 'Peter Veitch'

Several fast-growing hardy hybrids were raised by the Veitch Nurseries in Exeter in 1907. These plants arose as seedlings from a *Magnolia campbellii* crossed with *Magnolia denudata*. One of the best selections, 'Peter Veitch', was named after the man who propagated it. It is a medium to large tree with pale purplish-pink flowers appearing before the leaves.

Magnolia × veitchii was subsequently crossed again with *Magnolia liliiflora* 'Nigra', to produce the cultivar '**Peppermint Stick**', by D.Todd Gresham in 1961. It picks up features of *Magnolia campbellii* in having 12 tepals, and *Magnolia liliiflora* 'Nigra' in the prominent flush of dark pink on the outside of the flower.

Growth: 3-6-8. Hardiness: 50%. Choice: 1.

'Sayonara'

'Rustica Rubra'

Magnola × veitchii 'Peter Veitch'

'Peppermint Stick'

'Merrill'

'Leonard Messel'

Yellow Cucumber Tree

'Norman Gould'

Magnolia stellata

Magnolia sargentiana

Magnolia × *thompsoniana*

var. *robusta*

Magnolia × loebneri

This group of distinctive deciduous trees originally came from Max Loebner and the Wilhelm Kordes Nursery in early twentieth-century Germany. Crossing *Magnolia kobus* with *Magnolia stellata*, they selected five outstanding floriferous seedlings. Further hybridizing has taken place, notably in America. These plants are ideal in sheltered gardens, tolerating both acid and alkaline soils and semi-shade or full sun.

The cultivar '**Leonard Messel**' is a bushy plant flowering in early spring. It originated in the garden of Colonel Leonard Messel at Nymans, Sussex. In this instance the *Magnolia stellata* parent was 'Rosea'. In contrast '**Merrill**' is a big vigorous white-flowered tree raised in 1939 at the Arnold Arboretum, Boston, Massachusetts.

Growth: variable. Hardiness: 40-50%. Choice: 1.

Yellow Cucumber Tree *Magnolia cordata*

Discovered near Augusta, Georgia in the late 1700s, this species was sent to France in 1803. It requires moisture and some shelter in northern gardens but is tolerant of acid or alkaline soil conditions.

Growth: 3-6-10. Hardiness: 40%. Choice: 1.

Magnolia × thompsoniana

A hybrid between *Magnolia tripetala* and *Magnolia virginiana*, two American species, this plant was raised at Mile End, in London, by Archibald Thompson in 1808. It is a deciduous or semi-evergreen sun-loving shrub up to 4m tall, with wavy edged glossy green silvery-backed leaves. The fragrant flowers occur at intervals throughout the summer.

Growth: 2-3-4. Hardiness: 40%. Choice: 1.

Magnolia stellata 'Norman Gould'

This particularly floriferous form of the ubiquitous 'Star Magnolia' was first raised artificially at Wisley in the 1950s. It bears numerous white 15cm 'star' flowers.

Growth: 2-3-4. Hardiness: 50%. Choice: 1.

Magnolia sargentiana

Native of Yunnan and Szechuan in China, this magnolia was discovered by the French missionary Armand David in 1869. It is potentially a very large tree, 24m tall in the wild. The variety **robusta** is the most hardy garden form. The scented flowers tend to droop downwards as they open.

Growth: 3-16-24. Hardiness: 40-50%. Choice: 1 (requires space).

Magnolia sinensis

A spreading Chinese shrubby tree with fragrant drooping spring and autumn flowers. The red stamens are a prominent feature. It needs rich moist soil, full sun and shelter from strong winds.

Growth: 2-4-8. Hardiness: 40%. Choice: 1.

Magnolia globosa

There are at least two distinct types of this Himalayan mountain species. Before the fragrant white summer flowers open they resemble eggs, which is why in Nepal this tree is called the 'Hen Magnolia'. In northern Europe rich, organic, moisture-retaining soil and shelter give the best results.

Growth: 2-6-8. Hardiness: 30-40%. Choice: 1.

Magnolia sinensis

Magnolia globosa

Magnolia × *soulangiana*

fruit

'Lennei Alba'

'Lennei'

North Japanese Magnolia

ripe fruit

new leaf

Japanese Willow-leaf Magnolia

Magnolia × *soulangiana* 'Lennei'

Magnolia sprengeri var. *elongata*

Magnolia × soulangiana 'Lennei'

'**Lennei**' was one of the original nineteenth-century Italian hybrid clones, selected from a *Magnolia denudata* × *Magnolia liliiflora* cross. It is a small tree often with several stems. Plants raised vegetatively are particularly prized because they begin flowering as soon as they are established. The large goblet-shaped flowers are creamy-white with variable amounts of purplish streaks and shading mostly on the outside. '**Lennei Alba**' is a pure white-flowered form. Both these clones have been used as parents in subsequent Magnolia breeding programmes.

Growth: 3-7-8. Hardiness: 40-50%. Choice: 1.

North Japanese Magnolia
Magnolia kobus var. *borealis*

This Japanese forest tree was introduced first to North America in 1861 then to Europe in 1865. The variety occurs naturally in the region of Hokkaido. The performance of garden specimens appears to depend very much on the provenance of source material. This is a plant that tolerates lime-rich soils.

Growth: 3-10-15. Hardiness: 50%. Choice: 1.

Japanese Willow-leaf Magnolia
Magnolia salicifolia

This variable plant grows naturally in the semi-shade of broadleaved forest on Honshu and other nearby Japanese islands. It was first introduced to America and England in the early 1890s by Sargent and Veitch respectively. The deciduous foliage smells of aniseed if lightly crushed. The spring flowers are also scented. They prefer moist acid soils.

Growth: 3-8-10. Hardiness: 50%. Choice: 1.

Magnolia sprengeri var. *elongata*

This magnificent early-flowering deciduous species consists of 2 varieties, the well-known pink *diva* and this white-flowered Chinese tree introduced by Ernest Wilson in 1900.

Growth: 3-7-10. Hardiness: 50%. Choice: 1.

Yulan, or Lily Tree *Magnolia denudata*

This central Chinese tree has for centuries been cultivated in Buddhist temple gardens. In the Tang Dynasty the flowers were regarded as a symbol of purity. They are pure white and scented of lemon. Moist acid soils are needed in a sheltered frost-free place.

Growth: 4-12-15. Hardiness: 40-50%. Choice: 1, 4.

Magnolia liliiflora

The wild distribution of this plant has been obscured by centuries of cultivation in China and Japan. It is a slow-growing deciduous, shade tolerant shrub which flowers in early summer. The best known and most hardy form is probably 'Nigra' which has later purplish-red flowers. The scientific names of this and the previous species have been challenged by some horticulturalists recently, the names used here are the oldest valid names on record, published by Desrousseaux in 1791.

Growth: 2-3-4. Hardiness: 50%. Choice: 1.

Yulan

Magnolia liliiflora

Magnolia campbellii

closed flower

Magnolia campbellii

subsp. *mollicomata*

var. *alba*

Umbrella Magnolia

Umbrella Magnolia

Fraser Magnolia

Magnolia campbellii

In cultivation this is a big tree (27m in England, with a trunk over 1m thick). The large pink flowers, which only appear on seedlings after 20 years, come out in early spring before the leaves. The prominent grey-green velvety winter flower buds are a distinctive feature. The subsp. *mollicomata* is from south-east Tibet, north Burma and neighbouring regions of China. The purplish-pink flowers develop a 'cup-and-saucer' appearance, a ring of flat petal-like tepals round a central upright cluster. There is a pure white-flowered variety **alba**.

Growth: 4-18-25. Hardiness: 50%. Choice: 1 (requires space).

Umbrella Magnolia *Magnolia tripetala*

The scientific name refers to the three petal-like sepals, or tepals, on the flower which open before the rest. This is a very hardy tree or large branchy shrub from eastern North America, where it is typically a plant of humid stream-sides and woodland ravines, growing in semi-shade. It was introduced to Britain by the eighteenth-century American plant collector John Bartram. The deciduous ovate leaves are huge, up to 50cm long and 25cm wide. It makes a very satisfactory umbrella if the rain shower is brief. The large, cream-coloured strongly scented three tepal 'goblet' flowers appear in early summer. Acid soil is essential for healthy growth.

Growth: 3-10-12. Hardiness: 50-60%. Choice: 1, 4.

Fraser Magnolia *Magnolia fraseri*

This North American species from the Appalachian region was discovered in 1776 and named after John Fraser a Scottish plant collector. It is a medium-sized fast-growing tree which thrives in the shade of woodland. The distinctive big deciduous leaves have ear-like lobes. It is called 'earleaf cucumber tree' and 'earleaf umbrella tree' in America. The late spring flowers are milky white with a somewhat 'clinical' smell. Moist acid soil is required.

Growth: 3-10-15. Hardiness: 50%. Choice: 1.

Sweet Bay Magnolia *Magnolia virginiana*

In North America this variable semi-evergreen tree or shrub grows particularly well on the coastal plains. It likes wet swampy ground, an alternative American name is 'Swampbay'. It tolerates a wide range of soil types and is resistant to wind and sea spray. This was the first American magnolia to arrive in Britain (1688). It is not a strong grower in cultivation but the creamy-white short-lived summer flowers are delightfully scented, and appear over a long period. Early American colonists called this 'Beaver Tree', as the fleshy roots were used to bait beaver traps.

Growth: 3-12-18. Hardiness: 50%. Choice: 1, 2, 3.

Wilson's Magnolia *Magnolia wilsonii*

Named after Ernest Wilson this small spreading Chinese tree has fragrant white upside-down 10cm flowers. Each has a ring of densely packed maroon stamens inside. The flowers are best seen from below so plants need early upward training to achieve enough height. In gardens it should be planted in semi-shade especially against an east wall.

Growth: 3-7-8. Hardiness: 40%. Choice: 1.

Sweet Bay Magnolia

Wilson's Magnolia

Tulip Tree

fruit

seed

'Aureomarginatum'

autumn

Chinese Tulip Tree

Tulip Tree

seedling

436

Tulip Tree *Liriodendron tulipifera*

This pyramidal tree can exceed 35m in height and 25m in width, but it is very worthwhile planting where space permits. The deciduous pea-green leaves are unlike those of any other temperate tree: they seem to have been cut off across the top. The largest are around 18cm long with a truncate base and an acute lobe on each side. After about 15 years (from seed) erect 4-5cm solitary flowers are produced in early summer all over the tree, even on low branches. They have six overlapping petals resembling a tulip except for the additional ring of prominent deflexed sepals. The petals are pale greenish-white with a faint orange blotch towards the base. The inside is filled with numerous yellow stamens and an enlarged pistil, consisting of about 70 densely packed carpels.

This is a stately tree with light grey corky bark. In old age it often forms an intricate lattice pattern of vertical ridges. The autumn foliage colour is outstanding, especially when trees are planted close to water and where autumn mists are common. Colour develops over 2-3 weeks, from soft yellow to gold and then to a subtle shade of golden-brown. Such a large tree carpets the ground over a wide area with its fallen leaves.

In the wild this species extends through North America from Nova Scotia to Florida. It is common along riversides, probably because the seed floats in water. Its date of introduction to Europe is uncertain but John Tradescant is believed to have brought it to England in the mid-seventeenth century. It was recorded at Fulham Palace, in London, in 1688. This tree needs moist fertile heavy soil to thrive. Some shade at first is an advantage. It is generally a good town tree being indifferent to air pollution. Above all it requires an enormous amount of space.

There are several cultivated forms including a variegated type '**Aureomarginatum**', produced in 1903. It grows to around 15-20m tall. The upright form '**Fastigiatum**' is about the same height but requires less space.

Growth: 3-15-30. Hardiness: 50%. Choice: 1 (requires space). Wood: 1, 3, 4.

Chinese Tulip Tree *Liriodendron chinense*

A medium-sized tree from south-east Asia, introduced to Europe by Ernest Wilson in 1901. It is rare in cultivation and is very difficult to distinguish from the American species. Even the more deeply-lobed leaves are not a constant feature.

Growth: 3-10-20. Hardiness: 50%. Choice: 1 (requires space). Wood: 1, 3, 4.

'**Fastigiatum**'
autumn

'**Aureomarginatum**'

old bark

Spur Leaf

♂ flowers

Spur Leaf

fruit

Gutta-percha Tree

leaf showing latex strands

Gutta-percha Tree

438

LAUREL FAMILY · Lauraceae

Gutta-percha Tree
Eucommia ulmoides (Eucommiaceae)

For centuries in China this tree has been cultivated for its medicinal properties and as an attractive plant. It is the only temperate tree which contains rubber. If a leaf is gently pulled in half latex strands will hold the two halves together. When confronted by this tree, which is superficially like an elm, leaf tearing is a useful aid to its true identity. Specimens 15m tall are known with spreading branches and pale grey bark. The deciduous leaves are up to 16cm long and 10cm wide sometimes offset at the base. The fruits, on separate female trees are similar to elm but more elongated. The native status of this species within China is unknown, it has been completely obscured by cultivation. The first plants were introduced to Europe around 1896.

Growth: 2-8-15. Hardiness: 40-50%. Choice: 1, 3.

Spur Leaf *Tetracentron sinense* (Tetracentaceae)

Only one species remains in this primitive genus, which has wood closely resembling that of the conifers. The foliage has some resemblance to the Katsura tree (p. 441), but the completely different hermaphrodite flowers are in long catkins, and the outline of the tree is upswept and rather gaunt. In its native Himalayas to central China it grows in temperate woodland on low slopes and in deep valleys. Ernest Wilson introduced it to Europe in 1901 but it remains obscure and confined to specialist collections.

Growth: 2-6-12. Hardiness: 40-50%. Choice: 1.

Bay Tree *Laurus nobilis* (Lauraceae)

There are only two species of true 'Laurel' the ceremonial plant of early civilizations. *Laurus nobilis* the 'Bay Laurel' from southern Europe was used by the Ancient Greeks and Romans to reward victors and athletes and adorn nobility and bay leaves have long been used for flavouring food. As a living plant this is a strong-growing, but slightly tender, evergreen which is tolerant of clipping and withstands salty coastal conditions. Plants 15m tall are known, but in the north they may have been cut back to the base several times in their lifetime by severe winter weather. Modern plants were re-introduced to northern Europe in 1562. In Britain, from the evidence of Roman burials in London live trees were flourishing there in the third century.

The cultivar '**Aurea**' is a golden-leaved form which looks good in winter but not so good in late summer, when it appears to have some mineral deficiency or disease. The Willow-leaved Bay '**Angustifolia**' is an interesting aromatic evergreen with tough narrow, pointed wavy-edged leaves on stiff branches.

Growth: 2-9-15. Hardiness: 40%. Choice: 1, 2, 3. Wood: 1 (species).

Bay Tree

'**Aurea**'

'**Angustifolia**'

Fig

leaf variation

var. *magnificum*

Katsura Tree

autumn

♀ flower ♂ flower

Katsura Tree
autumn

'Pendulum'

Katsura Tree

Cercidiphyllum japonicum (Cercidiphyllaceae)

Usually this is a small tree 10-15m tall, but occasional 30m specimens have been recorded. It comes from southern Japan and China and was introduced to America in 1865 and to Europe in 1881. In cultivation this species is grown as an individual specimen or in small groves, so that male and female trees can be planted together. The tiny bright red flowers appear on spur shoots in late winter before the leaves. They are followed on female trees by clusters of 1-2cm pea-pods containing winged seeds. The thin deciduous leaves are heart-shaped and 5-10cm long. They are glaucescent on the underside, purplish-pink when young, and subtle shades of pale yellow and pink in the autumn. As the leaves fall they produce an elusive smell of burnt sugar or caramel.

The variety **magnificum** is confined to Honshu Island in Japan. It is a rare tree with smooth bark, larger more coarsely toothed leaves and seeds with a wing at both ends. A larger variety is *sinense*, introduced from its native China by Ernest Wilson in 1907, some individual trees have reached 40m in height. The cultivar '**Pendulum**' is a weeping form, possibly a hybrid between these two varieties. It has been in cultivation for a long time and is also said to occur spontaneously in Japan.

Growth: 3-12-25. Hardiness: 50%. Choice: 1 (requires space).

Fig *Ficus carica* (Moraceae)

Originally from western Asia, this species has now been cultivated all over the temperate world. It is a close relative of the rubber plant *Ficus elastica* (see p. 785). It makes a spreading deciduous tree 10-15m tall, with a stem up to 60cm across which generally needs some support in order to sustain upward growth. The green shoots are stout with big leaf scars which persist for years on the pale grey wrinkled bark. The flowers are formed inside the shoot tips, their presence only indicated by a small hole. They are pollinated exclusively by a specialist burrowing beetle which rears its young inside the hidden flower. In cold countries where the beetle cannot survive the fruit is always infertile. Fortunately there are cultivars such as 'Nottingham', 'Brunswick' and 'Brown Turkey' which set fruit without the need for pollination. Fig trees were introduced to England by Cardinal Pole in 1550.

Growth: 3-6-12. Hardiness: 30-40%. Choice: 3.

Katsura Tree

seed
fruit
Sassafras
var. *molle*
autumn

seedling

Sassafras

Californian Laurel

Sassafras *Sassafras albidum* (Lauraceae)

This eastern North American deciduous tree has provided useful products to Indians and colonists alike for hundreds of years. The roots yield an aromatic oil which is used to perfume soap and cosmetics. Tea and root beer are also flavoured with it. For a time it was thought to cure every conceivable ailment though some of these magical powers are questioned today. It is certainly not poisonous because there are still people around who enjoy chewing the twigs for their spicy taste. Like the mulberries, Sassafras has a diverse range of leaf shapes. Healthy leaves are between 6 and 12cm long, sometimes elliptical, sometimes oval and sometimes with up to three large lobes. They are pale green with entire margins, turning to yellow and orange in the autumn. Trees seldom exceed 15m in height, and plants often become multi-stemmed thickets. The yellow-green terminal flowers develop, on female trees, into 1cm elliptical glossy blue-black berries, each held on a bright red fleshy stalk.

Sassafras has a broad natural range across North America from Ontario to southern Maine southwards to central Florida and west to Texas. It grows in the Appalachian Mountains to 1500m. The first introductions to Europe were in 1633. The variety ***molle*** is similar to the species but has silky hairy young shoots and leaf veins. It was first cultivated in 1930.

Growth: 2-9-18. Hardiness: 40-60%. Choice: 3.

Californian Laurel
Umbellularia californica (Lauraceae)

The Laurel family (Lauraceae), of which this species and Sassafras are part, are mostly tropical plants. Californian Laurel is an aromatic evergreen tree up to 25m tall in favourable conditions. It has a natural range from California into Oregon State. The thick glossy dark green 8-10cm leaves are oblong-lanceolate and pointed at both ends. The small umbels of flowers are about 1.5cm across developing into ovoid fruits which turn yellowish-purple at maturity in late autumn.

The decorative wood, 'Pepperwood', is pale brown with dark brown streaks in the grain. It is used for veneers, high quality furniture and craft work. The natural oils in it give a superb polished finish. The aromatic foliage can bring on a severe headache on hot summer days.

Growth: 3-10-20. Hardiness: 30-40%. Choice: 4. Wood: 1.

Californian Laurel

seed

fruit

Sweet Gum

seedling

'Variegata'

'Silver King'

Chinese Sweet Gum

Formosana group

Monticola group

Oriental Sweet Gum

autumn

old bark

Sweet Gum

444

WITCH-HAZEL FAMILY · Hamamelidaceae

Sweet Gum *Liquidambar styraciflua*

The genus Liquidambar consists of only four species, but they extend round the whole north temperate world. They mostly have five-lobed star-shaped shining green deciduous leaves. These differ from maples in that they are alternate on the shoot and not opposite. The North American species *Liquidambar styraciflua* is an important timber tree. Its heartwood is known in the furniture trade as 'satin walnut'. The living tree is particularly ornamental in the autumn, when a whole range of brilliant foliage colours may be produced. This does depend on the site and soil conditions which should ideally be acid. Plants were introduced to Europe in 1681, but it has never been easy to grow. Many provenances are frost tender and young saplings are difficult to transplant.

There are a range of ornamental forms of Sweet Gum. '**Variegata**' has normal leaves spotted and splashed with yellow in a random fashion. This cultivar is probably the same as 'Aurea'. Variegation is taken further in the cultivar '**Silver King**' which has much more yellow, particularly around the edges of the lobes and between the veins. This form has leaves with all the points directed forwards. Other yellow-leaved forms are '**Moonbeam**' which is variegated but has soft edges between pale yellow and green and '**Golden Treasure**' which is deeper yellow. These both produce good red and purple autumn colour. The very best autumn colour is to be found on the cultivar '**Lane Roberts**' and '**Worplesdon**' which were specially selected for this feature.

Growth: 3-14-30. Hardiness: 60%. Choice: 1 (requires space). Wood: 1, 2 (species).

Chinese Sweet Gum *Liquidambar formosana*

The species is tender away from its natural range in southern China and Taiwan. The 'Monticola group' (formerly var. *monticola*) is more robust. They generally have three-lobed leaves, which are relatively large on new shoots and coppice. The species was introduced to Europe in 1884 and the 'Monticola group' was brought into cultivation by Ernest Wilson in 1908.

Growth: 3-14-30. Hardiness: 30%. Choice: 1. Wood: 1, 2.

Oriental Sweet Gum *Liquidambar orientalis*

This slow-growing small tree or large bush has five-lobed leaves reminiscent of Field maple (p. 625). Each lobe is further divided to produce additional broad teeth. The autumn colour is particularly good. This species was introduced to Europe from its native Asia Minor in 1750.

Growth: 2-7-15. Hardiness: 40-50%. Choice: 1. Wood: 1.

'Lane Roberts' autumn

'Worplesdon'

'Moonbeam'

'Golden Treasure'

'Lane Roberts' autumn

Persian Ironwood

fruit

'Pendula'

Persian Ironwood
spring

446

Persian Ironwood *Parrotia persica*

F.W. Parrot, the German surgeon, explorer and naturalist, is commemorated in the name of this plant from the eastern Caucasus and northern Iran. Parrot, 1792-1841, was also the first person credited with climbing to the summit of Mount Ararat in Turkey in 1829. Noah is said to have arrived there by boat many centuries before.

Persian Ironwood is a highly ornamental tree or large shrub and has been in cultivation since 1840. It makes a year-round feature with something to offer in every season. In winter the bark on mature specimens, which is grey-brown, exfoliates in thin scaly plates like a plane tree's, to reveal red or orange-brown patches of colour underneath. In late winter or early spring the flowers appear. They are small and have no petals, but occur in profusion. The red anthers of the males appear directly out of brown velvety buds like tiny jewels among a dark tangle of bare winter twigs. In summer the lustrous green deciduous leaves obscure every branch. They are oval to obovate, roughly toothed on the upper half and terminate in a short point. The most luxuriant may be 12cm long and around 6cm wide. Under a lens, scattered stellate pubescence can be seen on them, tiny silver hairs in clusters like stars.

The autumn colour of this species is quite outstanding: vibrant yellows, reds and purples, all enhanced by the shiny upper surface of the leaves. In contrast the underside of each leaf exhibits the same colours with a pale-grey cast, giving cream, pink and lilac hues. The fruits are 8mm shiny nuts enclosed in a tough brown tomentose husk.

In cultivation, this tree, which is a woodland species in parts of its native range, is somewhat variable. In Britain trees in the drier east develop stems while specimens in the moist west of the country usually branch at or near ground level. Both forms produce a tangled dome of foliage 8-10m high and wide in around 100 years.

As a young plant in the garden Persian Ironwood is very rewarding. Although it grows relatively slowly, the summer foliage is vibrant and strong and from an early age an impressive annual display of autumn colour can be relied upon, well into November.

The cultivar '**Pendula**' is a strongly weeping form up to about 3m high and eventually somewhat wider. It has all the same excellent features of the species, especially the autumn colour. Any kind of soil is tolerated, but side shelter is essential for symmetrical development. It seems very likely that the stemless old trees found in western England were originally this selection, but with age some have reached 7m in height and an even greater spread.

Growth: 3-10-15. Hardiness: 50%. Choice: 1. Wood: 1.

'Pendula'

autumn leaves

fruit

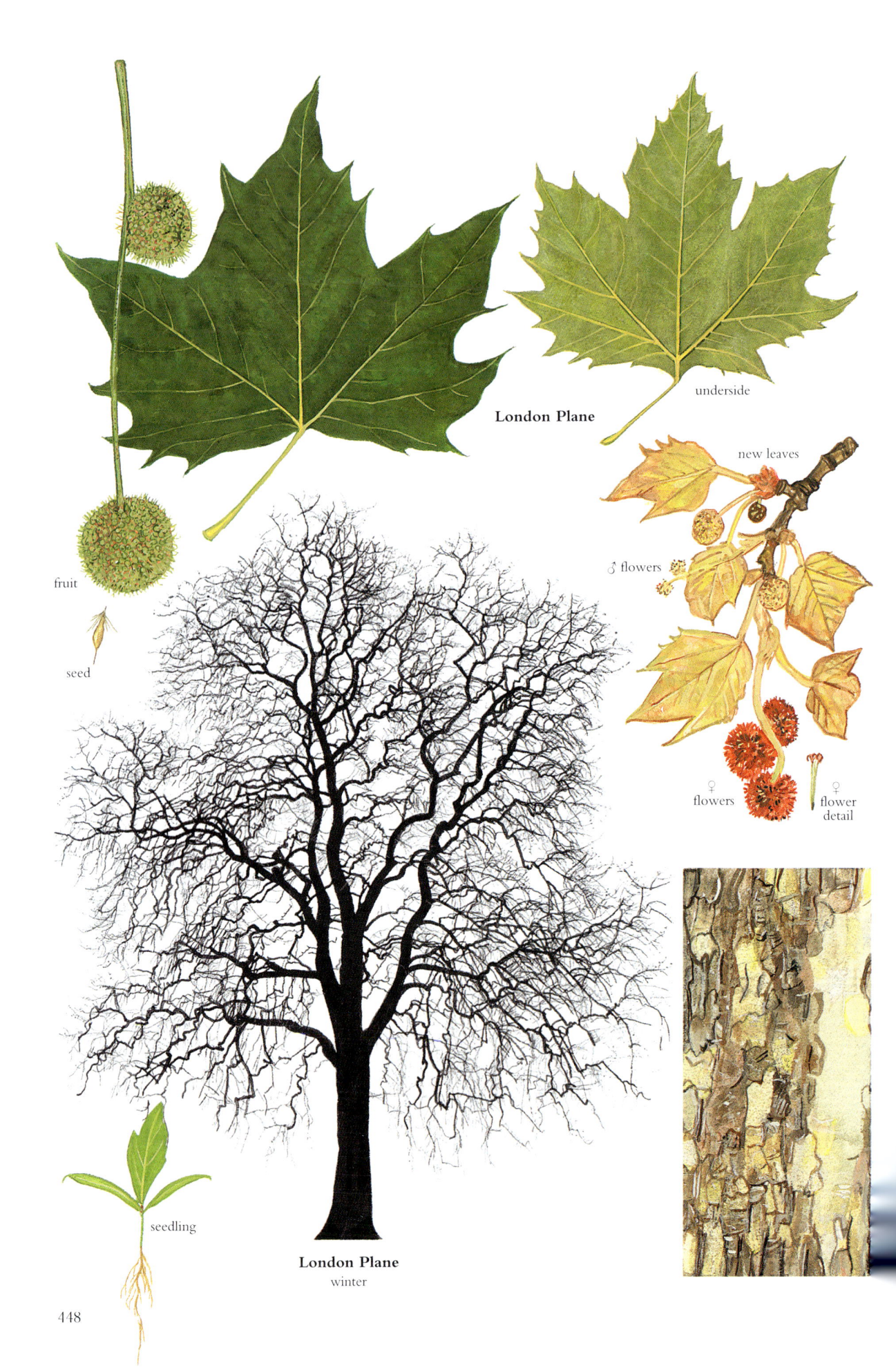

seed

London Plane

underside

new leaves

♂ flowers

♀ flowers

♀ flower detail

seedling

London Plane
winter

PLANE FAMILY • Platanaceae

London Plane *Platanus* × *hispanica*

Some of the thin olive green and grey bark of London Plane exfoliates randomly in hand-sized plates each year to reveal patches of creamy yellow underneath. In this way the tree sheds city dirt and soot and is able to breathe again through its stem. Flaking bark usually falls away after the main growing season in mid-summer. Some years this may be limited to a few scattered patches and in other years whole sheets of new pale stem are revealed. Deciduous thick leathery plane leaves are palmately-lobed and have a long petiole. They are about 20cm long and wide. The triangular lobes may be shallow or deep according to the origin of the plant. Winter buds form inside the base of the leaf stalk, where they remain hidden for several months. Trees up to 40m tall are known with spreading rounded tops over 25m wide. Although terminal buds are not formed on planes, the stems are usually long and straight and seldom fork below the base of the crown. The lower branches on old trees have a tendency to droop; consequently in towns they are mostly pruned off. Fruits, in tight round clusters 2.5cm across, hang down on slender threads singly or up to four in a string. They remain on the tree long after the leaves have fallen.

London Plane is one of the largest ornamental urban trees available to town planners. Considerable space is required if it is to develop properly. In the past it was often used as a street tree and pollarded annually. Few civic authorities can afford to do this now. Clonal populations of any sort are vulnerable to disease. Anthracnose caused by the fungus *Apiognomonia veneta* and canker caused by a *Ceraatocystis* fungus are lethal to some clones of London Plane.

In addition to its obvious ornamental value this is a productive timber tree. Stems 1m thick may take only 100 years to grow. The wood, known in the trade as 'lacewood' is highly ornamental. It is golden brown with an intricate continuous pattern of small brown flecks. As a veneer it was used on a large scale in the early twentieth century. Although still very expensive it is less fashionable today.

The beautiful cultivar '**Suttneri**' is a fairly large and rare tree. It is easy to overlook it when there are no low branches in view. The green leaves are variously marked with spots of yellow and white which in autumn turns to yellow and orange.

Growth: 4-18-35. Hardiness: 50%. Choice: 2. Wood: 1.

'**Suttneri**'

autumn

Platanus 'Augustine Henry'

hood

underside

bud detail

'Pyramidalis'

seedling

Platanus 'Augustine Henry'

Platanus orientalis 'Mirkovec'
underside

Plane hybrids and cultivars

London Plane is itself considered a hybrid between Oriental Plane and American Sycamore (p. 453). It was first recorded in Britain in 1663 and is now planted in cities world-wide from Mexico to China. It seems rather odd that in cooler conditions, for example around London, the hybrid thrives very well but the supposed American parent will hardly grow at all. Young American Sycamore plants are repeatedly stunted by frost and soon succumb to disease and die. London Plane, on the other hand, is a fertile tree which often seeds freely and regenerates on river sides, wet mud and disturbed gravel. It also grows extremely easily from vegetative reproduction, so huge clonal populations have arisen – which in some areas have become susceptible to disease.

Platanus 'Augustine Henry'

This artificially selected cultivar is considered to be a form of London Plane by some authorities but that is not certain. A form of *Platanus racemosa* is suggested as an alternative theory. Whatever its origin this is a huge 40m tree with deeply divided, 'hooded' 3-5 lobed leaves. It originated in southern California and was first cultivated in 1870, adding weight to the *Platanus racemosa* argument. The lower branches on old trees are pendulous and the stem exfoliates freely.
Growth: 3-15-40. Hardiness: 40-50%. Choice: 2.

Platanus × *hispanica* cultivars

'**Pyramidalis**' is a conical tree at first but it tends to become spreading and untidy with age. It is very easy to grow from cuttings so nurseries have reproduced it in large numbers since 1850. The bark does not exfoliate as readily as 'Augustine Henry'. The Cambridge Plane '**Cantabrigiensis**' has smaller leaves than other cultivars. They are five-lobed and similar to Oriental Plane. The vigorous upright clone '**Tremonia**' makes a good street tree. It was produced in the Dortmund Botanic Garden in 1951.
Growth: variable. Hardiness: 50%. Choice: 1.

Platanus orientalis 'Mirkovec'

Coloured leaves in planes are rare but this strange and unusual cultivar has foliage which is brownish-purple, especially when young and growing in full light.
Growth: 3-12-25. Hardiness: 50%. Choice: 1.

'Cantabrigiensis'
leaf variations

'Tremonia'

Oriental Plane

bud covered by leaf petiole

var. *insularis*

fruit

♂ flowers

♀ flowers

underside

Oriental Plane
winter

var. *insularis*

452

Oriental Plane *Platanus orientalis*

Most ornamental examples of this superb tree are massive spreading specimens with long sinuous heavy gold-flecked branches which occasionally bend and twist down to the ground and take root. A multiple layered tree at Corsham in southern England in 1990 measured 200m round the periphery. Originally from south-east Europe, Oriental Plane has been in general cultivation since the early 1600s. In parts of its natural range it is an upright tree 25-30m tall. The 15-20cm leaves are variable but mostly deeply-lobed and leathery. The leaf stalks have a swollen reddish base which encloses the following years bud throughout the summer. No terminal buds are formed so every year new shoot growth starts off at a tangent. The flowers are in tightly packed globular 2cm clusters. When mature up to four of these spheres of interlocking seeds hang on a slender thread.

The variety **insularis**, the Cyprian Plane, is a smaller tree which has remarkable palmate leaves with extended narrow lobes. Each of these resembles a finger if additional points and subdivisions are absent. This variety, formerly called *digitata*, was introduced in 1842.

Growth: 3-12-25. Hardiness: 50%. Choice: 1 (requires space), 2. Wood: 1.

American Sycamore *Platanus occidentalis*

In its native eastern North America this makes a large 30-40m tree with a stem often up to 1.2m thick. Relics of a previous generation of trees remain in America, with stems up to 4.6m across. Present-day trees are used for flooring and functional furniture such as kitchen units and chopping blocks. Low-grade wood is used for pulp and fibreboard. The live tree is used in city and park landscaping. All plane trees cast a dense cool shade and they are relatively free of insect pests.

American Sycamore, also called Buttonwood, has bark which is smooth and pale, exfoliating in large and small flakes to expose patches of even lighter colour. Very old stems gradually become darker with deep rugged fissures and wide ridges. The leaves are 10-22cm long and wide with 3-5 shallow lobes interspersed with occasional widely spaced teeth. At first they are softly felted on both sides but at maturity they are only pubescent along the veins on the underside. The compact 3cm spheres of dry fruits are mostly solitary, hanging on a thread-like stalk. In Europe, where it was introduced in 1636, it seldom grows well, and in Britain it invariably fails to grow at all.

Growth: 3-12-25 (40 in native range). Hardiness: 60-70%. Choice: 1, 4. Wood: 1, 2, 4.

Oriental Plane
autumn

American Sycamore

Medlar

Common Quince

underside

Common Quince

underside

Medlar

Medlar
autumn

Himalayan Tree Cotoneaster

ROSE FAMILY · Rosaceae

Medlar *Mespilus germanica*

This deciduous shrub or small tree is grown chiefly for its fruit. It comes from south-east Europe to western Asia and has been cultivated for centuries well beyond this natural range. *Mespilus* is the name given to the tree by Theophrastus. *Germanica* means German or from Germany, which is certainly not strictly true in the modern sense. The 3-4cm white flowers occur in early summer but they are not showy. The fruits are globular or pear-shaped, 3cm across, with a persistent calyx reminiscent of Diospyros (p. 765). The dull brown fruits do not look appetizing, and they are indeed most disagreeable until after incipient decay begins. After that they develop a sharp acid taste.

Growth: 2-6-12. Hardiness: 50%. Choice: 3.

Common Quince *Cydonia oblonga*

The Common Quince is another ancient fruit tree from western Asia with a long history of cultivation. It is a shrubby deciduous tree sometimes reaching up to about 7m in height. The white or palest pink single flowers are 4-5cm across. The 10cm long fruit is roughly pear-shaped, bright yellow and aromatic. The leaves remain on the tree until early winter before turning yellow and falling. There are several choice named cultivated fruiting varieties. The genus name *Cydonia* is Latin for an apple tree from Cydon, on the island of Crete.

Growth: 2-6-10. Hardiness: 50%. Choice: 3.

Himalayan Tree Cotoneaster *Cotoneaster frigidus*

This untidy shrubby garden tree has tight clusters of creamy white flowers, bright green, sometimes semi-evergreen leaves, and in the autumn numerous heavy bunches of bright red twin seeded 7mm berries. After mid-winter these are taken by birds. This species is sometimes planted as an informal flowering hedge. It responds well to being cut back and still manages to fruit freely. It originated in the Himalayas and was introduced to Europe around 1824. The name *Cotoneaster* means quince-like; *frigidus* refers to its coming from a cold place.

Most tree-like Cotoneastesters in Britain are hybrids between this species and one or two others. They are collectively called *Cotoneaster × watereri*. The original was probably the clone 'John Waterer', produced by the nurseryman of that name in 1928. Since then it has hybridized wildly with several compatible species and even become naturalized in some places. Some chance hybrid seedlings make excellent garden plants. Berries may be orange or red, and leaves evergreen or deciduous (or somewhere in beweeen). Good red autumn colour may occur on plants that drop their leaves.

Growth: 3-5-8. Hardiness: 50%. Choice: 2, 3.

Himalayan Tree Cotoneaster
trained single stem

Common Quince

Downy Hawthorn

Hungarian Hawthorn leaf variations

Azarole leaf variations

Oriental Thorn

Tansy-leaved Thorn

Hybrid Cockspur Thorn

'Carrierei'

'Carrierei' bark

456

Thorn Trees *Crataegus*

In European folklore the thorn tree is generally considered unlucky. It is associated with the month of May and the goddess Maia, whose son Hermes conducted souls to Hades. Marriages in the month of May are still considered unlucky in some European countries. However, thorns are highly ornamental, providing scented spring blossom and good autumn foliage and fruit colours. A few species retain their berries (haws) until mid-winter.

Hybrid Cockspur Thorn *Crataegus × lavallei*

A small tree which is ultimately 6-7m tall and almost as wide. It flowers in mid-summer and produces 2cm haws which stay on well into the winter. The name was given to a single tree in the Segrez Arboretum in France, in 1880. A second, virtually identical plant, '**Carrierei**', originated in Paris three years later. One parent was *Crataegus mexicana*, the other might have been *Crataegus crus-galli*.

Growth: 2-5-7. Hardiness: 70%. Choice: 1, 3. Wood: 5.

Downy Hawthorn *Crataegus mollis*

This wide-spreading sage green tree is 9-12m tall, native from Quebec to Nova Scotia and southwards to West Virginia, Alabama and Texas. It was introduced, as 'White Thorn', to European gardens in 1683. The incised leaves are soft and downy, and the 2.5cm summer flowers are creamy-white with reddish centres. The dark red-brown haws are also downy.

Growth: 2-6-12. Hardiness: 60-70%. Choice: 1, 3. Wood: 5.

Hungarian Hawthorn *Crataegus nigra*

Native of Hungary, this felty grey-twigged tree was introduced to West European gardens in 1819. The late flowers, which are often obscured by the fully expanded leaves, are white at first then pink tinted as they age. The soft black haws are often slightly flattened.

Growth: 2-5-7. Hardiness: 60-70%. Choice: 1, 3. Wood: 5.

Azarole *Crataegus azarolus*

Sometimes called the Mediterranean Medlar, this 9m tree bears apple-flavoured edible fruits. It is native to southern Europe, North Africa and western Asia and has been cultivated as far north as England since the seventeenth century.

Growth: 2-7-9. Hardiness: 40-50%. Choice: 1, 3. Wood: 5.

Oriental Thorn *Crataegus laciniata*

Introduced from the Orient in 1810, this often thornless 6-7m tree is a popular garden plant. It has a neat round or flat head of branches usually on a single clear vertical stem. The deeply cut grey-green leaves are felted on the under-side.

Growth: 2-5-7. Hardiness: 50%. Choice: 1, 3. Wood: 5.

Tansy-leaved Thorn *Crataegus tanacetifolia*

A small, virtually thornless tree introduced from Asia Minor in 1789. Closely related to *Crataegus laciniata*, it has variable but deeply cut leaves. The mid-summer clusters of creamy-white 2.5cm flowers are fragrant.

Growth: 2-7-10. Hardiness: 50%. Choice: 1, 3. Wood: 5.

Black Hawthorn *Crataegus douglasii*

This hardy mountain tree occurs from Alaska and British Columbia southwards to central California at up to 1800m. The white flowers are showy and the glossy leaves colour well in the autumn. It was discovered by, and named in honour of, David Douglas in the nineteenth century.

Growth: 2-8-12. Hardiness: 70%. Choice: 1, 3. Wood: 5.

Scarlet Thorn *Crataegus pedicellata*

This tree has 5cm shiny brown thorns which protect its rough glabrous foliage. It grows to 6m in its native eastern North America. The white flowers have attractive light red centres.

Growth: 2-5-7. Hardiness: 60-70%. Choice: 1, 3. Wood: 5.

Black Hawthorn

Scarlet Thorn

thorn

Midland Hawthorn

Common Hawthorn

old twig

Common Hawthorn   'Pendula Rosea'   'Stricta'

Midland Hawthorn *Crataegus laevigata*

The name 'midland' refers to central England where this tree is a native species and an indicator of old woodland. It is also native of large areas of Europe. *Crataegus* means 'strong' and is a reference to the hard wood, *laevigata* means smooth or polished, a distinguishing feature of the foliage when compared to common hawthorn (*Crataegus monogyna*). Midland thorns are totally hardy. They grow very well in some shade but flower best in full sun. The scented white flowers occur in small clusters in late spring. The fruits or 'haws' of this species each contain two hard seeds. The Common Hawthorn has only one.

The cultivar '**Paul's Scarlet**' is a fine garden tree covered in late spring and early summer with tight clusters of deep pink double flowers. Each individual flower is like a minute 2cm rose. The cultivar '**Rosea Flore Plena**' is another double form, an ideal small tree for town parks or gardens. It is said to be a parent of 'Paul's Scarlet' and was first cultivated as long ago as 1832. All of these trees tolerate a wide range of soils, they can be hard pruned if necessary, grow slowly, and do not get very large.

Growth: 3-8-12. Hardiness: 60%. Choice: 1, 2, 3.
Wood: 3, 5.

Common Hawthorn *Crataegus monogyna*

In cultivation this European native tree is most commonly used as a hedging plant, and seldom occurs as a garden specimen in its own right. The 1.5cm flowers in tight clusters, are creamy-white and delightfully scented. They occur in late spring. In England a popular common name is 'May', a reference to the month when it is in flower. The haws contain only one seed, hence the species name. Open grown trees usually develop a twiggy roundish head of thorny branches on a stout often straight stem. They flower and fruit best in full sun. Almost any kind of soil is tolerated, even dry soils over chalk, or heavy wet clay. Plants can be pruned hard at almost any time of year, so they make an ideal impenetrable hedge.

Hawthorn since very early times has figured in superstition and folklore. It was thought to be able to ward off evil spirits but, strangely, flowers were not allowed inside the dwelling. In Ireland, particularly venerable thorns are still reckoned to be meeting places for the fairy folk. In the past all parts of the foliage were used medicinally.

The cultivar '**Stricta**' has erect branches and is a perfect thorn tree in a place where space is limited. '**Pendula Rosea**' is a delightful small tree with pendulous branches wreathed in pink flowers in late spring.

Growth: 3-12-15. Hardiness: 60%. Choice: 2, 3.
Wood: 3, 5.

'Rosea Flore Plena'

'Paul's Scarlet'

Midland Hawthorn

Common Hawthorn

'Lutescens'

'Variegata'

'Aurea'

var. *eriocarpa*

'Plena'

'Rosea'

'Gireoudii'

'Punicea'

var. *aurea*

f. *rosea*

'Bicolor'

Cockspur Thorn

Cockspur Thorn
spring

Cockspur Thorn

autumn

460

Crataegus laevigata cultivars

Midland thorn has a long history of cultivation which has given rise to numerous decorative forms. '**Gireoudii**' is an old variegated plant cultivated by Späth's Nursery in 1899. It is seldom seen these days. In summer the second flush of leaves are mottled pink and white. '**Plena**' is a floriferous double-flowered white cultivar. The flowers turn to pale pink as the they mature. It was first cultivated in the 1700s. '**Punicea**' is a rose pink single-flowered type. It was raised at Loddiges Nursery. The form *rosea* is a wild pink-flowered tree which is quite variable. The variety *aurea* is also occasionally found growing wild, it has yellow berries. These are all excellent hardy small park and garden trees, ideal as lawn specimens and for open spaces.

Growth: variable. Hardiness: 60%. Choice: 1, 3.

Crataegus monogyna cultivars

The common hawthorn has produced many different sports and forms over a very long period of time in cultivation. '**Variegata**' has leaves splashed and blotched with creamy-white. '**Lutescens**' has leaves that are light yellowish-green, whereas '**Aurea**' has green leaves but yellow fruit. The variety *eriocarpa*, originally from Poland, has deep red fruits that are woolly at first. The cultivar '**Rosea**' has delicate single pink flowers. Natural populations of plants similar to this are often seen in the countryside with pinkish flowers. The best of all single-flowering hawthorns is probably the German cultivar '**Bicolor**', which has white petals with a deep pink broad margin reminiscent of Dianthus.

Growth: variable. Hardiness: 60%. Choice: 1, 3.

Cockspur Thorn *Crataegus crus-galli*

In cultivation this is a popular broad-headed tree around 6m tall with viciously sharp 8cm slightly curved woody thorns. It is an east and central North American tree introduced to Europe in 1691. The creamy-white flowers in early summer occur freely in clusters. The glossy scarlet haws stay on the tree well into winter. There are several ornamental cultivars and varieties.

Growth: 2-5-7. Hardiness: 60-70%. Choice: 1, 3. Wood: 5.

Broad-leaved Cockspur Thorn
Crataegus prunifolia

Another North American thorn closely related to the Cockspur Thorn, this splendid garden tree is under 6m tall with a compact rounded outline. The brilliant autumn foliage colour coincides with numerous plump glossy orange-red berries. This is a tree for open spaces in full sun, a feature plant of outstanding quality for late spring and for the autumn.

Growth: 2-5-6. Hardiness: 50%. Choice: 1, 3. Wood: 5.

autumn

Broad-leaved Cockspur Thorn

autumn

thorn

Crataegus oresbia

Crataegus atrorubens

Crataegus maineana

Crataegus macrocarpa

Crataegus macrocarpa leaf variations

Crataegus flabellata

Crataegus songorica

Crataegus × *durobrivensis*

Rare Thorns

Some very rare species are illustrated here. **Crataegus oresbia** is a mountain form which has largely been replaced in horticulture by *Crataegus pedicellata* and *Crataegus prunifolia* (p. 461). **Crataegus atrorubens** is an uncommon, 6-10m, virtually thornless tree from the Mississippi bottom-lands. The 1cm, 4-5 seeded haws are shed very quickly. **Crataegus maineana** is a segregate of *Crataegus pruinosa* from the state of Maine in the USA. It produces good orange-red autumn foliage colour. **Crataegus macrocarpa** (*laevigata* var. *macrocarpa*) is a kind of Midland Hawthorn (p. 459) found in southern France and Switzerland. It was described as a species in its own right by Hegetschweiler in 1840, and then as a variety by Rouy and Camus in France in 1901. **Crataegus flabellata** is a large thorny tree 6-8m tall with vicious 6-10cm, slightly curved spines. The 12mm oval crimson haws contain 3-5 seeds. **Crataegus songorica** is an obscure south-east Asian species closely related to the thornless *Crataegus wattiana*. Its leaves are cut half way to the midrib. **Crataegus chlorosarca** is a small rare Asiatic pyramidal tree usually without thorns. Its ragged-edged leaves are 5-10cm long and the 8cm corymbs of whitish flowers are followed by clusters of black fruits.

Growth: variable. Hardiness: 50%. Choice: 1, 3.

Crataegus × durobrivensis

An ornamental hybrid from the northern United States, this shrub is a cross between *Crataegus pruinosa* and *Crataegus punctata*, first discovered on the Genesee River, Rochester, New York. The deep red glossy fruits stay on for most of the winter.

Growth: 2-5-6. Hardiness: 50-60%. Choice: 1, 3.

Crataegus pinnatifida

This small 6-8m Chinese tree has either very short thorns or none at all. The 5-8cm deeply cut leaves have exceptionally long petioles. The 2cm early summer flowers are white. The variety *major* is larger and brighter as a garden tree. The glossy red fruits are covered with minute dots.

Growth: 2-5-6. Hardiness: 50%. Choice: 1, 3.

Crataegus wilsonii

This tree is morphologically similar to many American thorns, but comes from China. The spines are short and thick and the glossy lobed leaves are 5-10cm long. The flowers are white and produced in early summer in crowded clusters, followed by small glossy red fruits which are only 8mm across.

Growth: 2-5-6. Hardiness: 50%. Choice: 1, 3.

Crataegus chlorosarca

Crataegus pinnatifida

Crataegus wilsonii

buds

Rowan

flower detail

Rowan

'Xanthocarpa'

'Aspleniifolia'

seed

Rowan   'Fastigiata'   'Dirkenii'

Sorbus serotina bark

Rowan *Sorbus aucuparia*

The Rowan is an attractive slender tree with silvery-brown bark, creamy-white spring flowers, and clusters of brilliant orange to scarlet autumn berries. It is hardy especially in northern Europe and Asia where it inhabits upland areas and mountainsides. Rowan is environmentally useful in that it provides a valuable crop of berries in early winter which are taken by birds, especially migrating thrushes such as fieldfares. The scented flowers also attract numerous insects.

This tree has an established place in folklore, being central to several superstitious beliefs and magical stories. Trees often reach 15-20m in height in sheltered places, but much less in exposed situations. They may stay no more than gnarled bushes when they cling precariously to almost bare mountain rocks. For this reason they make good alpine rockery subjects in cold situations when starved of soil. As garden trees they prefer sandy slightly acid soils. They thrive best away from hot dry conditions. *Sorbus* is the Latin name for the Service Tree, another member of the same genus. *Aucuparia* means 'of bird catchers', as the fruit was used as bait for this in former times.

The cultivar '**Aspleniifolia**' has deeply incised serrate leaflets giving the foliage a delicate feathery effect. It bears large drooping clusters of red berries. '**Beissneri**' has densely packed upright branches which are reddish-brown when young. Its main stem is also coppery-red to some extent and the foliage is variable but similar to that of 'Aspleniifolia'. The cultivar '**Fastigiata**' is a distinctive upright narrow-crowned tree, bearing particularly bright red berries. For many gardens its minimal need for space, and fairly slow growth, are positive assets. The cultivar '**Xanthocarpa**', meaning 'yellow seeds' has amber-yellow berries.

'**Dirkenii**' is a small upright tree with delicate pale yellow foliage in spring and early summer, accompanied at first by flat clusters of creamy-white flowers. Before mid-summer the leaves turn green and unspectacular clusters of orange-red berries begin to develop. Autumn colour is not striking. This obscure cultivar, raised around 1850, is rare in cultivation and not much sought-after.

Growth: 3-8-15. Hardiness: 90% (species). Choice: 1, 2, 3.

Sorbus serotina

An unusual small upright tree thought to have come originally from Japan and Korea. It is closely related to *Sorbus commixta* (p. 469) and like that species produces spectacular autumn colour. The fruits are small but bright red. The species name means late, a reference to the slow seasonal progress of this tree when compared to *Sorbus commixta*.

Growth: 2-6-8. Hardiness: 50%. Choice: 1, 3.

Sorbus serotina

Sorbus pohuashanensis

underside

Sorbus japonica

autumn

Sorbus pohuashanensis

'Pagoda Red'   autumn

bud   underside   **Sorbus rupicola**

Sorbus × meinichii

Sorbus pohuashanensis

This small deciduous tree from China has pale woolly pubescent twigs and buds. The leaves are pinnate with 11-15 elliptic oblong 3-6cm leaflets, and a greyish pubescence on the underside. The white 1cm flowers in dense clusters occur in late spring. The fruits, less than 1cm across, are orange-red. This is a good garden tree when it is young. The pubescent silvery foliage can then be fully appreciated at eye level when standing by the tree.

Growth: 3-9-14. Hardiness: 50-60%. Choice: 1, 3.

Sorbus japonica

This substantial south-east Asian tree grows up to 20m tall with pinnate 10cm pale-backed leaves, and dense clusters of creamy-white flowers. In the autumn scarlet brown-spotted 1.2cm berries are accompanied for a time by yellow leaves. The variety *calocarpa* has white-backed leaves and larger fruits. It is probably a better garden plant, especially for autumn colour. '**Pagoda Red**' is another brilliantly-coloured tree in the autumn.

Growth: 3-14-20. Hardiness: 50%. Choice: 1, 3.

Sorbus rupicola

This rare plant is usually shrubby and less than 2m tall. It resembles Whitebeam and is probably only a microspecies in the *Sorbus aria* group. It is native to Europe, including Britain, and Scandinavia. The ovate-oblong fruits are reddish with brown dots and a paler or light green shaded side.

Growth: 1-2-2. Hardiness: 60%. Choice: 1, 3.

Sorbus × meinichii

A hybrid between Whitebeam and Rowan, this obscure plant comes from southern Norway. It is usually an upright-branched broad-headed tree which closely resembles Rowan. The pinnate leaves have 4-6 pairs of robust deep green leaflets, fused towards the tip. Clusters of red berries are produced in the autumn. It is a tough hardy plant with a preference for cool, open situations and slightly acid soils.

Growth: 2-5-6. Hardiness: 80%. Choice: 1, 3.

Sorbus caloneura

This rare hardy Chinese shrubby tree has dark twigs and branches and ovate toothed leaves – similar to those of *Sorbus rupicola* but with more (9-13) pairs of parallel veins. The white flowers occur in dense 7cm clusters. The stamens are purplish before they mature. The pear-shaped 1cm berries are dull brown.

Growth: 2-5-6. Hardiness: 50%. Choice: 1, 3.

Sorbus xanthoneura

The species name, meaning yellow, is a reference to the leaf stalk and midrib, on what is essentially a Chinese form of *Sorbus pallescens*. The leaves are 10-13cm long with 16-20 glabrous parallel veins and double-toothed margins. They have strikingly white undersides. The 8mm depressed-globose fruits, by contrast, are red.

Growth: 2-6-8. Hardiness: 50%. Choice: 1, 3.

Sorbus caloneura (autumn)

Sorbus xanthoneura

'Pagoda Red'

autumn leaflet

Japanese Rowan

Sorbus wilfordiana

Sorbus aucuparia subsp. *sibirica*

Sorbus amurensis var. *rota*

autumn leaflet

Japanese Rowan *Sorbus commixta*

In Japan and Korea this is a variable shrub or small tree. Cultivated plants of wild origin are also variable but some specimens can be remarkably beautiful. The autumn colour is the main horticultural feature. In late summer numerous clusters of berries ripen to orange-scarlet and in time their colour is augmented by leaves that glow orange red and finally purple. After 10 days or so the leaves fall but the berries stay on the tree until birds eventually take them. The largest garden specimens reach up to 8m in height. Japanese rowan was first cultivated in America and Europe around 1880.
Growth: 2-6-8. Hardiness: 50%. Choice: 1, 3.

Sorbus amurensis var. *rota*

This little known tree was introduced to Europe from north-east Asia in 1907. The parent species is extremely hardy. The variety *rota* has beautiful incised leaf margins and clusters of bright orange-red fruit.
Growth: 2-5-6. Hardiness: 80%. Choice: 1, 3.

Sorbus wilfordiana

An extremely rare tree in cultivation, this close relative of *Sorbus aucuparia* has dark glossy leaves with paler net-veined undersides. The buds are crimson-coloured and sticky. Young vigorous shoots have elongated lenticels giving them a kind of winged appearance. Again, the red autumn colour combination of leaves and berries is superb.
Growth: 2-6-8. Hardiness: 80-90%. Choice: 1, 3.

Sorbus aucuparia subsp. *sibirica*

This is a tough northern form of the European rowan with 4-5cm leaflets which are glabrous on both sides.
Growth: 2-5-6. Hardiness: 100%. Choice: 2.

Sorbus americana 'Belmonte'

The American Rowan *Sorbus americana* was introduced to Europe in 1782. Its native range is west Ontario to Newfoundland and south as far as Georgia. It grows to 1800m in the southern Appalachian Mountains. It is a fine hardy ornamental tree of 9m with a spreading crown, but has a tendency to produce multiple stems. It grows best in the company of coniferous trees on poor moist soils. The cultivar 'Belmonte' was selected for its neat single-stemmed habit. The symmetrical branches have an up-swept tendency and the foliage is light-coloured and open. Numerous clusters of bright red fruits are borne in the autumn, when the leaves turn golden yellow and rosy pink.
Growth: 3-7-9. Hardiness: 90%. Choice: 1, 2, 3.

winter

autumn leaflet

Sorbus americana 'Belmonte'

Sorbus 'Ghose'

Sorbus wardii

Sorbus aronioides

Sorbus keissleri

underside

Sorbus 'Signalman'

'Hilling's Spire'

Sorbus 'Ghose'

A small upright rowan similar in many respects to *Sorbus insignis*, 'Ghose' originated as a chance seedling. It was from a batch of Himalayan seed sent to the Hillier Nurseries by the Indian nurseryman Ghose of Darjeeling. The berries are pink maturing to light red. This tree is hardier than most of the other *Sorbus insignis* cultivars and forms.

Growth: 2-6-8. Hardiness: 40-50%. Choice: 1, 3.

Sorbus wardii

This quick-growing whitebeam of the *Sorbus thibetica* type is another numbered introduction from Frank Kingdom-Ward (KW 21127). The species name commemorates Kingdom-Ward. Plants also exist in cultivation that are not reproduced from this individual, but these tend to be variable on account of the tree's extensive and diverse natural range in Tibet and Bhutan. The columnar shape of KW 21127 makes it useful for streets and planting in limited spaces. The flowers are creamy-white in terminal flat clusters. Smallish bunches of 12mm grey-dotted yellow-brown fruits follow.

Growth: 3-6-8. Hardiness: 40-60%. Choice: 1, 3.

Sorbus aronioides

This very rare tree, probably part of the *micromeles* group, was identified in the early part of the twentieth century by Alfred Rehder. Then it appears to have been lost to cultivation, at least in Britain and North America. New wild source material has been collected during the recent Guizhou expedition to China.

Growth: 2 - -. Hardiness: 40-50%. Choice: 4.

Sorbus keissleri

Another Ernest Wilson introduction from China in 1907, this rare 12m tree is also in the *micromeles* section of *Sorbus*. It is a curiosity, in many respects similar to *Malus*. The clusters of fruits are like crab-apples, green at first with a gradually extending blushed cheek on the sunny side.

Growth: 3-8-12. Hardiness: 40-50%. Choice: 1, 3.

Sorbus 'Signalman'

An artificial product of the Hillier Nurseries, this tree was cultivated at Eastleigh, Hampshire, in 1968. It was especially bred from *Sorbus aucuparia* 'Fastigiata' using *Sorbus domestica* to improve the quality, vigour and strength of the fastigiate tree. The objectives were achieved in this good columnar specimen with rich green foliage and bright orange clusters of berries.

Growth: 3-7-9. Hardiness: 80%. Choice: 1, 3.

Sorbus auccuparia 'Hilling's Spire'

This popular garden form of Rowan has tight upswept branches and produces abundant nodding clusters of scarlet fruit in the autumn.

Growth: 3-6-8. Hardiness: 80. Choice: 1.

'Hilling's Spire' *Sorbus keissleri* *Sorbus* **'Signalman'**

Sorbus harrowiana

Sorbus insignis

flower detail

Kashmir Rowan

Sorbus esserteauiana

Sorbus commixta **'Jermyns'**

type

'Flava'

Sorbus insignis

This superb but slightly tender Mountain Ash from Assam is a very worthwhile tree for any sheltered garden. The foliage turns from rich green to fiery red in a good autumn. The large bunches of oval pink berries are seldom taken by birds and usually stay on all winter. Most cultivated specimens have been raised from a single plant collected by Frank Kingdom-Ward in 1928, and numbered by him KW 7746. It is upright, shapely and not more than 6m tall.

Growth: 2-5-6. Hardiness: 40%. Choice: 1, 3.

Sorbus harrowiana

Closely related to *Sorbus insignis*, this small pink-fruited tree has remarkably big leaves, each with up to 9 leaflets 15-18cm long. It is tender in northern Europe. The original plants in cultivation, introduced from Yunnan by George Forrest in 1912, have not survived in many places. A later introduction by Frank Kingdom-Ward has fared rather better, and grown up to 13m tall as far north as southern England.

Growth: 2-7-13. Hardiness: 30-40%. Choice: 1, 3.

Kashmir Rowan *Sorbus cashmiriana*

In spite of its warm place of origin this tree grows well in northern Europe, although canker and die-back can affect it if environmentally stressed. The flowers in early summer are in clusters of palest pink, followed in autumn by big pure white berries in weighty bunches. Birds usually ignore these, so they last a long time and contrast well with the big red winter buds. It makes a stiff upright tree and grows to around 8m. It has been cultivated in European gardens since 1934.

Growth: 2-5-8. Hardiness: 50%. Choice: 1, 3.

Sorbus commixta 'Jermyns'

Named after Jermyns House in Hampshire, former home of the great nurseryman Sir Harold Hillier, this chance seedling originated from a consignment of *Sorbus sargentiana* seed. It has outstanding autumn colour and amber berries which gradually turn orange.

Growth: 2-6-8. Hardiness: 50%. Choice: 1, 3.

Sorbus esserteauiana 'Flava'

The cultivar 'Flava' has bright yellow berries in dense bunches, whereas the species has red fruits. It is a small tree not over 10m tall, and one of the best yellow-berried rowans.

Growth: 2-5-8. Hardiness: 40-50%. Choice: 1, 3.

Sorbus scalaris

This spreading tree with bold foliage was discovered by Ernest Wilson in West China in 1904. Each leaf has over 30 leaflets which are grey-felted on the back. They turn brilliant red and purple in autumn.

Growth: 2-5-6. Hardiness: 50%. Choice: 1, 3.

Sorbus vilmorinii

An ideal tree for the small garden, this species has small ferny leaves and seldom exceeds 5m in height. The 3-5mm berries are very striking as they develop in late summer from rose pink to bright mauve. The autumn foliage is dark purplish-brown. In winter the berries fade almost to white. Although small for rowan they occur in quite large clusters. This tree was discovered in West China by the French missionary Father Armand David in 1889.

Growth: 2-4-5. Hardiness: 50%. Choice: 1, 3.

Sorbus scalaris **Sorbus vilmorinii** (autumn leaflet) **Kashmir Rowan**

underside

Sargent's Rowan

autumn leaflet

Sargent's Rowan

Sorbus × kewensis

ripening fruit

unripe fruit

Sorbus forrestii

Chinese Mountain Ash

type

'Rufus'

underside

'November Pink'

Chinese Mountain Ash

Sargent's Rowan *Sorbus sargentiana*

A woodland tree from the mountains of south-west China, Sargent's Rowan was introduced to western gardens in 1908. It makes a splendid neatly rounded specimen tree, 8-10m tall. The crimson winter buds are prominent and sticky like a horse chestnut's. The substantial clusters of tiny flowers develop into huge bunches of orange berries – frequently well over 300 to a bunch. The foliage also colours to orange in the autumn.

Growth: 2-7-9. Hardiness: 40-50%. Choice: 1, 3.

Sorbus × kewensis

Another orange-fruited rowan which produces huge bunches of berries in the autumn. Occasionally so much fruit, in fact, that weaker branches break under the weight of it. Birds such as fieldfares and redwings on their southern winter migration are attracted to this rich harvest. An artificial hybrid between *Sorbus pohuashanensis* from China and *Sorbus aucuparia*, this tree originated at Kew Gardens.

Growth: 2-8-10. Hardiness: 50%. Choice: 1, 3.

Sorbus forrestii

This uncommon Chinese tree, closely related to *Sorbus hupehensis*, was introduced from Yunnan Province by George Forrest in 1921. It was eventually named in his honour in 1980.

Growth: 2-6-. Hardiness: 40-50%. Choice: 1, 3.

Chinese Mountain Ash *Sorbus hupehensis*

A distinctive tree with blue-green-backed leaves and white or palest pink berries. Birds tend to leave them until late winter, so trees festooned with white 'pearls' are often seen at Christmas time, long after the leaves have blackened and fallen. The species, from a wide area in China, is variable, and named forms have been cultivated mostly from the variety *obtusa*. The cultivar '**Rufus**' has beautiful rose-pink berries and delicate pinnate leaves with 11 leaflets on each. The cultivar '**November Pink**' is a lovely small tree with deep pink berries and bright golden yellow autumn foliage.

Growth: 3-8-14. Hardiness: 50%. Choice: 1, 3.

Sorbus 'Joseph Rock'

The garden tree 'Joseph Rock', originally collected from Yundshi Mountain in Yunnan in 1932, remains fairly small with light airy foliage and prominent clusters of amber berries in the autumn. It is a form of the Chinese species *Sorbus rehderiana*. Unfortunately it has become very susceptible to the disease fireblight in recent years. The similar-looking resistant cultivar 'Golden Wonder' should possibly be planted instead in fireblight areas.

Growth: 2-6-8. Hardiness: 50%. Choice: 1, 3, 4.

Sorbus commixta 'Embley'

Of all the Japanese Rowan cultivars 'Embley' makes probably the best autumn feature. The shining scarlet berries and glowing gold, red, claret and purple foliage colours are quite outstanding. The display may last for a full two weeks in a good year. 'Embley' stands some shade and benefits from some side shelter.

Growth: 2-6-8. Hardiness: 50%. Choice: 1, 3.

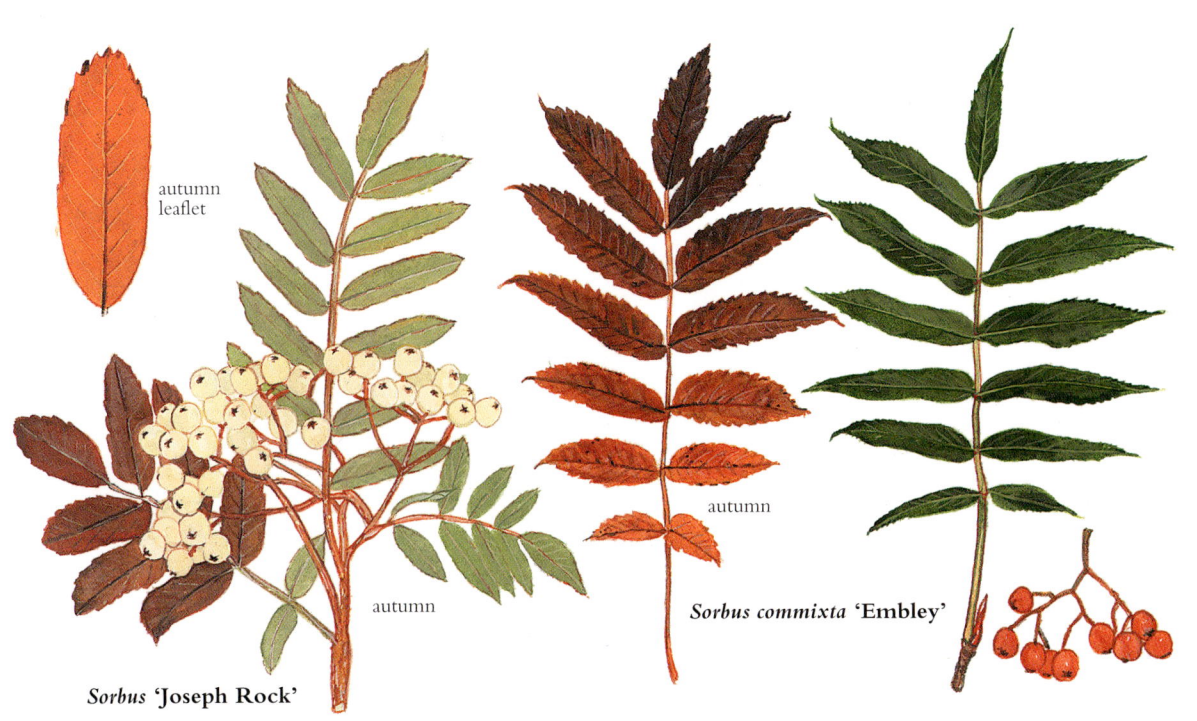

Sorbus megalocarpa

Sorbus 'Winter Cheer'

Showy Mountain Ash

Sorbus 'Sunshine'

Sorbus randaiensis

underside   *Sorbus* 'Tundra'

Sorbus megalocarpa

This small tree or large shrub has stout spreading branches. The broad obovate leaves are coarsely toothed and usually colour well to red in the autumn. Corymbs of cream flowers appear just before the leaves unfold, they have a slightly unpleasant smell. The conspicuous 2-3cm ovoid fruits are russet-brown to buff with minute pale dots. From western China, this species was introduced to Britain in 1903 and America in 1908.

Growth: 2-5-7. Hardiness: 40-50%. Choice: 1, 3.

Sorbus 'Winter Cheer'

Raised at Eastleigh, Hampshire, in 1959 from a *Sorbus esserteanana* 'Flara' × *Sorbus pohuashanensis* cross, this outstanding seedling retains its fruit for most of the winter. The berries, in big clusters, are cadmium yellow at first becoming flushed with orange and eventually turning orange-red.

Growth: 2-6-8. Hardiness: 50%. Choice: 1, 3.

Showy Mountain Ash *Sorbus decora*

Showy, or ornamental, alludes to the bright red fruit (see also p. 479)

Sorbus 'Sunshine'

This selected seedling from Sorbus 'Joseph Rock' has been in cultivation since 1968. The fruits are spectacular clusters of deep yellow berries which gradually become tinted orange. As with 'Joseph Rock' this plant may become infected with fireblight.

Growth: 2-6-8. Hardiness: 50%. Choice: 4.

Sorbus randaiensis

Most of the existing specimens cultivated in gardens under this name are actually narrow-leaved forms of *Sorbus commixta*. The true species, which is a native of Taiwan, has recently been re-introduced to western botanic gardens. It is probably less attractive than the imposter.

Growth: -. Hardiness: 40%. Choice: -.

Sorbus 'Tundra'

'Tundra' is probably a seedling of *Sorbus* 'Joseph Rock', but because seed does not always come true the exact parentage of this plant is uncertain. It is reminiscent of *Sorbus vilmorinii* and *Sorbus koehneana*. 'Tundra' is a small fairly fastigiate tree with delicate greyish-backed leaves that colour well in the autumn. The unusual fruits are pale green at first, gradually changing to white in a curious way. They remain on the tree well into winter because birds are not usually attracted to them.

Growth: variable. Hardiness: 50%. Choice: 4.

Sorbus 'Leonard Messel'

A fine garden form of Mountain Ash, 'Leonard Messel' produces a neat crown of foliage on a tree up to 10m tall. The leaves are large, with 7-11 leaflets which may themselves exceed 10cm long. The big clusters of creamy-white flowers are followed by distinctive pink berries. The cultivar was raised by and named in honour of Leonard Messel in England in 1949.

Growth: 2-7-10. Hardiness: 60%. Choice: 1, 3.

underside

Sorbus 'Leonard Messel'

Sorbus × *hybrida* 'Gibbsii'

autumn

underside

Sorbus lancifolia

fruit

Showy Mountain Ash

Sorbus meliosmifolia

Sorbus × *hybrida* 'Gibbsii'
autumn

Showy Mountain Ash

winter

Sorbus meliosmifolia
leaf variation

478

ROWANS

Sorbus × hybrida 'Gibbsii'

This is a selected clone of the hybrid between *Sorbus aucuparia* and *Sorbus rupicola*. It comes true from seed. Technically it is a tetraploid apomict, which can produce seed without the need for sexual fertilization. *Sorbus × hybrida* originated spontaneously in Scandinavia where it makes a tree 10m tall. The cultivar 'Gibbsii' originated in England before 1924. In cultivation it is frequently confused with *Sorbus × thuringiaca*, a *Sorbus aria × aucuparia* cross which is fertile so it does not come true from seed.

Growth: 2-7-10. Hardiness: 60%. Choice: 1, 3.

Sorbus lancifolia

This tough little tree seldom over 4m tall in cultivation and often less in the wild comes from Norway close to the Arctic Circle and has attractive deeply-lobed leaves and clusters of 9mm bright red berries.

Growth: 1-3-4. Hardiness: 90%. Choice: 1, 3.

Sorbus meliosmifolia

One of the earliest flowering whitebeams in cultivation, this small tree has ascending stiff purple-brown branches. The flowers are white and the fruit consists of 12mm globose red-brown berries. The leaves are reminiscent of a chestnut (*Castanea*), 10-18cm long, sometimes with a more ragged edge. The tree was introduced to European gardens from west China in 1910 by Ernest Wilson. It is often confused in cultivation with another Wilson plant *Sorbus caloneura*.

Growth: 2-6-10. Hardiness: 40-50%. Choice: 1, 3.

Showy Mountain Ash *Sorbus decora*

One of the few American rowans, this 10m tree is close to *Sorbus americana* in the wild, but is possibly of hybrid origin in cultivation. It comes from the United States and Eastern Canada, and was introduced to Europe in 1636. It produces impressive tight clusters of red berries which stay on well into winter. The leaves have 11-17 lanceolate leaflets each 7cm long (see also p. 477).

Growth: 2-7-10. Hardiness: 90%. Choice: 1, 3.

Sorbus tamamschjanae

This is one of a series of apomictic hybrids between *Sorbus rupicola* and *Sorbus aucuparia* which reproduce as clones. It occurs wild in Soviet Armenia. Others appear in Scotland (*Sorbus arranensis*) and Wales (*Sorbus minima*).

Growth: 1-4-6. Hardiness: 80%. Choice: 3.

Sorbus folgneri

This elegant small spreading tree with white-backed leaves and felted shoots at first colours well in the autumn and produces drooping clusters of 13cm globular dark red berries. The species was introduced from Central China in 1901. A yellow-berried form 'Lemon Drop' was introduced by the Hillier Nurseries before 1950.

Growth: 2-6-8. Hardiness: 50%. Choice: 1, 3.

Sorbus tamamschjanae   underside   *autumn*   **Sorbus folgneri**
Sorbus folgneri

True Service Tree

var. *pomifera*

var. *pyrifera*

True Service Tree

winter

True Service Tree *Sorbus domestica*

This is a stately open branched tree some 20m tall with 'Mountain Ash' (Rowan) flowers and leaves, but rough bark like a pear tree. It is native to southern and central Europe, North Africa and western Asia. In former times it was cultivated for its edible fruits and juice, from which a type of cider was produced. The 1.5cm flowers occur in broad panicles 10cm across, in late spring. They are creamy-white. The deciduous foliage consists of alternate 20cm pinnate leaves with 11-21 ovate, parallel-sided, toothed, 5-8cm leaflets. In winter the buds are distinctly sticky. The fruits are around 3cm across. In the variety **pomifera** they resemble small clusters of little apples, light green in colour with a brownish-red side facing the light. The variety **pyrifera** has vaguely pear-shaped fruits which are brighter red.

In the garden these trees require a lot of room but they are attractive and support a wide variety of wildlife. Grass will grow reasonably well under a single specimen on a lawn.

In Britain this tree is of particular interest to naturalists and historians for its antiquity in cultivation, harking back perhaps to times when the edible fruit was highly prized. Some isolated populations in the west of the British Isles are considered to be actually of native origin.

Growth: 3-9-18. Hardiness: 50%. Choice: 1 (requires space). Wood: 1, 5.

Sorbus × *thuringiaca*

A hybrid between *Sorbus aria* (Whitebeam) and *Sorbus aucuparia* (Rowan), this tree brings together some of the most ornamental features of each parent. It develops into a compact branchy-topped tree of upright habit. The 1.2cm flowers are creamy-white in clusters, appearing in late spring and followed by glossy red 1cm berries, similar to holly. The leaves are like whitebeam except that the tip of the leaf narrows, and the two basal pairs of lobes are split to the midrib.

The cultivar '**Fastigiata**' has distinctive, neat, closely-packed upright branches, pale-backed leaves, and dark red berries. It was raised in York in 1907.

The parents of *Sorbus* × *thuringiaca* tend to produce occasional spontaneous hybrids in the wild. These have resulted in some interesting isolated populations of apomictic variants which have become established over time as microspecies. A similar rare plant occurs in central Ireland where *Sorbus hibernica* has crossed with Rowan.

Growth: 2-7-10. Hardiness: 60%. Choice: 1, 3.

Sorbus × *thuringiaca* '**Fastigiata**'

detail

Whitebeam

Whitebeam

underside

underside

'Majestica'

Sorbus 'Wilfrid Fox'

underside

'Lutescens'

'Magnifica'

Whitebeam *Sorbus aria*

This fine ornamental garden, park and street tree is a native species in north and central Europe, including Britain and Ireland. It grows best on lime-rich soils and will thrive on chalk. The branches are upright and then spreading with age. At first the glossy twigs are coated with pale grey mealy down. The leaves too are downy on both sides at first. The upper surfaces soon shed their hairs but the undersides remain permanently felted and brilliantly white. The terminal clusters of 1.5cm creamy-white flowers give way to bunches of 12mm red berries in late summer. In former times these were eaten once they had begun to rot and become sweet. Also in the past the heavy white wood was used for chairs, beams, cogs and wheels in machinery and vehicles.

The cultivar '**Majestica**' frequently still referred to as 'Decaisneana' is a larger tree in every respect than the species. It can grow up to 20m tall with a stem 60cm across. The same kind of white-backed leaves as the species are 10-15cm long with double or multiple toothed margins. It was first cultivated in France in 1880.

'**Lutescens**' is a normal-sized whitebeam which is something of a disappointment. The name implies that it should be golden yellow. Although the hairs on the young leaves are indeed creamy-white the foliage is a poor apology for yellow. Superficially this cultivar resembles the ordinary species with orange-red berries and fairly early dull yellow and grey-brown autumn foliage colour.

'**Magnifica**' is a fine upright tree that spreads in a picturesque fashion in middle to old age. It has the smooth light grey-brown bark of the other whitebeams. The leathery white-backed leaves develop a good glossy green upper surface. The fruits in small bunches, are around 15mm across and bright red in the autumn. This cultivar was produced in 1917 in Germany.

Growth: 3-8-15. Hardiness: 50%. Choice: 1, 2, 3. Wood: 1.

Sorbus 'Wilfrid Fox'

This hybrid between *Sorbus aria* and *Sorbus vestita* was produced at the Hillier Nurseries before 1920. It was named after the founder of the Winkworth Arboretum in Surrey who was a close friend of the Hillier family. This columnar and then broad-crowned tree produces a dense tangle of ascending branches reaching 12m in height. The large 15-20cm leathery, double toothed, dark glossy green leaves are pale grey-felted on the underside. The fruits are green, ripening to amber with tiny grey dots. They are around 2cm across and occur in small bunches. The *Sorbus vestita* parent is the Himalayan Whitebeam previously called *cuspidata*.

Growth: 2-7-10. Hardiness: 60%. Choice: 1, 3.

'Majestica'

spring

Whitebeam

Sorbus vexans

Greek Whitebeam

Sorbus thibetica **'John Mitchell'**

Himalayan Whitebeam

Sorbus thibetica **'John Mitchell'**

Himalayan Whitebeam
young tree

Himalayan Whitebeam *Sorbus vestita*

Formerly called *Sorbus cuspidata*, this is a magnificent smooth-barked tree up to 23m tall, with big 18-25cm grey-green elliptic or oblong leaves. The creamy-white flowers are in flattened terminal clusters which develop into smallish bunches of rock hard, 2cm, green to orange-brown fruits. It has been in cultivation in Europe and America since about 1820.
Growth: 3-9-23. Hardiness: 40-50%. Choice: 1, 3.

Sorbus vexans

In Britain this is a very local apomictic microspecies confined to a small area in North Devon. It was described by E. F. Warburg in 1957. Unlike most of the other English hybrid whitebeams it thrives on neutral to acid soils.
Growth: 1-4-6. Hardiness: 40-50%. Choice: 3.

Sorbus thibetica 'John Mitchell'

One of the finest big whitebeam trees ever selected, 'John Mitchell' has 20cm oval to almost round grey-backed leaves. Nicely proportioned, it can grow to over 15m in height with wide spreading branches. It is named in honour of William John Mitchell the one-time curator of Westonbirt Arboretum who selected it from a batch of Himalayan seed, presumably of *Sorbus vestita*, and planted it in the collection in 1938.
Growth: 3-8-15. Hardiness: 40-50%. Choice: 1 (requires space).

Greek Whitebeam *Sorbus graeca*

More properly called *Sorbus umbellata* var. *cretica* this is a small untidy tree with somewhat dense branches from Greece, Syria, Asia Minor and parts of central Europe. It has brilliant white-backed leaves and clusters of fruits which are greenish-brown flushed with red when they ripen. It appears to have been in cultivation since 1830, but has long been confused with *Sorbus aria*. The whitebeams of Eastern Europe and Asia Minor, including *Sorbus umbellata*, are geographic races of *Sorbus aria*, so this is not surprising.
Growth: 2-5-7. Hardiness: 40-50%. Choice: 1, 3.

Sorbus mougeotii

This beautiful medium-sized whitebeam is closely related to the Service Tree of Fontainebleau, *Sorbus latifolia*. It comes from the European Alps and the Pyrenees. The 8mm fruits which occur in bunches are bright red, and edible. *Sorbus mougeotii* might be of hybrid origin, possibly a cross between *Sorbus latifolia* and *Sorbus intermedia*. It is apomictic and comes true from seed.
Growth: 2-8-20. Hardiness: 50-60%. Choice: 1, 2, 3. Wood: 1, 5.

Sorbus × paucicrenata

This small tree has no particular garden merit but it is a complex hybrid curiosity that might appeal to serious plant collectors. It is a backcross that has occurred spontaneously where the parents grow together in Central Europe. One of these is *Sorbus × decipiens*, which is itself a hybrid between *Sorbus aria* and *Sorbus torminalis* and is totally sterile. The other parent is *Sorbus aria* which, because *Sorbus × decipiens* can not produce viable seed, has to be the mother tree.
Growth: 2-7-8. Hardiness: 50-60%. Choice: 4.

Sorbus mougeotii

Sorbus × paucicrenata

Sorbus alnifolia

var. *macrophylla*

var. *longifolia*

Sorbus takhtajan

underside

underside

Sorbus alnifolia

underside

Sorbus umbellata

Sorbus alnifolia
summer

Sorbus hajastana

underside

Sorbus zahlbruckneri

486

Sorbus alnifolia

This is a large deciduous tree 20m tall in the wild, but generally it is much less in cultivation. The upright branches support a neat rounded top. The 1cm single white flowers, in terminal clusters, appear in spring. Bunches of 1cm round berries turn from olive-green through dull orange to red with tiny brown dots. The ovate to elliptic toothed leaves turn bright yellow, orange and red in the autumn. The varieties **macrophylla** and **longifolia** are superior garden forms with larger and longer leaves respectively.
Growth: 2-8-20. Hardiness: 50%. Choice: 1, 3.

Sorbus takhtajanii

Strikingly white woolly-backed leaves are a feature of this rare western Asian species of whitebeam. It is particularly good in early spring when the buds break and the rolled new leaves resemble upright silver candles.
Growth: 2-5-7. Hardiness: 40-50%. Choice: 1, 3.

Sorbus umbellata

This shrubby plant from south-east Europe and Asia Minor is closely related to *Sorbus aria*. It has almost round 5cm silver-backed leaves which are incisely-lobed. The creamy-white flowers are in flat terminal clusters. The fruits are orange-red, oval and slightly flattened.
Growth: 2-5-7. Hardiness: 50-60%. Choice: 1, 3.

Sorbus hajastana

Important as a native species in western Asia, but very rare in cultivation, this is probably an eastern extension of *Sorbus aria*. The leaves are neatly serrate and silver-backed. It is a difficult plant to obtain in Europe where most nurseries only stock the similar-looking ordinary European Whitebeam.
Growth: 2-5-8. Hardiness: 40-50%. Choice: 4.

Sorbus zahlbruckneri

This obscure Chinese species appears to be different in the wild to cultivated plants. It seems that the name has been used for two quite different plants. The tree cultivated under this name is usually, but not always, found to be *Sorbus alnifolia* var. *submollis*. Both it and the true species are broadly similar to *Sorbus aria* and only have garden value as curiosities.
Growth: -. Hardiness: -%. Choice: 4.

Sorbus alnifolia
autumn

Sorbus zahlbruckneri
autumn

Wild Service Tree

Swedish Whitebeam

underside

autumn

Wild Service Tree

Swedish Whitebeam

Wild Service Tree

WHITEBEAMS

Wild Service Tree *Sorbus torminalis*

This is an environmentally important large suckering tree up to 25m tall with rugged cracking bark. The flowers in terminal clusters occur in early summer and they are followed by russet brown edible fruits. It is native to Europe and as far south as North Africa. Ancient wild populations still survive that have considerable conservation significance. New research is under way investigating the potential timber value of this species. The wood is hard, strong and pale-coloured, reminiscent of Sycamore (p. 633). Choice lengths have a wavy grain, and a silvery sheen when cut on the radius.

Wild Service usually makes a shapely specimen with rich golden-brown autumn foliage colour. It requires light and plenty of space to develop to its full capability.

Growth: 3-10-25. Hardiness: 50%. Choice: 2, 3. Wood: 1.

Swedish Whitebeam *Sorbus intermedia*

This is one of the most important trees for decorative and shelter planting in the far North of Europe. It tolerates severe climatic conditions, notably in Norway, Denmark and Scotland. And it is the only broadleaved tree that really thrives on Orkney and Shetland. It is equally at home further south, though, and is grown on numerous European city streets. The lobed leaves are silvery-green. Dull white branching corymbs of scented flowers appear in late spring. The oval fruits, in conspicuous bunches, are brownish then red.

Growth: 3-8-15. Hardiness: 70%. Choice: 2, 3. Wood: 5.

Service Tree of Fontainebleau

Sorbus latifolia

This is a 20m tree in France, with smooth grey bark cracking vertically only in old age. The triangular-lobed leaves are shining green above and tomentose grey-green underneath. Clusters of short-stalked flowers are followed by 12mm globular edible twin seeded fruits that are reddish with scattered minute brown dots. It is an apomictic species that always comes true from seed. Presumably it originated as a hybrid involving *Sorbus torminalis* and a form of *Sorbus aria*. Individual specimens near to the Forest of Fontainebleau exhibit very constant botanical features.

Growth: 2-8-20. Hardiness: 50%. Choice: 1, 2, 3. Wood: 1, 5.

Sorbus latifolia microspecies

Of considerable botanical and conservation interest but limited garden merit are a number of rare endemic British Isles microspecies.

In the *Sorbus latifolia* aggregate is **Sorbus devoniensis**, a tree up to 15m tall which is native only to south-west England and parts of Ireland. **Sorbus bristoliensis** occurs on the River Avon gorge near Bristol. **Sorbus × vagensis** (*torminalis × aria*) is a rather variable and not always apomictic hybrid. Fertile and sterile trees are known within its limited range in south-east Wales and along the adjacent English border. In the *Sorbus intermedia* aggregate is **Sorbus anglica**, a shrubby tree seldom more than 3m tall, which is local in isolated parts of the British Isles as far west as North Kerry.

Service Tree of Fontainebleau

Crab Apple

young fruit

underside

spring **Crab Apple** winter

490

APPLES

Crab Apple *Malus sylvestris*

This small 9m tree is native to Europe, including the British Isles, Scandinavia, and parts of Asia Minor. Everywhere it is confused with domestic apple trees which have escaped from cultivation and become naturalized. The fruit of the true Crab Apple is 2-3cm across, yellow-green, flushed with light red and often speckled with tiny white spots. The sepals of its flowers are not deciduous. Although juicy, it is never sweet, even when over-ripe. Nevertheless, it has always been an important source of food and was also used to make a particularly harsh kind of cider. Pips will grow, although they may take a leisurely 18 months to germinate – and 12-15 years to fruit. Crab Apple was one of several species used in the development of hybrid domestic apples and seedlings were cultivated for use as under-stocks on which to graft orchard apples. In Ireland a yellow dye was extracted from the bark to colour wool.

It is often a shapeless tree with several stems and a bushy top. Some branches, especially towards the base, develop short sharply pointed spur shoots. Trees up to 200 years old are known. The subspecies *mitis*, which is similar but not spiny, appears to have been used most often in breeding orchard apples.

Growth: 3-7-9. Hardiness: 80%. Choice: 3. Wood: 1, 5.

Orchard Apple *Malus domestica*

The Orchard Apple is not a true species in the strict botanical or horticultural sense. It has no wild predecessor, but is wholly man-made by selection and breeding. It is thought that *Malus sylvestris* subspecies *mitis*, *Malus dasphylla* and *Malus praecox* were used as parents, but other Asiatic species, such as *Malus sieversii*, may also have been involved. Centuries of development, and a few 'happy accidents' have resulted in sweet eating apples and sharp fruit for cooking and for cider. It is reckoned that over 1000 species have been named. However, modern legislation and mass-production have reduced diversity. Just a handful of good-looking cultivars now dominate the market and many fine-tasting varieties have become very rare. The ordinary garden with an old named apple tree in it is increasingly important for the future conservation of obscure threatened cultivars.

The British countryside in particular is littered with 'apple core progeny' – trees that have grown from discarded cores of apples eaten many years ago. Abandoned rural railway lines and country lanes are common locations and even urban roadsides still support a few trees. Most are of little consequence, but some bear very acceptable fruit.

Growth: 3-7-10 variable. Hardiness: 50-70%. Choice: 3. Wood: 1, 5.

Orchard Apple

seed

'Joan'

'Yellow Siberian'

Malus × robusta

Malus brevipes

Malus × zumi var. calocarpa

Malus halliana

Malus kirghisorum

Chinese Crab Apple

Malus spectabilis 'Riversii'

Malus × robusta

This vigorous and hardy hybrid between *Malus baccata* (p. 501) and *Malus prunifolia* (p. 505) is a large upright shrub or small tree with slightly pendulous branch tips. The leaves are 8-11cm long and bright green. The 3-4cm flowers occur in clusters, pink in bud then white with just a hint of pink. The fruit is globular to ellipsoid and only 1-3cm across; it turns yellow and red in the autumn. The cultivar '**Joan**' has larger early white flowers and red fruits produced in profusion, usually every other year. '**Yellow Siberian**' is a well-known yellow-fruited heavy-cropping cultivar.

Growth: 2-6-9. Hardiness: 80%. Choice: 1, 3.

Malus × zumi var. calocarpa

This spreading bushy small tree is a 1905 Japanese cross between *Malus baccata* var. *mandshurica* and *Malus sieboldii*. The flowers are pale pink in bud and white when fully open. The abundant 1.5cm apples are orange-red and remain on the tree until the winter. Calocarpa means beautiful fruit – and they are.

Growth: 2-4-6. Hardiness: 70%. Choice: 1, 3.

Malus brevipes

Brevipes means short-stalked, a reference to the leaf stalks. This compact little tree produces abundant almost pure white flowers with orange stamens. The bright red fruits are roundish and 1-3cm across. Its origin is unknown but it is closely related to *Malus floribunda* (p. 495).

Growth: 2-4-6. Hardiness: 50%. Choice: 1, 3.

Malus kirghisorum

A rare species, similar to *Malus × robusta,* with numerous compact clusters of flowers. It makes a rounded tree about 5m tall and wide. It is no longer widely available in the nursery trade.

Growth: 2-4-5. Hardiness: 70%. Choice: 1, 3.

Malus spectabilis 'Riversii'

This cultivar of the **Chinese Crab Apple** is an admirable tree, usually less than 8m tall with spreading branches. The flowers are deeper pink than the species, and it is one of the best dark pink crab apple cultivars available at present. The fruits are of no real ornamental significance. It was raised, however, in England before 1864 and widely distributed in Europe through Booth's Nurseries near Hamburg.

Growth: 2-6-8. Hardiness: 60%. Choice: 1, 3.

Malus halliana

Around 5m tall this old cultivar has now largely been superseded by modern more flamboyant purple-leaved forms. The young shoots are purplish-brown and the leaves are often purplish tinted green with a minute crimson margin. The flowers are deep pink in bud, opening to paler pink, with long dark purple-brown stalks. The 1cm fruits are reddish-brown with a deciduous calyx, and extraordinarily large seeds. This Chinese and Japanese garden tree is now unknown in the wild. It was introduced to America from Japan in 1863.

Growth: 2-4-5. Hardiness: 50%. Choice: 1, 3.

'Joan'
spring

Malus kirghisorum
spring

Sweet Crab Apple

autumn

fruit enlarged

'Charlottae'

Japanese Crab Apple

Japanese Crab Apple

Malus hupehensis

Malus hupehensis

Malus hupehensis
spring

Sweet Crab Apple *Malus coronaria*

This North American tree, introduced to Europe in 1724, is still uncommon in cultivation. Up to 9m tall, it flowers in late spring with violet-scented white blossoms, flushed rose-pink in bud, on long slender shoots. The leaves are distinctly lobed. The 3cm fruits are green, ripening to pale yellowish-green. Alfred Rehder and Charles Sprague Sargent described the lobed-leaf form (illustrated) as var. *elongata* and the species as having entire, coarsely serrate leaves. Cultivation in Europe appears to have confused this distinction. The wood is decorative, heavy but soft, light-red in the centre and yellow towards the bark.

The beautiful cultivar '**Charlottae**' has semi-double flowers and larger, more deeply-lobed leaves. It retains the delightful scent of violets and in autumn it has good foliage colour. The original plant was found as a spontaneous seedling in Illinois in 1902.

Growth: 2-5-9. Hardiness: 70%. Choice: 1, 3. Wood: 1.

Japanese Crab Apple *Malus floribunda*

This tree was introduced to Europe and America in 1862 from Japan but it does not have any known wild distribution there. It has become very popular in cultivation, and is one of the most floriferous of apples, the whole tree changing from pink to white as the flowers mature in mid-spring. The tiny 1cm fruits are yellow. A fully mature specimen growing in the open is likely to spread wider than it is tall, to about 8m.

Growth: 2-5-6. Hardiness: 60-70%. Choice: 1, 3.

Malus hupehensis

A fine garden feature for all seasons, this apple has widely spreading branches, good flowers, and decorative fruit. It originated in Central China where the local people used to make a kind of tea from the leaves. The long-stalked spring flowers, in nodding clusters, are white with a hint of pink while in bud. By late summer the whole tree is covered with cherry-like translucent red 1.5cm apples. These are eventually accompanied by reasonably good coloured autumn foliage. The seeds come true, as this is an apomictic triploid (see glossary) and does not rely on sexual means of reproduction.

There is a pink-flowered cultivar 'Rosea' which is a useful substitute for a flowering cherry, where cherries are difficult to grow.

Growth: 2-5-8. Hardiness: 60%. Choice: 1, 3.

Sweet Crab Apple

Japanese Crab Apple

Pillar Apple

Pillar Apple

Malus transitoria

Malus 'Magdeburgensis'

Oregon Crab Apple

leaf variation

Malus trilobata

Oregon Crab Apple

496

APPLES

Pillar Apple *Malus tschonoskii*

An erect tree up to 12m tall from Japan, this species was discovered by western plant collectors near Mount Fujiyama in 1897. As a garden specimen it is usually planted for its upright stature. It has unusual grey-backed green summer leaves, and glorious autumn foliage colour. Its pinkish-white blossom is fairly ordinary, and its fruits insignificant.
Growth: 3-8-12. Hardiness: 50%. Choice: 1. Wood: 5.

Malus transitoria

This species is closely related to *Malus toringoides*. They are both rare Chinese bushy trees, usually with distinctively lobed leaves. The 2cm flowers are white, appearing in mid to late spring. The globose or slightly elongated 1cm fruits are light orange-red. The autumn foliage colour can be excellent. *Malus transitoria* came originally from Kansu Province in north-east China.
Growth: 2-5-8. Hardiness: 50%. Choice: 1, 3.

Malus 'Magdeburgensis'

This is possibly a hybrid between a crab apple and an orchard apple but its exact parentage is uncertain. It was raised in Germany before 1900, and is closely related to *Malus spectabilis* (p. 499). The large clusters of 5cm semi-double 'orchard apple' flowers are carmine in bud, becoming pale pink as they open. The 3cm round apples are yellow-green with a red or red-brown sunny side. In cultivation 'Magdeburgensis' is prized for its lovely flowers which give the feeling of a traditional apple orchard in spring.
Growth: 2-5-9. Hardiness: 60%. Choice: 1, 3.

Oregon Crab Apple *Malus fusca*

(See also p. 499). A native of the north-west Pacific coast of America, this woodland tree has a huge natural range from southern Alaska to north-west California. Such an extensive north to south distribution gives rise to great variation. Ultimate height, for instance, may be anything between 4m and 12m. The leaves are entire or three-lobed but frequently a mixture of both. The flower clusters are white but slightly pink in bud. The fruits come in a range of colours, they are elongated and up to 4cm long.
Growth: 2-7-12. Hardiness: 50-60%. Choice: 3, 4.

Malus trilobata

This unusual apple with lobed maple-like leaves was originally classified as a species of thorn. It is a small narrow-crowned tree, native to Syria and the eastern Mediterranean. In cultivation it is quite rare and slightly tender. The white flowers are 3.5cm across in clusters. The fruits are elongated or slightly pear-shaped. They contain 'stone cells' which more usually occur in pears. In a good season the autumn foliage can turn bright red.
Growth: 2-4-6. Hardiness: 50%. Choice: 1, 3.

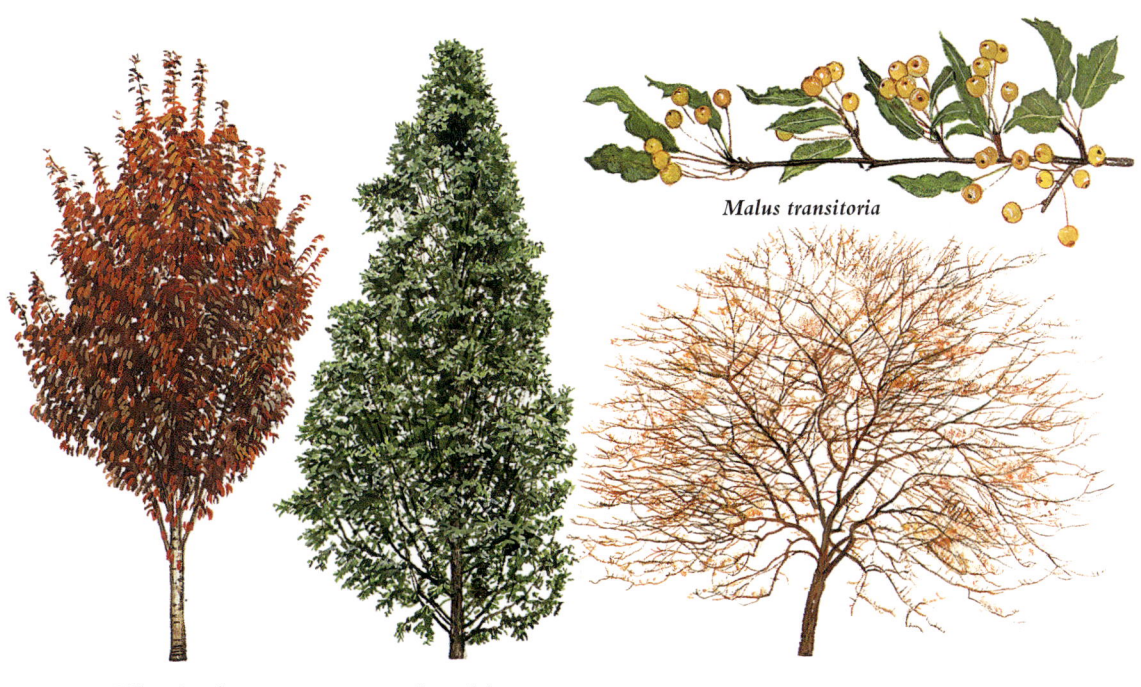

Pillar Apple autumn

Malus trilobata

Malus transitoria

Oregon Crab Apple

Chinese Crab Apple

Malus lancifolia

Malus orthocarpa

Malus lancifolia

Oregon Crab Apple

Oregon Crab Apple *Malus fusca*

This species is described on p. 497.

Malus lancifolia

A 6-8m tree with long flowering branches and spiny side shoots. It is native to the United States, especially in Missouri and Illinois, and in southern Canada. In America it is usually regarded as a form of *Malus coronaria* (p. 495). The clusters of 3-4cm flowers are pale pink providing a lovely garland effect on the extended shoots. The narrow leaves are more or less lanceolate but can be variable in shape, and some are occasionally lobed. The round 3cm apples are waxy green on thread-like stalks.

Growth: 2-6-8. Hardiness: 50-70%. Choice: 1, 3.

Chinese Crab Apple *Malus spectabilis*

This decorative 6-9m Chinese garden tree has been in cultivation so long that no wild distribution is known. It produces a huge accumulation of semi-double 5cm shell pink flowers in mid-spring with the fresh young leaves. The prominent mass of yellow 2.5cm globular apples is a valuable early winter feature. The tree has been in Europe at least since 1780. A single-flowered form was also noted in 1825, but it is probably no longer in cultivation.

Growth: 2-6-8. Hardiness: 60%. Choice: 1, 3.

Malus orthocarpa

From China, this shrub or small tree has the palest of pink flowers. Unfortunately it is now extremely rare in cultivation. The bright orange-red apples are mostly held in an upright position.

Growth: 2-4-5. Hardiness: 50%. Choice: 3, 4.

Malus prattii

Discovered by A.E. Pratt in China, and introduced by Ernest Wilson for the Veitch Nursery, in 1904, this lovely tree is closely related to *Malus yunnanensis* (p. 505). It is native to Szechuan Province. Reminiscent of a Japanese flowering cherry, it grows into an upright specimen some 7-8m tall with slightly spreading branches. The white flowers are 2cm across in clusters. The 3cm apples, on thick fairly rigid stalks, are round or pear-shaped turning through yellow to red, and covered with minute white dots. They contain gritty cells like a pear. The 6-15cm leaves are large for an apple, especially those on vigorous young shoots. They are slightly red veined through the summer and generally give a good show of autumn colour.

Growth: 2-6-8. Hardiness: 50%. Choice: 1, 3.

Malus prattii

Malus prattii

Siberian Crab Apple

var. *mandshurica*

'Jackii'

Malus 'Lady Northcliffe'

var. *mandshurica*

Siberian Crab Apple

Siberian Crab Apple

Siberian Crab Apple *Malus baccata*

This is a very hardy 8-14m tall tree, starting off with a narrow rounded crown but spreading out widely with age. It is native to a large area of north-east Asia and northern China and was introduced to Kew Gardens in London in 1784. The 3-4cm single fragrant white flowers, occurring in mid-spring with the fresh glossy green leaves, are reminiscent of a pear tree. The fruits are small with a hollowed base and deciduous calyx. They turn from yellow to red in the autumn, or sometimes remain bi-coloured. Although tediously small to collect the apples make a delicious jelly. The name *baccata* is a reference to the fleshy fruit. The true species is uncommon in horticulture. Many early plants were in fact hybrids with *Malus prunifolia* which generally have larger fruit (see *Malus* × *robusta*, p. 493). These included 'Red Siberian' and 'Yellow Siberian', which appeared shortly after 1850.

The cultivar '**Jackii**' from Korea, was introduced in 1905. It is another free flowering tree with single ivory-white blossoms and golden stamens. The leaves are deep green and the 1cm fruits are glossy red.

The variety **mandshurica** has early 4cm fragrant white flowers and larger 1.2cm red fruits on long stalks. Its natural range runs through eastern Siberia, south to central China and across Japan. It was introduced to the west in 1825 and was noted at Kew in 1874, but wrongly named *Malus baccata*. The genuine variety was reintroduced by Ernest Wilson to the Veitch Nursery in 1901.

Growth: 3-8-12. Hardiness: 80%. Choice: 1, 3. Wood: 5 (species).

Malus 'Lady Northcliffe'

This hybrid, of uncertain origin, was raised at Aldenham, in Hertfordshire in the 1920s and appears to have characteristics of *Malus baccata*. It flowers abundantly, pink in bud and white on opening, at the same time as the fresh green leaves appear. The fruits are yellow to russet-brown with a deciduous calyx. This is a short but fairly wide densely 'twiggy' plant which can be quite spectacular when covered in spring blossom. All of the forms of Siberian Crab Apple, and the species itself, deserve to be more widely planted. They are extremely hardy and make excellent additions to an exposed landscaped area or as a decorative component of a shelterbelt. They will tolerate most soil types and urban conditions.

Growth: 2-6-8. Hardiness: 70%. Choice: 1, 3.

Siberian Crab Apple bark

spring

***Malus* 'Lady Northcliffe'**

Malus baccata var. *himalaica*

Malus × *hartwigii*

Malus prunifolia var. *rinki* bark

Malus × *sublobata*

Malus sargentii

Malus prunifolia var. *rinki*

Malus sargentii

502

Malus baccata var. *himalaica*

This is a southern race of the Siberian Crab Apple which varies widely according to local provenance but is never very different to the species. Some individuals have more coarsely toothed leaves. The flower buds are often flushed with pink but the single flowers are white. It was introduced around 1910 by George Forrest, and also Frank Ludlow and George Sherriff working in Tibet and Bhutan.

Growth: 2-7-10. Hardiness: 50-70%. Choice: 4.

Malus prunifolia var. *rinki*

The species and the variety are both of garden origin. **Malus prunifolia** (p. 505) is thought to have been introduced from north-east Asia in 1753. Its variety *rinki* is extensively cultivated in China for its edible fruit. Ernest Wilson found apparently wild plants of it there, but it was first introduced to Europe from Japan, around 1850, by the German plant collector Philipp Franz von Siebold. There are pink-flowered forms and paler types. There are also red-fruited and yellow-fruited trees.

Growth: 2-5-7. Hardiness: 70%. Choice: 1.

Malus × *hartwigii*

Although the origin of this tree is unknown it is thought to be a hybrid between *Malus halliana* and *Malus baccata*. It was introduced to Germany from Asia by August Karl Julius Hartwig in 1906. It is a fine spreading tree with dark twigs and 6-8cm ovate leaves. The semi-double flowers are pink in bud emerging white as the leaves unfold. The greenish-yellow 1cm fruits are roughly pear-shaped.

Growth: 2-5-7. Hardiness: 50%. Choice: 1.

Malus × *sublobata*

This hybrid between *Malus sieboldii* and *Malus prunifolia* var. *rinki* was first described at the Arnold Arboretum, Massachusetts, USA. It is an unpredictable plant probably because of the variable nature of *Malus prunifolia*. The 4-8cm leaves tend to be narrower than most other apples and slightly lobed on vigorous young growth, hence the name *sublobata*. The shaggy 4cm flowers are pink in bud opening to very pale pink.

Growth: variable. Hardiness: 50-60%. Choice: 4.

Malus sargentii

This shrubby Japanese plant, not more than 3m tall but often wide spreading, has densely packed twigs which are frequently spiny. The 5-8cm toothed leaves have woolly backs and can develop one or two lobes. The 3cm flowers are single and white with prominent golden stamens, and the 1cm fruits which follow are bright red with a deciduous calyx. Plants were sent to Kew Gardens from the Arnold Arboretum by Professor Sargent in 1908. The tree was discovered in Japan by Sargent himself in 1892 but it now seems doubtful whether it is a true species. Hybrid status would perhaps be more appropriate, but botanists are still discussing this.

Growth: 1-2-3. Hardiness: 50%. Choice: 1.

Malus prunifolia
spring

Malus × hartwigii
spring

Malus florentina

autumn

fruit enlarged

Malus prunifolia

Toringo Crab Apple

'Plena'

Malus ioensis

Malus florentina

From northern Italy and the Balkans, this small tree has upright branches but a rounded outline. The pale furry-backed, often truncate, leaves are broadly ovate, 3-7cm long and deeply incised into several pairs of toothed lobes like hawthorn with reddish stalks and main veins. The autumn foliage colour is bright orange and scarlet. Pure white flowers occur on second year spur shoots all along the branches. It was introduced to England by H. Groves in 1886 from near Florence, Italy, hence the species name. It is rare in cultivation but deserves to be planted more widely.

Growth: 2-4-5. Hardiness: 50%. Choice: 1.

Malus prunifolia

Although this small hardy tree is well known in cultivation it is of uncertain Asiatic origin. It has 3cm fragrant white flowers in terminal clusters. The 2cm slightly ovoid fruits turn from yellow to red with a persistent calyx and remain on the tree well into winter. The name means having leaves like those of a plum tree.

Growth: 2-5-6. Hardiness: 70%. Choice: 1.

Toringo Crab Apple Malus sieboldii

This small shrubby tree, rarely over 4m tall, is from Japan. The leaves are extremely variable, from oval to lobed and up to 6cm long. The slender-stalked flowers are rose pink and short-lived. Tiny pea-sized yellow fruits follow which acquire a russet or rosy side by early winter. The plant was introduced by Philipp Franz von Siebold to Berlin in 1856. Toringo means 'Chinese apple' in Japan. Siebold's original tree appears to have had larger 3cm fruits.

Growth: 1-3-4. Hardiness: 50%. Choice: 1.

Malus ioensis

This hardy 10m tree from the USA – the name meaning 'from Iowa' – is the common crab apple of the Mississippi area. The fresh green leaves are coarsely toothed, often partially incised on the most vigorous growth. The 4cm flowers are single, pale pink, and appear in terminal clusters, scented like violets. The globular 3cm fruits are waxy green and yellow with a persistent calyx. A double-flowered form '**Plena**', the Bechtel Crab Apple, is one of the very best ornamental flowering apples. The pink early summer flowers are up to 6cm across and also have the smell of violets. It was introduced into cultivation by Messrs Bechtel, nurserymen of Illinois, USA, in 1891.

Growth: 2-6-10. Hardiness: 90%. Choice: 1. Wood: 5.

Malus yunnanensis

From Yunnan in west China this 10m tree was discovered by Father Jean Marie Delavay, a missionary working in China. It was introduced to the west by Ernest Wilson in 1908. The tree has slightly lobed or very coarsely toothed 6-12cm leaves with pale brown felted backs. The young shoots are tomentose. The flowers are palest pink and very small, in dense clusters reminiscent of a thorn tree. A more common plant in cultivation is the variety **veitchii**. It colours well in the autumn with orange leaves and tight bunches of 1cm bright red fruits.

Growth: 2-6-10. Hardiness: 50%. Choice: 1.

Malus florentina

Malus yunnanensis

var. **veitchii**
autumn

Malus 'Lemoinei'

Malus 'Liset'

Malus 'Profusion'

Malus × *purpurea*

'Aldenhamensis'

Malus 'Laxton's Red'

Malus 'Lemoinei'

This deep pink French flowering crab apple, a favourite with gardeners, is probably of similar parentage to *Malus × purpurea*. Catalogues began to list it from around 1922. It is a dark-leaved tree which remains fairly small, seldom over 6m tall, with a broad slightly ragged head of branches. The stunning purple-crimson flowers occur with the bronze-brown leaves in spring. The summer foliage is sombre greenish-purple then in autumn the tree produces masses of little round very deep red apples on long stalks like cherries.

Growth: 2-5-7. Hardiness: 50%. Choice: 1.

Malus 'Liset'

'Liset' is another garden favourite like 'Lemoinei', but generally larger and brighter. The summer leaves are dark glossy green, tinted purplish-bronze. It is an artificial hybrid between *Malus sieboldii* (p. 505) and *Malus* 'Lemoinei'.

Growth: 2-5-6. Hardiness: 50%. Choice: 1.

Malus 'Profusion'

Like the previous two trees this medium-sized spreading plant has purple-bronze foliage and deep pink flowers. The leaves on vigorous shoots are often lobed. Older specimens develop pendulous branches. The flowers fade as they mature to paler pink, but they retain a delicate scent. The apples are small and something of a disappointment.

Growth: 2-6-8. Hardiness: 50%. Choice: 1.

Malus × purpurea

This is a hybrid between *Malus × atrosanguinea* and *Malus niedzwetzyana* which produces huge numbers of strong pink single flowers on long stalks. It makes a rounded mound of a tree 5-7m tall. Cultivated in France before 1900 this hybrid has been widely planted in gardens, parks and streets, and many named cultivars have been developed from it. The clusters of 2cm apples are dark brownish-red. The twigs are purplish-brown and even the wood is sometimes stained red. The cultivar '**Aldenhamensis**' is one of the best known forms with mostly semi-double flowers appearing in late spring, often with a limited second flush in autumn. The tree was cultivated at Aldenham, Hertfordshire, in 1922. The 2.5cm brownish-red apples are slightly flattened and their pulp is also stained red.

Growth: 2-6-7. Hardiness: 50%. Choice: 1.

Malus 'Laxton's Red'

The name Laxton is usually associated with domestic orchard apples, 'Laxton's Superb' being one of the finest of all eating apples. This diversion by the Laxton nurseries from orchard apples is a lovely little tree related to *Malus × purpurea*, but with lighter-coloured foliage. Unfortunately it is no longer generally available in the nursery trade.

Growth: 2-5-7. Hardiness: 50%. Choice: 1.

Malus 'Laxton's Red'

Malus 'Profusion'

Malus 'Butterball'

Malus 'Crittenden'

Malus 'Golden Hornet'

Malus 'John Downie'

Malus 'Butterball'

A relatively new cultivar produced in 1961, very similar to 'Golden Hornet', producing numerous 2.5cm round apples which are bright yellow and lightly flushed with orange on the sunlit side. It makes a small spreading tree with drooping branches and bright green leaves. The flowers are pink in bud opening to white. It is ideal for the small garden as something a little different to the ubiquitous 'Golden Hornet', below.

Growth: 2-4-6. Hardiness: 50%. Choice: 1.

Malus 'Crittenden'

Noted for its numerous tiny 1-2cm glossy scarlet apples which hang on for most of the winter, from a distance this small tree resembles a hawthorn laden with late haws. The mid-spring flowers are palest pink. The original plant was sent to B. P. Tompsett of Crittenden House, Kent, from Japan in 1921. It is possibly related to the red-fruited form of *Malus prunifolia* var. *rinki* (p. 503).

Growth: 2-4-5. Hardiness: 50%. Choice: 1.

Malus 'Golden Hornet'

This is now probably the favourite and most planted garden crab apple of all. It bears numerous little 2cm yellow apples in the autumn. These will usually stay on the tree until mid-winter when there is hardly any other bright colour left in the garden. 'Golden Hornet' was produced by Waterer's Nursery before 1949. The exact parentage is unknown but the tree has a lot in common with the yellow-fruited *Malus prunifolia* var. *rinki* (p. 503).

Growth: 2-6-8. Hardiness: 60%. Choice: 1.

Malus 'John Downie'

'John Downie' is a strong-growing apple tree, which bears numerous 3-4cm round or conical apples. They are pleasant to eat when fully ripe and are also ornamental, being bright yellow to orange, with a rosy-red flushed sunny side, hanging in clusters on slender stalks. The flowers are pink in bud and then white, appearing in late spring. This cultivar was raised by E. Holmes of Lichfield in 1875. John Downie was his friend and a fellow nurseryman from Scotland.

Growth: 2-7-9. Hardiness: 50%. Choice: 1.

Malus 'Dartmouth'

This cultivar produces beautiful pure white 3.5cm single flowers in late spring accompanied by fully extended fresh green leaves. The rather angular 4cm edible apples are bloomed wine-red. It is a vigorous plant raised in New Hampshire, USA, around 1883. An ideal garden tree for both spring and autumn interest.

Growth: 2-5-7. Hardiness: 50%. Choice: 1.

Malus 'Eleyi'

This well known small tree with deep pink flowers was raised by Charles Eley in England before 1920. The purplish-red fruits are more decorative than most of the other deep pink-flowered crab apples. It is said to be a hybrid between *Malus niedzwetzkyana* and *Malus spectabilis*. It is known that Mr Eley produced many seedlings. Although only one was named 'Eleyi' several of them still appear to be in cultivation.

Growth: 2-5-7. Hardiness: 50%. Choice: 1.

Malus 'Dartmouth'

Malus 'Eleyi'

Malus 'Red Jade'

Malus 'Red Sentinal'

Malus 'Royalty'

Malus 'Van Eseltine'

Malus 'Coralburst'

Malus 'Mary Potter'

510

Malus 'Red Jade'

Thought to be a seedling of the weeping crab apple 'Exzellenz Thiel', this small tree has drooping branches. It appeared in Brooklyn Botanic Gardens, USA, in 1935. The leaves are finely toothed and have slender stalks. The spring flowers are pure white after being flushed with pink in bud. The 1.5cm fruits are bright red and persist in huge numbers on the tree well into the winter.

Growth: 2-4-4. Hardiness: 50-60%. Choice: 1.

Malus 'Red Sentinal'

This 1959 selection of the hybrid *Malus × robusta* (p. 493) was produced by Notcutts Nursery. The flowers start pink and turn white as they open. The numerous 2.5cm deep glossy red fruits are globular and slightly ribbed. They remain on the tree at least until mid-winter.

Growth: 2-5-7. Hardiness: 50%. Choice: 1.

Malus 'Royalty'

Grown for its foliage and flowers this small tree was raised by W.L. Kerr in Saskatachewan, Canada, in 1962. The leaves are purple, turning fiery red in the autumn. The large 5cm flowers are deep pink, appearing with the leaves in mid to late spring. The apples are very dark red.

Growth: 2-4-5. Hardiness: 60%. Choice: 1.

Malus 'Van Eseltine'

This narrow-crowned tree is an ideal plant for the small garden requiring very little space. It was raised by the New York Department of Agriculture Experimental Station between 1930 and 1941. The semi-double flowers are red in bud then shell pink with paler pink central petals. They occur in clusters with the leaves in spring. The 2cm fruits are yellow, occasionally with a light red flush on the sunny side.

Growth: 2-4-5. Hardiness: 50-60%. Choice: 1.

Malus 'Coralburst'

A low-growing tree recently raised in America. It has numerous clusters of pink blossom. The single flowers are paler on the tops of the petals than the back, giving a two-tone effect. It is another compact tree which needs very little space.

Growth: 2-4-5. Hardiness: 50%. Choice: 1.

Malus 'Mary Potter'

Often a small shrubby tree, this was selected in 1939 from a *Malus × atrosanguinea* crossed with *Malus sargentii* 'Rosea'. It has blush-pink flower buds opening to white with golden yellow stamens. The numerous 1cm fruits are red like small hard cherries.

Growth: 2-3-4. Hardiness: 50%. Choice: 1.

Malus 'Royalty'
spring

Malus 'Coralburst'
emerging flowers

Wild Pear

Wild Pear

Pyrus serrulata

Pyrus regelii

twig of Wild Pear

Pyrus betulifolia

Wild Pear

Pyrus amygdaliformis

Wild Pear *Pyrus pyraster*

The status of this plant is uncertain. In Britain it is regarded generally as the form of *Pyrus communis* (p. 519) most likely to be from wild stock. A thorny tree often of great age and substantial size.
Growth: 3-9-12. Hardiness: 60%. Choice: 3. Wood: 1.

Pyrus serrulata

This rare tree in cultivation was introduced in 1917 from central China. It is a plantsman's tree with little popular appeal. The 5-11cm ovate-oblong pointed and neatly toothed leaves are its best feature.
Growth: 2-5-6. Hardiness: 50%. Choice: 4.

Pyrus betulifolia

This slender 6-10m tree from northern China was introduced to France in 1863, to America around 1865, then eventually to England in 1882. It is used in China mostly as a rootstock for orchard pears. The young branches and twigs are covered with thick grey felt, and the leaves resemble birch (the Himalayan sort) as indicated by the species name. They are 4-7cm long and distinctly toothed. White 2cm single flowers are produced on long slender stalks in mid to late spring. The brown fruits are tiny with pale dots.
Growth: 2-6-9. Hardiness: 60-70%. Choice: 1, 2.

Pyrus regelii

This small spiny tree is variable with both deeply cut and shallowly-lobed leaves often on the same branch. The 2-2.5cm white flowers are infrequent in sparse corymbs and are followed by 2-3cm globose pears. The plant was introduced from Turkestan in 1891 by Albert Regel, and raised in Germany.
Growth: 2-5-8. Hardiness: 50%. Choice: 1.

Pyrus amygdaliformis

Unlike most pears, dry arid soils suit this species very well. It grows in association with olives and almonds in southern Europe and Asia Minor, and extends into high mountainous situations. The species name means 'like an almond tree'. It was introduced to Britain in 1810 but is not widely grown in gardens. Although usually a small spiny shrub, trees 8m tall are known, the branches spreading outwards in a dense tangle of foliage. Flowers occur in clusters of 8-12 followed by subglobose 2-3cm pears.
Growth: 2-4-6. Hardiness: 50%. Choice: 1, 3.

Pyrus elaeagrifolia

This species is like *Pyrus nivalis* (p. 515) but has narrower, grey leaves and comes from further east in Asia Minor. It was introduced into cultivation in the British Isles in 1800 and was one of the first trees to be planted in the Irish National Botanic Garden, at Glasnevin, founded in 1789. It is a small thorny tree with grey tomentose shoots, grey-green leaves, and hard brown cream-dotted pears.
Growth: 2-4-6. Hardiness: 60-70%. Choice: 1, 3.

Pyrus amygdaliformis

Pyrus elaeagrifolia

Pyrus cossonii

Snow Pear

Pyrus cossonii

Pyrus bretschneideri

Snow Pear

underside

Pyrus cossonii

Snow Pear

Pyrus cossonii

Formerly called *Pyrus longipes*, this is an unusual pear tree from north-west Africa, in particular the Batna area of Algeria. It was introduced to America shortly before 1875 and to Europe in that year, but it does not thrive in the north and often remains small and bushy. The twigs have many spur shoots but they are almost thornless. Clusters of 3cm flowers start off pale pink in bud and turn to white on opening. The orbicular-ovate leaves seldom exceed 5cm in length. Globose 1.5cm slender-stalked brown pears, covered with tiny scattered dots, occur in the autumn.
Growth: 2-4-6. Hardiness: 30-40%. Choice: 3.

Snow Pear *Pyrus nivalis*

This central and south-east European 10-16m tree was introduced to England in 1826. Although it is virtually thornless it usually produces a dense impenetrable tangle of twigs. The 3cm flowers are pure white, single, with five petals. The stamens are yellow with red anthers. Elongated pears 5cm long are sparingly produced. The striking feature of this tree is its light silvery-grey-backed leaves. They turn from summer grey-green, to wine-red in the autumn but still retain their pale, now glaucous-pink, backs. It is a hardy tree, ideal for a garden with a grey or white theme. It can be pruned to size or shape but preferably only in summer so as to minimize the risk of infection from silverleaf disease, *Chondrostereum purpureum*.
Growth: 3-8-15. Hardiness: 50%. Choice: 1, 2, 3.

Pyrus bretschneideri

This medium-sized upright tree has been cultivated in northern China for its juicy edible fruit for centuries. Although introduced in 1882 it is rare in cultivation in the west. It is closely related to *Pyrus usssuriensis* var. *ovoidea* (see also p. 517) from a more northerly region in eastern Asia. The 5-11cm leaves are oval to almost round with a short abrupt pointed tip. The 2.5cm flowers are white in loose clusters. They occur in spring with the leaves. The small greenish-yellow pears are oval to globose, up to 3cm long.
Growth: 3-8-16. Hardiness: 50%. Choice: 1, 3. Wood: 1, 5.

Pyrus bretschneideri

Manchurian Pear

Manchurian Pear

Pyrus × canescens

Willow-leaved Pear

Willow-leaved Pear

var. *hondoensis*

Manchurian Pear
spring

var. *hondoensis*
spring

516

Manchurian Pear *Pyrus ussuriensis*

A 15m, vigorous, hardy, tree from north-east Asia, extensively planted in temperate gardens worldwide. It appears to have arrived in the USA in 1855. Seed was then sent to Berlin in 1859, and the tree was introduced to Britain in 1865. The deciduous leaves are rounded-ovate to oval, 5-10cm long, glabrous, with a kind of waxy feel on both sides. In the autumn they turn to rich red-brown and are almost black before falling. The single flowers are white with yellow stamens and purplish red anthers, occurring in terminal clusters on side shoots in early spring. This is one of the first pears to come into flower at the same time as early orchard apples and plum trees.

The globose pears are greenish-yellow 3-4cm long. They are hard and not good to eat. Some individuals crop very heavily, completely covering the ground with ripe pears in the autumn. Even these seem reluctant to rot down or ferment.

The variety **hondoensis** comes from central Japan and was introduced in 1917. It has pretty rust-coloured tomentum on the young emerging leaves and the foliage colours well in the autumn. The variety *ovoidea* has ovoid fruit on long stems.

Growth: 3-9-15. Hardiness: 60-70%. Choice: 1, 3. Wood: 1.

Willow-leaved Pear *Pyrus salicifolia*

One of the best silver-grey trees available to gardeners at present, widely available and frequently planted. It makes a good centre-piece on a lawn or can be used as a feature at the end of a vista. The species, which is up to 8m tall, was introduced from its native Caucasus in 1780. The pointed leaves are narrow-lanceolate 3-9cm long and only 1-2cm wide. They are white silky tomentose when young, becoming almost glabrous and grey-green later. The 2cm flowers are creamy-white with dark anthers, which show up as a red spot as the flowers begin to open. A heavy crop of flowers or emerging fruit can actually spoil the glaucous effect of the foliage for a time. Most of this falls off in due course to leave just a few 2-3cm bottle-green inedible pears. The cultivar 'Pendula' is exactly the same except for its exaggerated downward-pointing shoots.

Growth: 3-7-9. Hardiness: 60%. Choice: 1.

Pyrus × canescens

A grey-green-leaved hybrid between Willow-leaved Pear and *Pyrus nivalis* (p. 515), this tree probably arose in Germany before 1830. The 6-8cm leaves are elliptic and often twisted. Silvery grey adpressed hairs cover it at first, especially on the underside. A tree at Kew in London grew to 9m in just 30 years. The pears are short-stalked and pale green.

Growth: 2-6-10. Hardiness: 50%. Choice: 3, 4.

spring

summer

Willow-leaved Pear

Pyrus × canescens spring

Common Pear

Plymouth Pear

'Beech Hill'

Common Pear
spring

twig of 'Beech Hill'

spring

'Beech Hill'
late autumn

518

PEARS

Common Pear *Pyrus communis*

The Common Pear originated, possibly as a hybrid, in Europe and western Asia but virtually all the 'wild pears' encountered today have escaped from cultivation and become naturalized. In Britain trees considered to be of uncultivated origin are usually called *Pyrus pyraster* and have thorny branches. Common Pear was cultivated in Sennacherib's gardens in Nineveh as long ago as 700 BC. The earliest recorded named varieties were selected by Jean Robin, arborist to Henri III of France, in 1611. John Tradescant introduced pears from there to England. The fruit garden at Versailles, in France, was another source of great orchard pear diversity from 1677. Such a confused origin has made the Common Pear difficult to identify with precision.

It is a substantial tree, ultimately from 15m to over 20m tall, with a broad pyramidal crown. Spur shoots may be pointed but genuine spines are rare. The leaves are bright and glossy, the single flowers are white, and the variable fruits are yellowish to russet. '**Beech Hill**' is a narrow-crowned cultivar which colours well in the autumn to bronze-yellow.

Growth: 3-9-15 (species). Hardiness: 70%. Choice: 3.
Wood: 1.

Pyrus calleryana

This is a thorny Chinese tree introduced to the west in 1908, but little known in gardening circles as a species. However, two cultivars of it are very well known indeed and are among the best garden, street and park trees developed in the twentieth century.

One of them, '**Bradford**', is a thornless rounded tree which flowers profusely in spring and colours to brilliant orange and red in the autumn. It originated in the USA at Maryland in 1920. It produces small oval 1.5cm pears that are golden brown with darker dots.

The other cultivar is the world famous American pear '**Chanticleer**', a narrow conical tree ideal for street planting and for confined spaces. The flowers appear very early in the spring and it is extremely floriferous. The foliage colours to carmine-red in the autumn. This tree is completely hardy and also withstands harsh city conditions.

Growth: 2-7-14. Hardiness: 50%. Choice: 1, 2, 3.
Wood: 1 (species).

Plymouth Pear *Pyrus cordata*

This rare thorny suckering shrub is native to parts of southern Europe and south-west England, notably round the city of Plymouth. It grows vigorously but seldom exceeds 3-4m in height. The long-stalked oval sub-cordate leaves are deep glossy green. The profuse white single flowers are small and the pears ripen to brownish-red.

Growth: 2-3-4. Hardiness: 40%. Choice: 3.

'Chanticleer'   *Pyrus calleryana*   'Bradford'

Pyrus korshinskyi

Sand Pear

Pyrus korshinskyi

Pyrus balansae

Pyrus pashia

Pyrus fauriei
autumn

Pyrus korshinskyi
autumn

Pyrus pashia

Pyrus korshinskyi

This high-elevation mountain species from Turkestan is not widely available in cultivation. It varies according to which part of its natural range cultivated material originated in. A tall tree form was collected for Kew Gardens in London in 1891, but material obtained by Späth's Nursery in Germany in 1900 turned out to be a shrubby sort. The species is closely related to the Common Pear of Europe and is probably a regional fringe population adapted to a particularly harsh environment. When taken into cultivation such genotypes often behave differently to in the wild.

Growth: variable. Hardiness: 60-70%. Choice: 4.

Sand Pear or Oriental Pear *Pyrus pyrifolia*

The species name, meaning 'pear-leaved', harks back to the time when the genus *Pyrus* also included apples and whitebeams. The wild form of this species is very rare. It was introduced to America from China by Ernest Wilson in 1909. Some of the cultivars and forms, however, are better known in cultivation than the species itself. This is the domestic pear of the Orient and many hundreds of them have been selected for their soft juicy fruit. Introductions of the var. *culta* began to arrive in America from China and Japan before 1850. Inevitably the Asiatic and European orchard pears have hybridized many times since 1850. Excellent eating pears such as the variety *lecontei* and the cultivar 'Kieffer' have resulted from this. Like most pears the deciduous leaves turn deep red in the autumn and then almost black.

Growth: 3-5-10. Hardiness: 50%. Choice: 3. Wood: 1.

Pyrus balansae

An Asiatic variant of *Pyrus communis*, this species has ovate to almost round 5-10cm leaves and golden-brown 3-4cm edible pears. It was introduced into cultivation in 1866 but has little merit as a garden tree, and is rarely grown.

Growth: 3-9-15. Hardiness: 70%. Choice: 4. Wood: 1.

Pyrus fauriei

This species is closely related to *Pyrus calleryana* (p. 519), which is usually a shrubby, densely twiggy, spiny plant. The ovate toothed leaves are 2.5-5cm long, colouring well in autumn. It was introduced to the west from Korea in 1918 but remains very rare in cultivation.

Growth: 2-3-5. Hardiness: 50-60%. Choice: 4.

Pyrus pashia

This 12m vigorous suckering tree has tangled spiny branches. The twigs are woolly at first. The big 12cm ovate-oblong, pointed leaves are occasionally three-lobed on sucker shoots. Compact clusters of 2-2.5cm white flowers appear with the leaves in spring. Each one has 25-30 yellow stamens with purplish-red anthers until the golden pollen is shed. The 2cm pears are brown with 2-3cm stalks. It was first introduced from south-east and central Asia in 1825 and reintroduced by George Forrest from Yunnan in 1908. The original plant was probably var. *kumaoni* which has thornless glabrous twigs and is more common in cultivation. This is a good spring-flowering and autumn colour (yellow to wine-red and black) tree in the garden, but the suckers may become a nuisance.

Growth: 3-8-12. Hardiness: 50%. Choice: 1, 4.

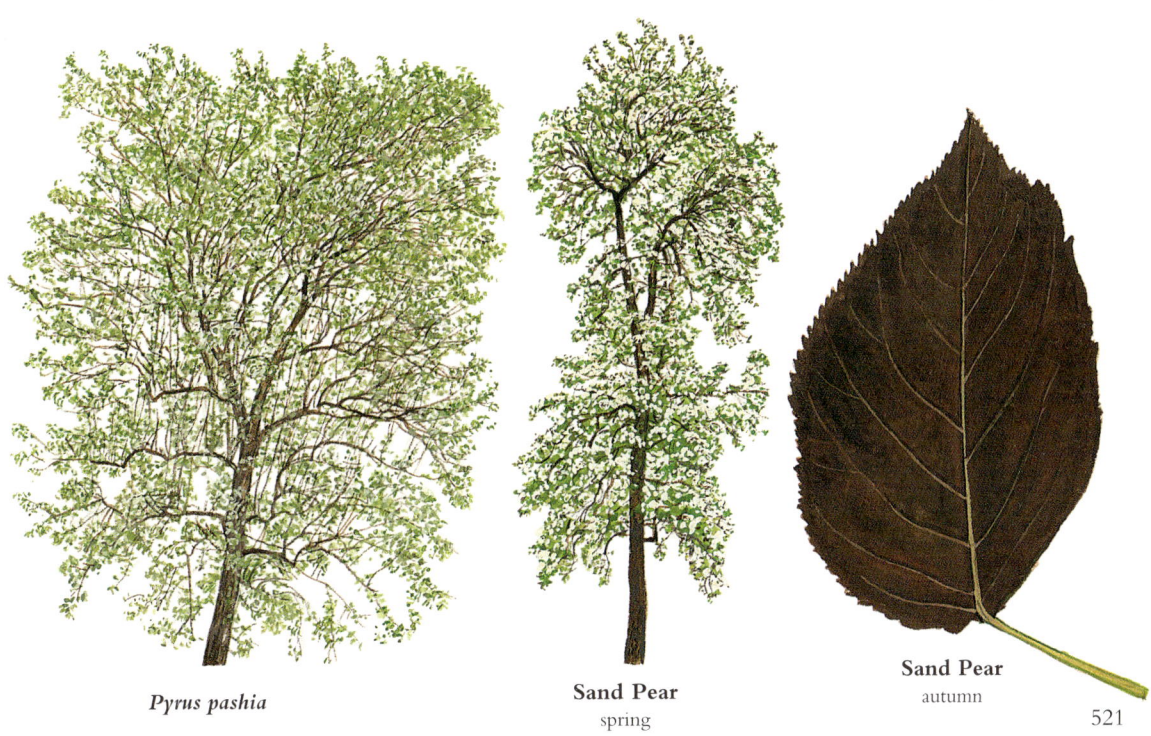

Pyrus pashia

Sand Pear
spring

Sand Pear
autumn

European Bird Cherry

underside

'Colorata'

'Watereri'

subsp. *borealis*

fruit stone

Blackthorn

'Purpurea'

shrub form

fruit stone

Blackthorn

CHERRIES

European Bird Cherry *Prunus padus*

This is a small to medium-sized hardy deciduous tree from Europe and parts of northern Asia. The 1cm fragrant white flowers occur in 15cm racemes of 10-40, first spreading then drooping. They are followed by a smaller number of glossy black ovoid bitter fruits which are quickly taken by birds, hence the name. The leaves usually turn to orange-red in the autumn. Bird Cherries need full sun to flower well but they will grow on very poor infertile soils.

The cultivar '**Plena**' has semi-double flowers. '**Watereri**' is a larger tree than the species with racemes of white flowers up to 20cm long. Specimens are known 18 metres tall and 70cm through the stem.

A very beautiful form, '**Colorata**', has plum-purple shoots and pale pink flowers. Its young leaves unfold purplish bronze, becoming green with reddish backs. The wild subspecies ***borealis*** is a tough shrub from the mountains of Europe and Scandinavia.

Growth: 3-7-10. Hardiness: 90%. Choice: 3.

Blackthorn or Sloe *Prunus spinosa*

Common in the north European countryside: densely branched spiny shrubs or small trees bearing numerous 1cm single white flowers before the leaves in early spring. The globose fruits are bloomed blue-black. They are astringent to taste but can be cooked to produce delicious jam or jelly, and can also be used to make sloe-gin.

The cultivar '**Purpurea**' is spiny and smaller with purplish-green leaves and light pink flowers. Blackthorns are hardy throughout Europe. They grow best in full sun on any kind of soil, and withstand sea winds and salt spray very well.

Growth: 3-6-7. Hardiness: 70%. Choice: 3.

Garden Plum *Prunus domestica*

(See also p. 531). This is a variable rounded tree 10-15m tall. There are numerous cultivated forms. Although the blossom is attractive plums are of course usually grown for their edible fruit which may be yellow, orange-red or bloomed purple. Trees planted on stony ground produce the best fruit. Any pruning should be done in summer to reduce the risk of 'silver leaf' (*Chondrostereum purpureum*) infection. Many modern plums are grafted or budded on to dwarfing rootstocks to keep the fruit within reach of the ground for easy picking.

Growth: 3-8-10. Hardiness: 70%. Choice: 3. Wood: 1.

'Watereri'

fruit section

Garden Plum

old bark

Purple-leaved Cherry

Cherry Plum

'Nigra'

Cherry Plum

fruit section

Purple-leaved Cherry

Cherry Plum

Purple-leaved Cherry

524

Cherry Plum or Myrobalan Plum
Prunus cerasifera

This is an untidy tree with deep green young shoots and very early small white flowers that appear almost before the end of winter. It is similar to Blackthorn (*Prunus spinosa*) but is less thorny and flowers earlier. There are numerous cultivated forms and garden escapes so the true species, which is native to western Asia and south-east Europe, is seldom seen. Naturalized escaped plants occur in hedgerows, especially around cities such as London. They can usually not be recognized until their incredibly early flowers appear before the winter is over, or until fruit of some sort appears. Some trees produce yellow fruit (var. *divaricata*), others have red. These are all edible and around 2.5cm across. The name *cerasifera* means 'bearing cherry-like fruits'. Young plants are often used as understocks for grafting domestic plums.

Growth: 3-6-8. Hardiness: 80%. Choice: 3.

Purple-leaved Cherry *Prunus cerasifera* 'Pissardii'

This cultivar was introduced to France in 1880. It was obtained from the Shah of Iran's head gardener Monseigneur Pissard at Tabris. It has dark purple-brown leaves and very pale pink flowers, but seldom in profusion. It is extremely – some would say far too – popular as a garden and street tree, and it can be clipped into an unusual hedge. The cultivar '**Nigra**' is better in many respects. It has darker foliage and blackish-purple shoots. The single flowers are deep blush-pink and more numerous. It was developed in the USA in 1916. Certainly this is one of the best small "purple" trees for those who like them. It is totally hardy and tolerates almost any kind of soil.

Growth: 3-8-10. Hardiness: 70-80%. Choice: 1.

Prunus cerasifera 'Rosea'

'Rosea' is like the purple-leaved cherries at first, but the foliage becomes green as it matures in summer. The flowers are pink fading to pale pink. It was raised in Holland and is believed to be a cross between *Prunus cerasifera* 'Nigra' and Blackthorn.

Growth: 2-6-8. Hardiness: 80%. Choice: 1.

Prunus cerasifera 'Lindsayae'

The foliage of 'Lindsayae' is similar to 'Rosea' but greener. The bark and shoots are almost black. It was introduced from Iran by Miss Nancy Lindsay to near Oxford before 1935. It makes a graceful garden tree with bright pink spring flowers.

Growth: 2-6-8. Hardiness: 70%. Choice: 1.

Prunus × *blireana*

The initial contrast between the big 3-4cm solitary flat pink semi-double flowers and the emerging copper leaves of this hybrid is outstanding, but the foliage later turns muddy green. The plant was developed around 1895 by Lemoine in France. At about the same time Moser at Versailles developed the cultivar 'Moseri' which is an even stronger tree but has slightly smaller flowers. Both plants are hybrids with the same parents, Purple-leaved Cherry × *Prunus mume* 'Alphandii'.

Growth: 2-6-8. Hardiness: 60%. Choice: 1.

Prunus cerasifera '**Lindsayae**'

Prunus cerasifera '**Rosea**'

Prunus × *blireana*

Black Cherry

old bark

fruit stone

Black Cherry

var. *salicifolia*

'Rhexii'

Double Sour Cherry

Black Cherry
spring

'Pendula'

526

Black Cherry *Prunus serotina*

This is not the familiar edible black cherry, but a form of North American bird cherry. Its range includes the east and central USA and also extends into Mexico and Guatemala. The fruits were once used to flavour rum, which gave rise to an alternative name 'Rum Cherry'. After its introduction to Europe in 1629 it was extensively grown in some countries as a timber tree. The variety *salicifolia* 'Capulin Black Cherry' arose in Central and South America including Peru and was introduced to Europe in 1820. The lanceolate leaves are willow like. The cultivar '**Pendula**' is a weeping form. The bark on all of these has a distinctive and rather unpleasant smell if scratched. White flowers 8mm across occur in tightly packed 10-14cm racemes.

Growth: 4-18-25. Hardiness: 80%. Choice: 3.
Wood: 1, 5.

Double Sour Cherry *Prunus cerasus*

Originally from south-east Asia, Sour Cherry has become naturalized in parts of Europe. It is one of the parents of morello cherry and has been cultivated for centuries. '**Rhexii**' is an old garden form cultivated in England since the sixteenth century. The neat round 2.5cm double white daisy flowers appear in mid-spring. Although trees 8m tall are known, growth is usually slow.

Growth: 2-5-7. Hardiness: 80%. Choice: 1.

St Lucie Cherry *Prunus mahaleb*

This central and southern European timber tree has a long history of cultivation for decorative wooden items such as smokers' pipes and fancy walking sticks. It was introduced to England in 1714 and was widely used in horticulture particularly as a rootstock for other cherries. As a result of this it escaped from cultivation and has become naturalized in parts of North America. It makes a 12m tree on a good site, with racemes of tiny white fragrant flowers. The leaves are like domestic pear except for two glands on the stalk. This tree survives on poor sandy soil but it needs plenty of moisture. It is very hardy but grows best with some side shelter.

Growth: 2-7-10. Hardiness: 50%. Choice: 1, 3.
Wood: 1, 5.

American Red Plum *Prunus americana*

This hardy North American fruit tree, seldom planted in Europe, grows to 12m in height with a billowing head of branches. The oblong-ovate abruptly pointed leaves are 6-10cm long. There are deliciously scented white single flowers, but they are not the main attraction. This is primarily a fruit tree bearing subglobose 3cm edible plums. On the wild plant they turn red but in over 200 years of cultivation many different colours have been developed. Unfortunately, for some unknown reason most of these do not seem to thrive away from America.

Growth: 3-8-12. Hardiness: 80%. Choice: 3, 4.
Wood: 1, 5.

St. Lucie Cherry

American Red Plum

Wild Cherry

'Plena'   'Plena'   'Decumana'   'Salicifolia'   'Rubrifolia'

Wild Cherry
spring

Wild Cherry *Prunus avium*

The genus name *Prunus* is the classical name for the plum to which the cherry is closely related. *Avium* is a reference to birds, which are attracted to the fruit as soon as it ripens. This is not such a bad thing because seed is naturally dispersed by birds, the stones passing unharmed through their digestive tract. This tree is Europe's largest cherry, up to 25m tall. It is uncertain whether it is a European native species in the strict sense, or a pre-historic, or even pre-glacial introduction from western Asia. It has been cultivated for food, timber and fuel wood for many centuries. Cherry firewood burns well, wet or dry, with perfumed smoke smelling faintly of the blossom. If left alone a wild cherry tree will sucker over a wide area and may become a nuisance: given space uncontrolled suckers eventually grow into a forest of trees. These begin to produce their 2cm scented white flowers when only 2m tall, but as clonal thickets are really all one plant they are usually self sterile. It is one of the parents of numerous edible forms of domestic cherry and is also widely used as an understock for grafted orchard trees and flowering ornamentals.

The cultivar '**Plena**', the Double White Cherry, is perhaps the finest of all big white spring-flowering trees, becoming a mass of 2cm blossom when tulips and spring bedding plants are at their best. It has been cultivated in England since around 1700, tolerates heavy clay soils, is completely hardy but seldom produces fruit.

The cultivar '**Decumana**' has big 20-30cm leaves and 2.5cm flowers. It is of French origin and has been grown since the beginning of the nineteenth century. It is also known as the Tobacco-leaved Cherry. The purple-leaved Wild Cherry '**Rubrifolia**' is another French plant produced after 1892. It is uncommon in cultivation, possibly out-classed by purple forms of *Prunus cerasifera* (p. 525). The cultivar '**Salicifolia**' is a narrow-leaved plant, its leaves incised but less deeply than those of 'Asplenifolia' the cut-leaved cherry.

The weeping tree '**Pendula**', another French introduction from 1825, is a delightful symmetrical shape when it grows well, though many specimens, become untidy or one sided with straight outgrowths. It may require frequent pruning to keep it in order. The dwarf form '**Nana**' has acceptable white flowers but is a peculiar little plant of no particular merit. It was cultivated in England, presumably from a witches broom, in 1914.

Growth: 4-18-25 (species). Hardiness: 80%. Choice: 2, 3. Wood: 1, 2, 5 (species).

'Pendula'

'Nana'

Almond

fruit stone   seed

'Roseoplena'

'Albaplena'

underside

Almond

Apricot

Apricot

Almond
spring

Almond *Prunus dulcis*

Originally from western Asia and North Africa, the Almond has been cultivated since pre-history for its edible seed. In the Middle East some veteran trees are claimed to be far over 1000 years old. It is a tree of myth and mythology: the rods of Moses and Aaron were of Almond and are considered to be the origin of the crozier or pastoral staff of bishops. In addition to its wood and the fruit, however, it makes a very ornamental tree with narrow willowy leaves and lovely pink blossom. Flowers on the species are 5cm across, single but in clusters. There is a double-flowered pink form '**Roseoplena**' and a double white '**Albaplena**'. There are also early flowering, erect, weeping and bitter-fruited examples. As a tree it is fairly tender and is prone to disease when planted in places not climatically suitable for it. In southern Europe it makes a tree 8-10m tall but in the north it is much less.

Growth: 2-6-9. Hardiness: 40-50%. Choice: 3.

Apricot *Prunus armeniaca*

A 10m round-headed tree in its native Asiatic range, the Apricot has been cultivated and 'improved' for its fruit for centuries. In northern Europe it can only be grown in the shelter of a sunny wall or under glass. The solitary 2.5cm single flowers are white or palest pink, followed by blushed golden-yellow 3-4cm fruits. The fairly flat stones have a thickened keel on the edge. Apricots have been cultivated in China for at least 2000 years. There are also variegated, weeping and double-flowered forms.

Growth: 3-7-10. Hardiness: 50%. Choice: 3.

Bullace *Prunus insititia*

This name covers a range of small-fruited European and western Asian plums which are closely related to the domestic plum. The Bullace itself is up to 6m tall with 2cm single white flowers. The dark grey-brown branches are sometimes spiny. Sweet subglobose 3-4cm plums are produced in the autumn, often in large numbers, purplish-black with a grey bloom. The Bullace and the feral **Damson** (strictly *Prunus domestica* subsp. *insititia*, see p. 523) are almost indistinguishable, but several cultivars of Damson have been selected and grown for their superior fruit, for example 'Farleigh', 'Merryweather' and the 'Prune Damson'. The name damson comes from Damascus where the tree is commonly grown. The **Greengage**, *Prunus domestica* subsp. *italica*, has sweet green fruit. It too is available under a range of heavy cropping cultivar names. The yellow forms of Bullace, *Prunus domestica* subsp. *syriaca*, produce fruit which is similar to an apricot but smaller. There are several hardy cultivars of it known collectively as '**Mirabelle**'. Some carry the place of origin in the name, for example 'Mirabelle de Nancy'.

Growth: 3-5-6. Hardiness: 70%. Choice: 3. Wood: 1, 5.

Peach

'Klara Mayer'

Peach

var. *nectarina*

'Prince Charming'

'Sagami-shidare'

'Kurokawa-yaguchi'

Peach
spring

'Stellata'

'Albo Plena'

532

Peach *Prunus persica*

The peach tree grows to around 8m tall with fairly erect branches and bears big round 5-7cm velvety edible fruit. The stone is large, pale brown, and distinctly pitted. Peaches probably originated in China but have been cultivated for so long that their actual origin is obscured. The leaves are oblong to elliptic, widest above the middle and 8-15cm long. The single pink flowers are mostly solitary. Fruiting peach trees are tender and need the protection of a south facing wall or conservatory in cold areas. The fungus *Taphrina* causes a disorder known as peach leaf curl. This spoils the tree and the fruit, and can kill young or weak plants. A copper based fungicide spray in autumn or late winter may prevent re-infection.

In addition to fruit trees there are many forms of peach that have been cultivated primarily for their flowers. The most popular is probably '**Klara Mayer**' a bright pink 4cm double-flowered tree first cultivated in 1890 in Germany, at the Späth Nursery, Berlin. The cultivar '**Prince Charming**' has similar flowers on a more erect plant. There are two deep pink, almost red types, '**Kurokawa-yaguchi**' is a standard tree, and '**Sagami-shidare**' is a strongly weeping form. '**Stellata**' has tightly-packed 'star-like' blossom. Semi-double snow-white flowers occur on '**Albo Plena**', and '**Alba**' is a single white form. Numerous varieties have been cultivated with every kind of flower colour from red through pink to white. The variety **nectarina** with its popular smooth skinned fruit also comes in a range of cultivated edible forms.

Growth: 3-6-8. Hardiness: 40%. Choice: 1, 3.

Japanese Apricot *Prunus mume*

A lovely range of small rounded garden forms, most of which flower very early before the leaves appear, are available. The twigs are strikingly dark green to black. The leaves are broadly ovate, 4-10cm long and sharply toothed. Trees have been cultivated in Japan for centuries but they probably originated in China and Korea. Plants were first introduced to Europe in 1844. The fruit, which is only produced in mild areas, is round, up to 3cm across, greenish-yellow and slightly pubescent. It usually tastes bitter, but can be pickled or made into a sweet liqueur. In Japan this is a favoured bonsai tree. The flowers are sweetly scented.

One of the best single deep pink cultivars is '**Omoi-no-mama**', '**Benishidori**' is similar but pure white and '**Alphandii**' is a well known early flowering double pink form. There are also several white single and double types. The Japanese Apricots are a little more hardy than most peaches, but they flower at a harsh time of year and are frequently spoiled by frost.

Growth: 2-7-10. Hardiness: 40-50%. Choice: 1, 3.

'Omoi-no-mama'

'Benishidori'

'Alphandii'

Japanese Apricot

'Kurokawa-yaguchi'
spring

'Sagami-shidare'
spring

Peach

Manchurian Cherry

Sargent's Cherry

autumn

Prunus × schmittii

Fuji Cherry

Manchurian Cherry *Prunus maackii*

This substantial tree, up to 15m tall, has a thick stem and decorative shiny brownish-yellow bark, eventually flaking into horizontal strips. It is native to Manchuria, eastern Russia and Korea. Cultivated plants were introduced to western Europe through St. Petersburg in 1910. It is a large form of bird cherry with 1.5cm single white flowers in tight 6-8cm racemes. The stamens are more prominent than the petals, so from a distance the blossom looks yellowish. The emerging young foliage is also yellowish-green.

Growth: 3-8-15. Hardiness: 90-100%. Choice: 1, 2. Wood: 1, 5.

Sargent's Cherry *Prunus sargentii*

Though probably the best large pink cherry in cultivation, this tree is not suitable for small gardens. Ultimately it may reach 20m in height and 12-15m in width. In spring it produces a great unmistakable cloud of brilliant rose-pink 3-4cm single flowers. In the autumn the whole tree becomes a ball of fiery-red and orange foliage. It is also one of the few flowering cherries that regularly produces some fruit: 1cm long-stalked gems of glossy yellow, orange, red and purple-black. It originated in Japan, Sakhalin and Korea but was named and distributed widely in 1890 from America. Charles Sprague Sargent, who is commemorated in the species name was Director of the Arnold Arboretum, Massachusetts, USA.

Growth: 3-10-18. Hardiness: 70%. Choice: 1 (requires space).

Prunus × *schmittii*

A fast-growing hybrid between Wild Cherry, *Prunus avium* (p. 529) and *Prunus canescens* (p. 517), this is a lovely shrubby Chinese tree with dark mahogany brown bark. The cross first appeared in cultivation in 1923. It picks up the vigour of one parent (*Prunus avium*) and the richly-coloured bark of the other to produce a fine conical tree over 10m tall. The pale pink flowers are less of a feature than the bark. It is scarce in cultivation, but deserves wider use in garden situations.

Growth: 3-9-10. Hardiness: 60%. Choice: 1. Wood: 1, 5.

Fuji Cherry *Prunus incisa*

This delicate twiggy small rounded tree is an early spring-flowering plant which requires close examination to appreciate its real charm. It has deeply incised leaves which colour well in the autumn. The flowers are small and white, emerging from pink buds. Old collections still contain typical semi-pendulous trees grafted at head height on excessively fat overgrown stems. The grafts were always incompatible because of the slow growth rate of the Fuji cherry scion. It was first cultivated in 1910 from trees growing in the Hondo Region of Japan. There are several named cultivars, mostly developed for early flowering. 'Umineko' (p. 555) is a *Prunus incisa* hybrid, crossed with the ancient Oshima Cherry (*Prunus speciosa* p. 545).

Growth: 2-6-10. Hardiness: 50%. Choice: 1.

old tree in spring   young tree in autumn

Sargent's Cherry

Prunus × fontanesiana

Himalayan Bird Cherry

occasional off-set leaf base

underside

Prunus padus var. *commutata*

Prunus padus 'Purple Queen'

Prunus × *fontanesiana*

This hybrid between Wild Cherry (*Prunus avium*) and the Saint Lucie Cherry (*Prunus mahaleb*) grows rapidly to around 12m tall. The foliage resembles Wild Cherry but with a downy leaf stalk and main veins. The 2cm white flowers are in small racemes of between 5 and 10. Deep red cherries are produced, tasting bitter. This hybrid seems to have occurred in Greece long ago and was introduced to horticulture in Paris before 1834.

Growth: 3-10-12. Hardiness: 60-70%. Choice: 3.

Himalayan Bird Cherry *Prunus cornuta*

The eastern representative of *Prunus padus*, this tree is native to the Himalayas as far as western China and tends to grow larger than the European species. Trees 18m tall are known in the wild. The white flowers are early, and appear in dense racemes 10-20cm long, followed by drooping clusters of 8mm fruits resembling small bunches of grapes. By late summer they are deep red, eventually turning to dark brownish-purple.

Growth: 3-8-12. Hardiness: 60%. Choice: 3.

Prunus padus 'Purple Queen'

The purple-leaved forms of bird cherry are a source of great taxonomic confusion. Purple foliage sports appear to have arisen and been described at various times and in various places. The best known cultivar is 'Colorata' which originated in Sweden in 1953. It has carmine pink flowers and coppery-purple young leaves. The foliage turns muddy brown later in the year. 'Purple Queen' is similar but apparently not synonymous. It is a smaller tree, less than 7m tall, with pale pink clusters of flowers and purplish leaves. The loose bunches of 8mm cherries are dark maroon.

Growth: 3-6-7. Hardiness: 80%. Choice: 1.

Prunus padus var. *commutata*

This is a wild form of bird cherry from Manchuria. It flowers 10-15 days ahead of the European tree. The 1.5cm flowers appear in tightly packed 15cm racemes. The leaves are larger and coarser than the species and fringed with conspicuous teeth. The variety has been in cultivation since 1880.

Growth: 3-8-10. Hardiness: 80-90%. Choice: 3.

Prunus sargentii 'Columnaris'

One of several fastigiate forms of Sargent's Cherry, this cultivar originated at the Arnold Arboretum in the USA in 1914. It is less widely available in Europe than 'Rancho', recently introduced from America, or 'Spire', a seedling of 'Columnaris' propagated by the Hillier Nursery. They all appear to be very similar.

Growth: 4-12-18. Hardiness: 70%. Choice: 1, 2.

Prunus cuthbertii

An American bird cherry related to Black Cherry (*Prunus serotina* p. 527), this tree grows wild in the State of Georgia in woods and thickets. Multiple stems often occur and growth is slow. Cultivated since 1912, it is a rare curiosity rather than a good ornamental tree.

Growth: 2-4-6. Hardiness: 40-50%. Choice: 4.

Prunus padus* 'Purple Queen'**   ***Prunus sargentii* 'Columnaris'**   ***Prunus cuthbertii

Spring Cherry bark

'Pendula Rosea'

Spring Cherry

'Pendula'

'Stellata'

'Omoigawa'

'Flore Pleno'

'Pendula'
old tree in spring

'Pendula Rosea'
old tree

Spring Cherry *Prunus subhirtella*

There are a number of cultivars derived from the original Japanese species first introduced to Europe in 1894. It is probably unknown in the wild and could actually be a hybrid between *Prunus incisa* and *Prunus subhirtella* var. *ascendens*, which in Japan is a small bushy tree with upright branches, much smaller than cultivated specimens in Europe. All of the forms flower in winter or early spring making them an essential choice of the winter garden. They are small twiggy trees seldom over 8m tall. In Japanese temples venerable specimens exist that are said to be up to 1800 years old and 30m wide, having been lovingly rejuvenated over centuries by careful pruning and training.

The cultivars look their best planted in a mixed group (together with 'Autumnalis', p. 541), at about 4m spacing. Their flowers appear over a long period, so – as with all flowering cherries – a continuous winter and spring feature can be created. The weeping forms benefit from pruning to lift the drooping branches which would otherwise drag on the ground.

The common weeping form '**Pendula**' is a free-flowering domed 'mushroom' of a tree introduced to the west in the 1860s via the Arnold Arboretum in America. The Japanese name for it is 'Ito Zakura'. Ito means a thread, a reference to the pendulous thread-like branchlets that reach down to the ground. Trees are often grafted on to a wild cherry root stock at 1.5-2m. Western cultivated plants are said to have been raised originally from seed, so it is doubtful whether they were exactly like the original plants. European plants produce rather small insignificant flowers.

'**Pendula Rosea**' is similar in size and form but has rose pink buds which fade to paler pink as the single flowers open in great profusion. There is also a semi-double form, '**Pendula Rubra**', which has carmine red buds and deeper pink flowers. A well shaped mature specimen can be a stunning 'eyecatcher' in the urban landscape. The flowers are of better quality and more densely packed along the fine weeping branches than other cultivars.

The cultivar '**Stellata**' is an upright branchy tree raised in California. The flowers are clear pink with incised pointed petals giving a star-like effect. They occur in clusters all along the light sinuous branches.

The cultivar '**Omoigawa**' is a graceful spreading floriferous form which typifies the classical cherry tree shape in Japanese art.

'**Flore Pleno**' is an unusual double-flowered form with bright pale pink 2.5cm long lasting flowers in spring. It develops into a small pendulous tree about 5m tall. The autumn foliage colour is yellow turning to red.

Growth: 2-5-8. Hardiness: 50%. Choice: 1.

'Pendula Rubra' 'Flore Pleno' 'Omoigawa'

Prunus × **hillieri** 'Spire'

Prunus 'Accolade'

'Autumnalis Rosea'

new leaves

autumn

underside

540 *Prunus* × **hillieri** 'Spire'
spring

'Autumnalis Rosea'

Prunus × hillieri 'Spire'

In 1929 the Hillier Nursery near Winchester produced a hybrid between *Prunus incisa* and *Prunus sargentii* (p. 535). This resulted in a fine round-headed bright pink-flowering tree which combined the best features of each parent. In 1956 a narrower form of the same thing was produced. It was named 'Spire' and became a favourite tree for restricted areas and roadside planting. It is a slender-crowned 8m tall tree seldom reaching 4m in width. If the lowest branches are retained it produces a solid pillar of pink spring blossom from ground level to the topmost branch.
Growth: 3-6-8. Hardiness: 60%. Choice: 1.

Prunus 'Accolade'

This hybrid combines early flowering of *Prunus subhirtella* with the bright pink blossom and good autumn colour of *Prunus sargentii*. The semi-double flowers are 3.5cm across in dense clusters. Usually this is the first strong pink colour to appear in the garden in spring. As it matures the tree spreads sideways faster than it grows upwards. This well liked garden cherry was produced at Knaphill Nursery in 1952. Its early flowers respond favourably to some side shelter and last longest in a dry mild spring.
Growth: 3-6-8. Hardiness: 50-60%. Choice: 1.

Prunus subhirtella 'Autumnalis'

The familiar small twiggy winter flowering tree 'Autumnalis' was introduced to Europe in 1901. Small semi-double light pink flowers, 2cm across, occur randomly along the slender shoots. They start to appear in the autumn and keep going through the winter during mild intervals. At maturity 'witch's brooms' and other twisted growths start to occur among the branches.

'**Autumnalis Rosea**' is a deeper pink-flowered form which brightens up the dull days of winter. These trees are best seen at close quarters they are not spectacular from a distance.
Growth: 2-6-10. Hardiness: 50-60%. Choice: 1.

Prunus subhirtella 'Fukubana'

'Fukubana Higan Zakura' to give it its full name, was brought to England by Captain Collingwood Ingram in 1927. Not from Japan on this occasion but from California. This fairly small, 7m tree produces a mass of daisy-like deep pink flowers with narrow notched petals. They occur in mid-spring in clusters along the upright branches. With age the tree becomes spreading and untidy.
Growth: 2-6-7. Hardiness: 50-60%. Choice: 4.

Prunus subhirtella
spring

Prunus subhirtella 'Fukubana'
spring

Prunus subhirtella
spring leaves

Prunus triloba 'Multiplex' 'Petzoldii'

Holly-leaved Cherry underside

Prunus campanulata

'Okame'

'Kursar'

Pin Cherry

'Schubert'

Choke Cherry

Prunus triloba 'Multiplex'

This is a form of flowering almond which has 3-6cm, very coarsely toothed, almost three-lobed, leaves. It is a shrubby plant seldom over 4m in height. The beautiful double flowers, produced in great profusion, are 2.5cm clear pink rosettes, borne in small clusters or pairs. 'Multiplex' was introduced from China in the mid nineteenth century. The cultivar '**Petzoldii**' is similar except that it has broad elliptical leaves which are not lobed. The rose pink flowers are semi-double with about 10 petals.

Growth: 2-3-4. Hardiness: 50%. Choice: 1.

Prunus incisa × *campanulata* 'Okame'

This is one of the finest examples of a well-tried hybrid cross. It has deep pink early flowers with incised petals, which appear before the leaves. The flowers also have a deep red-brown calyx which further enhances the colour effect. This is a small tree under 5m tall. The original plant was produced by Captain Collingwood Ingram in 1947.

Growth: 2-4-5. Hardiness: 50%. Choice: 1.

Prunus kurilensis × *sargentii* 'Kursar'

Another of Collingwood Ingram's excellent hybrids. 'Kursar' has numerous single deep rose pink flowers in early to mid-spring, before the leaves. An ideal garden tree because of its small size and early flush of colour.

Growth: 2-4-5. Hardiness: 60%. Choice: 1.

Prunus 'Asano'

This is a small form of *Prunus serrulata* with ascending sinuous branches and numerous pink flowers that are double but not compact. They give a light fluffy open appearance to the whole tree in spring.

Growth: 2-5-6. Hardiness: 60%. Choice: 1.

Holly-leaved Cherry *Prunus ilicifolia*

This is the dense evergreen Californian shrub or small tree after which Hollywood is named. It seldom exceeds 6m in height, with an untidy outline. The glossy glabrous ovate leathery leaves are around 5cm long with distinctive hard teeth like holly. The flowers are small and white in short racemes occurring in mid-summer.

Growth: 2-4-6. Hardiness: 30%. Choice: 1, 3.

Pin Cherry *Prunus pennsylvanica*

Another North American species, this hardy tree grows rapidly to around 10m in height in the wild state but usually much less in cultivation. It has small white or faintly pink late spring flowers 1.5cm across in clusters or short racemes of 4-8. It is rare in European gardens but makes a good shelter tree, and deserves wider use. The pea-sized fruits are sometimes prolific.

Growth: 3-8-10. Hardiness: 90%. Choice: 2, 3.

Choke Cherry *Prunus virginiana*

This small North American tree or large shrub has elliptic to obovate glossy green leaves 5-11cm long. The tiny flowers, under 1cm across, occur in dense racemes. It is very hardy and worthy of wider garden use. The fruits are dark purplish-red. The cultivar '**Schubert**' is a purple-leaved form.

Growth: 2-6-8. Hardiness: 90%. Choice: 1.

Prunus 'Asano'   **Prunus kurilensis × sargentii 'Kursar'**   **Prunus incisa × campanulata 'Okame'**

trees in spring

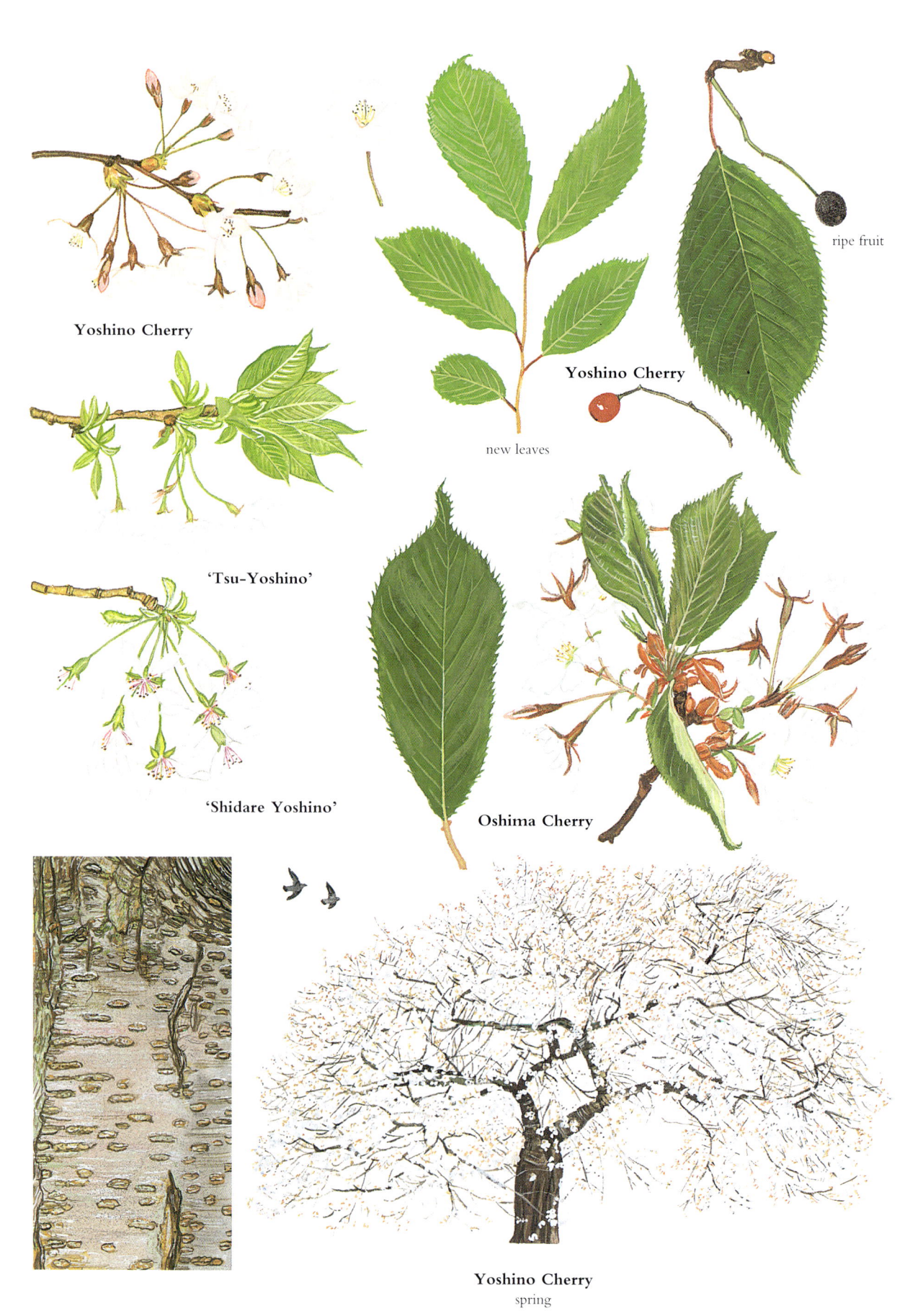

Yoshino Cherry

Yoshino Cherry

new leaves

ripe fruit

'Tsu-Yoshino'

'Shidare Yoshino'

Oshima Cherry

Yoshino Cherry
spring

Yoshino Cherry *Prunus × yedoensis*

This is a cultivated tree that does not appear to occur anywhere in the wild. It is thought to be a hybrid between *Prunus speciosa* and *Prunus subhirtella* 'Rosea' (p. 539). Yoshino is a district in southern Japan but the tree does not grow there much now. Around Tokyo however, there are said to be around 50,000 living specimens. Consequently the name 'Tokyo Cherry' is often used for it. Plants appeared in Europe in 1902, and in America in 1912. Thousands have been planted around Washington DC. The single pale pink spring flowers develop a purplish centre as the stamens mature, giving a unique bi-colour effect. The autumn foliage changes from yellow-green through orange to bronze-red.

There are notable named cultivars such as '**Tsu-Yoshino**' which is a splendid white-flowered tree with spreading branches. As the Japanese name suggests 'like the wings of a bird'.

Another well known × *yedoensis* cultivar is the graceful weeping '**Shidare Yoshino**' introduced to Europe in 1910. It is usually grafted on to a tall standard stem. The flowers are almost white with pink stamens. They hang down in slender-stalked clusters. The *subhirtella* parent of this cultivar was presumably 'Pendula'.

Growth: 3-8-10. Hardiness: 50%. Choice: 1.

Oshima Cherry *Prunus speciosa*

Originally this was a Chinese plant but it has long been cultivated in Japan. From ancient times it has held an important place in classical Japanese gardening. The hawthorn scented flowers are pure white with golden stamens and maroon-brown sepals. They emerge in clusters from bunches of reddish bracts and bud scales. The leaves at this time are slightly bronzed green. In old age the tree may spread to twice its height of 4-6m. Plants were introduced to Europe in 1882. These days it is used by nurserymen as an understock for more showy cultivars. It is less vigorous than *Prunus avium* for this purpose and does not sucker so freely.

Oshima cherries should not be planted and then neglected. They need to be pampered and lightly pruned at frequent intervals to produce strong foliage, good flowers and a pleasing shape. As with all Japanese cherries, pruning of any kind should only be done in mid-summer to reduce the risk of disease infection.

Growth: 2-5-6. Hardiness: 50%. Choice: 1, 3, 4.

Oshima Cherry
spring

'Tsu-Yoshino'
spring

Tibetan Cherry

Tibetan Cherry

Korean Hill Cherry

Japanese Hill Cherry

new leaves

Japanese Hill Cherry autumn

Japanese Hill Cherry
spring

Tibetan Cherry bark

546

Tibetan Cherry *Prunus serrula*

The unique bark for which this tree is well known resembles polished mahogany with a satin finish. It develops from around 5-10 years of age and lasts for around 60 years before being increasingly divided up horizontally and reduced by bands of rougher dull brown corky material.

Tibetan cherry is an ideal subject for the winter garden but the foliage and flowers are of little consequence, and the total height is seldom over 6m. Nurserymen have attempted to increase its value by grafting stronger flowering cultivars on to 2m stocks, providing both brilliant flowers and bright bark but the join seldom looks other than painfully obvious and artificial.

Growth: 3-5-6. Hardiness: 50%. Choice: 1.

Korean Hill Cherry

Prunus serrulata var. *pubescens*

This is a wild form, closely related to the Chinese and Japanese Hill Cherries, from which many cultivated ornamental cherry trees have come. This variety is distinctive in that the underside of the leaf and the stalk is hairy. The single blushed-white blossoms occur in numerous semi-pendulous clusters in early to mid-spring with the pale bronze emerging leaves.

Growth: 2-6-10. Hardiness: 50%. Choice: 1.

Japanese Hill Cherry

Prunus serrulata var. *spontanea*

Although the name suggests a spontaneous wild Japanese plant, some botanists think this tree actually originated in China. It has been growing in Japan for 2000 years so its status and natural distribution have been confused by centuries of cultivation. It is a variable tree but exquisite forms have been discovered and developed. The foliage emerges deep coppery-red and the flowers, often with incised petals, have the faint scent of almonds.

Growth: 3-8-12. Hardiness: 50%. Choice: 1.

Chinese Hill Cherry

Prunus serrulata var. *hupehensis*

The wild form was collected and introduced to Britain in 1822, but cultivated Chinese plants, collected by Ernest Wilson, only arrived from 1900 onwards. Originally taken from a variable natural population, cultivated material contained enormous potential for selection. Bright pink and white flowering trees have resulted, mostly upright specimens around 6m tall but some individuals develop a spreading tendency. The young foliage is glabrous and richly copper-coloured.

Growth: 3-8-12. Hardiness: 50%. Choice: 1.

spring

underside

Chinese Hill Cherry

Prunus lannesiana **'Shizuka'**

Prunus lannesiana **'Yaebeni-Ohshima'**

forma *contorta*

'Tsukubane'

Prunus lannesiana forma *contorta*
spring

Prunus lannesiana **'Tsukubane'**
spring

Prunus lannesiana Ornamental Cherry cultivars

There is some confusion about the species name *lannesiana*. It was extensively used by Ernest Wilson in 1916 but subsequently went out of favour in Britain. However, it is widely used again now by the Flower Association of Japan in their *Manual of Japanese Flowering Cherries* published in 1982.

Prunus lannesiana 'Shizuka'

This is an erect round-topped tree reaching 8-12m in Japan. The branches and stem have grey-brown bark. The greenish-bronze 18cm leaves appear before the flowers and become deep green at maturity with numerous distinct teeth. Blush pink 5-6cm double flowers occur in corymbs of 4-5 blooms in mid-spring. They are fragrant and have roundish notched petals. This tree was bred by Masatoshi Asari in 1960 by crossing 'Erecta' and 'Amayadori'. The Japanese name 'Shizuka' means quiet fragrance.
Growth: 3-8-10. Hardiness: 50%. Choice: 1.

Prunus lannesiana 'Yaebeni-Ohshima'

In Japan this is a large tree with shiny brown bark and numerous sinuous branches. The bronze-green leaves appear before the flowers. They turn to deep glossy green and become broadly-elliptic up to 12cm long. Corymbs of slightly fragrant 3-4cm double pink flowers occur in mid-spring. The cultivation of this tree can be traced back to Izu-oshima Island, Tokyo. Most of the sato-zakura trees were saved from extinction by the Takagi family and planted by the Arakawa River in Tokyo in 1886.
Growth: 3-7-8. Hardiness: 50%. Choice: 1.

Prunus lannesiana forma *contorta* ('Fukurokuju')

This is a saucer-shaped tree in Europe but it is more erect and up to 10m tall in Japan. The 8-12cm leaves occur with the flowers. They are bronze at first then deep green above and light brown below, ovate-elliptic in shape and conspicuously serrated with glandular teeth. The 5cm double flowers open out flat. They are slightly fragrant with wrinkled petals, hence the name *contorta*. This form was cultivated before 1916 in America but is probably much older in Japan.
Growth: 3-8-9. Hardiness: 50%. Choice: 1.

Prunus lannesiana 'Tsukubane'
Hirano-tsukubane

When fully grown this is an erect cup-shaped, 6-12m tree with dark glossy bark. The leaves, occurring before the flowers, are double serrate and up to 14cm long. Corymbs of drooping pink double flowers are red in bud. An ancient cherry of the chrysanthemum-flower type with over 100 petals, this cultivar is found in the famous cherry forests of the Hirana Shrine in Kyoto.
Growth: 3-8-9. Hardiness: 50%. Choice: 1, 3.

***Prunus lannesiana* 'Shizuka'**
spring

***Prunus lannesiana* 'Yaebeni-Ohshima'**
spring

Prunus lannesiana 'Sarasa'

Prunus lannesiana 'Beni-yutaka'

Prunus lannesiana 'Beni-shigure'

new leaves

Prunus lannesiana 'Tsyu-kosade'

new leaves

Prunus lannesiana 'Hanagasa'

new leaves

Prunus lannesiana 'Beni-tama-nishiki'

Prunus lannesiana Matsumae cultivars

This species name is used by Japanese botanists and horticulturalists for a number of hybrid flowering cherries. Several of these appear in western reference books as *speciosa* or *serrulata*. The Matsumae cultivars are mostly modern selections grown in the famous Matsumae Cherry Tree Gardens in Hokkaido. Matsumae is often used by growers as a prefix in the cultivar name.

Prunus lannesiana 'Sarasa'

A superb rounded tree over 6m tall, 'Sarasa', produces huge clusters of 5-6cm double pink blossoms in spring. This tree was produced in Japan by Masatoshi Asari around 1980, by crossing 'Minakami' with 'Kechimyaku-zakura'. It is a triumph of late twentieth-century cherry-breeding but remains very rare in the west.

Growth: 3-5-7. Hardiness: 40%. Choice: 1, 4.

Prunus lannesiana 'Beni-yutaka'

An earlier Asari hybrid cultivar produced in 1961, this is a cup-shaped 10-15m tree with multiple greyish branches. The serrate leaves are 12-14cm long. The drooping double pink spring flowers are red in bud.

Growth: 3-9-12. Hardiness: 50%. Choice: 1.

Prunus lannesiana 'Beni-shigure'

This is an 8-10m erect open-topped tree with shiny purple-brown branches and large 10-14cm leaves which are bronze-brown at first. In spring the 5cm double flowers are deep pink in bud, becoming a little paler as they open. Each of the petals is notched. This tree was bred by Masatoshi Asari in Japan from 'Azuma-nishiki' crossed with *Prunus verecunda*, both very rare plants in the west.

Growth: 3-8-9. Hardiness: 40%. Choice: 1, 4.

Prunus lannesiana 'Tsyu-kosade'

This obscure cultivar appears to have come from the Matsumae Cherry Tree Collection in Hokkaido. It is a single pink-flowered tree with distinctly notched petals. The flowers are dark pink in bud and emerge at the same time as the bronze-green leaves. Later the foliage is bright green, each obovate leaf is distinctly serrate.

Growth: 3-7-8. Hardiness: 50%. Choice: 1.

Prunus lannesiana 'Hanagasa'

This 10-15m tall umbrella-shaped tree has bronze-brown leaves in the spring, accompanied by corymbs of drooping semi-double 5-6cm pink flowers with petals at first reddish and wrinkled. The cultivar was developed by Masatoshi Asari in 1963.

Growth: 3-10-12. Hardiness: 40%. Choice: 1.

Prunus lannesiana 'Beni-tama-nishiki'

The Japanese name means 'red-ball brocade' which is a reference to the distinctive globular buds. The tree is round-topped, 8-10m tall, and has dull purplish-brown branches. The leaves appear before the flowers and are briefly tinted bronze. The 4cm double pink flowers in mid to late spring mostly face downwards. This is another Asari tree developed in 1963 at Matsumae in Hokkaido.

Growth: 3-8-10. Hardiness: 40%. Choice: 1.

***Prunus lannesiana* 'Sarasa'**
spring

***Prunus lannesiana* 'Beni-yutaka'**
end of flowering

***Prunus lannesiana* 'Tsyu-kosade'**
spring

autumn

Prunus 'Kanzan'

glands →

Apple Blossom Cherry

Prunus 'Kanzan'

Prunus 'Cheal's Weeping'

Prunus 'Kanzan' old tree in late spring

Prunus 'Kanzan' bark

CHERRIES

Prunus 'Kanzan'

Kanzan is the name of a mountain in China, also called Sekiyama. This cherry has been popular in Europe ever since it was introduced in 1913. It has become one of the most familiar – and hardly subtle – trees planted in western parks and gardens. It becomes an urn-shaped 6-10m plant with upright branches and a wide top. In mid to late spring it is wreathed in large double pink flowers. There are several cultivated forms: the variety 'Kirin' is a slower-growing, smaller, broad-topped tree with the same garish pink blossom.

Growth: 3-11-14. Hardiness: 50%. Choice: 1 (requires space).

Prunus 'Cheal's Weeping'

The Japanese name for this plant, 'Kiku Shidare Zakura', means 'weeping chrysanthemum cherry'. The 3cm double late spring flowers are deep pink in dense clusters ranged all along the sinuous arching branches. The individual petals are narrow and pointed, slightly reminiscent of a double pink daisy. Trees are usually trained up to 2-4m tall, or grafted on a long stock, and then allowed to weep downwards. If not pruned they will soon reach the ground to form a delightful 'tent' of spring flowers. This is a perfect tree for a small garden, the centre of a lawn, or a fairly confined space.

Growth: 3-4-4. Hardiness: 50%. Choice: 1.

Apple Blossom Cherry
Prunus 'Amanogawa'

The Japanese name means 'celestial river', which aptly describes this rigidly narrow fastigiate plant. Trees up to 6-8m tall may be only 50cm wide. When the clusters of pale pink flowers adorn this improbable structure in late spring the celestial river analogy becomes very plausible. The blossom is strongly scented of hawthorn.

In order to reduce the risk of snow or wind damage branches should be retained and encouraged right down to the base of the stem. In the event of disastrous damage, which does tend to happen, the lower branches can be trained up to form a replacement tree. This cultivar is a challenge for garden designers, as such a tall thin plant looks incongruous in most situations. Triangular groups of three or more may be easier to work with.

Growth: 3-7-8. Hardiness: 50%. Choice: 1.

trees in spring

Prunus 'Kanzan'
young tree

Apple Blossom Cherry

Prunus 'Cheal's Weeping'

Prunus × *juddii*

Prunus 'Pandora'

Prunus 'Umeniko'

Japanese Alpine Cherry

Prunus 'Umeniko'
spring

Japanese Alpine Cherry
spring

Prunus × juddii

This is a hybrid between *Prunus sargentii* and *Prunus × yedonesis*, two of the best flowering cherries in cultivation. It was produced artificially at the Arnold Arboretum, Boston, Massachusetts in 1914. It resembles *Prunus sargentii* (p. 535) but is a smaller tree. The leaves emerge coppery-brown in mid-spring with the vibrant pink fragrant flowers. In autumn the foliage is brilliant deep red.
Growth: 3-7-10. Hardiness: 50%. Choice: 1.

Prunus 'Pandora'

A complicated hybrid between *Prunus subhirtella* 'Ascendens Rosea' and *Prunus × yedonesis*, 'Pandora' was produced at Waterer's Nursery in England before 1939. It has the upright habit of 'Ascendens Rosea', but also picks up the flexible shoot tips of *Prunus × yedonesis*. The profuse, but solitary, flowers are white with just a suspicion of pink. The leaves emerge green in spring and turn to pale yellow in the autumn. The bark of young trees is lustrous brown. Hybrid vigour ensures rapid growth, but ultimate size seldom exceeds 6m high and wide. Young trees are best, in old age 'Pandora' gets very straggly and has a tendency to produce 'witch's brooms' among the branches.
Growth: 3-8-7. Hardiness: 50%. Choice: 1.

Prunus 'Umeniko'

The pure white blossom gives this medium-sized tree its Japanese name which means 'seagull'. It is an upright hybrid between *Prunus incisa* and *Prunus speciosa*. The 3cm single flowers occur in abundance in spring. They have attractive crimson stamens with golden-yellow anthers. The leaves colour well in the autumn.

This is an ideal, but not well-known, flowering cherry for the smallish garden. Its main branches naturally develop into an upswept outline which can be easily maintained by minimal side pruning in summer. In the past it was often called 'Moerheimii' and can still be found labelled as such in some collections.
Growth: 3-7-8. Hardiness: 50%. Choice: 1.

Japanese Alpine Cherry *Prunus nipponica*

A north Japanese mountain species around 4-5m tall this shrubby tree grows very slowly but is completely hardy. An ideal cherry for cold exposed places where cherries would not normally be considered at all, and a good plant for the larger rockery or alpine garden. Planting in groups of about five at close 1-2m spacing is very effective. The small flowers are blushed white.

Growth: 2-4-5. Hardiness: 50-60%. Choice: 1.

trees in spring

Prunus 'Pandora'

Prunus × juddii

Prunus 'Ariake'

Prunus 'Washi-no-o'

Prunus 'Shogetsu'

Prunus 'Ariake'

Prunus 'Mikuruma-gaeshi'

Prunus 'Ariake'
spring

Prunus 'Mikuruma-gaeshi'
spring

Prunus 'Ariake'

A vigorous robust broad-headed tree 6m tall, this plant is hardy enough for most north European gardens. The Japanese name 'Ariake' means 'dawn'. It was introduced to Europe early in the twentieth century. The numerous flowers are mostly single but some have an extra petal or two in the centre. They begin pale pink in bud opening to faintly blushed white in mid-spring. The petals of the individual 5cm flowers are held fairly flat, like a wild rose. The emerging leaves are greenish-bronze.

Growth: 3-5-6. Hardiness: 50%. Choice: 1.

Prunus 'Washi-no-o'

Another Japanese cherry in the *Prunus serrulata* group, this tree is fast-growing and fairly hardy, with a broad open head of branches. Many gardens are not large enough to accommodate its ultimate 8m of height and even greater spread. The 4cm single flowers are delightfully scented like hawthorn with five ragged edged petals. The Japanese name means 'eagle's tail' which is probably a reference to this. Flowers are numerous and occur all over the tree in clusters. They are blush pink in bud and nearly white when fully out. The young foliage, which follows the early flowers, is bronze-green. In a favourable season, yellow autumn foliage colour can be expected.

Growth: 3-7-8. Hardiness: 40-50%. Choice: 1.

Prunus 'Shogetsu'

The taxonomy of this cultivar is confused. Until recently it was listed by nurseries as 'Shimidsu Zakura'. It is another early twentieth-century introduction in the *Prunus serrulata* Japanese cherry group. Flower buds are pink and the semi-double flowers in late spring are white, about 5cm across, and held in pendulous clusters. The foliage starts off bronze, turns green in summer, and then red and orange in the autumn.

Growth: 3-7-8. Hardiness: 50%. Choice: 1.

Prunus 'Mikuruma-gaeshi'

This grand Japanese name means 'the royal carriage returns'. It is said that a passing Emperor of Japan turned his carriage back especially to look at a flowering specimen a second time because he liked it so much. Eventually it is a 6m tall upright open branched tree, with single pink spring flowers, tightly packed along the branches on short spur shoots. They are scented like apple blossom. The foliage emerges bronze and turns green in summer.

Growth: 3-4-6. Hardiness: 50%. Choice: 1.

Prunus 'Washi-no-o'
spring

Prunus 'Pink Perfection'

Mount Fuji Cherry

young leaf

Prunus 'Ukon'

Mount Fuji Cherry

Prunus 'Ukon'
spring

Prunus 'Ukon'

Prunus 'Pink Perfection'

This tree was found as a chance seedling from 'Shimidsu Zakura' ('Shogetsu', p. 557), in 1935 at Waterer's Nursery. It appears that the pollen parent was 'Kanzan' (p. 553). 'Pink Perfection' develops a broad top, 7m tall and wide, and becomes slightly pendulous in old age. The double, or semi-double, mid-spring flowers are bright pink and borne on long drooping stalks. They give an impression of being two shades of pink as they move freely in the wind. This has a particularly delightful effect against blue sky, or a dark evergreen background, further enhanced by the emerging bronze-coloured bracts and green leaves.

Growth: 3-6-7. Hardiness: 50%. Choice: 1.

Mount Fuji Cherry *Prunus* 'Shirotae'

Another fine example of a sato-zakura Japanese cherry derived from *Prunus serrulata*, the Oriental Cherry, this is a pure white form. The Japanese name means 'snow white'. Clusters of 5cm semi-double flowers hang all the way along the spreading branches in mid-spring, representing 'fingers' of snow in the deep gullies around the top of Mount Fujiyama. They are scented like hawthorn blossom. The leaves are large, 12cm long, deeply incised, and colour well in the autumn.

This vigorous tree develops a flat top in middle age. During its most rapid growth stage some of the flowers are single. It is an ideal plant where great height is not required but there is plenty of room for it to spread sideways.

Growth: 3-6-7. Hardiness: 50%. Choice: 1.

Prunus 'Ukon'

This favourite garden tree is the nearest thing in cultivation to a yellow-flowered cherry. The Japanese name 'Ukon' means 'yellowish' which is exactly the colour of the semi-double flowers. They appear translucent in late spring sunshine, and acquire a pinkish tinge before the petals fall. The leaves are orange-red to purplish-brown in the autumn. Trees 6-8m tall are common and some spread out to as much as 10m wide. Not a tree for a confined space or small garden, but a good colour contrast with strong-growing pink varieties, such as 'Kanzan' in a woodland grove of cherry trees.

It also excels when planted against a backdrop of evergreens, such as Juniper or Yew. The first trees to appear in the west arrived around 1905 when 'fashionable' gardeners were desperately seeking a yellow-flowered cherry. The only other cultivar with yellowish flowers is 'Gioiko', introduced in 1914.

Growth: 3-7-8. Hardiness: 50-60%. Choice: 1 (requires space).

trees in spring

Mount Fuji Cherry

***Prunus* 'Pink Perfection'**

Prunus 'Oshokun'

Prunus 'Shimidsu Zakura'

Prunus 'Oshokun'

Prunus 'Jo-nioi'

Prunus 'Jo-nioi'
spring

Prunus 'Oshokun'

This is a slightly tender, weak, spreading tree needing a sheltered location and much loving care to achieve success in the garden. It was named after an extremely beautiful Chinese courtesan. Once established it produces numerous clusters of apple blossom scented pink flowers in mid to late spring. The foliage at this time is emerging brownish-green. It is not a long lived tree, and a new one should be established from time to time in anticipation of the older plant's demise.
Growth: 3-4-5. Hardiness: 30-40%. Choice: 1.

Prunus 'Shimidsu Zakura'

A cultivar of *Prunus serrulata* produced around 1930 the taxonomy of this plant has always led to confusion. Alternatively it is referred to as *Prunus serrulata longipes* or 'Shogetsu'. The Japanese name means 'moon hanging low by a pine tree'. It is a compact rounded little tree with numerous clusters of pendulous semi-double 5cm pale pink flowers reminiscent of fuchsia. The deeper pink buds give it a two-colour effect when flowering begins in late spring. This is always a small tree less than 5m tall with pendulous branch tips.

For best effect it is worthwhile heeding the old Japanese name and planting a specimen in front of a pine tree — better still, several pine trees — to contrast with the pale colours and form of the cherry.
Growth: 3-4-4. Hardiness: 50%. Choice: 1.

Prunus 'Jo-nioi'

'Jo-nioi' is one of the most strongly scented cherries. The fragrance of the blossom is similar to hawthorn or almonds. It is a medium-sized spreading tree which can exceed 10m in height, but seldom does. The individual single or semi-double white spring flowers are small, but they occur in great numbers. The sepals by contrast with the petals are purplish-brown, and the young leaves are golden brown. This is a cultivar of *Prunus serrula* introduced around 1900, it is uncommon in cultivation, but is worth looking out for on account of its delightful scent.
Growth: 3-6-7. Hardiness: 50%. Choice: 1.

These small cherry trees, and those on p. 563, all have broadly similar flowers but flowering times vary slightly. It is worth planting several cultivars together to extend the display of spring blossom over a long period. Planting 3-5 trees of each sort, if space permits, at about 4m spacing, intensifies the effect.

Prunus 'Oshokun'   **Prunus 'Shimidsu Zakura'**

trees in spring

Prunus 'Takasago'

Prunus 'Hokusai'

Prunus 'Ichiyo'

Prunus 'Horinji'

Prunus 'Ichiyo'
spring

Prunus 'Horinji'
spring

CHERRIES

Prunus 'Takasago'

One of the first Japanese flowering cherries to arrive in Europe, 'Takasago' is a broad-headed tree about 8m tall. It will live for 50-60 years in most garden situations. The Japanese name means 'good health and long life'. It was introduced to Europe, probably as *Prunus sieboldii*, in about 1864 by Philipp Franz von Siebold, a Bavarian eye doctor working in Japan. He was only allowed into Japan on account of his profession. Fortunately for the rest of the world he was also a plant collector. The light pink flowers are semi-double, about 4.5cm across, produced in mid-spring. The young leaves are bronze-green turning to light green. They are distinctly silky-hairy on both sides. The short leaf stalks have two glands on them, which is unusual in sato-zakura cherries but is a feature of other groups of *Prunus*.

Growth: 3-6-8. Hardiness: 50%. Choice: 1.

Prunus 'Hokusai'

Many nurserymen suggest 'Hokusai' as a "better quality" replacement for 'Takasago'. It certainly grows faster, and the similar-looking flowers remain fresh for a long time, up to three weeks. They are scented like Chinese peonies (*Paeonia lactiflora*). The name commemorates the great Japanese painter Hokusai Katsushuka (1760-1849). This plant was another von Siebold introduction of around 1866.

Growth: 3-8-9. Hardiness: 50%. Choice: 1.

Prunus 'Ichiyo'

Strangely this splendid tree is uncommon in European gardens, but it is popular in Japan. It is vigorous, free-flowering, spreading – up to 7m tall and wide. The shell-pink double flowers often produce a leafy bract in the centre. They are long lasting, from mid to late spring.

Growth: 3-6-7. Hardiness: 40%. Choice: 1.

Prunus 'Horinji'

This is a classic Japanese temple cherry named after an ancient buddhist holy place in Kyoto. It has the most beautiful 5cm semi-double pink flowers, the fringe a deeper colour than the centre, festooning the stiff upright branches in spring. The whole plant seldom exceeds 5m in height. Its open branch structure lends itself to formative pruning, particularly as a component in the creation of a Japanese garden. The tree was first introduced to Europe around 1905.

Growth: 3-5-5. Hardiness: 40%. Choice: 1.

Prunus 'Takasago' **Prunus 'Hokusai'**

trees in spring

Great White Cherry

Prunus **'Shirofugen'**

Flag Cherry

Great White Cherry

old tree   young tree

Great White Cherry *Prunus* 'Tai-haku'

In 1923 Captain Collingwood Ingram, the English cherry enthusiast, was shown a magnificent white cherry in a garden in Sussex. It had the largest pure white flowers of any he had seen, 6cm across. He immediately propagated the tree without knowing what it was. Some years later when in Japan he was shown an eighteenth-century book of paintings by a Mr. Funatsun. To his astonishment his Sussex cherry was in it, 'Tai-haku' named by a Japanese Prince Tsukasa in ancient times. So far as was known the tree had been extinct for hundreds of years. How it managed to re-appear in Sussex is uncertain, but from this single plant, gardens the world over have been restocked.

'Tai-haku' is without doubt the finest snow-white cherry there is. It has low spreading branches filled with clusters of 6cm flowers and bronze-red unfolding leaves in spring. It is hardy, and undemanding with regard to soil. It will grow and flower perfectly well in semi-shade or full sun. The flowers are faintly scented of gorse (*Ulex europaeus*), or warm almonds.
Growth: 3-7-8. Hardiness: 50%. Choice: 1.

Prunus 'Shirofugen'

This is a vigorous tree up to 8m wide and almost as tall. The Japanese name means 'white god' and is a reference to the colour of the fully open flowers. These begin pale pink in bud, become pure white, and turn back to pale purplish-pink just before the petals fall. In the garden the great value of this tree is its late flowering. It extends the spring cherry blossom season into early summer. The centre of the flower often develops into a leafy bract.

This is a good garden tree, tolerant of a wide range of soil types. Its white flowers and deep bronze young leaves make it an ideal lawn specimen. By the time it flowers in early summer the weather is usually good enough for the garden chairs to be set out in its shade.
Growth: 3-7-8. Hardiness: 50%. Choice: 1.

Flag Cherry *Prunus* 'Hatazakura'

So called because the petals have tattered edges like a well used flag, this is an early flowering very pale pink cultivar. The faintly scented single flowers soon fade nearly to white and are quickly spoiled by cold spring rain. The young leaves are bronze-green, appearing after the flowers. It is not a widely grown form, and it has become rare in cultivation.
Growth: 3-6-7. Hardiness: 40%. Choice: 1.

***Prunus* 'Shirofugen'**   **Flag Cherry**

trees in spring

Cherry Laurel

Cherry Laurel

'Rotundifolia'

'Camelliifolia'

'Schipkaensis'

'Otinii'

'Magnoliifolia'

'Serbica'

'Bruantii'

Cherry Laurel *Prunus laurocerasus*

The common name Cherry Laurel, and the appetizing glossy black fruit, belie the poisonous nature of this plant. Even the evergreen leaves are poisonous, being rich in cyanide. Not a tree to plant where there are young children or pets, such as horses. It is not a suitable subject where under-planting is required either. Nothing will grow under the poisonous drips of rain-water from laurel leaves. It is said that the laurel is an evergreen because the Greek god Apollo loved the beautiful nymph Daphne. She disliked him but he pursued her relentlessly. When he finally cornered her she cried out for help and was immediately changed into a laurel tree. Apollo embraced the tree and declared that it would always remain fresh and green and, like his love, would never die. The off-white spring flowers are densely packed in upright or nodding racemes. They are strongly scented and attract numerous insects.

In cultivation the wild form, from western Asia, is almost unknown. There are, however, numerous horticultural selections. '**Rotundifolia**' is a French cultivar produced at Fontenay-aux-Roses in 1865. The short rounded leaves are less glossy than most of the other forms. '**Camelliifolia**' is a vigorous large shrub 3-4m tall. It was produced in 1901 and is very commonly grown in English gardens particularly as a tall evergreen hedge.

A smaller but more hardy plant is '**Schipkaensis**' from the Schipka Pass (1333m) in Bulgaria. It was introduced by Späth in Berlin in 1889. A similar but smaller type called '**Compacta**' was developed in Austria.

Probably the most common form in cultivation '**Latifolia**', has bright glossy leaves 20-25cm long. It is tall, vigorous, and very shade tolerant. The original plant was produced at Versailles, France, in 1869. It has been extensively used on shooting estates as cover and as a food source for pheasants. The cultivar '**Otinii**' is a vigorous but compact tree with big dark green pendulous leaves up to 25cm long. It was cultivated at St. Etienne, in France, but is tender in northern Europe.

A large shrub with very large leaves is '**Magnoliifolia**'. The tough dense cultivar '**Serbica**' is a very hardy plant. It has 10-14cm leaves which are less glossy green. It originated in the Balkans and was introduced to northern Europe via Germany in 1877. The cultivar '**Bruantii**' is another French selection made before 1913. It is tender but makes a small tree or large shrub 4m tall with upright branches in mild districts.

Growth: 4-6-6. Hardiness: 40-50%. Choice: 2, 3.

'Magnoliifolia'

new leaves

Judas Tree

leaf variation

Judas Tree

seed pods

'Bodnant'
(reduced)

seed pod

autumn leaflet

Yellow-wood

fruit

Chinese Yellow-wood

568

PEA FAMILY · Fabaceae

Judas Tree
Cercis siliquastrum (Caesalpiniaceae)

This distinctive rounded deciduous tree is prized by gardeners for its numerous bright purplish-pink pea flowers in early summer. These occur in clusters along the branches even if they are frequently and heavily pruned. The Judas Tree originated in south-east Europe and western Asia, but has been cultivated for centuries throughout Europe and much of the rest of the temperate world. In North America its place is usually taken by *Cercis canadensis*, Redbud (p. 571). The genus name comes from the Greek 'kerkis' which, strangely, appears to mean poplar. The thin rounded leaves do vaguely resemble some poplars.

If allowed to grow freely and un-pollarded, Judas trees may reach 10m. Old specimens often lean at an angle, fall down, or recline on the ground, but nearly always continue to grow vigorously and flower profusely. In the autumn fairly good yellowish-brown autumn foliage colour is produced. This is a plant for hot sunny dry stony places. It is tolerant of acid or alkaline soils but does not transplant well. There is a white-flowered form *albida*. The pre-1914 cultivar '**Bodnant**' is a superior floriferous type with deep pink flowers.

Growth: 2-6-10. Hardiness: 40%. Choice: 1, 2.

Cladrastis (Fabaceae)

There are only four deciduous species in this genus from North America and eastern Asia. The name is from the Greek 'kiados' meaning branch, and 'thraustos' fragile, a reference to the weak twigs and branches. These trees are hardy in Europe but require protection in the exposed north and east.

Yellow-wood *Cladrastis kentukea (lutea)*

In America this tree grows to 20m in height but in cultivation in Europe it remains much smaller. It has alternate pinnate leaves which turn clear gold in autumn. In summer fragrant white pea flowers occur in panicles 25-40cm long. It does not flower freely in cold areas. The bark is smooth and pale grey, and the wood is bright yellow.

Growth: 2-7-15. Hardiness: 70%. Choice: 1. Wood: 1.

Chinese Yellow-wood *Cladrastis sinensis*

This less hardy species from China has greyish-green leaves and produces broad 12-30cm panicles of white or pinkish-white 1.2cm flowers late in the summer. Yellow-woods are seldom planted in gardens but they are good shade trees requiring only a sheltered site and rich moist soil. Growth is generally slow and the ultimate size remains easily manageable. Trees can be pruned back to make them safe and maintain a predetermined shape and size.

Growth: 2-5-9. Hardiness: 50%. Choice: 1, 2. Wood: 1.

Yellow-wood

flowers on bole →

Judas Tree
flowering

Eastern Redbud

'Forest Pansy'

Eastern Redbud

Cercis racemosa

underside

Cercis racemosa

Silk Tree

'Rosea'

Silk Tree

Eastern Redbud
Cercis canadensis (Caesalpiniaceae)

This deciduous tree rarely exceeds 10m in height. It comes from south and east North America and north-east Mexico. The rounded heart-shaped leaves are 10cm wide and long. They are bright green, smooth, and paper thin. In spring new growth is bronze to deep brown. In the popular cultivar '**Forest Pansy**' early reddish-bronze colour persists all season. Eastern Redbud tends to flower less well in northern Europe than it does in its native America. It is tolerant of a range of soil types and withstands drought. It is hardy but spring frosts can cause superficial damage to the flowers and foliage.

Growth: 2-6-10. Hardiness: 60%. Choice: 1, 2.

Cercis racemosa

This Chinese species is closely related to the European and American trees. The 10cm leaves are hairy underneath, which is unusual in *Cercis*. The 10cm long racemes of flowers (as opposed to clusters in other species) appear on old wood in early summer. The seeds are produced in flat green pea pods tinged with red-brown as they mature. It is rare in cultivation but a worthwhile addition to a sheltered garden for its delicate flowers.

Growth: 2-5-10. Hardiness: 30%. Choice: 1.

Silk Tree *Albizia julibrissin* (Mimosaceae)

Albizia is a genus of about 150 species usually represented in temperate gardens by just one or two. The Silk Tree is doubtfully hardy in much of Europe, although it thrives in the south. It is native to Asia from Iran to Japan. The name commemorates the eighteenth-century Florentine nobleman Filippo Degli Albizzi who brought it into cultivation. It makes a rounded tree up to 10m high with spreading branches. The light green deciduous leaves are bipinnate with around 24 minor leaflets about 1cm long on each of 12-14 main leaflets. The early summer flowers, closely resembling a red mimosa, occur in racemes. Each 'flower' is in fact a cluster of smaller rudimentary flowers. Seed occurs in 15cm pea pods in autumn.

Once established the Silk Tree will survive minor frosts, but in colder areas it is usually grown inside as a conservatory plant. It requires strong sunshine to flower in summer and is tolerant of drought. The cultivar '**Rosea**' is less vigorous but has deeper red flowers. It is said to be slightly more cold resistant. There is also a rare white-flowered form.

Growth: 2-7-9. Hardiness: 20-30%. Choice: 1. Wood: 1.

Silk Tree
flowering

Eastern Redbud
spring

Silver Wattle
young bark

Silver Wattle

fruit

Green Wattle

fruit

Pale Hickory Wattle

Silver Wattle
young tree flowering

fruit

adult leaves

intermediate leaves

juvenile leaves

Blackwood

Silver Wattle or Mimosa

Acacia dealbata (Mimosaceae)

In the wild state in Australia this is a 30m tree with stems around 1m thick. The shoots and leaves are covered with silvery down, giving an overall frosted appearance. The fragrant sulphur-yellow flowers occur in panicles 10cm across in late summer – in Europe, winter. When cultivated in the northern hemisphere it survives out of doors in mild regions but will only thrive in a conservatory. In southern Europe it can be cut down by a frost but will then often recolonise the ground from a mass of root-suckers.

Growth: 3-5-5. Hardiness: 0-10%. Choice: 1.
Wood: 2, 3, 4 (tannins), 5.

Green Wattle

Acacia decurrens var. *mollis* (syn. *mearnsii*)

An evergreen tree to 18m tall, Green Wattle has dark foliage consisting of fine pinnate leaves with 16-70 pairs of leaflets. Flowers occur in racemes followed by flat seed pods 10cm long.

Growth: 3-5-5. Hardiness: 0-10%. Choice: 1.

Pale Hickory Wattle *Acacia falciformis*

This tender species is from south-east Australia. It has undivided leaves and scented spring flowers which occur in profusion in the leaf axils and also in terminal panicles.

Growth: 4-5-5. Hardiness: 0%. Choice: 1.

Blackwood *Acacia melanoxylon*

This evergreen tree exceeds 25m in the wild, but much less in cultivation. It is native to Tasmania and southern Australia but tolerates the milder parts of Europe. The distinctive foliage consists of a mixture of adult and juvenile leaves, and also has an intermediate stage. The flowers occur in small axillary clusters in spring. The 7-10cm long seed pods are often curved or distorted.

Growth: 4-5-5. Hardiness: 0-10%. Choice: 1.
Wood: 1, 2, 3, 4 (tannins).

Mount Etna Broom *Genista aetnensis*

Although this is a Mediterranean broom, it grows to tree size as far north as the milder parts of northern Europe. Specimens in southern England, for example, have reached 18m with stems over 35cm in diameter. It thrives in seaside areas, but having only rudimentary leaves it gives little shelter from the wind. It is native to Sicily and Sardinia, but is naturalized on rocky hillsides and cliffs all over southern and western Europe. The fragrant yellow flowers occur in profusion on thin, almost leafless bright green straight shoots.

Growth: 4-8-15. Hardiness: 40-50%. Choice: 1.

Mount Etna Broom

Black Locust

bud detail

fruit

Black Locust

'Tortuosa'

Black Locust *Robinia pseudoacacia*

This North American species is both ornamental in the garden and useful as a timber producer. It was named in honour of Jean and Vespasien Robin who were sixteenth-century herbalists to the French Royal Household. British colonists in America discovered the species in 1607 at Jamestown Virginia. American Indians made bows from the strong flexible wood and cultivated straight trees specially for this purpose.

Black Locust is potentially large, around 25m tall and over 1m through the stem. It should only be planted where there is plenty of open space because it spreads almost indefinitely by sprouting from the extensive surface root system. Care must always be taken to ensure that sucker shoots, resulting in further trees, do not encroach upon neighbouring property. Black Locust is hardy throughout most of Europe, but old trees tend to become hollow and unsafe in strong winds. Small branches and twigs are armed with flat razor sharp thorns in pairs on either side of each alternate bud. The 25cm pinnate leaves have 7-19 pairs of opposite, oval untoothed 4cm leaflets. The fragrant white flowers, in lax or pendent 10-20cm racemes, appear with the leaves in early summer. This tree is late coming into leaf and it drops its poorly-coloured leaflets early in the autumn.

There are a large number of cultivated forms, '**Frisia**' was raised at the Jansen Nursery, Holland, in 1935, and is now very popular. Its yellow foliage is striking through the summer and then it takes on a glowing golden hue in the autumn (see also next page).

An unusual slow-growing form is '**Tortuosa**'; it has a compact head of twisted branches that tend to droop.

Though not particularly pretty, the cultivar '**Pyramidalis**' ('Fastigiata') is a tough columnar tree with the considerable horticultural advantage of having no thorns. It originated before 1850 but is still very much under used.

The Weeping Black Locust, '**Rozynskyana**' is another cultivar which is much less popular than it deserves to be. First cultivated in 1920, it makes a delightful tree with pendulous branch tips and large 25-40cm leaves.

See p. 579-581 for other Black Locust cultivars.

All Black Locusts transplant well and tolerate almost any kind of soil. Their wide spreading roots and late leafing out makes them particularly tolerant of drought.

Growth: 3-9-25. Hardiness: 70-80%. Choice: 1, 4. Wood: 1, 2, 3 (species).

'Pyramidalis'   'Frisia'   'Rozynskyana'

'Frisia'

Clammy Locust

Robinia × *holdtii*

leaflet

Rose Acacia

One-leaved Black Locust

leaf variations

One-leaved Black Locust

Robinia pseudoacacia 'Frisia' (see p. 575)

Clammy Locust *Robinia viscosa*

First cultivated in 1791, this small tree up to 12m tall is from the south-eastern part of the United States. The dark red branches, and the leaf and flower stalks, are glandular and sticky. A most unpleasant tree to touch, not only is it sticky but it is often armed with small but very sharp spines. The pretty pea flowers are pale pink with a yellow blotch on the top petal (the standard) and a red calyx. There are 6-16 2cm flowers to each pendulous raceme. The 5-8cm seed pods are also glandular.

Growth: 3-8-12. Hardiness: 50-60%. Choice: 1.

Robinia × *holdtii*

This hybrid between Black Locust and *Robinia luxurians* (p. 579) originated before 1890, in the region of Colorado. It makes a substantial tree similar to Black Locust but with light rose-pink flowers. The leaves are slightly larger with 4-5cm leaflets. The seed pods are slightly glandular.

Growth: 3-8-14. Hardiness: 60-70%. Choice: 1, 4.

Rose Acacia *Robinia hispida*

The Rose Acacia is a lovely shrub or very small tree but it has no respect for space or boundaries. It is stoloniferous, and spreads far and wide by constantly throwing up new stems from its extensive surface root system. The foliage is glandular and sticky. Flowers 2-5cm across occur in short racemes with particularly bristly (hispid) stalks. In America it is sometimes called Moss Locust. The petals are rose-coloured or pale purple with a red calyx. The plant, from Virginia and Kentucky south to Georgia was brought into cultivation in 1758. The variety *macrophylla* has somewhat larger leaves and flowers, but it lacks the density of sticky bristles. Stems appear to be brittle and frequently snap off in strong winds or snow.

Growth: 1-1-2. Hardiness: 50%. Choice: 1, 4.

One-leaved Black Locust

Robinia pseudoacacia 'Unifolia'

Often known as 'Monophylla' this fairly big, often rather gaunt tree looks at first sight as if it suffers from a dreadful foliage disease. This is because the familiar pinnate *Robinia* leaves with many leaflets are reduced to just 3-5 or sometimes only one. It originated in Europe in 1855 and in America in 1858.

Growth: 3-9-20. Hardiness: 70%. Choice: 4.

Mop-head Acacia

Robinia pseudoacacia 'Umbraculifera'

This is a curiosity that is worthy of a place in the specialist plant collector's garden. It is small but has architectural impact. Unfortunately it is very slow-growing and patience will be needed before the effect can be seen. The tightly packed thornless branches seldom leave room for any flowers to be produced, but are a feature in their own right. The tree was first cultivated in 1811 and has often been wrongly sold under the name 'Inermis'. Real 'Inermis' is another thornless cultivar, but it lacks the distinctive foliage of 'Umbraculifera', which gives the impression of having just been neatly clipped with shears.

Growth: 1-4-6. Hardiness: 60%. Choice: 1.

Mop-head Acacia

young tree

old tree

'Coluteoides'

'Hillieri'

Robinia × *slavinii*

'Aurea'

'Coluteoides'

'Monophylla Fastigiata'

'Aurea'

Robinia pseudoacacia cultivars

The cultivar '**Coluteoides**' is a small densely-twigged tree that takes on a rugged appearance in old age. The flowers are numerous though the racemes are hardly showy. It is a good plant for the small garden provided that any suckers that might appear can be removed. This is probably best done by surrounding the tree with grass and mowing it frequently. Unfortunately this cultivar is seldom available now in the nursery trade. Another interesting tree is '**Aurea**' which grows as large as the species (over 20m) and is often mistaken for it. The characteristic soft yellow foliage only occurs in early summer and is easily confused with ordinary yellowish unfolding Black Locust leaves, or a possible nutrient deficiency. It was first cultivated in 1864 but has now been largely replaced in the trade by 'Frisia'. The unusual tree '**Monophylla Fastigiata**' is now rarely seen. It is an upright form of the 'One-leaved Black Locust' (p. 577). A gaunt-looking plant with a mixture of single or tri-foliate leaves. Another cultivar which is sadly very difficult to come by now is '**Glaucescens**'. It has delicate soft grey-green foliage (Other Black Locust cultivars are illustrated on pages 579-581).

Growth: variable. Hardiness: 50-70%. Choice: 1, 4.

Robinia × slavinii

This hybrid between *Robinia pseudoacacia* and *Robinia kelseyi*, was first cultivated in 1915 in the USA. It is intermediate between the parents, but has broader leaflets than *Robinia kelseyi*. The foliage is bristly but not glandular like *kelseyi* – which incidentally is known in America as 'Allegheny Moss'. The flowers, which are also on hairy-stalked racemes, are lilac to rose pink. The seed pods are roughened by very small tightly packed tubercles.

A fine cultivar of this hybrid, '**Hillieri**', has numerous purplish bristly foliage hairs and rose-pink, slightly fragrant flowers. The leaves, with 7-11 leaflets each around 3cm long, are pea-green with paler undersides. This small rounded, shapely tree was raised at the Hillier Nurseries in 1933, and has now more or less replaced the original hybrid in cultivation in Europe.

Growth: 2-6-10. Hardiness: 50-60%. Choice: 1, 4.

Robinia luxurians

This small tree up to 10m tall is from the southern United States and north Mexico. It has relatively large leaves, each consisting of 15-21 elliptic-oblong 2-3.5cm leaflets. They are silky-pubescent on the underside at first. Each petiole and rachis is glandular. Vicious stipular spines, in threes, protect the luxuriant foliage from browsing animals. The flowers are rose-pink fading to almost white, about 2cm across, in dense 15-20cm long racemes. Seeds are in glandular sticky pods up to 10cm long. Although it was brought into cultivation in 1881 this is still an unusual plant in horticulture.

Growth: 2-6-10. Hardiness: 60-70%. Choice: 1, 4.

'Monophylla Fastigiata'

'Glaucescens'

leaves to scale

Robinia luxurians

'Appalachia'

Robinia pseudoacacia 'Rehderi'

Robinia × holdtii 'Britzensis'

Robinia pseudoacaci 'Bessoniana'

Robinia pseudoacacia 'Appalachia'

Robinia pseudoacacia 'Rehderi'

Robinia pseudoacacia 'Bessoniana'

LOCUST TREES

Robinia × *holdtii* 'Britzensis'

The flowers of the hybrid (described on p. 577) are almost white with only a hint of pink. The leaves are green at first becoming grey-green as they mature. This similar-looking cultivar is a rare plant in cultivation. It appears to have been first grown as a garden tree sometime between 1893 and 1900.
Growth: 3-9-18. Hardiness: 60%. Choice: 1, 4.

Robinia pseudoacacia 'Rehderi'

This small bushy tree with its compact thornless branches has more erect twigs than the otherwise similar Mop-Head Acacia (p. 577). It was first cultivated in 1859 and is usually grown on its own roots (not grafted).
Growth: 1-2-2. Hardiness: 60-70%. Choice: 1.

Robinia pseudoacacia 'Appalachia'

Usually this makes an upright tree but, as the illustration shows, it can spread quite widely. It has been largely replaced in cultivation in Europe by other cultivars.
Growth: 2-7-9. Hardiness: 60%. Choice: 1.

Robinia pseudoacacia 'Bessoniana'

In recent times this cultivar has become recognized as an ideal street tree. It is compact, flowers well, is not particularly large, has small leaflets and no spines. The taxing environment of paving and vehicle exhaust fumes appears to suit it perfectly well. The leaves are rich green and accompanied by white flowers in summer. The rough bark does not accommodate carved graffiti or suffer serious damage from minor traffic 'bumps' and pinned up notices. 'Bessoniana' was first cultivated in America in 1864 and introduced to Europe in 1871.
Growth: 3-9-15. Hardiness: 60-70%. Choice: 1, 2.

Robinia 'Idahoensis'

A great deal of complex breeding has gone into producing this splendid but little-used cultivar. The flowers are pink to pale lavender, and backed by strong green foliage. It is a very robust hardy tree which originated as a selection from crosses between Black Locust and *Robinia viscosa*. From the same parentage and more available in Europe is 'Bella-Rosea'.
Growth: 3-8-10. Hardiness: 70-80%. Choice: 1.

Caspian Locust *Gleditsia caspica*

Closely related to Japanese Honey Locust (p. 583) this 12m tree is very spiny and has pinnate leaves with up to 20 leaflets, though some are bi-pinnate with up to 8 subdivisions. It is native to parts of Asia Minor including northern Persia and Azerbaijan and was first cultivated in the west in 1822.
Growth: 3-7-12. Hardiness: 40-60%. Choice: 1.

Robinia 'Idahoensis'

Caspian Locust

Chinese Honey Locust

var. *koraiensis*

Japanese Honey Locust

Chinese Honey Locust   new leaves   **Chinese Honey Locust**

582

Chinese Honey Locust
Gleditsia sinensis (Caesalpiniaceae)

An old name for this 1774 introduction from China, *Gleditsia horrida*, describes Karl Willdenow's initial reaction when he first described it, no doubt on account of the viciously sharp branched spines. It is no accident that Carl Thunberg and Tomitaro Makino gave the same species name to another *Gleditsia*, Japanese Honey Locust. The Chinese tree is a moderately large specimen growing to around 15m tall with delicate pinnate leaves 12-18cm long with up to 18 leaflets. They are dull yellowish-green and 3-8cm long. The insignificant racemes of greenish-white flowers develop into 12-24cm long straight pea-pods.

Growth: 2-8-15. Hardiness: 40-50%. Choice: 1, 4. Wood: 3, 5.

Japanese Honey Locust *Gleditsia japonica*

This beautiful but well armed tree has ferny 30cm pinnate and bi-pinnate leaves and grows to a substantial size, 20-25m tall. Its vicious flattened thorns are 5-10cm long and often branched. The flowers occur in slender racemes and produce twisted seed pods 25-30cm long. Japanese honey locust also occurs in China. It was introduced to western horticulture around 1800. The variety **koraiensis**, sometimes listed as a species in its own right is a Korean segregate of *Gleditsia japonica*.

Growth: 3-9-20. Hardiness: 50%. Choice: 1, 4. Wood: 3, 5.

Honey Locust *Gleditsia triacanthos*

This 24m spreading thorny tree is from east and central North America, from southern Ontario to Florida and west to south-east Texas. In America it is also called 'Sweet Locust' because the seed pods contain sweet pulp relished by most wildlife. It was sent to London in the year 1700 and many cultivated forms have arisen from it since then. (See also the illustration on p. 585). There is also a desirable thornless form, f. *inermis*.

Growth: 4-10-20 (45 in native region). Hardiness: 60-70%. Choice: 2. Wood: 3, 5.

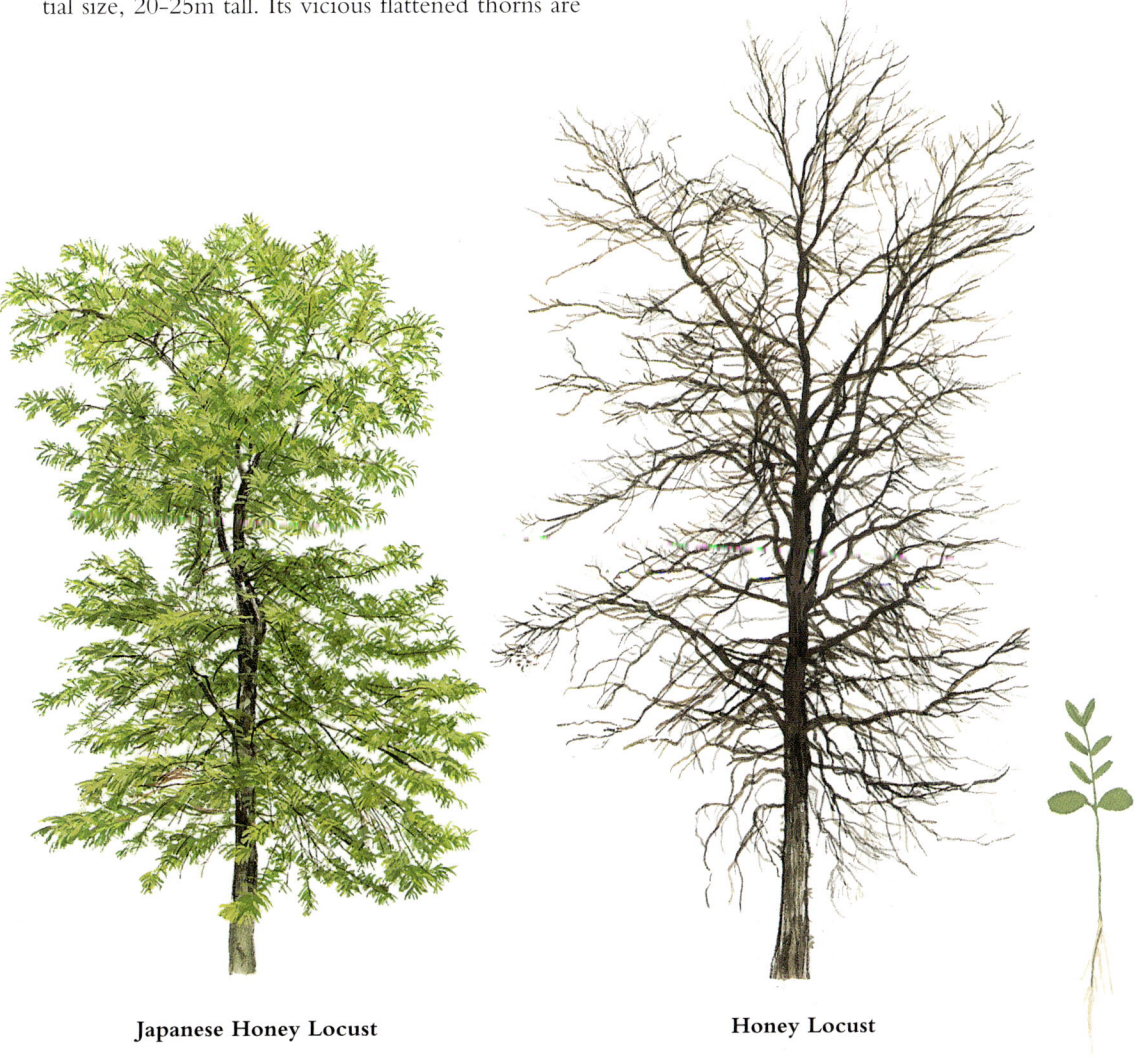

Japanese Honey Locust

Honey Locust

Honey Locust

bi-pinnate leaves

pinnate leaves

Honey Locust

'Skyline' spring leaves

Gleditsia triacanthos 'Skyline'

young tree

'Imperial'

Gleditsia triacanthos 'Imperial' young tree

Gleditsia triacanthos 'Bujotii'

'Sunburst'

Gleditsia triacanthos × *texana*

Gleditsia triacanthos 'Variegata'

Pagoda Tree

autumn

Gleditsia triacanthos 'Sunburst'

'Elegantissima' autumn

Gleditsia triacanthos 'Elegantissima'

Pagoda Tree 'Pyramidalis'

Pagoda Tree bark

Gleditsia triacanthos cultivars

Considerable effort has been put into developing urban shade trees from this species. '**Skyline**' is the epitome of this, a monopodial, conical, straight specimen, 15m tall, with good yellow spring foliage colour.

'**Imperial**' is a shorter, wider spreading town park tree. Some of the new American cultivar names say it all, e.g. 'Shademaster', 'Skymaster' and 'Trueshade'.

'**Bujotii**' is a small plant with slender pendulous branchlets. '**Variegata**' is one of several weakly variegated cultivars. The natural hybrid between *Gleditsia aquatica* and this species is × **texana**, a big tree without spines.

Finally, '**Elegantissima**' is a slow-growing, more or less thornless, shrubby tree with densely twiggy branches and fern-like foliage.

'**Sunburst**' is a sport from the form *inermis*, the thornless American Honey Locust. Few trees have become as popular as this golden-leaved plant, first cultivated in 1953, which makes an ideal town tree. It is tolerant of air pollution and withstands hot dry conditions. Even mown grass around its base does not seem to present any problems for its roots. Although optimum size has probably not yet been reached it does not appear to be an excessively large tree. The leaflets are small and do not cause a great deal of nuisance when they fall. There are no serious pathological problems and trees hardly ever blow down.

Growth: variable. Hardiness: 60%. Choice: 1.

Pagoda Tree *Sophora japonica*

This graceful 25m tree has a rounded top and spreading branches. Its young shoots are vivid green and completely glabrous. The pinnate leaves are 15-25cm long with around 15 ovate leaflets which are 3-5cm long. The upper sides of these are dark green and they are glaucous beneath. The pretty white pea-flowers are in terminal panicles up to 30cm long appearing in summer and often hidden by luxuriant foliage high up in the tree. It flowers best in a very hot dry season.

The exact range of the Pagoda Tree has been confused by centuries of cultivation. It may only be wild in the Chihli Province of northern China, but it grows all over China and also in Japan. It was introduced to France in 1747 and soon spread to all the botanic gardens of Europe. A favourite location for this species has been in Universities and other places of learning. An alternative name for it is the Chinese Scholar Tree, suggesting a very long historical precedent for this practice.

The cultivar '**Pendula**' was first seen in Shanghai by Robert Fortune in 1853. It was grafted above head height and had weeping shoots down to the ground. It makes a good garden tree with twisted pendulous branches but does not appear to flower. '**Pyramidalis**' is a narrow upright form also in cultivation under the variety name *columnaris*. It is now seldom seen and has mostly been replaced by the newer cultivar 'Princeton Upright'.

Growth: 3-9-25 (species). Hardiness: 60-70%. Choice: 1, 3.

fruit

Pagoda Tree

'**Pendula**'

Voss's Laburnum

Scotch Laburnum

Common Laburnum

Adam's Laburnum

Voss's Laburnum

bud detail

Scotch Laburnum

'Aureum'

Adam's Laburnum

Voss's Laburnum

Scotch Laburnum

586

Laburnum

There are two species, a hybrid and several cultivated forms of Laburnum. They all originated in southern Europe or western Asia. The deciduous foliage is trifoliate and the inflorescences are pendulous yellow racemes of late spring pea flowers. The small hard seeds occur in flat pods which hang in clusters and turn from green to dark brown. All Laburnums, especially their seeds, should be regarded as seriously poisonous.

Voss's Laburnum *Laburnum × watereri*

A hybrid raised in Holland in the late nineteenth century and now widely planted for its profusion of golden yellow 30cm racemes of flowers. It tolerates chalky soils and remains fairly small.
Growth: 3-7-10. Hardiness: 60%. Choice: 1, 4. Wood: 1.

Scotch Laburnum *Laburnum alpinum*

When a hardy ornamental plant is required for an exposed area this species from the mountains of southern Europe is one of the best. The later flowers are fragrant, in racemes up to 45cm long.
Growth: 2-7-14. Hardiness: 60-70%. Choice: 1, 4. Wood: 1.

Common Laburnum *Laburnum anagyroides*

This European tree may grow to 9m tall and wide. The leaves have distinctive grey-green backs and 25cm golden inflorescences. It tolerates lime-rich soils. The wood has a long history of use in fine furniture making. It is dark brown with a narrow pale yellow sapwood border. There is a rather insipid yellow-leaved form '**Aureum**' which boasts the name Golden-leaved Laburnum, but tends to revert if green growths are not constantly cut out.
Growth: 2-6-9. Hardiness: 50%. Choice: 1, 4. Wood: 1.

Adam's Laburnum +*Laburnocytisus adamii*

This small tree is an entirely artificial plant called a graft hybrid or 'chimaera'. It was created in Paris in 1825. The inner stem is Common Laburnum and the outer part is Purple Broom (***Cytisus purpureus***). The tree produces flowers of both species and intermediate forms simultaneously.
Growth: 3-6-9. Hardiness: 50%. Choice: 1.

Maackia chinensis

Unlike Laburnum the leaves of this small, 8m, rounded tree are pinnate, 20cm long with up to 13 leaflets. The racemes of pea flowers stand upright on the shoot tips. They are dull creamy-white and appear in late summer. A highly ornamental species, introduced from its native China in 1908 by Ernest Wilson.
Growth: 2-6-8 (23 in native region). Hardiness: 40-50%. Choice: 1. Wood: 1, 3.

Adam's Laburnum

Cytisus purpureus

Maackia chinensis

autumn leaflet

old American tree in summer

underside

winter

Kentucky Coffee Tree

588

Kentucky Coffee Tree

Gymnocladus dioicus (Caesalpiniaceae)

The seeds of this big 17m tree are said to have been roasted to make a sort of coffee by early European pioneers in America. Raw seeds, however, are poisonous, although the unripe seeds were once used in homoeopathic medicine. The huge bi-pinnate deciduous leaves are up to 1m long with as many as 140 leaflets. Each leaflet is ovate, entire and abruptly pointed. The base is irregularly rounded or slightly offset, according to its position on the leaf. The whole structure flushes out pink, soon becoming bronze-green, then bright green and lustrous on the upper side. Thin grey tomentum on the underside gradually wears off as the leaves mature, but the colour remains paler yellow-green. The autumn foliage colour is bright clear yellow, the leaflets and the rachis then falling separately.

There are panicles of greenish-white fragrant flowers but these are seldom seen in cold northern areas. There are separate male and female trees, but occasionally male flowers occur on the lower branches of female trees. The seeds are in 15-25cm brownish, leathery, hanging pods which remain unopened on the tree through the winter. The individual bean-like seeds are separated and insulated by a thick layer of sweet-tasting pulp.

The bark becomes rough and fissured with age and branches develop a gaunt outline. The genus name is from the Greek for 'naked branch'; the tree spends a long time in the leafless winter state.

The wood is relatively soft but heavy and durable, especially in contact with wet ground. It is light brown with a red cast on good lengths, with a thin creamy-white layer of sapwood. It prefers moist, fertile, sheltered sites, in sun or shade. The natural habitat of this tree is fairly wet alluvial 'bottom-lands' in a vast area of central North America, from southern Ontario to New York and west to Oklahoma and Minnesota.

The cultivar '**Variegata**' has leaflets blotched with pale yellow and white. It is a rather sickly plant which has a diseased look about it.

Growth: 3-9-17 (30 in native region). Hardiness: 40%. Choice: 1 (requires space), 3. Wood: 1, 2, 3, 5.

'Variegata'

fruit

Kentucky Coffee Tree

young tree

fruit

Euodia

fruit detail

var. *lavallei*

Japanese Cork Tree
underside

fruit

Amur Cork Tree

underside

Euodia
bark

autumn

Euodia

590

ORANGE FAMILY · Rutaceae

Euodia *Tetradium daniellii*

Originally introduced as two distinct species under the genus name Euodia (sometimes spelt Evodia) this small deciduous tree has a natural range across northern China and Korea. The Chinese form, introduced as *Euodia hupehensis*, is a larger tree up to 20m tall. The 3-4mm scented flowers are whitish in corymbs 10-16cm across. Euodia is the Greek word for 'pleasant odour'. The opposite pinnate leaves have 7-11 ovate pointed leaflets which are 5-10cm long. They are distinctly pale green on the underside. The fruits consist of small 8mm red pods each with a short curved point, containing 1-2 shiny black seeds.

The identity and introduction of this species has been complicated by taxonomic uncertainty. *Euodia daniellii* arrived in the west in 1905 probably from Korea, while *Euodia hupehensis* came from China in 1907. Whatever its origin, this is a good ornamental plant in cultivation with sweetly scented flowers and yellow autumn foliage accompanied by red fruits.
Growth: 3-8-20. Hardiness: 50%. Choice: 1.

Amur Cork Tree *Phellodendron amurense*

One of about ten species, this 14m tree comes from Japan, Korea, parts of China and eastern Asia. It takes its name from the Amur region where it is a mixed deciduous woodland species in mountainous areas. The bark is corky and is harvested locally. In cultivation it makes a highly decorative and moderately hardy specimen tree. The soft lattice of ridged pale buff to brown bark is of special interest after trees exceed 25 years of age. The outline of the branches is neatly rounded, usually on a straight stem. Pinnate deciduous leaves, up to 40cm long each have 7-11 leaflets and resemble ash (*Fraxinus*). They colour to pale yellow in the autumn, contrasting beautifully in good years with clusters of black 1cm fruits on female trees.

The Amur Cork Tree was introduced to the west in 1856. The variety **lavallei**, introduced six years later from Japan as a separate species, is a smaller tree seldom over 10m tall. The bark is slightly less corky and the leaves are dull yellowish-green.
Growth: 3-8-14. Hardiness: 70-80%. Choice: 1, 3. Wood: 4 (cork).

Japanese Cork Tree *Phellodendron japonicum*

Closely related to the Amur Cork Tree this 10m tall individual is from central Japan. The dark brown bark is less thick, but still relatively soft and warm to the touch. The 6-10cm leaflets are felted grey-green on the underside. It was introduced in 1863.
Growth: 2-6-10. Hardiness: 60-70%. Choice: 1, 3. Wood: 4 (cork).

Amur Cork Tree

Tree of Heaven

underside

Downy Tree of Heaven

fruits

Tree of Heaven

TREE OF HEAVEN FAMILY • Simaroubaceae

Tree of Heaven *Ailanthus altissima*

This fast-growing tree originated in northern China, where it had been extensively cultivated and widely distributed long before it was discovered by western plant hunters. Its exact natural distribution remains in some doubt. Father d'Incarville, a Jesuit missionary, introduced it to the Chelsea Physic Garden in London from Nanking in 1751. The name Tree of Heaven is a Chinese reference to the speed this tree grows up towards the sky: native and cultivated specimens rapidly exceed 30m in height. The bark is smooth and grey, similar to common ash. The 30-60cm leaves, which emerge pink, are pinnate with up to 20 pairs of leaflets. The bottom pair each have an oil gland or nectary which, on a hot day, gives off a strong and rather unpleasant smell. The greenish-white male flowers, on separate trees, also have a disagreeable smell which can cause sore throats and nausea. The fruits consist of keys in clusters each with a 1cm seed fixed in the centre. As they ripen they turn from green to bright red and finally brown. During the two week 'red stage' whole trees take on a distinctive and surprising rosy appearance.

This species is tolerant of poor air quality and indifferent to dry soils, but it suffers from frost and cold wind exposure. Unfortunately it produces new shoots from root suckers as much as 30m from the original plant on occasions. Felled trees regenerate themselves from suckers with renewed vigour and refuse to go away. In parts of North America it has become an invasive weed.

Growth: 5-22-30. Hardiness: 60%. Choice: 4. Wood: 1, 4.

Downy Tree of Heaven
Ailanthus vilmoriniana

Otherwise essentially the same as the ordinary Tree of Heaven, this species has bristly hairs on the shoots and downy leaves. It was introduced from west China by Père Farges in 1897.

Growth: 3-12-20. Hardiness: 40-50%. Choice: 4. Wood: 1, 4.

Picrasma *Picrasma quassioides*

Closely related to *Ailanthus*, this small, 10-12m, rounded, often multi-stemmed tree, produces brilliant orange and red autumn foliage colour. It is native over a wide area of the Himalayas, east to Taiwan and south into India. The 20-30cm leaves are pinnate with 7-13 pointed oval leaflets. The flowers in open rather lax 15cm axillary corymbs are yellow and occur in late spring. They produce ovoid berries which ripen through orange to red. The bark is dark brown to almost black and rough. It is bitter to taste (not recommended), the scientific name is a reference to this, from 'Picris', which was Theophrastus' name for a bitter herb.

Growth: 2-6-10. Hardiness: 40-50%. Choice: 1.

Picrasma

fruit

Picrasma
leaf variation

Varnish Tree

fruit

Potanin's Sumach

Varnish Tree   Stag's-horn Sumach   Potanin's Sumach

SMOKE BUSH FAMILY · Anacardiaceae

Varnish Tree *Rhus verniciflua*

Traditional Chinese lacquer is obtained from the sap of this substantial 15-22m tree. Almost everything about the plant is poisonous and some people are so allergic to it that simply brushing against it will cause a reaction. Growth in cultivation is vigorous, a conical outline quickly developing, then trees become rounded with age. The branches are open and sparse, rapidly spreading upwards and outwards. The 30-60cm pinnate leaves have 9-19 leaflets each with a slender point and a short stalk. The upper surfaces are glossy green and the undersides are downy. In the autumn good red foliage colour may be expected. Drooping panicles of yellowish-white flowers appear in mid-summer, followed by flattened 8mm pale yellowish-brown berries. The natural range of this species includes China, Japan and the Himalayas. It was cultivated in the west some time before 1862.
Growth: 4-9-20. Hardiness: 50%. Choice: 1, 3, 4. Wood: 4.

Potanin's Sumach *Rhus potaninii*

This Chinese tree was discovered by Augustine Henry in 1888 and introduced to the west by Ernest Wilson in 1902. It also has poisonous sap which can cause an allergic reaction in some people. Trees 20m tall are known but in cultivation it is a much smaller suckering plant, often with multiple main stems and untidy spreading branches. The autumn foliage colours are brilliant pink and red. The pinnate leaf stalks completely cover the following year's buds. The flowers are in 10-18cm terminal panicles. Each one has cream petals and deep purple stamens. They produce clusters of downy red berries.
Growth: 3-7-16. Hardiness: 50%. Choice: 1, 4.

Stag's-horn Sumach *Rhus typhina*

This familiar garden shrub or small suckering tree has thick densely hairy shoots reminiscent of a deer antler in velvet. It will not be confined in one place for long and soon spreads over a wide area by producing suckers from its surface roots. The autumn foliage colour is quite outstanding. Upright female crimson flowers, on separate trees, develop into distinctive 'drum stick' fruits which are retained on the bare branches well into the winter. First cultivated in 1629, this is an east North American plant. '**Dissecta**' is a cut-leaved female form with fern-like leaves, which colour brilliantly in the autumn.
Growth: 3-4-4. Hardiness: 70%. Choice: 1, 4.

Smooth Sumach *Rhus glabra*

Another wide spreading shrubby tree, introduced from North America a little earlier in 1620, Smooth Sumach is like the previous species except for its hairless stems. The autumn foliage colours are equally as good.
Growth: 3-4-4. Hardiness: 90%. Choice: 1, 4.

Stag's-horn Sumach   **'Dissecta'**   **Smooth Sumach**

Common Box

fruit
♂ flowers
immature fruit

Common Box

seeds

Balearic Box

'Latifolia Bullata' 'Aureovariegata'

'Marginata'

Himalayan Box

Dwarf Box

'Pyramidalis'

var. *sinica*

'Rotundifolia'

Common Box

'Rosmarinifolia'

'Angustifolia'

BOX FAMILY · Buxaceae

Common Box *Buxus sempervirens*

Most wild box trees are multi-stemmed and less than 8m tall. They are native across a huge range in temperate Europe and Asia, usually growing under large deciduous trees to which they remain subordinate. This tough evergreen plant is extremely shade tolerant; it also re-grows from broken stumps and once established is almost indestructible.

There are several distinct groups of Common Box cultivars, 'Latifolia' covers all the broad-leaved individuals. '**Latifolia Bullata**' has broad but blistered leaves which give it a diseased look. '**Latifolia Maculata**' substitutes blisters with dull yellow blotches. However, the new growth in spring, or after clipping, is flecked with bright yellow. '**Aureovariegata**' has similar-coloured foliage but it is a more vigorous bush and the leaves are smaller. Even more vigorous is '**Marginata**' which combines blisters with flecks and margins of pale yellow. Closer in appearance to common box with 2-3cm leaves is '**Gold Tip**'. It has bright yellow edges towards the ends of some young leaves. This kind of variation is often seen on isolated shoots of wild box trees.

There is a complete range of leaf shapes in box cultivars. '**Rotundifolia**' is virtually round, '**Angustifolia**' is narrow, and '**Rosmarinifolia**' is almost linear. In addition to bushy plants there are box trees selected for their particular shape. '**Pyramidalis**' is naturally upright even when it is not clipped and '**Pendula**' is a good evergreen weeping tree although without training it becomes prostrate.
Growth: 2-6-8. Hardiness: 50-60%. Choice: 2. Wood: 1.

Balearic Box *Buxus balearica*

Introduced before 1780 this tender tree, up to 10m in height, has relatively large 5cm long oval leathery leaves. As well as the Balearic Islands it occurs in southern Spain and North Africa.
Growth: 3-8-10. Hardiness: 20-30%. Choice: 2. Wood: 1.

Himalayan Box *Buxus wallichiana*

This fairly tender small tree has tough evergreen 6cm long lanceolate leaves. It was introduced to Europe from its native India and the north-west Himalayas in 1850 but remains uncommon in cultivation.
Growth: 2-2-3. Hardiness: 30%. Choice: 2.

Dwarf Box *Buxus microphylla*

Most small Box plants encountered in gardens today are cultivars of this Japanese species. They were introduced to Europe in 1860 particularly for edging parterre boarders. The evergreen elliptic leaves are less than 1.5cm long. The Chinese variety **sinica** introduced in 1900 has rounded leaves.
Growth: 1-1-1. Hardiness: 50-60%. Choice: 1, 2.

'Gold Tip'

'Latifolia Maculata'

'Pendula'

old bark

Common Holly

leaf from top of tree

'Aurea Marginata'

'Argentea Marginata'

'Recurva'

'Golden Milkboy'

'Handsworth New Silver'

'Ferox'

'Ferox Argentea'

'Ovata'

'Amber'

'Flavescens'

Common Holly

HOLLY FAMILY · Aquifoliaceae

Common Holly *Ilex aquifolium*

This familiar tree has a smooth silver-grey stem and dense shade-tolerant prickly foliage. It grows naturally in mixed woodlands throughout Europe, western Asia and North Africa, often as an under storey to large deciduous trees such as oak. Lower leaves are sharply spined but many of the upper leaves are entire except for a spine tip.

There are a large number of cultivars of Common Holly in the nursery trade. Most of the variegated forms have green glossy leaves with some form of yellow margin. '**Aurea Marginata**', '**Argentea Marginata**' and '**Handsworth New Silver**' are good examples. They are all free-fruiting female plants. The yellow variegation is more random on '**Golden Milkboy**', a male clone which tends to revert to green, and '**Flavescens**', the Moonlight Holly, which is especially pale-coloured in mid-winter.

Variable leaf forms are common in cultivated hollies. '**Recurva**' has backward-facing spines on 3-4cm leaves. It is a slow-growing male plant with purple shoots. Although small and bushy it is exceedingly spiteful. The Hedgehog Holly, '**Ferox**', is quite unmistakable. The small deformed leaves have concentrations of spikes emanating from the margin and across the upper surface. There is a pale yellow variegated form of the same thing, '**Ferox Argentea**', which has been cultivated since 1662. They are both male plants up to 5m tall.

The male cultivar '**Ovata**' has almost oval leaves with evenly spaced, short spines round the margins. It grows slowly and seldom exceeds 2m in height. The shoots are deep purple for the first years.

Alternative berry colours in holly include yellow and orange. Before 1955 the Hillier Nurseries produced '**Amber**', which has large bronze-yellow berries. Pure yellow fruits, often in profusion, appear in early winter on '**Bacciflava**', the Yellow-fruited Holly. It is a large tree exactly like the species (except when in fruit) with sharply spined glossy green leaves. This cultivar is still occasionally listed as 'Fructu Luteo'.

There are two thick-leaved variegated hollies. '**Ovata Aurea**' is a strong plant with particularly thick 5-7cm short-spined leaves. It is a male clone so no berries are produced, but the young shoots are deep purple. '**Crispa Aurea Picta**' is another male cultivar with hard thick twisted leaves, mostly without spines. Unlike 'Ovata Aurea' its yellow variegation is towards the centre of each leaf.

Growth: 2-8-15 (species): (cvs variable). Hardiness: 50%. Choice: 1, 2. Wood: 1 (species).

Common Holly bark

'Bacciflava'

'Ovata Aurea'

'Crispa Aurea Picta'

Ilex aquifolium cultivars

'J.C. van Tol' 'Crassifolia' 'Aurifodina' 'Nellie R. Stevens'

'Laurifolia' 'Pyramidalis' 'Scotica' 'Angustifolia'

'Alaska' 'Lichtenthalii'

Ilex × *altaclerensis* cultivars

'Golden King' 'Camelliifolia' 'Hodginsii'

HOLLIES

Ilex aquifolium cultivars

Most cultivars of Common Holly have the distinctive evergreen holly leaf shape. Some look very similar to one another and are difficult to identify. It is helpful to look for berries in early winter or check the sex of the spring flowers. Hollies are mostly dioecious, which means that they are separate male or female trees, and the sex of vegetatively produced clones is defined.

One of the few exceptions to this rule is '**J.C. van Tol**', which is self-pollinating. Berries do not indicate a female clone here. They are produced in profusion with glossy green, usually spineless leaves. Berries, however, are never seen on '**Crassifolia**', Saw-leaved Holly, which is male. It is an early cultivar produced in the eighteenth century. The narrow leaves are hard, thick and narrow with vicious spines. The shoots are deep purple on the sunny side and green below. The cultivar '**Aurifodina**', formerly called 'Goldmine', has green shoots and golden variegated leaves. It is female and produces bright scarlet berries. '**Nellie R. Stevens**' is a hybrid cultivar between Common Holly and *Ilex cornuta*. It is a female American plant with leathery three-spined shining leaves and large numbers of orange berries. '**Laurifolia**' is a male clone planted for its glossy deep green spineless leaves and bright purple shoots. An upright selection of ordinary Common Holly is '**Pyramidalis**'. It is female and bears a heavy crop of scarlet berries most years. '**Scotica**' is a fairly large bush around 8m tall. It has small twisted leaves with only occasional irregular spines. Although it is female it bears fruit only sparingly. A more pyramidal bush is '**Angustifolia**'. Growth is slow but the foliage is distinctive. Narrow hard glossy leaves with up to 17 sharp spines accompany purple shoots and red berries. Similar narrow leaves occur on the female cultivar '**Lichtenthalii**' but this is a semi-prostrate bush. '**Alaska**' has shorter leaves and makes a compact hardy plant with numerous red berries.

Growth: variable. Hardiness: 50%. Choice: 1.

Highclere Holly *Ilex × altaclerensis* cultivars

Highclere Holly originated in England as a hybrid between the Madeira Holly *Ilex perado*, including the Canary Islands variety *platyphylla*, and Common Holly. A large number of cultivars have been selected from these crosses. '**Golden King**' is one of the best variegated forms. It arose as a sport on 'Hendersonii' in Edinburgh in 1884. For reasons only known to the taxonomists it is actually a female clone. '**Camelliifolia**' is a large tree produced in 1865 with glossy 'Camellia' leaves and red berries. '**Hendersonii**' is a big broad-leaved female specimen tree cultivated in Ireland in the early 1800s. '**Hodginsii**' is similar in size and shape but it is male, although a female form of it exists. By contrast '**Wilsonii**' is a compact rounded bush with large scarlet berries. The broad glossy leaves, with or without spines, are typical of Highclere Holly. It was raised in the 1890s and has always been popular. See also pp. 605, 607.

Growth: variable. Hardiness: 50%. Choice: 1.

Ilex × altaclerensis cultivars

'Hodginsii'

'Wilsonii'

'Hendersonii'

underside 'Crispa' 'Donningtonensis' 'Beetii'

'Heterophylla' 'Foxii' 'Latispina'

'Hastata' 'Ferox Aurea' 'Gold Flash'

'Ciliata Major'

HOLLIES

Ilex aquifolium cultivars (continued)

There are many small-leaved and contorted hollies which make excellent foliage plants and hedging. One of the less attractive, though, is '**Crispa**' with screwed-up and twisted leathery leaves. It is a male sport of 'Scotica' (p. 601). The leaves of '**Donningtonensis**' are less contorted but viciously spined. They are flushed with purple when young. The new growth is also dark purplish-black, becoming green as it matures. '**Beetii**' has almost round but very sharply spined leaves. These three are all male clones so no fruits are produced on them.

'**Heterophylla**' now refers to several different plants, all with variable spined and un-spined leaves. The original cultivar 'Heterophylla' is now called 'Pyramidalis'. '**Foxii**' is a narrow-leaved clone with numerous sharp points. The young shoots are bright purple. Two cultivars '**Hastata**' and '**Latispina**' are closely related or may be forms of the same thing. Both have very sharply spined leaves but the spines are often few and far between or limited to the basal half of the leaf. 'Hastata' is usually male.

A rare but unique cultivar is '**Ciliata Major**' which has smallish leaves with spines all in one plane and inclined forward. It is a female clone, producing scarlet berries. The young stems are purple and the whole bush is neat and compact.

Growth: variable. Hardiness: 50%. Choice: 1.

Weeping Holly *Ilex aquifolium* 'Pendula'

Although there are several forms of weeping Common Holly the original cultivar is a female clone. It forms a small 2-4m rounded bush with long trailing shoots which bend outwards and down to the ground. On the lower shoots the leaves turn 180° to face up to the light. Berries are produced each year, but sparingly, along the shoot. The spined leaves are very dark glossy green. The variegated form, Perry's Silver Weeping Holly, '**Argentea Marginata Pendula**', is also female and fruits more freely. It is an extremely popular shrub in cultivation but is less popular with florists because the leaves are mostly twisted round to face backwards.

The Golden Hedgehog Holly '**Ferox Aurea**' is a deeper yellow colour than the silver form (p. 599). As it is a male clone no berries are ever produced.

'**Gold Flash**' has its yellow variation in the centre of the leaf. It is reminiscent of variegated Elaeagnus, having oblong entire leaves.

Growth: 3-4-4. Hardiness: 60%. Choice: 1.

Weeping Holly   **'Argentea Marginata Pendula'**   **'Donningtonensis'**

'Nigrescens'

'Atkinsonii'

Ilex cornuta

'Belgica Aurea'

'W.J. Bean' underside

Ilex × *beanii*

Ilex ciliospinosa

Ilex 'Lydia Morris'

'Shiro-Fukurin'

Japanese Holly

Ilex × *altaclerensis* cultivars (continued from p. 601)

The precise origin of the cultivar '**Nigrescens**' is known, it is one of the Highclere hollies bred from *Ilex perado* var. *platyphylla*, the Canary Island Holly. It is a large tree around 10m tall with strong purple shoots and broad glossy leaves. Most are entire or have a limited number of sharp teeth. This is a male clone but it is no longer in cultivation. Another male clone '**Atkinsonii**' is similar except that it has green shoots.

There are also a few variegated Highclere hollies. '**Belgica Aurea**' is one of the best; furthermore it is female and produces scarlet berries. The leaves, each one up to 10cm long, are green and grey with a bright yellow margin. The origin of the cultivar '**W. J. Bean**' is uncertain. It can easily be mistaken for a Common Holly, a compact bush with spiny leaves and red fruits. Finally '**Mundyi**' is a vigorous green-stemmed cultivar, which has typical large glossy green leaves. They are evenly toothed with short sharp spines. See also p. 607.

Growth: variable. Hardiness: 50%. Choice: 1.

Ilex cornuta

From Eastern China, this shrubby plant has extraordinary stiff leaves with only 3-5 spines. The 8-10mm fruit is bright red, in clusters. First introduced to Europe in 1846.

Growth: 1-2-3. Hardiness: 40%. Choice: 1.

Ilex × *beanii*

This early twentieth-century hybrid between Common Holly and Himalayan Holly, *Ilex dipyrena*, tends to be variable. It makes a broad shrub 5-7m tall with fairly uninteresting foliage. The teeth are small or absent.

Growth: 2-5-6. Hardiness: 40-50%. Choice: 1.

Ilex ciliospinosa

Also related to *Ilex dipyrena*, this 6m shrub has yellowish-backed elliptic-ovate weakly spined leaves and red ovate berries. It was introduced in 1908 from west China but has never been popular in cultivation.

Growth: 2-5-6. Hardiness: 40%. Choice: 4.

Ilex 'Lydia Morris'

This compact upright shrub, around 2m tall, is unlike conventional holly. It is a hybrid between *Ilex cornuta* 'Burfordii' and *Ilex pernyi*. The small deep glossy green leaves are squarish with a pointed tip and spines in each of the other four corners. It is female and sparingly produces large bright red fruits. In general appearance it resembles *Ilex cornuta*.

Growth: 2-2-2. Hardiness: 40%. Choice: 1.

Japanese Holly *Ilex crenata*

Seldom over 5m in height, this small-leaved shrub has 5mm glossy black berries. On first sight it is not obviously a holly at all, and the alternative name for it, 'Box-leaved Holly', reflects this. It makes a good formal evergreen hedge and was first cultivated in Europe in 1864. The native range is limited to Sakhalin Island, Japan and Korea. Of the many cultivated forms of Japanese Holly '**Shiro-Fukurin**' is one of the best, with dark stems and gold-edged foliage.

Growth: 2-4-5. Hardiness: 40-50%. Choice: 1.

'Nigrescens'

'Mundyi'

'Lawsoniana' 'Howick' 'Balearica' 'Purple Shaft'

Tarajo *Ilex × koehneana* *Ilex kingiana* Himalayan Holly (leaf variation)

var. *veitchii* 'Indian Chief' 'Drace' Himalayan Holly

Perny's Holly

Ilex × *altaclerensis* cultivars (continued)

Two popular vigorous female variegated clones are '**Lawsoniana**' and '**Howick**'. They are both sports of the old Irish cultivar 'Hendersonii' (p. 601). The green cultivar '**Balearica**' is a medium-sized erect tree. Red berries are produced, often in great quantities. '**Purple Shaft**' is a vigorous sport of 'Balearica'. It has scarlet berries and deep purple shoots.

Growth: variable. Hardiness: 50%. Choice: 1.

Tarajo *Ilex latifolia*

Native Chinese and Japanese trees are large but in cultivation they seldom exceed 6m in height. The big leaves are ovate-oblong and up to 18cm long. The margins are evenly toothed with short spines. The berries are orange. ***Ilex* × *koehneana*** is a red berried hybrid between this species and Common Holly. It was introduced some time before 1890.

Growth: 2-5-6 (20 in native region). Hardiness: 30%. Choice: 1.

Ilex kingiana

The big leaves of this species may be over 22cm long with evenly spaced saw teeth like Chestnut (*Castanea*). The berries in large groups along the shoot are bright red and up to 1cm across. The whole plant is around 5m tall.

Growth: 2-4-5. Hardiness: 40%. Choice: 1.

Himalayan Holly *Ilex dipyrena*

This substantial tree is 15m tall in its native range which extends from the eastern Himalayas to western China. The 6-11cm elliptic leaves are finely toothed or more or less entire and the fruits are red.

Growth: 3-9-15. Hardiness: 30-40%. Choice: 1. Wood: 5.

Perny's Holly *Ilex pernyi*

The small 1-3.5cm leaves on this Chinese species are distinctive. They are abruptly angular with 3-7 vicious points. The variety ***veitchii***, also from western China, has larger even more spiny leaves. It arrived in the west in 1912 four years after the species. There are two superb female garden hybrids of Perny's Holly crossed with *Ilex cornuta*: '**Drace**' is a clone raised in America with angular glossy leaves and '**Indian Chief**' has similar-looking leaves on long shoots punctuated with small clusters of red berries.

Growth: 3-8-10. Hardiness: 40-50%. Choice: 1.

American Holly *Ilex opaca*

Native from Massachusetts to Florida and Texas, this 15m tall tree looks very similar to Common Holly in Europe. The leaves are less glossy but the clusters of berries are brilliant red in winter. Forma **xanthocarpa** has yellow berries.

Growth: 3-10-15. Hardiness: 50%. Choice: 1.

Canary Island Holly

Ilex perado subsp. *platyphylla*

This tender plant was introduced in 1842. The large leaves may be up to 15cm long. It is one parent of the many cultivars of *Ilex* × *alterclerensis*.

Growth: 2-4-5. Hardiness: 20-30%. Choice: 1.

Ilex pedunculosa

Charles Sprague Sargent introduced this large acid-loving shrub from south-east Asia in 1893. The wavy-edged leaves are elliptic and entire. The scarlet berries occur on long slender stalks (peduncles).

Growth: 2-8-10. Hardiness: 40-50%. Choice: 4.

American Holly forma ***xanthocarpa*** **Canary Island Holly** *Ilex pedunculosa*

fruit

Norway Maple

flower detail

autumn

Norway Maple

MAPLE FAMILY · Aceraceae

Norway Maple *Acer platanoides*

This hardy tree has a broad natural range from southern Scandinavia across Europe to the Caucasus. In its wild state it is a woodland species but recently it has become much more familiar in parks and large gardens. Specimens often exceed 25m in height with a crown spread of over 20m. Huge stems may be 1.3m in diameter but they are usually short and soon divide into massive upswept branches. The bark is beautifully patterned with vertical and interlaced ridges. In spring, before the leaves appear, most trees are completely covered in corymbs of golden yellow flowers. On some the flowers are tinted crimson. The leaves are similar in shape to those of the Plane (p. 449) but not so leathery and a little smaller, very like the stylized Maple leaf on the Canadian flag. They are palmate and about 15cm long, and wide, with a small number of prominent teeth. The 10-20cm petioles are pink and green and produce milky sap if cut or broken. In the autumn the foliage colour is yellow, occasionally finishing with orange. The effect is always spectacular because of the sheer size of the tree.
Growth: 4-12-25. Hardiness: 80%. Choice: 1 (requires space). Wood: 1, 4, 5.

Acer platanoides 'Cleveland'

Produced in Cleveland, Ohio, before 1948, this 10-12m tree has an oval outline and up-swept branches, which makes it a good street tree in urban areas. The leaves are similar to the species but with a hint of red on them as they emerge. A still more improved American shade tree clone with a narrower habit and more compact branches is called 'Cleveland Two'.
Growth: 3-9-12. Hardiness: 70%. Choice: 1.

Acer platanoides 'Columnare'

This 1878 French selection has fastigiate branches but seldom confines itself to producing a single stem. For this reason it is usually grafted on to a Norway Maple standard. The steep branch angle is a disadvantage in urban situations because the weak forks are inclined to eventually break: a serious problem on a tree up to 20m tall. The deep green foliage is similar to that of the species.
Growth: 3-11-20. Hardiness: 70%. Choice: 4.

***Acer platanoides* 'Cleveland'**   young tree in autumn   ***Acer platanoides* 'Columnare'**   old tree

Acer platanoides cultivars

'Drummondii'

'Laciniatum'

'Cucullatum'

'Dissectum'

'Walderseei'

'Oekonomierat Stoll'

'Globosum'
young tree

'Globosum'

610

Acer platanoides cultivars

There are around 90 named cultivars of Norway Maple, which fall into three broad categories of leaf colour, leaf shape and tree outline.

Variegated leaves occasionally occur spontaneously as sports or seedlings of this species. '**Drummondii**' is probably the best known cultivar. It grows to over 12m in height with a broad head of upswept branches. The Drummond Nursery at Stirling in Scotland produced it but it was named in Germany in 1910. '**Heterophyllum Aureo-variegatum**' an old, 1880, French cultivar has similarly-coloured leaves but they are small and deformed. More subtle variegation is to be found on the 1904 German cultivar '**Walderseei**', which has tiny white and cream dots on the leaves.

Cut-leaved Norway Maples are common in cultivation. '**Laciniatum**' (see also p. 615) has deeply cut lobes almost to the petiole and greatly exaggerated teeth. '**Dissectum**', an 1834 German clone, takes the cut-leaf effect to its limits. Each lobe has a short stalk of its own reminiscent of a compound leaf.

Distorted leaves give some Norway Maple cultivars special curiosity value. '**Cucullatum**' is an 1866 French clone with crumpled leaves often bunched tightly together. Although trees grow to over 10m in height they always have a diseased look about them. Even more deformed and generally unhealthy in appearance is '**Dilaceratum**', an 1885 German clone. The small, lacerated and screwed up leaves are often blotched with yellowish-green – most unattractive.

'**Globosum**' has normal foliage but the tree is stunted. When grafted on to a Norway Maple standard it makes quite a good 'toy' specimen tree for a site where space is severely restricted. It was produced and first described in Belgium in 1873.

Norway Maple comes in just about every shade of purple, with foliage ranging from brownish-green as in the 1888 German clone '**Oekonomierat Stoll**', to virtually black, as in 'Faassen's Black' (not illustrated).

An outstanding big tree in this group is the old 1869 German clone '**Schwedleri**', a towering 20-25m mass of bright brownish-purple foliage when seen against strong sunlight. '**Goldsworth Purple**' is another fairly large cultivar produced in England in 1947. It has been less successful in the horticultural trade than the French 1937 clone '**Crimson King**' produced in the USA from 1948. This 12-15m tree and the very similar 'Royal Red' have cornered the market in deep purple-leaved Norway Maples for city gardens world-wide.

Growth: variable. Hardiness: 70%. Choice: 1.

Acer platanoides cultivars

'Superform'

'Meyering'

'Deborah'

'Deborah'
spring

'Erectum'

'Crimson Sentry'

'Olmsted'

Acer platanoides cultivars (continued)

'**Superform**' was selected in Oregon, and named in 1968. The horticultural objective was to ensure that a near-perfect tree could always be used where perfection was demanded, notably in American city parks and private gardens. By providing a clonal plant with known performance, uniformity could be assured and unacceptable variation avoided. This is a straight, fast-growing specimen 20-22m tall with tough hard leaves. They emerge early in the spring.

The 1958 Dutch clone '**Meyering**' is a 10-15m tree with leaves that flush out bronze-purple and turn to green in the summer. The autumn foliage colour is orange to deep red. A more upright form of the same kind of tree is '**Deborah**', a Canadian cultivar named in 1975. It arose as a seedling of 'Schwedleri' and reaches 15m in height.

'**Erectum**' is another 15m tall tree with short branches giving an neat erect outline. It was discovered in a New York cemetery and named in 1931. The leaves are light yellowish-green but similar in size and shape to the species.

Another clone selected as a street tree in America is '**Olmsted**'. It was discovered in Rochester, New York, and named in 1955, although Olmsted is in Ohio. The outline of the branches is fairly narrow and growth is fast up to a height of about 18m. An ideal tree where quick cover is required and for screening in car parks and shopping centres. The short branches are an advantage in these situations and on streets. The foliage is exactly like that of the species.

'**Crimson Sentry**' is a distinctive cultivar which arose as a stunted branch sport on 'Crimson King'. Although the deep purple colour is retained the leaves are smaller and the shoots are short and compact. Trees seldom exceed 9m in height with a fairly narrow outline. This plant arose in Fairview, Oregon, in 1974 and has been patented in the United States.

Growth: variable. Hardiness: 70%. Choice: 1, 2.

Acer campestre '**Elsrijk**'

Selected in 1953 in Holland from an existing group of established city trees, this cultivar makes an ideal street and park specimen. Seldom over 10m in height, it has short twiggy branches and dense green foliage. The 4-6cm leaves turn to warm golden yellow in the autumn. See also p. 625.

Growth: 3-6-10. Hardiness: 70%. Choice: 2.

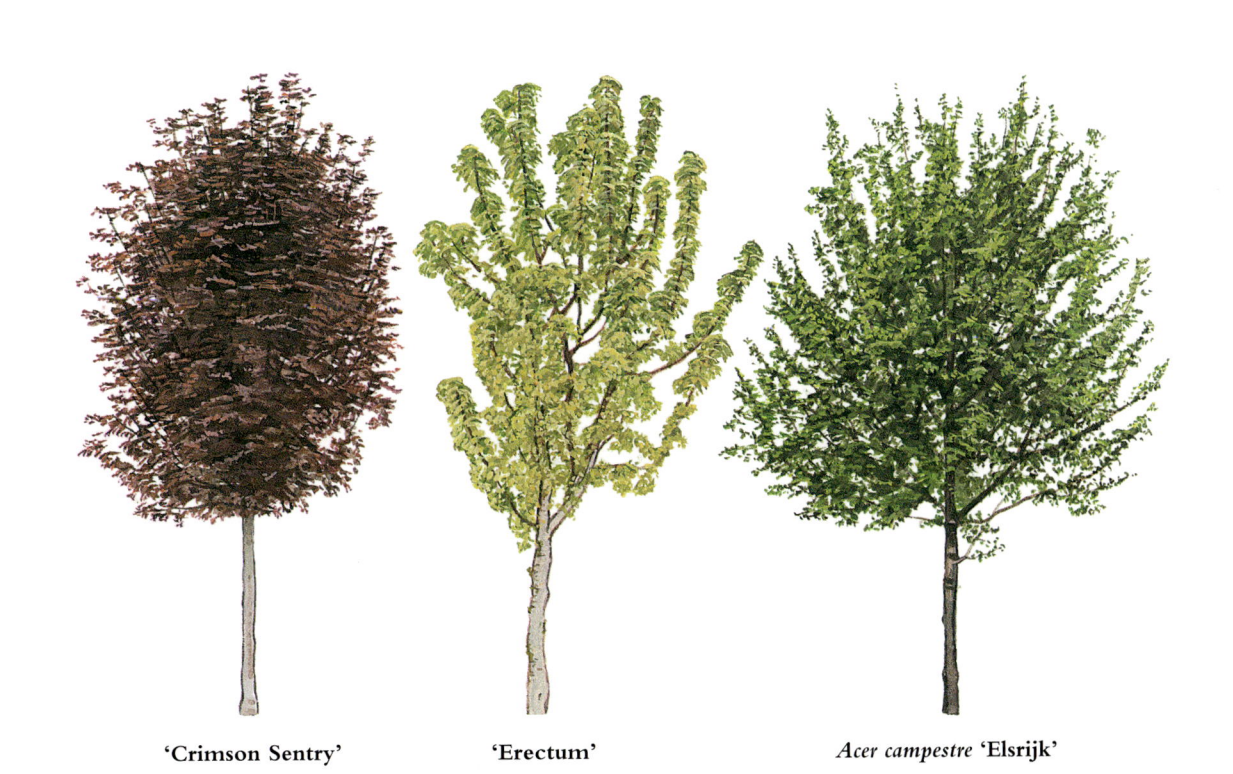

'**Crimson Sentry**'   '**Erectum**'   *Acer campestre* '**Elsrijk**'

Acer × *dieckii*

'Maculatum'

'Pyramidale Nanum'

'Laciniatum'

'Pyramidale Nanum'

Acer × dieckii

Although the parentage of this hybrid is uncertain it has a great deal in common with Norway Maple. Some authorities describe it simply as a form of *Acer platanoides*. It was named in honour of Georg Dieck, the German botanist and explorer, in 1893. Sometimes this is a large tree 25m tall. The leaves are variable, from 12 to 25cm across, with 3-7 triangular lobes. In the autumn a good display of butter-yellow foliage colour can be relied upon.

Growth: 4-12-25. Hardiness: 60%. Choice: 1, 2.

Acer platanoides cultivars (continued)

'**Laciniatum**' (see also p. 611) has deeply cut leaves on a tree around 12m tall. The original clone was named in 1683 but it is probably no longer in cultivation having been obscured by more recent cut-leaved seedlings. The 1942 American name 'Eagle Claw' is a selection from this group, which is commonly used to describe all cut-leaved Norway Maples.

The British cultivar '**Maculatum**' was described in 1881. It is slower-growing than the species and has variegated foliage. The deep green leaves are finely spotted with creamy-yellow. This clone is similar to 'Walderseei' (p. 611), but there are fewer teeth on the leaves and they are shorter.

'**Pyramidale Nanum**' is a very slow-growing plant first described in 1877 in Belgium. It grows to around 5m in height in the first 20 years and then remains more or less that size. Occasional long shoots will be produced, pointing in any direction, and then in subsequent years the tree will build up a mass of short twigs around them. The leaves, on relatively long petioles, are like the species but one third of the normal size.

An important large dark-leaved form of Norway Maple is '**Reitenbachii**', a Russian cultivar named in Germany in 1874 and introduced into cultivation in Belgium in 1880. The young leaves emerge deep wine red and then turn dark green through the summer casting deep cool shade on hot days. Trees 20m tall are known with a broad-spreading picturesque outline.

'**Summershade**' is an American cultivar selected especially for its ability to provide shade. The large green leaves are leathery and resist strong sunlight when other trees all around begin to shrivel. Originally it was a seedling of 'Erectum' (p. 613), so it retains a tall columnar outline and grows quickly. It was named and patented in 1958 by Princeton Nurseries, New Jersey.

Growth: variable. Hardiness: 70%. Choice: 1, 2.

'Reitenbachii' underside

'Summershade'

'Reitenbachii'

fruit

Acer × dieckii

Miyabe Maple

Paperbark Maple

underside

Nikko Maple

underside

Montpelier Maple

autumn

Rough-barked Maple

Vineleaf Maple

Miyabe Maple *Acer miyabei*

The 3-5-lobed leaves on this tall Japanese tree resemble those of Norway Maple (p. 609). The species is now divided into several slightly different subspecies. There is also a smaller Chinese type with small 3-5cm wide leaves. Introduced in 1892 by Charles Sprague Sargent, director of the Arnold Arboretum, this tree remains rare in cultivation.

Growth: 3-12-24. Hardiness: 50%. Choice: 4. Wood: 1.

Paperbark Maple *Acer griseum*

Since its introduction from China by Ernest Wilson in 1901 this tree has become a great garden favourite. It remains fairly small and in a short time produces paper-thin curls of cinnamon-coloured bark on the stem and main branches. These are translucent against the light. The trifoliate grey-backed leaves colour red and orange in the autumn.

Growth: 3-7-8. Hardiness: 50%. Choice: 1.

Nikko Maple *Acer maximowiczianum*

Still known as *Acer nikoense* in many tree collections, this small rounded tree from Japan and central China has been widely planted in the west. Its trifoliate leaves are softly downy, giving brilliant but beautifully diffused autumn colours and remaining on the tree late in the year when most other trees' foliage has blown away. Both names for this species originated in 1867 but *'nikoense'* was a confusion with an entirely different plant.

Growth: 3-10-15. Hardiness: 50%. Choice: 1.

Montpelier Maple *Acer monspessulanum*

This is another maple which has now been split into several regional subspecies which vary slightly from each other. True Montpelier Maple is from southern Europe along the Mediterranean coast, particularly of northern Italy, France and Spain. It has small 4cm three-lobed leathery leaves. In mild seasons some remain in place throughout the winter. Trees up to 12m tall occur in favourable conditions but in exposed places it generally makes only a densely-twigged shrub.

Growth: 2-7-10. Hardiness: 50%. Choice: 1.

Rough-barked Maple *Acer triflorum*

Although this small tree has trifoliate leaves the species name actually refers to the flowers, which also occur in threes. It is not in great demand and now very rare in cultivation. It closely resembles Paperbark Maple without the benefit of decorative peeling bark. It was introduced from northern China in 1923, but also grows in Korea.

Growth: 3-7-8. Hardiness: 50%. Choice: 4.

Vineleaf Maple *Acer cissifolium*

The trifoliate leaves of this maple are carried on slender petioles and are delicately toothed, often with long trailing points. In the autumn they colour well to orange and yellow. The 8-12m tree is from mountainous forests in Japan and prefers moist conditions and slightly acid soils. Originally described in 1854 as Ashleaf Maple (p. 661), it was re-classified in 1864. Male and female flowers occur on separate trees and most cultivated plants are female.

Growth: 2-6-10. Hardiness: 40-50%. Choice: 1.

Nikko Maple
young tree

Paperbark Maple
old tree

Horned Maple

forma *purpurascens*

Acer × coriaceum

Acer morifolium

Horned Maple

Shandong Maple
(distorted leaf)

Acer argutum

Acer divergens

Acer divergens

Horned Maple *Acer diabolicum*

Also known as the Devil's Maple because of the horn-shaped remnants of the female flower retained between each pair of seed-wings, this 15m tall upland forest tree is native in parts of Japan. It was described in 1864 and introduced to Britain in 1881 by Charles Maries. Most specimens grow poorly in cultivation. The form **purpurascens** described in 1914 has purplish-red young foliage.

Growth: 3-10-15. Hardiness: 50%. Choice: 3. Wood: 1, 5.

Acer × coriaceum

This natural hybrid between *Acer monspessulanum* (p. 617) and *Acer opalus* subsp. *obtusatum* (p. 627), is a small 8-10m tall tree with mostly three-lobed 5-8cm wide leaves. It holds the somewhat infamous record of having been given 16 different botanical names since 1792.

Growth: 3-8-10. Hardiness: 50%. Choice: 1. Wood: 1, 5.

Acer morifolium

This rare grey-green snake-bark maple, a 10-12m tree, is not in cultivation in Europe or North America except for a single tree in Westonbirt Arboretum and a few seedlings in Holland. The species name refers to the leaves, which resemble mulberry.

Growth: 2-7-12. Hardiness: 40-50%. Choice: 4.

Acer argutum

Charles Maries introduced this neat little tree from its native Japan in 1881. The young shoots are bright red, developing thin white 'snake-bark' markings for several years. The 6-12cm five-lobed palmate leaves are sharply toothed.

Growth: 2-5-6 (12). Hardiness: 50%. Choice: 1.

Shandong Maple *Acer truncatum*

The wide natural distribution of this species includes northern China, Manchuria, Korea and Japan. It is a small 8-10m tall forest tree with tangled branches, rough bark and dense foliage. It was described in 1833 but not brought into cultivation until 1881.

Growth: 3-8-10. Hardiness: 50%. Choice: 1.

Acer cappadocicum subsp. *divergens*

For the sake of simplicity this large shrub is still referred to as **Acer divergens.** It has glossy 3-5-lobed leaves, like some cultivars of *Acer mono* (p. 623). The subspecies name refers to the divergent wings on the pairs of seeds.

Growth: 3-5-6. Hardiness: 50%. Choice: 1.

Wilson's Maple *Acer wilsonii*

This small tree from south-west China was named after Ernest Wilson in 1908. It is thought to be a subspecies of *Acer campbellii*. The three-lobed 8-10cm leaves have rounded bases.

Growth: 2-6-7. Hardiness: 40%. Choice: 1.

Acer davidii subsp. *grosseri*

Named after the German botanist W. C. H. Grosser (1869-1924) this small green snake-barked maple was discovered in China and described in 1902. It reached Europe via the USA in 1927. Many authorities still regard it as a species, *Acer grosseri*. In cultivated maple collections it appears to hybridize freely with other snake-bark maples to produce a bewildering array of intermediate forms.

Growth: 3-9-12. Hardiness: 50%. Choice: 1.

Wilson's Maple

Acer davidii subsp. ***grosseri***

Cappadocian Maple

new leaves

'Rubrum'

'Aureum'

Cappadocian Maple
autumn

'Aureum'

MAPLES

Cappadocian Maple *Acer cappadocicum*

Milky latex sap in the foliage distinguishes this species from most other maples. Its native range extends through northern Turkey, Iran and the Caucasus. It makes a big round-headed tree up to 30m tall. Frequent root suckers always appear around the base of the stem and out to the limit of the surface root system. The 5-10cm clean-cut palmate leaves emerge reddish, turn brilliant green in summer and colour to butter-yellow in the autumn. The first plants arrived in western Europe in 1838. It is common in large gardens and parks and tolerates a wide range of soil and climatic conditions. Although fertile seed is produced most propagation is achieved by transplanting root suckers.

The cultivar '**Rubrum**' was produced by Booth's Nursery in Germany in 1842 quite soon after the introduction of the species. It differs only in the colour of the foliage which is purplish-red at first, later turning green. The autumn colour is good yellow. '**Aureum**' is another German plant. Although smaller than the species it has the same rounded spreading outline. Young foliage is purple, becoming yellow and then pale green. In the autumn it fades to light brown.

Growth: 3-17-30. Hardiness: 40-50%. Choice: 1, 4. Wood: 1.

Lobel Maple *Acer cappadocicum* subsp. *lobelii*

Named after the French botanist Matthias de L'Obel (1538-1616) this 15-20m tree has upright branches and a narrow columnar outline. It was introduced in 1865 and has been given various scientific names including the familiar and still widely used species designation *Acer lobelii*. In many respects it is similar to *Acer platanoides* (p. 609). The shoots are green with a distinct bluish bloom on them. The five-lobed wavy edged leaves are 10-15cm long and wide, glabrous except for the vein axils, and deep green. They colour to yellow and sometimes orange in the autumn but can not be relied upon to colour well. This subspecies occurs naturally high up in the mountains of southern Italy, so it is hardy in much cooler northern regions.

Growth: 3-10-20. Hardiness: 30-40%. Choice: 2. Wood: 5.

underside

Lobel Maple winter summer

Acer sterculiaceum subsp. *thomsonii*

Acer cappadocicum subsp. *sinicum*

forma *ambiguum*

Acer mono

Acer × *rotundilobum*

Acer caudatum subsp. *ukurunduense*

Velvet Maple

Acer sterculiaceum subsp. *thomsonii*

This deciduous 20m tall species from the Himalayas is confusingly divided into three indistinct subspecies. The better-known synonymous name *Acer villosum* is still used in many collections. Subspecies *thomsonii*, named in honour of Thomas Thomson, curator of Calcutta Botanic Garden, has huge leaves, up to 30cm across, and is one of the rarest maples in cultivation.

Growth: 3-10-20. Hardiness: 40%. Choice: 1.

Acer cappadocicum subsp. *sinicum*

The Chinese end of the range of Cappadocian Maple (p. 621) is represented by this subspecies. It is a large tree with dense branches and a rounded outline. The golden yellow autumn foliage colour is outstanding. Ernest Wilson introduced it in 1911 and George Forrest made later collections of provenances from different regions.

Growth: 3-10-20. Hardiness: 40-50%. Choice: 1.

Acer × *rotundilobum*

Modern specimen trees listed under this name are probably not the original named plant which is barely more than a large shrub, a hybrid between *Acer monspessulanum* (p. 617) and *Acer opalus* subsp. *obtusatum* (p. 627), produced in Muskau Arboretum in Germany. It was described by Count Fritz von Schwerin in 1894. The three-lobed leaves are rounded and around 6cm across. This is an extremely rare plant which is probably no longer available in the nursery trade.

Growth: 2-2-2. Hardiness: 50%. Choice: 4.

Acer caudatum subsp. *ukurunduense*

Ukurundu is a region in China where this rare tree comes from. It seldom exceeds 8m in height with sparse uneven branches. The leaves are soft and hairy and colour yellow in the autumn. It is often mistaken in cultivation for Mountain Maple (*Acer spicatum*).

Growth: 2-6-8. Hardiness: 50-60%. Choice: 1.

Velvet Maple *Acer velutinum*

This is a fast-growing, huge tree, rapidly exceeding 25m in height, found in the Caucasus and Iran. It is used in Russia as a park and street tree but is rare in Western Europe and America. The 15-25cm palmate leaves have velvety tomentum on them especially along the veins on the underside.

Growth: 4-18-25. Hardiness: 40-50%. Choice: 2.
Wood: 1, 5.

Acer mono forma *ambiguum*

Acer mono, the Painted Maple, from eastern Asia and Japan, is divided into several regional forms. *Ambiguum* is closely related to the species but has rougher bark. Some authorities suggest that it only exists in cultivation. The original specimens no longer survive and even the name of this form means 'doubtful'.

Growth: variable. Hardiness: 50%. Choice: 4.

Acer × *rotundilobum*

Acer cappadocicum subsp. *sinicum*

Field Maple

corky twig

twig cross section

underside

new leaves

Field Maple

autumn

624

Field Maple *Acer campestre*

This hedgerow and underwood species has a huge natural distribution throughout most of Europe, southern Scandinavia and western Asia. The best specimens may exceed 25m in height but most are under 18m. Some ancient pollards and coppice rootstocks could be over 600 years old. As a tree the outline is irregular with burrs and epicormic shoots on the stem. The dense twiggy shoots have corky bark, which is exaggerated on young saplings and on hedge regrowth a year or two after cutting. The five-lobed 7cm leaves are bright green with entire ciliate margins. In the autumn they turn to golden yellow, suffused with pale orange on some individuals. The corymbose clusters of greenish-yellow flowers are erect in spring when they first appear, becoming pendent as they develop into bunches of paired wide winged seeds. Although this tree prefers dryish stony ground it is tolerant of most soil conditions provided that acidity is not excessive. Trees will tolerate some shade when young but full light is required later on. Growth may be rapid up to 4-5m but then it usually slows down. The wood is of high quality but mostly produced in small diameters. It is largely ignored by the timber trade now in favour of other high-production maple species. The burrs produce excellent 'birds eye' maple which, before 1850, was extensively used in furniture manufacturing and for veneers. Wavy grained material from roots and compression wood was also highly sought after by craftsmen.

A golden form, '**Postelense**', originally from Poland, was described in 1896 and introduced, first in Germany, by Friedrich Lauche. It is usually a small tree with yellow young leaves which turn pale green by mid-summer. It can be grafted on to a standard stock to give it greater height.

Also from Germany, probably the Muskau Arboretum, is '**Pulverulentum**', a white and green variegated cultivar. Some leaves are just speckled, while others develop whole white lobes or broad patches. Reversion to green foliage is a problem and neglected plants are soon lost.

The Hesse Nurseries in Germany are responsible for introducing the popular upright cultivar '**Schwerinii**'. It was described by Hermann Hesse himself in 1897. The young leaves are purple and the form is good, with short side branches and a stem around 6m in height. See also p. 613 and p. 641.

Growth: 2-8-14. Hardiness: 50-60%. Choice: 1. 2, 3. Wood: 1, 5 (species).

summer

'Postelense' spring

'Pulverulentum'

'Schwerinii'

'Postelense' spring

Italian Maple

leaf variation

Cretan Maple

Amur Maple

Italian Maple
flowering in spring

Italian Maple *Acer opalus*

There are three major regional subspecies of Italian Maple, covering between them the whole of central Europe from Spain (subsp. *hispanicus*) to the Caucasus. *Acer opalus* subsp. *opalus*, the Italian Maple, occurs in Switzerland, France, Corsica, Italy and parts of North Africa. In France it can be found up to 1000m. It was described in 1768, some 16 years after it was introduced into cultivation. Most specimens are medium-sized, 10-13m rounded trees. The leaves are like small 10-12cm crinkled sycamore leaves with 3-5 lobes. The autumn colour is burnished bronze-brown often finishing with a brief flush of red. The species name is a misspelling of 'opulus', an old name for *Acer*, as used in *Viburnum opulus*, which has maple-like leaves.

Growth: 2-7-12. Hardiness: 50%. Choice: 1. Wood: 1.

Bosnian Maple *Acer opalus* subsp. *obtusatum*

Originally, in 1806, this tree was considered to be a true species. Since 1925 it has been regarded only as a subspecies. It is a multi-stemmed shrub or a tree with multiple branches. The leaves are smaller than the species usually with three lobes. The natural range extends from Hungary to the Balkans, southern Italy and North Africa. It was first cultivated as an ornamental tree in 1805.

Growth: 2-4-6. Hardiness: 50%. Choice: 1.

Cretan Maple *Acer sempervirens*

This shrubby tree, one of very few evergreen maples, has small variable 2-4cm leathery leaves, mostly with three lobes. Its natural range includes the Mediterranean Islands and coast from Crete to the Lebanon. Although challenged many times by taxonomists, the original name given to this plant by Linnaeus in 1767 still stands. It has been recorded in cultivation since 1752.

Growth: 2-5-7. Hardiness: 30-40%. Choice: 1.

Amur Maple *Acer ginnala*

This large shrub or small tree from south-east Asia should more properly be called *Acer tataricum* subsp. *ginnala*. 'Ginnala' is the common name for it in Manchuria and northern China. The 4-8cm narrow leaves have three or more lobes and a long terminal point. The brief autumn colour is bright red. Variegated leaves appear on many specimens from time to time.

Growth: 2-4-6. Hardiness: 50-60%. Choice: 1.

Bosnian Maple

new leaves

Sugar Maple

autumn

Sugar Maple

old bark

Sugar Maple
winter

'Temple's Upright'   'Newton Sentry'

Sugar Maple *Acer saccharum*

Originally from eastern and central North America, this huge 30-40m tall tree has been extensively planted in parks and large gardens since 1753. It is valued particularly for its brilliant autumn foliage colours – red, yellow, orange and scarlet. The outline is rounded with long upswept branches which bend outwards and then upwards again at the extremities. Stems are usually straight and can be almost 1m thick at the base. The hard wood, called rock maple, is prized by the furniture industry and is used for all kinds of high quality internal woodwork. 'Birds-eye' maple is also cut from burrs, and some stems have highly decorative wavy grained wood known as 'fiddleback maple'. In America the boiled sap eventually becomes maple syrup: further refinement will produce a pure kind of sugar. The palmate leaves are variable, anything between 8 and 15cm long. The lobes have long points similar to the European Norway Maple (p. 609).

Several subspecies are recognized, particularly towards the edges of the natural distribution, for example subspecies *floridanum* in the south-east. The Bigtooth Maple, subsp. *grandidentatum*, and Chalk Maple, subsp. *leucoderme*, are treated on p. 631.

Black Sugar Maple, subspecies **nigrum**, has leaves somewhat like Sycamore (p. 633) in size. It occurs in eastern and central North America but is rare in cultivation except for the cultivar named '**Temple's Upright**'. This columnar clone is an ideal city landscaping tree from Rochester, New York only described in 1954 but cultivated since 1887. The autumn foliage colour is spectacular in America but is sometimes disappointing in Europe. '**Newton Sentry**' is another upright form of Sugar Maple but it is quite unlike 'Temple's Upright'. It lacks a persistent single stem and the main branches are all fastigiate. Growth is slow and side shoots are very short. The overall effect is like a pillar of solid vegetation in summer. It may produce spectacular colour in the autumn if the season has been good. The type specimen of it has survived in Newton cemetery Massachussetts since around 1890, the cultivar was first introduced in 1871.

Growth: 3-15-30. Hardiness: 80%. Choice: 1 (requires space), 3. Wood: 1 (species).

subsp. *nigrum*

underside

Sugar Maple
summer

Acer saccharum
subsp. *grandidentatum*

Oregon Maple

Balkan Maple

Rock Maple
subsp. *douglasii*

Acer saccharum
subsp. *leucoderme*

Oregon Maple
winter

summer

Oregon Maple

630

Acer saccharum subspecies (continued)

Sugar Maple, *Acer saccharum* is illustrated and described on p. 629. Its subspecies **grandidentatum**, the Bigtooth Maple, occurs in the Rocky Mountains to 2500m and in Utah, Texas, Oklahoma and south to Mexico. It is a small tree seldom over 10m tall but varies widely according to the origin of the seed. The 5-8cm leaves are shining green with five lobes and entire margins (see also p. 629). They change to glorious reds and orange in the autumn. The subspecies **leucoderme**, the Chalk Maple, is from the southern United States from Florida to North Carolina and west to Louisiana. *Leucodermis* means with white skin which is a reference to the pale grey bark. This is a generally small tree 6-8m tall with 3-5-lobed downy leaves up to 8cm long and wide. The autumn colour is pale yellow to orange.

Growth: variable. Hardiness: 70%. Choice: 1.

Oregon Maple *Acer macrophyllum*

Large leaves, as the species name suggests, are a feature of this tree. They are up to 25cm long and wide with five main lobes further indented with prominent teeth. They are deep lustrous green and colour orange and yellow in the autumn. This big 15-25m tall tree is from western North America from British Columbia to California. It was discovered in the late 1700s by Archibald Menzies and successfully introduced to Britain by David Douglas in 1826. An earlier introduction in 1812 all died. See also p. 655.

Growth: 3-10-25. Hardiness: 40-50%. Choice: 1 (requires space), 3. Wood: 1.

Rock Maple *Acer glabrum*

This North American shrub or small tree grows on river sides and in moist woodland situations in the Rocky Mountains and the Black Hills of South Dakota. The subspecies **douglasii** has leaves with three lobes whereas the species leaves usually have five. The reddish-grey twigs are especially attractive in winter. The commercial timber called 'Rock Maple' is not this species, it is actually *Acer saccharum* (p. 629).

Growth: 2-5-8. Hardiness: 50%. Choice: 3.

Balkan Maple *Acer hyrcanum*

Named after the province of Hyrcania in Persia this small 8-12m tree from south-east Europe and Asia Minor was first cultivated in 1865. Its taxonomy is obscure because it has confusing botanical similarities with Field Maple (p. 625) and other European species. The autumn foliage colour is yellow.

Growth: 2-6-10. Hardiness: 40%. Choice: 1.

Tatarian Maple *Acer tataricum*

In central Europe, from Austria to the Balkans and east to the Ukraine, this is an undershrub species of dry warm woodlands. The distinctive adult leaves are unlobed or lobulate and 8cm long. They fall early before good autumn colour can be produced. There are several regional subspecies.

Growth: 2-5-10. Hardiness: 60%. Choice: 1.

Tatarian Maple

underside **Balkan Maple**

Balkan Maple

♂ flowers

Sycamore

♂-♀ flowers

fruit

♂-♀ flower detail

seedling

Sycamore

summer

winter

632

Sycamore *Acer pseudoplatanus*

The original natural distribution of Sycamore has been obscured by widespread cultivation. It probably extended over the European mountain ranges from the Pyrenees through the Alps to the Carpathians. Although its range was across southern Europe its preference for alpine habitats has ensured that it is hardy enough to survive as far north as Scandinavia and Scotland. The clean white wood is about equal in strength to oak but it is far less durable. Its lack of any taste or resins make it ideal for use in contact with food. It also takes dye well and was a favourite material for children's toys and beads before plastic took its place. The wavy grain, fiddleback wood which occasionally appears in a sawn log is of great value but it can not be reliably detected until after the tree has been cut down.

Sycamore is particularly resistant to atmospheric pollution and salt spray. It is also wind firm, so it can not be surpassed as a wind break close to the sea. The greenish-grey bark is smooth for many years becoming scaly in old age. The palmate leaves are about 20cm long and wide. Flowers hang down in yellow racemes as the bronze-green young leaves emerge. Paired seeds occur in bunches which break up in the autumn and begin to germinate as soon as they touch the ground. This species was introduced to northern Europe at an early date. The first record of it in England was 1280 but it probably arrived with Celtic people in Wales before then. This is the largest of all the maples. Trees 40m tall are known and the largest diameter stems exceed 220cm.

The cultivar '**Erectum**' is a narrow tree up to 20m tall. It originated at The Hague in Holland around 1934 and came into cultivation in 1949. Several other different erect clones have been introduced from time to time and inevitably they are sometimes confused with each other.

The variegated sycamore '**Variegatum**' is no longer considered to be an individual cultivar. Many different seedling forms appear in the population. Some, as illustrated, are fine shapely trees, but others are weedy individuals barely clinging on to life. The amount of leaf variegation differs widely, from over half the foliage being yellow to just an occasional splash of pale colour here and there (see p. 635).

Growth: 4-16-35 (species). Hardiness: 60%. Choice: 2, 3. Wood: 1 (species).

'Erectum'
young tree

'Variegatum'

'Atropurpureum' underside

'Variegatum'

'Brilliantissimum'
spring

'Worley'

'Nizetii'

'Negenia'

'Simon Louis Frères'

forma *erythrocarpum*
fruit

Acer pseudoplatanus cultivars

The clone '**Atropurpureum**', cultivated in 1883, is almost impossible to separate from similar spontaneous seedlings with purple-backed leaves. These can be found in gardens and arboreta everywhere and also in the open countryside. The best examples have stunning, almost synthetic colour but it is only seen when the wind blows the leaves over to show the undersides.

There is a wide range of variegated Sycamore cultivars. Some of them, such as '**Variegatum**' (p. 633), have been adulterated by similar-looking variegated sports which often occur. '**Brilliantissimum**' is a 1905 British plant which flushes out orange in the spring and gradually transforms to yellow and pale green through the summer. Slow-growing and compact, it is best grafted on to a standard rootstock. It makes a good formal garden plant, a real pleasure when reflected in water on a sunny day. '**Worley**', or '**Worleeii**', is an 1893 German cultivar with yellow emerging leaves which turn green during the summer months. It is a counterpart of the seventeenth century Scottish clone 'Corstorphinense'.

Yellow variegation and purple-backed leaves come together on the 1887 French selection '**Nizetii**'. This combination is repeated in '**Prinz Handjery**', but the leathery long pointed lobes on the leaves are quite different. Unless grafted on to a standard stock 'Prinz Handjery' becomes a spreading bushy plant. Named in 1883 it was introduced in Germany in 1890.

Another slow-growing variegated Sycamore is '**Simon Louis Frères**' a French selection named in 1881. The mostly three-lobed green leaves emerge pink and are then marked with stripes and blotches of creamy-white. '**Leopoldii**' is a large tree with yellowish-white mottled leaves. It originated in Belgium and was named in honour of King Leopold I of Belgium in 1864. Its integrity is often obscured by the huge number of similar-looking seedlings that have appeared since then.

The wild Sycamore, forma *erythrocarpum*, is a native species in the Bavarian and Swiss Alps. In summer the seed wings are distinctly red. In cultivation most plants have originated from the 1727 French cultivar 'Erythrocarpum', which was selected especially for its bright red seed wings.

In 1948 the Dutch Horticulture Selection Service nominated the best example of Sycamore available to them in Holland for urban use. It was called '**Negenia**', a large 25m specimen tree which is particularly resistant to poor air quality and impoverished or re-formed soils. Its deep green foliage provides excellent shade.

Growth: variable. Hardiness: 60%. Choice: 1.

'Leopoldii'

'Prinz Handjery'

Zoeschen Maple

Greek Maple

new leaves

autumn

van Volxem's Maple

Zoeschen Maple

van Volxem's Maple

636

MAPLES

Zoeschen Maple *Acer × zoeschense*

The common and species names commemorate a German village where this hybrid (*Acer campestre × Acer cappadocicum* subsp. *lobelii*) was produced by Schwerin's Nursery, although the plant had originated around 1880 in Copenhagen, Denmark. Initially it was named as a variety of Field Maple (p. 625), which it closely resembles. It is a medium-sized, 15m tall, tree with spreading branches. The 5-7-lobed leaves are 8-18cm across with acuminate points. The corymbs of flowers are erect at first. A well known cultivar of this hybrid 'Annae' is described on p. 659.

Growth: 3-8-15. Hardiness: 50-6-%. Choice: 1, 2. Wood: 1, 5.

Greek Maple *Acer heldreichii*

Also known in some countries as Heldreich's Maple, this handsome, smooth-stemmed relative of the sycamore is a spreading tree which reaches over 15m in height. The 3-5-lobed thin leaves are deeply cut and up to 16cm long and wide. In the autumn they turn yellow and golden brown. In northern Greece, Albania, the Balkans and Bulgaria this is usually a mountainside species.

Growth: 3-8-15. Hardiness: 50%. Choice: 2. Wood: 1.

van Volxem's Maple

Acer velutinum var. *vanvolxemii*

This superb variety collected by G. van Volxem in 1873 near Lagodechi in the Caucasus, has overshadowed the species *velutinum* (p. 623) in cultivation. It is closely related to sycamore but larger in all its parts. Clonal material is often grafted on to sycamore and the graft union is generally almost perfect, even 70 years later. On good ground the tree often exceeds 25m in height and nearly as much in width, leaves 25cm across are commonplace.

Growth: 4-16-25. Hardiness: 50%. Choice: 1 (requires space). Wood: 1.

Redbud Maple *Acer heldreichii* var. *trautvetteri*

Named, for a long time as a species, after E. R. von Trautvetter (1809-1889), director of St Petersburg Botanic Garden, this 20-25m tree has deeply-lobed, 12-15cm leaves. The petioles (leaf stalks) are strikingly red. Fruits with red wings up to 7cm long hang in pendulous bunches in late summer. Winter buds are almost black. The native range extends from eastern Turkey to the Caucasus up to 2500m. It was discovered in 1864 and introduced into cultivation in 1866. Hybrids between this variety and sycamore vary and tend to confuse gardeners and botanists alike.

Growth: 3-8-15. Hardiness: 50%. Choice: 1. Wood: 1.

Redbud Maple

Greek Maple

Acer × *hillieri*

Lime-leaved Maple

Acer franchetii

Acer micranthum forma *candelabrum*

Hawthorn-leaved Maple

underside

Hawthorn-leaved Maple

Acer × *hillieri*

This hybrid, described by Roy Lancaster at the Hillier Nurseries in 1979, is a hybrid between *Acer miyabei* (p. 617) and the golden form of Cappadocian Maple (p. 621). It arose as a seedling from a mixed maple collection at Kew Gardens in London before 1930. The original plant was named 'West Hill' and is now recognized as a cultivar. Another golden cultivar, 'Summergold', was produced in the same way at Hergest Croft Gardens in Herefordshire.

Growth: 2-7-12. Hardiness: 50%. Choice: 1.

Lime-leaved Maple *Acer distylum*

From the northern part of Honshu in Japan this rare shrubby tree was introduced to the west in 1879 by Charles Maries. It is unique among maples for its 10-15cm unlobed leaves which resemble Common Lime (p. 683). They are greyish and tinted pink when young.

Growth: 2-8-15. Hardiness: 30-40%. Choice: 1. Wood: 1.

Acer franchetii

Now more properly considered to be a subspecies of *Acer sterculiaceum*, this 15m tall tree is from China and the adjacent Himalayas. It was introduced to the west by Ernest Wilson in 1901 and named in honour of the French botanist Adrien Franchet. The 10-15cm palmate leaves are cordate and have distinctly pointed lobes. Male and female flowers occur on separate trees.

Growth: 2-6-15. Hardiness: 40%. Choice: 1. Wood; 1.

Acer micranthum

This small Japanese tree has thin twigs and small deeply toothed five-lobed leaves not more than 6cm long. The very small flowers, in terminal racemes, appear with the leaves in spring. There is a specimen of *Acer micranthum*, forma **candelabrum,** in the Hillier Arboretum. It produces small clusters of flower racemes. Although larger than the species it is probably only an isolated variant. The autumn colour is reliably bright orange and red.

Growth: 2-5-7. Hardiness: 50%. Choice: 1.

Hawthorn-leaved Maple *Acer crataegifolium*

This is another Japanese plant introduced in 1879 by the Veitch Nursery plant collector Charles Maries. It is a small bushy tree with upright branches and small variable leaves. The bark is attractively marked with white vertical stripes on a green, brown or purplish background. The variegated *crataegifolium* cultivar 'Veitchii' is described on p. 641.

Growth: 2-5-9. Hardiness: 40-50%. Choice: 1.

Trident Maple *Acer buergerianum*

The species name commemorates J. Buerger (1804–1858) the Dutch plant hunter. The common name describes the shape of the three-lobed leaves. Taxonomists have recently divided this species into regional subspecies. The Chinese plants are broadly similar but the Taiwanese subspecies *formosanum* has only slightly-lobed or sometimes unlobed leaves. In China and Japan this is an important ornamental tree, a role usually filled in the west by *Acer palmatum*.

Growth: 2-5-8. Hardiness: 40-5-%. Choice: 1.

new leaves

Trident Maple

Acer caesium
subsp. *giraldii*

Acer longipes
subsp. *longipes*

Birch-leaved
Maple

var. *tiliifolium*

Acer pectinatum
subsp. *laxiflorum*

Acer crataegifolium
'Veitchii'

Acer campestre
'Nanum'

MAPLES

Acer caesium subsp. *giraldii*

This Chinese tree is around 10m tall, reminiscent of a small sycamore. The species *caesium* is split into regional subspecies which vary only slightly. The subspecies *giraldii*, from north-west China, was named after Giraldi, an Italian missionary. Young shoots are covered in a bluish-white bloom.
Growth: 2-5-10. Hardiness: 40-50%. Choice: 1.

Acer longipes subsp. *longipes*

Originally called *Acer fulvescens* by Alfred Rehder in 1911, this 18m tall Chinese tree is rare in cultivation. The species *longipes* is divided into several regional subspecies. This one is probably the nearest to the true species in China. It is a round-topped tree superficially similar to Norway Maple (p. 609) on to which it is sometimes grafted. The leaves are as illustrated or palmate with the slender points more widely spread out.
Growth: 2-5-7 (18 in native range). Hardiness: 50%. Choice: 4.

Birch-leaved Maple *Acer stachyophyllum*

Known until recently as *Acer tetramerum*, the Birch-leaved Maple is an erect tree to about 8m, often with multiple stems. The 6-8cm leaves are ovate with a pair of small indistinct lobes. The subspecies *betulifolium* has much smaller leaves rather like Silver Birch. Once established, it produces suckers from its surface roots. Ernest Wilson introduced it in 1901 but it remains rare in cultivation. This variable species produces many foliage types which have all been allocated names in the past, for example var. ***tiliifolium*** (lime-leaved).
Growth: 2-5-8. Hardiness: 40-50%. Choice: 4.

Acer campestre 'Nanum'

This British cultivar of Field Maple was described in 1839. It is a mop-headed tree less than 3m tall with a tangled mass of branches. The leaves are similar in shape to the species but smaller in size. If not trained it remains a prostrate bush. There is always a tendency to revert to vigorous growth, which should be cut out before the plant is overwhelmed. See also p. 625.
Growth: 2-3-3. Hardiness: 60%. Choice: 1.

Acer pectinatum

There are several subspecies of this complex maple; most of them were formerly given full species rank. They are from a limited but diverse area in China and the differences that occur in cultivation are unpredictable. Subspecies *forrestii* was introduced in 1906 and ***laxiflorum*** in 1908. They are small 7-12m tall trees with decorative bark and lax foliage.
Growth: variable. Hardiness: 50%. Choice: 4.

Acer crataegifolium 'Veitchii'

The Hawthorn-leaved Maple, *Acer crataegifolium* (p. 639), has small bunched leaves and tightly packed shoots. There is probably only one cultivar 'Veitchii', although many other fancy names have been ascribed to it. It has pink, white, and green foliage and was first described in Britain in 1881.
Growth: 2-5-9. Hardiness: 40-50%. Choice: 1.

Acer oliverianum

This beautiful small Chinese species develops into a neat round-headed tree. The deep green 3-5-lobed palmate leaves are mostly less than 10cm across. There are regional subspecies which vary only slightly. **Formosanum** is a larger tree with reddish shoots and leaves with lobes up to 10cm long and coarse teeth.
Growth: 2-5-8. Hardiness: 50%. Choice: 1.

Acer oliverianum

subsp. *formosanum*

underside

flower detail

'Vitifolium'

Full Moon Maple
autumn

'Aconitifolium'
autumn

'Aureum'

Vine Maple
autumn

Korean Maple

Full Moon Maple *Acer japonicum*

Introduced in 1864 from Hokkaido and Honshu in Japan, this 8-15m tall tree, often with more than one stem, has produced some of the finest garden cultivars of 'Japanese Maple' in the nursery trade. However, the true species itself is seldom seen in western gardens. Its 8-12cm leaves are rounded, with 9-11 short pointed lobes. Attractive drooping corymbs of small purplish-red flowers appear before the leaves in spring. Autumn colour starts early and runs for 4-5 weeks, covering every shade from cream to wine red.

The Vine-leaved Japanese Maple, '**Vitifolium**', named in 1876 in Britain, has larger leaves than the species and in ideal conditions grows to a larger size. It is the finest of all multi-coloured autumn foliage trees, holding leaves that are green, yellow, orange, red and claret all at the same time and over a period of several weeks. The cut-leaved form of *Acer japonicum* '**Aconitifolium**' is a slightly smaller, but even more spreading tree with aconite-like leaves. A good well positioned specimen will produce the best pure scarlet autumn colour of any maple.

The Golden Japanese Maple '**Aureum**', now called *Acer shirasawanum* 'Aureum' (see also p. 645) is a compact shrubby tree developing a crooked mass of stems and branches. The leaves are mostly around 7cm across and resemble those of *Acer japonicum* but are yellow all summer.

Growth: 2-7-10. Hardiness: 50%. Choice: 1.

Korean Maple *Acer pseudosieboldianum*

This underwood species has a wide natural distribution from Korea and north-east China northwards along the Pacific coast of Russia. It seldom grows taller than 8m and thrives in partial shade. The leaves are similar to Japanese Maples with 7-9 distinct toothed lobes. In the autumn they turn brilliant orange and red.

Growth: 2-6-8. Hardiness: 50%. Choice: 1.

Vine Maple *Acer circinatum*

Usually this is a dense shrub with sticky glutinous shoots and bright red corymbs of flowers in spring. The 7-9-lobed leaves are almost round and distinctly double-toothed. In the autumn they turn brilliant orange and red. The seeds, which also turn bright red as they develop, are in opposite almost horizontally opposed pairs. In its native western North America this plant forms thickets along river valleys, extending as high as 2000m into the Cascade Mountains. David Douglas introduced it to Europe in 1826.

Growth: 3-8-12. Hardiness: 50%. Choice: 1.

'Aconitifolium'

'Vitifolium'
autumn

Henry's Maple

fruit enlarged

autumn

Shirasawa Maple

new leaves

autumn

Acer sieboldianum

'Shishigashira'

'Volubile'

'Shishigashira'

Henry's Maple *Acer henryi*

Augustine Henry, the Irish plant collector and writer, discovered this small rounded tree, and it was introduced to England in 1903. Its natural distribution is confined to central China, where it is the counterpart of the Japanese Maple *Acer cissifoliuim* (p. 617). The leaves are trifoliate, more or less entire and 5-10cm long. They change to glorious shades of red in the autumn.

Growth: 2-6-8. Hardiness: 50%. Choice: 1.

Shirasawa Maple *Acer shirasawanum*

In cultivation this is a small tree or a large bush, but in the wild state it grows up to 15m in height. Its range is limited to southern Honshu and neighbouring districts of Japan. In cultivation it is often confused with some cultivars of Japanese Maple, *Acer palmatum*. Unlike them, the flowers and fruits stand upright on the shoots. See also p. 643.

Growth: 2-7-10. Hardiness: 50%. Choice: 1.

Acer sieboldianum

This 10m tree is a close relative of the Japanese Maple *Acer japonicum* (p. 643). One of its Japanese names, Ko-hau-uchiwa Kaede, means 'small-leaved form'. It was named in honour of Philipp von Siebold and first cultivated in the west in 1880. In its native Japan it is a tough mountainside tree which makes it a very hardy garden plant.

Growth: 2-7-10. Hardiness: 50%. Choice: 1.

Smooth Japanese Maple *Acer palmatum*

In cultivation this species is almost entirely represented by literally hundreds of named cultivars. It is difficult now, outside of Japan, to be certain as to the form of a wild *Acer palmatum*. In its native Japan '**Shishigashira**' is usually a bushy shrub or tree with small five-lobed deep green contorted leaves. In many collections it is still listed with the 1888 German name 'Ribesifolium', recalling its similarity to the Currant (*Ribes alpinum*). '**Volubile**' is a German cultivar described in 1893. It is an upright bushy tree occasionally reaching 6m in height. The leaves are seven-lobed and irregularly cut producing a ragged but lacy effect. Well known in cultivation now is the strangely attractive clone '**Butterfly**'. The small five-lobed leaves are variegated creamy-white and green, and each one is shaped differently. In the autumn the white areas turn pink and the green parts change to red. This plant was originally described in Japan in 1882. Also described in 1882 was '**Seiryu**' a cut-leaved upright form up to 5m tall which produces good purple autumn colour. '**Katsura**' is a deeply divided leaf form which flushes out pale orange in the spring, turning yellow by early summer. '**Nicholsonii**' is a 5m tall 1893 German tree with a rounded outline which produces stunning autumn colour. Finally '**Tana**' is a pale green small upright shrub which colours brilliantly in the autumn.

Growth: variable. Hardiness: 40-50%. Choice: 1.

Acer palmatum **cultivars**

Acer palmatum
variable leaf forms

autumn

'Atropurpureum'

new leaf

'Heptalobum'

'Dissectum Rubrifolium'

'Dissectum'

'Osakazuki'

autumn

'Ornatum'

Acer palmatum

'Sangokaku'

Acer palmatum cultivars (continued)

Genetically unstable, the species is in a constant state of evolution. Each new generation of seedlings is certain to produce different forms which range from large spreading trees to compact bushes. Leaves too, although based on a palmate theme, vary enormously in shape, size and colour.

'**Atropurpureum**' which was described before 1910 has now become something of a collective name in the nursery trade for a host of vaguely purple-leaved plants. Some of these are individually named, but even if they are not, they can be relied upon to produce deep summer shade and vivid red autumn colour. A typical cut-leaved purplish form is the 1867 French selection '**Ornatum**'.

'**Heptalobum**', the seven-lobed type of *Acer palmatum*, was recognized as a cultivar in 1938 but many different plants now appear under this name, which is often given variety or group status. The original 'Heptalobum' is a 10m tree with yellow or orange tinted autumn colour. '**Osakazuki**' also has seven-lobed leaves. The true 1882 cultivar, a 6-8m rounded tree, is the best of all Japanese Maples for red autumn colour. Unscrupulous nurserymen have been known to collect seed from it for sale under the same cultivar name instead of propagating from cuttings. Less than 5 in every 100 seedlings come true to type.

'**Dissectum Rubrifolium**' is a cut-leaf bushy maple which flushes out purple but then fades to muddy green and produces no autumn colour at all. The ordinary green cut-leaf maple '**Dissectum**' is a more attractive plant. It makes a neat mushroom of lacy foliage seldom more than 4m tall in 100 years. The autumn colour is straw-yellow.

The variable-leaved cultivar '**Sangokaku**' (Senkaki), 'Coral-barked Maple', produces incredibly bright carmine-red shoots. These can be perpetuated by periodically lightly pruning them back. '**Hessei**' is an 1893 German plant with deeply divided leaves and distinct teeth. These flush out purple then change to green through the summer. '**Oshio Beni**' is a similar plant produced in Japan in 1898, although this cultivar name appears to have been applied to several quite different things.

The distinctive narrow clean-cut lobes of '**Linearilobum**' set it apart from other forms of *Acer palmatum*, although named forms of it do exist. The original clone was Dutch, described in 1867, but there was almost certainly a Japanese plant in existence before that.

Finally '**Cuneatum**', another product of the golden age of German Maple cultivation in 1893, has seven-lobed leaves with more or less cuneate (wedge-shaped) bases. Its identity has been more or less swallowed up in the 'Heptalobum' complex, now more sensibly described as the Heptalobum group or the Elegans group.

Growth: variable. Hardiness: 40-50%. Choice: 1.

'**Sangokaku**' leaf forms

'**Hessei**'

'**Cuneatum**'

'**Linearilobum**'

'**Oshio Beni**'

'Madeleine Spitta'

Acer rufinerve 'Albo-limbatum'

Acer 'Silver Vein'

Acer barbinerve

Acer davidii 'Madeleine Spitta'

Acer pycnanthum

Hornbeam-leaved Maple

Acer davidii 'Madeleine Spitta'

This 12m upright tree was raised at the Winkworth Arboretum and described in 1950. It was named in honour of the lady who helped to plan the Arboretum.

Growth: 2-7-12. Hardiness: 50%. Choice: 1.

Acer rufinerve 'Albo-limbatum'

Described by Joseph Hooker while he was Director of Kew Gardens in London in 1869, this is a slightly variegated form of the species. The bark is less 'snake-barked' but the leaves develop white margins and occasional splashes of grey and white. Trees often revert to only green leaves.

Growth: 2-4-6. Hardiness: 50%. Choice: 1.

Acer 'Silver Vein'

The bark of this 8-10m tree has one of the finest 'snake-bark' effects of any maple. The ground colour is blue-green overlaid with a tracery of discontinuous vertical white stripes. It was produced by the Hillier Nurseries in 1961. An artificial cross between *Acer pectinatum* subsp. *laxiflorum* and *Acer davidii* 'George Forrest'. It is claimed by some authorities that *Acer pensylvanicum* is included in the parentage.

Growth: 2-5-9. Hardiness: 40%. Choice: 1.

Acer barbinerve

This small tree, usually under 10m tall, is from Manchuria, northern China and Korea. The 6-12cm leaves are downy with tufts of hairs in the vein axils on the underside. The species name means 'bearded veins'. Male and female flowers occur on separate trees. Although discovered in 1867 it is rare in cultivation.

Growth: 2-5-9. Hardiness: 50%. Choice: 4.

Acer pycnanthum

It is difficult to separate this Japanese tree from the American Red Maple. Only the chromosome numbers, which are slightly different, can settle the matter in cultivated plants. It is slightly less colourful than Red Maple in the autumn.

Growth: 2-6-10. Hardiness: 50%. Choice: 4.

Hornbeam-leaved Maple *Acer carpinifolium*

Botanists are easily fooled at first by this species which superficially resembles Hornbeam (p. 325) except for its opposite leaves. It is from high elevations in Japan and was introduced to the west in 1879 by Charles Maries a plant collector for the Veitch Nurseries.

Growth: 2-6-10. Hardiness: 50%. Choice: 1.

Acer mono var. *mayrii*

Heinrich Mayr, professor of forestry in Munich, discovered this 10-25m tall tree in northern Japan in 1886. It is extremely hardy and snow tolerant. The thin leaves turn yellow in the autumn.

Growth: 3-10-15. Hardiness: 70%. Choice: 1.

Acer tegmentosum

From riverside locations in Russia through Asia to Manchuria and Korea, this small tree has purplish grey-green bark with white vertical markings and distinctive blue-green shoots. The 3-5-lobed leaves are up to 18cm across with a 3-7cm petiole. They appear with the flowers early in the year and are often damaged by frost in cultivation.

Growth: 2-6-10. Hardiness: 60-70%. Choice: 1. Wood: 1, 5.

Acer mono var. **mayrii**

Acer tegmentosum

Her's Maple

Red Snake-bark Maple

Moosewood

Acer rufinerve

leaf variations

Père David's Maple

young bark

Her's Maple *Acer grosseri* var. *hersii*

Since its discovery in 1902 in the Shaanxi Province of China, this small tree, seldom over 10m tall, has been a problem for taxonomists. Even the name used here is disputed now in favour of *Acer davidii* subspecies *grosseri* var. *hersii*. A rather complicated substitute for the once familiar '*Acer hersii*' which is still written on most existing arboretum labels. The best, but not completely foolproof, means of identification is to remember that everything about this tree is green. This includes the beautiful snake-bark, the seeds and the foliage including the leaf petioles which in so many other taxa have some red coloration.

Growth: 2-6-10. Hardiness: 50%. Choice: 1.

Red Snake-bark Maple *Acer capillipes*

Introduced from its native Japan by Charles Sprague Sargent in 1892, this small tree has light red, brown and green bark with white vertical markings. The 6-12cm leaves are 3-5-lobed, with reddish petioles. The small pairs of seeds are also flushed red as they ripen.

Growth: 2-6-10. Hardiness: 50%. Choice: 1.

Moosewood *Acer pensylvanicum*

In America the common name for this 6-8m tall tree is Striped Maple, which aptly describes the shoots, branches and young stems. They are bright green at first, becoming reddish-brown finely marked with pale grey vertical lines. In its native eastern North America moose actually do eat the bark. The species was introduced to Europe in 1755. It prefers moist acid soils and some shade. The bright pink barked form '**Erythrocladum**' is a popular garden cultivar but it is not very robust. To promote brightly-coloured new shoots it is best pollarded or coppiced on a 3-5 year cycle.

Growth: 2-5-8. Hardiness: 80%. Choice: 1, 2.

Acer rufinerve

This small Japanese tree resembles Moosewood and also to some extent *Acer capillipes*. They are part of a group of snake-bark maples which are difficult to separate, furthermore in cultivation intermediates often occur. *Acer rufinerve* produces good red and yellow autumn colour in favourable conditions. See also p. 649.

Growth: 2-6-12. Hardiness: 50%. Choice: 1.

Père David's Maple *Acer davidii*

Central China is home to this attractive little tree. It is a snake-bark maple with green, brown and pale grey bark. The bright green foliage colours well in the autumn. It was introduced to the west in 1879 by Charles Maries and is named in honour of the French missionary Father Armand David. There are two subspecies and numerous variations in cultivation. The cultivar 'Ernest Wilson' arose at the Edinburgh Botanic Garden in 1907. Unfortunately seed has been grown from it under the same cultivar name and the identity of the original has become confused. The clone 'George Forrest' has suffered the same fate. Horticulturists are continuing to select and name new forms of *Acer davidii* and the subject has become very specialized.

Growth: 3-8-15. Hardiness: 50%. Choice: 1.

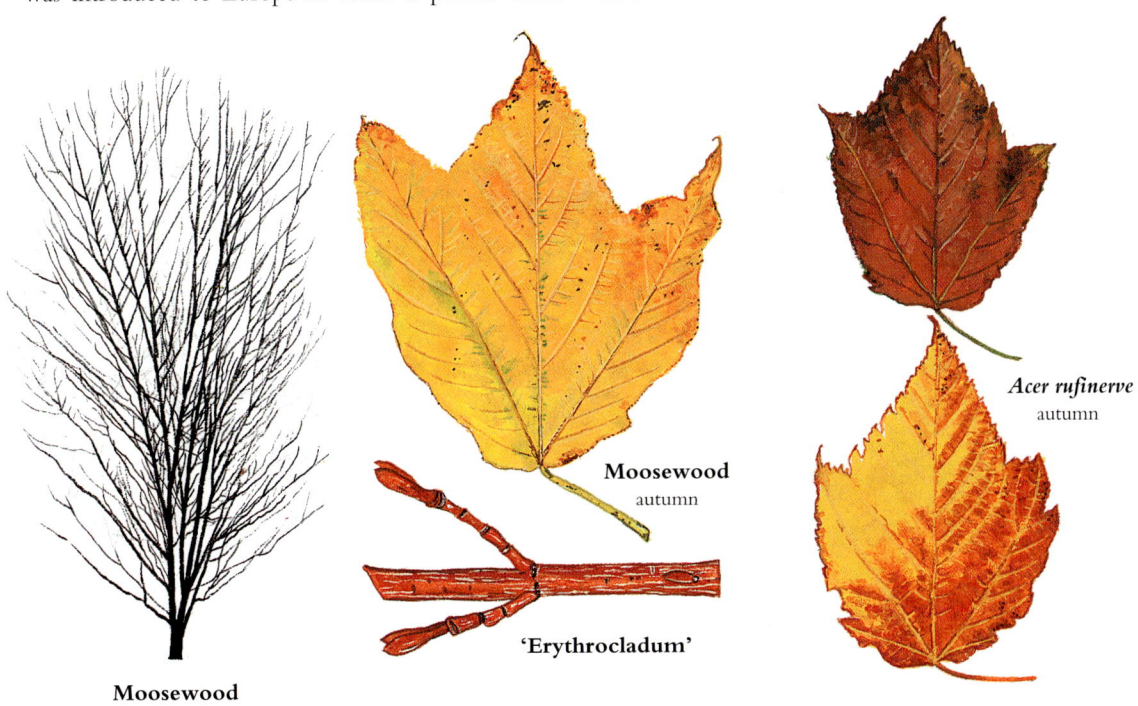

Moosewood

Moosewood autumn

'**Erythrocladum**'

Acer rufinerve autumn

Red Maple

'Schlesingeri'
autumn

underside

fruit

autumn

Red Maple

'Columnare'

♂-♀ flowers

♂ flowers

Red Maple *Acer rubrum*

First cultivated in Europe in 1656, this east and central North American tree, with its rounded or narrow compact outline, can grow up to 40m tall. It is well named Red Maple because red colour in some form is evident on it all year long – from winter twigs to brilliant corymbs of male or female flowers in early spring and culminating in spectacular red autumn foliage. The leaves are palmate or tri-lobed, 6-10cm long, with variable teeth and margins. Some have small rounded lobes, while others are sharply pointed and irregular. The upper surface is always dark matt green but the underside can be grey-green to almost white, adding an additional pink and cream dimension to the superb red and orange autumn tints. In its natural environment this is a tree of moist mixed deciduous woodlands. It can survive reasonably well on dry sites but is slower-growing and less productive. In Europe the autumn colour is disappointing, particularly on dry lime-rich soils.

The cultivar '**Schlesingeri**' was found by Charles Sprague Sargent in a United States garden. It was introduced into cultivation in Berlin in 1888 and named in 1896. It is a particularly good autumn feature with deep red wavy-edged leaves.

'**Scanlon**' is a compact upright tree which also colours well in the autumn, from deep red to purple. The effect can be like a column of fire. It was described in Ohio, in 1956 and is widely available in the nursery trade. Upright trees of this sort are still listed as '**Columnare**' in some collections, although this clone is no longer in cultivation since newer fastigiate cultivars have replaced it.

Growth: 3-12-30 (40 in native range). Hardiness: 70-80%. Choice: 1, 2, 3. Wood: 1, 4, 5 (species).

Acer rubrum var. *trilobum*

This variety, named and described in 1853, is represented in the south-east of the native Red Maple range, mainly in Florida. It is very rare in cultivation. The leaves are three-lobed with finely pointed teeth.

Growth: 2-8-20. Hardiness: 40-50%. Choice: 4.

Acer rubrum var. *drummondii*

The leathery rounded leaves of this variety are mostly three-lobed. Each lobe has a short blunt point. It grows along the lower Mississippi and in neighbouring states. First described as a cultivar, it was subsequently changed to variety status in 1884. It is very rare in cultivation possibly because in some collections it is wrongly labelled just as *Acer rubrum*.

Growth: 2-7-18. Hardiness: 30%. Choice: 4.

Acer rubrum var. *trilobum*

'Scanlon'

'Columnare'

Acer rubrum var. *drummondii*

'Scanlon'

underside

'Tricolor'

Florida Maple

Acer rubrum 'October Glory'

underside

'Seattle Sentinel'

'Seattle Sentinel'

Acer macrophyllum cultivars

There are four named cultivars of Oregon Maple, *Acer macrophyllum* (p. 631). '**Tricolor**' is an old German selection made in 1893. The original is probably no longer in cultivation. It had leaves marked with red and splashed with white. Variegated forms can also still be found in collections bearing the invalid name 'Variegatum'. Another completely different cultivar, the fastigiate American tree '**Seattle Sentinel**' was named in 1954. The green leaves are large like ordinary Oregon Maple.

Growth: variable. Hardiness: 50%. Choice: 1.

Florida Maple *Acer barbatum*

Many authorities now only list this species name as a synonym for a southern subspecies of Sugar Maple, *Acer saccharum* (p. 629). This spreading rounded tree reaches up to 18m in height with a stem 60cm in diameter. The 5cm leaves are 3-5-lobed but are blunt ended and wavy. The autumn colour is mostly yellow finally turning red. The rough bark is pale grey. It is a tree of moist low ground and upland valleys. The natural range includes Virginia and Florida west to the borders of Texas and Oklahoma and it does intergrade with other Sugar Maple subspecies. It was described and named by the French botanist André Michaux in 1810 but the name was changed to *Acer saccharum* var. *rugelii* in 1900. The validity of this remains uncertain so *Acer barbatum* is retained here. Unfortunately *barbatum* has been used by various authors to describe several different maples causing great confusion in the process.

Growth: 2-10-18. Hardiness: 30%. Choice: 4. Wood: 1.

Acer rubrum 'October Glory'

Numerous selections of Red Maple, *Acer rubrum* (p. 653) have been introduced, particularly in the second half of the twentieth century. '**October Glory**' named in 1961 by Princeton Nurseries in New Jersey, has been selected for its outstanding autumn foliage colour. This develops from yellow, through deep orange to fiery red and lasts a particularly long time. It is a big upright tree when grown on deep fertile soil.

Growth: 2-8-20. Hardiness: 60%. Choice: 1.

Acer rubrum 'Red Sunset'

A selection made and patented by J. Frank Schmidt of Oregon in 1966. It is likely to make a big tree when it reaches maturity. The large leaves are reminiscent of Silver Maple (p. 657) suggesting possible hybrid origin. The fiery red autumn foliage colour is exceptional.

Growth: 2-8-20(?). Hardiness: 60%. Choice: 1, 2.

underside

Acer rubrum 'Red Sunset'

Silver Maple

bark with epicormic shoots

underside

'Laciniatum Wieri'
leaf reduced

'Laciniatum Wieri'
young tree

Silver Maple

656

Silver Maple *Acer saccharinum*

In nature and in cultivation this is usually a healthy, fast-growing large tree. Specimens over 25m tall are known with crowns spreading out to 20m wide. The branches are graceful and arching with light foliage which allows the sun to shine through to the ground below. The deeply cut five-lobed deciduous 8-15cm irregular saw-toothed leaves are green on the upper surface and silvery-white on the underside. The long petioles allow them to flutter in the slightest breeze, giving a shimmering green and white effect. In the autumn the foliage turns yellow with a paler shade retained on the underside of each leaf. An attractive pattern of yellow and creamy-white fallen leaves is produced on the ground under each tree.

Many specimens are prone to developing thin whiskery epicormic shoots on the main stem. In the timber these cause the 'bird's eye' effect for which maple wood is well known. It is a tree of moist ground especially river sides and flood plains. It also grows in mixed damp woodland. Its natural range covers a huge area in North America from Ontario to New Brunswick, south to Florida and west to the Mid West States, including Oklahoma. In America and Europe it is a popular park tree and has been extensively used for street planting. However, in streets and built up areas it rapidly out-grows its allotted space and also tends to shed its brittle branches, so this use is falling out of favour.

Silver Maple was introduced to Europe in 1725 by Sir Charles Wagner and was described and named by Linnaeus in 1753. Although extremely beautiful, this species should only be used with caution because of its tendency to drop branches, its instability and its reputation for clogging up drains with its roots.

There are a large number of cultivars of Silver Maple available including many new ones. A feature much exploited by plant breeders is exaggerated lobes on the leaves. Several of these 'cut-leaved' forms, '**Laciniatum**', are individually named in cultivation. The most popular one was produced in Britain and named in 1875 '**Laciniatum Wieri**', but it is sold under various names including 'Wieri', 'Aspleniifolium' or simply 'Laciniatum'. The latter is now considered to be a collective name for all cut-leaved Silver Maples.

Growth: 3-12-30 (40 in native range). Hardiness: 80%.
Choice: 1 (requires space), 2, 3, 4. Wood: 1 (species).

underside

autumn

'Laciniatum'

Nippon Maple

Acer pectinatum subsp. *maximowiczii*

Acer acuminatum

'Annae'

Acer campbellii subsp. *flabellatum*

var. *yunnanense*

Nippon Maple *Acer nipponicum*

This rare Japanese tree is from mountainous areas between 900 and 1800m high. It is unlike any other maple, with huge, very shallow 3-5-lobed leaves up to 25cm across. Most characteristic, though, are the panicles of up to 500 flowers; they can be 40cm long, developing into large trusses of winged fruits.
Growth: 2-7-16. Hardiness: 50%. Choice: 1.

Acer pectinatum subsp. *maximowiczii*

From the Hubei, Gansu and Sichuan regions of China, this rare small tree or large shrub has greenish bark with pale grey vertical stripes. The 3-5-lobed leaves are quite variable but have long points and quite distinct teeth. Most of them are around 6cm long. Originally named as a species in 1889, this plant was reduced to subspecies status in 1977.
Growth: 2-5-6. Hardiness: 40%. Choice: 1.

Acer acuminatum

Nepal, West Pakistan and Kashmir make up the natural range of this slender tree or large shrub, which seldom grows taller than 6m. Its 10cm leaves usually have three lobes with very acuminate points. The young shoots are reddish-purple and slightly downy. The species was introduced into cultivation through the Calcutta Botanic Garden and described by David Don, professor of botany at Kings College, London in 1825.
Growth: 2-4-6. Hardiness: 20%. Choice: 1.

Acer × *zoeschense* cultivars

Zoeschen Maple (p. 637) has a few named cultivars. '**Annae**' is a German form described by Count Fritz von Schwerin in 1908. It is a rounded 10m tree with dark green densely packed foliage. The five long lobes on each 8cm leaf are distinctly wavy and acutely pointed. In spring they are deep purple as they emerge. The cultivar '**Elongatum**', from the same source, has distinctive three-lobed leaves which are slightly wavy and broadest towards the tip. It is probably no longer available in the nursery trade.
Growth: variable. Hardiness: 50%. Choice: 1.

Acer campbellii subsp. *flabellatum*

This small 8m tall tree is from the Hubei and Sichuan provinces of China. The variety **yunnanense** is from the Yunnan and Burma. It is more tender and has sharp bristle tipped teeth along the leaf margins, reminiscent of some *Acer palmatum* cultivars (p. 645). It was described in 1905 and introduced to the west in 1907 by Ernest Wilson.
Growth: 2-6-8. Hardiness: 20-30%. Choice: 1.

'**Elongatum**'

Acer pectinatum subsp. *maximowiczii*

'Giganteum'

subsp. *californicum*

shoot

'Violaceum'

'Elegans'

Ashleaf Maple

'Auratum'

'Variegatum'

Ashleaf Maple *Acer negundo*

Also known in America as Boxelder and Manitoba Maple, this 18m dioecious species has a huge natural range across North America, with subspecies extending into areas where the normal type does not occur. It is classified as a maple because it has paired winged seeds, but the leaves are pinnate with up to 9 leaflets. The name Boxelder refers to the wood, which is white like box, and the leaf which is like elder (*Sambucus*). It was introduced to Europe sometime around 1688.

The subspecies **californicum** is a tree up to 25m tall with mostly trifoliate leaves covered with whitish hairs. It occurs in central southern California and into Arizona where there is sufficient moisture. It is widely cultivated there for shelter and as a city park tree. Where this subspecies extends into Texas it is referred to as var. *texanum*.

Growth: 3-10-18. Hardiness: 80%. Choice: 1, 2. Wood: 1, 3, 5.

Acer negundo cultivars

'**Giganteum**' is a selection of the above with huge leaves up to 40cm long, named in Germany in 1893. It is similar in size and shape to the species. Quite different is the Franco-German selection '**Elegans**' named in 1901. This is a slow-growing female plant less than 7m tall with densely packed creamy-yellow margined leaflets.

'**Violaceum**', produced before 1826, is a British plant up to 20m tall. Some authorities consider it to be a natural variety growing in the mid-west states of the U.S. The shoots are bloomed purple and the leaves have silky hairs on the underside. In spring it produces an abundance of pendulous crimson flower tassels.

'**Auratum**' is a 6m shrub with golden-yellow leaves when grown in full light. It is a product of the Späth Nursery in Germany named in 1891, but it was originally found as a sport in France.

One of the most widespread Ashleaf Maples in cultivation is '**Variegatum**', a rather weak rounded tree seldom over 8m tall. The variable and often distorted leaflets are splashed cream and green. At first the emerging foliage is pink and almost white. It is a female tree but the fruit is always sterile. Vigorous green reversions are common and if unchecked they can soon eliminate all the variegated foliage.

The superb Dutch clone '**Flamingo**' is a superior form of the same thing with deep pink buds and young emerging leaves, and bluish bloomed shoots. In summer the leaves turn green with creamy-white variegation suffused with pale pink. This small 6m tree was described in 1976.

Growth: variable. Hardiness: 50-70%. Choice: 1.

'Flamingo'
spring

leaflet in summer

Ashleaf Maple

Common Horse Chestnut

underside

Common Horse Chestnut

662

HORSE CHESTNUT FAMILY • Hippocastanaceae

Common Horse Chestnut
Aesculus hippocastanum

The familiar European Horse Chestnut tree is a delightful sight in spring when its huge billowing crown is packed with 'candles', the 20cm upright white flower panicles. Unfortunately in cultivation this tree is far too large for most gardens, ultimately reaching 36m in height and 25m wide, with a stem around 220cm in diameter. It grows easily in urban situations from any stray discarded seed (conker), often against paths or buildings. It soon becomes a tree almost before anyone realizes what damage it can do by growing in the wrong place. Once a young plant begins to flower, after only 6-8 years, people become attached to it and its place is often assured, even if this will eventually lead to expensive removal costs when it outgrows its space. Remedial work by a tree surgeon will be necessary if it becomes dangerous. Worse still, the cost of building repairs due to root damage is likely to be immense. So this is not a tree to be planted casually, or nurtured in an unsuitable place where it has regenerated by itself. Horse Chestnuts should not be grown closer than 30m from any solid structure, path or road. Where they can be grown safely they are effective in isolated groups associated with wide expanses of grass. For instance playing fields, parks and golf courses.

Although Common Horse Chestnut is originally from south-east Europe, it is relatively hardy. It was introduced to Vienna via Constantinople in 1576 and reached Britain around 1615. Trees grow best where there is good soil moisture, fertility, and full sun. They live for 150 years, but tend to drop their brittle branches after about 80 years. In winter the big sticky buds and 'horseshoe nail marks' on the leaf scars are of interest.

The cultivar 'Baumannii' which was raised from a sport around 1820 and formerly called 'Flore Pleno', is another potentially big tree. It is usually grafted on to Common Horse Chestnut. The double flowers are white and tightly packed in upright panicles. So far as is known it does not set fertile seed.

Growth: 4-14-28 (species 36). Hardiness: 60-70%.
Choice: 1 (requires space), 2, 3. Wood: 3, 4.

autumn

Common Horse Chestnut

Cut-leaved Horse Chestnut
'Laciniata' group
leaf variations

'Digitata'

Aesculus hippocastanum **'Pyramidalis'**

Cut-leaved Horse Chestnuts

Aesculus hippocastanum 'Laciniata' group

There are several named plants with incised leaves in this group. These vary from deeply cut, almost to the midrib of each leaflet, to only partially cut margins, hardly more than exaggerated teeth. New cut-leaved 'sports' still appear on healthy trees from time to time, usually as a single branch or small section of twig like a 'witch's broom'. Cultivated plants are usually grafted on to Common Horse Chestnut rootstocks but they tend to lack vigour and may become incompatible. Any shoots that are allowed to grow up from the root rapidly dominate the scion.

The cultivar '**Digitata**', formerly called 'Pumila', is a dwarf form with deformed and stunted leaflets. The branches are crooked and weak giving a haggard appearance to this already unhealthy looking plant. The vogue for producing horticultural curiosities of this sort has now largely died out in the nursery trade.

Growth: variable. Hardiness: 50%. Choice: 4 (requires space).

Aesculus hippocastanum 'Pyramidalis'

Originally described as a variety by Augustine Henry the British dendrologist, this cultivar has a compact pyramidal outline. The main branches ascend almost vertically to a maximum height of 30m. Trees were originally propagated by grafting, but over the years upright seedlings have confused the integrity of the initial selection. In Britain it is no longer in commercial cultivation.

Growth: 3-12-30. Hardiness: 50%. Choice: 4.

Aesculus hippocastanum 'Pendula'

Only old specimens of this cultivar remain. It was distributed by the Puvilland Nursery in France around 1800, but does not appear to be available in cultivation now. Almost invariably old Horse Chestnut trees develop branch extremities with a weeping habit so there is little point in having a particular plant which does this. Furthermore, the wood of Horse Chestnut is brittle and high level grafts, which are necessary to produce pendulous branched trees, are prone to incompatibility and eventually breakage.

Growth: 2-4-5. Hardiness: 50%. Choice: 4.

'Laciniata' group

ature*Aesculus hippocastanum* 'Pendula'
old tree

'Umbraculifera'

'Hampton Court Gold'
summer

'Memmingeri'

Dallimore's Horse Chestnut

Aesculus × *bushii*

Texas Buckeye

Aesculus hippocastanum cultivars

Common Horse Chestnut (p. 663) has been cultivated for its flowers and shady foliage for 400 years. Many different trees of all sizes and colours have resulted from this. The unusual cultivar '**Memmingeri**' has leaves that are speckled with white briefly when young. Another form, '**Umbraculifera**', was formerly named by the English dendrologist, Augustine Henry, as a variety in the early twentieth century. It is now regarded as a cultivar. It is a small 'mop-headed tree with deep green leaves. Yet another cultivar '**Hampton Court Gold**' is a relatively new plant with greenish-yellow foliage.

Growth: variable. Hardiness: 60%. Choice: 1.

Dallimore's Horse Chestnut
Aesculus + dallimorei

This curious graft hybrid between Common Horse Chestnut and American Yellow Buckeye (p. 671) is now very rare in cultivation. It is an unpredictable plant, showing features of both or either parent species, notably both yellow and white inflorescences. The white flowers have maroon spots and the yellow ones have deep yellow-ochre spots inside. Joseph Sealy from Kew Gardens in London named it in honour of his friend William Dallimore who became curator of Kew.

Growth: 2-5-6. Hardiness: 50%. Choice: 4.

Aesculus × bushii

A hybrid between *Aesculus glabra* and *Aesculus pavia*, this plant is thought to be synonymous with *Aesculus × mississippiensis*. It produces superb yellow, pink and red flowers all in the same inflorescence and makes a low spreading domed tree seldom over 7m tall.

Growth: 2-4-7. Hardiness: 50%. Choice: 1.

Texas Buckeye *Aesculus glabra* var. *arguta*

Also known in many collections as *Aesculus arguta*, this plant should more properly be called a variety of Ohio Buckeye (p. 673). It is a bushy 6m plant with narrow double toothed leaflets. The flowers are creamy-yellow.

Growth: 2-5-6. Hardiness: 40%. Choice: 1.

Wilson's Horse Chestnut *Aesculus wilsonii*

This large 25m tree has a thick stem and broad spreading crown of branches. The flowers are white with yellow spots inside the upper petals and a red centre which shows up as decline sets in. It is a rare tree, introduced to the west from China by Ernest Wilson in 1908.

Growth: 3-12-25. Hardiness: 40%. Choice: 1, 3.

Wilson's Horse Chestnut

Red Horse Chestnut

'Briotii'

'Plantierensis'

Red Buckeye

autumn

Red Horse Chestnut old bark

HORSE CHESTNUTS

Red Horse Chestnut *Aesculus × carnea*

There are many different examples of this hybrid between the Common Horse Chestnut (p. 663) and Red Buckeye *Aesculus pavia*, varying widely in flower quality, susceptibility to branch damage and swelling caused by a genetic abnormality which results in bud proliferation and subsequent death.

It makes a spreading tree seldom over 20m in height. The branches and foliage tend to be dark-coloured, the spring flowers range from rose pink to deep red, in upright panicles 12-20cm long. The light brown fruit is 3-4cm across, either slightly prickly or lacking any spines. The seeds are glossy chestnut brown. Some clones seed freely and are fertile, producing plants which may begin flowering in only five years, others seem reluctant to produce any seed at all.

Established trees tolerate urban situations and drought, but they are often disfigured by abnormal stem and branch growths. Shoots have a tendency to become pendulous at the tips. There is a variety *pendula* which has a semi-weeping habit.

The brightest red flowers occur on a French cultivar **'Briotii'**, which is a strong-growing compact tree to around 15m tall. The cultivar **'Plantierensis'** is a backcross to common horse chestnut. It has almost white flowers with just a hint of pink. The fruits are prickly like Common Horse Chestnut. None of the Red Horse Chestnuts are particularly good garden or park trees, except for the short flowering period they are fairly uninteresting and oppressive. There is virtually no autumn foliage colour.

Growth: 3-9-18. Hardiness: 70%. Choice: 4.

Red Buckeye *Aesculus pavia*

This is a small tree from Florida to Texas and north to Illinois. It grows to around 8m in the wild and in cultivation. The showy flowers are brilliant red in early summer, borne in open 10-16cm panicles. The petals do not open widely so they have a spiky appearance. The palmately compound leaves are small, only 8-12cm across with five oblong-obovate toothed leaflets. The light brown fruits are without prickles and are more or less pear-shaped. In a good season the foliage colours very well to orange and red in the autumn.

This is a splendid tree for sheltered sunny gardens. It is tolerant of a wide range of moist soil types, and remains fairly small. American Indians used to throw dried powdered seeds and branch wood into pools of water to stupefy fish and make them easier to catch. And American pioneers somehow used the roots as a kind of soap substitute.

See also *Aesculus splendens* on p. 675.

Growth: 2-6-9. Hardiness: 40-50%. Choice: 1.

'Briotii'   **Red Horse Chestnut**

'Sydney Pearce'

autumn leaflet

Yellow Buckeye

Indian Horse Chestnut

Yellow Buckeye

underside

'Sydney Pearce'

Indian Horse Chestnut old bark

Indian Horse Chestnut *Aesculus indica*

This is one of the best hardy horse chestnuts in cultivation, though it requires a lot of space. On a good site in northern Europe it will grow to 24m tall and 18m across. In its native Himalayan forests it reaches 30m in height. The deep green leaves are flushed bronze on opening. Flowers, which are late for a horse chestnut, appear in mid-summer. They occur in 25cm upright panicles, each individual is white with the uppermost inside lip blotched cadmium yellow, and the lower part rose pink. The fruits appear late in the season and do not fall until the onset of winter. This species is closely related to *Aesculus californica*, which has fragrant white to rose pink flowers but, coming from the misty coastal hillsides of California, is more tender and soon looks miserable in a hot summer.

The cultivar of Indian Horse Chestnut '**Sydney Pearce**' is an outstanding, large, floriferous selection with darker green leaves, upright branches and a rounded outline. It was raised at Kew Gardens in London in 1928 and some fine early specimens of it are still there. The huge flower panicles may be 30-40cm long. Ordinary Indian Horse Chestnut grows easily from seed, but 'Sidney Pearce' must be raised vegetatively by budding in mid-summer or by grafting in early spring. It is best to plant out small-sized trees and avoid any root severance. Good moist soil, and partial shade at first, should ensure success.

Growth: 3-10-24 (30 in native range). Hardiness: 30-50%. Choice: 1, 2, 3. Wood: 4, 5.

Yellow, or Sweet Buckeye *Aesculus flava*

Flava, meaning yellow, is a reference to the 3cm late spring to early summer flowers. They occur in upright panicles 15cm long and have four unequal frilly-edged butter yellow petals, with a distinctive pink blotch inside the hooded upper part. The fruits, usually in twos, are encased in smooth rounded 6cm greenish-brown scaly husks. The tree is native to the south-east United States, where it becomes very large, up to 30m tall. In cultivation in Europe it is generally much less. The compound leaves, each with five leaflets, are dark green above and pubescent yellowish-green below; they colour well in the autumn. In northern Europe Yellow Buckeye needs some shelter to become established; and flowers best when the top is in full sun. The old name *Aesculus octandra* still persists in some text books and nursery lists.

Growth: 3-8-16 (30 in native range). Hardiness: 80%. Choice: 1. Wood: 3, 4, 5.

summer

winter

Yellow Buckeye

new leaf

cross section of fruit

Japanese Horse Chestnut

underside

Ohio Buckeye

Sunrise Horse Chestnut

Japanese Horse Chestnut *Aesculus turbinata*

The Japanese Horse Chestnut looks much the same as the common European Horse Chestnut. It is a very large tree, up to 30m tall, and like European Horse Chestnut is only suitable for cultivation where there is plenty of space. The palmately compound leaves are almost identical or a little larger than the common species grown on moist fertile ground. The less showy flowers are about 1.5cm across, creamy white with a red spot inside, in panicles 15-25cm tall. The fruits are more or less pear-shaped, about 5cm across with few, or no spines. The spherical seeds, about 3cm across, have an extended pale grey-brown hilum (point of attachment to the husk) which takes up almost half the surface area.

Growth: 3-15-30. Hardiness: 50%. Choice: 2. Wood: 3.

Ohio Buckeye *Aesculus glabra*

From Ohio and Oklahoma this small hardy tree, up to 10m tall, has superb 2-3cm yellowish flowers in early summer. Even trees under 5m tall can produce a spectacular display of flowers in cultivation, vertical panicles like tallow candles between 10-15cm long. The fruit is obovoid, 3-5cm across, containing one or two glossy chestnut seeds. These seeds, the bark and the young foliage are all poisonous. As the common name suggests, this tree is native in the United States: and is the state tree of Ohio. The variety **sargentii** is a shrubby form with narrower leaflets than the species but similar flowers.

Growth: 2-7-10. Hardiness: 50-70%. Choice: 1.

Sunrise Horse Chestnut
Aesculus × neglecta 'Erythroblastos'

This cultivar, developed at Behnsch, Germany in 1935, is a great pleasure to grow. Given shelter it makes a small tree, seldom more than 7m tall, which erupts into a billowing cloud of salmon pink foliage in spring. Over about 3-4 weeks the colour changes through orange-yellow to lime green. Throughout the summer the foliage is not spectacular and there is no display of autumn colour. The flowers of *Aesculus × neglecta (flava × sylvatica)* are yellowish suffused with red, and the smooth fruits are 4cm across. Specimens of 'Erythroblastos' rarely flower and do not appear to set fertile seed.

Growth: 2-5-7. Hardiness: 40-50%. Choice: 1.

Japanese Horse Chestnut

Sunrise Horse Chestnut
spring

Aesculus glaucescens

Aesculus splendens

Dwarf Horse Chestnut
forma *serotina*

Aesculus assamica
leaf variations

Aesculus glaucescens

This species and the synonymous *Aesculus sylvatica* are segregates of Sweet Buckeye (p. 671). They were named in America by Charles Sprague Sargent and John Bartram respectively. By 1914 the two were considered to be the same and listed as close relatives of *Aesculus octandra* (now *Aesculus flava*) by Alfred Rehder in 1940.

Growth: 2-7-12. Hardiness: 60%. Choice: 1.

Aesculus splendens

This shrubby 4m plant from Alabama and Mississippi has stunning red panicles of flowers. It was introduced in 1911 and named by Charles Sprague Sargent. Modern taxonomists regard it as part of *Aesculus pavia* (p. 669).

Growth: 2-4-4. Hardiness: 30-40%. Choice: 4.

Dwarf Horse Chestnut *Aesculus parviflora*

Introduced to Europe from the south-east USA in 1785 this is a suckering shrub which spreads over a wide area but seldom exceeds 4m in height. The spectacular mid-summer flowers, in 20-30cm panicles, are white with red exserted anthers. The leaves unfold deep bronze. The form **serotina** is usually considered to be identical to the species.

Growth: 3-4-4. Hardiness: 40%. Choice: 1.

Aesculus assamica

This obscure 25m tree comes from Bhutan, Sikkim and North Vietnam. It has lustrous green leaves with up to 7 leaflets. The flowers are white with a rose-pink centre developing into ovoid fruits without spines.

Growth: 2-6-15 (25 in native range). Hardiness: 20-30%. Choice: 4. Wood: 3, 5.

Aesculus × hybrida

From the Alleghany mountain range in the USA, this hybrid between *Aesculus flava* (p. 671) and *Aesculus pavia* (p. 669) is a small tree. It has intermediate characteristics between the parent species, including red and yellow flowers in the same inflorescence. It was formerly called *Aesculus × discolor*, and still is in some collections, but confusingly the name *discolor* was also given to the species, *pavia*.

Growth: 2-5-10. Hardiness: 60%. Choice: 4.

Chinese Horse Chestnut *Aesculus chinensis*

This 30m tree is from northern China. It was introduced to western cultivation first in 1877 then again in 1882 and 1912. In Europe it tends to grow slowly and never reaches its potential size. Most provenances are completely hardy but little is known about the species as a whole. The flowers are white with slightly exserted stamens. The subglobose fruits are thick skinned and up to 2.5cm in diameter. It is often confused in collections with *Aesculus wilsonii*.

Growth: 2-5-15 (30 in native range). Hardiness: 50%. Choice: 4. Wood: 3, 5.

Aesculus × hybrida

Chinese Horse Chestnut

'Rubra' twig

Large-leaved Lime

flower detail

underside

'hood'

Large-leaved Lime

'Laciniata'
flowering

MALLOW FAMILY · Malvaceae

Large-leaved Lime *Tilia platyphyllos*
This lime is native to much of Europe including southern Britain and south-west Sweden in the north and western Ukraine in the east. Subspecies are recognized across this extensive range (p. 679). It is a large, 35m, spreading round-topped tree, growing to as much as 25m across in an open situation. Many specimens produce a straight stem frequently over 1m in diameter at the base. At maturity the lower branches arch outwards and droop towards the extremities. It is not a constant species throughout its whole diverse range: three subspecies are recognized, botanically by the amount of pubescence on the foliage and geographically by the regions they occupy. The 10-15cm long leaves are sharply toothed and distinctly heart-shaped at the base. In hot or dry weather they tend to droop a little and take on a 'hooded' appearance. Flowers appear in clusters of 3-6 early in the summer, earlier than most other limes. This is one of the parents of the ubiquitous Common Lime, *Tilia × europaea* (p. 683).

In cultivation *Tilia platyphyllos* '**Rubra**', the Red-twigged Lime, is becoming more popular than the species. As it is usually reproduced vegetatively, individual trees grow at a uniform speed to more or less the same ultimate shape and size (20-24m). This makes it ideal for avenues and formal plantings. The red twigs provide winter interest and in summer the large leaves cast good shade. In the past this cultivar has been listed under several different names, including 'Corallina'. It also occurs naturally in the wild and is an indicator of ancient woodland.

The cut-leaved cultivar '**Laciniata**' is a variable form of Large-leaved Lime with irregular mutilated leaves. Some branches produce more deeply cut leaves than others and reversion occurs frequently. A selection from 'Laciniata' called 'Aspleniifolia' is a small tree with more deeply cut and twisted leaves.

Another curious and unattractive cultivar with curved twigs and distorted leaves is '**Tortuosa**', which originated as a sport in a nursery at Chiswick, London, in 1888. It was described, first as a variety, in 1902. The variety *vitifolia*, now also presumed to be a cultivar, has leaves which have around three extended teeth. It was described by the Hungarian botanist Lajos Simonkai around 1900 but is now rare in cultivation.

Growth: 3-18-35 (species). Hardiness: 70%. Choice: 2, 3. Wood: 1, 3, 4, 5 (species).

'Tortuosa'

'Laciniata'

var. *vitifolia*

Tilia platyphyllos subsp. *pseudorubra*

Tilia platyphyllos subsp. *cordifolia*

underside

'Örebro'

'Örebro'

'Aurea' shoot

Tilia platyphyllos subsp. *pseudorubra*

This subspecies is often seen throughout the south-eastern part of the range of Large-leaved Lime (p. 677). It extends eastwards into the Ukraine, Romania and Bulgaria. Although broadly similar to western trees it has almost no pubescence on the upper side of the leaf and a minimal amount on the underside. A foliage sample taken out of context looks exactly like *Tilia × europaea* (p. 683).
Growth: 3-18-35. Hardiness: 70-80%. Choice: 2, 3. Wood: 1, 3, 4, 5.

Tilia platyphyllos subsp. *cordifolia*

Trees towards the northern part of the species range are represented by this subspecies. It is very similar to the central European population (in the strict sense subspecies *platyphyllos*) having pubescent leaves and young shoots. In this respect it is more constant than subspecies *platyphyllos* in which pubescence density varies from tree to tree.
Growth: 3-18-35. Hardiness: 70%. Choice: 2, 3. Wood: 1, 2, 3, 5.

Tilia platyphyllos cultivars

Broad-leaved Lime has been used to create ornamental cultivars for many years (see also p. 677). Selections have been made to display twig colour, crown shape and leaf outline. '**Örebro**' is a Swedish selection made in 1935. It is a large columnar tree up to 30m tall with upright and then horizontally spreading branches.

The cultivar '**Fastigiata**' is another very upright form with dense foliage and a conical top. It does not make a good urban street tree because it becomes infested with aphids and drops honeydew on everything below it.

An interesting winter feature tree, particularly if it is pollarded low down, is '**Aurea**'. Its young shoots are bright yellow for the first year, becoming olive green as they mature. The yellow and the green can be seen very well together on branches which are 3-4 years old.

The cultivar '**Princes Street**' is a strong-growing narrow-crowned cultivar with ascending branches and reddish winter twigs. Its exact origin (the name suggests Edinburgh) is uncertain and it could be a hybrid with another species, or a form of *Tilia × europaea*.
Growth: variable. Hardiness: 70%. Choice: 1, 2.

'Fastigiata'
young tree

'Princes Street'

underside

Crimean Lime

underside

leaf variations

Tilia laetevirens

Crimean Lime

Begonia-leaved Lime

LIMES

Crimean Lime *Tilia × euchlora*

It is suggested that the origin of this hybrid was a spontaneous cross between Small-leaved Lime (p. 685) and the Crimean species *Tilia dasystyla*, which occurred somewhere in the Crimea around 1860. It was collected, propagated and distributed by Booth's Nursery of Hamburg. Trees were generally grafted on to Common Lime which sends up bushy shoots from the rootstock, but young plants on their own roots are known.

This is an unmistakable tree with brilliant glossy deep green leaves and pendulous lower branches. It seldom exceeds 15m in height but may be wider than that in ideal conditions. The creamy-yellow drooping flowers in clusters of 3-8 appear in midsummer, but seeds are not usually produced. The foliage does not suffer from aphid infestations resulting in black fungus-infested honeydew which makes a mess on city pavements and parked cars. Over-indulgent bees may become intoxicated with an excess of nectar from the flowers, but most of them survive.

Growth: 3-12-15. Hardiness: 50%. Choice: 2, 3. Wood: 1, 4.

Tilia laetevirens

This close ally of *Tilia chinensis* (p. 689) is rare in its native China and very rare in cultivation. It was discovered by William Purdom in 1911 and described and named in America soon afterwards. Trees seldom reach 8m in height and the leaves are up to 6cm long, with reticulate veins and grey downy undersides. Flowers appear in clusters of 1-3.

Growth: 2-6-8. Hardiness: 30-40%. Choice: 4.

Begonia-leaved Lime *Tilia begoniifolia*

In its native southern Russia and Iran this heavily branched tree reaches up to 25m in height. It was introduced to Britain in 1972 by Roy Lancaster but has not yet had time to prove its worth.

Hardiness: 40-60%. Choice: 4.

Tilia insularis

Wild specimens of this tree grow up to 35m, but in cultivation it usually remains fairly small. It is native only to the Korean island of Cheju Do, and was introduced to the west by Ernest Wilson in 1919. The foliage is similar to its close relative *Tilia japonica* (p. 689) except many of the 8-10cm leaves develop one or two exaggerated points called denticles. Including the well developed tip some leaves take on a distinctly trident shape. The pendulous flowers are fragrant and in clusters of 30 or more, attracting large numbers of bees.

Growth: 3-8-12 (35 in native range). Hardiness: 40%. Choice: 1. Wood: 1, 4.

Begonia-leaved Lime

leaf variations

Tilia insularis

underside

flower detail

Common Lime

Common Lime

Common Lime *Tilia × europaea*

The hybrid between Small-leaved Lime (p. 685) and Large-leaved Lime (p. 677) has occurred naturally in Europe for a very long time where the ranges of these species overlap. It was first noticed and brought into cultivation in the seventeenth century. For some reason, which is not entirely understood, this hybrid, unlike either of its parents, produces epicormic shoots in profusion. These develop round the base of the tree at first and then higher up the stem among the branches, sometimes producing a huge unsightly mass of tangled twigs. It was learned at an early date that the basal shoots, particularly when the tree was cut down, would grow easily when layered. A large number could be pegged down all round a stump to produce new plants easily and cheaply. Consequently this plant was over produced and soon earned the name 'Common'. Probably only a small number of clones are represented in cultivation and inevitably these are the ones with epicormic growths. However, there is sufficient clonal variation to produce trees of different sizes and outlines. Many avenues of Common Lime fail as a landscape feature because of mixed-up clonal stock, which is a pity because it would be so easy to produce identical trees for an individual avenue from a single source (see p. 687).

In addition to its variable shape, unpredictable size and twiggy epicormic growth, this tree suffers badly from predation by sap-sucking aphids. In summer these produce a shower of ejected sticky 'honeydew' which is a dismal nuisance. Furthermore this sugar rich substance is rapidly colonized by 'sooty moulds' which coat everything with a black glutinous film. It is particularly unsightly on the lower leaves of the tree itself and makes them dysfunctional.

Productive clones of Common Lime may tower up to 45m in height with a stem diameter of over 2m. The smooth bark is dull grey-brown on young stems becoming vertically fissured with age. Burrs often form with or without epicormic growths. The leaves are rounded with an oblique-cordate base and an abrupt tip. They are edible when very young, a fact which does not escape the notice of numerous insect predators. The autumn foliage colour is dull yellow, but it is valued for its lateness. Flowers are in clusters of 4-10, appearing in mid-summer.

Growth: 3-20-40. Hardiness: 60-70%. Choice: 2, 3, 4. Wood: 1, 3, 4, 5.

autumn

seedling

Common Lime

winter

underside

Small-leaved Lime

underside

Small-leaved Lime
flowering

Small-leaved Lime *Tilia cordata*

The extensive range of this old world species includes the whole of Europe and much of Russia, from Spain to Siberia and from Scandinavia to the Crimea and the Caucasus. In England it is regarded as a heritage tree, part of the English rural culture, and an indicator of ancient woodland. Since pre-history it has been managed as coppice to produce 'bast', the inner bark from young poles, which consists of rope and fabric quality fibres. When coppice stumps are 'cut over' they rejuvenate almost indefinitely. Each time a stump or 'stool' is cut it re-grows slightly larger than it was before. Stools 16m in diameter are known and it is estimated that they are over 2000 years old, or perhaps even as old as the re-colonization by this species in Europe following the last ice age 6500 years ago.

A typical Small-leaved Lime tree has a columnar outline usually with a very straight vertical stem. Average specimens reach around 24m in height with a rather ragged pale greenish-yellow crown. The leathery leaves are heart-shaped (cordate) and between 3cm and 8cm long and wide. Some individuals have very small 2-4cm leaves. The flowers appear, often in profusion, in mid-summer in open clusters of 4-15. Bees are attracted to them and they are not harmed in any way by the nectar. After 10-20 years the coppice develops very distinctive vertical gun barrel stems often standing close together. Neglected coppice produces a wall of stems with light or non-existent branches except near the very top. This is a shade tolerant species which grows in close proximity with other species in dense woodland. In northern areas seed is only produced following a good summer, so many populations have remained static for hundreds of years and the species has been reluctant to spread to new locations.

There are several cultivated forms of Small-leaved Lime (see also p. 687). '**Pyramidalis**' is a rare cultivar usually with a narrow crown and delicate foliage. It is of German origin and was described by Max Wittmack (1839-1919).

Growth: 3-12-24. Hardiness: 70%. Choice: 1 (cvs), 2, 3. Wood: 1, 3, 4, 5 (species).

'Pyramidalis'

'Pallida'

autumn

'Zwarte Linde'

'Wratislavensis'

'Rancho'

'Wratislavensis'

Tilia × *europaea* cultivars

The hybrid European lime has the potential to produce numerous seedling forms resembling either species parent (see p. 683). Once a good cultivar is recognized its proliferation by vegetative propagation is reliable and relatively easy. German nurserymen in particular have led the way in producing successful decorative lime trees. '**Pallida**', known as Kaiserlinde, is a conical tree with pale green foliage. The leaves are yellowish on the underside. In winter the warm brown twigs combine with bright red buds to produce a pleasing overall colour. In summer this clone flowers freely, producing drooping clusters of 7-9 pale yellow blossoms. '**Wratislavensis**' is also pale-coloured in the spring and autumn: the foliage begins and ends each season bright yellow. Although cultivated in the early 1900s at Wroclaw (Breslau) in Poland, this plant has only become popular in recent years. The cultivar '**Zwarte Linde**', the Black Lime, is a big round-topped tree with dark green leaves in summer. In winter the twigs and buds give a deep wine-red effect.

Growth: variable. Hardiness: 70%. Choice: 1.

Tilia cordata cultivars

Small-leaved Lime (p. 685) has been 'improved' for various horticultural purposes. Most of the emphasis has been on producing narrow-crowned trees which are suitable for urban situations. The earliest of these was named 'Swedish Upright'. It was selected by Alfred Rehder in Sweden in 1906 and developed in America at the Arnold Arboretum. In 1961 the improved form '**Rancho**' was developed. It is a smaller tree with short horizontal or pendulous branches and dense foliage. The leaves are small, around 4cm long and wide. Probably the ultimate narrow Small-leaved Lime is '**Greenspire**' raised in America in 1961. It has upright branches and a very narrow crown. If limes have any place in town parks and streets this is the most suitable cultivar to use. It is very wind-firm, the fallen leaves rot down quickly and the stem can be pruned above head height without any risk of disease. There are other named cultivars with a narrow outline, 'Erecta' for example, but there is little to choose between them.

Growth: variable. Hardiness: 70%. Choice: 1.

'Rancho'

'Greenspire'

Chinese Lime

leaf variation

underside

Tilia tomentosa
'Varsaviensis'
leaf variations

Japanese Lime
leaf variations

Tilia tomentosa
'Varsaviensis'

Chinese Lime *Tilia chinensis*

This Chinese tree grows up to 15m tall in ideal conditions. Usually it is much less, but keeps a neat outline. The broad ovate deciduous leaves are 6-10cm long, finely toothed and thinly covered with grey tomentum (felt) on the underside. In cultivation some specimens produce an abundant crop of early summer, scented, flowers. The olive-green bark is smooth at first, becoming flaky and grey-brown at maturity. Closely related to *Tilia maximowicziana* (p. 701), it was introduced in 1925.
Growth: 2-7-15. Hardiness: 50%. Choice: 1.

Tilia tomentosa 'Varsaviensis'

Formerly thought of as a hybrid between this species and *Tilia platyphyllos* (p. 677), this plant originated spontaneously around 1824 at the Warsaw Botanic Gardens. It was introduced to Britain by Tony Schilling in 1978 but remains rare in cultivation. In America, where it has been grown since 1965, it is distributed under the name *Tilia* 'Mrs Stenson'. The form grown in Canada has large leaves, up to 10cm long.
Growth: 3-15-. Hardiness: 70%. Choice: 4.

Japanese Lime *Tilia japonica*

A small tree, seldom reaching 20m in height, Japanese Lime, which is native to Japan and eastern China, is probably an eastern segregate of European Small-leaved Lime (p. 685). The 5-8cm cordate leaves are almost identical to the European species, with an abruptly pointed tip. Numerous scented flowers occur in compact bunches of up to 40. This species was introduced, first as a variety of *Tilia cordata* then as a species in its own right in 1875.
Growth: 3-9-20. Hardiness: 50%. Choice: 3. Wood: 1, 3, 4, 5.

Tilia kiusiana

Superficially this shrubby species is unlike most other limes. It has fine branches and small 4-5cm pale green almost 'birch-like' leaves. The flowers hang down in bunches of 20-35. It is closely related to *Tilia japonica*. As a distinct species it was described in 1900 and brought into cultivation in 1930. This is one of the best lime species for a small garden and city open spaces.
Growth: 2-5-5. Hardiness: 30-40%. Choice: 1.

Tilia kiusiana

White Basswood

underside

Henry's Lime

White Basswood

Mongolian Lime

690

White Basswood *Tilia heterophylla*

An alternative American name for this species is 'Beetree Linden', reflecting the importance of its nectar to bees and bee keepers. It comes from an extensive range in the eastern United States. Although it was first cultivated in 1755 it was not given its current scientific name until 1800, by Etienne Ventenat in Paris. In 1838 it was suggested that variety status *Tilia americana* var. *heterophylla* would be more appropriate, indeed there is some affinity with *Tilia americana* (p. 693), but this was subsequently rejected. The silver-backed leaves are coarsely-toothed and variable in shape; the largest may be up to 13cm long. The flowers which open in early summer are in clusters of 10-20.

Growth: 3-12-20. Hardiness: 50%. Choice: 3.
Wood: 1, 3.

Henry's Lime *Tilia henryana*

This rare Chinese tree seldom grows taller than 13m. The broad ovate 8-12cm leaves have distinctive bristle-tipped teeth. The flowers, in clusters of around 20, are very pale, almost white. They hang down among the leaves in early summer. This species was discovered by Augustine Henry in central China in 1888 and introduced to the west by Ernest Wilson in 1901. In cultivation it grows disappointingly slowly but its uniquely toothed leaves make it worthwhile in sheltered situations.

Growth: 2-7-12. Hardiness: 50%. Choice: 3.

Mongolian Lime *Tilia mongolica*

There are a small number of slow-growing trees that are ideal for gardens and confined spaces. This is certainly one of them: it seldom reaches 10m in height and is completely hardy. Its native range is Mongolia, eastern Russia and northern China, mostly between 1200 and 2200m. In cultivation specimens usually develop a compact, twiggy head of branches and a rounded outline. In winter the reddish shoots show up very well. In spring delightful bronze and then glossy deep green leaves on reddish stalks appear. These are small, 4-7cm long, and reminiscent of maple or ivy, having 3-5 irregular lobes and coarse teeth. In the autumn a spectacular display of golden-yellow foliage can usually be relied upon. The greenish-white flowers occur in clusters of 6-20. Mongolian Lime was discovered by Abbé David in 1864 but was not described until 1880, when it was introduced to the Jardin des Plantes in Paris.

Growth: 2-5-10. Hardiness: 60-70%. Choice: 1.

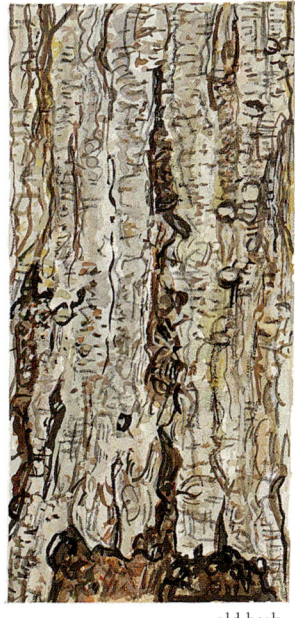

fruit

Mongolian Lime

old bark

underside

American Lime

'Dentata'

(flower enlarged)

American Lime

692

American Lime *Tilia americana*

The huge range of this species, from south-east Canada through the eastern and central United States to Oklahoma and North Carolina, has resulted in considerable variation between cultivated strains depending on where the seed was originally collected. A fairly standard tree may be between 24m and 27m tall; a good one may reach 40m. For a lime the leaves are large, usually up to 18cm long and almost as wide. The teeth are often distinct and triangular. Once mature, the thin leaves have no hairs on the upper surface and only small tufts in the vein axils on the underside. In the autumn they turn yellow to brown. Not brilliant colours but often produced in large amounts on big trees, which can be spectacular. The flowers tend to droop in tight or widely spaced clusters of 5-15 attached to a bract around 12cm long.

In America this is a valuable timber tree. Although the wood is soft and non-durable it has straight grain and is easy to work. In Europe, where it was introduced into cultivation in 1752, it has so far only been used as an ornamental tree. It is very important for growers to choose an appropriate strain to suit their local climatic and site conditions. Many early introductions were unsuitable in this respect and the results have been disappointing. If trees from different regions had been introduced, the reputation of the species might have been better and it would have certainly become more popular, even as a broad-leaved timber-producing plantation tree in parts of Europe.

Growth: 3-12-25 (40 in native region). Hardiness: 80%. Choice: 2, 3. Wood: 1.

Tilia americana ornamental cultivars

Three important clonal selections have been produced. '**Dentata**' is a vigorous 30m tree with coarsely toothed leaves and good flowers. 'Fastigiata', a clone raised in America in 1927, has a narrow crown and upswept branches. The foliage is similar to that of the species. Finally '**Redmond**', which could be of hybrid origin, is a small conical tree with compact twiggy branches and copious flowers in summer.

Growth: variable. Hardiness: 80%. Choice: 1.

underside

'**Redmond**'

young tree

underside

underside

Silver Pendent Lime

autumn

Silver Pendent Lime

694

Silver Pendent Lime
Tilia tomentosa 'Petiolaris'

This cultivar makes an even larger tree than the species (p. 699). Heights between 30 and 40m are common. A huge stem supports massive arched branches which resemble the vaulted ceiling of a vast cathedral when viewed from below. This impressive structure supports a vigorous covering of reflective white-backed green foliage. The leaves are dark green with silver tomentum on the underside. Being woolly they are less likely to be infested with aphids than many other limes. Towards the extremities of the crown curtains of weeping shoots hang down vertically: it is a matter of some speculation how a tree with such lax shoots achieves such staggering heights. The flowers, in clusters of 3-10, are creamy-white and strongly scented. In summer the presence of a flowering tree can be recognized long before it comes into sight by its smell and sound, the hum of bees. Although this is a valuable bee tree and the honey from it is superb, it does tend to overcome indulgent bees. The cultivar does not consist of a single clone, although there is little apparent variation. Some individuals, however, are sterile and others seed freely. Early specimens were usually grafted anywhere between 2m and 5m above ground. Stocks of various species were used and the less vigorous of these have produced a discrepancy in trunk diameter to scion, often resulting in a huge aerial lump on a more modest stem, sometimes with several major limbs emanating from it. The cultivar was first described by the Swiss botanist Alphonse de Candolle in 1864, at first as a species, but it was not introduced into horticulture until 1889. For a time it was mistakenly thought to be a form of American Lime.

Growth: 3-18-30. Hardiness: 50%. Choice: 2, 3. Wood: 4.

Moltke's Lime   *Tilia × moltkei*

Silver Pendent Lime and American Lime (p. 693) have combined to create this hybrid. Examples of it are rare in cultivation although it appears that the cross has occurred several times. Features vary from one specimen to another, particularly details of the foliage. It is a big tree, up to 22m tall, with a broad head of arching branches but without the silvery foliage of 'Petiolaris'. The leaves which resemble those of American lime are 14-20cm long and glabrous except for sparse grey tomentum on the underside. The fragrant flowers, in clusters of 6-10, attract bees but in excess the nectar is narcotic and does kill some of them. This hybrid cultivar was named in Germany in 1880.

Growth: 3-15-22. Hardiness: 50%. Choice: 2, 3, 4. Wood: 4.

Moltke's Lime

Tilia paucicostata

underside

Miquel's Lime

new leaves

underside

Oliver's Lime

underside

Caucasian Lime

Oliver's Lime

Oliver's Lime bark

Oliver's Lime *Tilia oliveri*

Also known as Chinese White Lime, this 20m tree may be tall and domed with a single stem, or low and wide-spreading. The silver-grey bark is clean and smooth, giving the tree a light healthy appearance. The large leaves, up to 14cm long, are glabrous mid-green on the upper side and covered with pure white felt underneath, fluttering in the wind alternately green and white in a characteristic way. The pendulous cream flowers, in clusters of around 10, appear in early summer. Discovered by Augustine Henry in 1888 and introduced to the west by Ernest Wilson in 1900.

Growth: 2-8-20. Hardiness: 50%. Choice: 1 (requires space). Wood: 1.

Tilia paucicostata

This close relative of Small-leaved Lime (p. 685) occupies a huge natural range in central and western China. It was introduced to America in 1901 but not planted in Europe until 1934. So far no specimens over 12m tall are known. The flowers occur in clusters of 7-15.

Growth: 2-7-12. Hardiness: 60-70%. Choice: 4.

Miquel's Lime *Tilia miqueliana*

Fredrich Miquel (1811-1871) was born in Hanover and became professor of botany in Utrecht, Holland. The lime named in his honour is a sacred plant traditionally grown in the grounds of Buddhist temples. It seldom exceeds 12m in height and has small, 10cm, grey-backed leaves. The inflorescence is relatively large, with flowers in clusters of 10, sometimes up to 20, produced in mid-summer. They are very fragrant and attract bees in huge numbers, producing copious amounts of scented honey. Although native to China this species has been cultivated in Japan for centuries. Introduced to the west between 1900 and 1904.

Growth: 2-8-14. Hardiness: 50%. Choice: 1, 3.

Amur Lime *Tilia amurensis*

Usually a small tree, this Chinese species may in exceptional circumstances attain 20m in height. It also occurs in Manchuria and Korea and was introduced to America in 1909. In Europe, where it arrived around 1925, it does not thrive particularly well.

Growth: 2-7-15. Hardiness: 50%. Choice: 4.

Caucasian Lime *Tilia caucasica*

This vigorous tree from the Caucasus and northern Iran may reach 30m on a fertile sheltered site. The robust 10-14cm leaves are roundish, each with a distinctly toothed margin and a short point. They are dark lustrous green on the upper side and lighter below, with tufts of pale hairs in the primary vein axils. Flowers, and subsequently the fruits, are in clusters of 3-7. Closely related to *Tilia dasystyla* (see p. 681), this species was first described by the German doctor and botanist, Franz Joseph Ruprecht, and later brought into cultivation in England in 1880.

Growth: 9-16-30. Hardiness: 50%. Choice: 2. Wood: 1.

Amur Lime

Caucasian Lime

old bark

Silver Lime

underside

underside

'Szeleste'

Silver Lime
winter

'Szeleste'

698

Silver Lime *Tilia tomentosa*

Called 'Silver' because of its white-backed leaves and felted shoots, this large tree may exceed 30m in height and over 20m in width. It usually develops heavy spreading branches and drooping shoot-tips but is quite variable in this respect. The most pendulous individuals are generally regarded as the cultivar 'Petiolaris' (p. 695). The aphid-resistant leaves are 5-10cm long and almost as wide, their cordate and oblique shape makes them so unstable that they flutter in the slightest breeze. Sometimes the bi-serrate margins produce an occasional enlarged pair of teeth or a small lobe. The flowers in clusters of 5-10 are creamy-yellow and appear after mid-summer.

The nectar is a valuable source of honey, particularly in the south of the range, but unfortunately some bees find it narcotic in excess, and many die by being trampled on or predated when lying intoxicated on the ground. Others may indulge themselves to such an extent that they die anyway. Honey bees appear to be less likely to do so than bumble bees.

Silver Lime is native in western Asia, the Balkans, Hungary and western Russia. It has been cultivated for a long time in most of Europe. The introduction date to Britain and America is believed to be 1767. It was described and named by the German professor of Botany in Marburg, Conrad Moench. Invalid species names such as *alba* and *argentea*, reflecting on the white or silver foliage, have been used in the past.

Such a decorative plant has not escaped the notice of nurserymen wishing to 'improve' it. Named cultivars are still being released, especially in Holland and America. 'Brabant' is a 1970 Dutch clone with upright branches and a strong persistent stem. 'Green Mountain', 'Princeton', 'Sterling Silver' and **'Szeleste'** are cultivars with names that describe the plants themselves or recall their place of origin. Many nurseries are aiming at the street tree market with new narrow-crowned, decorative aphid-free limes of small to medium size.

Growth: 3-20-30. Hardiness: 70%. Choice: 2, 3. Wood: 4.

Silver Lime

underside

Silver Lime
summer

Tilia
'Harold Hillier'

'Glenleven'

Tilia × *flavescens*

Tilia × *flaccida*

'Diversifolia'

Tilia 'Harold Hillier'

This superb hybrid between *Tilia insularis* (p. 681) and *Tilia mongolica* (p. 691) was raised in England in 1973 by Nigel Muir. He named it in honour of the late Sir Harold Hillier of Jermyns House, Hampshire. The very decorative leaves retain the distinctive points (denticles) of *Tilia insularis*, some of which become exaggerated into maple-like lobes. The autumn colour, which is golden-yellow, is also outstanding.

Growth: 2-6-10. Hardiness: 40%. Choice: 1.

Tilia × flavescens

In 1836 this hybrid, presumed to be between the American and Small-leaved Limes, was created at Karlsruhe in Germany. It was described by Alexander Braun, professor of botany in Berlin in 1843. Most specimens today seem to closely resemble Small-leaved Lime and may grow up to 30m in height. Some have been given cultivar names such as 'Dropmore', 'Wascana' and '**Glenleven**', which show varying amounts of *Tilia americana* in their appearance.

Growth: 3-12-25. Hardiness: 50%. Choice: 2. Wood: 4.

Tilia × flaccida

The Karlsruhe Nursery in Germany also produced this hybrid between American Lime and *Tilia platyphyllos* (p. 677). It appeared in cultivation around 1830 but has never been popular. Tall specimens with pendulous extremities have been described. The cultivar '**Diversifolia**' is a form with grossly exaggerated teeth on the leaves. Some become completely divided down to the petiole in an unpredictable way reminiscent of *Tilia platyphyllos* 'Laciniata'.

Growth: 3-12-25. Hardiness: 50%. Choice: 1, 4. Wood: 4.

Tilia maximowicziana

The heady scent of lime blossom is never stronger than from this Japanese species on early summer evenings. The tree is rounded and spreading, 30m tall in Japan but considerably less in cultivation. It was introduced to America in 1880 and Britain 10 years later. The inflorescences are up to 15cm long with flowers in clusters of 3-20, from seed these take many years, 25 or more, to appear. To overcome this problem cultivated plants are generally grafted.

Growth: 3-1-17. Hardiness: 50%. Choice: 1, 3.

underside

autumn

Tilia maximowicziana

French Tamarisk bark

Tamarix ramosissima 'Rubra'

French Tamarisk

shoot detail · fruit · seed

flower details

Tamarix canariensis

seedling

French Tamarisk

Tamarix canariensis

702

TAMARISK FAMILY • Tamaricaceae

Tamarisk or Salt Cedar *Tamarix*

Of the 50 or so species in the genus *Tamarix*, only two or three are extensively planted as ornamentals or encouraged as shelter trees. They are feathery plants with plumes of tiny pink flowers in spring or summer. The shoots are slender but very wind resistant, hence the tree's use in wind-breaks. Furthermore they are tolerant of maritime conditions making them an ideal first line of defence against gales blowing in from the sea. The roots go deep into sandy soils seeking out deep reserves of moisture during the summer when drought conditions are likely. The foliage is rudimentary, so actual requirements for water are quite modest.

Tamarix ramosissima

Also known as *Tamarix pentandra* until quite recently, this Asiatic species is a popular late summer flowering garden plant. The flowers, in profusion, occur on the current seasons growth as it begins to harden off. Young shoots are yellowish-green, quickly maturing to red-brown. Stems proliferate from near ground level on most individuals to produce a sprawling bushy tree up to 6m tall. Plants with a single stem have usually been pruned or grazed to that particular shape. There are two well known deep pink cultivars: '**Rubra**' formerly called 'Summer Glow' and 'Rosea' which dates back to 1883. 'Pink Cascade' has been selected for its ability to flower so thickly that the foliage is completely obscured.

Growth: 2-4-5. Hardiness: 80-90%. Choice: 1, 2.

French Tamarisk *Tamarix gallica*

This common species is very similar to *Tamarix ramosissima* except that the foliage is slightly more glaucous and the stems are purplish-brown. It is widely used for coastal protection, notably in the Channel Islands. It flowers in late summer. Originally from south-west Europe, it has become naturalized as far north as Britain.

Growth: 2-5-9. Hardiness: 50%. Choice: 1, 2.

Tamarix canariensis

This is a bushy tree with dense foliage and pale pink flowers. It is from southern Europe and the Canary Islands but is tender elsewhere.

Growth: 2-4-5. Hardiness: 10%. Choice: 1.

Tamarix canariensis
young tree

French Tamarisk
flowering

street tree

fruit

'Plena'

Eucryphia glutinosa

Eucryphia cordifolia 'Ulmo'

Eucryphia × *intermedia* 'Rostrevor'

Eucryphia lucida

Eucryphia milliganii

EUCRYPHIA FAMILY · Eucryphiaceae

Eucryphia glutinosa

This species from Chile, is a multi-stemmed 5m bush or small tree. It has pinnate semi-evergreen or deciduous leaves which colour well in the autumn. The 5cm, fragrant, mid to late summer flowers have four white petals and a dense central ring of yellowish stamens with tiny red anthers. This is a forest species which requires lime-free soil and semi-shade to thrive. It appears to do best in high rainfall areas. The cultivar '**Plena**' has been selected for its double flowers.
Growth: 2-6-10. Hardiness: 50%. Choice: 1.

Eucryphia cordifolia 'Ulmo'

This tender fastigiate tree or large upright shrub has single white flowers in summer. Each one has four petals and a central ring of orange-tipped stamens. The simple evergreen leaves are pale green, backed with netted veins. Another Chilean forest species, it likewise requires moist acid soil and semi-shade.
Growth: 2-10-20. Hardiness: 30%. Choice: 1.

Eucryphia × intermedia 'Rostrevor'

This popular hybrid between *Eucryphia glutinosa* and *Eucryphia lucida* was raised in Northern Ireland. It is a free flowering vigorous form with variable intermediate characteristics of the parents. It has an upright tendency which requires little space.
Growth: 2-7-15. Hardiness: 40%. Choice: 1.

Eucryphia lucida

The 5cm single white flowers of this Tasmanian species are fragrant and often face downwards on the slender shoots. The pink tipped stamens appear before the bud fully opens. The narrow leaves are willow-like with pale backs. A tender tree, growing best in moist shady areas with acid soil.
Growth: 2-6-12. Hardiness: 30-40%. Choice: 1.

Eucryphia milliganii

Introduced from Tasmania in 1929 this narrow grey-green-leaved species has ivory-white flowers. The prominent buds are sticky. It is frequently cut back by cold weather in Europe.
Growth: 2-4-6. Hardiness: 20%. Choice: 1.

Eucryphia × nymansensis

A garden hybrid between *Eucryphia cordifolia* and *Eucryphia glutinosa*. The flowers, in great profusion, occur in mid-summer when little else is flowering in north European gardens. They are shining white, backed by dark evergreen leaves. The cultivar 'Nymansay' is a fast-growing upright form raised in England in 1915. It requires semi-shade and neutral to acid soil.
Growth: 2-9-18. Hardiness: 30%. Choice: 1.

Eucryphia 'Penwith'

A cross between *Eucryphia cordifolia* and *Eucryphia lucida* which occurred in Cornwall produced this beautiful but tender hybrid. It makes a 15m columnar evergreen tree with 5cm single white flowers. The wavy edged leaves are dark glossy green with glaucous backs.
Growth: 2-6-15. Hardiness: 30%. Choice: 1.

Eucryphia × nymansensis

Eucryphia 'Penwith'

Japanese Stewartia

Korean Stewartia

fruit

autumn

Tall Stewartia

Chinese Stewartia

fruit

Silky Camellia

TEA FAMILY · Theaceae

Japanese Stewartia *Stewartia pseudocamellia*

A tender 10-20m tall Japanese tree with upright branches, summer flowers, bright autumn colour and interesting winter bark. On the stem and main limbs this is grey-brown and flakes off to reveal irregular patches of pale brown and light red reminiscent of some Eucalyptus trees. The deciduous leaves are alternate, pointed, elliptic to ovate and up to 10cm long. They colour well in the autumn from orange and fiery-red to vibrant purple. Flowers occur singly over a period of three weeks in mid-summer; they are white, 6cm across, cup-shaped and single. The five white petals are fused at the base, and when the flower is finished it falls in one piece. The numerous anthers are a conspicuous bright orange-yellow.

Stewartias are difficult to transplant and establish. The genus name recalls John Stuart, Earl of Bute, a patron of botany in England in the eighteenth century. The species name is a reference to the flowers which resemble those of single camellias. It was introduced to America in 1874 and to Europe soon after.
Growth: 2-6-15. Hardiness: 30%. Choice: 1.

Tall Stewartia *Stewartia monadelpha*

Introduced in 1903 from Japan this tree can in theory grow up to 20m in height. It seldom does in cultivation and is tender in northern Europe. The flowers have white silky petals and violet anthers on yellow-stalked stamens. The deep green leaves are velvety and colour well in the autumn. The bark is smooth, bright orange-brown and peels in paper thin flakes. This tree prefers cool acid shaded soil, but only flowers well if its top is in full sun.
Growth: 2-5-12. Hardiness: 20-30%. Choice: 1.

Korean Stewartia
Stewartia pteropetiolata var. *koreana*

The flaking bark of this 6-8m tree is smooth grey-green and pale orange-brown. It is fairly tender and sensitive to exposure and severe cold. It requires moist peaty soil but good drainage. The deciduous leaves and flowers are similar to Japanese Stewartia.
Growth: 2-5-7. Hardiness: 20-30%. Choice: 1.

Chinese Stewartia *Stewartia sinensis*

Introduced from China in 1901 this species only makes a large shrub in cultivation. Its ornamental flaking brown bark is most effective when coppiced. The 5-10cm deciduous leaves colour well in the autumn. The 5cm single white fragrant flowers have numerous yellow and orange stamens.
Growth: 2-4-4. Hardiness: 20-30%. Choice: 1.

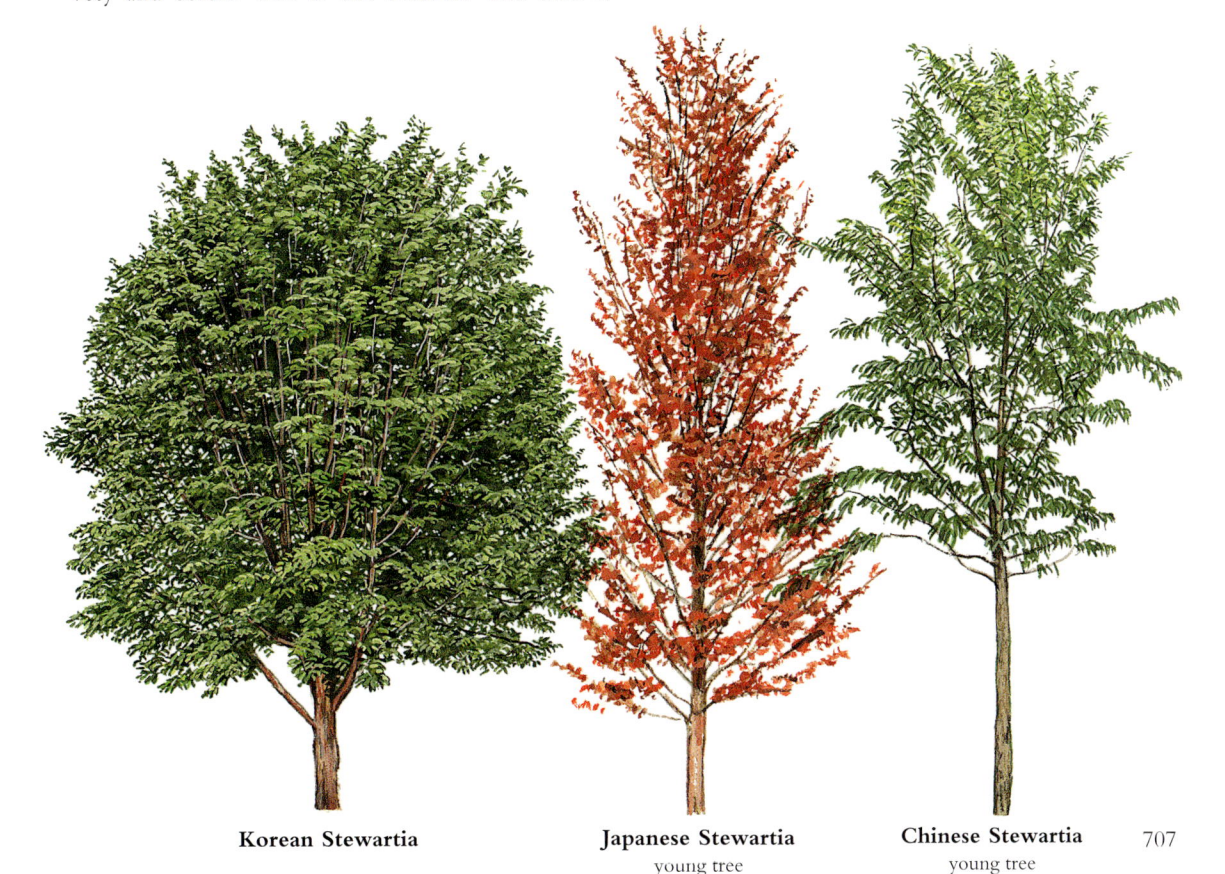

Silky Camellia *Stewartia malacodendron*

This tender Japanese shrub, seldom over 5m tall, is particularly floriferous and has beautiful red to deep purple autumn foliage. The twigs and young 6-10cm leaves are pubescent. The large 8-10cm flowers are creamy-white with purplish-blue stamens.
Growth: 2-4-4. Hardiness: 20-30%. Choice: 1.

Korean Stewartia **Japanese Stewartia** **Chinese Stewartia**
young tree young tree

Prickly Caster-oil Tree

var. *maximowiczii*

Chinese Cedar

Prickly Caster-oil Tree

Chinese Cedar

Prickly Caster-oil Tree
Kalopanax septemlobus (Araliaceae)

Better known to most collection holders as *Kalopanax pictus*, this 15-25m tree is curious for several reasons. The deciduous palmate leaves resemble some maples or ivy, although at 10-20cm long and broad they are much larger than ivy. The small flat clusters of white flowers develop into 5mm blue-black berries which also resemble ivy. The shoots are bloomed green at first becoming brown and after 3-4 years develop sharp thorns which are retained for many more years. This species is native to eastern Asia, including central and northern China, Korea, Japan and parts of Russia. It was introduced to the west in 1865. The variety **maximowiczii** has leaves with 5-7 deeply divided lobes.

Growth: 3-8-18 (30 in native region). Hardiness: 60-70%. Choice: 1. Wood: 1 (Japanese Ash).

Chinese Cedar *Toona sinensis* (Meliaceae)

This deciduous tree grows to around 20m in height and comes from north and west China. The foliage resembles the Tree of Heaven (p. 593) except that the 10-24 leaflets are toothed and not entire. The leaves are used as a vegetable in China, tasting of onion, though when picked they have a rather unpleasant smell. Young trees produce stout straight stems which mature to pinkish-grey with a neat head of foliage. However, with age any symmetry is soon lost and the outline becomes ragged and gaunt. The flowers, in terminal 40-50cm panicles, are white and scented and followed by clusters of winged seeds. It was introduced in 1862 as *Cedrela,* a genus which is now known to be restricted to tropical South and Central America. The cultivar 'Flamingo' emphasizes a feature of this species, bronze-pink emerging leaves.

Growth: 3-7-18. Hardiness: 50%. Choice: 1. Wood: 1 (Chinese mahogany).

Idesia polycarpa (Flacourtiaceae)

From Japan, Taiwan and the adjacent mainland of south-east Asia this deciduous 20m tree has huge 15-20cm leaves like those of some oriental poplars. The shoots are grey-green, becoming pinkish-grey, and the bark is rough on the main stem like an oak's. The long leaf stalks are bright red with a pair of glands near the leaf blade and others half way along. These are said to attract ants which in turn discourage leaf-eating predators. Flowers occur on separate male and female trees. They are followed by huge hanging clusters of 8-10mm red berries. The first introductions to the west were in 1864 and many years later Ernest Wilson brought a Chinese variety back with him in 1908.

Growth: 2-9-20. Hardiness: 40-50%. Choice: 1.

Chinese Cedar

underside

Idesia polycarpa

Golden Rain Tree

flower detail

fruit

var. *apiculata*

fruit (enlarged)

Golden Rain Tree 'Fastigiata'

SOAPBERRY FAMILY • Sapindaceae

Golden Rain Tree *Koelreuteria paniculata*

Also called 'Pride of India' or 'China Tree' this east Asian species is particularly valued for its golden-yellow mid-summer flowers. The four tiny 0.5cm petals back a minute cluster of red stamens. Flowers occur, up to 100 at a time, in huge terminal panicles 35-45cm long all over the tree. Each flower develops into a 3-sided papery straw-coloured, or faintly pink-tinted, capsule containing three hard black seeds. The Chinese used to make necklaces of these decorative seeds and used the flowers medicinally. The unique pinnate leaves are easy to identify, they are large, up to 45cm long, with deeply divided leaflets. The midrib is often pink and contrasts with the rich green leaflets. The tree, frequently over 10m tall, and 8m wide, has rough fissured purplish-brown bark. *Koelreuteria* commemorates the eighteenth-century professor of natural history at Karlsruhe, in Germany, Joseph Koelreuter. *Paniculata* and 'golden rain' are references to the inflorescence.

Without doubt this is one of the best summer feature trees for a sunny garden. It is hardy in southern England and it does not grow excessively large. Although it likes full sun, plenty of moisture is required round the roots. Fertile soil and shelter are also definite advantages.

There are several variants of the Golden Rain Tree, the cultivar '**Fastigiata**' is an unusual, small, slow-growing columnar form which originated in 1888. '**Variegata**' has variegated foliage, but it is not very robust. The variety *apiculata* has all bipinnate leaves and often flowers more freely than the species. It was introduced from China in 1904.

Two rare minor species of Koelreuteria, *bipinnata* and *integrifolia* are usually listed as synonymous, which is strange because the names suggest opposing things. **Koelreuteria bipinnata**, the Chinese Flame Tree, has 40cm bipinnate leaves with 4-10cm deeply serrate leaflets. It was introduced from western China in 1900. Trees there exceed 18m in height. The fruit capsules are usually tinted rose pink. **Koelreuteria integrifolia** has no bipinnate leaves, but its exact taxonomic status is uncertain.

Growth: 2-9-10. Hardiness: 50%. Choice: 1.

Koelreuteria integrifolia

underside

'Variegata'

Koelreuteria bipinnata

fruit

Manna Ash

flower detail

Manna Ash

Fraxinus holotricha

fruit

Fraxinus holotricha

Manna Ash

712

OLIVE FAMILY · Oleaceae

Manna Ash *Fraxinus ornus*

This species is one of a botanical subsection of ash trees called Euornus 'Flowering Ashes'. They have late spring flowers in dense terminal panicles. The petals are 6mm long, creamy-white and very narrow. They are fragrant, like new mown hay, and attract large numbers of early bees and other insects. The bunches of winged seeds which follow are 2-3cm long, bright green in summer, then brownish-yellow when they ripen in the autumn. The pinnate compound leaves usually have seven stalked oblong to ovate 4-8cm leaflets. Side leaflets sometimes have an oblique base extending closer to the rachis on the lower side.

Manna Ash is a pretty, billowing round-headed tree with fresh green summer foliage. Specimens over 20m tall are known but many are much shorter with a thick stem often forking at low level. Many old trees were grafted and the graft unions have often become grossly incompatible. Originally from southern Europe and western Asia this tree was in general cultivation by around 1700. The cultivar '**Arie Peters**' is a fairly broad-leaved clone specially bred for use in urban situations. There are also upright forms but they are rare in cultivation.

Growth: 2-8-16. Hardiness: 50%. Choice: 1 (requires space).

Fraxinus holotricha

Apparently from south-east Europe, this small tree has grey-green foliage with downy young shoots and leaves. It is very rare in cultivation and its status in the wild is uncertain.

Growth: 2-6-12. Hardiness: 50%. Choice: 4.

Chinese Flowering Ash *Fraxinus mariesii*

Of all the Flowering Ashes this must be the best park and garden tree. The flowers are creamy-white appearing a little later than Manna Ash. The pinnate leaves have 5-7 leaflets which are dark green above and bright silvery-green on the underside like Balsam Poplar (p. 271). They are 4-8cm long, virtually stalkless, ovate to elliptic, and have such shallow teeth they give the impression of being entire. The shoots are olive green to pale brown with thin discontinuous silvery skin at first and short brown pubescence. The very distinctive buds appear to be covered with grey-brown velvet, which has a bloomed or frosted appearance. Charles Maries, after whom Joseph Hooker, director of Kew Gardens in London, named the tree, brought material back to the Veitch Nursery in 1878.

Growth: 2-6-8. Hardiness: 40%. Choice: 1.

fruit

Chinese Flowering Ash

'Arie Peters'

young tree

fruit

Manchurian Ash

Blue Ash

stem cross-section

Littleleaf

Black Ash

Fraxinus chinensis var. *acuminata*

Chinese Ash

Blue Ash *Fraxinus quadrangulata*

The immediately obvious feature of this 15-20m North American tree is its distinctly four-angled winged shoots. It has a narrow crown of rather sparse branches. The compound pinnate leaves are 20-30cm long with 7-11 long pointed serrate leaflets. Flowers occur in early spring, they are insignificant and bisexual, which is unusual in American Ashes. The natural range extends along fragmented dry rocky hillsides in the centre of the United States from Ohio to Georgia and Oklahoma to Wisconsin. Blue in the name refers to a dye made from the inner bark by early settlers in America.

Growth: 3-9-18. Hardiness: 70-80%. Choice: 1, 3. Wood: 1, 5.

Black Ash *Fraxinus nigra*

Black heartwood gives this tree its common name. It is the most northerly ash in eastern North America extending to Newfoundland and north-west to Manitoba. The bark at maturity produces grey corky scales. In nature this is a wetland tree. It was introduced in 1800 but has never become popular and seldom thrives out of its native range.

Growth: -25 in native range. Hardiness: 90%. Choice: 4. Wood: 1, 5.

Manchurian Ash *Fraxinus mandshurica*

This is the equivalent of Common Ash in north-east Asia, and it also closely resembles Black Ash in America. Its range extends through Manchuria to Korea and Japan where it was once common in Hokkaido. In Europe it seems to have arrived from St Petersburg between 1882 and 1891, but like so many Manchurian trees it suffers from early spring frost damage.

Growth: -30 in native range. Hardiness: 80%. Choice: 3, 4. Wood: 1, 5.

Littleleaf *Fraxinus greggii*

Also known as Gregg Ash (after Josiah Gregg, 1806-1850, who discovered it) this tree is confined to Trans-Pecos Texas and north-east Mexico. Extremely rare in cultivation and unlikely to thrive in cold northern areas.

Growth: 2-7-10. Hardiness: 20%. Choice: 4.

Chinese Ash *Fraxinus chinensis*

A feature of this medium-sized 15m tall tree in winter is its plump brownish-black buds. They are covered in pale velvet pubescence which gives the appearance of frost. The shoots are olive-grey, bearing 12-18cm compound pinnate leaves which sometimes colour well in the autumn. The species was introduced to Europe in 1891, ten years after its subspecies **rhyncophylla** from north-east Asia which is a better tree and probably more common in cultivation. Further introductions of the subspecies were made in 1892 so individual trees in collections vary. The variety **acuminata** is a native Chinese form with long narrow, finely pointed leaflets. Chinese Ash is closely related to *Fraxinus ornus* so showy flowers are produced in summer. The cultivar '**Floribunda**' has been selected for its exceptionally good flowers.

Growth: 2-7-15. Hardiness: 50%. Choice: 1 (requires space). Wood: 1, 5.

underside

'Floribunda'

Fraxinus chinensis subsp. *rhyncophylla*

♀ flowers

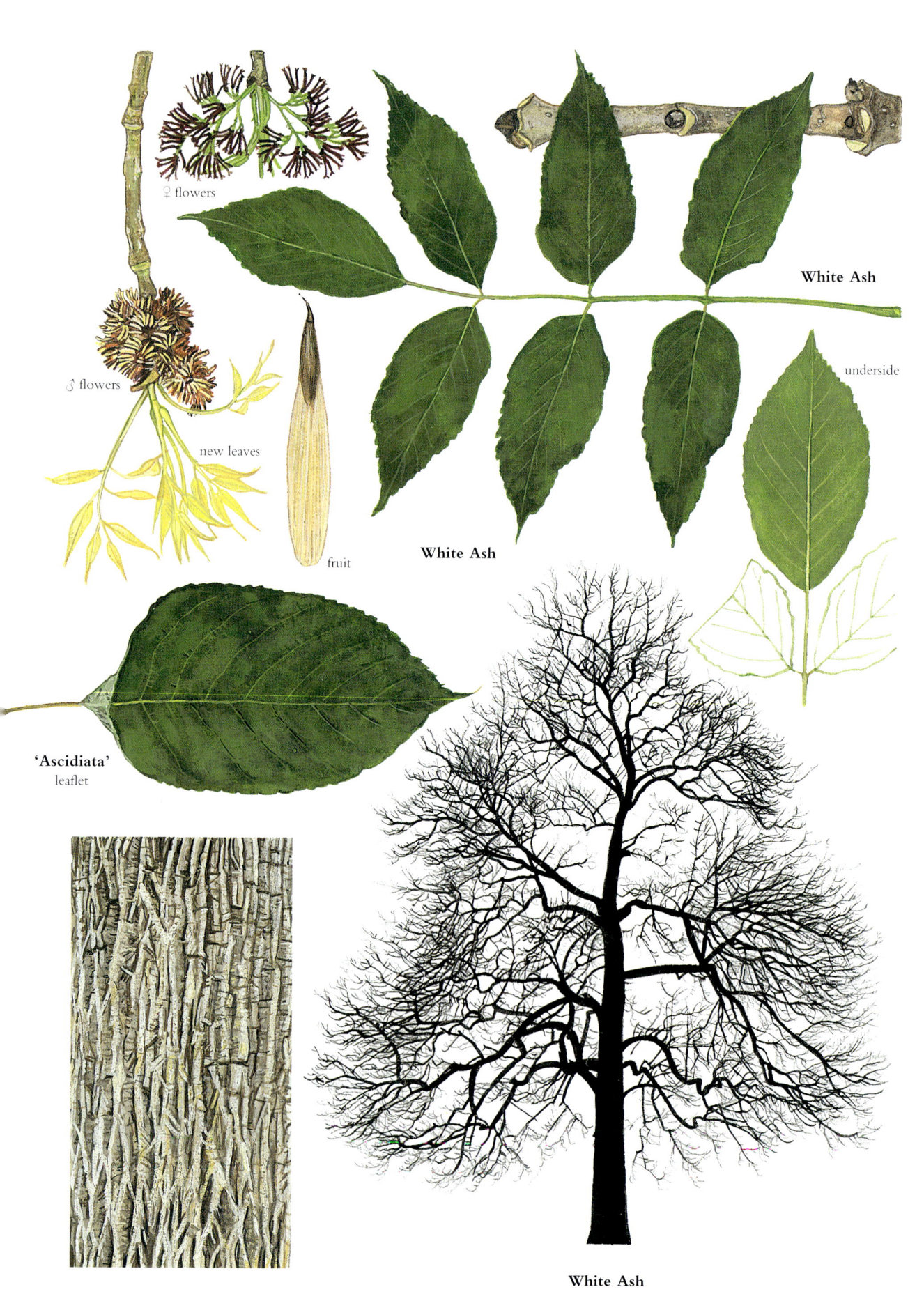

♂ flowers

new leaves

fruit

White Ash

underside

White Ash

'Ascidiata' leaflet

White Ash

716

White Ash *Fraxinus americana*

In its native North America this 24m tall ash tree produces the wood for the finest baseball bats. It is also favoured for other sports equipment such as polo mallets, hockey-sticks and oars because of its great strength and elasticity. Untreated it is not durable, so most of the products made from it for outdoor use are varnished or painted. Stems are usually straight and true and if grown in plantations for timber they benefit from early side branch pruning. This eliminates knots in the stem which is the most valued section of wood. Like most ash trees in woodland conditions trees must never be shaded out, otherwise growth almost stops. Winter buds are rusty brown on green shoots that turn grey after two years. The foliage is strong and luxuriant. Each 20-30cm compound pinnate leaf has around seven short-stalked leaflets which are themselves up to 12cm long and 6cm wide. The upper surface is dark green and the underside is almost white, the rachis (central stalk extension) is pale yellow. In the autumn the leaves turn to a pleasant purplish-cream colour before falling. The maroon flowers on separate male and female trees are small and appear before the leaves in spring. The fruits, in crowded pendulous clusters, are winged seeds 3-5cm long and quite narrow.

This species has a broad natural distribution across eastern and central North America from Cape Breton Island to the north-west Florida border then extending westwards to southern Ontario and Texas. It appears to have been introduced into cultivation in America and Europe in 1724.

The peculiar cultivar '**Ascidiata**' is similar to the White Ash species except the leaflets are pitcher-shaped at the base. It was described by George H Shull in America in 1906 and first appeared in 1910 but is extremely rare and not in general cultivation. The 1800 Dutch cultivar '**Juglandifolia**' cultivated by Lombarts Nursery, at Zundert in Holland, is probably a subspecies which grows wild in the northern part of the White Ash range. As a variety it was described in 1906 as having more distinctly toothed leaflets with pubescent undersides. There are also a couple of selections of White Ash made for their purple autumn colour. 'Autumn Purple' discovered on the campus of the University of Wisconsin, and introduced in 1956, is reddish-purple and 'Rosehill' (p. 721) has a more bronze tint.

Growth: 3-12-24 (40 in native region). Hardiness: 80%. Choice: 3. Wood: 1, 5 (species).

'Juglandifolia'

♂ flowers

♀ flowers

Green Ash

fruit

var. *subintegerrima* leaflet

Green Ash

Biltmore Ash

Green Ash *Fraxinus pennsylvanica*

Throughout central and eastern North America this is the most common and probably most planted of all the ash species. Its natural range extends from Alberta to Cape Breton Island, south along the Atlantic coast to the north Florida border and then west to within sight of the Rocky Mountains. Often cultivated as a fast-growing component of shelter-belts and also in plantations on reclaimed land. Where appropriate it is also used as an urban tree although it does not cast dense shade. On a good site with plenty of moisture in the soil trees rapidly grow to around 18m in height. The opposite compound pinnate leaves are 15-25cm long with 5-9 leaflets. They are shiny green above and pale with some pubescence on the undersides.

There is also a glabrous form identified by some authorities since 1947 as variety **subintegerrima**. The twigs are olive-green becoming grey after 1-2 years and the winter buds are dull brown. Flowers appear in early spring before the leaves. Male and female are on separate trees. Fruits in bunches are yellowish-grey with a narrow 4-6cm wing. The seeds germinate easily without going into a long period of dormancy. Green Ash was introduced to Europe in 1783 but it is not common and is easily mistaken for some other American and Asiatic species.

Growth: 3-9-20. Hardiness: 90-100%. Choice: 3. Wood: 1, 5.

Biltmore Ash
Fraxinus americana var. *biltmoreana*

The exact origin and natural range of this large American tree are uncertain. Some authorities regard it as a natural hybrid between White Ash and Green Ash. It is a handsome tree around 20m tall with a billowing outline and bark which is sometimes like that of Black Walnut (p. 295). The leaflets are very pale like White Ash's. The terminal leaflet is on a long stalk and unequal at the base. In a favourable year autumn colour is particularly good. In cultivation it is easily confused with other American Ashes, and may be quite rare.

Growth: 3-10-20. Hardiness: 60-70%. Choice: 1, 4. Wood: 1, 5.

underside

Biltmore Ash

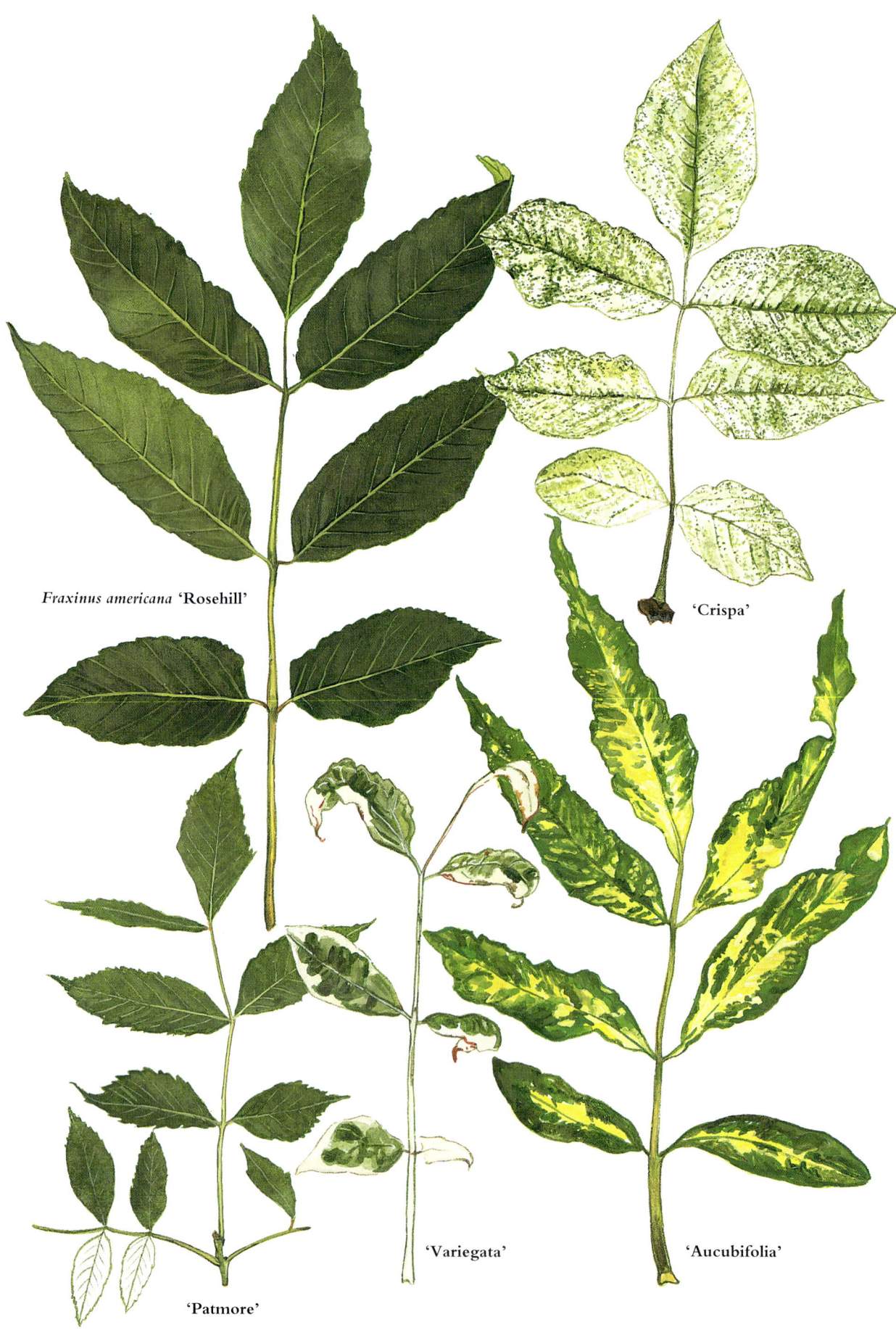

Fraxinus americana 'Rosehill'

'Crispa'

'Patmore'

'Variegata'

'Aucubifolia'

720

Fraxinus americana 'Rosehill'

This hardy cultivar is fast-growing with a vigorous persistent stem and bold foliage. The compound pinnate leaves with 5-9 leaflets are dark green above and almost white on the underside. In the autumn the foliage all turns through red to bronze-purple before falling. This is a good town tree where space permits and one of the best autumn colour White Ashes. It was selected by Evert Asjes of Rosehill Gardens, Kansas City, Missouri and patented in 1966.
Growth: 3-7-12. Hardiness: 40-50%. Choice: 1, 2.

Fraxinus pennsylvanica cultivars

Green Ash, or Water Ash as it is also known in its native North America, (p. 719) has produced several good decorative cultivars. '**Crispa**' a rare variegated form with crimped leaflets is not in cultivation. It should not be confused with *Fraxinus excelsior* 'Crispa', which has dark green deformed leaves. '**Patmore**' is a fastigiate form selected especially for urban planting. It usually has a straight stem and a narrow crown. Quite different are the cream and green leaflets of '**Variegata**'; they tend to be small and often deformed. However, the colours are bright and the tree remains fairly small. '**Aucubifolia**' is more vigorous with larger strongly pointed leaflets. It has deep yellow and green variegation.
Growth: variable. Hardiness: 90%. Choice: 1.

Pumpkin Ash *Fraxinus profunda*

Wrongly named *Fraxinus tomentosa* in 1813 this American floodplain tree develops into a venerable 24m tall specimen with massive buttresses and swollen appendages from which heavy low spreading branches emerge. The opposite, deciduous pinnate leaves are 20-40cm long with 7-9 large leaflets up to 18cm long. These are short-stalked but not always exactly in opposite pairs. Some individuals have almost no teeth and others have forward pointing saw teeth with fine points. The undersides are yellowish green and softly pubescent. Winter buds are brown and the stout young shoots soon turn from green to pale grey in the first year. The insignificant male flowers are yellow and the females are green produced before the leaves appear in spring on separate trees. The fruits, in pendulous bunches, are up to 7.5cm long. This fairly rare tree is a native species on wet ground from southern Maryland to north Florida and west to Illinois and Louisiana. It was introduced to European horticulture in 1912.
Growth: 3-12-24. Hardiness: 50%. Choice: 3. Wood: 5.

underside

Pumpkin Ash

♂ flowers

Oregon Ash

♀ flowers

Oregon Ash

fruit

fruit

Oregon Ash

Arizona Ash
young tree

722

Oregon Ash *Fraxinus latifolia*

Ash in north-west North America is represented by this single species. It is a valuable hardwood timber tree around 25m tall with a straight stem and usually a compact narrow outline. The natural distribution includes parts of Washington State, Oregon and south to central California. This range is extended by extensive planting along the Pacific coast for decoration and shade. In this role it is completely wind firm and the fallen leaves are small and not much of a nuisance. The compound pinnate leaves are 15-30cm long with 5-7 more or less untoothed or coarsely toothed leaflets. The undersides are distinctly hairy with pale stellate hairs especially along the veins in summer. Oregon Ash, originally called *Fraxinus oregona* in 1849, was discovered by David Douglas the Scottish plant collector in 1825 on the Columbia River. It was first recorded in Europe, at Berlin Botanic Garden, in 1872. In some parts of America it is said that where this tree grows, poisonous snakes, especially rattlesnakes, will not go.

Growth: 3-12-25. Hardiness: 30-40%. Choice: 3. Wood: 1, 5.

Arizona Ash *Fraxinus velutina*

A more apt name for this species, often used in its native North America, is Velvet Ash. The shoots, leaf rachis and leaflets are all covered in dense white pubescence on typical trees, although occasional ones may be glabrous. The native range is quite restricted, extending in two narrow strips from the Mexican border to central California and from Trans-Pecos Texas to Utah. It is planted as a shade tree in California but the foliage is light and it affords little shade. Often the leaves consist of only three mealy-green leaflets on a short 6-8cm winged rachis. The first tree on record in Europe was the 1891 planting at Kew Gardens in London.

Growth: 2-7-15. Hardiness: 30%. Choice: 1. Wood: 5.

Texas Ash *Fraxinus texensis*

Hot dry rocky Texas hillsides, especially on lime-rich geology, suit this species very well. It is not a large tree, specimens 12m tall are as good as it gets, but it has a dense crown of lush foliage. The leaflets are unusually broad for an ash. Usually they are in fives. The terminal one may be up to 10cm long and 7cm wide and the others are often 8cm long and 5cm wide. The flowers on separate male and female trees are purple and appear before the leaves in spring. Texas Ash was discovered by Dr. J M Bigelow in 1852 and sent to Europe in 1901.

Growth: 2-7-12. Hardiness: 20-30%. Choice: 1. Wood: 5.

Arizona Ash

underside

Texas Ash

♂ flowers

Common Ash

old bark

♀ flowers

fruit

'Pendula'

Common Ash

Common Ash *Fraxinus excelsior*

The Common Ash extends throughout Europe from the Mediterranean coast to Norway and eastwards to the Caucasus and western Russia. In the north it is a large tree over 30m tall but in the hot dry south it is often reduced to a shrubby bush. It can be distinguished from most other ash trees by its black velvety buds on light grey shoots. These are opposite and decussate and in terminal clusters. Sometimes the vigorous shoot regrowth on coppice stools is purplish or green for a time before taking on its characteristic silver-grey colour in 2-4 years. As trees mature the bark develops a fine lattice pattern of ridges and fissures but remains pale-coloured, grey or buff. The pinnate compound leaves have 6-12 pairs of unstalked elliptic-ovate shallowly toothed leaflets. Before falling they turn to a warm dusty gold. The flowers in dense axillary panicles are maroon to black but very small and insignificant appearing well before the leaves in late winter. Some trees are male or female but others are bisexual. They appear to be able to change their gender status year by year. The 4-5cm winged seeds are in pendulous bunches. Sometimes they will stay on the leafless tree all winter but then take two years to germinate.

In the past Common Ash was economically the most valuable of all European trees, but with its timber, quality was dependent upon the type of soil on which it was grown. Ash plantations also have to be managed properly; for example crowns must never be shaded by other trees, even other ash trees. Timber trees must never be left standing too long. Wood quality peaks at between 50 and 70 years of age. It is then white, tough and elastic but not durable so it should not be used in contact with the soil. As laminated timber it is ideal for functional furniture and shop or office fittings.

The Weeping Ash '**Pendula**' has occurred repeatedly in cultivation and in nature. The first recorded plant appeared near Cambridge around 1760. Many early trees survive in gardens. They are usually grafted on to a Common Ash stock as much as 5m above the ground.

The Golden Ash '**Jaspidea**' has yellow twigs and is a most effective winter feature while it is relatively small. It grows rapidly and soon exceeds 10m in height. The foliage is also yellow in the autumn. This clone should not be confused with 'Aurea' (p. 729) which, according to the Hillier Nursery, is a dwarf plant.

Growth: 3-15-30 (species). Hardiness: 70-80%. Choice: 3. Wood: 1, 5.

'Jaspidea'

autumn

'Eureka'

'Nana'

var. *dumosa*

Syrian Ash

Afghan Ash

'Eureka'

Afghan Ash

726

Fraxinus excelsior cultivars

'**Eureka**' is a cultivar from around 1940 with bold foliage, a neat outline while young, and usually a straight stem. Although developed in Holland as a street tree it is still not in general cultivation in the British Isles however, plants as far apart as western Ireland and London are growing well. The Common Ash cultivar '**Nana**' is scarcely more than a rather untidy bush. Quite often the foliage is weak and yellowish green.

Growth: variable. Hardiness: 60%. Choice: 1.

Syrian Ash Fraxinus angustifolia subsp. *syriaca*

This rare tree is from western and central Asia. The leaves are pale green, relatively small and somewhat crowded together. It was first cultivated as a species, *Fraxinus syriaca*, in 1880 but remains rare in cultivation.

Growth: 2-6-10. Hardiness: 40-50%. Choice: 4.

Afghan Ash Fraxinus xanthoxyloides

Often only a shrubby bush this small-leaved ash is from Afghanistan and the western Himalayas. The 5-9 leaflets are only 3-5cm long and glabrous. In order to create an ornamental tree from this shrub many early specimens were grafted on to a standard rootstock. The variety **dumosa** has compound pinnate leaves not more than 4cm long with 5-7 tiny leaflets. Some authorities suggest this variety is of hybrid origin. It was introduced in 1865.

Growth: 2-4-7. Hardiness: 40-50%. Choice: 1.

Caucasian Ash

Fraxinus angustifolia subsp. *oxycarpa*

Selected for planting in urban areas for its outstanding shape and fine delicate foliage, this subspecies is almost identical to the species (p. 731). The lanceolate pointed leaflets are 4-7cm long and sharply serrate. From southern Europe, Persia and the Caucasus it was introduced originally, as *Fraxinus oxycarpa* in 1815. It is usually represented as the cultivar 'Raywood' which has bronze-purple autumn colour (below).

Growth: 3-7-10. Hardiness: 50-60%. Choice: 2.

Fraxinus angustifolia 'Raywood'

Formerly a cultivar of *Fraxinus oxycarpa* this tree was selected in 1928 for its outstanding bronze-purple autumn foliage colour. It is an ideal town tree, having a compact habit and very small leaflets which do not block drains or make a huge mess. In summer it is bright green with typical 'Narrow-leaved Ash' lacy foliage (p. 731). Where room permits this is a good garden tree, but it should not be planted within 15m of a building.

Growth: 3-7-10. Hardiness: 50-60%. Choice: 1, 2.

Caucasian Ash

Fraxinus angustifolia '**Raywood**'
autumn

fruit

'Diversifolia Pendula'

'Elegantissima'

'Scolopendrifolia'

forma *diversifolia*

leaf variations

'Elegantissima'

forma ***diversifolia***

Fraxinus excelsior cultivars (continued)

The old cultivar '**Elegantissima**' selected from *Fraxinus excelsior* var. *angustifolia* in 1906, is a narrow-leaved form which has largely been superseded by newer types of *Fraxinus angustifolia*. In most respects it is exactly like the Common Ash species. The peculiar tree '**Scolopendrifolia**' has broad, almost round leaflets often with notched ends like Common Alder (p. 317). This plant is not in cultivation and the integrity of its name is dubious.

The 'One-leaved Ash', *Fraxinus excelsior* forma ***diversifolia***, is a variable foliage type which grows into a large 15-20m tall tree. Compound pinnate leaves are reduced to three leaflets or to a single leaf. The teeth are usually much exaggerated, so from a distance it is sometimes difficult to say the foliage is not Common Ash. The general spiky appearance and outline of the tree are exactly the same. This form has arisen independently several times since it was first noted in cultivation in 1789. In 1804 it was named *monophylla* by René Desfontaines in Paris and in the same year *heterophylla* by Martin Vahl in Copenhagen. An excellent single-leaved form was discovered in 1830 near Hillsborough in Ireland. This actual plant was widely distributed and is probably still in cultivation as 'Diversifolia'. A weeping form of 'One-leaved Ash' named '**Diversifolia Pendula**' is also in cultivation. Like most pendulous ash trees it is a curiosity but not a particularly good feature.

A selection of ordinary 'Weeping Ash' (p. 725), '**Pendula Wentworthii**' was once a popular cultivar in Britain, but it finally went out of cultivation in 1998. It is almost impossible to separate this clone from the other Weeping Ashes.

The little shrub '**Aurea**' is another almost forgotten cultivar. According to Hilliers Nursery it is a slow-growing plant and quite distinct from the Golden Ash 'Jaspidea' (p. 725). This is a poor specimen which is probably no longer available in the nursery trade. Elwes and Henry in 1906 were clearly referring to 'Jaspidea' when they described the variety *aurea* of Loudon.

Growth: variable. Hardiness: 60-70%. Choice: 1.

'Aurea'
late spring

'Pendula Wentworthii'

'Diversifolia Pendula'

bark grafted on Common Ash bole

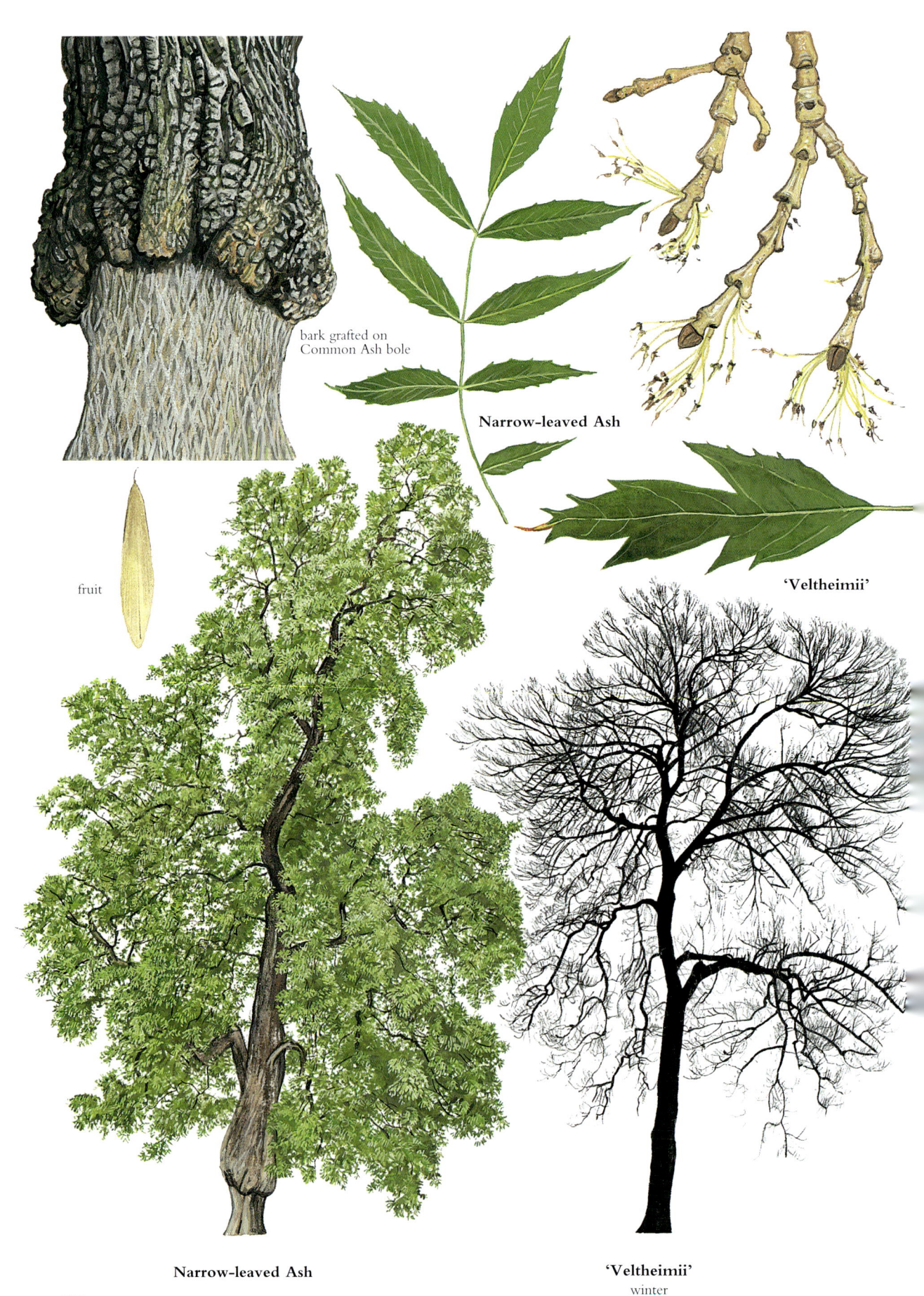

Narrow-leaved Ash

fruit

'Veltheimii'

Narrow-leaved Ash

'Veltheimii'
winter

Narrow-leaved Ash *Fraxinus angustifolia*

This vigorous tree from southern Europe and western Asia has very narrow leaflets which are extremely decorative. It was introduced in 1800 and has been subjected to rigorous selection for urban planting in recent years. The species itself is probably less often planted now than some of its well known cultivars. It is a big tree around 25m tall with dark brown winter buds and rugged mature bark. Early specimens were often grafted on to Common Ash but the Narrow-leaved species usually out-grows the rootstock and becomes grossly incompatible.

The cultivar '**Veltheimii**' is unlike any ash. It has single, not pinnate, glabrous leaves which are more regular in shape and less diverse than the 'one-leaved' Common Ash (p. 725). Each one is 8-12cm long on a 4-6cm slender petiole. There are about 8 pairs of large saw-teeth which occasionally split to form a pair of pointed lobes. Originally named var. *monophylla*, this superb tree was introduced in 1885.

'**Obliqua**' is an obscure tree brought into cultivation from western Asia in 1834, but it is probably no longer available. Originally it was thought to be a species in its own right. The 7-11 strongly toothed leaflets are 4-8cm long, but the terminal one may exceed 12cm, and be oblique at the base.

The best known selections of Narrow-leaved Ash are 'Raywood' and subspecies *oxycarpa* (p. 727), listed for many years as *Fraxinus oxycarpa*.

Growth: 3-12-25. Hardiness: 40-50%. Choice: 3 (species), 1 (cvs). Wood: 1, 5 (species).

Fraxinus pallisae

Closely related to *Fraxinus holotricha* (p. 713), this very rare tree comes from the Balkan Peninsular. Its compound pinnate leaves consist of 5-11 stalkless leaflets which are ovate-lanceolate and remotely toothed and pointed. They are small at the base of the leaf and gradually become larger towards the tip. The fruits, in pendulous clusters, are 4-5cm long with a single stiff wing. The introduction date is thought to be 1840 but very little is known about this obscure tree. It is no longer in cultivation.

Growth: 2-6-12. Hardiness: 50%. Choice: 4.

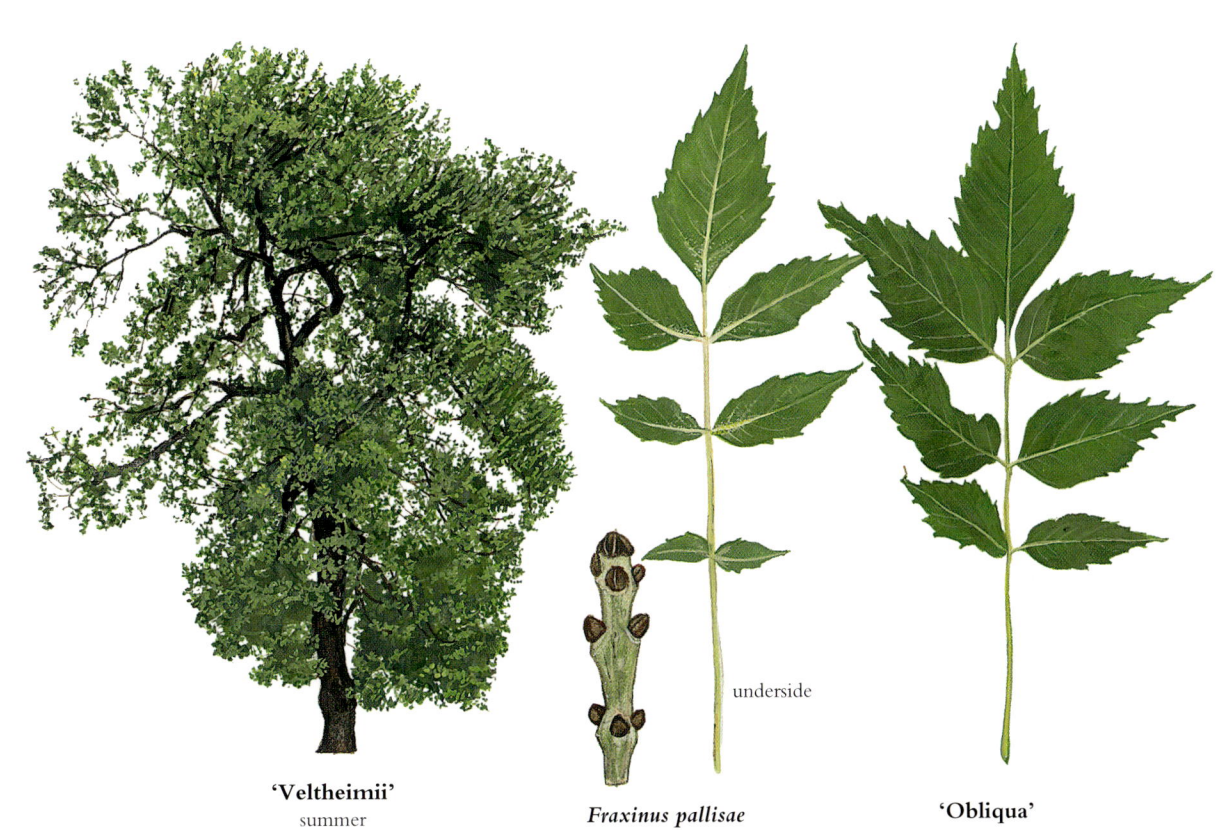

'Veltheimii'
summer

Fraxinus pallisae

'Obliqua'

Kohuhu

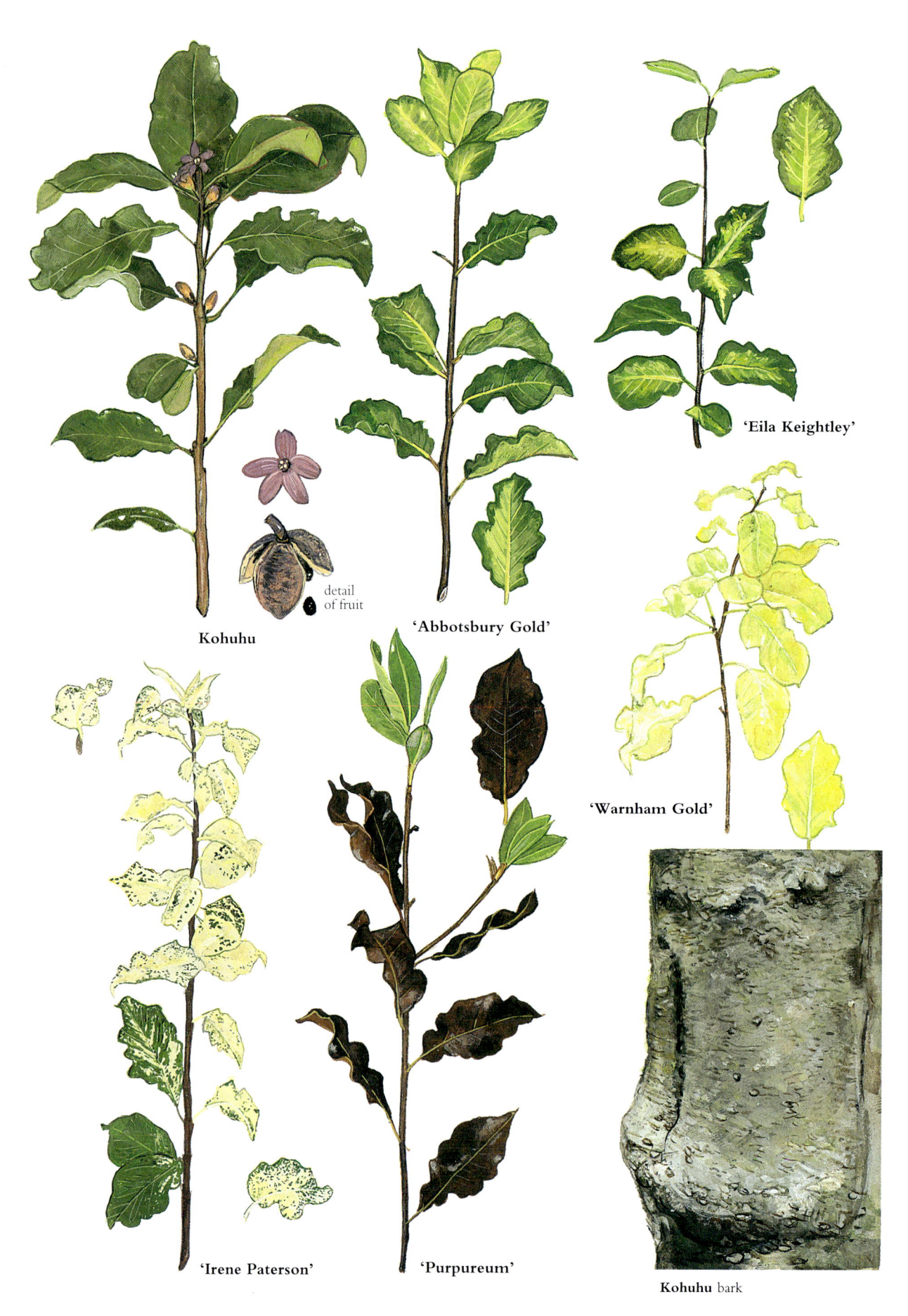

detail of fruit

'Abbotsbury Gold'

'Eila Keightley'

'Warnham Gold'

'Irene Paterson'

'Purpureum'

Kohuhu bark

PITTOSPORUM FAMILY · Pittosporaceae

Kohuhu *Pittosporum tenuifolium*

In its native New Zealand this can become a tree to 30m in height. In cultivation it is more likely to be a large shrub or clipped hedge. It has a soft columnar outline with numerous twiggy branches. The bark is dark grey-brown or almost black. The evergreen oblong, obovate and elliptic leaves (all on the same plant) are up to 10cm long. The entire margins undulate, which causes light from any direction to reflect from their lustrous leathery surface. This and the pale green colour give the whole plant a bright airy appearance. The flowers are purplish-brown, solitary or in small terminal or axillary clusters. They appear in spring and are sweetly scented.

In cool temperate regions this species can only be grown in very sheltered places or close to the sea. It seems to thrive in sandy coastal situations and is benefitting from recent climate change to warmer conditions in Northern Europe. The foliage is used in floristry where the contrast between the dark bark and the pale leaves is much appreciated.

Growth: 2-4-5. Hardiness: 30-40%. Choice: 1.

Pittosporum cultivars

'**Abbotsbury Gold**', which was noticed as a sport on the species at sub-tropical Abbotsbury Gardens on the south coast of England in 1970, is a variegated form with golden young leaves which become green as they mature. '**Eila Keightley**', formerly called 'Sunburst' has blotched yellow and green leaves. It appeared in 1964 as a sport on the round-leaved form 'Rotundifolium'. '**Irene Paterson**' is a dwarf shrub from New Zealand. The leaves are creamy-white at first, maturing to mottled green with a pink tinge in winter. It was discovered in the wild in 1970. '**Purpureum**' is a fine garden plant with shining deep brownish-purple mature foliage. '**Warnham Gold**' is a cultivar with young butter yellow leaves that mature to golden yellow. They do not turn green as so many other golden forms of Pittosporum do. It was discovered at Warnham Court in southern England in 1959. The cultivar '**Variegatum**' is probably not pure *Pittosporum tenuifolium*. It has cream edged leaves. '**Garnettii**' is a hybrid between *tenuifolium* and *Pittosporum ralphii*. A good bushy greenish-grey-leaved shrub or small tree which is variegated in a subtle way with cream and light pink leaf markings.

Growth: variable. Hardiness: 30-40%. Choice: 1.

'Variegatum'   'Garnettii'   Kohuhu

Tupelo

♂ flowers

♀ flowers

Swamp Tupelo
autumn

Nyssa sinensis

fruit

Tupelo
winter

Tupelo
autumn

734

TUPELO FAMILY • Nyssaceae

Tupelo *Nyssa sylvatica*

Also known as Black Gum, this ornamental tree is of particular environmental value, providing fruit for birds and nectar for bees. It is native in a huge area of eastern North America from Ontario to the borders of Mexico, usually as a component of mixed woodlands. It grows to between 15m and 30m in height with 5-12cm elliptical-oblong deciduous leaves. Its ornamental strength is outstanding autumn colour, unrivalled fiery reds and orange. The fruits, on separate female trees, are juicy and reminiscent of a wild cherry but bitter to the taste.

Growth: 2-8-20. Hardiness: 60-70%. Choice: 1, 3.
Wood: 1, 2, 4, 5.

Swamp Tupelo *Nyssa sylvatica* var. *biflora*

Inevitably Tupelo, with such a wide geographic range, will evolve differently on extreme sites. This variety occupies wet lands between North Carolina, Florida and Louisiana. It has slightly narrower leaves. The rather flat berries are usually produced in pairs.

Growth: 2-7-18. Hardiness: 40%. Choice: 1, 3.
Wood: 1, 2, 4, 5.

Nyssa sinensis

A 20m tree from central China with deciduous elliptic 15cm leaves. The fruits are bluish, 1.5cm long usually occurring in pairs on short stalks. In cultivation it is often shrubby but the red autumn colour, and red-coloured young growths are superb. It was first cultivated in Europe in 1902 but remains rare.

Growth: 2-8-20. Hardiness: 30-40%. Choice: 1.
Wood: 1, 2, 4, 5.

Water Tupelo *Nyssa aquatica*

This is a large narrow tree, 30m tall in America, with a vertical stem often developing a swollen base. The deciduous ovate leaves are 14–18cm long with a few large teeth or small lobes and longer stalks than other tupelos. The flowers are pale green developing, on female trees, into fleshy 2.5cm purple berries. The stones are deeply ridged. This is a wetland species, even seasonally flooded ground is tolerated. Its natural range extends from northern Florida to southern Illinois and in a fragmented distribution to south-east Texas.

Growth: 2-7-18. Hardiness: 30-40%. Choice: 1.
Wood: 1, 2, 4, 5.

Ogeechee Tupelo *Nyssa ogeche*

Usually an untidy shrubby tree with a leaning or crooked stem, this plant originated in northern Florida, South Carolina and south Georgia. It has typical Nyssa foliage which colours well. An occasional lobe appears randomly on some leaves. The flowers are greenish and about 0.5cm across. The fruit, on female trees, is a dull red berry up to 4cm long. It has sour pulp and a deeply ridged stone. To grow properly this tree needs wet soils, a similar habitat to the Water Tupelo.

Growth: 2-6-8. Hardiness: 30%. Choice: 1. Wood: 5.

Water Tupelo

Ogeechee Tupelo

juvenile leaves

Mountain Gum

Mountain Gum bark variants

Mount Wellington Peppermint

fruit

adult leaves

Shining Gum

juvenile leaves

Mountain Gum

Shining Gum

MYRTLE FAMILY • Myrtaceae

Mountain Gum *Eucalyptus dalrympleana*

This tree is a subalpine species from New South Wales, Victoria and Tasmania. On Mainland Australia it grows up to elevations of 1300m. In its natural habitat it can be a tree or just a shrubby bush, depending on the prevailing climatic conditions. In cultivation, particularly in mild localities, it grows rapidly to a huge size with a straight stem. A tree in Ireland has exceeded 34m in height with a stem 94cm in diameter. The bark exfoliates to reveal a range of brightly-coloured patches including cream, blue-grey, pink and brown. Even where stems are large the timber quality is poor. This species is susceptible to silverleaf disease (*Chondrostereum purpureum*) in cultivation so it should only be pruned in the summer.

Growth: 4-22-30. Hardiness: 20-30%. Choice: 3. Wood: 3, 5.

Mount Wellington Peppermint
Eucalyptus coccifera

A variable subalpine tree from Tasmania, this species is one of the most hardy Eucalyptus. It varies from a twisted bush to a 20m straight tree. The smooth bark is white with pale grey patches eventually stripping off vertically. The bluish-green 5-7cm adult leaves have a peppermint scent. A plant is on record in Scotland over 28m tall.

Growth: 3-18-25. Hardiness: 30%. Choice: 3. Wood: 3, 5.

Shining Gum *Eucalyptus nitens*

This fast-growing tree is a 'blue gum' from New South Wales and Victoria in Australia. It makes a 40m tall slender tree on good moist soil in a sheltered position. It withstands some snow but can not be described as hardy. The 10-25cm leaves start purplish grey and turn grey-green as they develop. The juveniles are opposite and the adult leaves are alternate. The bark is mostly smooth but shreds in a characteristic way. Long thin vertical sheets are exfoliated and immediately roll up in the sun. Many hang on by a thread covering the lower stem and looking like organ pipes until they are blown away by the wind. Unlike many Eucalyptus this species does not coppice.

Growth: 3-8-15 (40 in native region). Hardiness: 20%. Choice: 3. Wood: 2, 3, 5.

Spinning Gum *Eucalyptus perriniana*

Spinning Gum, a species from south-east Australia and Tasmania, is a small 10m tree in the 'white gum' group. It is a popular ornamental curiosity because of the pairs of opposite juvenile leaves, which are connate (fused around the stem). Once they become dysfunctional, they cling to each other and spin round the branch in the wind. When they do fall off the leaf scars, and possibly the effect of the spinning, results in branches which are ringed at short intervals like a truncated bamboo.

Growth: 3-8-10. Hardiness: 30-40%. Choice: 1, 3.

Alpine Snow Gum

Urn Gum

fruit

underside

juvenile leaves

fruit

Urn Gum

seedling

Alpine Snow Gum

fruit

young tree

Urn Gum

Alpine Snow Gum

Eucalyptus pauciflora subsp. *niphophila*

This alpine form of Snow Gum is confined to high elevation locations in south-east Australia and Tasmania. It reaches higher into the mountains than any other Eucalyptus, and withstands deep snow and temperatures down to -22°C. Most specimens are bushy with long bending stems and branches. Typically these are brilliant white and smooth until pinkish-brown patches of bark develop and then exfoliate.

The species was described in 1929. Originally *niphophila* was regarded as a species name, the subspecies designation is relatively recent. Experimental plantations have been established in Britain but they tend to demonstrate hardiness rather than productivity. In the European context this species with its white bark and grey leaves does not fit easily into the landscape. It also tends to become unstable and lean or fall over.

Growth: 3-10-18. Hardiness: 50%. Choice: 1. Wood: 5.

Urn Gum *Eucalyptus urnigera*

This species is restricted to Mount Wellington in central Tasmania. It has been planted commercially for wind-breaks and as an ornament over a much wider area. It is a small tree or large bush usually with drooping branches. The flowers are relatively large and showy for a Eucalyptus. The leaves are waxy and narrow, 8-15cm long and glossy green. The name refers to the fruit capsules which are around 16mm long and 9mm wide and distinctly urn-shaped, something like poppy seed heads. They occur in small clusters of 3. This species was discovered in the early nineteenth century and described at Kew Gardens in London in 1842 although it was apparently not growing in Britain until 1860. Fine ornamental specimens can be found growing in the cool moist climate of western Ireland.

Growth: 4-20-25. Hardiness: 30%. Choice: 1, 2, 3. Wood: 3, 4, 5.

Tingiringi Gum *Eucalyptus glaucescens*

This small tree, usually about 4-10m tall, occurs high up, 1400-1600m, in the mountains of south-east Australia. Odd specimens have recently been discovered that are 45m tall and 30m trees have now been found on Mount Erica in Victoria. The foliage is silvery blue-green and the bark is smooth and white until it becomes rough with age. This species was first described in 1929. Its potential as a forest species or a tree for decorative planting outside Australia has yet to be investigated.

Growth: 3-9-15 (variable). Hardiness: 30-40%. Choice: 1, 3. Wood: 3, 4, 5.

late juvenile leaves

adult leaf

Tingiringi Gum

juvenile leaves

juvenile leaves

mature leaves

intermediate leaf

Tasmanian Blue Gum

juvenile leaves

Cider Gum

Cider Gum

seedling

Tasmanian Blue Gum

fruit

seedling

Cider Gum

fruit

Tasmanian Blue Gum *Eucalyptus globulus*

This very fast-growing but somewhat tender tree is the floral emblem of Tasmania. It also comes from the State of Victoria. Trees with straight stems up to 60m tall are to be found. The timber is used for construction work and is available in generous thicknesses and long lengths. Dense crowns give mature trees a healthy vigorous appearance. Juvenile leaves are grey-green and have become well known as garden plants in summer bedding schemes. The dark green adult leaves are large and leathery, up to 40cm long and 6cm wide. The bark is a mixture of patchy blue-grey, yellow and brown, becoming deciduous with age and falling off in ribbons.

Growth: 4-22-30. Hardiness: 20%. Choice: 3.
Wood: 2, 3, 4, 5.

Cider Gum *Eucalyptus gunnii*

The natural range of this species is upland Tasmania at around 1200m. It is usually a tall tree with a straight vertical stem. The illustration shows a plant which has re-grown after being eaten, burned or cut down: a frequent occurrence because this species is often predated by animals. The foliage has almost no repellent Eucalyptus smell. The bark is variable, smooth patchy olive green and grey, or stringy pale brown, yellow and grey.

In 1846 this was the first native Australian tree to grow in the open air in Britain. Although the timber is of relatively low value, cider gum is planted as a forest tree throughout the temperate world. The subspecies *archerii* is even hardier and shows great promise for forest use. The roundish powder-blue juvenile leaves of cider gum are extensively used in floristry.

Growth: 4-22-30. Hardiness: 40%. Choice: 1 (requires space).
Wood: 2, 3, 4, 5.

Silver Gum *Eucalyptus cordata*

Of all the gums grown in the temperate zone this 15-25m tree is one of the most tender. It is from Tasmania, where it was discovered in 1792 and introduced to Europe before 1840. The main use for it today is as a summer bedding plant in municipal gardens and parks. In a matter of weeks after sowing 10-20cm seedlings are fit to plant out. During the summer season they will grow to around 1m tall with a profusion of silvery-grey stalkless juvenile leaves. Unfortunately the first autumn frost will scorch them or kill them off. As a fully grown tree, in mild districts, this species has attractive white and grey bark. The slender heart-shaped adult leaves retain a glaucous appearance. The flowers, which in Europe often appear in winter, are showy and numerous.

Growth: 3-16-20. Hardiness: 10%. Choice: 1, 3.
Wood: 2, 3, 4, 5.

Cider Gum bark

young tree

frost-damaged leaves

Silver Gum

fruit

Tasmanian Yellow Gum

fruit

a *Eucalyptus* hybrid

seedling

Tasmanian Yellow Gum

juvenile leaves

a *Eucalyptus* hybrid

742

Eucalyptus hybrids

The *Eucalyptus*, part of the Myrtle family, contains about 600 species. They are widely distributed in Australia, often confined to isolated creeks and river valleys in the centre of the country. Many are only species because they have been in isolation for so long. They are genetically compatible so, given the opportunity, they are capable of hybridizing. When moved into close proximity, in collections for example, a bewildering range of hybrids occur. Identity and nomenclature are thrown into chaos.

Growth: variable. Hardiness: 10-30%. Choice: 1 (require space). Wood: 3, 5.

Tasmanian Yellow Gum

Eucalyptus johnstonii

Botanically this is classified as a true gum. It is from Tasmania, growing up to 1000m. Opinion is divided about its hardiness but cultivated strains from high elevations are clearly more hardy than those from lower down. It is a large tree, 40m may be expected on a moist sheltered site and 60m trees have been recorded in Tasmania. In Ireland growth over 2m a year occurs. The stem is very straight, like a huge flag pole, with blue-grey young bark which turns brown with age and exfoliates in a pile at the base of the stem. Tree tops are usually narrow and dense. The 10cm lanceolate evergreen leaves are glossy green on distinctive deep red young shoots. The seed capsules, in threes, are around 1cm long and stalkless. This is a fairly recent introduction to horticulture.

Growth: 4-26-40 (60 in native region). Hardiness: 30%. Choice: 1 (requires space), 3. Wood: 1, 2, 3, 4, 5.

Black Sallee *Eucalyptus stellulata*

This is a small 6-10m spreading tree in the 'ash' group (nothing to do with the genus *Fraxinus*). It is moderately hardy and withstands winter snow. From the Australian States of Victoria and New South Wales this tree has a preference for wet sites. The bark is smooth, greyish to olive green, and rough towards the base. The leaves are narrow and elliptic, leathery, evergreen and up to 8cm long and 3cm wide. It is the flower buds that give this plant its species name. They are sharply pointed and arranged in sessile clusters of 7-16 which resemble stars. The flowers are prolific and provide a good source of nectar for bees. Fruit capsules, which are up to 8mm long, also occur in conspicuous clusters.

Growth: 3-8-10. Hardiness: 30-40%. Choice: 1, 3. Wood: 5.

Black Sallee

old bark

Handkerchief Tree

flower bract

fruit

undersides

var. *vilmoriniana*

Handkerchief Tree

Handkerchief Tree

fruit (enlarged)

DAVIDIA FAMILY • Davidiaceae

Handkerchief Tree *Davidia involucrata*

The Handkerchief, or Dove Tree, is a favourite temperate garden specimen world-wide. It is large and vigorous and on a good site might reach half its ultimate height in only 25 years. It will grow to over 20m in mild sheltered localities. It is native to China where it was discovered by the Jesuit plant collector and missionary the Abbé Armand David in 1869. It was subsequently named in his honour, and introduced to Europe by Ernest Wilson in 1904.

The main attraction of the Handkerchief Tree is its late spring display, not of flowers, but of pure white ovate pointed bracts surrounding the flowers. These are in unequal-sized pairs, the longest being up to 20cm and the short one usually under 10cm. They hang down on a slender stalk shielding the insignificant globular 2cm clusters of dark greenish male or female flowers. The whole structure is aerodynamically unstable and constantly moves even in the lightest wind. From seed it may take 20 years to flower, but the strong bold foliage and usually impressive form of the young plant is in itself garden-worthy. The anticipation of flowers in the future is a source of interest and much discussion among growers. It is possible to buy grafted plants or saplings raised from cuttings which will flower earlier because material can be used which is already mature and in a flowering state. The dangers of this are possible graft incompatibility, and a tendency for graft scions, or cuttings, not to grow upwards.

Handkerchief Trees require moist fertile soil, and some shelter to thrive. They are especially rewarding if well spaced out, especially in association with other large trees. Extremes of climate, for instance drought and sun scorch, and spring or autumn frost, can cause damage. Exposure to cold or drying winds will disfigure or even kill foliage and branches, and ruin the flowers.

The variety **vilmoriniana** is very similar to the species in every other respect, but it lacks the downy backs to the leaves. It is equally good as a garden tree. Many cultivated specimens are in fact this variety.
Growth: 3-10-20. Hardiness: 50%. Choice: 1.

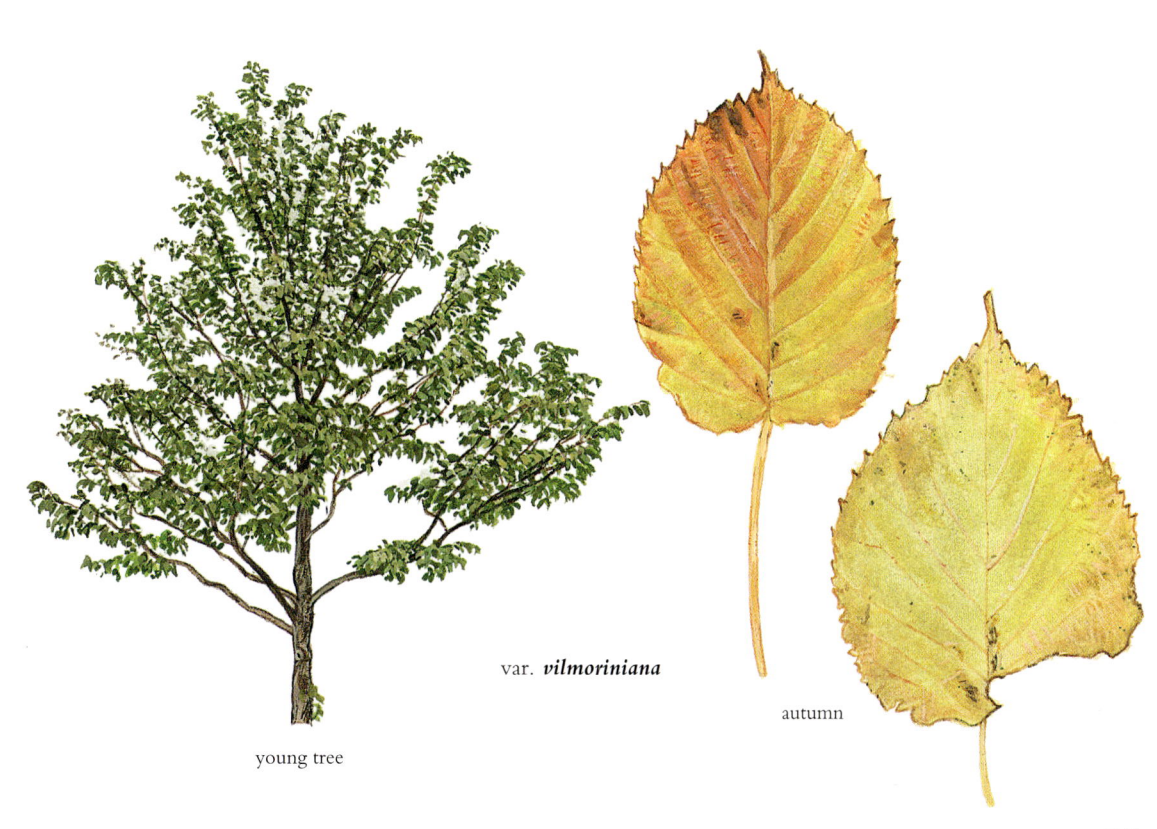

var. *vilmoriniana*

autumn

young tree

old bark

Pacific Dogwood

autumn

Pacific Dogwood

'Gold Spot'

Cornus 'Eddie's White Wonder'

autumn

Pacific Dogwood
winter

fruit

flower bud

746

DOGWOOD FAMILY · Cornaceae

Pacific Dogwood *Cornus nuttallii*

There are basically two kinds of dogwood flower. One has distinctly large bracts and the other has not. This species is in the first category. Although potentially a big tree up to 20-25m tall, Pacific Dogwood is more often seen in cultivation as a large multi-stemmed shrub. It is native to woodlands in western North America, and it is also widely planted there in parks and gardens. It tends to be tender and short lived in northern Europe and eastern North America. The 4-7 creamy-white flower bracts are up to 7cm long, oval to obovate with an abrupt point. As they age they become flushed with pink. The flowering season is late spring. In the autumn the foliage turns to brilliant orange and scarlet.

The cultivar '**Gold Spot**' is a distinctive form with variegated leaves that become more spectacular late in the year as they mature.

Growth: 2-6-10 (25 in native region). Hardiness: 30%. Choice: 1.

Cornus 'Eddie's White Wonder'

This hybrid between *Cornus florida* and *Cornus nuttallii* was produced artificially in America, uniting eastern and western species. The bracts, mostly in fours, are white, or occasionally slightly flushed with pink. The foliage colours very well in the autumn.

Growth: 2-6-10. Hardiness: 40%. Choice: 1.

Alternate-leaved Dogwood *Cornus alternifolia*

This species is peculiar for a dogwood because of its alternate leaves (most other species are opposite). These are ovate and may be up to 12cm long. The flattened 8cm inflorescences superficially resemble elder and do not have large showy bracts. They are creamy-white in early summer but of little significance.

From the whole of eastern North America, Newfoundland to Florida and Georgia, this small tree was introduced to Europe in 1760. One of its American names, Pagoda Dogwood, reflects the tiered effect produced by upward-facing flowers massed along horizontal branches. In a good dry season reasonable autumn foliage colour can be produced.

The cultivar '**Argentea**' has silvery-cream edged fairly narrow green leaves. It tends to develop vertical stems with tiered horizontal branches and a flat top. Usually it is more of a shrub than a tree, seldom over 3m in height. It was produced in the USA around 1900.

Growth: 2-5-8. Hardiness: 70-80%. Choice: 1.

'Argentea'

fruit

Alternate-leaved Dogwood

Flowering Dogwood

autumn

fruit

'White Cloud'

'Cherokee Chief'

'Variegata'

underside

Table Dogwood
summer

Table Dogwood

Flowering Dogwood *Cornus florida*

Although this can be a tree up to 6m tall it is usually much less in cultivation away from its native eastern North America. Its date of introduction to Europe is uncertain but it was recorded flowering in Enfield, north London, in 1759. The flower bracts, in fours, develop in the autumn and remain wrapped round the flower cluster all winter protecting it from the cold. In spring they open out, become heart-shaped and expand to around 5cm long. The tips are often notched and discoloured pink and pale brown at the point where they were joined. A good plant will produce countless thousands of white bracts in spring before the leaves emerge.

'**Cherokee Chief**' is a selected pink form with narrower more distinctly notched bracts. It was raised in the USA in 1958. The cultivar '**White Cloud**' is more of a pure white form than the species. It was also raised in the USA, but ten years earlier in 1948. Flowering Dogwood occasionally occurs in the wild with pink bracts. Pink forms in cultivation are described as forma *rubra*. There is a reference to them as early as 1770 but they were not brought into cultivation until around 1889. These dogwoods thrive in strong sunshine as experienced in Massachusetts and Florida, but they like their roots in cool shaded soil. The strange cultivar '**Plenifolia**' produces 6-8 normal-sized but screwed up bracts and several more smaller ones round each flower. It was first cultivated in 1914. There are also weeping and variegated forms of Flowering Dogwood. They make excellent garden plants giving early summer interest and autumn foliage colour. But in cold wet soil conditions they are prone to disease.

Growth: 2-5-6. Hardiness: 40-60%. Choice: 1.

Table Dogwood *Cornus controversa*

Like *Cornus alternifolia* (p. 747) this species has alternate leaves. It is a larger tree, though, reaching 20m in its native south-east Asia but less in cultivation. The name Table Dogwood refers to the symmetrical flattened horizontal tiered branches. The ovate leaves are distinctly wedge-shaped towards the base with around eight pairs of parallel veins. With a lens it is possible to see that the remarkable hairs on the underside are joined to the leaf half way along their length. Numerous small creamy-white flowers are produced in flattened cymes up to 18cm across. The fruit is a 1cm blue-black berry. The cultivar '**Variegata**' is a slower-growing form introduced by Veitch's Nursery before 1890. The leaves are narrower, not over 4cm wide, with a cream border.

Growth: 3-8-14. Hardiness: 50%. Choice: 1.

Flowering Dogwood type

'Plenifolia'

forma *rubra*

'Variegata'

Cornus **'Porlock'**

Cornus walteri

Cornus **'Porlock'**

fruit

Cornus macrophylla

var. *chinensis*

underside

Japanese Strawberry Tree
spring

underside

Japanese Strawberry Tree

Japanese Strawberry Tree *Cornus kousa*

This hardy shrub or small tree is not usually more than 6m tall. It is slow-growing, becoming nicely rounded and densely twiggy at maturity. A very useful garden plant in a confined space. The flowers are small and held together in tight clusters. Each one is protected by four upward facing finely pointed 7.5cm ovate bracts. These are yellowish-white at first, then tinted or spotted with pinkish-brown as they mature and decline. A good specimen will be completely covered by fully open bracts every year in early summer. The unique fruits are round, strawberry red and in fused clusters 2-3cm across.

The variety **chinensis** is a larger tree in every respect. It was introduced to America in 1907 by Ernest Wilson, and arrived in England from there in 1910. Both Wilson and Augustine Henry claimed that the fruit was sweet to eat. These trees have the advantage of flowering later than most other spring-flowering subjects in the garden.

Growth: 2-4-6. Hardiness: 50%. Choice: 1.

Cornus 'Porlock'

This plant originated as a self sown hybrid between *Cornus capitata* and *Cornus kousa*. It is like *kousa* but has superior pink-tipped cream-coloured bracts which turn completely pink with age. In a good year this cultivar also fruits well.

Growth: 2-4-6. Hardiness: 50%. Choice: 1.

Cornus walteri

From China, this is a tree of medium stature, up to 12m tall. It was introduced by Ernest Wilson in 1907. The wavy edged leaves are oval 5-12cm long and pointed at both ends. Each of the tiny flowers has four slender white petals less than 1cm long, and prominent yellow stamens. They occur in loose flattened terminal clusters and are superseded by bunches of small 6-7mm hard black berries.

Growth: 2-7-12. Hardiness: 50%. Choice: 1.

Cornus macrophylla

This is a rare late flowering dogwood similar to *Cornus walteri* but it has larger 16cm leaves. It was introduced from the Himalayas to Britain in 1827, and widely distributed, often as a gift to notable gardens, by the Veitch Nursery.

Growth: 2-6-15. Hardiness: 40%. Choice: 1.

Bentham's Cornel *Cornus capitata*

Unfortunately this rare evergreen Himalayan tree, which is so beautiful, is very tender. In most of northern Europe it is only possible to grow it as a south facing wall shrub. It was originally introduced in 1825. A later introduction from China in 1937 has survived rather better in Britain as far north as Edinburgh. The early summer flowers are protected by 4-6 light yellow 5cm bracts. The agglomerated fruits are on long hanging stalks like those of *Cornus kousa*.

Growth: 2-4-6. Hardiness: 10-20%. Choice: 1.

Japanese Strawberry Tree
summer

Bentham's Cornel

old bark

young bark

'Integerrima'

underside

flower detail

seedling

'Rubra'

Strawberry Tree

Madrona

752

HEATHER FAMILY • Ericaceae

Strawberry Tree *Arbutus unedo*

A most beautiful evergreen tree able to grow to a height of 10m, but generally gnarled and twisted into a lesser size. It is native to Cork, Kerry and Sligo Countries in Ireland, and western France, Iberia, and the Mediterranean coast to Lebanon and Israel. Strangely this member of the heather family tolerates lime in the soil. In parts of Ireland it appears to grow on almost bare limestone rock. The tough glossy 5-10cm serrate leaves are deep green and more or less elliptical. The 6mm flowers are translucent creamy-white often with a warm pink tinge. They open in late summer. The fruits, which look superficially like strawberries, are red when they ripen, which takes a whole year. Strawberry Trees bear fruit all year round including the time when the following years flowers appear, which is very unusual. The berries are technically edible, the orange flesh is pulpy and full of seeds. Opinions vary as to the taste, but the species name *unedo* means 'I eat one' implying that one is quite enough.

Like *Eucalyptus*, this tree grows from a lignotuber which is an adaptation of the base of the trunk enabling it to survive total destruction above ground. After serious top damage the lignotuber, which contains dormant buds, will sprout and produce new stems indefinitely. Cultivars or forms available for garden use include '**Integerrima**', a slow-growing shrubby plant with white flowers and mostly entire leaves and '**Rubra**' which has pink or deep pink flowers. It has been cultivated since 1835. These trees all need a plentiful supply of water, good drainage and full sun.

Growth: 2-7-10. Hardiness: 40%. Choice: 1, 3.

Madrona *Arbutus menziesii*

The Pacific Madrone (Madrona is the Mexican Spanish name) was discovered by and named after Archibald Menzies (1754-1842) and introduced to Britain by David Douglas in 1827. It seldom reaches 20m in cultivation, but may be considerably more in the wild. Its main feature, the bark, starts off coarse and flaking into curly plates, and then develops smooth vertical patches of red, rusty-brown, cinnamon and grey-green reminiscent of *Eucalyptus*. The white flowers occur in spring and early summer at the same time as the previous years orange-red 1.5cm inedible fruits begin to ripen. The 5-12cm leaves are variable elliptic, oval or ovate and mostly entire. They are shining green above and glaucous beneath. Trees from the south of the natural range, California, Sierra Nevada and Santa Cruz Island are tender. In cultivation Madrona requires acid soil and full sun to thrive.

Growth: 2-7-16. Hardiness: 40-50%. Choice: 1, 3.

young bark

fruit

underside

old bark

Madrona

Grecian Strawberry Tree

Grecian Strawberry Tree

fruit

Hybrid Strawberry Tree

Hybrid Strawberry Tree

Grecian Strawberry Tree *Arbutus andrachne*

Also known as the Cyprus Strawberry Tree, this 6-12m tender evergreen plant is a native species in south-east Europe. It is a domed tree often with several main stems – an ornamental bonus where bark colour is so important. This is smooth at first then peels to reveal pale patches of greenish-grey. With age, areas of bright red, cream and brown develop. The white 6mm heather-like flowers occur on previous years shoots in loose panicles. The fruits ripen in one season. They are rough red spheres about 1.2cm across, which are edible but unpleasant. The leaves are thick and leathery. The Grecian strawberry tree was introduced into cultivation in 1724 and although it will tolerate either lime-rich or acid soils it is not resistant to frost or cold winds.
Growth: 2-5-10. Hardiness: 20%. Choice: 1, 3.

Hybrid Strawberry Tree
Arbutus × andrachnoides

This spontaneous cross between the Irish Strawberry Tree (p. 753) and the Grecian species occurs naturally in Greece. It is also planted in parks and gardens over a wide area. The Irish species brings a degree of hardiness into the hybrid progeny that the Greek species alone does not have. The bark is an important decorative feature, especially the twisted cinnamon-coloured young growths. The top of the tree is domed but seldom exceeds 10m in height. The 4-12cm stiff evergreen leaves on red-brown shoots are variable, glossy-green with a yellowish midrib. Flowers occur both in autumn and in spring, so some flowers are present when the tree bears ripe fruit.
Growth: 2-5-10. Hardiness: 30%. Choice: 1, 3.

Canary Island Strawberry Tree
Arbutus canariensis

Although it was described before 1781, the origin of this species is uncertain; it may be a segregate of the mainland European Strawberry Tree. It is a tender 5-10m bushy plant with oblong-lanceolate leaves that are strongly toothed and have glaucous undersides. The flowers occur in loose erect panicles. They are 1cm across and greenish-white, eventually tinged with pink. The fruit ripens in early summer, it is bright orange, granular and has a rough warty surface. Away from the Canary Islands this plant only thrives in a mild climate.
Growth: 2-5-8. Hardiness: 10-20%. Choice: 1, 3.

Grecian Strawberry Tree

Canary Island Strawberry Tree

flower detail

Sorrel Tree

autumn

Tree Rhododendron
deep red form

Sorrel Tree

Tree Rhododendron

Sorrel Tree *Oxydendrum arboreum*

This member of the heather family can only be grown on acid soils. It originated in eastern North America and thrives best in hot sunshine. It is a deciduous tree reaching 16m in height with whitish terminal panicles of small fragrant summer flowers. These often stick out above the leafy canopy which is a useful identification feature – even in winter when the flowers themselves have finished but the stalks remain. The flowers are a good source of nectar for bees.

Although introduced in 1752 this species remains rare in cultivation, probably due to its intolerance of lime and shade. As a garden tree in very sunny areas it is prized for its glorious red, yellow and purple autumn foliage colour. The name is from the Greek 'oxys' meaning sour (the commercial timber name is sourwood), and 'dendron' – tree, a reference to the sour acid taste of the leaves which is similar to the herbaceous plant Sorrel (*Rumex*). In America the strong hard, heavy wood was traditionally put to various specialist uses, such as wooden bearings and sled runners. It is shock-resistant and has straight grain but is difficult to season.

Growth: 3-8-16 (25 in native region). Hardiness: 40%. Choice: 1. Wood: 1.

Tree Rhododendron *Rhododendron arboreum*

Several species and hybrids of Rhododendron attain the dimensions of a tree, but in northern Europe only this species does it all the time, often reaching 10m in height with a woody stem over 30cm thick. It is a variable evergreen plant originally from the Himalayas, south-west China and Sri Lanka. It was the first rhododendron to be introduced to Europe from the Himalayas in about 1810. The clusters of 5cm bell-shaped flowers occur in late winter and early spring. Confusingly, they may be white, pink or even deep red. These may be called by their respective cultivar names of 'Album', 'Roseum' and 'Blood Red'. Intermediates and hybrids also occur. The tough, thick, leathery leaves are variable, with distinctive felted backs which range from silvery grey to rusty brown. This species has been widely used as a parent in breeding big hardy hybrid rhododendrons. It likes to grow in semi-shade, especially under large deciduous trees, and must have moist acid soil to thrive.

Growth: 3-8-10. Hardiness: 50%. Choice: 1, 4.

pink form

underside

Tree Rhododendron

Snowdrop Tree

Bigleaf Storax

fruit

Epaulette Tree

Hemsley's Storax

fruit

Snowbell Tree

fruit

STORAX FAMILY • Styracaceae

Snowdrop Tree *Halesia carolina*

This is a lovely spreading tree up to 10m tall. The elliptic to ovate-oblong leaves arc 5-10cm long with a finely tapered point. In mid to late spring, as the leaves emerge, clusters of white or creamy-pink 3cm flowers like bells on slender stalks emerge. The contrasting stamens are bright orange. An alternative and apt name for this species is 'Silverbell Tree'. The fruits are not decorative, but do add interest. They are yellowish-green 2-3.5cm oblong capsules with four curious papery wings and a slender 'beak' on the end. As the species name suggests the snowdrop tree is from the south-east United States. *Halesia* commemorates the Rev. Stephen Hales (1677-1761) a writer on plants. Trees thrive best on lime-free soils.
Growth: 2-7-10. Hardiness: 50%. Choice: 1.

Bigleaf Storax *Styrax obassia*

Originally from Japan, Korea and north-east China, this is a large shrub or small tree rarely over 10m tall. The deciduous dark green leaves are variable, elliptic to almost round and up to 20cm across, with an abrupt small point. The fragrant 2.5cm bell flowers, in slender racemes 10-20cm long, have spreading petals and point downwards like snowdrops. This is definitely a plant to be seen from below; otherwise the leaves hide the flowers from view. In the wild state Bigleaf Storax grows in mixed forest, usually as an under-storey, it prefers moist soil and semi-shade.
Growth: 2-7-10. Hardiness: 50%. Choice: 1.

Hemsley's Storax *Styrax hemsleyana*

This excellent plant, introduced in 1900 from China by Ernest Wilson, is a shrubby bush or upright 10m tree. The flowers in terminal racemes, are more or less erect. The prominent yellow stamens show up very well against the white petals. This species thrives in cool shady moist situations in open woodland.
Growth: 2-5-8. Hardiness: 50%. Choice: 1.

Snowbell Tree *Styrax japonica*

The Japanese Snowbell has small 2-8cm leaves arranged in threes so they appear to be trifoliate. The 1.5cm white flowers occur in small clusters or singly on long slender stalks all along the branches. They always hang down like delicate bells with a bright yellow 'clapper' of stamens. This is a spreading, often leaning, tree 6-10m tall. It grows best in semi-shade and prefers moist fertile soil.
Growth: 2-6-8. Hardiness: 50-60%. Choice: 1.

Epaulette Tree *Pterostyrax hispida*

This is a tree 15m tall in its native south-east Asia, but it is usually a lot less in cultivation. It is open-headed with spreading slender branches. The deciduous dark green 'lop-sided' leaves are obovate-oblong 7-17cm long. They colour well in the autumn. The fragrant creamy-white summer flowers are small (8-10mm) in clusters on drooping panicles. The stamens project beyond the end of the bud before it opens. The cylindric 1cm bristly fruits are ribbed. In some specimens these ribs become enlarged to form wings. The genus name comes from the Greek word 'pteron' meaning wing.
Growth: 2-8-15. Hardiness: 50%. Choice: 1.

spring

Snowdrop Tree

old bark

Olive

flower detail

fruit

Wild Olive

Olive

Chinese Privet
flowering

Olive *Olea europaea* (Oleaceae)

This medium-sized tender tree grows in southern Europe. It has been cultivated for its fruit and oil for so long that its natural range has become obscured. However, ancient specimens over 1000 years old occur and some of these are likely to be native trees. The stems are often forked and become gnarled with age. The opposite grey-green, silvery-backed, leaves are evergreen, tough and leathery. The fragrant racemes of white cruciform flowers occur in late summer. Purple black olives with glossy skins are then produced in abundance. The stone is narrowly oval and grooved. Olive wood, although seldom available, is of high quality, exceptionally durable and hard. In Greek mythology it is said that Hercules' club was made from the wood of wild olive. The wild (uncultivated) form does grow in lowland regions of Greece. This tree is benefitting from current climate change and surviving further north in Europe than 30 years ago.

Growth: 2-6-8. Hardiness: 0-10%. Choice: 1, 3. Wood: 1.

Chinese Privet *Ligustrum lucidum* (Oleaceae)

Sir Joseph Banks of the Royal Botanic Gardens, Kew brought this tree out of China in 1794 while on Captain Cook's expedition to the Far East. London still has several good 12m tall ornamental specimens although they are not original. This tree thrives in urban conditions and seems to survive on compacted dry and even eroded soil. It will withstand damage and abuse by people, domestic dogs and grass cutting machines, and also tolerates high levels of air pollution and even proximity to the sea. As an ornament its deep green very glossy pointed evergreen leaves are reminiscent of tropical rain forest species. Its scented upright panicles of tiny creamy-white flowers occur over a long period from mid-summer until the autumn. These mostly stand up above the outline of the foliage. In mild areas they develop into 1cm blue-black berries in clusters, like stiff upright bunches of small grapes. The timber of Chinese Privet, although seldom seen, is hard and heavy, pale yellow-brown and can be worked to a smooth finish.

The cultivar '**Excelsum Superbum**' is like the species but has golden-yellow edged leaves which fade to creamy-white. '**Tricolor**', first cultivated in 1895, has narrow leaves marked with grey-green: they are flushed pink at first with pale pink edges which gradually develop into yellow and finally creamy-white as they age.

Growth: 2-7-10. Hardiness: 10-20%. Choice: 1. Wood: 1 (species).

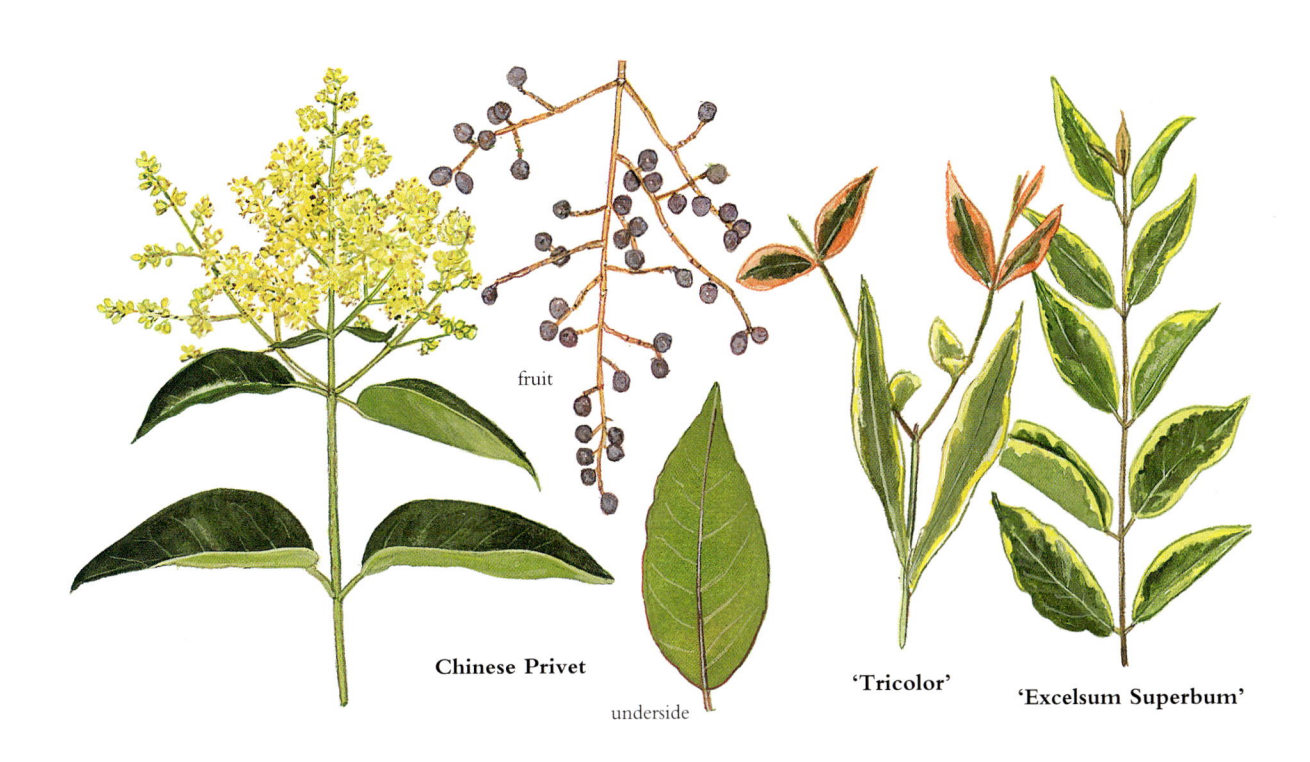

Fringe Tree

Fringe Tree
fruit

Chinese Fringe Tree

Chinese Fringe Tree

Fringe Tree
bush form, flowering

Fringe Tree *Chionanthus virginicus* (Oleaceae)

This member of the Olive family can be a large shrub or small tree up to 10m tall. It has narrow elliptic entire 10-20cm long leaves on short 2cm petioles. The slightly fragrant flowers are showy in loose 20cm panicles, with a cluster of bracts or small leaves at the base of each one. The 5 or 6 creamy-white feathery petals on each flower are up to 3cm long but only 2mm wide. Fruits, produced by separate female plants, are dark blue and bloomed, reminiscent of olives, they are up to 2cm long. Introduced to Europe in 1736, the natural range of this species includes New Jersey, Florida and Texas.

Growth: 2-7-10. Hardiness: 40%. Choice: 1, 3.

Chinese Fringe Tree
Chionanthus retusus (Oleaceae)

Native to China, Korea and Japan, this plant was introduced in 1845 by Robert Fortune. It is a spreading shrub which seldom exceeds 6m in height. The narrow ovate leaves are usually around 6cm long and entire. The flowers in 6-10cm panicles appear in early summer. They are similar to the American species but a little smaller with broader petals and they come out slightly later. The most spectacular flowers occur on male plants but fruit is only produced by females. Whole plants can be completely obscured by white flowers for more than two weeks in a good season.

Growth: 2-4-6. Hardiness: 50%. Choice: 1, 3.

Phillyrea *Phillyrea latifolia* (Oleaceae)

There are four species of evergreen Phillyrea, all originally from around the Mediterranean coast. They have flexible leathery salt-resistant foliage and tolerate high levels of salinity in the soil. They also thrive in sandy places such as stabilised dunes. *Latifolia* is a spreading plant up to 10m tall. The thick leaves are elliptic-ovate, 3-6cm long, with prominent but blunt teeth. They are deep glossy green above and have light matt green undersides. The tiny pale yellowish-white flowers occur in small tight clusters in the leaf axils. These are followed by round blue-black 6mm fruits.

This species' natural range includes most of southern Europe and eastwards to Asia Minor. It has been in cultivation at least since 1597 and is extensively used for coastal protection, decorative qualities and as a wind break. It also makes a good evergreen hedge in city and maritime conditions. Summer clipping does not cause any problems. It seems to positively thrive on de-icing salt spread on roads and pavements. It also makes a good landscape substitute for Holm Oak (p. 373) where space is limited. There are round-leaved and narrow-leaved forms.

Growth: 2-7-10. Hardiness: 30%. Choice: 2. Wood: 1.

fruit

Phillyrea

Persimmon

underside

Persimmon

underside

'Lycopersicum'

seed

Persimmon

'Hachiya'

Chinese Persimmon

EBONY FAMILY · Ebenaceae

Diospyros

There are around 200 species in this genus, which is closely related to ebony. Most of them are tropical and sub-tropical, and they have world-wide distribution. Dios is from the Greek for divine and pyros means grain. 'Divine fruit' aptly describes the juicy edible berries produced by some species. Male and female flowers occur on separate trees. Vegetative propagation by cuttings or layers is essential if the sex of young plants needs to be predetermined.

Persimmon *Diospyros virginiana*

This is a round-headed deciduous tree ultimately with drooping branches, reaching 15-30m in its native southern United States from Connecticut to Kansas and Texas. The flowers open in mid-summer followed by astringent 2.5-5cm orange to orange-brown fruits which ripen, and sweeten, in the autumn. They contain 4-8 flattened 1cm brown seeds. The withered brown calyx remains fixed to the ripe fruit. This is a distinctive feature of Persimmon. To thrive the tree requires a warm dry site, it is not hardy in northern Europe. The dark brown, almost black, wood is strong and elastic with wavy grain. It is famously used for golf 'woods'.

Growth: 2-7-18. Hardiness: 50%. Choice: 1, 3. Wood: 1.

Kaki or Chinese Persimmon *Diospyros kaki*

This small tree is a garden favourite in Europe. Cultivation from ancient times in south-east Asia has obscured its exact origin. It forms a large bushy plant seldom over 10m high. In a sunny position female trees bear 7.5cm roundish juicy orange-yellow fruits, though the flesh is mouth-puckering until really soft. The deciduous foliage turns to orange, red and purple in the autumn. The bark is scaly and ridged greyish-brown but is less rough than the American species. Numerous forms have been cultivated commercially for persimmon or sharon fruit. '**Lycopersicum**' and '**Hachiya**' are particularly good plants. When in production these trees need special protection from birds and animals.

Growth: 2-7-10. Hardiness: 30-40%. Choice: 1, 3. Wood: 1.

Date Plum *Diospyros lotus*

In north European gardens this is a rare stately deciduous tree valued for its stature rather than for its fruit. In sheltered conditions on good moist soil it can attain heights of 15-24m, with a billowing crown around 10-15m wide. It originated in Asia and Iran where it is still widely cultivated for its fruit. 'Orchards' are common in warm places as far apart as China and Italy.

Growth: 2-8-15. Hardiness: 40-50%. Choice: 1 (requires space), 3. Wood: 1.

Date Plum

Indian Bean Tree

flower detail

underside

young pod

old pod

seed

Indian Bean Tree

BIGNONIA FAMILY · Bignoniaceae

Indian Bean Tree *Catalpa bignonioides*

'Indian' here is a reference to North American Indian. The tree is from the southern United States of Georgia, Florida, Alabama and Mississippi. Catalpa comes from the American Indian name for this tree 'kutuhlpa'. It is ultimately a broad-headed specimen 15-20m tall and wide. The large deciduous ovate leaves are 10-25cm long by 8-15cm across. Although they arrive late in the season their accumulated weight can pull down and even snap off big branches in the summer. Large urban trees might need cable bracing or frequent cutting back. They respond favourably to pruning, and even to pollarding if necessary.

Since the nineteenth century this has been a favourite town centre tree, absorbing dirt and dust. There is even a row of venerable specimens by the Houses of Parliament in London, making them some of the most photographed trees in the world. The roots seem to enjoy creeping about in the damp conditions under pavements and roads. This is a very decorative shade tree, in mid-summer the frilly flowers, 4-5cm across, occur in upright panicles 20cm long. The petals are white with two short yellow stripes inside, and a central concentration of purplish-brown blotches. The distinctive fruits are narrow pendulous green bean pods, up to 40cm long in hanging clusters. They turn brown and hang on the bare branches in winter until the weather breaks them up and the seeds are dispersed.

The cultivar '**Nana**' is a 'mop-head' tree, well suited to a small garden where space is restricted. The Golden Catalpa '**Aurea**', first cultivated in 1877, is a really magnificent tree. It is wide spreading, but less tall than the species. Its leaves are soft greenish-gold. They are very thin and translucent so sunlight shines through them in early summer to bathe everything below in golden light.

Catalpas are tolerant of all sorts of soil but do best on moist fertile loams. Industrial air pollution is tolerated, so they serve as good city trees. In the garden the potential size and tendency to split branches must be carefully considered before planting close to paths or structures. None of the species should be planted in windy places because the leaves tear easily.

Growth: 2-8-15. Hardiness: 70%. Choice: 1, 2, 4. Wood: 1, 2, 3, 4, 5.

'Nana'

'Aurea'

flower detail

Western Catalpa

fruit

var. *duclouxii*

new leaves

Western Catalpa

Western Catalpa *Catalpa speciosa*

In its native North America, Western Catalpa is a timber tree up to 30m tall. It is pyramidal at first, with a single stem eventually spreading out with old age. The wood is prized for its durability in damp conditions, especially as untreated fence posts in wet soil. The bark is grey brown, vertically fissured, and broken into rough scales. The deciduous leaves are 15-30cm long, bright green and often occurring in whorls of three. The 6cm creamy-white flowers are widely spaced out, in 15cm panicles. Each has two indistinct yellow stripes inside and faint lines of purplish spots. The fruit (green bean pods) may be 40cm long but are only about 1.5cm thick. They ripen in one season, turn brown, then remain on the tree until the following year. In cultivation this is not a tree for the small garden, it can grow rapidly to a large size and casts dense shade that will kill out grass or summer bedding plants. Of course if shade is required then it is ideal.

Growth: 3-14-30. Hardiness: 70%. Choice: 1, 3. Wood: 1, 2, 3, 4, 5.

Farge's Catalpa *Catalpa fargesii*

This substantial 20m tree from western China is widely cultivated in America and Europe. The downy-backed ovate leaves are 8-14cm long with acuminate tips, sometimes shallowly 1-3-lobed on young trees and vigorous regrowth. Superb rosy-pink 4cm bell-shaped flowers occur in dense clusters of 7-15 in corymbose racemes. Each flower has purple-brown dots and a yellow patch inside a shallow throat. They appear in late spring, before most of the other catalpas and while the emerging leaves are still bronze-green. In summer the 45cm beans hang down in bunches. The most common form in cultivation in Europe is var. ***duclouxii*** introduced in 1907 by Ernest Wilson. This has hairless leaves and rose pink flowers marked with orange and purplish brown. The often slightly-lobed leaves are brownish-black when they first emerge.

Growth: 3-10-20. Hardiness: 50%. Choice: 1, 3. Wood: 1, 2, 3, 4, 5.

flower detail

underside

new leaf

Farge's Catalpa

old bark

flower detail

Catalpa × *erubescens* 'Purpurea'

fruit

seed

flower cluster

new leaves

Catalpa × *erubescens* 'Purpurea'

Yellow Catalpa bark

CATALPAS

Catalpa × *erubescens* 'Purpurea'

This selected hybrid between *Catalpa bignonioides* and *Catalpa ovata* was first cultivated in 1886. Now it is often planted in large gardens both for its interesting almost black young foliage and its outstanding flowers. The thin deciduous 20-30cm heart-shaped leaves are either entire or 1-3-lobed. They start off dark purple or almost black in the spring and slowly turn to pale green as the summer advances. A conspicuous display of black foliage can be produced by cutting back to ground level or to a pollarded stem each year. Pruning in winter will encourage abundant new dark-coloured spring growth but will restrict free flowering.

The flowers are in terminal panicles like those of *Catalpa bignonioides*, but usually more numerous. They have frilly white petals which are liberally spotted on the inside with tiny purple dots. The throat is brownish-purple and there are two yellow marks on the lower lip. Flowers appear in late spring as the leaves begin to turn from black to green, providing an unusual effect. The ripe bean pods split open to shed the seed at the end of the year but remain on the tree in tatters throughout the winter. The best green-leaved garden form of this hybrid is the sterile *Catalpa* × *erubescens* 'J. C. Teas', first raised in Indiana. It has fragrant but fairly small flowers.
Growth: 3-8-10. Hardiness: 60%. Choice: 1.

Yellow Catalpa *Catalpa ovata*

This small, rare, Chinese tree seldom exceeds 7m in height. The 2.5cm flowers are yellowish-white reminiscent of Common Horse Chestnut (p. 663). They open in mid to late summer in upright panicles 10-25cm long. The resulting 30cm bean pods hang down in bunches and turn from green to dark brown in the autumn. They remain on the tree all through the following winter. The thin deciduous leaves are mostly three-lobed. This is a better town tree than the ubiquitous Indian Bean (p. 767) and should be more widely used.
Growth: 3-5-7. Hardiness: 60-70%. Choice: 1.

Catalpa bungei

From northern China this small pyramidal tree has triangular-ovate to oblong 15cm leaves. The 3cm flowers in 3-12-flowered racemes are white with purple spots inside. The hanging bunches of beans can be up to 35cm long. A form with distinctly toothed leaves *Catalpa bungei* var. *heterophylla* is also known.
Growth: 2-6-9. Hardiness: 50%. Choice: 1.

fruit

Yellow Catalpa

Catalpa bungei

underside

mature leaf

mature fruit　seed

fruit

Foxglove Tree
winter

'Coreana'

FOXGLOVE FAMILY · Scrophulariaceae

Foxglove Tree *Paulownia tomentosa*

This potentially large deciduous tree has big opposite broadly ovate leaves. These may be 50cm across on young vigorous shoots or coppice re-growth. Strong-growing leaves often develop shallow lobes. The foliage and shoots are densely clothed with glandular hairs which trap aphids and other small winged insects. The main feature of this tree in the garden is its beautiful pale violet early spring flowers. They are funnel-shaped and campanulate, in terminal panicles, with darker spots and yellow streaks inside. Unfortunately the flower buds are present throughout the winter and the flowers open before the leaves appear, so in cold areas they are usually spoiled. The soft pithy shoots of young plants are also frequently damaged by frost. A well established plant will react to being frosted by growing new shoots or suckers at a furious rate, often over 2.5m in one season.

This is a south-east Asian species, widely used in China on farms where its aphid-trapping 'fly-paper' leaves are valued and it was extensively cultivated for shade by Buddhist monks. It was introduced to France from Japan in 1834 and to Chiswick, London, in 1838. The plant in the Jardin des Plantes, Paris, began flowering in 1841 and over 20,000 plants were raised from the seed.

In America it has often escaped from cultivation and in some areas it is naturalized. The American plants, introduced by Ernest Wilson in 1907, were from West Hupeh in China and are thought to be variety *lanata*.

The genus name commemorates Anna Paulowna, princess of the Netherlands, 1795-1865. The species name is a reference to the hairy leaves and shoots. Foxglove Trees grow best on deep moist loams, preferably with side shelter in exposed areas. The variety *lanata* probably has the best flowers but they are usually concentrated almost out of sight at the top of the tree. The cultivar '**Coreana**' has woolly-backed, yellow-tinted leaves and violet flowers.

Growth: 3-9-18. Hardiness: 40-50%. Choice: 1 (requires space), 3. Wood: 1.

Paulownia fortunei

A Chinese, 20m tall tree with 12cm lustrous leaves, tomentose on the underside and stellate-hairy along the young shoots. The compact fragrant foxglove-like flowers are pale cream, flushed with mauve on the outside.

Growth: 3-9-18. Hardiness: 40%. Choice: 1. Wood: 1.

spring flowers

Foxglove Tree

Paulownia fortunei

Canary Island Palm

leaf detail

frond detail

♂ flowers

♀ flower

Fan Palm

Fan Palm

774

PALM FAMILY · Palmae

Canary Island Palm *Phoenix canariensis*
The magnificent Canary Island Palm is a large, fast-growing tree with a long clear stem up to 1.5m in diameter near the ground. The foliage consists of a graceful branchless crown of curving pectinate evergreen leaves up to 5m long. The yellowish flowers on a huge cluster of twigs up to 2m long occur in spring, followed on female trees by heavy bunches of purplish-brown fruits. These look like edible dates but they are not good to eat.

Phoenix theophrasti is a similar-looking but smaller tree, native to Crete. Unfortunately the male flowers have an unpleasant smell. Nevertheless this is a useful coastal fringe tree often growing in tight clusters and affording much needed shelter.

Growth: 6-16-20. Hardiness: 10-20%. Choice: 1, 2.

Fan Palm *Trachycarpus fortunei*
This 10-15m palm extends further into cool temperate zones than any other true palm. Since 1836 it has been widely planted in European coastal gardens and parks.

The distinctive soft fibrous stem is made up of discarded leaf bases. Each leaf, held on a long petiole, is 60-80cm across and roundish but divided almost to the base into narrow pleated strips. The much-branched flower clusters, male and female on separate trees, develop on females into great bunches of 2cm bloomed purple fruits.

Growth: 5-10-14. Hardiness: 40%. Choice: 1, 2.

Cabbage Palm *Cordyline australis* (Agavaceae)
The forked suckering stems of this palm-like member of the Lily family terminate in an evergreen cluster of stiff greyish 40-80cm slender sharply pointed leaves. The fragrant creamy-white 1cm flowers are spectacular in early summer, occurring in erect branched clusters up to 1m long. Dead twiggy flower-stalks often hang on the tree over winter, long after the bloomed 6mm berries have gone.

Originally from New Zealand, this tree, introduced in 1823, is widely planted near the coast in mild areas. Its situation has dramatically improved in Northern Europe as a result of climate change. Specimens are flowering strongly on a regular basis and the range where the tree reliably survives is rapidly extending.

Growth: 4-10-12. Hardiness: 30%. Choice: 1.

Cabbage Palm

Date Palm

fruit

Petticoat Palm

fronds removed

Chilean Wine Palm

Petticoat Palm

Spanish Bayonet

detail of leaf margin

Dragon Tree

Cabbage Tree

Dragon Tree

Spanish Bayonet
young plant

Cabbage Tree

Spanish Bayonet
old plant

Date Palm *Phoenix dactylifera*

Cultivated for at least 5,000 years, this suckering tree has a clear stem and feathery top. The leaves are pinnate, 3-5m long, with a hard curving rachis and numerous strap-like, 40cm, leathery leaflets. The base of the petiole is spiny, making the top of the stem formidable to predators. Flowers are dioecious, males small in upright clusters, females pendulous with brown petals. The familiar fruit is a 1-seeded berry, 3-7cm long, edible and sweet.

Growth: 10-25-35. Hardiness: 0%. Choice: 2.

Petticoat Palm or Desert Fan Palm
Washingtonia filifera

A popular ornamental, this slender tree from Central America often develops a characteristic swollen base to the stem. The bark is grey, between horizontal rings of brown leaf scars. Leaves are palmate, deeply divided into narrow lobes, partially joined by white thread-like fringing. The base and underside of the petiole is toothed. A bunch of dead leaves persists below the live crown (the petticoat) obscuring the top of the branch-free stem. Flowers in 3m pendulous clusters are white, bell-shaped, with 3 petals and 3 outer sepals fused together. Fruit is 6mm across, ripening to black.

Growth: 8-15-15. Hardiness: 10%. Choice: 1.

Chilean Wine Palm *Jubaea chilensis*

Noted for its very thick stem, up to 2m in diameter. The bark is dark grey with horizontal, smooth, close-spaced leaf scars. Pinnate leaves are 4-5m long, arching and not spined. Purplish-brown flowers occur in dense clusters up to 1.5m long. The fruit, a globose berry, is 4-5cm long, fleshy and yellowish-brown.

Growth: 5-18-30. Hardiness: 20-30%. Choice: 1.

Dragon Tree *Dracaena draco* (Agavaceae)

From the Canary Islands and Madeira, a multiple-stemmed, forked, giant palm-like tree. It has thick woody-purplish or silver-grey branches. Living trees reputed to be 6000 years old are known. Stems were formerly a source of 'dragon's blood', a red resin from the bark, used as a pigment in varnish. Many trees are fluted and buttressed. The leaves in dense rosettes are evergreen and strap-like, 50cm long, flattened, pointed and blue green. Flowers are in branchy, upright panicles often held above the foliage, each individual flower like a greenish-white lily. The fruit is a 1cm orange berry.

Growth: 8-15-18 (40 in the wild). Hardiness: 0%. Choice: 1.

Cabbage Tree *Cordyline indivisa*

Introduced in 1850 from New Zealand, this tree is more tender than *Cordyline australis* (p. 775). The leaves are broad, 1-2m long by 10-15cm wide, lanceolate, glaucous, with conspicuous often red veins. Flowers are in 160cm, compact clusters. Individual flowers 8mm across, dull white, flushed with purple. There are foliage colour variations in cultivation: 'Rubra' is red and 'Purpurea' is purple.

Growth: 3-8-8. Hardiness: 10%. Choice: 1.

Spanish Bayonet *Yucca aloifolia*

One of the largest species of *Yucca*, with a simple or branched stem up to 8m long, topped by a dense tuft of pungent foliage, consisting of 60cm, stiff, flat leaves and long flexible flower spikes. Flowers are rounded, bell-shaped, 5-10cm long, creamy white with 6 purple tinged lobes. They are fragrant at night to attract pollinating moths. The dark purple, almost black, fruit has purplish flesh that is said to be edible. Originally from southern North America, this species is extensively planted and has become naturalized in dense thickets. Subsp. *draconis* has a more divided branchy outline. **Yucca elephantipes** is similar but larger with 10m forked stems. More hardy than these species is **Yucca gloriosa**, the Spanish Dagger or Palm Lily. From the south-east USA it is a low branchy shrub up to 3m tall with spine-tipped stiff leaves and 4m spikes of flowers. There are variegated, glaucous and distorted leaf forms in cultivation.

Growth: 4-8-9. Hardiness: 0-10%. Choice: 1.

Yucca elephantipes

Yucca gloriosa

Canary Island Pine

Canary Island Pine

Montezuma Cypress

Montezuma Cypress

seeds

Montezuma Cypress
autumn

Canary Island Pine

Caribbean Pine

778

SOME SOUTHERN TREES

Canary Island Pine *Pinus canariensis*
(Pinaceae, pp. 204-59)

This tender pine, native in the Canary Islands, grows in the mildest parts of Europe, particularly along the dry slopes of the Mediterranean coast. For many years it is a straight-stemmed narrow conical tree, its branches in whorls representing annual growth. In old age the top gradually becomes irregular, often on a clear, knot-free stem. Branch tips droop under the weight of the long 20-30cm floppy needles in bunches of 3, bright green after a glaucous-green start, and lasting 3-5 years. Juvenile foliage on seedlings is quite different, soft short 3-5cm blue-green tightly packed single needles. The bark is thick, rugged, dark reddish-brown and scaly; yellowish-brown and smooth on young branches. The woody cones are 10-20cm long by 6cm thick (closed), singly or in whorls on the shoot. Typically they are one-sided, with strongly developed scale bosses only on the sunlit side. The timber is good quality but the risk of forest fire in tourist areas is high because of the thick resinous foliage.

Growth: 7-22-60. Hardiness: 20%. Choice: 2. Wood: 2,3.

Caribbean Pine or Cuban Pine *Pinus caribaea*

A potentially large tree (up to 30m tall), originally from Central America and the West Indies. The needles are usually in bunches of 3 but in regional forms (Bahamas and Honduras) they may be in 4 or 5s. Each needle is 15-25cm long, held in lax clusters. Although there are indistinct greyish stomatal lines on all surfaces, the overall colour is bright or olive green. The 10cm long stout woody cones are red-brown with hard flat scale ends each armed with a small central spine. Grey-brown stems are smooth at first, becoming scaly and exfoliating with age.

Growth: 4-12-30. Hardiness: 0-10%. Choice: 4. Wood: 2,3.

Soft Tree Fern *Dicksonia antarctica* (Dicksoniaceae)

Although not strictly a tree, now much planted in mild or protected places. It does best where rainfall is plentiful, depending as it does on moisture channelled down the fronds into the root-filled stem. Ancient plants in its native Australia are 15m tall with stems 60cm in diameter. The 'bark' consists of red-brown fibrous frond bases. The foliage, which is confined to the top of the stem, fans out radially, regenerating itself from the centre like a palm. The 2m fronds are pinnate, splitting 2-3 times but always facing up to the light. Reproduction is through microscopic spores produced on the underside of the fronds. It is advisable not to inhale spore-filled air during the shedding period.

Growth: depends on moisture and plant size. Hardiness: 20-30%. Choice: 1.

Montezuma Cypress *Taxodium mucronatum*
(Taxodiaceae; other *Taxodium*, p. 103)

This species is similar to Swamp Cypress (p.103) except for shorter needles that are more or less persistent, often changing from green to brown but overwintering in mild areas. Branches flex and bend downwards, the extremities of the foliage droop. It is native in southern North America and Mexico where trees 45m tall are known. The timber is strong and rot resistant.

Growth: potentially 45m. Hardiness: 20%. Choice: 1.

Caribbean Pine

Soft Tree Fern

Avocado Pear

fruit section

underside

Winter's Bark

Red Bay

Myrtle Oak

Himalayan Oak

underside

Kermes Oak

Kermes Oak

Quercus iberica

Winter's Bark *Drimys winteri* (Winteraceae)

An aromatic tree from western South America, introduced in 1827. The shoots often have a reddish sunlit side. The fruit is a glossy black berry. This primitive genus produces wood without vessels (pores). It is pale brown and soft but has many uses.
Growth: 4-10-15. Hardiness: 30-40%. Choice: 1. Wood: 1,2.

Avocado Pear *Persea americana* (Lauraceae)

Probably Central American. Various forms are now grown and orchard trees remain quite low. The leaves are leathery, glabrous, and aromatic from oily glands. The wood is hard, heavy, fragrant and lustrous. *Growth: 6-9-10 (18 where native). Hardiness: 0%. Choice: 2. Wood: 1,2.*
Red Bay *Persea borbonia* is another decorative aromatic flowering tree, producing valuable wood for fine furniture and, in America, timber. From southern North America, it has been in Europe since at least 1739. The leaves flavour food. Bark becomes vertically fissured like Common Oak (p. 383).
Growth: 6-9-18. Hardiness: 20%. Choice: 2. Wood: 1.

Kermes Oak *Quercus coccifera*
(Fagaceae; other *Quercus*, pp. 351-93)

Native to the Mediterranean on dry rocky ground and host to the Kermes beetle, from which cochineal used to be obtained, this small dense tree has ascending branches smooth bark, pinkish-grey shoots and evergreen leaves like a Holm Oak (p. 373) with abrupt unevenly-spaced spiny teeth. The acorns, which need 2 years to ripen, are larger than most of the leaves and spine-tipped; their cups are armed with hard reflexed spines. In south-west Europe subsp. *calliprinos*, the Palestine Oak, replaces the species in the east.
Growth: 2-4-6. Hardiness: 50%. Choice: 2,3.

Myrtle Oak *Quercus myrtifolia*

An ideal oak for mild seaside locations, from the southern USA, this is relatively wind and salt tolerant though often remains stunted and bushy when too exposed. The branches and twigs form a dense domed top. The leaves' undersides at first have a distinctive reddish-orange pubescence. Acorns are ovoid, about 1cm long in pubescent cups with overlapping scales. *Growth: 2-3-6. Hardiness: 20-30%. Choice: 3.*
Himalayan Oak *Quercus semicarpifolia* A relatively small tree from Afghanistan to western China, but Roy Lancaster has recently collected forms that seem superior. Leaves 9-11cm, leathery, evergreen rounded-oblong, entire on old wood but spine-edged in the juvenile state. Undersides are brownish-felty. Acorns 2-3cm long, frequently in pairs in shallow cups. *Growth: 4-9-15 (30 where native). Hardiness: 40%. Choice: 1,3.*
Quercus iberica is a close relative of Sessile Oak (p. 381) but smaller, and not from Iberia at all, but from the Balkans and west Asia. It is cultivated here as it withstands hot dry conditions. Acorns are often in clusters of 2 or 3, their cups softly pubescent with adpressed scales. *Growth: 3-8-20. Hardiness: 50-60%. Choice: 3. Wood: 3.*

Horse-tail She Oak *Casuarina equisetifolia*
(Casuarinaceae)

A salt-tolerant, shelter tree adapted to heat and drought, introduced from south-east Asia and Australia for sea and river erosion control. It has a very hard timber called Red Beefwood. Superficially like a Pine, the evergreen foliage is reduced to needle-like jointed flexible shoots. As branches expand they become grooved and ribbed to conserve moisture and provide protection from strong light. Grey-brown bark strips vertically. Fruits grey-brown and woody.
Growth: 6-15-20 (site sensitive, 35 where native). Hardiness: 10%. Choice: 1,2,3. Wood: 1,2,5.

fruit

stem detail

Winter's Bark

Horse-tail She Oak

Golden Chestnut

underside

Golden Chestnut
leaf variation

Ombu Tree

fruit

flower detail

Ombu Tree

Loquat

SOME SOUTHERN TREES

Golden Chestnut *Chrysolepis chrysophylla* (Fagaceae)

Potentially a large tree, this Californian species was introduced in 1844 and is occasionally planted in the mildest parts of Europe for ornament. The edible nuts are infrequent and small. Bark is grey-brown, becoming vertically fissured with age, the inner bark is bright red. Young shoots are golden-yellow and hairy. Leaves are also yellowish-green with a scaly golden pubescent underside, evergreen, 13cm long with a 5mm petiole, oblong-lanceolate with slightly rolled-back entire margins. Terminal panicles of slender yellowish-white scented catkins appear in mid-summer followed by 4cm spiked husks protecting the fruit which takes 2 years to ripen.

Growth: 3-6-16 (very site sensitive, 25 in native range). Hardiness: 40%. Choice: 1, 4 (flower odour). Wood: 3,4,5.

Ombu Tree *Phytolacca dioica* (Phytolaccaceae)

Potentially this is a large tree with a thick stem and vigorous, evergreen or semi-evergreen foliage, common in Mediterranean countries but originating in South America. The shoots are fleshy and basal epicormic growths frequently occur. Leaves alternate, elliptic to ovate, 6-15cm, with a distinct pale coloured midrib and parallel veins. Any deciduous foliage colours yellow to purple before falling. Flowers on separate male and female trees are in spiky greenish racemes, around 6cm long. Individual male flowers have 20-30 stamens and 5 petal-like (no real petals) segments, females are a little larger up to 1.5cm across. The berry-like fruit is fleshy, 7cm across and produced in pendulous clusters. They yield a dye and have medicinal properties but in Europe, especially areas such as Gibraltar, this tree is planted for shade.

Growth: 4-7-20. Hardiness: 10-20%. Choice: 3. Wood: 1.

Loquat *Eriobotrya japonica* (Rosaceae)

Originally from China and southern Japan this fruit tree is now established in commercial orchards in California, Florida and southern Europe. It will only fruit in the mildest areas because the erect fragrant panicles of white flowers appear in the autumn. The fruit sets over winter and ripens in the spring. A wild plant produces a round or pear-shaped yellow fruit about 4cm in diameter. Selected clones produce much larger fruits up to 8cm across. The flesh is edible raw but tastes acid. It is much better cooked or preserved as jam or jelly. The tree is evergreen with a rounded outline. Young branches are downy, leaves are 25cm long, narrow-oblong glossy and pointed. The undersides are felted at first.

Growth: 3-5-7. Hardiness: 20-30% (0% for fruit). Choice: 2.

Kiwi Fruit *Actinidia deliciosa* (*chinensis*) (Actinidaceae)

This woody, scrambling, tree-like climber produces the commercial fruit known as Chinese Gooseberry or Kiwi. It will easily reach 8m in height and probably more if it has adequate support. The deciduous alternate leaves are 8-12cm long, more or less oval, with a cordate base. Buds are totally enclosed in the base of the petiole like the Plane tree's (p. 449). Shoots are pubescent with reddish-brown hairs. Flowers are 4cm across in clusters, emerging creamy and darkening at maturity. There are 5 petals and numerous stamens. The familiar fruits are ovoid, up to 6cm long, brown and hairy. Inside the edible flesh is pale green with a gooseberry flavour. Small dark-coloured seeds radiate from the centre.

Growth: 6-8-8. Hardiness: 40%. Choice: 2.

Loquat

seeds

Kiwi

Rubber Tree

Azara microphylla

Azara microphylla

Moreton Bay Fig

underside

Sycamore Fig

Moreton Bay Fig

Moreton Bay Fig

SOME SOUTHERN TREES

Rubber Tree *Ficus elastica*
(Moraceae; other *Ficus*, p. 441)

In northern Europe this is a familiar house plant in its juvenile state, but in parts of the south it is hardy outside and can make a tall, evergreen, shade tree. It is native to Java and south-east Asia. In natural conditions it will buttress freely and produce aerial roots resembling multiple stems. Formerly it was cultivated as a source of inferior natural rubber. The leaves are pointed oblong 30cm long by 15cm wide (less on very old specimens). Fruits, around 1cm long, are globular, green figs with yellowish flecks that occur in pairs. There are many cultivars available in the nursery trade.

Growth: 5-25-60 (in native range). Hardiness: 0%. Choice: 1,3.

Moreton Bay Fig or Australian Banyan Tree
Ficus macrophylla

A giant in its native Australia, this tree has to be given plenty of room and sited carefully in cultivation. Like an ordinary Banyan it develops a twisted mass of vertical stems and aerial roots. It tends to be a epiphyte, at first rapidly smothering its host before standing up on its own. The 20cm evergreen leaves are glabrous green, paler on the underside, elliptic to ovate with an abrupt tip and a cordate or rounded base. The 1-2cm figs, in pairs, are green then purplish with random yellowish markings. The bark remains fairly smooth and pinkish grey.

Growth: unpredictable (55m in native range). Hardiness: 0%. Choice: 4.

Sycamore Fig *Ficus sycomorus*

From north-east Africa and Asia. It is a thick stemmed, often buttressed tree with a wide spreading crown but relatively thin bark. The deep green leaves are entire but wavy-edged, 15cm long, ovate or nearly round with an abrupt pointed tip and heart-shaped base. The surface is distinctly rough to touch. Figs are 8-10cm long, obovoid yellowish or brownish red and finely pubescent.

Growth: 4-8-25. Hardiness: 10%. Choice: 4.

Azara microphylla (Flacourtiaceae)

Introduced from its native Argentina to Europe in 1861, this small evergreen tree has remained a favourite with gardeners with limited space. Although the vanilla-scented yellow spring flowers are small and have no petals, they are its best feature. Leaves are obovate to rounded, entire or remotely and irregularly toothed, seldom over 1.5cm long. Stipules at the base of the short petiole are persistent. The fruit is a bright orange-red berry only 3mm in diameter. There is a variegated form in cultivation. The smaller tender **Azara petiolaris** introduced 3 years earlier from Chile has slightly larger 7cm leaves and (black) fruit. The yellow flowers in short racemes are equally fragrant. **Azara serrata** from Chile is a shrubby tree up to 4m tall with sharply toothed glossy 6cm narrowly oblong leaves. The fruit is black about 7mm across. **Azara dentata** is a more tender plant with yellow fruit, fragrant flowers and small glossy evergreen toothed leaves. **Azara lanceolata** is a shrubby tree with coarsely toothed, evergreen, lanceolate leaves up to 6cm long. Axillary flowers are in crowded clusters, followed by striking violet berries.

Growth: 2-6-8. Hardiness: 30-40%. Choice: 1.

immature fruits

Azara lanceolata   *Azara dentata*   *Azara petiolaris*   *Azara serrata*

African Tamarisk

Sapodilla Plum

fruit section

Storax

Christmas Berry

Victorian Box

SOME SOUTHERN TREES

African Tamarisk *Tamarix africana* (Tamaricaceae; other *Tamarix*, p. 703)

This and *T. canariensis* (p. 703) are often grown in the western Mediterranean, with *T. dalmatica* more common in the east. A feathery, small spreading tree with minute 2-4mm alternate leaves clasping the slender shoot like a Cypress. Each 2-3mm pale pink flower has 5 petals. They appear densely packed together along side shoots in early summer and persist for a long time. The fruit is a tiny capsule. In exposed coastal areas thickets of reddish-black stems are often conspicuous in winter.

Growth: 6-8-8. Hardiness: 20-30%. Choice: 3.

Sapodilla Plum *Achras (Manilkara) zapota*

A large evergreen fruit tree with milky sap, extensively grown on fertile, sandy loams. Leaves elliptic, papery and almost hairless. Flowers solitary, with 6-7 lobes in leaf axils, the edible fleshy fruit with up to 8 glossy pips in granular yellow-brown, sweet pulp, is called Chiku in Mexico and Central America and the latex (Chicle) was an early component of chewing gum. The genus also has high quality timber trees, e.g. Nkunya (*M. cuneifolia*) from Uganda.

Growth: 8-15-30. Hardiness: 0%. Choice: 2. Wood: 1,2.

Storax *Styrax officinale* (Styracaceae; other *Styrax*, p. 759)

A small flat-topped tree, on lime-free soil, native to the Mediterranean fringe and Asia Minor. Its bark yielded a valuable form of vanilla-scented balsam and the dried fruits were used in rosaries. It often makes a flat-topped, branchy tree that has smooth grey bark for many years. Leaves alternate, 4-7cm, fresh green above and glaucous below. Drooping clusters of fragrant, white, waxy flowers each have 5 recurved lobes, giving a ballerina or bell-like effect. The fruit is a roundish, fleshy drupe set in a pubescent calyx like an 'elf's hat', on a slender stalk. Oddly, the last recorded account of resin being collected by monks was in 1755. It may be that the ancients confused this species with *Liquidambar orientalis* (p. 445), also said to be the source of Storax resin.

Growth: 3-5-7. Hardiness: 20%. Choice: 1.

Christmas Berry *Photinia serratifolia* (Rosaceae)

More often a large shrub than a tree, but it can reach 12m. *P. × fraseri* is its hybrid with *P. glabra*, with various cultivars, such as 'Red Robin'. Leaves start reddish-bronze in spring, turn glossy-green and remain in place for up to 3 years. Flowers dull white, the fruits red haws. Lime tolerant. Introduced from China in 1804.

Growth: 4-8-12. Hardiness: 40%. Choice: 1.

Karo *Pittosporum crassifolium* (Pittosporaceae; other *Pittosporum*, p. 733)

A tender evergreen ornamental shrub or small tree from New Zealand, often planted instead of its hardier cousin (*P. tenuifolium* p. 733). Several cultivars exist. Bark grey, tomentose at first, then black. Leaves alternate, wavy-edged, undersides white-felted at first. Scented flowers, in tight stalked clusters, have 5 dark red petals. Males and females on separate trees, females producing globose, fruits that become woody, each with 3 shiny black seeds.

Growth: 3-7-10. Hardiness: 20%. Choice: 1.

Victorian Box *Pittosporum undulatum*

From Australia in 1789. Shining green, 7-15cm, leathery leaves, creamy-white fragrant flowers in terminal clusters and berries in pairs, coated in sticky resin (Greek Pittos meaning pitch). The wood is occasionally used for inlay work. This species is frequently used as a rootstock for grafting ornamental forms, like 'Variegatum' with white-edged leaves.

Growth: 3-8-14. Hardiness: 10%. Choice: 1. Wood: 1.

Karo

Christmas Berry

Carob fruit

Evergreen Sophora

Carob

Red Powder Puff Tree

fruit enlarged

Kowhai

Carob

Wirilda

SOME SOUTHERN TREES

Carob *Ceratonia siliqua* (Leguminosae)
A domed, evergreen tree on dry arid ground from the Mediterranean to south-west Asia. The leathery, glossy green leaflets are 4-6cm long, oval with a notched tip. Usually no terminal leaflets. Small greenish or red tinted flowers occur in tightly packed upright spikes consisting entirely of prominent stamens or a style. The soft pea-pod fruit with white pulp is used as a cattle food. The hard white seeds were the original 'carat' weight of goldsmiths, and ground up as a substitute for flour.
Growth: 3-8-10 (occasionally more). Hardiness: 0-10%. Choice: 2.

Red Powder Puff Tree *Calliandra haematocephala*
Large shrub or small tree from South America, planted extensively. Bi-pinnate evergreen leaves are up to 45cm long, lustrous green above and paler beneath. The 'shaving brush' flowers, bisexual or male, appear to consist entirely of long stamens, white at the base and bright red towards the tip, in tight clusters on downy side shoots in late winter.
Growth: 2-4-6. Hardiness: 0%. Choice: 1.

Evergreen Sophora *Sophora microphylla*
A small ornamental New Zealand tree. Foliage is dense, often tangled with dark green pinnate leaves, each with around 30 opposite pairs of 1cm oval leaflets. The golden-yellow spring flowers droop downwards so as not to trap raindrops. Often seen as the early-flowering cultivar, 'Sun King'.
Growth: 3-6-9. Hardiness: 20-30%. Choice: 1.

Kowhai *Sophora tetraptera* 'Grandiflora'
This semi-evergreen species is most often seen as the fairly robust cultivar 'Grandiflora', the national flower of New Zealand. The bark is purplish-brown with yellowish-grey tomentum on the young shoots. The twigs are slender and tend to droop and the flowers golden-yellow, pea-like, each on a slender, curving, yellowish-brown, 3cm stalk. Flowers occur in spring before the leaves are far advanced. The fruit is a curious four-winged pod of small seeds. The wood, hard, durable and elastic, is used for cabinet work and tool handles. The species is native in New Zealand and Chile so it was well established before the earth's tectonic movement formed the Pacific Ocean.
Growth: 2-5-12. Hardiness: 20%. Choice: 1. Wood: 1,3.

Mimosas or **Wattles** *Acacia* species
Several species of this large genus (see also p. 573) have been introduced to Europe from various parts of Australia. They generally have a smooth, grey-green bark and evergreen foliage. The leaves are much reduced to modified petioles to conserve moisture, flowers are small but numerous in deep yellow spikes. They often throw profuse root-suckers and when cut down by frosts will re-establish themselves. **Sydney Golden Wattle** *A. longifolia* from south-east Australia has been used in south-west Europe for dune fixing and municipal planting. *Growth: 5-8-8 (occasionally 10). Hardiness: 10%. Choice: 1,3.*

Wirilda or **Swamp Wattle** *Acacia retinoides*, a wetland species and more lime-tolerant than others, is widely planted for shelter and erosion control. Fruits are pea pods with red stalks. *Growth: 4-6-6. Hardiness: 30%. Choice: 3.*

Black Wattle *Acacia mearnsii* has been extensively planted along watercourses and areas subject to erosion. *Growth: 6-10-15. Hardiness: 30%. Choice: 3.*

Golden Wreath Wattle *Acacia saligna* from Western Australia is semi-pendulous and suckering, often becoming invasive but liked by florists for the dense, bright yellow flowers. The seed stalks are white and the seeds themselves brown with pale margins. The bark, like Black Wattle's, can be used for tanning leather.
Growth: 5-6-6 (occasionally 10). Hardiness: 10%. Choice: 1,2,3.

Sydney Golden Wattle   **Black Wattle**   **Golden Wreath Wattle**

Swamp Mahogany

juvenile leaf

Swamp Mahogany

flower buds

fruit

seedling

seedling

Tuart

flower buds

juvenile leaf

fruit

Tuart

Red Mahogany

fruit

juvenile leaf

flower buds

seedling

Red Mahogany

Tuart *Eucalyptus gomphocephala*
(Myrtaceae; other *Eucalyptus*, pp. 737-43)

Over 520 species and 120 varieties of Eucalyptus have been identified. They all pass through 3 stages of development, juvenile, with strikingly different foliage, intermediate and mature. This species is ultimately a 40m tall spreading tree with fibrous grey bark from Western Australia. Juvenile leaves are ovate, alternate with a cordate or rounded base, adult leaves are lanceolate 9-16cm long, and drooping. Axilliary flowers mostly in umbels of 7 are creamy-white with prominent stamens. Fruit is bell-shaped, 1-2cm long, also in clusters of up to 7. Buds are distinctive, usually in 3s, shaped like an emerging mushroom. In Australia and southern Europe this is a short-lived pioneer forest tree.

Swamp Mahogany *Eucalyptus robusta*

This Eucalypt prefers wet ground and will grow close to the sea. The bark is fibrous red-brown. Flowers and fruits occur in umbels of 10-15.

Red Mahogany *Eucalyptus resinifera*

A giant tree, 45m tall in its native Queensland and New South Wales. Bark and foliage are similar and flowers occur in umbels of 7-11. The wood is very strong, heavy and hardens with age. It is used for industrial and domestic construction work.
Growth: 9-20-35 (45 in native range). Hardiness: 20%. Choice: 2. Wood: 1,2,3,4,5. (Tuart 4 only).

Luma *Amomyrtus luma (Myrtus luma)*

There is uncertainty in the botanical world about the scientific name of this plant. For many years it was *Myrtus luma* which confusingly was also a former name for *Luma apiculata*. This small evergreen tree is best known for its year-round display of smooth exfoliating bark, in patches of cinnamon-brown, pale grey and cream. Flowers, in open racemes, are generally produced in profusion. They are fragrant, with short rounded 5mm petals framing numerous yellow stamens (up to 300 have been counted). The 1cm diameter fleshy fruit ripens to dark purple. Leaves are dark green, leathery, 2-4cm long, oval with an abrupt point. They are aromatic if crushed. Originally from Chile, introduced in 1843, this plant has been extensively cultivated in mild parts of Europe, where several ornamental cultivars have been produced by the nursery trade.
Growth: 2-5-6 (10 in natural range). Hardiness: 20%. Choice: 1.

Luma

Myrtle

Crimson Bottlebrush

Broadleaf

Apuka

Pomegranate

Pomegranate

seeds

Myrtle *Myrtus communis*

Native to the Mediterranean region and west Asia, the exact range of this species is uncertain, but it has been cultivated since pre-history, and was said to be sacred to Aphrodite. For centuries escapes from cultivation have naturalized and it is common in maquis, particularly near the sea, but generally stunted as it prefers shade. The evergreen, aromatic foliage is dense and twiggy. Each leaf has tiny transparent scent glands. The flowers may be white to pale pink and the fruit is a purple-black, sometimes bloomed berry containing many seeds. Several cultivars have been produced including double flowered 'Flore Pleno' and small leaved 'Microphylla' forms. Subsp. *tarentina* has pinkish flowers and white berries.
Growth: 2-4-5. Hardiness: 20-30%. Choice: 1.

Crimson Bottlebrush *Callistemon citrinus*

Introduced from its native Australia in 1788 this evergreen curiosity has become a familiar component of European gardens in mild areas. The shoots are silky-pubescent at first, lax and arched, the leaves rigid and narrow, 8-10cm long, pale grey-green and lemon-scented if crushed. The flowers are dense cylindrical spikes of fine red stamens produced over a long period in summer and followed by distinctive woody capsules containing seeds. The outline of a good tree is pyramidal but most are ragged and shapeless. The slender stem has grey-brown bark.

Callistemon viminalis, the **Weeping Bottlebrush** is a small tree around 6m tall from New South Wales, with 8-10cm lanceolate leaves that emerge bronze-green. The slender branches flex downwards, showing off the ornamental red flowers to perfection. Each one has a mass of stamens up to 3cm long. The fruits are globose and woody. This species is extensively planted in California and Florida and is suitable for similar climatic conditions in Europe
Growth: 4-6-7. Hardiness: 0-10%. Choice: 1.

Pomegranate *Punica granatum* (Punicaceae)

Cultivated for so long, the original 'wild' Pomegranate once had a huge geographic range from the Mediterranean to the Himalayas. Escapes from gardens and plantation for fruit or ornament have obscured the original distribution and spread it all round the warm temperate world, including South America, China and southern North America. This small tree has stiff branches and thorns. The original colour of the flowers was probably orange but cultivated forms range from red to white. There are distinctive pale orange, leathery, bell-shaped, 5-7 pointed sepals behind each flower. The familiar edible fruit is a large berry divided inside into angular compartments, each containing sweet watery-pink juice and a seed. It was formerly used to cure tapeworms and is still used in the tanning industry, giving Morocco leather its characteristic yellow colour.
Growth: 2-6-8. Hardiness: 10%. Choice: 1,2.

Broadleaf *Griselinia littoralis* (Cornaceae)

Closely related to Dogwoods (p. 747-751), this drought- and salt-tolerant evergreen from New Zealand is much planted for ornamental coastal shelter and hedging. Several cultivars have yellowish or variegated foliage, 'Dixon's Cream' and 'Variegata'.
Growth: 3-7-8. Hardiness: 30%. Choice: 1,3.

Apuka *Griselinia lucida*

Similar to *G. littoralis* but with larger leaves, often with an oblique base. The plant itself is often lax and shrubby. It is said to be epiphytic in warm moist conditions in sub-tropical New Zealand.
Growth: 2-4-5. Hardiness: 10-20%. Choice: 1.

Weeping Bottlebrush

Broadleaf

Jerusalem Thorn

Common Jujube

dried fruit

Ziziphus lotus

flower detail

fruit

Silky Oak

Silky Oak

SOME SOUTHERN TREES

Jerusalem Thorn *Paliurus spina-christi* (Rhamnaceae)

A straggling small semi-evergreen tree with vicious straight and hooked thorns in unequal pairs. It is native from southern Europe to northern China and was first cultivated here in 1597. The foliage is angular, flexible and dense. Leaves are alternate, ovate, 2-4cm long, toothed or entire, with thorns at the base of the petiole. Flowers are in axillary clusters. Each one has 5 greenish-yellow small twin-lobed petals. The fruit is a hard, round, red, flattened disk with an undulating membranous 2-3cm wing surrounding it.

Growth: 2-6-7. Hardiness: 30%. Choice: 3.

Common Jujube or Chinese Date
Ziziphus (Zizyphus) jujuba

Cultivated for centuries by the Chinese as a dessert fruit, this small spiny tree is widely naturalized in southern Europe. It appears to have been introduced from Asia at the time of Augustus. There are now extensive commercial orchards, mostly on lime-rich soils. The leaves, glossy green above and slightly pubescent on the underside, have only 3 parallel veins and 5 glandular teeth. The flexible shoots are green at first then purplish-grey. The spines in pairs may be straight or curved. The fruit is long, fleshy and dark reddish-brown when ripe. The similar, or possibly synonymus *Z. vulgaris*, is a rough-barked thorny tree with pale yellow flowers and slightly astringent olive-sized red fruit.

Growth: 2-5-8. Hardiness: 40%. Choice: 2.

Ziziphus (Zizyphus) lotus

Some authorities list this as an individual species, but the scientific name is questionable. It is reputed to be the source of the legendary liqueur that induced the forgetfulness of the 'Lotus-eaters' in Greek mythology. The dried fruit was ground and made into a kind of bread that formed a staple part of the food for the poor. The word lotophagi, lotus-eaters, became synonymous with poverty.

Silky Oak *Grevillea robusta* (Proteaceae)

A massive genus of 250 species mostly from Australia, and nothing to do with Oak (p. 351). This is an upright thinly-branched tree that is resistant to drought and salt but requires good drainage and full light. The foliage is pubescent (silky) when young. The pinnate leaves are evergreen, about 20-30cm long. The flowers are yellow to orange in pairs on a one-sided raceme and the fruit is a 2-3cm long woody capsule. As pollination is very specialized, seed is seldom produced away from the tree's natural habitat. This species has been taken round the warm temperate and tropical world as a windbreak and in America and southern Europe it is used as a shade tree. The name commemorates C.F. Greville (1749-1809) founder member of the Royal Horticultural Society in London.

Growth: 8-20-30. Hardiness: 20%. Choice: 2,3.

Oleaster *Elaeagnus angustifolia* (Elaeagnaceae)

A large shrub, occasionally a spreading spiny deciduous tree, with striking silvery-green foliage. Introduced from west Asia in the sixteenth century, it is frequently planted on sea and river sands and gravel. It is naturalized in southern Europe. Leaves have copious silver scales, especially on the under side. Strongly scented, even the flowers are dusted with silvery scales. The 1cm olive-like fruit is amber to orange-brown. The raw pulp is edible and sweet; when dried the berries are called Trebizond grapes.

Growth: 2-6-7 (occasionally 12). Hardiness: 50-60%. Choice: 1.

Oleaster

Pepper Tree

Indian Bead Tree

Mastic Tree

Pepper Tree fruits

young fruit

Pistachio

Turpentine Tree

Pistachio nut

Pepper Tree

Mastic Tree *Pistacia lentiscus* (Anacardiaceae)

Mastic is a pale yellow high grade resin coated with a white bloom, exuded in pea-sized droplets by this small bushy tree. It is native to the Mediterranean, North Africa and the Canary Islands. In southern Europe it is most common on dry rocky sites, growing in isolation or amongst scrub. The bark is grey-brown, smooth at first, becoming rough with age. Pinnate leaves with 3-5 pairs of evergreen 1.5-4.5cm oblong-lanceolate leaflets are glossy green and alternate. The rachis and the petiole are winged. The small dioecious flowers have no petals and the globose fruit is aromatic, red at first then black, and end with a pointed tip.

Growth: 2-4-5. Hardiness: 10-20%. Choice: 2.

Turpentine Tree *Pistacia terebinthus*

Often a stunted, gnarled maquis shrub, in summer a source of turpentine, so it is a contributor to raging heath fires in summer. It is native to southern Europe, Asia Minor and North Africa. Usually it has a short trunk and thick, tangled, pubescent resinous twigs. The bark is grey becoming rough with age, it is suitable for tanning animal skins. The deciduous, aromatic foliage is glossy green and leathery. Leaves are 10-20cm long, pinnate, with 3-6 pairs of 4cm, oval-lanceolate, slender-tipped leaflets and a winged petiole. Flowers pink, in dense clusters in early spring, unisexual and without petals. The fruit, often in weighty bunches, is reddish- to purplish-brown with a hard wrinkled shell. It is around 8mm long, ovoid or spherical.

Growth: 4-8-10. Hardiness: 10%. Choice: 1.

Pistachio *Pistacia vera*

A small tree or large spreading shrub introduced from west Asia around 1770). Plantations are frequent, the trees liking hot dry conditions in summer, but cold winters. Only female trees bear fruit so one male is planted to every twelve females. They are 'alternate bearing' so heavy crops only occur every other year. In places it has escaped from cultivation and become naturalized. The bark becomes vertically ridged, the foliage brilliant red in the autumn. Flowers are small, in loose panicles of over 100 blooms, male and female on separate trees. The ovate fruit is green, ripening to reddish-brown, with the shelled nuts high in protein and low in sugar.

Growth: 5-8-10. Hardiness: 40%. Choice: 2.

Pepper Tree *Schinus molle*

In Central and South America the leaves are used for flavouring food and brewing an alcoholic drink, the dried fruit for pepper, and the sap as a resinous gum. Although the branches are slender, pendulous and elegant, the stem is often stunted in old age. The alternate, 10-30cm, pinnate leaves have up to 25 lanceolate leaflets and end in either a single leaf, a soft spine or a tendril. The small flowers are in drooping panicles and the reddish fruits contain glossy seeds.

Growth: 3-12-15. Hardiness: 10-20%. Choice: 1,2.

Indian Bead Tree or Persian Lilac
Melia azedarach (Meliaceae)

The bark and fruit have been used for medicinal purposes, but the fruit is poisonous in excess. *Melia* species have also been used to produce organic insecticide. Introduced from Asia in the sixteenth century and related to Mahogany, it thrives in hot, dry, rocky places. The bark, dark rusty-grey and ridged, is rich in tanic acid. Double pinnate leaves smell disagreeable when crushed but colour to a good autumn yellow, and the pale lilac flowers are fragrant. The hard ribbed nuts (beads) were used for rosaries.

Growth: 4-10-15. Hardiness: 10%. Choice: 1,2.

Pistachio

Indian Bead Tree

winged petiole

Seville Orange

Sweet Orange

Kumquat

Citrus × bergamia

winged petiole

Grapefruit

winged petiole

Lemon

Mandarin

Lemon

Citron

Oranges *Citrus* species *(Rutaceae)*

The genus of tender round-topped trees, most both flowering and fruiting simultaneously and throughout the year, often with spines among the glossy foliage that, crushed, smells of the fruit (botanically a berry).

Sweet Orange *Citrus sinensis*, the popular fruit tree grown commercially world-wide, is possibly a hybrid between *C. maxima* and *C. reticulata*. The foliage is compact, with angular twigs and sparse flexible spines. Leaves are ovate with an acute point and rounded base. The petiole is narrowly winged. Flowers are scented and white, in clusters on weak side shoots. Oranges have thick but fairly smooth peel.

Seville Orange *Citrus aurantium* is commonly grown for marmalade. A distillation of the flower is a constituent of Eau de Cologne. The fruit has rough orange rind and a dimple at the end and sour pulp. The variety *dulcis* is known as the sweet orange, the name also applied to *Citrus sinensis* above.

Bitter Orange *Citrus vulgaris* var. *bigaradia* is similar to Seville Orange, but grown in southern France, Calabria and Sicily to produce flowers for perfumery. It prefers dry soils on hot south-facing slopes.

Citrus × bergamia from south-east Asia is a natural hybrid between *C. aurantium* and the Lime *C. aurantiifolia* and has been cultivated in southern Europe at least since 1700. In Calabria it was grown for bergamot oil from its thick yellow peel. It is an untidy small tree with ovate-oblong leaves with long winged petioles. The flowers are deliciously fragrant and the fruits spectacular, up to 10cm long, with glossy yellow, pitted rind, like large pear-shaped lemons.

Florida Orange or **King Mandarin** *Citrus nobilis* (not illustrated) is possibly a hybrid between *C. reticulata* and *C. sinensis*, a small tree from Vietnam. It is a very popular fruit, mostly grown in California, though worthwhile anywhere, especially the cultivar 'Temple', its thin-peeled oranges are often patchy yellow and orange, sweet and juicy. The tree is ascending but spreads by suckering from the roots.

Mandarin, Satsuma, Tangerine and **Clementine** *Citrus reticulata*, from China and Japan, reached the Mediterranean in 1805. Intensive selection since has given rise to an array of different forms and names. The Satsuma, from the Japanese province of that name, has thin, bright orange skin, loose and 'ill fitting', but easy to peel. The Clementine is possibly of hybrid origin discovered by Père Clement in 1906. It is a favourite with French growers, and fruits early in the year.

Shaddock, Pampelmousse or **Pomelo** *Citrus maxima*. Close to the Grapefruit, this small tree has prodigious fruit, up to 25cm across and has pink flesh. It was named after Captain Shaddock who introduced it to Barbados before 1707.

Kumquat *Fortunella* species (*Citrus fortunella*) commemorates Robert Fortune who discovered the plant in China in 1847. There are now innumerable cultivars and hybrids. Most are pot plants but slow-growing, small trees do occur: *F. × crassifolia*, a hybrid with *C. aurantiifolia* is most vigorous with roundish fruit, and *F. margarita* is thick-peeled, sharp and spicy. There is also a "limequat" 'Eustis' with yellow fruit.

Grapefruit *Citrus × paradisi*, perhaps a hybrid between the Shaddock and *C. sinensis* came from the Antilles to Florida in 1814 and rapidly spread around the world. The juice of such cultivars as 'Ruby' and 'Foster' is deep red and fairly sweet.

Lemon *Citrus limon*, introduced to Greece from south-east Asia in the second century AD, was distributed throughout southern Europe by the eleventh century and introduced to California in 1858. Almost 50 varieties are currently grown. The roots and wood are of high decorative quality and strength, and polish well.

Lime *Citrus aurantiifolia*, introduced from Malaysia, via India, is more tender than most Lemons. Acidic, but there are also sweet limes in cultivation e.g. *C. limetta* and *C. limettoides* with yellowish fruit.

Citron *Citrus medica* Another ancient introduction from Persia and India and a possible parent of both the Lemon and Lime. Harvested for candied peel.

For *Citrus* species in general: *Growth: 2-4-5. Hardiness: 10%. Choice: 2.*

winged petiole

Shaddock

Lime

Hop Tree

'Aurea'

Devil Wood

Sweet Tea

Hop Tree
flowering

Tree Tobacco

SOME SOUTHERN TREES

Hop Tree *Ptelea trifoliata*

A small tree from southern North America and Mexico that has become naturalized in southern Europe. The bark is chestnut brown and the shoots are dark and glossy. Leaves are alternate, trifoliate, each leaflet is ovate to lanceolate, 4-12cm long, glandular-dotted and aromatic. Fragrant, yellowish flowers appear in early summer in cymose panicles followed by clusters of distinctive elm-like seeds. These are 2-3cm long, including a round, reticulate, flat wing notched at the base. There are ornamental forms such as '**Aurea**' with yellow leaves, 'Fastigiata' an 8m upright form, and var. *bailey* that has white bark.
Growth: 2-6-7. Hardiness: 30-40%. Choice: 1.

Trifoliate Orange *Poncirus trifoliata*

This curiosity, that just about clings to life in northern Europe, fares rather better in the mild south. Originally from China, introduced 1850, it produces 4cm, oval fruit resembling small oranges. The fruit is inedible but the peel has been processed in the past to produce an essential oil. It can be used as a *Citrus* rootstock and as a parent in hybridization to produce more hardy strains. The foliage is generally tangled and untidy, with stout, stiff green thorns. Leaves are trifoliate, with 5cm obovate-elliptic leaflets and a winged petiole. Flowers appear before the leaves in spring. They are waxy, white, solitary or in pairs with 5 petals and around 20 stamens. It is usually grown as an ornamental or thorny hedge.
Growth: 1-3-4. Hardiness: 50%. Choice: 1.

Sweet Tea or Fragrant Olive *Osmanthus fragrans* (Oleaceae)

Introduced to Europe in 1771, the exact origin of this Asiatic plant is uncertain. It is evergreen with opposite, oblanceolate, finely toothed or entire, 10cm, fragrant leaves. The small 4-petalled flowers are white and strongly scented. They occur in late summer and in China they are used to perfume tea. The olive-like fruit is a single seeded drupe. Forma *aurantiacus* has orange-yellow flowers. A similar species from North America is *O. americanus*, **Devil Wood**. Its creamy-white flowers appear in short panicles, situated in the leaf axils, and the fruits are deep blue.
Growth: 2-8-12. Hardiness: 10-20%. Choice: 1.

Tree Tobacco *Nicotiana glauca* (Solanaceae)

From Bolivia and Argentina, this ornamental tree has escaped from cultivation and become naturalized in southern Europe. It is slender-crowned, with flexible, drooping foliage. The leaves are up to 25cm long on a 10cm petiole, oval to elliptical, slightly glaucous and rubbery. Flowers are 3-4cm, slender yellow tubes with a bulbous, greenish base and a constricted end, terminating with 5 short lobes. They are non-seasonal. The fruit is an ovoid, 1.5cm long capsule that eventually splits into 4 parts.
Growth: 3-6-6 (10 in native range). Hardiness: 20-30%. Choice: 1.

Trifoliate Orange

Banana

Jacaranda

Boobyalla

leaflet

fruit

seeds

Jacaranda

Jacaranda

SOME SOUTHERN TREES

Banana or French Plantain *Musa × paradisiaca* (Musaceae)

Bananas have been cultivated since pre-history, and their origin is obscure. They are not strictly woody plant, though tree-like in appearance, with stems consisting of overlapping leaf bases and hollow (a pseudostem, unlike a palm. Leaves are around, 3m long, easily torn by the wind to horizontal shreds from the midrib to the margin. Manilla hemp is manufactured from them. The flowers are huge, produced in one year, 1.5m long and pendulous. The sterile male part towards the tip is covered by purplish-red bracts. Female flowers that develop without fertilization into familiar bananas are towards the base. The seedless fruit is yellow with buff-white flesh. They can be eaten unripe, when they are rich in starch.

Growth: 8. Hardiness: 0-10%. Choice: 1,2.

Japanese Banana *Musa basjoo*

This (unillustrated here) is the species commonly grown in warm areas of Europe for ornament, and is much smaller, though cultivated for fibre in its native Japan. The 7cm fruit, generally produced in Europe only under glass, is similarly yellow with white pulp. Certainly easier to manage as a garden tree than an ordinary Banana, it was introduced from the Ryukyu Islands in 1881 by Charles Maries. The leaves are up to 2m long and 70cm wide. The horizontal flowers are creamy-yellow, becoming pendulous and tinged with purple at maturity.

Growth: 4. Hardiness: 0%. Choice: 1. Wood: 4.

Boobyalla *Myoporum insulare* (Myoporaceae)

A small, bright green tree, originally from Australia, this species is used in southern Europe for shelter and fire resistance. It is evergreen with 7-8cm long, oblanceolate entire or randomly toothed alternate leaves. The bisexual flowers are in clusters of 2-4. They are tubular, 7mm across with 5 fused lobes, white with pink or purplish spots inside. The fruit is a purplish-blue globular drupe.

Growth: 2-8-10. Hardiness: 10%. Choice: 2.

Jacaranda *Jacaranda mimosifolia* (Bignoniaceae)

Originally from Argentina, this decorative tree is unpredictable in southern Europe. In one place it is a spreading invasive thicket, in another it is a substantial tree (it can grow to 50m tall in its native habitat). The foliage is feathery, semi-evergreen and tending to droop. The leaves are bi-pinnate, opposite and up to 45cm long. Each pinna can have up to 25 oblong 1cm leaflets along its length. When shedding, the leaves turn yellow. Flowers are mauve in erect 20cm conical clusters. Each bell-shaped 6cm bloom hangs down and has 5 spreading pointed lobes. Flowering often occurs twice a year. The fruit is an oval, 5-7cm, woody capsule containing numerous winged seeds. The timber is good.

Growth: unpredictable (up to 16m). Hardiness: 0%. Choice: 1. Wood: 2.

Jacaranda

Banana

GLOSSARY

Acidity. The acid reaction of the soil measured and expressed as pH (the hydrogen ion concentration). A reading of pH7 is neutral, a lesser number indicates greater acidity, each whole number represents a tenfold difference.

Acuminate. With a long tapering point.

Acute. Sharply pointed (leaf etc.).

Adpressed (hairs). Pressed against the stem or part of the foliage.

Agglomerated (fruits). Clustered together as in Plane or some Dogwoods.

Alkalinity. A measure of lime rich soil (see *Acidity*) a pH measurement above 7.

Anaerobic (soil). Lacking free oxygen, sour.

Angiospermae. Flowering plants bearing seeds within an enclosed structure.

Anthers. The fertile male pollen-bearing capsules borne on the stamens.

Apomictic. A plant that can produce fruit without the need for sexual fusion.

Auricles. Ear-like lobes.

Backcross. A result of hybrid progeny subsequently breeding with either one of the original parent species.

Berry. A fleshy fruit without a stone-like shell round the seed or seeds.

Bi-generic (hybrid). A cross between members of different genera.

Bisexual. A flower containing male and female sexual organs.

Bloom. A white powdery deposit.

Bract. A scaly or leafy appendage situated where a flower stalk (pedicel) leaves the stem.

Broadleaved. A tree usually with flat leaves (deciduous or evergreen) that is not a conifer.

Calyx. An outer whorl of leafy organs (sepals) at the base of a flower. A persistent calyx will remain on the top of a fruit permanently, a deciduous calyx will fall away as the fruit swells.

Canker. Enlargement, callousing and fissuring, often associated with a discharge of moisture or slime, on the stem or branches of a tree. It is caused by several kinds of fungal or bacterial infection.

Carpel. Division in a female flower or fruit.

Chimera. Two or more genetically different plants fused together by a mutation or deliberate grafting.

Clone. A single plant reproduced vegetatively.

Conifer. A cone-bearing tree with needle- or scale-like foliage.

Connate. Joined, e.g. some pairs of juvenile Eucalyptus leaves.

Coppice. A sustainable system of woodland management involving repeated cutting back to a stump at ground level, usually every 7-25 years.

Corolla. A complete set of petals.

Cotyledons. First or seed leaves on a new plant. They occur singly (monocotyledons), in twos (dicotyledons), or in clusters (as in many conifers).

Corymb (corymbose). A compound inflorescence with a central stem and spreading side branches producing a more or less flat top.

Crown (of a tree). The branches, twigs and foliage forming the whole upper part.

Cultivar. A variety or strain produced by human selection and propagated vegetatively.

Cuneate. Wedge-shaped (if a leaf, narrowest towards the base).

Cyme (cymose). An inflorescence with a terminal flower and replicated identical side shoots and subsidiary flowers.

Decussate. With opposite leaves, but each successive pair at right-angles to the preceding one.

Deciduous. Shedding, usually leaves in the autumn or bark in spring.

Deflexed. Bent abruptly down or back.

Dicotyledon. Plants with a pair of seed-leaves.

Die back. Shoot death from the tip downwards.

Dioecious. With separate male and female plants.

Drupe. A fleshy fruit with one or more seeds protected by a hard shell.

Ellipsoid. A solid body with a curved outline and elliptic shape.

Elliptic. Shaped like an ellipse, 2 or more times longer than wide.

Emarginate. Having a shallow notch at the apex.

Epicormic. Adventitious shoots which appear on the trunk of a tree.

GLOSSARY

Epiphyte. A plant that depends on another for sustenance or support.

Exfoliating. Shedding (usually bark).

Exserted. Protruding.

F1. Hybrids resulting from controlled crosses which can not be relied upon to produce further identical progeny.

F2. Second generation hybrids.

Fasciated. Flattened shoots growing together, from a genetic or chemical disorder.

Fastigiate. A very narrow upright tree, such as Lombardy Poplar.

Forma (f.). The recognized botanical category subordinate to variety.

Genotype. The classification of an organism based upon its genetic composition and not its morphological characteristics.

Glabrous. Having no hair.

Glandular. Having glands (secreting organs) usually on twigs and leaves.

Glaucescent. Becoming glaucous.

Glaucous. With a bluish bloom.

Globose. Vaguely spherical.

Globular. Spherical, or consisting of globules.

Heading back (pruning). Reducing top growth.

Hilum. The scar left on a seed when it becomes detached from the fruit.

Incised (leaves). Deeply toothed or lobed

Inflorescence. A cluster of flowers originating from a single point on the stem.

Internodal. The part of a stem between two adjacent nodes.

Lanceolate. Narrow, lance-shaped (leaf) broadest at a point just below the middle.

Lenticels. Lens-shaped spores.

Lignotuber. A woody swollen stem or root tuber bearing numerous fascicles of dormant buds.

Microclimate. The local climate, even in part of a garden, influenced by immediate surroundings.

Microspecies. A distinctive segregate of a true species, often originating as a hybrid which has resulted in apomictic progeny.

Monocotyledon. Plants with a single seed-leaf.

Monoecious. With male and female flowers on the same plant.

Monopodial. A stem in which growth is continued from year to year from the terminal growing point.

Monotypic. A single representative (e.g. a genus consisting of one species only).

Mucronate. With a short, narrow point.

Naturalised. A plant that has become established in an area beyond its native or natural distribution.

Nectary. The part of a flower which produces and secretes nectar.

Nectria (fungus). A common canker-forming fungus, especially in orchard trees, carried as spores in rain water or on the wind. It will penetrate the bark through any existing wounds.

Node. The point on a stem where one or more leaves arise.

Nomenclature. The naming of plants (classification is called Taxonomy).

Obovate (leaf). Egg-shaped, but broadest towards the tip.

Ovate (leaf). Egg-shaped, broadest towards the base.

Ovoid. Egg-shaped in three dimensions.

Palmate (leaf). Shaped like an open hand.

Panicle. An inflorescence, similar to a raceme but having branched stalks.

Pectinate. Comb-like.

Petiole. The stalk by which a leaf is attached to a stem.

Photosynthesis. The conversion of light energy from the sun into chemical energy (carbohydrates) using minerals from the earth and elements from the atmosphere, e.g. oxygen to produce plant food. This occurs in the green parts of the plant.

Pinnate. A compound leaf with more than 3 leaflets arranged in two ranks along a common axis (rachis).

Plumose. Feather-like.

Podocarp. A fruit with a stipe or stalk.

Pollarding. An ancient sustainable form of tree management involving the periodic removal of all the branches as an alternative to felling.

Provenance. A region within the natural distribution of a species.

Pubescent. Hairy (foliage).

Raceme. A spiked inflorescence with many individually stalked flowers all emanating directly from a central stem.

Rachis. The central rib of a pinnate leaf.

Radiation frost. Caused by heat loss from the ground by radiation – especially when no insulation layers of foliage or cloud are present.

Reflexed. Bent down or back.

Reticulate. Net-veined.

GLOSSARY

Root collar. The point, often clearly visible on young planting stock, where the root and the shoot meet at ground level.

Rootstock. The root on to which another plant is grafted.

Scion. A shoot or bud of one plant which is grafted on to another.

Sepal. A segment of a flower's outer whorl, often green and leaf-like.

Semi-double. A single flower with some additional petals but not enough to obscure the centre (stamens etc.)

Serrate. Toothed or saw-like (leaf margin)

Socketing. Caused when a poorly rooted or unsecured sapling blows about in the wind until an inverted cone-shaped hole develops round its base. This will cause the tree to lean over, or even die from subsequent root drying.

Squarrose. Rough from protruding tips of scales.

Stamens. The male parts of a flower supporting the anthers.

Stellate. Having star-shaped hairs (on foliage).

Stigma. The receptive female part of a flower.

Stipule. A leafy bract at the base of a leaf stalk.

Stoloniferous. Of a plant that produces creeping stems on or just below the soil from which frequent shoots may spring up.

Stomatal. With breathing pores on the surface.

Stone cells. Gritty cells found in the fruit of pears and similar species.

Subcordate. Somewhat heart-shaped.

Subglobose. Irregularly spherical.

Subspecies (subsp.). A taxonomic rank less than a species, usually originating as a regionally isolated natural population.

Suckers. Shoots produced from spreading surface roots.

Symbiotic (symbiosis). An intimate relationship between living organisms (including parasitism).

Taxonomy. The classification of organisms.

Tepals. Part of a flower, often mistaken for petals, and usually replacing any distinct calyx and corolla. Often brightly coloured as in tulips.

Tetraploid. A plant or other organism having cells with 4 times the usual number of chromosomes.

Tomentose (tomentum). Densely hairy or woolly.

Transpiration. Loss of moisture through the foliage.

Trifoliate. Having 3 leaflets on each petiole.

Triploid. A plant (or organism) having cells with three complete sets of chromosomes in each nucleus. Such plants are usually infertile.

Truncate. Flat at the base.

Tubercles. Warty projections.

Understock. (see rootstock)

Variety (var.). A taxonomic rank subordinate to species that originates as a spontaneous variant.

Vegetative propagation. Any method of reproducing plants other than by using seed, thus retaining its characteristics unmodified.

SHOOTS, BUDS AND LEAVES

The following pages offer an illustrated overview of the **shoots** and **buds** of representative (mainly deciduous) trees in this book. They tend to be neglected, but it is well worth making a habit of inspecting them. They are usually a valuable clue to at least the group's – sometimes the species' – identity, and have the added advantage of being there to see all round the year. The first point to notice is whether the tree bears its leaf-buds opposite each other or (much more commonly) arranged alternately up the stem. Those are followed by four pages of 72 distinctive **leaf-shapes**, coniferous and broadleaved.

SHOOTS – opposite buds

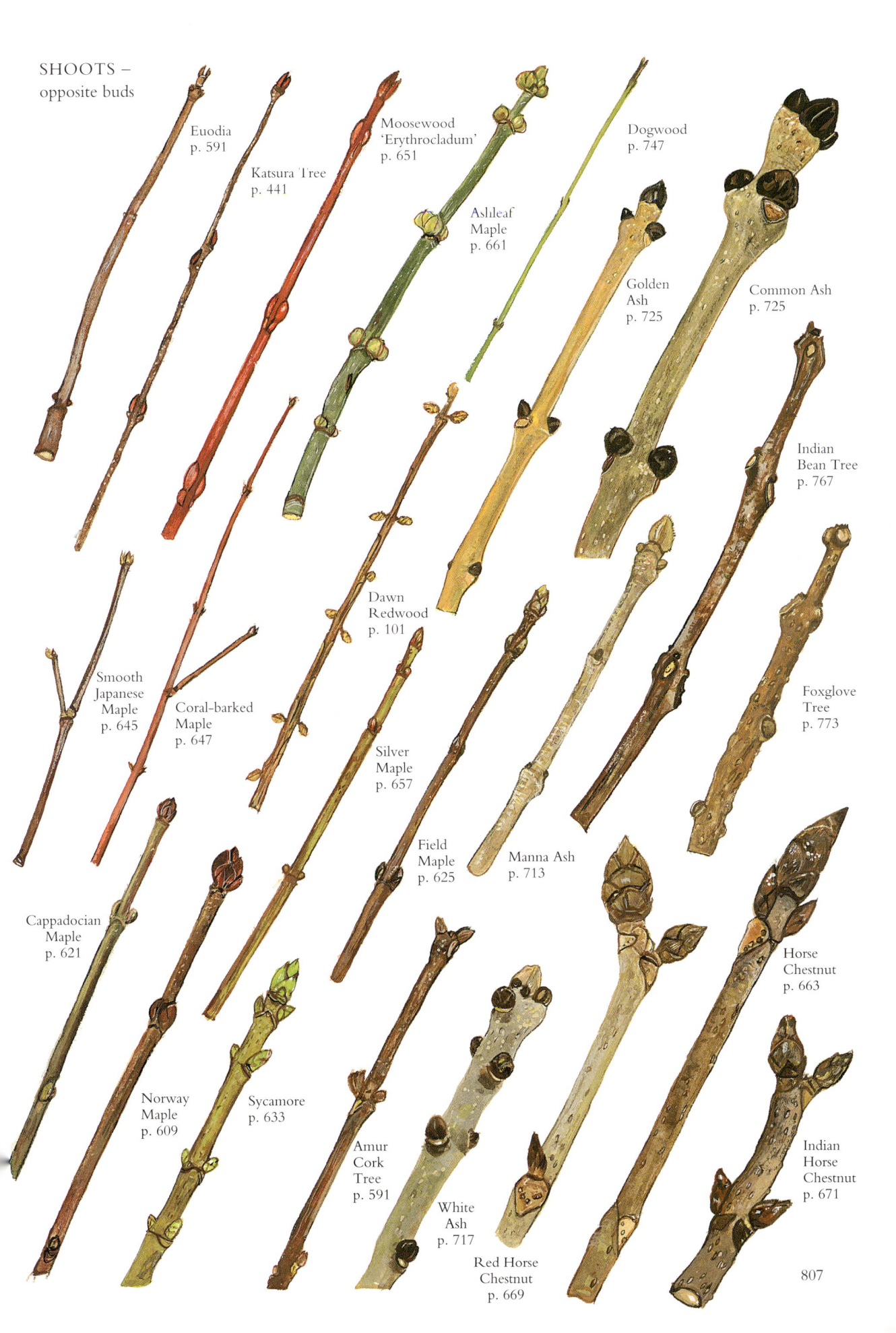

Euodia p. 591

Katsura Tree p. 441

Moosewood 'Erythrocladum' p. 651

Ashleaf Maple p. 661

Dogwood p. 747

Golden Ash p. 725

Common Ash p. 725

Indian Bean Tree p. 767

Smooth Japanese Maple p. 645

Coral-barked Maple p. 647

Dawn Redwood p. 101

Silver Maple p. 657

Foxglove Tree p. 773

Field Maple p. 625

Manna Ash p. 713

Cappadocian Maple p. 621

Horse Chestnut p. 663

Norway Maple p. 609

Sycamore p. 633

Amur Cork Tree p. 591

White Ash p. 717

Red Horse Chestnut p. 669

Indian Horse Chestnut p. 671

807

SHOOTS –
alternate buds

Coral-bark Willow p. 291

Grey Sallow p. 285

Weeping Willow p. 287

Crack Willow p. 287

Osier p. 289

Goat Willow p. 285

Caucasian Wingnut p. 293

Tamarisk p. 703

Snowbell Tree p. 759

White Poplar p. 263

White Willow p. 291

White Birch p. 315

Grey Poplar p. 263

Silver Birch p. 311

Cricket Bat Willow p. 291

Laburnum p. 587

Silver Willow p. 291

Paper Birch p. 315

Kentucky Coffee Tree p. 589

Stag's-horn Sumach p. 595

808

SHOOTS
alternate buds

Black Cherry p. 527

White Mulberry p. 421

'Chanticleer' Pear p. 519

Ginkgo p. 21

Black Mulberry p. 423

Wild Pear p. 513

Handkerchief Tree p. 745

Wild Cherry p. 529

Willow-leaved Pear p. 517

Plum p. 523

Aspen p. 265

Sweet Gum p. 445

Bird Cherry p. 523

Crab Apple p. 491

Black Poplar p. 275

Larch p. 155

Siberian Crab Apple p. 501

Persian Ironwood p. 447

Cherry 'Kanzan' p. 553

Orchard Apple p. 491

Balsam Poplar p. 271

Black Italian Poplar 'Regenerata' p. 279

SHOOTS
alternate buds

Japanese Larch p. 157

Swamp Cypress p. 103

London Plane p. 449

Common Walnut p. 295

Black Walnut p. 295

Common Alder p. 317

Italian Alder p. 321

Tulip Tree p. 437

Large-leaved Lime p. 677

Grey Alder p. 323

Turkey Oak p. 369

Hornbeam p. 325

Crimean Lime p. 681

Red Oak p. 363

Common Oak p. 383

Medlar p. 455

Common Beech p. 337

Sweet Chestnut p. 349

Small-leaved Lime p. 685

Hungarian Oak p. 377

SHOOTS
alternate buds

- Myrobalan Plum p. 525
- Purple-leaved Cherry p. 525
- Blackthorn p. 523
- Broad-leaved Cockspur Thorn p. 461
- Wild Service Tree p. 489
- Honey Locust p. 583
- Tree of Heaven p. 593
- Black Locust p. 575
- Hawthorn p. 459
- Wych Elm p. 399
- Rauli p. 335
- Hazel p. 333
- Turkish Hazel p. 333
- Rowan p. 465
- Golden Rain Tree p. 711
- *Magnolia campbellii* p. 435
- English Elm p. 395
- Caucasian Elm p. 415
- Roble Beech p. 335
- Judas Tree p. 569
- *Malus × purpurea* p. 507
- Swedish Whitebeam p. 489
- *Magnolia soulangiana* p. 429
- Shagbark Hickory p. 301
- Whitebeam p. 483
- Sargent's Rowan p. 475
- Japanese Rowan p. 469

811

CONIFER LEAVES

Yews
p. 23

Silver Firs
p. 109

Plum Yews
p. 33

Redwoods
p. 91

Hemlocks
p. 195

Junipers
p. 71

Monkey Puzzles
p. 37

Spruces
p 167

Japanese Cedars
p. 95

Redwoods
p. 93

Cypresses
p. 61

Thujas
p. 83

Lawson Cypresses
p. 41

Swamp Cypresses
p. 101

Dawn Redwoods
p. 101

Cedars
p. 147

Larches
p. 155

Pines
p. 205

2
3
5
needles

812

BROADLEAVES

Poplars
p. 263

Bays
p. 439

Willows
p. 285

Birches
p. 303

Medlars
p. 455

Alders
p. 317

Diospyros
p. 765

Beeches p. 337

Hornbeams
p. 325

Zelkovas
p. 415

Davidias
p. 745

Hazels
p. 333

Hackberries
p. 417

Box
p. 597

Southern Beeches
p. 335

Thorns
p. 457

Blackthorn
p. 523

Judas Tree
p. 569s

Katsura Trees
p. 441

Sweet Chestnuts
p. 349

813

BROADLEAVES

Limes
p. 677

Oaks
p. 351

Osage Orange
p. 425

Eucalyptus
p. 737

Magnolias
p. 427

Catalpas
p. 767

Whitebeams
p. 483

Elms
p. 395

Hollies
p. 599

Paulownias
p. 773

Eucryphias
p. 705

Laburnums
p. 587

Walnuts
p. 295

Golden Rain Tree
p. 711

BROADLEAVES

Tree of Heaven
p. 593

Ashes
p. 713

Rowans
p. 465

Locust Trees
p. 575

Pagoda Trees
p. 585

Hickories
p. 299

Caster-oil Tree
p. 709

Sweetgums
p. 445

Apples
p. 491

Wild Service Tree
p. 489

Maples
p. 609

Tulip Trees
p. 437

Planes
p. 449

Horse Chestnuts
p. 663

INDEX OF SCIENTIFIC NAMES

Abies
　alba 137
　　'Columnaris' 137
　　'Pyramidalis' 137
　amabilis 125
　balsamea 141
　bifida 121
　bracteata 139
　cephalonica 131
　　var. *apollinis* 131
　　var. *graeca* 131
　　var. *graeca* 135
　chengii 121
　chensiensis 111
　　salouenensis 111
　cilicica 109
　concolor 143
　　'Candicans' 143
　　f. *argentea* 143
　　var. *lowiana* 143
　　'Violacea' 143
　　'Wattezii' 143
　delavayi 117
　　var. *faxoniana* 117
　　var. *georgei* 117
　fabri 117
　　subsp. *minensis* 117
　fargesii 117, 119
　　var. *sutchuenensis* 113, 119
　faxoniana 117
　firma 121
　　'Tardina' 121
　forrestii 117
　　var. *smithii* 117
　fraseri 125
　gamblei 119, 129
　grandis 141
　homolepis 123
　　'Tomomi' 123
　holophylla 123
　kawakamii 119
　koreana 119
　lasiocarpa 139
　　'Compacta' 139
　　var. *arizonica* 139
　magnifica 125
　mariesii 113
　nebrodensis 133
　nephrolepis 133
　nordmanniana 135
　　var. *equi-trojani* 135
　numidica 131
　pindrow 129
　　var. *brevifolia* 129
　　var. *intermedia* 129
　pinsapo 133
　　'Glauca' 133
　procera 145
　　f. *glauca* 145
　recurvata 113
　religiosa 115
　sachalinensis 109
　　var. *mayriana* 109
　　var. *nemorensis* 109
　semenovii 109
　sibirica 109
　　var. *semenovii* 109
　spectabilis 127
　　var. *brevifolia* 127
　squamata 129
　veitchii 111
　vejari 115
　webbiana 127
　× *borisii-regis* 109
　× *bornmuelleriana* 135
　× *shastensis* 125
　× *vilmorinii* 133

Acacia
　dealbata 573
　decurrens
　　var. *mearnsii* 573
　　var. *mollis* 573
　falciformis 573
　longifolia 789
　mearnsii 789
　melanoxylon 573
　retinoides 789
　saligna 789

Acer
　acuminatum 659
　argutum 619
　barbatum 655
　barbinerve 649
　buergerianum 639
　　subsp. *formosanum* 639
　caesium
　　subsp. *giraldii* 641
　campbellii
　　subsp. *flabellatum* 659
　　var. *yunnanense* 659
　campestre 625
　　'Elsrijk' 613
　　'Nanum' 641
　　'Postelense' 625
　　'Pulverulentum' 625
　　'Schwerinii' 625
　capillipes 651
　cappadocicum 621
　　'Aureum' 621
　　'Rubrum' 621
　　subsp. *divergens* 619
　　subsp. *lobelii* 621
　　subsp. *sinicum* 623
　carpinifolium 649
　caudatum
　　subsp. *ukurunduense* 623
　circinatum 643
　cissifolium 617
　crataegifolium 639
　　'Veitchii' 641
　davidii 651
　　'Madeleine Spitta' 649
　　subsp. *grosseri* 619
　　subsp. *grosseri* var. *hersii* 651
　diabolicum 619
　　f. *purpurascens* 619
　distylum 639
　divergens 619
　franchetii 639
　fulvescens 641
　ginnala 627
　glabrum 631
　　subsp. *douglasii* 631
　griseum 617
　grosseri
　　var. *hersii* 651
　heldreichii 637
　　var. *trautvetteri* 637
　henryi 645
　hersii 651
　hyrcanum 631
　japonicum 643
　　'Aconitifolium' 643
　　'Aureum' 643
　　'Vitifolium' 643
　longipes
　　subsp. *longipes* 641
　macrophyllum 631, 655
　　'Seattle Sentinel' 655
　　'Tricolor' 655
　maximowiczianum 617
　micranthum 639
　miyabei 617
　mono
　　f. *ambiguum* 623
　　var. *mayrii* 649
　monspessulanum 617
　morifolium 619
　negundo 661
　　'Auratum' 661
　　'Elegans' 661
　　'Flamingo' 661
　　'Giganteum' 661
　　subsp. *californicum* 661
　　var. *texanum* 661
　　'Variegatum' 661
　　'Violaceum' 661
　nikoense 617
　nipponicum 659
　oliverianum 641
　　subsp. *formosanum* 641
　opalus
　　subsp. *hispanicus* 627
　　subsp. *obtusatum* 627
　　subsp. *opalus* 627
　palmatum 645
　　'Atropurpureum' 647
　　'Butterfly' 645
　　'Cuneatum' 647
　　'Dissectum' 647
　　'Dissectum Rubrifolium' 647
　　'Heptalobum' 647
　　'Katsura' 645
　　'Linearilobum' 647
　　'Nicholsonii' 645
　　'Ornatum' 647
　　'Osakazuki' 647
　　'Oshio Beni' 647
　　'Ribesifolium' 645
　　'Sangokaku' 647
　　'Seiryu' 645
　　'Shishigashira' 645
　　'Tana' 645
　　'Volubile' 645
　pectinatum 641
　　subsp. *forrestii* 641
　　subsp. *laxiflorum* 641
　　subsp. *maximowiczii* 659
　pensylvanicum 651
　　'Erythrocladum' 651
　platanoides 609
　　'Cleveland' 609
　　'Columnare' 609
　　'Crimson King' 611
　　'Crimson Sentry' 613
　　'Cucullatum' 611
　　'Deborah' 613
　　'Dilaceratum' 611
　　'Dissectum' 611
　　'Drummondii' 611
　　'Erectum' 613
　　'Globosum' 611
　　'Goldsworth Purple' 611
　　'Heterophyllum
　　　Aureo-variegatum' 611
　　'Laciniatum' 611, 615
　　'Maculatum' 615
　　'Meyering' 613
　　'Oekonomierat Stoll' 611
　　'Olmsted' 613
　　'Pyramidale Nanum' 615
　　'Reitenbachii' 615
　　'Schwedleri' 611
　　'Summershade' 615
　　'Superform' 613
　　'Walderseei' 611
　pseudoplatanus 633
　　'Atropurpureum' 635
　　'Brilliantissimum' 635
　　'Erectum' 633
　　f. *erythrocarpum* 635
　　'Leopoldii' 635
　　'Negenia' 635
　　'Nizetii' 635
　　'Prinz Handjery' 635
　　'Simon Louis Frères' 635
　　'Variegatum' 633, 635
　　'Worley' 635
　pseudosieboldianum 643
　pycnanthum 649
　rubrum 653
　　'Columnare' 653
　　'October Glory' 655
　　'Red Sunset' 655
　　'Scanlon' 653
　　'Schlesingeri' 653

INDEX OF SCIENTIFIC NAMES

var. *drummondii* 653
var. *trilobum* 653
rufinerve 651
  'Albo-limbatum' 649
saccharinum 657
  'Laciniatum' 657
  'Laciniatum Wieri' 657
saccharum 629
  'Newton Sentry' 629
  subsp. *floridanum* 629
  subsp. *grandidentatum* 629, 631
  subsp. *leucoderme* 629, 631
  subsp. *nigrum* 629
  'Temple's Upright' 629
  var. *rugelii* 655
sempervirens 627
shirasawanum 645
  Aureum' 643
sieboldianum 645
  'Silver Vein' 649
stachyophyllum 641
  subsp. *betulifolium* 641
  var. *tiliifolium* 641
sterculiaceum
  subsp. *franchetii* 639
  subsp. *thomsonii* 623
tataricum 631
  subsp. *ginnala* 627
tegmentosum 649
tetramerum 641
triflorum 617
truncatum 619
velutinum 623
  var. *vanvolxemii* 637
villosum 623
wilsonii 619
× *coriaceum* 619
× *dieckii* 615
× *hillieri* 639
× *rotundilobum* 623
× *zoeschense* 637, 659
  'Annae' 659
  'Elongatum' 659

Achras
zapota 787

Actinidia
deliciosa 783

Aesculus
+ *dallimorei* 667
arguta 667
assamica 675
californica 671
chinensis 675
flava 671
glabra 673
  var. *arguta* 667
  var. *sargentii* 673
glaucescens 675
hippocastanum 663
  'Baumannii' 663
  'Digitata' 665
  'Flore Pleno' 663
  'Hampton Court Gold' 667
  'Laciniata' 665
  'Memmingeri' 667
  'Pendula' 665
  'Pumila' 665

'Pyramidalis' 665
'Umbraculifera' 667
indica 671
  'Sydney Pearce' 671
octandra 671
parviflora 675
  f. *serotina* 675
pavia 669
splendens 675
sylvatica 675
turbinata 673
wilsonii 667
× *bushii* 667
× *carnea* 669
  'Briotii' 669
  'Plantierensis' 669
× *discolor* 675
× *hybrida* 675
× *mississippiensis* 667
× *neglecta*
  'Erythroblastos' 673

Ailanthus
altissima 593
vilmoriniana 593

Albizia
julibrissin 571
  'Rosea' 571

Alnus
cordata 321
cremastogyne 323
formosana 319
glutinosa 317
  'Aurea' 319
  'Fastigiata' 319
  'Imperialis' 317
  'Incisa' 319
  'Laciniata' 317
  'Pyramidalis' 319
  'Quercifolia' 317
hirsuta 319
incana 323
  'Angustissima' 323
  'Aurea' 323
  'Laciniata' 323
  'Pendula' 323
  'Ramulis Coccineis' 323
  subsp. *rugosa* 323
japonica 319
maximowiczii 321
nepalensis 323
rubra 323
sinuata 319
subcordata 321
viridis 321
× *spaethii* 321

Amomyrtus
luma 791

Araucaria
araucana 37
bidwillii 37
heterophylla 37

Arbutus
andrachne 755
canariensis 755
menziesii 753
unedo 753
  'Integerrima' 753
  'Rubra' 753

× *andrachnoides* 755

Athrotaxis
cupressoides 105
laxifolia 105
selaginoides 105

Austrocedrus
chilensis 39

Azara
dentata 785
lanceolata 785
microphylla 785
petiolaris 785
serrata 785

Betula
albo-sinensis
  var. *septentrionalis* 303
alleghaniensis 309
caerulea grandis 303
davurica 305
ermanii 303
  'Grayswood Hill' 303
  var. *japonica* 303
  'Fetisowii' 307
grossa 305
lenta 309
lutea 309
  var. *fallax* 309
mandshurica 307
maximowicziana 303
medwediewii 307
nana 307
neoalaskana 315
nigra 309
papyrifera 315
  var. *commutata* 315
  var. *humilis* 315
pendula 311
  'Birkalensis' 313
  'Dalecarlica' 311
  'Dentata Viscosa' 313
  'Fastigiata' 313
  'Gracilis' 313
  'Obelisk' 313
  'Purpurea' 311
  'Tristis' 313
  'Viscosa' 313
  'Youngii' 311
platyphylla 307
  var. *japonica* 305, 307
  'Whitespire' 307
populifolia 309
pubescens 315
szechuanica 315
utilis 305
  'Doorenbos' 305
  'Grayswood Ghost' 305
  'Inverleith' 305
  'Jermyns' 305
  'Moonbeam' 305
  'Silver Queen' 305
  'Silver Shadow' 305
  var. *jacquemontii* 305, 307
  var. *prattii* 307
× *caerulea* 303

Broussonetia
papyrifera 425

Buxus
balearica 597

microphylla 597
  var. *sinica* 597
sempervirens 597
  'Angustifolia' 597
  'Aureovariegata' 597
  'Gold Tip' 597
  'Latifolia' 597
  'Latifolia Bullata' 597
  'Latifolia Maculata' 597
  'Marginata' 597
  'Pendula' 597
  'Pyramidalis' 597
  'Rosmarinifolia' 597
  'Rotundifolia' 597
wallichiana 597
  'Latifolia Maculata' 597
  'Marginata' 597
  'Pendula' 597
  'Pyramidalis' 597
  'Rosmarinifolia' 597
  'Rotundifolia' 597

Calliandra
haematocephala 789

Callistemon
citrinus 793
viminalis 793

Calocedrus
decurrens 39
  'Aureovariegata' 39

Carpinus
betulus 325
  'Columnaris' 327
  'Fastigiata' 327
  'Frans Fontaine' 327
  'Incisa' 327
  'Pendula' 327
  'Pyramidalis' 327
  'Quercifolia' 327
caroliniana 329
cordata 331
fangiana 331
fargesiana 331
henryana 329
japonica 331
orientalis 331
polyneura 329
tschonoskii 329
turczaninowii 331
  var. *ovalifolia* 331
× *schuschuensis* 329

Carya
cordiformis 301
glabra 299
illinoinensis 299
laciniosa 299
ovata 301
tomentosa 299

Castanea
sativa 349
  'Albomarginata' 349
  'Heterophylla' 349

Casuarina
equisetifolia 781

Catalpa
bignonioides 767
  'Aurea' 767
  'Nana' 767
bungei 771

817

INDEX OF SCIENTIFIC NAMES

var. *heterophylla* 771
fargesii 769
  var. *duclouxii* 769
ovata 771
speciosa 769
× *erubescens*
  'J.C. Teas' 771
  'Purpurea' 771
Cedrus
atlantica 149
  'Aurea' 149
  f. *glauca* 149
  'Glauca Fastigiata' 149
  'Glauca Pendula' 149
brevifolia 153
deodara 151
  'Albospica' 153
  'Argentea' 151
  'Aurea' 151
  'Gold Mound' 153
  'Pendula' 153
  'Robusta' 153
  'Verticillata' 151
libani 147
  'Glauca' 147
Celtis
australis 417
bungeana 419
caucasica 419
koraiensis 419
laevigata 417
  smallii 417
occidentalis 417
  var. *cordata* 417
  var. *crassifolia* 417
sinensis 419
tournefortii 417
Cephalotaxus
fortunei 33
harringtonia 33
  var. *drupacea* 33
  'Fastigiata' 33
  var. *nana* 33
pedunculata 33
Ceratonia
siliqua 789
Cercidiphyllum
japonicum 441
  'Pendulum' 441
  var. *magnificum* 441
  var. *sinense* 441
Cercis
canadensis 571
  'Forest Pansy' 571
racemosa 571
siliquastrum 569
  'Bodnant' 569
  f. *albida* 569
Chamaecyparis
formosensis 55
lawsoniana 41
  'Albo-spica' 46
  'Alumnii' 43
  'Argenteovariegata' 46, 51
  'Aurea' 47
  'Blue Jacket' 46
  'Chilworth Silver' 47
  'Columnaris' 43

'Darleyensis' 51
'Elegantissima' 47
'Ellwood's Gold' 47
'Ellwoodii' 43
'Erecta Aurea' 46
'Erecta Filiformis' 49
'Erecta Glauca' 43
'Erecta Viridis' 43
'Filiformis' 49
'Fletcheri' 45
'Fraseri' 51
'Glauca Lombartsii' 41
'Golden King' 46
'Grayswood Pillar' 41
'Green Hedger' 47
'Green Pillar' 51
'Green Spire' 49
'Henry Dinger' 46
'Hillieri' 41, 45
'Hogger' 51
'Intertexta' 49
'Kestonensis' 49
'Kilmacurragh' 46
'Lombartsii' 41
'Lutea' 49
'Lutea Smithii' 51
'Lycopodioides' 46
'Merrist Wood' 51
'Moerheimii' 46
'Naberi' 51
'Pembury Blue' 51
'Pendula' 49
'Pottenii' 43
'Silver Tap' 47
'Slocock' 47
'Somerset' 45
'Stardust' 51
'Stewartii' 49
'Stricta' 43
'Stricta Glauca' 43
'Tamariscifolia' 47
'Triompf van Boskoop' 45
'Westermannii' 43
'Winston Churchill' 47
'Wisselii' 45
'Youngii' 45
nootkatensis 55
'Pendula' 55
'Variegata' 55
obtusa 57
'Argentea' 57
'Aurea' 57
'Crippsii' 57
'Filicoides' 57
'Lycopodioides' 57
'Tetragona Aurea' 57
pisifera 53
'Filifera' 53
'Filifera Aurea' 53
'Golden Spangle' 53
'Plumosa' 53
'Squarrosa' 53
'Squarrosa Aurea' 53
'Strathmore' 53
thyoides 55
'Glauca' 55
'Variegata' 55
Chionanthus
retusus 763

virginicus 763
Chrysolepis
chrysophylla 783
Citrus
× *paradisi* 799
aurantiifolia 799
aurantium 799
fortunella 799
limetta 799
limettoides 799
limon 799
maxima 799
medica 799
nobilis 799
reticulata 799
sinensis 799
vulgaris var. *bigaradia* 799
Cladrastis
kentukea (lutea) 569
sinensis 569
Cordyline
australis 775
indivisa 777
  'Rubra' 777
  'Purpurea' 777
Cornus
alternifolia 747
  'Argentea' 747
capitata 747
controversa 749
  'Variegata' 749
'Eddie's White Wonder' 747
florida 749
  'Cherokee Chief' 749
  f. *rubra* 749
  'Plenifolia' 749
  'White Cloud' 749
kousa 751
  var. *chinensis* 751
macrophylla 751
nuttallii 747
  'Gold Spot' 747
  'Porlock' 751
walteri 751
Corylus
avellana 333
  'Aurea' 333
  'Contorta' 333
  'Heterophylla' 333
  'Pendula' 333
colurna 333
maxima 333
  'Purpurea' 333
Cotoneaster
frigidus 455
× *watereri* 455
Crataegus 457
atrorubens 463
azarolus 457
chlorosarca 463
crus-galli 461
douglasii 457
flabellata 463
laciniata 457
laevigata 459
  f. *rosea* 461
  'Gireoudii' 461
  'Paul's Scarlet' 459

'Plena' 461
'Punicea' 461
'Rosea Flore Plena' 459
var. *aurea* 461
var. *macrocarpa* 463
macrocarpa 463
maineana 463
mollis 457
monogyna 459
  'Aurea' 461
  'Bicolor' 461
  'Lutescens' 461
  'Pendula Rosea' 459
  'Rosea' 461
  'Stricta' 459
  var. *eriocarpa* 461
nigra 457
oresbia 463
pedicellata 457
pinnatifida 463
prunifolia 461
songorica 463
tanacetifolia 457
wilsonii 463
× *durobrivensis* 463
× *lavallei* 457
  'Carrierei' 457
Cryptomeria
fortunei 99
japonica 95, 99
  'Ashio-sugi' 99
  'Aurescens' 95
  'Compacta' 97
  'Cristata' 95
  'Dacrydioides' 99
  'Elegans' 95
  'Ikari-sugi' 97
  'Kusari-sugi' 97
  'Lobbii' 99
  'Lycopodioides' 97
  'Pungens' 99
  'Pyramidata' 95
  'Sekkan' 97
  'Sekka-sugi' 95
  'Selaginoides' 97
  var. *radicans* 99
  'Viminalis' 97
  'Yoshino' 95
Cunninghamia
lanceolata 107
  'Glauca' 107
× **Cupressocyparis**
leylandii 59
  'Castlewellan' 59
  'Golconda' 59
  'Haggerston Grey' 59
  'Leighton Green' 59
  'Naylor's Blue' 59
  'Robinson's Gold' 59
  'Silver Dust' 59
Cupressus
abramsiana 65
arizonica 69
  var. *stephensonii* 65
cashmeriana 61
forbesii 65
funebris 61
glabra 69

INDEX OF SCIENTIFIC NAMES

'Conica' 69
'Pyramidalis' 69
goveniana 61
  var. *pygmaea* 61
guadalupensis 65
lusitanica 63
  'Glauca' 63
  'Glauca Pendula' 63
  var. *benthamii* 63
macrocarpa 67
  'Donard Gold' 67
  'Goldcrest' 67
  'Horizontalis Aurea' 67
  'Lutea' 67
nevadensis 63
nootkatensis 55
sargentii 63
sempervirens 65
  'Green Pencil' 65
  'Greenspire' 65
  'Swane's Golden' 65
  var. *horizontalis* 65
  var. *stricta* 65
torulosa 61

Cydonia
oblonga 455

Cytisus
purpureus 587

Davidia
involucrata 745
  var. *vilmoriniana* 745

Dicksonia
antartica 779

Diospyros
kaki 765
  'Hachiya' 765
  'Lycopersicum' 765
lotus 765
virginiana 765

Dracaena
draco 777

Drimys
winteri 781

Eleagnus
angustifolia 795

Eriobotrya
japonica 783

Eucalyptus
coccifera 737
cordata 741
dalrympleana 737
glaucescens 739
globulus 741
gomphocephala 791
gunnii 741
  subsp. *archerii* 741
johnstonii 743
nitens 737
pauciflora
  subsp. *niphophila* 739
perriniana 737
resinifera 791
robusta 791
stellulata 743
urnigera 739

Eucommia
ulmoides 439

Eucryphia
cordifolia
  'Ulmo' 705
glutinosa 705
  'Plena' 705
lucida 705
milliganii 705
  'Penwith' 705
× *intermedia*
  'Rostrevor' 705
× *nymansensis* 705

Euodia
hupehensis 591

Fagus
crenata 347
engleriana 347
grandifolia 347
japonica 347
lucida 347
moesiaca 345
orientalis 347
sylvatica 337
  'Albovariegata' 341
  'Ansorgei' 343
  'Argenteovariegata' 341
  'Aspleniifolia' 343
  'Aurea Pendula' 345
  'Cochleata' 339
  'Cockleshell' 345
  'Cristata' 339
  'Dawyck' 337
  'Dawyck Gold' 345
  'Dawyck Purple' 343
  'Grandidentata' 345
  'Luteovariegata' 341
  'Miltonensis' 345
  'Pendula' 337
  'Prince George of Crete' 345
  'Purpurea Pendula' 339
  'Purpurea Tricolor' 341
  'Quercifolia' 341
  'Remillyensis' 341
  'Riversii' 343
  'Rohan Gold' 339
  'Rohan Pyramid' 339
  'Rohanii' 343
  'Roseomarginata' 341
  'Rotundifolia' 345
  'Spaethiana' 343
  'Tortuosa' 339
  'Tricolor' 341
  'Zlatia' 337, 345
taurica 347

Ficus
carica 441
elastica 785
sycomorus 785
macrophylla 785

Fitzroya
cupressoides 69

Fortunella
× *crassifolia* 799
margarita 799

Fraxinus
americana 717
  'Ascidiata' 717
  'Autumn Purple' 717
  'Juglandifolia' 717
  'Rosehill' 717, 721
  var. *biltmoreana* 719
angustifolia 731
  'Obliqua' 731
  'Raywood' 727, 731
  subsp. *oxycarpa* 727, 731
  subsp. *syriaca* 727
  'Veltheimii' 731
chinensis 715
  'Floribunda' 715
  subsp. *rhyncophylla* 715
  var. *acuminata* 715
excelsior 725
  'Aurea' 729
  'Diversifolia Pendula' 729
  'Elegantissima' 729
  'Eureka' 727
  f. *diversifolia* 729
  f. *heterophylla* 729
  f. *monophylla* 729
  'Jaspidea' 725
  'Nana' 727
  'Pendula' 725
  'Pendula Wentworthii' 729
  'Scolopendrifolia' 729
greggii 715
holotricha 713
latifolia 723
mandshurica 715
mariesii 713
nigra 715
oregona 723
ornus 713
  'Arie Peters' 713
oxycarpa 727, 731
pallisae 731
pennsylvanica 719, 721
  'Aucubifolia' 721
  'Crispa' 721
  'Patmore' 721
  var. *subintegerrima* 719
  'Variegata' 721
profunda 721
quadrangulata 715
texensis 723
tomentosa 721
velutina 723
xanthoxyloides 727
  var. *dumosa* 727

Genista
aetnensis 573

Ginkgo
biloba 21
  'Sentry' 21
  'Variegata' 21

Glyptostrobus
pensilis 101

Gleditsia
caspica 581
horrida 583
japonica 583
  var. *koraiensis* 583
sinensis 583
triacanthos 583
  'Bujotii' 585
  'Elegantissima' 585
  f. *inermis* 583
  'Imperial' 585
  'Skyline' 585
  'Sunburst' 585
  'Variegata' 585
  × *texana* 585

Grevillea
robusta 795

Griselinia
littoralis 793
  'Dixon's Cream' 793
  'Variegata' 793
lucida 793

Gymnocladus
dioicus 589
  'Variegata' 589

Halesia
carolina 759

Idesia
polycarpa 709

Ilex
aquifolium 599
  'Alaska' 601
  'Amber' 599
  'Angustifolia' 601
  'Argentea Marginata' 599
  'Argentea Marginata Pendula' 603
  'Aurea Marginata' 599
  'Aurifodina' 601
  'Bacciflava' 599
  'Beetii' 603
  'Ciliata Major' 603
  'Crassifolia' 601
  'Crispa' 603
  'Crispa Aurea Picta' 599
  'Donningtonensis' 603
  'Ferox' 599
  'Ferox Argentea' 599
  'Ferox Aurea' 603
  'Flavescens' 599
  'Foxii' 603
  'Gold Flash' 603
  'Golden Milkboy' 599
  'Handsworth New Silver' 599
  'Hastata' 603
  'Heterophylla' 603
  'J.C. van Tol' 601
  'Latispina' 603
  'Laurifolia' 601
  'Lichtenthalii' 601
  'Nellie R. Stevens' 601
  'Ovata' 599
  'Ovata Aurea' 599
  'Pendula' 603
  'Pyramidalis' 601
  'Recurva' 599
  'Scotica' 601
ciliospinosa 605
cornuta 605
crenata 605
  'Shiro-Fukurin' 605
dipyrena 607
kingiana 607
latifolia 607
  'Lydia Morris' 605
opaca 607
  f. *xanthocarpa* 607
pedunculosa 607

perado
  subsp. *platyphylla* 607
pernyi 607
  'Drace' 607
  'Indian Chief' 607
  var. *veitchii* 607
× *altaclerensis* 601, 605, 607
  'Atkinsonii' 605
  'Balearica' 607
  'Belgica Aurea' 605
  'Camelliifolia' 601
  'Golden King' 601
  'Hendersonii' 601
  'Hodginsii' 601
  'Howick' 607
  'Lawsoniana' 607
  'Mundyi' 605
  'Nigrescens' 605
  'Purple Shaft' 607
  'Wilsonii' 601
  'W. J. Bean' 605
× *beanii* 605
× *koehneana* 607

Jacaranda
  mimosifolia 803
Jubaea
  chilensis 777
Juglans
  ailanthifolia 297
    var. *cordiformis* 297
  cathayensis 297
  cinerea 297
  elaeopyron 297
  major 297
  mandshurica 297
  microcarpa 297
  nigra 295
  regia 295
    'Laciniata' 295
    'Monophylla' 295
Juniperus
  chinensis 73
    'Albovariegata' 73
    'Argentea' 73
    'Aurea' 73
    'Blaauw' 79
    'Iowa' 73
    'Jacobiana' 73
    'Kaizuka' 73
    'Keteleeri' 73
    'Leeana' 73
    'Obelisk' 73
    'Variegata' 73
  communis 71
    f. *suecica* 71
    'Graciosa' 71
    'Hibernica' 71
    'Oblonga Pendula' 71
    'Pyramidalis' 71
    'Seil Island' 71
  deppeana 79
    var. *pachyphlaea* 79
  drupacea 75
  excelsa 75
  flaccida 75
  indica 77
  monosperma 79
  occidentalis 79

oxycedrus 77
recurva 77
  'Castlewellan' 77
  var. *coxii* 77
rigida 75
scopulorum
  'Skyrocket' 79
squamata 79
  'Meyeri' 79
  var. *fargesii* 79
virginiana 81
  'Burkii' 81
  'Canaertii' 81
  'Cupressifolia' 81
  'Glauca' 81
  'Globosa' 81
  'Pendula' 81
  'Pseudocupressus' 81
wallichiana 77
× *media* 79
  'Blaauw' 79
  'Blue and Gold' 79
Kalopanax
  pictus 709
  septemlobus 709
    var. *maximowiczii* 709
Koelreuteria
  bipinnata 711
  integrifolia 711
  paniculata 711
    'Fastigiata' 711
    var. *apiculata* 711
    'Variegata' 711
+Laburnocytisus
  adamii 587
Laburnum
  alpinum 587
  anagyroides 587
    'Aureum' 587
  × *watereri* 587
Larix
  decidua 155
    subsp. *polonica* 155
  gmelinii 163
    var. *japonica* 163
    var. *principis-rupprechtii* 163
  griffithiana 163
  kaempferi 157
    'Dervaes' 163
    'Pendula' 157
  laricina 159
  lyallii 159
  occidentalis 161
  potaninii 163
    var. *macrocarpa* 163
  russica 165
  × *eurolepis* 157
  × *marschlinsii* 157
  × *pendula* 161
Laurus
  nobilis 439
    'Angustifolia' 439
    'Aurea' 439
Ligustrum
  lucidum 761
    'Excelsior Superbum' 761
    'Tricolor' 761

Liquidambar
  formosana 445
  orientalis 445
  styraciflua 445
    'Golden Treasure' 445
    'Lane Roberts' 445
    'Moonbeam' 445
    'Silver King' 445
    'Variegata' 445
    'Worplesdon' 445
Liriodendron
  chinense 437
  tulipifera 437
    'Aureomarginatum' 437
    'Fastigiatum' 437
Luma
  apiculata 791
Maackia
  chinensis 587
Maclura
  pomifera 425
Magnolia
  acuminata 427
  campbellii 435
    var. *alba* 435
  cordata 431
  delavayi 427
  denudata 433
  fraseri 435
  globosa 431
  grandiflora 427
    'Exmouth' 427
    'Goliath' 427
  'Heaven Scent' 429
  hypoleuca 427
  kobus
    var. *borealis* 433
  liliiflora 433
    'Nigra' 433
  macrophylla 427
  officinalis
    var. *biloba* 427
  salicifolia 433
  sargentiana 431
    var. *robusta* 431
  sinensis 431
  sprengeri
    var. *diva* 433
    var. *elongata* 433
  stellata
    'Norman Gould' 431
  tripetala 435
  virginiana 435
  wilsonii 435
  × *loebneri* 431
    'Leonard Messel' 431
    'Merrill' 431
  × *soulangiana* 429
    'Brozzonii' 429
    'Lennei' 433
    'Lennei Alba' 433
    'Picture' 429
    'Rustica Rubra' 429
    'Sayonara' 429
  × *thompsoniana* 431
  × *veitchii* 427
    'Peppermint Stick' 429

  'Peter Veitch' 429
Malus
  baccata 501
    'Jackii' 501
    var. *himalaica* 503
    var. *mandshurica* 501
  brevipes 493
  'Butterball' 509
  'Coralburst' 511
  coronaria 495
    'Charlottae' 495
  'Crittenden' 509
  'Dartmouth' 509
  domestica 491
  'Eleyi' 509
  florentina 505
  floribunda 495
  fusca 497, 499
  'Golden Hornet' 509
  halliana 493
  hupehensis 495
    'Rosea' 495
  ioensis 505
    'Plena' 505
  'John Downie' 509
  kirghisorum 493
  'Lady Northcliffe' 501
  lancifolia 499
  'Laxton's Red' 507
  'Lemoinei' 507
  'Liset' 507
  'Magdeburgensis' 497
  'Mary Potter' 511
  orthocarpa 499
  praecox 491
  prattii 499
  'Profusion' 507
  prunifolia 505
    var. *rinki* 503
  'Red Jade' 511
  'Red Sentinal' 511
  'Royalty' 511
  sargentii 503
  sieboldii 505
  sieversii 491
  spectabilis 499
    'Riversii' 493
  sylvestris 491
    subsp. *mitis* 491
  transitoria 497
  trilobata 497
  tschonoskii 497
  'Van Eseltine' 511
  yunnanensis 505
    var. *veitchii* 505
  × *hartwigii* 503
  × *purpurea* 507
    'Aldenhamensis' 507
  × *robusta* 493
    'Joan' 493
    'Yellow Siberian' 493
  × *sublobata* 503
  × *zumi*
    var. *calocarpa* 493
Melia
  azedarach 797
Mespilus
  germanica 455

820

INDEX OF SCIENTIFIC NAMES

Metasequoia
  glyptostroboides 101
Morus
  alba 421
    'Pendula' 421
    'Pyramidalis' 421
    'Venosa' 421
  cathayana 423
  mongolica 421
    var. *diabolica* 421
  nigra 423
Musa
  × *paradisiaca* 803
  basjoo 803
Myoporum
  insulare 803
Myrtus
  communis 793
    'Flore Pleno' 793
    'Microphylla' 793
  luma 791
Nicotiana
  glauca 801
Nothofagus
  betuloides 335
  dombeyi 335
  nervosa 335
  obliqua 335
  procera 335
Nyssa
  aquatica 735
  ogeche 735
  sinensis 735
  sylvatica 735
    var. *biflora* 735
Olea
  europaea 761
Osmanthus
  americanus 801
  fragrans 801
Ostrya
  carpinifolia 331
Oxydendrum
  arboreum 757
Paliurus
  spina-christi 795
Parrotia
  persica 447
    'Pendula' 447
Paulownia
  fortunei 773
  tomentosa 773
    'Coreana' 773
    var. *lanata* 773
Persea
  americana 781
  borbonia 781
Phellodendron
  amurense 591
    var. *lavallei* 591
  japonicum 591
Phillyrea
  latifolia 763
Phoenix
  canariensis 775
  dactylifera 777

  theophrasti 775
Photinia
  × *fraseri* 787
    'Red Robin' 787
  glabra 787
  serratifolia 787
Phytolacca
  dioica 783
Picea
  abies 175
    'Argentea' 175
    'Cincinnata' 175
    'Cranstonii' 175
    'Cupressina' 175
    'Finedonensis' 175
    'Inversa' 175
    'Laxa' 175
    'Pendula' 175
    'Pendula Major' 175
    'Pyramidata' 175
    'Tuberculata' 175
    'Viminalis' 175
    'Will's Zwerg' 175
  alcoquiana 183
  asperata 173
  balfouriana 193
  bicolor 183
    var. *acicularis* 183
  brachytyla 173
    var. *complanata* 173
  breweriana 187
  engelmannii
    'Glauca' 189
    var. *mexicana* 169
  glauca
    var. *albertiana* 185
  jezoensis
    var. *hondoensis* 181
  koyamai 181
  likiangensis 193
    var. *yunnanensis* 193
  mariana 187
  maximowiczii 169
    var. *senanensis* 169
  montigena 171
  morrisonicola 181
  obovata 171
  omorika 179
  orientalis 179
    'Aurea' 179
    'Gracilis' 179
  polita 171
  pungens 189
    'Endtz' 189
    f. *glauca* 189
    'Koster' 189
    'Moerheim' 189
  purpurea 193
  rubens 185
  shirasawae 183
  schrenkiana 167
  sitchensis 191
  smithiana 167
    var. *nepalensis* 167
  spinulosa 169
  wilsonii 169
  × *fennica* 171
  × *hurstii* 187
  × *lutzii* 171

Picrasma
  quassioides 593
Pinus
  albicaulis 223
  aristata 207
    var. *longaeva* 207
  armandii 209
  attenuata 259
  ayacahuite 217
    var. *veitchii* 217
  balfouriana 207
  banksiana 249
  bhutanica 221
  brutia 231
  bungeana 213
  canariensis 779
  caribaea 779
  cembra 205
    'Aureovariegata' 205
    var. *chlorocarpa* 205
  cembroides 223
  contorta 255
    var. *bolanderi* 255
    var. *latifolia* 255
    var. *murrayana* 255
  cooperi 259
  coulteri 237
  densata 209
  densiflora 225
    'Aurea' 225
    'Oculus-draconis' 225
    'Umbraculifera' 225
  durangensis 249
  echinata 245
    × *rigida* 245
  edulis 223
  engelmannii 241
  excelsa 221
  flexilis 207
  gerardiana 239
  gregii 237
  griffithii 221
  halepensis 231
  hartwegii 257
  heldreichii 205
    var. *leucodermis* 247
  hwangshanensis 221
  jeffreyi 243
  koraiensis 239
  lambertiana 211
  monophylla 223
  montezumae 257
  monticola 211
  mugo 231
  muricata 251
  nelsonii 237
  nigra
    subsp. *laricio* 233
    subsp. *nigra* 235
    subsp. *pallasiana* 233
    subsp. *salzmannii* 235
    var. *caramanica* 233
    var. *maritima* 233
  parviflora 213
    'Glauca' 213
    'Saphir' 213
    'Tempelhof' 213
  patula 243
  peuce 215

  pinaster 215
    subsp. *atlantica* 215
  pinea 205
  ponderosa 241
  pumila
    'Compacta' 205
  radiata 253
  resinosa 253
  rigida 251
  rudis 257
  sabiniana 259
  sibirica 221
  strobiformis 237
  strobus 219
    'Contorta' 219
    'Fastigiata' 219
    'Radiata' 219
  sylvestris 227
    f. *aurea* 229
    'Fastigiata' 229
    subsp. *scotica* 229
    var. *engadinensis* 227
    var. *lapponica* 227
    var. *mongolica* 229
  tabuliformis 209
  taiwanensis 225
  thunbergii 239
  uncinata 231
    var. *rotundata* 231
  veitchii 217
  virginiana 249
  wallichiana 221
  washoensis 245
  × *holfordiana* 247
  × *schwerinii* 219
Pistacia
  lentiscus 797
  terebinthus 797
  vera 797
Pittosporum
  crassifolium 787
  ralphii 733
  tenuifolium 733
    'Abbotsbury Gold' 733
    'Eila Keightley' 733
    'Garnettii' 733
    'Irene Paterson' 733
    'Purpureum' 733
    'Variegatum' 733, 787
    'Warnham Gold' 733
  undulatum 787
Platanus
  'Augustine Henry' 451
  occidentalis 453
  orientalis 453
    'Mirkovec' 451
  × *hispanica* 449
    'Cantabrigiensis' 451
    'Pyramidalis' 451
    'Suttneri' 449
    'Tremonia' 451
Podocarpus
  acutifolius 35
  andinus 35
  hallii 35
  macrophyllus 35
    var. *maki* 35
  nubigenus 35

salignus 35
totara 35
Poncirus
trifoliata 801
Populus
acuminata 273
adenopoda 267
afghanica 275
　'Variegata' 275
alba 263
　'Pyramidalis' 263
　'Richardii' 263
balsamifera 271
　'Balsam Spire' 271
canadensis
　'Lloydii' 273
canescens
　'Macrophylla' 263
cathayana 269
deltoides 281
lasiocarpa 271
maximowiczii 267
　'Androscoggin' 267
nigra
　'Elegans' 277
　'Italica foemina' 277
　'Italica' 277
　'Lombardy Gold' 277
　'Plantierensis' 277
　'Variegata' 275
　'Vereecken' 275
　subsp. *afghanica* 277
　subsp. *betulifolia* 275
　var. *thevestina* 275
　'Oxford' 267
purdomii 267
simonii 269
　'Fastigiata' 269
　'Pendula' 269
szechuanica
　var. *tibetica* 269
tremula 265
　'Pendula' 265
tremuloides 265
trichocarpa 271
　'Fritzi Pauley' 271
　'Scott Pauley' 271
wilsonii 269
yunnanensis 267
× *berolinensis* 277
× *canadensis*
　'Eugenei' 281
　'Florence Biondi' 283
　'Marilandica' 281
　'Regenerata' 279
　'Robusta' 281
　'Serotina Aurea' 279
　'Serotina' 279
× *candicans* 271
　'Aurora' 271
× *canescens* 263
× *generosa* 273
　'Beaupre' 273
　'Boelare' 273
　'Interamericana' 273
Prumnopitys
andina 35

Prunus
'Accolade' 541
'Amanogawa' 553
americana 527
'Ariake' 557
armeniaca 531
'Asano' 543
avium 529
　'Decumana' 529
　'Nana' 529
　'Pendula' 529
　'Plena' 529
　'Rubrifolia' 529
　'Salicifolia' 529
cerasifera 525
　'Lindsayae' 525
　'Nigra' 525
　'Pissardii' 525
　'Rosea' 525
　var. *divaricata* 525
cerasus 527
　'Rhexii' 527
'Cheal's Weeping' 553
cornuta 537
cuthbertii 537
domestica 523
　subsp. *insititia* 531
dulcis 531
　'Albaplena' 531
　'Roseoplana' 531
'Hatazakura' 565
'Hokusai' 563
'Horinji' 563
'Ichiyo' 563
ilicifolia 543
incisa 535
　'Umineko' 535
insititia 531
　'Mirabelle' 531
　subsp. *italica* 531
　subsp. *syriaca* 531
'Jo-nioi' 561
'Kanzan' 553
'Kiku Shidare Zakura' 553
kurilensis × *sargentii*
　'Kursar' 543
lannesiana
　'Beni-Shigure' 551
　'Beni-tama-nishiki' 551
　'Beni-yutaka' 551
　f. *contorta* 549
　'Fukurokuju' 549
　'Hanagasa' 551
　'Sarasa' 551
　'Shizuka' 549
　'Tsukubane' 549
　'Tsyu-kosade' 551
　'Yaebeni-Ohshima' 549
laurocerasus 567
　'Bruantii' 567
　'Camelliifolia' 567
　'Magnoliifolia' 567
　'Otinii' 567
　'Rotundifolia' 567
　'Schipkaensis' 567
　'Serbica' 567
maackii 535
mahaleb 527
'Mikuruma-gaeshi' 557

mume 533
　'Alphandii' 533
　'Benishidori' 533
　'Omoi-no-moma' 533
nipponica 555
　'Oshokun' 561
padus 523
　'Colorata' 523
　'Plena' 523
　'Purple Queen' 537
　subsp. *borealis* 523
　var. *commutata* 537
　'Watereri' 523
'Pandora' 555
pennsylvanica 543
persica 533
　'Albo Plena' 533
　'Klara Mayer' 533
　'Kurokawa-yaguchi' 533
　'Prince Charming' 533
　'Sagami-shidare' 533
　'Stellata' 533
　var. *nectarina* 533
'Pink Perfection' 559
sargentii 535
　'Columnaris' 537
　'Rancho' 537
　'Spire' 537
serotina 527
　'Pendula' 527
　var. *salicifolia* 527
serrula 547
serrulata
　var. *hupehensis* 547
　var. *pubescens* 547
　var. *spontanea* 547
'Shimidsu Zakura' 557, 561
'Shirofugen' 565
'Shirotae' 559
'Shogetsu' 557
speciosa 545
spinosa 523
　'Purpurea' 523
subhirtella 539
　'Autumnalis' 541
　'Autumnalis Rosea' 541
　'Flore Pleno' 539
　'Fukubana' 541
　'Fukubana Higan Zakura' 541
　'Omoigawa' 539
　'Pendula' 539
　'Pendula Rosea' 539
　'Pendula Rubra' 539
　'Stellata' 539
'Tai-haku' 565
'Takasago' 563
triloba
　'Multiplex' 543
　'Petzoldii' 543
'Ukon' 559
'Umeniko' 555
virginiana 543
　'Schubert' 543
'Washi-no-o' 557
× *blireana* 525
× *campanulata*
　'Okame' 543
× *fontanesiana* 537

× *hillieri*
　'Spire' 541
× *juddii* 555
× *schmittii* 535
× *yedoensis* 545
　'Shidare Yoshino' 545
　'Tokyo Cherry' 545
　'Tsu Yoshino' 545
Pseudolarix
amabilis 165
Pseudotsuga
japonica 201
macrocarpa 203
menziesii 201, 203
　'Brevifolia' 203
　f. *caesia* 203
　'Fretsii' 203
　'Stairii' 201
　var. *glauca* 203
　var. *menziesii* 201
Ptelea
trifoliata 801
　var. *bailey* 801
Pterocarya
fraxinifolia 293
rhoifolia 293
stenoptera 293
× *rehderiana* 293
Pterostyrax
hispida 759
Punica
granatum 793
Pyrus
amygdaliformis 513
balansae 521
betulifolia 513
bretschneideri 515
calleryana 519
　'Bradford' 519
　'Chanticleer' 519
communis 519
　'Beech Hill' 519
cordata 519
cossonii 515
elaeagrifolia 513
fauriei 521
korshinskyi 521
longipes 515
nivalis 515
pashia 521
　var. *kumaoni* 521
pyraster 513, 519
pyrifolia 521
　'Kieffer' 521
　var. *culta* 521
　var. *lecontei* 521
regelii 513
salicifolia 517
serrulata 513
ussuriensis 517
　var. *hondoensis* 517
　var. *ovoidea* 517
× *canescens* 517
Quercus
acutissima 353
agrifolia 373
alba 389
　var. *latifolia* 389

INDEX OF SCIENTIFIC NAMES

aliena 353
  var. *acuteserrata* 353
alnifolia 379
bicolor 391
brachyphylla 375
canariensis 375
castaneifolia 365
  × *macranthera* 365
cerris 369
  f. *laciniata* 369
  subsp. *tournefortii* 369
  var. *austriaca* 369
  'Variegata' 369
coccifera 781
  subsp. *calliprinos* 781
coccinea 361
  'Splendens' 361
dentata 353
ellipsoidalis 357
falcata 357
  var. *pagodifolia* 357
frainetto 377
  'Hungarian Crown' 377
garryana 393
haas 387
iberica 781
ilex 373
  'Fordii' 373
  subsp. *rotundifolia* 373
imbricaria 359
ithaburensis 353
kelloggii 357
lanuginosa 353
laurifolia 357
libani 367
  var. *pinnata* 367
lobata 391
lyrata 355
'Macon' 379
macranthera 379
macrocarpa 389
macrolepis 353
marilandica 357
michauxii 393
mongolica 353
  var. *grosseserrata* 353
muehlenbergii 355
myrsinifolia 353
myrtifolia 781
nigra 355
palustris 361
pedunculiflora 387
petraea 381
  'Columna' 381
  'Insecata' 381
  'Laciniata' 381
  'Mespilifolia' 381
phellos 351
'Pondaim' 379
pontica 379
prinus 393
pubescens 375
  subsp. *palensis* 375
pyrenaica 377
  'Pendula' 377
robur 383
  'Argenteovariegata' 385
  'Atropurpurea' 385
  'Concordia' 385

  'Cristata' 387
  f. *fastigiata* 383
  'Fastigiata Grangei' 387
  'Filicifolia' 385
  'Granbyana' 387
  'Holophylla' 387
  'Hungarian' 383
  'Pendula' 387
  'Raba' 383
  'Strypemonde' 385
  'Tortuosa' 383
rubra 363
  'Aurea' 363
semicarpifolia 781
shumardii 357
  var. *texana* 357
stellata 355
suber 367
trojana 367
variabilis 353
velutina 359
  'Magnifica' 359
  'Nobilis' 359
virgiliana 375
warburgii 365
× *bushii* 355
× *falcata*
  var. *triloba* 355
× *heterophylla* 355
× *hispanica*
  'Ambrozyana' 367
  'Fulhamensis' 367, 371
  'Lucombeana' 371
× *leana* 359
× *ludoviciana* 351
× *rosacea* 385
× *schochiana* 351
× *turneri* 373

Rhododendron
arboreum 757
  'Album' 757
  'Blood Red' 757
  'Roseum' 757

Rhus
glabra 595
potaninii 595
typhina 595
  'Dissecta' 595
verniciflua 595

Robinia
'Bella Rosea' 581
hispida 577
  var. *macrophylla* 577
  'Idahoensis' 581
pseudoacacia 575
  'Appalachia' 581
  'Aurea' 579
  'Bessoniana' 581
  'Coluteoides' 579
  'Frisia' 575
  'Glaucescens' 579
  'Monophylla Fastigiata' 579
  'Pyramidalis' 575
  'Rehderi' 581
  'Rozynskyana' 575
  'Tortuosa' 575
  'Umbraculifera' 577
  'Unifolia' 577
viscosa 577

× *holdtii* 577
  'Britzensis' 581
× *slavinii* 579
  'Hillieri' 579

Salix
acutifolia 289
alba 291
  'Britzensis' 291
  f. *argentea* 291
  var. *caerulea* 291
  var. *sericea* 291
babylonica 287, 289
  'Crispa' 289
  'Tortuosa' 289
caprea 285
  'Kilmarnock' 285
cinerea 285
daphnoides 285
elaeagnos 289
fragilis 287
irrorata 289
matsudana 'Tortuosa' 289
oleifolia 285
pentandra 285
rosmarinifolia 289
triandra 285
viminalis 289
violacea 289
× *pendulina*
  'Blanda' 287
  'Elegantissima' 287
× *rubens* 287
  'Basfordiana' 287
× *sepulcralis*
  'Chrysocoma' 287
  'Erythroflexuosa' 289
  'Salamonii' 287

Sassafras
albidum 443
  var. *molle* 443

Saxegothaea
conspicua 39

Schinus
molle 797

Sciadopitys
verticillata 107

Sequoia
sempervirens 91
  'Adpressa' 91
  'Cantab' 91

Sequoiadendron
giganteum 93
  'Aureovariegatum' 93
  'Pendulum' 93

Sophora
japonica 585
  'Pendula' 585
  'Pyramidalis' 585
microphylla 789
  'Sun King' 789
tetraptera 789
  'Grandiflora' 789

Sorbus
alnifolia 487
  var. *longifolia* 487
  var. *macrophylla* 487
  var. *submollis* 487

americana
  'Belmonte' 469
amurensis
  var. *rota* 469
anglica 489
aria 483
  'Decaisneana' 483
  'Lutescens' 483
  'Magnifica' 483
  'Majestica' 483
aronioides 471
aucuparia 465
  'Aspleniifolia' 465
  'Beissneri' 465
  'Fastigiata' 465
  'Hilling's Spire' 471
  subsp. *sibirica* 469
  'Xanthocarpa' 465
bristoliensis 489
caloneura 467
cashmiriana 473
commixta 469
  'Embley' 475
  'Jermyns' 473
cuspidata 485
decora 477, 479
devoniensis 489
domestica 481
  var. *pomifera* 481
  var. *pyrifera* 481
esserteauiana
  'Flava' 473
folgneri 479
forrestii 475
  'Ghose' 471
graeca 485
hajastana 487
harrowiana 473
hupehensis 475
  'November Pink' 475
  'Rufus' 475
  var. *obtusa* 475
insignis 473
intermedia 489
japonica 467
  'Pagoda Red' 467
  var. *calocarpa* 467
'Joseph Rock' 475
keissleri 471
lancifolia 479
latifolia 489
'Leonard Messel' 477
megalocarpa 477
meliosmifolia 479
mougeotii 485
pohuashanensis 467
randaiensis 477
rupicola 467
sargentiana 475
scalaris 473
serotina 465
'Signalman' 471
'Sunshine' 477
takhtajanii 487
tamamschjanae 479
thibetica
  'John Mitchell' 485
torminalis 489
'Tundra' 477

INDEX OF SCIENTIFIC NAMES

umbellata 487
  var. *cretica* 485
vestita 485
vexans 485
vilmorinii 473
wardii 471
wilfordiana 469
'Wilfrid Fox' 483
'Winter Cheer' 477
xanthoneura 467
zahlbruckneri 487
× *decipiens* 485
× *hybrida*
  'Gibbsii' 479
× *kewensis* 475
× *paucicrenata* 485
× *thuringiaca* 481
  'Fastigiata' 481
× *vagensis* 489

Stewartia
malacodendron 707
monadelpha 707
pseudocamellia 707
pteropetiolata
  var. *koreana* 707
sinensis 707

Styrax
hemsleyana 759
japonica 759
obassia 759
officinale 787

Taiwania
cryptomerioides 101

Tamarix 703
africana 787
canariensis 703
dalmatica 787
gallica 703
pentandra 703
ramosissima 703
  'Rosea' 703
  'Rubra' 703
  'Summer Glow' 703
tetrandra 703

Taxodium
ascendens 103
  'Nutans' 103
distichum 103
  var. *nutans* 103
mucronatum 779

Taxus
baccata 23
  'Adpressa' 25
  'Adpressa Aurea' 25
  'Adpressa Variegata' 25
  'Aldenhamensis' 27
  'Aurea' 23
  'Aureovariegata' 26
  'Barronii' 25
  'Brevifolia' 25
  'Cheshuntensis' 27
  'Dovastoniana' 25
  'Dovastonii Aurea' 25
  'Erecta' 26
  'Fastigiata' 23
  'Fastigiata Aurea' 23
  'Fastigiata
    Aureomarginata' 23

  'Lutea' 23
  'Neidpathensis' 27
  'Paulina' 27
  'Rushmore' 27
  'Semperaurea' 26
  'Standishii' 26
  'Summergold' 26
  'Xanthocarpa' 23
canadensis 28
  'Variegata' 28
chinensis 28
cuspidata 28
× *hunnewelliana* 25
× *media* 29
  'Hatfieldii' 28
  'Hicksii' 29
  'Kelseyi' 29
  'Sargentii' 29
  'Skalborg' 29
wallichiana 29

Tetracentron
sinense 439

Tetradium
daniellii 591

Thuja
koraiensis 87
occidentalis 85, 89
  'Douglasii Pyramidalis' 85
  'Fastigiata' 85
  'Filiformis' 89
  'Holmstrup Yellow' 85
  'Lutea' 85
  'Spiralis' 85
  'Wareana Lutescens' 89
  'Waxen' 85
orientalis 85, 89
  'Bonita' 85
  'Elegantissima' 89
  'Flagelliformis' 89
plicata 83
  'Aurea' 83
  'Fastigiata' 83
  'Stoneham Gold' 83
  'Stricta' 83
  'Zebrina' 83
  'Zebrina Extra Gold' 83
standishii 87

Thujopsis
dolabrata 87
  'Aurea' 87
  'Variegata' 87

Tilia
americana 693
  'Dentata' 693
amurensis 697
begoniifolia 681
caucasica 697
chinensis 689
cordata 685
  'Pyramidalis' 685
  'Rancho' 687
  'Harold Hillier' 701
henryana 691
heterophylla 691
insularis 681
japonica 689
kiusiana 689
laetevirens 681
maximowicziana 701

miqueliana 697
mongolica 691
'Mrs Stenson' 689
oliveri 697
paucicostata 697
platyphyllos 677
  'Aspleniifolia' 677
  'Aurea' 679
  'Corallina' 677
  'Fastigiata' 679
  'Laciniata' 677
  'Örebro' 679
  'Princes Street' 679
  'Rubra' 677
  subsp. *cordifolia* 679
  subsp. *pseudorubra* 679
  'Tortuosa' 677
  var. *vitifolia* 677
tomentosa 699
  'Brabant' 699
  'Green Mountain' 699
  'Petiolaris' 695, 699
  'Princeton' 699
  'Sterling Silver' 699
  'Szeleste' 699
  'Varsaviensis' 689
× *euchlora* 681
× *europaea* 683
  'Greenspire' 687
  'Pallida' 687
  'Redmond' 693
  'Wratislaviensis' 687
  'Zwarte Linde' 687
× *flaccida* 701
  'Diversifolia' 701
× *flavescens* 701
  'Dropmore' 701
  'Glenleven' 701
  'Wascana' 701
× *moltkei* 695

Toona
sinensis 709
  'Flamingo' 709

Torreya
californica 31
grandis 31
nucifera 31

Trachycarpus
fortunei 775

Tsuga
albertiana 195
canadensis 197
  'Aurea' 197
  'Fremdii' 197
  'Macrophylla' 197
  'Microphylla' 197
  'Sargentii' 197
  'Taxifolia' 197
caroliniana 195
chinensis 199
diversifolia 199
dumosa 199
heterophylla 195

Ulmus
americana 397
bergmanniana 413
carpinifolia 405, 407
castaneifolia 413

davidiana 413
  'Dodoens' 405
glabra 399
  'Camperdownii' 401
  'Crispa' 401
  'Exoniensis' 401
  'Horizontalis' 399
  'Lutescens' 401
  'Nana' 401
japonica 411
  'Jacon' 411
  'Karagatch' 409
laciniata 413
laevis 395
'Lobel' 409
macrocarpa 413
minor
  'Dicksonii' 407
  'Louis van Houtte' 395
  'Sarniensis' 407
  'Silver Gem' 395
  subsp. *minor* 407
  var. *cornubiensis* 407
  var. *diversifolia* 405
  var. *lockii* 407
  var. *vulgaris* 395
  'Viminalis' 395
  'Viminalis Aurea' 395
montana 399
parvifolia 411
  'Plantjin' 405
  'Pinnato-ramosa' 409
procera 395
pumila 411
  var. *arborea* 409
racemosa 397
rubra 397
'Sapporo Autumn Gold' 411
thomasii 397
villosa 409
× *hollandica*
  'Dampieri' 403
  'Dampieri Aurea' 403
  'Groenveldt' 405
  'Major' 403
  'Vegeta' 403

Umbellularia
californica 443

Washingtonia
filifera 777

Xanthocyparis
nootkatensis 55

Yucca
aloifolia 777
  subsp. *draconis* 777
elephantipes 777
gloriosa 777

Zelkova
abelicea 415
carpinifolia 415
serrata 415
  subsp. *stipulacea* 415
sinica 415
× *verschaffeltii* 415

Ziziphus
jujuba 795
lotus 795
vulgaris 795

INDEX OF ENGLISH NAMES

The English names of cultivars are also included in the index of scientific names (pp. 816-24)

Acacia
　Mop-head 577
　Rose 577
Alder 317
　Caucasian 321
　Common 317
　　'Aurea' 319
　　'Fastigiata' 319
　　'Imperialis' 317
　　'Incisa' 319
　　'Laciniata' 317
　　'Pyramidalis' 319
　　'Quercifolia' 317
　Green 321
　Grey 323
　　'Angustissima' 323
　　'Aurea' 323
　　'Laciniata' 323
　　'Pendula' 323
　　'Ramulus Coccineis' 323
　Italian 321
　Red 323
　Sitka 319
Allegheny Moss 579
Almond 531
　'Albaplena' 531
　'Roseoplana' 531
Apple
　'Aldenhamensis' 507
　'Butterball' 509
　'Coralburst' 511
　'Crittenden' 509
　'Dartmouth' 509
　'Eleyi' 509
　'Golden Hornet' 509
　'Joan' 493
　'John Downie' 509
　'Rosea' 495
　'Lady Northcliffe' 501
　'Laxton's Red' 507
　'Lemoinei' 507
　'Liset' 507
　'Magdeburgensis' 497
　'Mary Potter' 511
　'Plena' 505
　'Profusion' 507
　'Red Jade' 511
　'Red Sentinel' 511
　'Royalty' 511
　'Riversii' 493
　'Van Eseltine' 511
　'Yellow Siberian' 493
　Crab 491
　　Bechtel 505
　　Chinese 493, 499
　　Japanese 495
　　Oregon 497
　　Siberian 501
　　　'Jackii' 501
　　Sweet 495

　'Charlottae' 495
　Toringo 505
　Oregon Crab 499
　Orchard 491
　Pillar 497
Apricot 531
　Japanese 533
　　'Alphandii' 533
　　'Benishidori' 533
　　'Omoi-no-moma' 533
Apuka 793
Arbor-vitae
　American 85
　　'Douglasii Pyramidalis' 85
　　'Fastigiata' 85
　　'Filiformis' 89
　　'Holmstrup Yellow' 85
　　'Lutea' 85
　　'Spiralis' 85
　　'Wareana Lutescens' 89
　　'Waxen' 85
　False 87
　Japanese 87
　Korean 87
Ash 713
　Afghan 727
　Arizona 723
　Biltmore 719
　Black 715
　Blue 715
　Caucasian 727
　Chinese 715
　　'Floribunda' 715
　Chinese Flowering 713
　Common 725
　　'Aurea' 729
　　'Diversifolia Pendula' 729
　　'Elegantissima' 729
　　'Eureka' 727
　　'Jaspidea' 725
　　'Nana' 727
　　'Pendula' 725
　　'Pendula Wentworthii' 729
　　'Scolopendrifolia' 729
　Flowering 713
　Golden 725
　Green 719
　　'Acubifolia' 721
　　'Crispa' 721
　　'Patmore' 721
　　'Variegata' 721
　Gregg 715
　Manchurian 715
　Manna 713
　'Arie Peters' 713
　Narrow-leaved 731
　　'Obliqua' 731
　　'Raywood' 727, 731
　　'Veltheimii' 731

　One-leaved 729
　Oregon 723
　Pumpkin 721
　Syrian 727
　Texas 723
　Velvet 723
　Water 721
　Weeping 725 709
　White 717
　　'Ascidiata' 717
　　'Autumn Purple' 717
　　'Juglandifolia' 717
　　'Rosehill' 717, 721
Aspen 265
　Chinese 267
　European 265
　Quaking 265
　Weeping 265
Australian Banyan Tree 785
Avocado Pear 781
Azarole 457
Balm of Gilead 271
Banana 803
　Japanese 803
Basswood
　White 691
Bay Tree 439
　'Angustifolia' 439
　'Aurea' 439
Bay
　Willow-leaved 439
　　'Angustifolia' 439
　　'Aurea' 439
Bean Tree
　Indian 767
Beech 335
　American 347
　Blue 329
　Chinese 347
　Cockscomb 339
　Common 337
　　'Albovariegata' 341
　　'Ansorgei' 343
　　'Argenteovariegata' 341
　　'Aspleniifolia' 343
　　'Aurea Pendula' 345
　　'Cochleata' 339
　　'Cockleshell' 345
　　'Cristata' 339
　　'Dawyck' 337
　　'Dawyck Gold' 345
　　'Dawyck Purple' 343
　　'Grandidentata' 345
　　'Luteovariegata' 341
　　'Miltonensis' 345
　　'Pendula' 337

　　'Prince George of Crete' 345
　　'Purpurea Pendula' 339
　　'Purpurea Tricolor' 341
　　'Quercifolia' 341
　　'Remillyensis' 341
　　'Riversii' 343
　　'Rohan Gold' 339
　　'Rohan Pyramid' 339
　　'Rohanii' 343
　　'Roseomarginata' 341
　　'Rotundifolia' 345
　　'Spaethiana' 343
　　'Tortuosa' 339
　　'Tricolor' 341
　　'Zlatia' 337, 345
　Copper 343
　Cut-leaved 341
　Engler 347
　Fern-leaved 343
　Golden 345
　Japanese 347
　Oriental 347
　Oval-leaved Southern 335
　Purple 343
　Roble 335
　Siebold's 347
　Water 329
　Weeping Purple 339
Beetree Linden 691
Birch 303
　Asian Black 305
　Blue 303
　Canoe 315
　Cherry 309
　Common 315
　Dwarf 307
　Erman's 303
　　'Grayswood Hill' 303
　Grey 309
　Himalayan 305
　　'Doorenbos' 305
　　'Grayswood Ghost' 305
　　'Inverleith' 305
　　'Jermyns' 305
　　'Moonbeam' 305
　　'Silver Queen' 305
　　'Silver Shadow' 305
　Japanese 305
　Japanese Cherry 305
　Manchurian 307
　　'Whitespire' 307
　Monarch 303
　Paper 315
　River 309
　Silver 311
　　'Birkalensis' 313
　　'Dalecarlica' 311
　　'Dentata Viscosa' 313
　　'Fastigiata' 313
　　'Gracilis' 313

825

INDEX OF ENGLISH NAMES

'Obelisk' 313
'Purpurea' 311
'Tristis' 313
'Viscosa' 313
'Youngii' 311
Transcaucasian 307
Weeping Silver 313
White 315
Yellow 309
Young's Weeping 311

Bitternut 301

Black Sally 573

Blackthorn 523
'Purpurea' 523

Blackwood 573

Boobyalla 803

Bottlebrush
Crimson 793
Weeping 793

Box 597
Balearic 597
Common 597
  'Angustifolia' 597
  'Aureovariegata' 597
  'Gold Tip' 597
  'Latifolia' 597
  'Latifolia Bullata' 597
  'Latifolia Maculata' 597
  'Marginata' 597
  'Pendula' 597
  'Pyramidalis' 597
  'Rosmarinifolia' 597
  'Rotundifolia' 597
Dwarf 597
Himalayan 597
Victorian 787

Broadleaf 793
  'Dixon's Cream' 793
  'Variegata' 793

Broom
Mount Etna 573

Buckeye
Ohio 673
Red 669
Sweet 671
Texas 667
Yellow 671

Bullace 531

Bunya-Bunya 37

Butternut 297

Buttonwood 453

Cabbage Tree 777

Camellia
Silky 707

Carob 789

Caster-oil Tree
Prickly 709

Catalpa 767
Farge's 769
Golden 767
Western 769
Yellow 771

Cedar 147
Atlas 149
Blue 149
'Aurea' 149
'Glauca Fastigiata' 149
'Glauca Pendula' 149
Chilean 39
Chinese 709
Cyprian 153
Deodar 151
'Albospica' 153
'Argentea' 151
'Aurea' 151
'Gold Mound' 153
'Pendula' 153
'Robusta' 153
'Verticillata' 151
Incense 39
'Aureovariegata' 39
Japanese 95, 99
'Ashio-sugi' 99
'Aurescens' 95
'Compacta' 97
'Crista' 95
'Dacrydioides' 99
'Elegans' 95
'Ikari-sugi' 97
'Kusari-sugi' 97
'Lobbii' 99
'Lycopodioides' 97
'Pungens' 99
'Pyramidata' 95
'Sekkan' 97
'Sekka-sugi' 95
'Selaginoides' 97
'Viminalis' 97
'Yoshino' 95
of Goa 63
of Lebanon 147
'Glauca' 147
Pencil 81
'Burkii' 81
'Canaertii' 81
'Cupressifolia' 81
'Glauca' 81
'Globosa' 81
'Pendula' 81
'Pseudocupressus' 81
Salt 703
Smooth Tasmanian 105
Summit 105
Tasmanian 105
Western Red 83
'Aurea' 83
'Fastigiata' 83
'Stoneham Gold' 83
'Stricta' 83
'Zebrina' 83
'Zebrina Extra Gold' 83
White 85, 69
'Douglasii Pyramidalis' 85
'Fastigiata' 85
'Filiformis' 89
'Holmstrup Yellow' 85
'Lutea' 85
'Spiralis' 85
'Wareana Lutescens' 89
'Waxen' 85

Cherry Laurel 567
'Bruantii' 567
'Camelliifolia' 567
'Magnoliifolia' 567
'Otinii' 567
'Rotundifolia' 567
'Schipkaensis' 567
'Serbica' 567

Cherry
'Accolade' 541
'Amanogawa' 553
'Ariake' 557
'Asano' 543
'Beni-Shigure' 551
'Beni-tama-nishiki' 551
'Beni-yutaka' 551
'Cheal's Weeping' 553
'Fukurokuju' 549
'Hanagasa' 551
'Hatazakura' 565
'Hokusai' 563
'Horinji' 563
'Ichiyo' 563
'Jo-nioi' 561
'Kanzan' 553
'Kiku Shidare Zakura' 553
'Kursar' 543
'Mikuruma-gaeshi' 557
'Okame' 543
'Oshokun' 561
'Pandora' 555
'Pink Perfection' 559
'Sarasa' 551
'Shimidsu Zakura' 557, 561
'Shirofugen' 565
'Shirotae' 559
'Shizuka' 549
'Shogetsu' 557
'Spire' 541
'Tai-haku' 565
'Takasago' 563
'Tsukubane' 549
'Tsyu-kosade' 551
'Ukon' 559
'Umeniko' 555
'Washi-no-o' 557
'Yaebeni-Ohshima' 549
Apple Blossom 553
Black 527
'Pendula' 527
Bullace 531
Capulin Black 527
Cherry Plum 545
'Lindsayae' 525
'Nigra' 525
'Pissardii' 525
'Rosea' 525
Choke 543
'Schubert' 543
Double Sour 527
'Rhexii' 527
Double White 529
European Bird 523
'Colorata' 523
'Plena' 523
'Purple Queen' 537
'Watereri' 523

Flag 565
Fuji 535
'Umineko' 535
Great White 565
Hill Cherry
Chinese 547
Japanese 547
Korean 547
Himalayan Bird 537
Holly-leaved 543
'Multiplex' 543
'Petzoldii' 543
Japanese Alpine 555
Manchurian 535
Matsumae 551
Mount Fuji 559
Myrobalan Plum 545
'Lindsayae' 525
'Nigra' 525
'Pissardii' 525
'Rosea' 525
Oshima 545
Pin 543
Purple-leaved 525
Rum 527
Sargent's 535
'Columnaris' 537
'Rancho' 537
'Spire' 537
Spring 539
'Autumnalis' 541
'Autumnalis Rosea' 541
'Flore Pleno' 539
'Fukubana' 541
'Fukubana Higan Zakura' 541
'Omoigawa' 539
'Pendula' 539
'Pendula Rosea' 539
'Pendula Rubra' 539
'Stellata' 539
St Lucie 527
Tibetan 547
Tobacco-leaved 529
Tokyo 545
Wild 529
'Decumana' 529
'Nana' 529
'Pendula' 529
'Plena' 529
'Rubrifolia' 529
'Salicifolia' 529
Yoshino 545
'Shidare Yoshino' 545
'Tokyo Cherry' 545
'Tsu Yoshino' 545

Chestnut, Horse
Chinese 675
Common 663
'Baumannii' 663
'Digitata' 665
'Flore Pleno' 663
'Hampton Court Gold' 667
'Laciniata' 665
'Memmingeri' 667
'Pendula' 665
'Pumila' 665
'Pyramidalis' 665

INDEX OF ENGLISH NAMES

'Umbraculifera' 667
Cut-leaved 665
Dallimore's 667
Dwarf 675
Indian 671
  'Sydney Pearce' 671
Japanese 673
Red 669
  'Briotii' 669
  'Plantierensis' 669
Sunrise 673
  'Erythroblastos' 673
Wilson's 667

Chestnut, Sweet 349
  'Albomarginata' 349
  'Heterophylla' 349
  Cut-leaved 349

China Tree 711

Chinese Date 795

Chinese Flame Tree 711

Chinese Scholar Tree 585

Christmas Berry 787
  'Red Robin' 787

Citrus fruits 799
  Bitter Orange 799
  Citron 799
  Clementine 799
  Florida Orange 799
  Grapefruit 799
  King Mandarin 799
  Kumquat 799
  Lemon 799
  Lime 799
  Mandarin 799
  Pampelmousse 799
  Pomelo 799
  Satsuma 799
  Seville Orange 799
  Shaddock 799
  Sweet Orange 799
  Tangerine 799

Cork Tree
  Amur 591
  Japanese 591

Cornel
  Bentham's 751

Cotoneaster
  Himalayan Tree 455

Cottonwood 271
  Eastern 281
  Lance-leaf 273

Crab 491

Cucumber Tree 427
  Earleaf 435
  Large-leaved 427
  Yellow 431

Cypress 39
  Arizona 69
  Bentham 63
  Chinese Weeping 61
  Cuyamaca 65
  Golden Hinoki 57
  Gowen 61
  Guadalupe 65
  Hinoki 57
    'Argentea' 57
    'Aurea' 57
    'Crippsii' 57
    'Filicoides' 57
    'Lycopodiodes' 57
    'Tetragona Aurea' 57
  Italian 65
    'Green Pencil' 65
    'Greenspire' 65
    'Swane's Golden' 65
  Kashmir 61
  Lawson 41
    'Albo-spica' 46
    'Alumnii' 43
    'Argenteovariegata' 46, 51
    'Aurea' 47
    'Blue Jacket' 46
    'Chilworth Silver' 47
    'Columnaris' 43
    'Darleyensis' 51
    'Elegantissima' 47
    'Ellwood's Gold' 47
    'Ellwoodii' 43
    'Erecta Aurea' 46
    'Erecta Filiformis' 49
    'Erecta Glauca' 43
    'Erecta Viridis' 43
    'Filiformis' 49
    'Fletcheri' 45
    'Fraseri' 51
    'Glauca Lombartsii' 41
    'Golden King' 46
    'Grayspire Pillar' 41
    'Green Hedger' 47
    'Green Pillar' 51
    'Green Spire' 49
    'Henry Dinger' 46
    'Hillieri' 41 25
    'Hogger' 51
    'Intertexta' 49
    'Kestonensis' 49
    'Kilmacurragh' 46
    'Lombartsii' 41
    'Lutea' 49
    'Lutea Smithii' 51
    'Lycopodioides' 46
    'Merrist Wood' 51
    'Moerheimii' 46
    'Naberi' 51
    'Pembury Blue' 51
    'Pendula' 49
    'Pottenii' 43
    'Silver Tap' 47
    'Slocock' 47
    'Somerset' 45
    'Stardust' 51
    'Stewartii' 49
    'Stricta' 43
    'Stricta Glauca' 43
    'Tamariscifolia' 47
    'Triompf van Boskoop' 45
    'Westermannii' 43
    'Winston Churchill' 47
    'Wisselii' 45
    'Youngii' 45
  Leyland 59 47
    'Castlewellan' 59
    'Golconda' 59
    'Haggerston Grey' 59
    'Leighton Green' 59
    'Naylor's Blue' 59
    'Robinson's Gold' 59
    'Silver Dust' 59
  Mendocino 61
  Mexican 63
    'Glauca' 63
    'Glauca Pendula' 63
  Monterey 67
    'Donard Gold' 67
    'Goldcrest' 67
    'Horizontalis Aurea' 67
    'Lutea' 67
  Montezuma 779
  Mourning 61
  Nootka 55
    'Pendula' 55
    'Variegata' 55
  Patagonian 69
  Piute 63
  Pond 103
    'Nutans' 103
  Rough-barked 69
  Santa Cruz 65
  Sargent 63
  Sawara 53
    'Filifera' 53
    'Filifera Aurea' 53
    'Golden Spangle' 53
    'Plumosa' 53
    'Squarrosa' 53
    'Squarrosa Aurea' 53
    'Strathmore' 53
  Smooth-barked Arizona 69
    'Conica' 69
    'Pyramidalis' 69
  Swamp 103
    Chinese 101
  Taiwan 55
  Tecate 65
  West Himalayan 61
  White 55
    'Glauca' 55
    'Variegata' 55

Damson 531

Devil Wood 801

Dogwood
  Alternate-leaved 747
  Flowering 749
  Pacific 747
  Pagoda 747
  Table 749

Dove Tree 745

Dragon Tree 777

Elm 395
  'Dodoens' 405
  'Karagatch' 409
  'Lobel' 409
  'Pinnato-ramosa' 409
  'Plantjin' 405
  'Sapporo Autumn Gold' 411
  American 397
  Camperdown 401
  Caucasian 415
  Chestnut-leaved 413
  Chinese 411
  Cornish 407
  Dutch 403
  English 395
    'Dicksonii' 407
    'Louis van Houtte' 395
    'Sarniensis' 407
    'Silver Gem' 395
    'Viminalis' 395
    'Viminalis Aurea' 395
  European White 395
  Exeter 401
  Field 407
  Fluttering 395
  Golden Cornish 407
  Golden Wych 401
  Guernsey 407
  Huntingdon 403
    'Dampieri' 403
    'Dampieri Aurea' 403
    'Groenveldt' 405
    'Major' 403
    'Vegeta' 403
  Japanese 411
    'Jacon' 411
  Large-fruited 413
  Lock's 407
  Plot's 407
  Rock 397
  Scotch 399
  Siberian 411
  Slippery 397
  Smooth-leaved 405, 407
  Soft 397
  Weeping Wych 399
  Wheatley 407
  White 397
  Wych 399
    'Camperdownii' 401
    'Crispa' 401
    'Exoniensis' 401
    'Horizontalis' 399
    'Lutescens' 401
    'Nana' 401

Epaulette Tree 759

Eucalyptus 737

Eucryphia
  'Penwith' 705
  'Plena' 705
  'Rostrevor' 705
  'Ulmo' 705

Euodia or **Evodia** 591

Fig 441
  Sycamore 785

Filbert 333
  'Purpurea' 333

Fir
  Algerian 131
  Alpine 139
    'Compacta' 139
  Balsam 141
  Bornmueller 135
  Bristlecone 139
  Californian Red 125

INDEX OF ENGLISH NAMES

Caucasian 135
Cheng 121
Chinese 107
  'Glauca' 107
Cilician 109
Colorado White 143
  'Candicans' 143
  'Violacea' 143
  'Wattezii' 143
Corkbark 139
Crimean 135
Delavay 117
Douglas 201
  'Brevifolia' 203
  'Fretsii' 203
  'Stairii' 201
  Bigcone 203
  Blue 203
  Fraser River 203
  Japanese 201
East Himalayan 127
East Siberian 133
Faber 117
Farges's 119
Flaky 129
Fraser's 125
Gamble 119
Grand 141
Greek 131
Himalayan 127
Khinghan 133
King Boris 109
Korean 119
Low's 143
Manchurian 123
Maries' 113
Min 113
Momi 121
  'Tardina' 121
Nikko 123
  'Tomomi' 123
Noble 125 125
Pindrow 129
Red 125
Rocky Mountain 139
Sacred 115
Sakhalin 109
Salween 111
Santa Lucia 139
Shensi 111
Siberian 109
Sicilian 133
Silver 111
  European 137
  'Columnaris' 137
  'Pyramidalis' 137
  Forrest's 117
  Pacific 125
  Veitch's 111
Spanish 133
  'Glauca' 133
Subalpine 139
Taiwan 119
Tienshan 109
Trojan 131
Vejar 115
Vilmorin's 133
West Himalayan 129

Foxglove Tree 773
Fragrant Olive 801
Fringe Tree 763
  Chinese 763
Ginkgo 21
  'Sentry' 21
  'Variegata' 21
Ginnala 627
Golden Chestnut 783
Golden Rain Tree 711
Greengage 531
Gum
  Alpine Snow 739
  Black 735
  Blue 737, 741
  Cider 741
  Mountain 737
  Shining 737
  Silver 741
  Spinning 737
  Tasmanian Blue 741
  Tasmanian Yellow 743
  Tingiringi 739
  Urn 739
  White 737
Gutta-percha Tree 439
Hackberry 417
  Japanese 419
  Mississippi 417
Handkerchief Tree 745
Hawthorn
  Black 457
  Common 459
    'Aurea' 461
    'Bicolor' 461
    'Lutescens' 461
    'Pendula Rosea' 459
    'Rosea' 461
    'Stricta' 459
  Downy 457
  Hungarian 457
  Midland 459
    'Gireoudii' 461
    'Paul's Scarlet' 459
    'Plena' 461
    'Punicea' 461
    'Rosea Flore Plena' 459
Hazel 333
  'Aurea' 333
  'Contorta' 333
  'Heterophylla' 333
  'Pendula' 333
  Corkscrew 333
  Turkish 333
Hemlock 195
  Carolina 195
  Chinese 199
  Eastern 197
    'Aurea' 197
    'Fremdii' 197
    'Macrophylla' 197
    'Microphylla' 197
    'Sargentii' 197
    'Taxifolia' 197
  Eastern Hymalayan 199
  Himalayan 199
  Hybrid American 197
  Japanese
    Northern 199
    Southern 199
  Mountain 197
  Western 195
Hiba 87
Hickory 299
  Shagbark 301
  Shellbark 299
Holly 599
  'Lydia Morris' 605
  American 607
  Box-leaved 605
  Canary Island 605, 607
  Common 599
    'Alaska' 601
    'Amber' 599
    'Angustifolia' 601
    'Argentea Marginata' 599
    'Argentea Marginata Pendula' 603
    'Aurea Marginata' 599
    'Aurifodina' 601
    'Bacciflava' 599
    'Beetii' 603
    'Ciliata Major' 603
    'Crassifolia' 601
    'Crispa' 603
    'Crispa Aurea Picta' 599
    'Donningtonensis' 603
    'Ferox' 599
    'Ferox Argentea' 599
    'Ferox Aurea' 603
    'Flavescens' 599
    'Foxii' 603
    'Gold Flash' 603
    'Golden Milkboy' 599
    'Handsworth New Silver' 599
    'Hastata' 603
    'Heterophylla' 603
    'J.C. van Tol' 601
    'Latispina' 603
    'Laurifolia' 601
    'Lichtenthalii' 601
    'Nellie R. Stevens' 601
    'Ovata' 599
    'Ovata Aurea' 599
    'Pendula' 603
    'Pyramidalis' 601
    'Recurva' 599
    'Scotica' 601
  Golden Hedgehog 603
  Hedgehog 599
  Highclere 601
    'Atkinsonii' 605
    'Balearica' 607
    'Belgica Aurea' 605
    'Camelliifolia' 601
    'Golden King' 601
    'Hendersonii' 601
    'Hodginsii' 601
    'Howick' 607
    'Lawsoniana' 607
    'Mundyi' 605
    'Nigrescens' 605
    'Purple Shaft' 607
    'Wilsonii' 601
    'W. J. Bean' 605
  Himalayan 607
  Japanese 605
    'Shiro-Fukurin' 605
  Moonlight 599
  Perny's 607
    'Drace' 607
    'Indian Chief' 607
  Perry's Silver Weeping 603
  Saw-leaved 601
  Weeping 603
  Yellow-fruited 599
Hop Tree 801
  'Aurea' 801
  'Fastigiata' 801
Hornbeam 325
  American 329
  Common 325
    'Columnaris' 327
    'Fastigiata' 327
    'Frans Fontaine' 327
    'Incisa' 327
    'Pendula' 327
    'Pyramidalis' 327
    'Quercifolia' 327
  European Hop 331
  Japanese 331
  Oak-leaved 327
  Oriental 331
  Weeping 327
Horse-tail She Oak 781
Indian Bead Tree 797
Jacaranda 803
Jerusalem Thorn 795
Judas Tree 569
  'Bodnant' 569
Jujube
  Common 795
Juniper 71
  Alligator 79
  Black 77
  Chinese 73
    'Albovariegata' 73
    'Argentea' 73
    'Aurea' 73
    'Blaauw' 79
    'Iowa' 73
    'Jacobiana' 73
    'Kaizuka' 73
    'Keteleeri' 73
    'Leeana' 73
    'Obelisk' 73
    'Variegata' 73
  Common 71
    'Graciosa' 71
    'Hibernica' 71
    'Oblongata Pendula' 71
    'Pyramidalis' 71
    'Seil Island' 71
  Drooping 77
    'Castlewellan' 77
  Flaky 77 59
  'Meyeri' 79

INDEX OF ENGLISH NAMES

Grecian 75
Himalayan 77
Hollywood 73
Mexican 75
Mexican Weeping 75
One-seed 79
Pencil Cedar 81
  'Burkii' 81
  'Canaertii' 81
  'Cupressifolia' 81
  'Glauca' 81
  'Globosa' 81
  'Pendula' 81
  'Pseudocupressus' 81
Prickly 77
Rocky Mountain 79
'Skyrocket' 79
Swedish 71
Syrian 75
Temple 75
Wallich 77

Kaki 765
  'Hachiya' 765
  'Lycopersicum' 765

Karo 787

Katsura Tree 441
  'Pendulum' 441

Keaki 415

Kentucky Coffee Tree 589
  'Variegata' 589

Kiwi Fruit 783

Kohuhu 733

Kowhai 789
  'Grandiflora' 789

Laburnum 587
  Adam's 587
  Common 587
    'Aureum' 587
  Golden-leaved 587
  Scotch 587
  Voss's 587

Larch 155
  Carpathian 155
  Chinese 163
  Dahurian 163
  European 155
  Golden 165
  Hackmatack 159, 161
  Himalayan 163
  Hybrid 157
  Japanese 157
    'Dervaes' 163
    'Pendula' 157
  Kurile 163
  Siberian 165
  Subalpine 159
  Tamarack 159
  Weeping 161
  Western 161

Laurel 439
  Bay 439
  Californian 443
  Cherry 567
    'Bruantii' 567

    'Camelliifolia' 567
    'Magniliifolia' 567
    'Otinii' 567
    'Rotundifolia' 567
    'Schipkaensis' 567
    'Serbica' 567

Leam 399

Lily Tree 433

Lime 677
  'Diversifolia' 701
  'Dropmore' 701
  'Glenleven' 701
  'Harold Hillier' 701
  'Mrs Stenson' 689
  'Wascana' 701
  American 693
    'Dentata' 693
    'Redmond' 693
  Amur 697
  Begonia-leaved 681
  Caucasian 697
  Chinese 689
  Chinese White 697
  Common 683
    'Greenspire' 687
    'Pallida' 687
    'Wratislavensis' 687
    'Zwarte Linde' 687
  Crimean 681
  Henry's 691
  Japanese 689
  Large-leaved 677
    'Aspleniifolia' 677
    'Aurea' 679
    'Corallina' 677
    'Fastigiata' 679
    'Laciniata' 677
    'Örebro' 679
    'Princes Street' 679
    'Rubra' 677
    'Tortuosa' 677
  Miquel's 697
  Moltke's 695
  Mongolian 691
  Oliver's 697
  Red-twigged 677
  Silver 699
    'Brabant' 699
    'Green Mountain' 699
    'Petiolaris' 695, 699
    'Princeton' 699
    'Sterling Silver' 699
    'Szeleste' 699
    'Varsaviensis' 689
  Silver Pendent 695
  Small-leaved 685
    'Pyramidalis' 685
    'Rancho' 687

Littleleaf 715

Locust
  'Bella Rosea' 581
  'Britzensis' 581
  'Idahoensis' 581
  'Hillieri' 579
  Black 575
    'Appalachia' 581
    'Aurea' 579

    'Bessoniana' 581
    'Coluteoides' 579
    'Frisia' 575
    'Glaucescens' 579
    'Monophylla Fastigiata' 579
    'Pyramidalis' 575
    'Rehderi' 581
    'Rozynskyana' 575
    'Tortuosa' 575
    'Umbraculifera' 577
    'Unifolia' 577
  Caspian 581
  Clammy 577
  Honey 583
    'Bujotii' 585
    'Elegantissima' 585
    'Imperial' 585
    'Skyline' 585
    'Sunburst' 585
    'Variegata' 585
  Chinese 583
  Japanese 583
  Moss 577
  One-leaved Black 577
  Sweet 583
  Weeping Black 575

Loquat 783

Luma 791

Madrona 753

Madrone
  Pacific 753

Magnolia 427
  'Brozzonii' 429
  'Heaven Scent' 429
  'Lennei' 433
  'Lennei Alba' 433
  'Leonard Messel' 431
  'Merrill' 431
  'Nigra' 433
  'Norman Gould' 431
  'Peppermint Stick' 429
  'Peter Veitch' 429
  'Picture' 429
  'Rustica Rubra' 429
  'Sayonara' 429
  'Wada's Memory' 429
  Bull Bay 427
    'Exmouth' 427
    'Goliath' 427
  Chinese Evergreen 427
  Fraser 435
  Japanese Big-leaf 427
  Japanese Willow-leaf 433
  North Japanese 433
  Sweet Bay 435
  Umbrella 435
  Veitch's Hybrid 427
  Wilson's 435

Mahogany
  Red 791
  Swamp 791

Maidenhair Tree 21
  'Sentry' 21
  'Variegata' 21

Maple 609
  Amur 627
  Ashleaf 661
    'Auratum' 661
    'Elegans' 661
    'Flamingo' 661
    'Giganteum' 661
    'Variegatum' 661
    'Violaceum' 661
  Balkan 631
  Bigtooth 631
  Birch-leaved 641
  Black Sugar 629
  Bosnian 627
  Boxelder 661
  Cappadocian 621
    'Aureum' 621
    'Rubrum' 621
  Chalk 631
  Cork-barked 647
  Cretan 627
  Devil's 619
  Field 625
    'Elsrijk' 613
    'Nanum' 641
    'Postelense' 625
    'Pulverulentum' 625
    'Schwerinii' 625
  Florida 655
  Full Moon 643
    'Aconitifolium' 643
    'Aureum' 643
    'Vitifolium' 643
  Golden Japanese 643
  Greek 637
  Hawthorn-leaved 639, 641
    'Veitchii' 641
  Henry's 645
  Her's 651
  Hornbeam-leaved 649
  Horned 619
  Italian 627
  Korean 643
  Lime-leaved 639
  Lobel 621
  Manitoba 661
  Miyabe 617
  Montpellier 617
  Moosewood 651
    'Erythrocladum' 651
  Nikko 617
  Nippon 659
  Norway 609
    'Cleveland' 609
    'Columnare' 609
    'Crimson King' 611
    'Crimson Sentry' 613
    'Cucullatum' 611
    'Deborah' 613
    'Dilaceratum' 611
    'Dissectum' 611
    'Drummondii' 611
    'Erectum' 613
    'Globosum' 611
    'Goldsworth Purple' 611
    'Heterophyllum Aureo-variegatum' 611
    'Laciniatum' 611, 615
    'Maculatum' 615

INDEX OF ENGLISH NAMES

'Meyering' 613
'Oekonomierat Stoll' 611
'Olmsted' 613
'Pyramidale Nanum' 615
'Reitenbachii' 615
'Schwedleri' 611
'Summershade' 615
'Superform' 613
'Walderseei' 611
Oregon 631 635
  'Seattle Sentinel' 655
  'Tricolor' 655
Painted 623
Paperbark 617
Père-David's 651
  'Madeleine Spitta' 649
Red 653
  'Columnare' 653
  'October Glory' 655
  'Red Sunset' 655
  'Scanlon' 653
  'Schlesingeri' 653
Red Snake-bark 651
Redbud 637
Rock 631
Rough-barked 617
Shandong 619
Shirasawa 645
  'Aureum' 643
Silver 657
  'Laciniatum' 657
  'Laciniatum Wieri' 657
'Silver Vein' 649
Smooth Japanese 645
  'Atropurpureum' 647
  'Butterfly' 645
  'Cuneatum' 647
  'Dissectum' 647
  'Dissectum Rubrifolium' 647
  'Heptalobum' 647
  'Katsura' 645
  'Linearilobum' 647
  'Nicholsonii' 645
  'Ornatum' 647
  'Osakazuki' 647
  'Oshio Beni' 647
  'Sangokaku' 647
  'Seiryu' 645
  'Shishigashira' 645
  'Tana' 645
  'Volubile' 645
Striped 651
Sugar 629
  'Newton Sentry' 629
  'Temple's Upright' 629
Tatarian 631
Trident 639
van Volxem's 637
Velvet 623
Vine 643
Vineleaf 617
Vine-leaved Japanese 643
Wilson's 619
Zoeschen 637 639
  'Annae' 659
  'Elongatum' 659

Mastic Tree 797
May Tree 459
Medlar 455
  Mediterranean 457
Mimosa 573, 789
Mirabelle 531
Mockernut 299
Monkey Puzzle Tree 37
Moosewood 651
  'Erythrocladum' 651
Moreton Bay Fig 785
Mountain Ash
  Chinese 475
    'November Pink' 475
    'Rufus' 475
  Ornamental 477
  Showy 477 459
Mulberry 421
  Black 423
  Chinese 423
  Paper 425
  White 421
    'Pendula' 421
    'Pyramidalis' 421
    'Venosa' 421
Myrtle 793
  'Flore Pleno' 793
  'Microphylla' 793
Nettle Tree 417
  Caucasian 419
Nutmeg
  Californian 31
  Japanese 31
  Spice 31
Oak 351
    'Ambrozyana' 367
    'Fulhamensis' 367, 371
    'Lucombeana' 371
    'Macon' 379
    'Pondaim' 379
  Algerian 375
  Armenian 379
  Bamboo-leaved 353
  Bartram's 355
  Basket 285
  Black 359
    'Magnifica' 359
    'Nobilis' 359
  Blackjack 357
  Bottomland Red 357, 363
  Burr 389
  Californian Black 357
  Cambridge 365
  Caucasian 379
  Cherrybark 357
  Chestnut 285
  Chestnut-leaved 365
  Chinese Cork 353
  Chinkapin 355
  Coast-Live 373
  Common 383
    'Argenteovariegata' 385
    'Atropurpurea' 385
    'Concordia' 385

    'Cristata' 387
    'Fastigiata Grangei' 387
    'Filicifolia' 385
    'Granbyana' 387
    'Holophylla' 387
    'Hungarian' 383
    'Pendula' 387
    'Raba' 383
    'Strypemonde' 385
    'Tortuosa' 383
  Cork 367
  Daimio 353
  Downy 375
  Fulham 367, 371
  Golden 385
  Golden Oak of Cyprus 379
  Himalayan 781
  Holm 373
    'Fordii' 373
  Hungarian 377
    'Hungarian Crown' 377
  Kermes 781
  Laurel 357
  Lea's Hybrid 359
  Lebanon 367
  Lucombe 371
  Ludwig's 351
  Macedonian 367
  Mirbeck 375
  Mongolian 353
  Mossycup 389
  Myrtle 781
  Northern Pin 357
  Oregon White 285
  Overcup 355
  Pin 361
  Possum 355
  Post 355
  Pyrenean 377
    'Pendula' 377
  Quercitron 359
  Red 363
    'Aurea' 363
  Sawtooth 353
  Scarlet 361
    'Splendens' 361
  Sessile 381
    'Columna' 381
    'Insecata' 381
    'Laciniata' 381
    'Mespilifolia' 381
  Shingle 359
  Shumard 357
  Spanish 357 343
  Stave 389
  Swamp Chestnut 285
  Swamp White 391
  Texas 357
  Turkey 369
    'Variegata' 369
  Turner's 373
  Valley 391
  Water 355
  Weeping 387
  White 389
  Willow 351
  Yellow 359

Oleaster 795
Olive 761
Ombu Tree 783
Orange, Bitter 801
Osage Orange 425
Osier
  Common 289
Pagoda Tree 585
  'Pendula' 585
  'Pyramidalis' 585
Palm
  Cabbage 775
  Canary Island 775
  Chilean Wine 777
  Date 777
  Desert Fan 777
  Fan 775
  Petticoat 777
Palm Lily 777
Paulownia
  'Coreana' 773
Peach 533
  'Albo Plena' 533
  'Klara Mayer' 533
  'Kurokawa-yaguchi' 533
  'Prince Charming' 533
  'Sagami-shidare' 533
  'Stellata' 533
Pear
  'Bradford' 519
  'Chanticleer' 519
  Common 519
  'Beech Hill' 519
  Manchurian 517
  Oriental 521
    'Kieffer' 521
  Plymouth 519
  Sand 521
    'Kieffer' 521
  Snow 515
  Wild 513
  Willow-leaved 517
Pecan 299
Pepper Tree 797
Peppermint
  Mount Wellington 737
Pepperwood 443
Persian Ironwood 447
  'Pendula' 447
Persian Lilac 797
Persimmon 765
  Chinese 765
Phillyrea 763
Picrasma 593
Pignut 299
Pine 205
  Akamatzu 225
  Aleppo 231
  Apache 241
  Arolla 205
    'Aureovariegata' 205
    'Compacta' 205

INDEX OF ENGLISH NAMES

Austrian 235
Bhutan 221
Big-cone 237
Bishop 251
Blackjack 241
Blue 221
Bosnian 247
Bristlecone 207
Calabrian 231
Canary Island 779
Caribbean 779
Chilgoza 239
Chinese Red 209
Chinese White 209
Colorado Pinyon 223
Cooper 259
Cow's Tail 33
Corsican 233
Crimean 233
Cuban 779
Digger 259
Dragon's-eye 225
Durango 249
Dwarf Mountain 231
Eastern White 219
  'Contorta' 219
  'Fastigiata' 219
  'Radiata' 219
Endlicher 257
Foxtail 207
Gaoshan 209
Gregg 237
Hartweg 257
Heidreich 205
Holford's 247
Huon 35
Jack 249
Japanese Black 239
Japanese Red 225
  'Aurea' 225
  'Oculus-draconis' 225
  'Umbraculifera' 225
Japanese Umbrella 107
Japanese White 213
  'Glauca' 213
  'Saphir' 213
  'Tempelhof' 213
Jeffrey 243
King William 105
Knobcone 259
Korean 239
Lacebark 213
Limber 207
Lodgepole 255
Macedonian 215
Maritime 215
Mexican Pinyon 223
Mexican Weeping 243
Mexican White 217
Mongolian Scots 229
Monterey 253
Montezuma 257
Mountain 231
Nelson Pinyon 237
Norfolk Island 37
Pitch 251
Ponderosa 241
Pyrenean 235
Red 253

Scots 227, 209
  'Fastigiata' 229
Scrub 249
Shore 255
Shortleaf 245
Siberian Stone 221
Single-leaf Pinyon 223
South-western White 237
Stone 205
Sugar 211
Swiss Stone 205
Taiwan Black 225
Umbrella 205
Washoe 245
Western Himalayan 221
Western White 211
Western Yellow 241, 243
Weymouth 219
  'Contorta' 219
  'Fastigiata' 219
  'Radiata' 219
Whitebark 223
Yunnan 209

Pistachio 797

Plane 449
  'Augustine Henry' 451
  Cambridge 451
  Cyprian 453
  London 449
    'Cantabrigiensis' 451
    'Pyramidalis' 451
    'Suttneri' 449
    'Tremonia' 451
  Oriental 453
    'Mirkovec' 451

Plum
  American Red 527
  Cherry 525
  Date 765
  Garden 523
  Myrobalan 525

Plum Yew 33
  'Fastigiata' 33
  Chinese 33

Podocarp
  Chilean 35
  Large-leaved 35
  Willow-leaf 35

Pomegranate 793

Poplar 263
  'Beaupre' 273
  'Boelare' 273
  'Fastigiata' 269
  'Interamericana' 273
  'Lloydii' 273
  'Oxford' 267
  'Pendula' 269
  Balm of Gilead 271
    'Aurora' 271
  Balsam 271
    'Balsam Spire' 271
  Berlin 277
  Black 275
    'Plantierensis' 277
    'Variegata' 275
    'Vereecken' 275
  Black Italian 279

    'Eugenei' 281
    'Florence Biondi' 283
    'Marilandica' 281
    'Regenerata' 279
    'Robusta' 281
    'Serotina' 279
    'Serotina Aurea' 279
    'Serotina de Champagne' 279
    'Serotina de Selys' 279
  Bolle's 263
  Canadian 279
  Chinese Necklace 271
  Grey 263
    'Macrophylla' 263
  Japanese Balsam 267
    'Androscoggin' 267
  Lombardy 277
    'Elegans' 277
    'Italica Foemina' 277
    'Italica' 277
    'Lombardy Gold' 277
  Picart's 263
  Prince Eugene's 281
  Swiss 279
  Western Balsam 271
    'Fritzi Pauley' 271
    'Scott Pauley' 271
  White 263
    'Pyramidalis' 263
    'Richardii' 263

Pride of India 711
  'Fastigiata' 711
  'Variegata' 711

Privet
  Chinese 761
  'Excelsior Superbum' 761
  'Tricolor' 761

Quince
  Common 455

Rauli 335

Red Bay 781

Red Powder Puff Tree 789

Redbud
  Eastern 571
  'Forest Pansy' 571

Redwood
  Coast 91
    'Adpressa' 91
    'Cantab' 91
  Dawn 101
  Sierra 93
    'Aureovariegatum' 93
    'Pendulum' 93

Rhododendron Tree 757
  'Album' 757
  'Blood Red' 757
  'Roseum' 757

Rowan 465
  'Aspleniifolia' 465
  'Beissneri' 465
  'Dirkenii' 465
  'Fastigiata' 465, 481
  'Flava' 473

  'Ghose' 471
  'Gibbsii' 479
  'Hilling's Spire' 471
  'Joseph Rock' 475
  'Leonard Messel' 477
  'Pagoda Red' 467
  'Signalman' 471
  'Sunshine' 477
  'Tundra' 477
  'Winter Cheer' 477
  'Xanthocarpa' 465
  American 469
    'Belmonte' 469
  Japanese 469
    'Embley' 475
    'Jermyns' 473
  Kashmir 473
  Sargent's 475

Rubber Tree 785

Sallee
  Black 743

Sallow
  Grey 285

Sapodilla Plum 787

Sassafras 443

Service Tree
  of Fontainebleau 489
  True 481
  Wild 489

Silk Tree (Albizia) 571
  'Rosea' 571

Silky Oak 795

Silverbell Tree 759

Sloe 523
  'Purpurea' 523

Snowbell Tree 759

Snowdrop Tree 759

Soft Tree Fern 779

Sophora, Evergreen 789
  'Sun King' 789

Sorrel Tree 757

Spanish Bayonet 777

Spanish Dagger 777

Spruce 167
  Alberta White 185
  Alcock's 183
  Balfour 193
  Black 187
  Blue Engelmann 189
  Brewer 187
  Candelabra 171
  Colorado 189
    'Endtz' 189
    'Koster' 189
    'Moerheim' 189
  Dragon 173
  Eastern 185
  Hondo 181
  Hybrid 187
  Hybrid American 171
  Japanese Bush 169
  Koyama 181
  Likiang 193

Maximowicz 169
Mexican 169
Morinda 167
Northern Sargent 173
Norway 175
 'Argentea' 175
 'Cincinnata' 175
 'Cranstonii' 175
 'Cupressina' 175
 'Finedonensis' 175
 'Inversa' 175
 'Laxa' 175
 'Pendula' 175
 'Pendula Major' 175
 'Pyramidata' 175
 'Tuberculata' 175
 'Viminalis' 175
 'Will's Zwerg' 175
Oriental 179
 'Aurea' 179
 'Gracilis' 179
Purple-cone 193
Red 185
Serbian 179
Schrenk 167
Siberian 171
Sikkim 169
Sitka 191
Taiwan 181
Tigertail 171
Wilson 169
Yellow 185

Spur Leaf 439

Stewartia 707
Chinese 707
Japanese 707
Korean 707
Tall 707

Storax 787
Bigleaf 759
Hemsley's 759

Strawberry Tree 753
 'Integerrima' 753
 'Rubra' 753
Canary Island 755
Cyprus 755
Grecian 755
Hybrid 755
Japanese 751

Sumach
Potanin's 595
Smooth 595
Stag's-horn 595
 'Dissecta' 595

Swampbay 435

Sweet Gum 445
 'Golden Treasure' 445
 'Lane Roberts' 445
 'Moonbeam' 445
 'Silver King' 445
 'Variegata' 445
 'Worplesdon' 445
Chinese 445

Oriental 445
Sweet Tea 801
Sycamore 633
 'Atropurpureum' 635
 'Brilliantissimum' 635
 'Erectum' 633
 'Leopoldii' 635
 'Negenia' 635
 'Nizetii' 635
 'Prinz Handjery' 635
 'Simon Louis Frères' 635
 'Variegatum' 633 615
 'Worley' 635
American 453

Tacamahacca 271

Tamarisk 703
 'Rosea' 703
 'Rubra' 703
 'Summer Glow' 703
African 787
French 703

Tarajo 607

Thorn 457
Broad-leaved Cockspur 461
Cockspur 461
Hybrid Cockspur 457
 'Carrierei' 457
Oriental 457
Scarlet 457
Tansy-leaved 457
White 457

Thuja
Chinese 85, 89
 'Bonita' 85
 'Elegantissima' 89
 'Flagelliformis' 89
Korean 87

Toona
 'Flamingo' 709

Totara 35
Acute-leaved 35

Tree of Heaven 593
Downy 593

Tree Tobacco 801

Trifoliate Orange 801

Tuart 791

Tulip Tree 437
 'Aureomarginatum' 437
 'Fastigiatum' 437
Chinese 437

Tupelo 735
Ogeechee 735
Swamp 735
Water 735

Turpentine Tree 797

Umbrella Tree
Earleaf 435

Varnish Tree 595
Victorian Box 787
 'Variegatum' 787
Walnut 295
Arizona 297
Black 295
Chinese 297
Common 295
 'Laciniata' 295
 'Monophylla' 295
Cut-leaved 295
Japanese 297
Manchurian 297
One-leaved 295
Wattle
Black 789
Golden Wreath 789
Green 573
Pale Hickory 573
Silver 573
Swamp 789
Sydney Golden 789
Wellingtonia 93
 'Aureovariegatum' 93
 'Pendulum' 93
Whitebeam 483
 'Decaisneana' 483
 'John Mitchell' 485
 'Lutescens' 483
 'Magnifica' 483
 'Majestica' 483
 'Wilfrid Fox' 483
Greek 485
Himalayan 485
Swedish 489
Willow
Almond-leaved 285
Bay 285
Caspian 289
Coral-bark 291
Corkscrew 289
Crack 287
 'Basfordiana' 287
Cricket Bat 291
Goat 285
 'Kilmarnock' 285
Golden 287
Hoary 289
Silver 291
Violet 285
Weeping 287
 'Blanda' 287
 'Crispa' 289
 'Chrysocoma' 287
 'Elegantissima' 287
 'Erythroflexuosa' 289
 'Salamonii' 287
 'Tortuosa' 289
White 291
 'Britzensis' 291
Wing Nut 293
Caucasian 293

Chinese 293
Hybrid 293
Japanese 293
Winter's Bark 781
Wirilda 789
Yellow-wood 569
Chinese 569
Yew
Canadian 25, 28
Chinese 28
Common 23
 'Adpressa' 25
 'Adpressa Aurea' 25
 'Adpressa Variegata' 25
 'Aldenhamensis' 27
 'Aurea' 23
 'Aureovariegata' 26
 'Barronii' 25
 'Brevifolia' 25
 'Dovastoniana' 25
 'Cheshuntensis' 27
 'Dovastoniana' 25
 'Dovastonii Aurea' 25
 'Erecta' 26
 'Fastigiata' 23
 'Fastigiata Aurea' 23
 'Fastigiata Aureomarginata' 23
 'Lutea' 23
 'Neidpathensis' 27
 'Paulina' 27
 'Rushmore' 27
 'Semperaurea' 26
 'Standishii' 26
 'Summergold' 26
 'Xanthocarpa' 23
Golden 23, 25
Fulham 26
Himalayan 29
Hybrid 29
 'Hatfieldii' 28
 'Hicksii' 29
 'Kelsyei' 29
 'Sargentii' 29
 'Skalborg' 29
Irish 23
Japanese 25, 28
Kelsey 29
Plum 33
 'Fastigiata' 33
 Chinese 33
Plum-fruited 35
Prince Albert's 39
Westfelton 25
Yulan 433
Zelkova 415
Chinese 415
Cretan 415
Cut-leaved 415